CONTENTS

Faced with the task of deciding who to include in this encyclopedia, we had to be selective. Of the 5,000 million people alive today, and 2,000 million from history, we had space to write about just over one thousand. We chose men and women whose achievements are famous worldwide. Almost every name will be familiar – but you may have forgotten why – and some will be quite new. In each entry we have given the person's full name, year of birth and death, and then concentrated on details of their achievements.

The encyclopedia is divided into six sections, covering famous people from all walks of life, and all times, from ancient civilizations through to the present day. The sections are:

1 People in the Arts (painters, sculptors, architects, musicians, and writers)
2 Scientists (including chemists, physicists, doctors and mathematicians)
3 People of Action (pioneers, explorers, fighters, adventurers)
4 Stars from the worlds of Sport and Entertainment (especially film, pop music, theatre and dance)
5 Thinkers and Inventors (including religious leaders, philosophers, inventors and engineers)
6 Leaders (emperors, monarchs, dictators, and politicians) from both past and present-day.

How to Use the Encyclopedia

Within each section, the entries are ordered chronologically, building up an on-going account of human development through the ages. To find a particular name – Julius Caesar, Florence Nightingale or Charlie Chaplin, for example – use the names index at the back of the book. If someone's name appears in **bold type** in the text, that person has his or her own entry in the encyclopedia. A note at the foot of the entry gives the appropriate page reference, so that you can browse, or leap exactly to the name you want. Specialist or unusual words in the text are explained in a glossary at the end of each section.

Acknowledgements

Dozens of people helped as we worked on this book. We should like especially to thank Sarah Robinson (who word-processed the text), Gill and Peter Gorton (who advised us on the science entries), Russ Shipton (who advised on pop), and Alison Pitt (who researched the sport and entertainment section). Other people – editor, artists, designers, picture researchers, and others – are mentioned on the acknowledgements page. We are grateful to them all.

Kenneth and Valerie McLeish
Spalding, Lincolnshire, 1990.

SECTION 1

THE ARTS

Artists,
Writers,
Composers ...

INTRODUCTION TO *THE ARTS*

The arts are such activities as story-telling, music-making, carving sculptures and making pictures. The first surviving signs of them came from the Stone Age, over 20,000 years ago. People then made music, danced, painted pictures and told stories for their own pleasure. But they also believed they were forms of magic. Singing and dancing were ways to communicate with the gods. Story-tellers used myths to explain how the world began, how the gods lived, what life was like in times and places no humans had ever experienced. Artists made images of the gods, and beautiful objects to please them and win their favour.

As communities became more settled and civilized, new forms of communication were invented. One was writing, on clay tablets (in Mesopotamia), bamboo strips (in China), and "paper" made from papyrus reeds (in Egypt). At first it was used mainly for lists (for example of goods in a storehouse). But gradually writers began to describe human life, making histories of their nation, and writing poems, plays and other works describing their fellow-citizens' good qualities and mocking their follies. Architects designed not only temples for gods but palaces for rulers and other buildings for humans. Artists and sculptors made images of people and their surroundings, and of nature itself. The arts were used for pleasure, and as a sign that people were "cultured": that is had more on their minds than fighting or labouring to survive.

In early times, people cared little about the survival of works of art. They lived in the present, and looked forward to the future. But views change, and, especially in the last few hundred years, people have wanted to learn about the arts of the past, and to preserve them, rather than to be surrounded only by artworks from their own time. In today's world we enjoy a huge range of ideas in the arts, some copied from the past, some up to the minute, and others *avant garde* – ahead of their time.

The arts are vitally important. Great artists are special, not just in their own countries during their own lifetimes, but to people everywhere, throughout history. Shakespeare's plays, for example, are translated and performed all over the world. Everyone agrees about the genius of Leonardo da Vinci. Someone, somewhere on Earth, is playing music by Mozart or Tchaikovsky every moment of every day. In other kinds of human activity – sport and exploration, say – new records are constantly created. But the greatest artists remain supreme. In their own fields, they show at its finest what the human mind can do.

This bust (head and shoulders statue) shows Homer as legend describes him: a blind, old man with a bushy beard.

HOMER (Homeros)

Greek story-teller and poet 8th century BC

Homer gathered together and retold two sets of stories, which are among the best-loved tales of ancient times.

The first set, the *Iliad*, takes place during the Trojan War, when the Greeks besieged Troy in Anatolia (Turkey) to win back Helen, their stolen princess. The main theme of the *Iliad* is the bitter quarrel between two heroes, Achilles (a Greek) and Hector (a Trojan). Achilles killed Hector and dragged his body three times round the walls of Troy.

The second set of stories, the *Odyssey*, tells of the ten-year-long adventures of the Greek hero Odysseus as he journeys home from Troy. On the way, he faces such monsters as the flesh-eating Cyclops Polyphemus and the enchantress Circe. The tale ends with Odysseus entering his own palace in disguise, to fight off a band of suitors who have been pestering his wife Penelope.

AESOP (Aisopos)

Greek story-teller 6th century BC

Legend says that Aesop was a slave living on the island of Samos who became popular for his stories, with which he entertained the royal courts.

The kind of story Aesop told was the "fable". This is a short tale or joke ending with a moral . Many of these are still used, such as "too many cooks spoil the broth" or "look before you leap". Aesop's tales were mainly about animals to whom he gave human failings in order to mock human behaviour.

Over a hundred of Aesop's fables are still told today. This illustration, from a book of Aesop's fables published 900 years ago, is of the thirsty crow. The bird could not reach the level of the water in the bucket. Cleverly, he dropped pebbles into the bucket until the water level was high enough for him to drink.

GREEK DRAMA

Over 2,500 years ago, drama flourished in ancient Greece – and some of the earliest Greek plays have survived. Serious plays used stories from myth, and comedies mocked ideas and people of the time. They were performed in huge open-air theatres, seating as many as 14,000 people. (The ruins of some can still be seen today.) Famous Greek dramatists are Aeschylus, Sophocles and Euripides, who wrote serious plays, and Aristophanes and Menander, who wrote comedies.

AESCHYLUS (Aiskhylos)

Greek playwright c 525-456 BC

Aeschylus was the first great playwright in history. He took his stories from Greek myths, and his plays include parts for gods, goddesses, giants and other supernatural beings.

Aeschylus wrote over a hundred plays, but only seven survive. Three

of the best known are together called *Oresteia* ("Story of Orestes"). They tell how King Agamemnon's wife, Clytemnestra, murdered him after the Trojan War, and how the gods spurred Agamemnon's son Orestes to take revenge.

SOPHOCLES

Greek playwright c 496-406 BC

Sophocles was interested in how belief in the gods affects the way humans behave. In his plays he liked to show people who could choose how to live their lives, and the results of the choice they made.

In *Antigone*, the heroine's brothers, one a hero and one a traitor, have both been killed, and Antigone is faced with a difficult decision. Should she obey her city's law (which says that only the "good" brother can be buried) or the gods' law (which says that both dead brothers are to be treated equally)?

In *King Oedipus*, a man hears a terrible prophecy – that he will live to kill his father and marry his mother. Instead of accepting the gods' will, he chooses to fight against it, but in so doing he brings about exactly the catastrophe he was trying to avoid.

MYRON

Greek sculptor c 490-430 BC

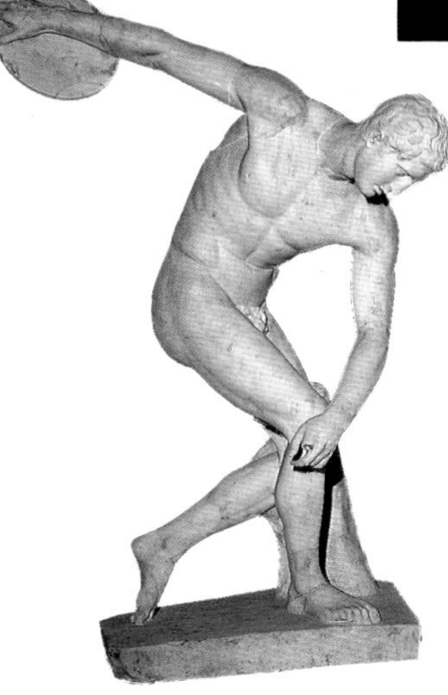

The discus-thrower. Myron's original statue is lost, and this copy comes from Roman times.

Until the fifth century BC, the people in most Greek sculptures looked stiff and unnatural, as if they were standing to attention. Myron pioneered a new style, putting his people into natural poses as if they had been frozen in mid-movement. *The Discus-thrower*, for example, shows a man leaning forward on one leg with the discus held high in the air behind his shoulder. He seems to be at the very last moment of upswing, just before whirling round and letting the discus fly.

EURIPIDES

Greek playwright c 480-406 BC

Euripides thought that what we do depends more on the sort of people we are than on any outside forces, including the gods. This was in line with the teaching of some of the most modern Greek thinkers of the time, such as **Socrates**, but it earned Euripides the reputation of being a dangerous, experimental writer.

Altogether, Euripides wrote over 90 plays, of which 18 survive. One of the best known is *Medea*, about a woman, abandoned by her husband, who turns to magic and murders her children. Another is the *Bacchae*, the story of King Pentheus who refuses to let his people worship the god Dionysus, and who is savagely punished for it.

This statue of the writer Euripides stands in the Naples Museum in Italy.

EURIPIDES: Socrates 326

HERODOTUS (Herodotos)

Greek historian c 484-420 BC

Until Herodotus, few Greeks wrote about history. Instead of describing facts, people told myths about gods, heroes and other superhuman beings. Herodotus, by contrast, wrote about real events: the invasion of Greece by the Persian armies under Darius and **Xerxes**, and the heroic Greek victory over an enemy many times its own army's size. He began by finding out every detail he could about these events, as if he were writing about scientific facts instead of about human lives. His *Historiai* ("researches") gave us the word history and earned Herodotus the nickname "the father of history".

Praxiteles' statue of Aphrodite, goddess of beauty, sculpted in 340 BC.

ARISTOPHANES

Greek playwright c 445-385 BC

Aristophanes wrote comedies which mocked the generals, priests and politicians of his city, Athens. His plays were filled with fantasy: people argue with frogs or turn into wasps, visit the Underworld (the kingdom of the dead) or fly up to Heaven to negotiate with the gods.

Eleven of Aristophanes' plays have survived. In one of the most famous, *Lysistrata*, the women of Greece grow so tired of a seemingly endless war that they refuse to make love with their husbands until peace is made.

Herodotus visited Egypt on his travels, and made notes for his book on Egyptian sights and customs.

PRAXITELES

Greek sculptor c 400-330 BC

Praxiteles earned his living by carving marble images of gods and goddesses for temples. Most sculpture until his time was in bronze; Praxiteles' preference for marble made it a popular material.

The Greeks thought of their gods as larger-than-life humans, with the same good and bad qualities magnified to superhuman scale. Praxiteles used this idea in his sculpture. He made his gods and goddesses look exactly like men and women, life-size or larger. He liked to show them naked, in natural poses as if carved in mid-movement. One famous example, the *Aphrodite of Cnidus*, shows the goddess of beauty taking off the last of her clothes ready to step into a pool to bathe.

VIRGIL (Publius Vergilius Maro)

Roman poet 70-19 BC

Virgil was a landowner in northern Italy who became a leading poet. His best-known work is the *Aeneid*, an epic poem (a long narrative or story) started soon after **Augustus** was made Emperor of Rome in 27 BC. Its central character is Aeneas, a mythical hero thought by Romans

HERODOTUS: Xerxes 412

to have been one of their most important ancestors. The story tells how Aeneas left the ruins of Troy (in Turkey) to find a new home for his people in Italy. It is filled with prophecies of Rome's future glory and power.

The *Aeneid* soon became one of the best known of all Roman books. Schoolchildren studied it, adults read it for pleasure, and its ideas and poetry influenced later writers for many centuries.

LIVY (Titus Livius)

Roman historian 59 BC- c AD 17

In 25 BC Livy began writing a history of Rome from its very beginnings, based on traditional stories such as those of Aeneas (see **Virgil**) and the story of Romulus and Remus (the twin brothers said to have founded Rome), right up to his own time. He finished his task 40 years and 142 volumes later. Only 35 volumes survive, and most of what we know of the legends of early Rome, and of Roman battles with **Hannibal**, comes from them.

ROMAN WRITERS

The ancient Romans particularly enjoyed reading poetry and plays. Some poets (Catullus, Horace) wrote about the countryside and about the pains and pleasures of love. Others (Apollonius, Virgil) wrote epics based on myth. Still others (Juvenal, Martial) wrote satires. Playwrights wrote tragedies (Seneca) and comedies (Plautus, Terence).

OVID (Publius Ovidius Naso)

Roman poet 43 BC - c AD 17

Ovid was a favourite poet at the court of Emperor **Augustus** in Rome. His best-known work today includes the light-hearted *Metamorphoses*, a collection of Greek and Latin folktales, and *Art of Love* – how to flirt and get away with it.

Right: This painting (on a stained-glass window) shows St Jerome working on his Bible translation.

JEROME (Hieronymus)

Christian writer AD 345-420

Jerome was a Christian priest who played an important role in the spread of Christianity. Following the declaration by the Emperor **Constantine** that the whole Roman Empire was to become Christian, a decision was made to use Latin as the official language of worship. Jerome set about translating the Bible into Latin from Greek, Hebrew, Aramaic and the other languages it was written in. His translation, the Vulgate ("common-language") Bible, was eventually used all over the world. Most later translations of the Bible, including **Luther**'s in German and the Authorized Version in English, were based on it.

VIRGIL: Augustus 416 LIVY: Hannibal 164 Virgil 6 JEROME: Constantine 419 Luther 338

Lady Murasaki, working on her book, as imagined by a modern artist.

MURASAKI, Shikibu

Japanese writer c 978-1026

Lady Murasaki spent her time imagining exciting adventures and flirtations, which she wrote as a novel entitled *The Tale of Genji*. It tells of a prince who won the heart of every lady he met, and it became so popular at court that Shoshi, wife of the Japanese emperor, asked Murasaki to be one of her ladies-in-waiting. Murasaki served the empress until she died, and wrote a diary about events at the emperor's court – a fascinating account of life in ancient Japan.

STURLUSON, Snorri

Icelandic writer and politician 1179-1241

Snorri collected ancient stories and myths and wrote them down as the *Prose Edda* and the *Verse Edda*. They tell of such events as the creation of the universe from the body of the giant Ymir, the adventures of Odin, Thor, Loki and the other gods, and the supernatural war between the Aesir and the Vanir – the two main races of god in Norse myth.

Snorri also wrote *Heimskringla* ("the orb of the world"), a set of biographies of Norway's ancient kings. In 1215, the Norwegians (who ruled Iceland at the time) made Snorri chief judge of the island, and he served for 26 years until he quarrelled with the Norwegian King Haakon IV and was put to death.

DANTE, Alighieri

Italian poet 1265-1321

Dante wrote books of many kinds, but he is best known for his poem *The Divine Comedy*. He admired **Virgil**'s *Aeneid*, and set out to write the sort of book Virgil might have written had he been a Christian. In the *Aeneid*, Virgil's characters visit the Underworld, and the poem describes the monsters they see and their reactions to them. In *The Divine Comedy* Dante describes a similar dream-journey through Hell and Purgatory, and finally to Paradise.

FOLK TALES

A thousand years ago, people particularly enjoyed reading collections of folk tales. Some tales (for example the legends of King Arthur or the Norse myths collected by Snorri Sturluson) were grand and impressive. Others (for example *The Arabian Nights*) were jokes or fantasies based on everyday life. Several writers made up stories of their own, using folk tale ideas: two of the most famous are Boccaccio and Chaucer.

Part of Dante's *Divine Comedy*, from a copy made in Dante's lifetime. The picture shows devils on the Burning Lake in Hell.

DANTE: Virgil 6

GIOTTO (Giotto di Bondone)

Italian artist and architect c 1266-1337

Giotto was one of the main Italian painters of the fourteenth century. He painted Christian saints and Bible characters in a realistic way, unlike the wooden, two-dimensional style of the time. He is particularly known for his frescoes (paintings made on wet plaster). In Assisi he painted frescoes showing the life of **St Francis**.

Giotto's greatest surviving work is in the Arena chapel in Padua, Italy, where he painted 39 scenes from the Bible. These are dramatic and very lifelike – he had great skill at making his characters seem real. Giotto also worked in Florence, and was made the city's architect in 1334. He carved many statues for the façade (front wall) of the cathedral, and designed the bell-tower. He is sometimes called the "father of Renaissance painting", as his work influenced many important artists after him.

NI TSAN

Chinese painter 1301-74

Ni Tsan is one of the best known of all Chinese painters. He and three colleagues (Huang Kung-Wang, Wu Chen and Wang Mang) were nicknamed "the four great landscape masters". They painted landscapes, brushing ink on to silk or bamboo. Chinese thinkers believed that human beings are part of a gigantic "wholeness" which includes rocks, sky, trees, animals – in fact everything in existence. They felt that by meditating (thinking quietly) about this, people might find calm in their otherwise busy lives.

Ni Tsan made pictures to help this meditation. As you look at his paintings of hills, plants and water, you gradually free your mind from the hustle and bustle of daily life.

One of Ni Tsan's peaceful landscape paintings which help you to relax your mind.

BOCCACCIO, Giovanni

Italian writer 1313-75

Boccaccio is best known for his book *The Decameron*, a collection of 100 short stories supposedly told by a group of ten friends staying in a country house during an outbreak of plague. Decameron means "ten days" – the time the friends spent together – and each friend told one tale each day. The stories come from many sources. Some are based on folktales; others are comic tales of young lovers, cunning servants, miserly old men, simpletons, crooks and rogues.

A detail from Giotto's picture of the Bible story of the Marriage at Cana, when Jesus turned water into wine.

GIOTTO: St Francis 335

Pilgrims riding to Canterbury, from a modern illustration of Chaucer's *Canterbury Tales.*

CHAUCER, Geoffrey

English poet c 1343-1400

Chaucer was first a soldier, then an ambassador to several European countries. He was fascinated by the folk-tales and poetry of the countries he visited, and set out to produce similar works in English. His best-known poems are *Troilus and Cressida*, a love-story set in the Trojan war, and *The Canterbury Tales.*

The people in *The Canterbury Tales* are pilgrims, riding from London to **St Thomas à Becket**'s shrine at Canterbury. To pass the time each of them tells a story. Some stories are funny, others serious; a priest preaches a sermon and Chaucer himself tells a tale making fun of knights and quests. His stories are written in rhyming verse, and are full of jokes and good humour and give insight into medieval life.

The Madonna and Child (Mary and Jesus), carved by Donatello.

DONATELLO (Donato di Niccolo di Betti Bardi)

Italian sculptor c 1386-1466

When Donatello learned his craft, European medieval sculptures of people looked stiff and unnatural. The aim was to show qualities of character (for example saintliness or courage) as much as people's actual looks. We can still see this style in the statues and carvings on medieval European tombs.

Donatello's work applied the ideas of such ancient Greek sculptors as **Myron** and **Praxiteles** to Christian, religious subjects, giving them human qualities but on a grand scale. Donatello's lifelike sculptures of prophets and saints showed how closely he had made studies of the human body.

One of Donatello's best-known works is a group of statues made to decorate the altar of the church of San Antonio in Padua, Italy. He made 7 bronze statues and 22 reliefs (carvings on flat surfaces), showing St Anthony's miracles. Whenever people looked at the altar, they were reminded of the life of the church's patron saint.

BOTTICELLI, Sandro (Alessandro di Mariano Filipepi)

Italian painter c 1445-1510

In his early years, Botticelli lived in Florence, painting large scenes from Greek and Roman myth for the city's leading family, the **Medicis**. One of his best-known paintings, *The Birth of Venus*, shows the Roman goddess of love being born from the foam of the sea-waves.

Botticelli's fame grew, and he was asked to make paintings for the Sistine Chapel in Rome for Pope Alexander VI (**Alexander Borgia**). For this he used scenes from the Bible and from stories of the lives of Christian saints.

Later, Botticelli returned to Florence and spent the rest of his life there. His art became more and more religious. One of his main works at this time was a set of illustrations for **Dante**'s poem *The Divine Comedy*.

CHAUCER: Becket 334 DONATELLO: Myron 5 Praxiteles 6 BOTTICELLI: Borgia family 432 Dante 8 Medici family 431

BOSCH, Hieronymus (Jerome van Aken)

Dutch painter c 1450-1516

Bosch's early paintings were of Bible scenes and stories, but he later became one of the world's greatest painters of fantasy. He painted vast, nightmare visions of such things as the end of the world, full of grinning skeletons, devils and the writhing, agonized people they are torturing. Such scenes were meant to warn people against doing wrong. Although sinister, the paintings are full of bright and brilliant colours. Bosch's best-known work is the triptych (painting on three panels) *The Garden of Earthly Delights*. Many of his paintings were bought by the Spanish king Philip II, and they later influenced the works of surrealist painters like Salvador **Dalí**.

LEONARDO DA VINCI

Italian artist and scientist 1452-1519

Leonardo was one of the most gifted people of the Renaissance. He was not only a great painter and illustrator, but also a brilliant sculptor, architect, scientist and engineer.

As an artist Leonardo worked for the dukes of Florence and Milan. Many of his paintings use Bible stories and ideas in a new and fascinating way. In *The Last Supper*, for example, he painted **Jesus** and his disciples at a long table facing us, as if we are on the other side of the table, sharing the meal.

Leonardo's style, like **Donatello**'s sculpture, was highly realistic, and he was expert at showing moving bodies – anything from a rearing horse to people in a crowd. His portraits show character as well as appearance – often in a tantalizing way.

Leonardo's reputation as one of the greatest geniuses in world history, however, comes also from his other many skills. He was interested in music and theatre; he wrote poetry; above all, he studied science and technology. He filled notebook after notebook with sketches and descriptions of rocks, plants, and the flow of water. He dissected corpses to learn about muscles and the way faces and bodies change as people age. He studied the physics of movement, and drew plans for all kinds of mechanical – and, in those days, technologically impossible – marvels including a submarine, a fixed-wing aircraft, a tank and a helicopter.

Who can tell what Mona Lisa is thinking, in Leonardo's famous picture? Her face is full of character – but what character?

BOSCH: Dalí 71 LEONARDO: Donatello 10 Jesus 329

This woodcut by Dürer shows the pig-herd in the Bible story of the Prodigal Son.

DÜRER, Albrecht

German artist 1471-1528

Dürer is best remembered today for his woodcuts and engravings on copper. He made thousands of pictures of this kind: illustrations for books, portraits of people, landscapes and pictures of mythical or Biblical stories. Dürer was a learned man, with both scientific and creative skills. His pictures are full of symbols of his ideas on the meaning of life. He was interested in the way the body works, in particular the bones and muscles, and worked to get every detail in his figure-drawings exactly right. He was one of the first artists ever to make accurate scientific drawings of plants and animals, and is considered one of the finest artists of the German Renaissance.

MICHELANGELO

Italian artist 1475-1564

Michelangelo's family name was Buonarotti, but he is known by his first names, Micaele and Angelo, run together. When he was 13 he began to learn how to paint frescoes. He also worked as a sculptor, and his talent impressed Duke Lorenzo de' **Medici** of Florence, who took him into his service.

Michelangelo spent the next three years studying and copying the sculpture of ancient Greece. He was a devout Christian, and from his teenage years onwards he tried to blend Bible themes with Greek ideas about making statues. His *David*, for example, shows the Biblical king not as a majestic ruler but as a naked youth, modelled on statues of

Apollo, Hermes and other Greek gods. It was the largest marble statue carved in Italy since the end of the Roman Empire.

As an adult Michelangelo spent much time in Rome. In 1508 Pope Julius II asked him to paint scenes from the Bible on the ceiling of the Sistine Chapel in the Vatican – a difficult task. It is now thought that Michelangelo had to lie on a scaffolding platform, painting above his head, to cover a ceiling twice as big as a tennis court. He painted many subjects from the Old Testament, including three of the most striking stories: the Creation, Adam and Eve, and Noah and the Flood. The work took three years, and has always been regarded as one of the world's masterpieces.

Michelangelo was also a great architect. Back in Florence he worked on several architectural projects for the Medici family. Then, when he was 59, he was recalled to Rome to paint the most awesome Bible scene of all: the Day of Judgement, when Christians believe that the world will end and God will judge the human race. The work, begun in 1536, took him five years. The picture is very different from his Sistine Chapel paintings. It shows scores of people being dragged into Hell by devils, writhing in torment or praying desperately for mercy.

Michelangelo spent the last years of his life in Rome. At the age of 71 he redesigned St Peter's, the world-centre of Roman Catholic worship, and made drawings of the Crucifixion. He also wrote poetry and spent much time praying and reading the Bible. When he died, aged 89, Michelangelo was regarded as one of the greatest artists of all time – a view many people still hold today.

The Creation of Adam: one of Michelangelo's most famous paintings from the ceiling of the Sistine Chapel in Rome.

MICHELANGELO: Medici family 431

The Virgin Mary, Jesus' mother, being presented in the Temple, as painted by Titian.

RAPHAEL (Raffaelo Sanzi)

Italian artist 1483-1520

When Raphael was 21 he showed his work to **Leonardo da Vinci** and **Michelangelo** in Florence, Italy. Leonardo encouraged him to spend more time on sketches, and to try out ideas in rough before beginning to paint. Raphael also admired and imitated Michelangelo's paintings of nudes. In 1508 he went to Rome, where Pope Julius II asked him to decorate the walls of the Vatican. He worked in Rome until his death, and painted hundreds of religious pictures.

People admire the naturalness of Raphael's characters. When he paints the Madonna and Child, for example, Mary is shown as an ordinary girl holding a chubby, struggling baby Jesus. Many critics also praise the way the beautiful curved forms in his paintings appear to be three-dimensional.

TITIAN (Tiziano Vecelli)

Italian painter c 1485-1576

Like many artists of his time, Titian made a good living painting portraits of monarchs and other rich people. For ten years he worked for Emperor **Charles V** in Spain, painting the court. Most of his best work was done in his native city, Venice, where he painted huge religious or mythical scenes. Like many painters of his day he often put into the pictures the people who had paid for them, showing them as watchers on the sidelines of the story.

RABELAIS, François

French writer c 1494-1553

Rabelais is famous for his comic story *Gargantua and Pantagruel*, about two giants. It begins with the birth and upbringing of Gargantua, then tells of the battles between the giants and their neighbours, and ends with accounts of Pantagruel's voyages to fabulous countries to find an answer to the question "Who shall I marry?"

Rabelais uses this story as a basis for satire, making fun of the priests, doctors, thinkers and lawyers of his time. His book is crammed with puns, jokes, funny lists and silly names: "a feast of mirth", he called it.

ITALIAN RENAISSANCE ARTISTS

Five hundred years ago, Italian artists began redeveloping the ancient Greek and Roman ways of paintings and sculpting. (Renaissance means "re-birth".) But as well as showing gods and characters from myth, they showed Bible scenes, especially the life of Jesus. The best-known artists are Botticelli, Giotto, Michelangelo, Leonardo da Vinci, Mantegna, Piero della Francesca and Raphael.

RAPHAEL: Leonardo 11 Michelangelo 12 TITIAN: Charles V 436

PALLADIO, Andrea

Italian architect 1508-80

Palladio studied as a stonemason, building and repairing churches in Vicenza, where he was brought up. In the 1540s he visited Rome and became fascinated by ancient Roman architecture. He began designing houses, theatres, churches, streets and squares in the ancient, Classical style. In 1570 he published his drawings and designs for villas and palaces as *Four Books on Architecture*, and for three centuries they were used by architects all over Europe and America.

Palladian buildings often have tall stone pillars to support the roof – like these from a London club.

BRUEGEL FAMILY

Flemish painters 16th-17th century

PIETER BRUEGEL THE ELDER (1525-69) and his sons PIETER THE YOUNGER (1564-1638) and JAN (1568-1625) were all painters. The two Pieters painted scenes of life in the farms and villages of their native Flanders. In *Children's Games* and *Netherlandish Proverbs*, for example, they crammed the canvas with people, each illustrating one game or proverb. *Peasant Wedding* shows dozens of people at a feast, drinking, dancing, joking and gossiping.

The two Pieters also painted many subjects from the Bible, concentrating on ordinary people. In *The Census*, for example, nearly 100 villagers are shown in winter, skating, snowballing, feasting and tramping through the snow. It is only when you look closer that you see Mary and Joseph arriving in the village on Christmas Eve, looking for shelter at the crowded inn.

Jan Bruegel painted flowers in vases or in leafy, summery landscapes. He also helped **Rubens**, and painted trees and flowers on some of Rubens' biggest pictures.

In the middle of this busy winter scene, painted by Pieter Brueghel, Mary and Joseph ride into the village to look for shelter.

EL GRECO (Domenikos Theotokopoulos)

Greek artist 1541-1614

El Greco ("the Greek") was born in Crete but spent most of his life in Toledo, Spain. He was a Christian, and painted Bible scenes in a style partly like that of the Italian painters **Titian** (who taught him) and **Michelangelo**, and partly like the *icons* (religious paintings) he would have known from his boyhood in Crete. He also painted people, but his style was very unusual. He distorted the figures into thin and twisted shapes and used bright colours. These portraits seem more like "modern" art than anything from his own Renaissance times, and influenced later artists, including **Picasso**.

BRUEGEL: Rubens 18 EL GRECO: Michelangelo 12 Picasso 60 Titian 14

As the windmill sails turn, Don Quixote mistakes them for giants waving their arms, and gallops to the attack.

CERVANTES SAAVEDRA, Miguel de

Spanish writer 1547-1616

Cervantes is remembered today for his novel *Don Quixote de la Mancha*, the tale of a foolish old man who spends so much time reading about the knights of the Middle Ages that he goes mad and imagines that he, too, is a knight. He finds himself a rusty spear, a trusty squire named Sancho Panza, and a bony nag called Rosinante, and he rides out to look for adventures. Since he is several hundred years out of date, and mad, the giants he fights are windmills, the armies are flocks of sheep, and his damsel in distress is Dulcinea, a dairy-maid. There is something very appealing about the idea of Don Quixote: his name and his adventures are known to millions of people all over the world who have never read Cervantes' book.

SHAKESPEARE, William

English playwright and poet 1564-1616

Shakespeare's father, a glove-maker, wanted his son to work in the family business. It is not certain that he did – many details of Shakespeare's life are a mystery – but it seems that for a time he lived quietly in his home town, Stratford-upon-Avon. He married Anne Hathaway and they had several children. But in his mid-20s, his life changed. The theatre was very popular entertainment at the time, and Shakespeare went to London to seek his fortune as an actor. He joined an acting company called The Lord Chamberlain's Men, which was favoured by Queen **Elizabeth I** and her courtiers.

As well as performing in plays Shakespeare began writing them, and his work was hugely successful. For the next 25 years, he stayed in London, only going home to Stratford at holiday times, when the theatres were closed and the royal court was out of town. He wrote 37 plays, a few with the help of other writers, and several books of poems. Then he retired, went back to Stratford as unexpectedly as he had left it, and died three years later at the age of 52.

Shakespeare wrote three main kinds of play. His Comedies are invented stories full of disguises, tricks and songs. His Histories are based on real-life characters (such as Julius **Caesar** and **Henry VIII**) and actual historical events. His Tragedies are serious plays dealing with such matters as nobility, trust, honour and duty. Most of the plays are in verse; some of them (including

SHAKESPEARE: Caesar 415 Elizabeth I 436 Henry VIII 435

Romeo and Juliet and *Antony and Cleopatra*, about doomed lovers, and also *Othello* and *King Lear*, about powerful men destroyed by failings in their own character) are magnificent poems written for the stage. His plays have been translated and performed around the world.

Among Shakespeare's Comedies, the best known are: *A Midsummer Night's Dream, Twelfth Night* and *As You Like It*; of the Histories *Henry V, Richard III* and *Henry IV Parts One and Two* (which include one of his finest comic characters, the fat boaster Falstaff). His best-known Tragedies – the plays for which he is probably most famous of all – are *Hamlet, Othello, Macbeth* and *King Lear*. At the end of his life he wrote *The Tempest*, about a group of people shipwrecked on a magic island. For many people, it is his finest play.

Shakespeare's best-known poems are a collection of over 100 *Sonnets* (short rhyming verses), mostly on the theme of love.

Top: Reconstruction of Shakespeare's Globe Theatre beside the Thames in London. The flag flew when a play was being performed. *Below, left:* The only drawing of Shakespeare thought to show what he really looked like.

MONTEVERDI, Claudio

Italian composer 1567-1643

Monteverdi began his career by playing, singing and composing works to entertain the Duke of Mantua, and became master of the duke's chapel. He wrote songs and madrigals (songs for groups of voices) in the usual sixteenth-century styles, but also worked in the new musical forms of the seventeenth century – above all opera, a fashionable invention of the 1590s. His *Orfeo*, about the Greek singer Orpheus who went to the Underworld to charm the gods of the dead, is one of the first and most striking operas ever composed.

In 1613 Monteverdi moved from Mantua to become musician-in-charge at St Mark's Cathedral in Venice. He wrote church works such as the *Vespers of the Blessed Virgin*, and although the words were sacred, he used voices in the same rich, emotion-packed way as in his operas and madrigals. His *Coronation of Poppea*, a fairly late opera, written in 1642, when he was 75, is considered to be another masterpiece.

A portrait of Claudio Monteverdi painted from a woodcut made of the composer in 1644.

Rubens loved to use rich, glowing colours in his paintings, which was very suitable for the luxurious clothing and surroundings of his subjects. His painting of Hélène Fourment and her Children was painted c 1636-40.

RUBENS, Peter Paul

Flemish painter 1577-1640

Rubens spoke six languages, and travelled all over Europe, going from town to town and from court to court, to paint portraits. He was soon rich and famous, and his paintings hung in the palaces of many European princes and monarchs.

At home in Antwerp, Rubens had a studio, like a factory or workshop. He would sketch out ideas for new paintings, and leave his assistants to work on them. Two of his helpers were Van Dyck, who painted faces and hands, and Jan **Bruegel**, who painted flowers and trees.

Rubens' studio specialized in huge pictures, big enough to fill whole walls. They showed battles, orgies, and other crowd scenes. He often chose stories from the Bible or ancient mythology, which allowed him to paint nudes: a good example is *The Rape of the Sabines*, from Roman legend. He is particularly famous for paintings of naked women. Nowadays they would seem fat, but in Rubens' time large size was a sign of wealth and prosperity. His second wife was young and beautiful, and he put her in as many paintings as he could, either nude, as a goddess or nymph in a myth-story, or shown as herself in silk dresses and feathery, flowery hats.

Rubens also painted landscapes, and made many sketches. The rich colour of his work influenced **Renoir**, 250 years later.

VELÁZQUEZ, Diego (Diego Rodrigo de Silva y Velazquez)

Spanish painter 1599-1669

When Velázquez was 24 he painted a portrait of King Philip IV, and the king liked it so much that he appointed Velázquez court painter. Today's monarchs use photographs to record details of their marriages, births, animals and members of their household. Velázquez's paintings did exactly the same job for the Spanish court. His best-known works are portraits of the royal children, a set of pictures of the royal maids, and another set of women weaving tapestries for the palace apartments.

RUBENS: Bruegel family 15 Renoir 47

Velázquez's royal work took up only part of each year, and left him free to paint pictures of other kinds: religious scenes, landscapes, and a huge panorama of the aftermath of a bloody battle (*The Surrender of Breda*).

After Velázquez's death, his pictures were forgotten for almost two centuries, until they were rediscovered during the 1850s. Impressionist painters such as **Renoir** and **Degas** imitated Velázquez's ideas (especially his flowing brush strokes and way of painting children). He is admired for the way he painted light, using shadows and bright shafts of sunlight, making his pictures very dramatic.

One of Velázquez's paintings of the Spanish royal family.

REMBRANDT (Rembrandt Harmensoon van Rijn)

Dutch painter 1606-69

By the time Rembrandt was 30 he was one of the most fashionable painters in Holland. Rich people flocked to have their portraits painted, wearing their most gorgeous clothes and laden with jewels, gold ornaments and medals. Rembrandt obliged; but he also indulged in sly humour at his sitters' expense. Their clothes might be dazzling, but they themselves were not: he put in every wrinkle, grey hair, skin blemish or frown. He also liked to paint groups, for example the crowd of well-dressed people watching a corpse being dissected in the *Anatomy Lesson of Doctor Tulp*.

People returned to Rembrandt, despite his cheekiness, because his work was magnificent. His mastery of *chiaroscuro* (strongly contrasting light and shade) was second to none. He imagined each painting as if lit by a single source of light, like a hidden spotlight; then he painted every tiny difference in light and shade.

In the 1650s Rembrandt began to fall out of fashion. Sitters complained that he was more interested in the details of his pictures than in painting people so that their friends could recognize them. Rembrandt turned to religious themes – and produced one of his best-known works, a scene from the Bible story *Saul and David*. He also made portraits of himself and his young son Titus, and fine landscape drawings and etchings.

For 150 years after Rembrandt's death, his reputation as an artist was not as high as he deserved. But in the nineteenth century, he was rediscovered as one of the world's greatest painters. People began searching for his work and, remarkably, more than 300 etchings, 2,000 drawings and 600 paintings were found.

Self-portrait by Rembrandt, painted when he was an old man.

VELÁZQUEZ: Degas 42 Renoir 47

This drawing of Milton comes from the title page of one of his books, and shows him as a man of about 30.

MILTON, John

English poet 1608-74

At university Milton was a brilliant classical scholar. He wrote verses in Greek and Latin, and poems in English which followed the style of the Italian Renaissance writers he admired. *Comus*, written in 1643, is a masque (poetic play), based on the style of **Sophocles**' plays.

In his 30s and 40s, Milton supported **Cromwell** in the English Civil War, opposing King **Charles I**, and wrote books and articles explaining republican ideas. When Cromwell took power he made Milton his secretary, but Milton's sight was failing, and he retired from politics and went back to poetry, dictating to secretaries.

Milton's finest works come from the last 20 years of his life. They include *Paradise Lost*, a poem in the style of **Virgil**'s *Aeneid* telling the Bible story of the battle between God and Satan.

MOLIÈRE

French actor and playwright 1622-73

When Jean-Baptiste Poquelin, a country boy, was 21, he took up acting as a career. He gave himself the stage-name Molière, gathered a company of actors and began touring local towns and villages. After 13 successful years the company moved to Paris, where Molière became a favourite of King **Louis XIV**.

Molière's best-known comedies include *Le bourgeois gentilhomme* ("The would-be gentleman"), about a rich man who tries in vain to learn the skills of polite society, *Le Tartuffe*, about a confidence trickster who poses as a holy man, and *Le malade imaginaire* ("The imaginary invalid"), about a hypochondriac (someone who is convinced that he or she has every illness possible).

VERMEER, Jan

Dutch artist 1632-75

A quiet man, Vermeer lived all his life in Delft in the Netherlands, and painted no more than two or three pictures each year. He was fond of painting people inside their own homes. The floors are tiles or marble, the ceilings are polished wood, the rugs and furniture are patterned and the windows are large, throwing a light across the picture like a spotlight. Vermeer liked to use yellows, blues and greys in his work, giving an impression of calm and peace. He also painted a few outdoor scenes, showing Delft's tranquil river, neat houses and peaceful fields.

Right: Vermeer's calm picture called *Girl Reading a Letter by an Open Window.*

MILTON: Sophocles 5 Charles I 442 Cromwell 442 Virgil 6 MOLIÈRE: Louis XIV 443

Left: St Paul's Cathedral in London: the finest building designed by Wren.

RACINE, Jean

French playwright 1639-99

Racine worked in Paris, and was one of **Louis XIV**'s favourite playwrights. He wrote tragedies, using stories from ancient myth. Some, for example *Iphigénie* and *Phèdre*, come from Greek myth, others, such as *Esther* and *Athalie*, use stories from the Bible. People admire Racine's "psychological insight": the way he understands his characters' feelings and the reasons for what they do. He is also praised for his flowing, dignified verse, some of the finest French ever written for the stage.

WREN, Christopher

English scientist and architect 1632-1723

Before Wren reached 30, he was Professor of Astronomy at the University of London and then at Oxford. Apart from astronomy, his other main interest was designing buildings. In 1666, parts of London were destroyed in what became known as the Great Fire, and Wren made plans for a magnificent new capital city, full of fine marble buildings and wide streets radiating from a central square like the spokes of a wheel. His plans were rejected as being too expensive, but he was asked to redesign 51 city churches, including St Paul's Cathedral, and 36 other public buildings. Wren gave up his scientific career, and designed buildings until he retired.

DEFOE, Daniel

English writer 1660-1731

Defoe spent most of his working life as a political journalist, and it was not until he retired that he turned to writing novels. He wrote many books, including his famous *Robinson Crusoe*, written in 1719 the story of a shipwrecked sailor who survives on a desert island. In the end, Crusoe is rescued with his servant Friday (whom he saved from cannibals), and he takes Friday home to England to show him what "civilized" life is like.

Crusoe in his island cave, dreaming of his long-lost home.

RACINE: Louis XIV 443

Left: This illustration from Swift's *Gulliver's Travels* shows what happened to Gulliver when he was shipwrecked in the land of Lilliput.

SWIFT, Jonathan

Irish priest and writer 1667-1745

Swift had two careers: churchman and journalist. He wrote satire, making fun of the thinkers, scientists and politicians of the time. In one article, for example, his mocking answer to the politicians' question: "What shall we do about Irish over-population?" was that babies are delicious, if properly cooked and served.

Nowadays, Swift is best known for his book *Gulliver's Travels*, about an explorer who sails to strange countries inhabited by midgets, giants and talking horses. The story is fun, but Swift's satire is sharp. Wherever Gulliver goes, he tries to persuade the inhabitants that life would be better if they learned the ways of educated English gentlemen of his time. The more he describes how so-called gentlemen behave in England, the more his listeners treat him as a dangerous barbarian.

VIVALDI, Antonio

Italian musician 1678-1741

The only known portrait of Vivaldi.

Vivaldi was the music-master of an orphanage, and wrote dozens of works for his pupils and operas for the theatre in Venice. He was one of the finest violinists of his time, and played all over Europe. He also studied to become a Roman Catholic priest. Despite this hectic life, Vivaldi still found time to write more than 1,000 works. He is especially remembered for his concertos. He wrote over 600, for almost every possible instrument. Some of his concertos are like musical stories: one, for example, tells of a storm, another of someone vainly trying to get to sleep. A well-known work is *The Four Seasons*, a set of four violin concertos painting sound-pictures of the changing weather and the activities of people in spring, summer, autumn and winter.

BACH: Vivaldi 22

BACH, Johann Sebastian

German composer 1685-1750

Bach's first training was from his father, a musician in Arnstadt, in Germany. He practised the harpsichord, violin and organ, and when he was old enough he became a choirboy, and learned composing from the church organist. At the age of 18, he became an organist in the Lutheran church. Many other musicians of the day – for example **Vivaldi** – became famous by performing all over Europe, but Bach remained a church musician, serving one community. At 38 he took the job of musician-in-charge at St Thomas' Church in Leipzig, where he stayed for the rest of his life.

Bach wrote two kinds of music: sacred (for church use) and secular (for concerts). For the church, he wrote hymn-tunes, anthems, masses (including the *B minor Mass* for soloists, choir and orchestra), passions and cantatas. For the concert-performer, he wrote sonatas, suites and concertos, including the six *Brandenburg Concertos.*

HANDEL, George Frederick

German/English composer 1685-1759

Handel was born in Germany, but spent little of his life there. At the age of 21 he worked in Italy as a composer and violinist in an opera house. Four years later, he was asked to write an opera to be produced in London. He spent the rest of his life in England and became a British citizen in 1726.

When Handel was a young man, opera was a favourite entertainment of rich people. Along with his other works (suites, sonatas, concertos), he always produced one or two new operas a year for London theatres. He also wrote music for grand state occasions – for example the *Fireworks Music*, written in 1749, to celebrate the signing of a peace-treaty between Britain and France.

By the time Handel was 50, the fashion for Italian opera was beginning to die, and he invented a new kind of music: oratorio (Bible stories arranged for soloists, choir and orchestra). For the rest of his life Handel wrote and directed a new oratorio every year, and his oratorios (for example *Messiah, Judas Maccabaeus* or *Jephtha*) are still among his best-known works. In the oratorio intervals, Handel used to play his own organ concertos – and he went on doing this even in the last seven years of his life, when he was completely blind.

Bach was a famous keyboard player, and wrote over 500 works for himself to play.

CANALETTO (Giovanni Antonio Canal)

Italian painter 1697-1768

Canaletto specialized in pictures of the waterways, palaces and churches of his native city, Venice. He captured the unusual quality of light in Venice, and took great care to get the scale and look of the places he painted accurate. Some paintings show sumptuous public occasions; others show ordinary people going about their business.

Canaletto went to England in 1746 to paint for the aristocracy, and did not return to Venice until 1755. Later, he found himself in debt and, through an English merchant, sold his library and many paintings of London and the river Thames to King George III. A great number of Canaletto's paintings and drawings thus became part of the English royal collection.

Canaletto's painting of the Rio Mendicante in Venice.

HAYDN, Franz Josef

Austrian composer 1732-1809

Haydn learned music as a choirboy at St Stephen's Cathedral in Vienna. He studied briefly with Nicola Porpora, an Italian composer and singing teacher, and gradually his music became known in Vienna. When he was 29, he joined the court of Prince Esterházy. The prince loved music, and had his own orchestra, church choir, opera company and military band. He built a magnificent country palace on the border between Austria and Hungary, where he and his musicians spent each summer. Haydn was a musician-in-chief. His tasks were to write works for the musicians to play, rehearse and conduct the orchestra, and supervise the purchase and repair of instruments.

Haydn worked for the Esterházy family for 30 years. He wrote symphonies and concertos for the Esterházy orchestra, operas, masses and other church works, and hundreds of sonatas, dance-suites, songs and other shorter pieces.

Prince Esterházy often invited important people, including aristocrats and politicians, from all over Europe. They admired Haydn's music, and soon Haydn was being showered with invitations to tour abroad. In 1790 he moved to Vienna, and from there toured France and Britain. Many of his best-loved works (including the "London" and "Oxford" symphonies, *The Creation* and *The Seasons*) were first played on these tours.

Most bullfighting pictures are grand and ceremonious. Goya concentrated on the cruelty in the people's faces, and on the agony of the bull.

GOYA, Francisco (Francisco Jose Goya y Lucientes)

Spanish painter 1746-1828

Until Goya was 28 he was an unknown, working mainly on book illustrations and religious paintings for churches. After an apprenticeship under a court painter, he went to Madrid to work in the royal tapestry factory, where he stayed from 1776 to 1791. He painted parks, fields, trees, and scenes from history, myth and daily life. His work was used as a model for enormous tapestries, woven to hang on the palace walls. In 1789 King Charles IV of Spain appointed Goya court painter, and over the next 20 years Goya painted scores of portraits of the royal family and their courtiers, and his employers' favourite scenes from mythology and the Bible. He was influenced by **Velázquez**, and his portraits used brighter colours than his earlier work.

In 1792 Goya suffered an ear-infection which left him stone deaf and changed his character, making him serious, gloomy and sad. His court pictures still glittered with colour and brightness, but the drawings, etchings and paintings made for himself often showed pain and suffering. From 1810-14, for example, after **Napoléon I** invaded Spain, Goya made a set of etchings called *The Horrors of War*. They show battles, torture, suffering and death. He also painted grim scenes of occupied Spain – *The Shootings of May 3rd 1808* is one of the best known of all his paintings.

GOETHE, Johann Wolfgang von

German writer 1749-1832

In his mid-20s Goethe was already famous, for the play *Ironhand*, about a swaggering, sixteenth-century soldier, and *The Sorrows of Young Werther*, a novel about a young man passionately and hopelessly in love.

In 1776, aged 27, Goethe was made a privy counsellor (court official) to the Duke of Weimar, which he remained for the rest of his life. He had a variety of jobs: he worked as a politician, scientist (supervising a geological survey of the area) and manager of the state theatre. Above all, he wrote poetry, plays and novels. His plays range from a version of the Greek myth *Iphigenia in Aulis*, to Shakespearean tragedies set in Renaissance Italy (*Tasso*) and the sixteenth-century civil war in Flanders (*Egmont*, for which **Beethoven** later wrote incidental music). His novels include *The Apprenticeship of Wilhelm Meister*, and *Elective Affinities*, a book in letter-form about some friends who decide to have an adulterous love-affair.

By his 60s Goethe was the "grand old man" of German literature. People made pilgrimages to Weimar to visit him, and he was regarded as one of the world's greatest literary geniuses, rivalled only by such writers as **Dante** or **Shakespeare**.

Goethe's best-known works today are his love-poems and a long verse-play called *Faust*. Its hero is a medieval alchemist, who spends his life trying to discover the secrets of the universe and who almost loses his soul to the Devil.

This illustration to Goethe's *Faust* shows Faust in a magic circle drawn on the floor, muttering a spell to make the Devil come to him.

GOYA: Velázquez 18 Napoléon 451 GOETHE: Beethoven 28 Dante 8 Shakespeare 16

MOZART, Wolfgang Amadeus

Austrian composer 1756-91

Mozart could play the harpsichord when he was 3 years old. Before he was 5 he began making up music, and by the time he was 6 he was giving concerts all over Europe. He grew up playing (piano or violin) or conducting at concerts, teaching harpsichord and piano, writing and conducting operas and other musical works for anyone who would pay him.

When Mozart was 31 his father died. Mozart and his wife Constanze found themselves heavily in debt. He was constantly overworked – as well as travelling to dozens of cities each year to play and conduct, he was pouring out new compositions, sometimes at the rate of one a week. On top of this stressful existence, he was in poor physical health and in 1791, aged only 35, he died.

During his short, hectic life, Mozart wrote over 150 orchestral works – symphonies, serenades and concertos – as well as sonatas, string quartets and other chamber music. He wrote nearly a dozen operas, including *The Marriage of Figaro, Don Giovanni* and *The Magic Flute*, and also masses and other works for the church. For many music lovers he is the finest classical composer who ever lived.

This famous painting shows the 6-year-old Mozart (sitting at the keyboard), with his violinist father and his sister, then aged 12.

SCHILLER, Johann Christoph Friedrich von

German playwright and poet 1759-1805

As a young man, Schiller worked as a medical orderly in the army. But when he was 23 his first play, *The Robbers*, was performed, and he left the army to take a job writing for the theatre. Schiller was soon one of Germany's leading dramatists.

Schiller's plays are about personal freedom, the struggle we have to follow our own ideas when other people disagree with them. He chose stories from history which fitted his theme, and wrote in grand, sonorous verse, so that his plays are like a blend of the histories and tragedies of his favourite writer, **Shakespeare**. His best-known plays include *Maria Stuart*, about **Mary** Queen of Scots, *The Maid of Orleans*, about **Joan of Arc**, and *William Tell*, about the legendary Swiss freedom-fighter. Many of his plays were later turned into operas: one of the finest is *Don Carlos*, set to music by **Verdi**. German children also know Schiller as a poet; they learn his poems (such as *The Diver* and *Polycrates' Ring*) by heart. One of his finest poems, *Ode to Joy*, was set to music by **Beethoven** in his Ninth Symphony, and is now used as the anthem of the European community.

SCHILLER: Beethoven 28 Joan of Arc 170 Mary, Queen of Scots 438 Shakespeare 16 Verdi 37

HOKUSAI, Katsushika

Japanese artist 1760-1849

Hokusai was expert at making colour prints, and liked to make striking contrasts of colour. This, and his genius for capturing a scene in a few simple lines, influenced many French artists in the nineteenth century, including **Gauguin**.

Hokusai published books of witty prints showing people enjoying themselves, and others of children's rhymes and proverbs. He also made 15 volumes of *Random Sketches*, which show ordinary people shopping, gossiping, eating etc, and which have been called an encyclopedia of Japanese life. Outside Japan, Hokusai is probably best known as a landscape artist.

The Wave, one of Hokusai's most famous prints.

JAPANESE COLOUR PRINTS

Japanese eighteenth- and nineteenth-century artists specialized in making colour prints from carved wood blocks. Their pictures showed scenes from everyday life, or landscapes, flowers, birds, fish and other creatures. Famous painters include Hiroshige, Hokusai, Masonobu and Utamaro. Their work was unknown outside Japan until almost the end of the nineteenth century, when European painters such as Toulouse-Lautrec began to use ideas from it.

WORDSWORTH, William

English poet 1770-1850

Wordsworth lived near Grasmere in the English Lake District with his wife, Mary, and his sister, Dorothy. He believed that city-living was bad for creative people, and that artists, writers and musicians had greatest success when they tried to equal the beauty or harshness of nature in their work. This was a Romantic idea (see **Romanticism**), and Wordsworth's friends included leading English Romantic writers (such as Coleridge) and painters of the time.

Wordsworth's own favourite among his poems was *The Prelude*, a long account of his childhood and growing up, but his most famous work is a shorter poem: *To Daffodils* ("I wander'd lonely as a cloud...").

Wordsworth, and a peaceful Lake District scene near Grasmere.

HOKUSAI: Gauguin 48 WORDSWORTH: Romanticism 31

Beethoven, composing music at the piano. The artist has tried to show not just what Beethoven looked like, but the power and passion he put into his work.

BEETHOVEN, Ludwig van

German composer 1770-1827

Until Beethoven was over 30, he was chiefly famous as a pianist, especially for improvising (making up music on the spot). Afterwards, he would often write down these improvisations (for example, the two piano sonatas later nicknamed "Moonlight" and "Pastoral"). He also composed symphonies, concertos and string quartets.

As early as 1798 Beethoven's doctors told him that he was going deaf, and that in a few years he would hear no sounds at all but whining and thudding noises inside his head. Beethoven and his doctors tried various means to save his hearing, but all failed: by the time he was 50 he was practically stone deaf. People had to write down any remarks they made to him, and he could hear none of his music being performed.

Like all musicians, Beethoven was able to "hear" music in his mind, and so he could carry on composing. But his music changed. He still tried to express feelings and emotions in sound, but now he stretched the usual ideas of harmony, melody – even how the instruments should be played. His music became inward-looking and meditative, like a private world of its own, and at the time the critics hated it. Gradually, though, people began to understand and appreciate it, as if they too shared Beethoven's feelings while they listened. He came to be considered one of the greatest artistic geniuses in history, a musical equivalent of such giants as **Shakespeare** or **Leonardo**. His 9 symphonies, 5 piano concertos, 16 string quartets and 32 piano sonatas are among the most often performed and best loved of all classical music.

SCOTT, Walter

Scottish writer 1771-1832

Scott was fascinated by the folktales of Scotland, and thought that they would make magnificent poems. He wrote ballads in the style of medieval minstrels, and his poems (for example *The Lay of the Last Minstrel*) were soon popular all over Europe.

In 1814 Scott began a series of novels treating Scottish and then English history in the same swash-buckling, romantic style as his poetry. They became best-sellers, and some of them, including *Rob Roy, The Heart of Mid-Lothian, The Bride of Lammermoor*, and *Ivanhoe* (about Saxon and Norman England) are among the best-known of all nineteenth-century novels.

AUSTEN, Jane

English novelist 1775-1817

Austen was a vicar's daughter, and lived all her life quietly with her family; she never married, never moved from her parents' home.

BEETHOVEN: Leonardo 11 Shakespeare 16

Although her parents were not rich, they were respected in society, and their friends included lords and ladies, leaders of fashion and good taste. Austen watched their dances, tea-parties, theatre-trips and endless gossip about marriages and fortunes with sharp amusement, and put her observations into six witty novels. One of the most popular is *Pride and Prejudice*, about the efforts of a mother to find "good" husbands (by which she meant well-born, charming and rich) for her five daughters.

TURNER, Joseph Mallord William

English painter 1775-1851

As a teenager Turner sold prints in his father's barber-shop, earning enough money to finance sketching tours. He travelled round Britain, making drawings of rivers, mountains, forests and ruined abbeys or castles. By the time he was 25 he was famous.

In 1802 Turner made his first trip to Europe, and was amazed by the Swiss mountains and the unusual light of Venice. His landscapes became more Romantic – dramatic and full of emotion. He liked to begin each picture with a precise charcoal or pencil sketch, then scrub and rub paint on the canvas in a blur of dazzling colours. Turner believed that everything could be shown as light and colour, rather than by line and shape. One of his most famous pictures, *Rain, Steam and Speed,* shows a steam-engine crossing a bridge over the river Thames on a stormy day – but is chiefly a swirl of cloudy, half-seen shapes, an impression of the enormous power of weather, river and machine.

When Turner died he left his paintings to the British nation. But the London art authorities stored all but the most famous of his pictures in a cellar, leaving them unexhibited for over a century. The few paintings that were known were greatly admired outside Britain, especially in France. French painters such as **Monet** were inspired by Turner's ideas and from this the art style of Impressionism was developed.

Jane Austen, from an engraving made in her lifetime.

Turner's famous painting *Rain, Steam and Speed.*

TURNER: Monet 46

Like all Constable's paintings of landscape, this one tries to suggest feelings and emotions to us. The more we look at it, the more it affects our mood.

CONSTABLE, John

English painter 1776-1837

In the 1790s, when Constable began working as a painter, the people who bought art were chiefly interested in pictures of themselves, their families and their pets. Constable, however, painted landscapes, especially the fields, woods and streams of Suffolk, the English county where he was born. He was fascinated by the way light changes as clouds pass across the sky, and liked to show dramatic sky-scenes in his painting. He made careful studies of the shapes and form of clouds, and often spent days on a single patch of sky, getting the colours exactly right.

There are nearly always small figures in Constable's paintings, but he concentrated on the landscape. Like many Romantic artists and writers of his time, Constable believed that nature can reflect and focus our moods, that we have sympathy with landscape as we do with friends. He never went abroad, and his finest landscapes are of Suffolk and Hampstead, the areas he knew and loved best. But his ideas strongly influenced French Romantic painters and later the French Impressionists, such as **Monet**.

GRIMM, Jakob Ludwig Carl

German writer 1785-1863

and

GRIMM, Wilhelm Carl

German writer 1786-1869

The Grimm brothers wrote reference books on mythology, folklore, and law. The brothers are most famous, however, for their collection of folktales and legends now known as *Grimms' Fairy Tales*. They visited German villages and farms, asking people to tell stories they remembered hearing as children, which the brothers wrote down. The Grimms intended their book for adults, but the *Fairy Tales* became some of the best-loved children's stories ever published. There can be few European children who have never heard of Rumpelstiltskin, the Frog Prince, or the tailor who kills seven flies with one blow and then goes hunting giants.

Right: Little Red Riding Hood and "Granny", from one of the fairy tales collected by the Brothers Grimm.

CONSTABLE: Monet 46

ROSSINI, Gioacchino

Italian composer 1792-1868

Rossini wrote his first successful opera at the age of 18, and from then until he was 37 he composed two or three new operas every year. Some were grand and serious (for example *William Tell*); but most were comedies, whose musical wit few other composers have equalled. (Two of the best, and best known, are *Cinderella* and *The Barber of Seville*.)

In 1829 Rossini retired from opera-writing, and spent his time (and the fortune he had made from music) enjoying the good things of life. He wrote only songs and piano pieces until he was 70. Then he gathered his energy and composed one last large-scale work: *Petite messe solennelle* ("Little Solemn Mass"). In it, he set religious words to the same kind of uncomplicated, tuneful music as in his operas.

Every Rossini comic opera has a scene where all the characters line up at the front of the stage, singing about their feelings. This scene is from *The Barber of Seville*.

ROMANTICISM

Many nineteenth-century artists, composers and writers were Romantics. They put "romance" (fantasy) into their work, letting it go wherever their imagination led, as unpredictable and changing as people's emotions are in real life. Famous Romantic writers include the English poets Keats, Byron and Shelley, and the German poet and playwright Goethe. Turner and David are famous Romantic painters, while Beethoven and Berlioz are leading Romantic composers.

KEATS, John

English poet 1795-1821

Keats was one of the first Romantics, believing that writers should describe their emotions and feelings, and show the world through their own eyes. Whereas earlier poets had described such things as sunsets, flowers or storms just as they saw them, Keats' poems expressed the feelings the sights aroused in him, and how those sights fitted his own moods. His best-known poems are his odes: short lyric poems on one subject, including *Ode To Sleep*, *Ode to a Nightingale*, and *Ode on a Grecian Urn*. Many of his longer poems, for example *La belle dame sans merci* or *The Eve of St Agnes*, are also on the same theme: hopeless love.

A Greek urn (vase), the subject of one of Keats' most famous poems.

SCHUBERT, Franz

Austrian composer 1797-1828

Schubert learned music as a choirboy in Vienna, and at 16 became a teacher, like his father and brothers. But he soon gave up teaching and for the rest of his life he made a living by writing songs and piano music. He was often poor, and only survived thanks to loans from generous friends.

Schubert admired **Beethoven** and, like him, wrote symphonies, piano sonatas and string quartets. But most of his music is of a completely different kind. All through his life, he spent three or four evenings each week with friends – eating, playing games and, above all, singing and playing music. People called the parties "Schubertiads" after him. For the Schubertiads, Schubert wrote short piano pieces and songs. He wrote over 600 songs, and some – *The Erlking; The Trout; Hark, Hark, the Lark; To Music* – are among the best-loved of all his works.

BALZAC, Honoré de

French writer 1799-1850

Balzac wanted to write novels and stories to include every single kind of person, with an exact description of each one's appearance, way of life and character. He called the whole project *The Human Comedy*, and it contains over 50 volumes. His best-known book is *Father Goriot*, about an old man ill-treated by his daughters and left to die in a Paris lodging-house.

Left: Schubert wrote this joke piece for a violinist friend. People said in those days that violin strings were made from catgut – which explained the noise they made.

DUMAS, Alexandre, "Père"

French writer 1802-70

and

DUMAS, Alexandre, "Fils"

French writer 1824-95

DUMAS *père* (father), as he was called, wrote historical adventure novels. His heroes fight duels, foil villains and rescue beautiful ladies in distress. His best-known books are *The Count of Monte Cristo* and *The Three Musketeers*.

DUMAS *fils* (son) wrote plays and novels. His most famous work is *The Lady of the Camellias*, a sad story of a dying woman who gives up the man she loves. The composer **Verdi** made it into an opera, *La Traviata*, and in that form it remains one of the best-known love-stories ever told.

Two famous French writers: Dumas *père* (above) and *fils* (below).

HUGO, Victor-Marie

French writer 1802-85

Hugo won prizes for poetry while still at school, and was first successful with his plays, including *Hernani, Le*

SCHUBERT: Beethoven 28 DUMAS: Verdi 37

Left: The slums of Paris looked like this in the time of the writers Balzac and Hugo.

roi s'amuse and *Lucretia Borgia*. But he became more famous for his novels. *Notre Dame de Paris* is about Quasimodo, a deformed bell-ringer at the cathedral of Notre Dame, and Esmeralda, the beautiful gypsy girl he loves. *Les misérables* is about an innocent man condemned to life imprisonment. The novel, full of harsh descriptions of the suffering of the poor in 1850s Paris, was made into a highly successful 1980s musical on the London stage.

Other Hugo novels include *1793*, set during the French Revolution, and *The Toilers of the Sea*, about life in the fishing villages of eighteenth-century Guernsey, one of the islands in the Channel off the coast of France.

HAWTHORNE, Nathaniel

American novelist 1804-64

Hawthorne wrote short stories and children's books, including *A Wonder Book* and *Tanglewood Tales*, retelling stories from Greek myth. But he is best known for his adult novels about a community of Puritan settlers (like his own ancestors), in New England, USA. His most famous book is *The Scarlet Letter*, a savage story about a woman tormented by local people after she has an illegitimate child, and about her husband's efforts to make the child's father (a local minister) publicly admit his "guilt".

ANDERSEN, Hans Christian

Danish writer 1805-75

Andersen is best known for a set of fairy tales for children. He took ideas from folk tales, and adapted them into 168 new stories of his own. Two favourites are *The Snow Queen*, about a boy, kidnapped by the wicked Snow Queen, who is saved when kindness melts the ice-splinter she has lodged in his heart, and *The Ugly Duckling*, about a little bird who hates himself because he is so ugly, compared with other ducklings, but who grows into a beautiful swan.

This illustration shows the moment in Hans Andersen's story when the Ugly Duckling, now grown up, realizes that he is a swan after all.

MENDELSSOHN (BARTHOLDY), (Jacob Ludwig) Felix

German composer 1809-47

Mendelssohn began to show musical genius at the age of 10, playing piano and violin, conducting orchestras and composing. When he was 16 he wrote an Octet which to everyone who heard it was the finest piece of chamber music since **Mozart**'s time. A year later he composed an overture to **Shakespeare**'s play *A Midsummer Night's Dream*, which carried his fame as a composer all over Germany.

Mendelssohn's travels around Europe inspired many of his best-known works, for example the "Italian" and "Scottish" symphonies and the *Hebrides* overture, a musical picture of the sea. Soon after these successes, he was appointed conductor of the orchestra in Leipzig, Germany. He conducted new works by the best living composers, and rediscovered and played music by earlier musicians, especially **Bach**, **Handel** and Mozart, which had been long neglected. He organized concerts, played the piano and gave lessons. Once or twice a year he went on concert tours. The strain of this hectic life wore Mendelssohn out, and he had a fatal stroke.

Left: Fingal's Cave off the coast of Scotland: the scenery which gave Mendelssohn the idea for his *Hebrides* Overture.

POE, Edgar Allan

US poet and writer 1809-49

Poe was admired as a poet as well as a writer and successfully published a collection of poems, *The Raven and Other Poems*. But he is best known for his mysteries and horror-stories.

Poe liked to set his stories in dark, lonely houses at night or during storms, with people being buried alive, going mad or unexpectedly meeting supernatural and ghastly beings. Many of his stories have been turned into terrifying films, such as *The Pit and the Pendulum* (about a prisoner being psychologically tortured by a blade swinging like a pendulum above him), and *The Fall of the House of Usher* (about a madman who buries his sister alive).

Edgar Allan Poe.

CHOPIN, Fryderyk (Frédéric)

Polish/French musician 1810-49

Chopin trained as a pianist and composer, and by the age of 19 he was giving concerts throughout Europe. Although he seldom went back to Poland, he remembered his homeland with affection, filling his music with sounds based on Polish folksongs and dances.

Chopin wrote two piano concertos and three sonatas but, apart from these, most of his works are short, like poems in sound: nocturnes, études ("studies"), waltzes, preludes, mazurkas and polonaises.

MENDELSSOHN: Bach 22 Handel 23 Mozart 26 Shakespeare 16

SCHUMANN, Robert

German composer 1810-56

and

SCHUMANN, Clara

German pianist and composer 1819-96

As a young man, ROBERT SCHUMANN went to study with a famous piano teacher of the time, lodged in the man's house – and fell in love with his daughter CLARA, a girl of 11 who was also studying to be a concert pianist. They had to wait a dozen years before they could marry, and in the meantime Robert became a music critic and composer instead of a pianist. He wrote dozens of works for piano, which Clara played on world-wide concert tours.

Robert and Clara Schumann, from a drawing made before Robert's tragic illness.

All his life, Robert Schumann suffered from depression. In 1854 he tried to commit suicide, and was put in a mental asylum, where he died two years later. His death left Clara with seven children to bring up, as well as her musical career touring, teaching and playing. She was one of the finest – and busiest – of all nineteenth-century pianists, but still insisted on spending three months each summer and three months each winter at home with her family.

Robert Schumann composed symphonies, sonatas, choral works, songs, and many piano works, including sonatas and a concerto for his beloved wife.

LISZT, Ferenc (Franz)

Hungarian musician 1811-86

Liszt gave his first public piano-recital at the age of 9; by 15 he was famous all over Europe, and for the next twenty years he led a life as busy and glamorous as that of any twentieth-century pop star. Few pianists have ever equalled him. Cartoonists of his day showed him as a lion-tamer making the piano beg, or as a magician conjuring flowers and butterflies from the keyboard.

But there was more to Liszt than showmanship. In 1848 he retired from concert-giving for nearly fifteen years, and became musician-in-charge at the royal court at Weimar (now in East Germany), conducting the orchestra and composing. Other composers (such as **Wagner**) admired the way he experimented with ways to make orchestral sound suggest emotion, and imitated it. Musicians today respect him chiefly for those experiments. Other people remember him as a piano genius, and his piano works (a sonata, two concertos, and pieces picturing everything from waterfalls and gardens to lovers whispering and devils dancing) still delight and amaze most people who hear them.

LISZT: Wagner 36

Charles Dickens writing at his desk.

DICKENS, Charles John Huffham

English writer 1812-70

Dickens began his writing career as a law reporter for a London paper. In 1837 he published his first novel, *The Pickwick Papers*, about a group of friends led by a fat, cheerful character called Mr Pickwick. It was so popular that Dickens was able to give up journalism and become a full-time novelist.

Dickens wrote a best-seller each year for several years. Often, he based his characters on people he had met or seen as a reporter. The hero of *Oliver Twist* lives in the London underworld, learning to be a pickpocket yet trying to stay honest even though he knows hardly anyone but beggars and criminals. The hero of *Nicholas Nickleby* begins as a teacher in a grim boarding school, then becomes an actor and finally a clerk in a counting-house. With stories like these Dickens gave vivid pictures of the best and worst aspects of the life of his time. Many middle-class people were made to realize for the first time that poverty, cruelty and suffering existed in nineteenth-century Britain.

As Dickens' fame grew, he began to tour Britain and the USA, reading to audiences, to raise money for charity. He planned new novels while he travelled, and wrote them down each summer, when touring ended. Some of his finest books were written in this way, including the novel he thought was his masterpiece: *David Copperfield*, about an unhappy, ill-treated boy who grew up to become a successful writer.

The Valkyries riding to war, to carry the bodies of dead warriors to feast with the gods.

WAGNER, Richard

German composer 1813-83

Wagner admired **Shakespeare**'s plays and **Beethoven**'s symphonies, and set out to equal them. He wrote plays based on German folk-tales and myths, and set them to music in which the orchestra was not just an accompaniment for the singers (as in many other operas of the time), but had important musical things to say, as vital to the drama as any of the people on the stage.

Wagner's "music-dramas" (as he called them) were never popular enough to pay their way. He had to raise money by giving concerts, performing extracts from his music-dramas, such as the triumphant *Ride of the Valkyries* (a musical picture of warrior goddesses galloping to battle).

WAGNER: Beethoven 28 Shakespeare 16

Wagner dreamed of a theatre of his own, specially constructed for performances of his masterpiece, the 15-hour long *Ring of the Nibelungs*, whose cast included gods and giants as well as mortals, and whose orchestra was twice the normal size. In 1876, after ten years' work, the theatre, built at Bayreuth in Germany, was complete. It is the home of a huge festival every year.

The overwhelming power of Wagner's music, and his strong views, not only about music and drama but on such matters as race, sex, religion and politics, made him as many enemies as friends. People still tend to love or loathe his works. But whatever people's reactions, no one now doubts that in his music-dramas he rivalled Shakespeare and Beethoven, exactly as he planned.

This scene, from Verdi's opera *Nabucco*, shows the Israelite slaves kept by the cruel king in Babylon. The opera shows how God released the slaves and punished the king.

VERDI, Giuseppe

Italian composer 1813-1901

As a boy Verdi learned singing, organ-playing and composition, and by the time he was 18 he was in charge of all the musical activities in his local town (Busseto). He worked as a church musician and band conductor for ten more years, until the third of his operas, *Nabucco*, about the mythical Old Testament king **Nebuchadnezzar**, was a success and he decided to make opera-writing his career. In the next eleven years he wrote twenty more operas, and they made him world-famous. Many used stories from history, for example *Joan of Arc*; others, including the most popular – *Rigoletto, Il Trovatore, La Traviata*, were based on books or plays.

In 1860 Verdi slowed down the pace of his opera-writing. He took up other things – for five years, for example, he was a member of parliament – and after only three more operas (including *Aida*, performed to celebrate the opening of the Suez Canal in 1870) he announced his retirement. Fifteen years later, however, when he was over 70, his publisher persuaded him to write two more operas, the comedy *Falstaff* and the tragedy *Othello*. They were based on two plays by **Shakespeare** – *The Merry Wives of Windsor* and *Othello* – and they renewed Verdi's fame as the greatest opera-composer of his time.

VERDI: Nebuchadnezzar 410 Shakespeare 16

Portrait of Charlotte Brontë, by J H Thompson. (© The Brontë Society)

BRONTË SISTERS

English writers 19th century

There were three sisters: CHARLOTTE (1816-55), EMILY (1818-48) and ANNE (1820-49). They lived with their father and brother in the vicarage of the lonely moorland village of Haworth in Yorkshire, England. From an early age, Charlotte and Emily made up stories, wrote them in tiny books (the size of matchboxes) and illustrated them with their own drawings. When they grew up they worked as teachers, but went on writing and published novels, poems and stories to earn money.

Between them the sisters wrote some of the finest nineteenth-century English novels. Charlotte Brontë's best-known book is *Jane Eyre*, about a lonely governess who falls in love with her employer. Emily's masterpiece was *Wuthering Heights*, about a tempestuous and unhappy love-affair. It was her only novel – she died of tuberculosis in 1848. Anne wrote two short novels, *Agnes Grey* and *The Tenant of Wildfell Hall*, but she too died of tuberculosis before she could equal her sisters' work.

At the time when the Brontës wrote, publishers preferred books to be written by men, not women, and so the sisters used male pen-names. Charlotte called herself Currer Bell, with the initials C.B., just like her own, Emily was Ellis Bell and Anne was Acton Bell.

Moby-Dick taking his revenge on the whalers who hunt him down.

ELIOT, George

English writer 1819-80

"George Eliot" was the pen-name of Mary Ann Evans. She was one of the most forward-looking thinkers of her time, disbelieving in God, saying that women and men were equal and that life in the slums of nineteenth-century industrial England was degrading and pitiful. She put these and other ideas into novels, which were among the most powerful and political of her time. They are also full of exact detail of people's lives: reading them is like looking through a window into nineteenth-century England and seeing just what life was like. Her best-known novels are *The Mill on the Floss, Middlemarch, Adam Bede* and *Silas Marner*.

MELVILLE, Herman

US novelist 1819-91

Melville admired the fine language of the Bible and **Shakespeare**, and set out to imitate it in his novels. Most are sea-stories: powerful tales of humans pitting themselves against

MELVILLE: Shakespeare 16

waves, storms and the terror of being lost at sea. His best-known book, considered one of the finest of all American novels, is *Moby-Dick*. It tells of Ahab, the captain of a whaling ship the *Pequod*, who is obsessed by the need to hunt down and kill a huge white whale that has bitten off his leg. In Melville's mind the whale stands for fate, and Ahab's battles against it stand for the struggle all human beings face in life.

Left: The writer Gustave Flaubert.

FLAUBERT, Gustave

French writer 1821-80

Flaubert set out to write in a calm, unflurried style: he thought that a writer's words should flow as easily as a stream, neither hurrying nor drowning the reader. He filled his books with descriptions of scenery, houses and furniture, so that his readers could imagine the exact background to each of his characters' lives.

This gentle, quiet writing contrasts magnificently with the tempestuous events in Flaubert's stories and the torrents of emotion which engulf his characters. His best-known book is *Madame Bovary*, about a country doctor's wife who becomes bored and seeks a lover – with disastrous results.

DOSTOEVSKY, Fyodor Mikhailovich

Russian writer 1821-81

Until Dostoevsky was 40, he led a miserable life. His father was murdered; he himself was sentenced to death for being a revolutionary, and only at the last moment sent to prison in Siberia instead. He wrote about his prison experience in a book called *The House of the Dead*. On his release, finding himself in debt, he took to gambling, and in 1867 he had to move abroad to escape the people to whom he owed money.

It is perhaps not surprising that Dostoevsky's novels deal with the unhappy side of human life. He believed that there are two sides to every person's nature, dark and light, and that they are constantly battling for control. His writing showed how well he understood human feelings. One of his finest novels is *Crime and Punishment*, which shows the conflict between dark and light in the mind of a penniless student. The student nerves himself to commit a murder, and is then punished – not by being arrested but by having to live with the memory of what he has done and by guilt-feelings which drive him near to madness.

The sad, grim Dostoevsky, drawn when he first went to live abroad.

At the dances where the Strauss family played, people wore gorgeous clothes and danced the fashionable, swirling waltz.

STRAUSS FAMILY

Austrian musicians and composers 19th-20th centuries

The Strauss family lived in Vienna, at a time when it was one of the busiest cities in Europe, and the heart of the glittering Austro-Hungarian Empire. The Strausses made fortunes providing light music for people's enjoyment. They hired out dance-bands and orchestras, conducted them and wrote music – chiefly waltzes and polkas, the fashionable dances of the time.

The most talented composer in the family was JOHANN STRAUSS II (1825-99), so-called to distinguish him from his father JOHANN I (1804-49). He wrote mainly waltzes, and earned the nickname "The Waltz King". His 400 waltzes include such favourites as *The Blue Danube, Roses from the South* and *The Emperor Waltz*. He also wrote polkas, with novelty effects to tickle people's ears: the *Champagne Polka* is full of popping corks; in the *Pizzicato Polka* the string players pluck their instruments instead of bowing; and the *Explosions Polka* uses fireworks.

Other well-known composers in the family were Johann's brothers JOSEF (1827-70) and EDUARD (1835-1916).

IBSEN, Henrik Johan

Norwegian playwright 1828-1906

Ibsen's first two successful plays were *Brand*, a tragedy modelled on those of **Shakespeare**, *and Peer Gynt*, about a man's encounters with trolls, witches and devils, who is saved from Hell only by the love of the woman he has ignored all his life. *Peer Gynt* is well known partly because Edvard Grieg (1843-1907) wrote music for it.

After *Peer Gynt* Ibsen began to write plays about the life and ideas of his time. He set his stories in ordinary Norwegian towns, and based his characters on exactly the sort of people who were his audience. His dramas were like real life, and the subjects he dealt with were the problems people might read about in newspapers or discuss with friends, but hardly expected to see acted in the theatre. *A Doll's House* is about women's rights; *Ghosts* is about a family destroyed by guilt over the sexually transmitted disease syphilis;

IBSEN: Shakespeare 16 Shaw 50

An Enemy of the People is about a man who fights to end bribery and corruption in his local town.

Ibsen also wrote about the private unhappiness of his characters. The heroine in *Hedda Gabler* is a woman driven mad by the need to dominate every man she meets, while the hero of *The Master Builder* comes to realize that his lifelong success is because he is a bully and a coward, not the genius he once thought himself.

Ibsen had a stroke in 1900, which ended his writing, but his work influenced many other European writers including **Shaw**.

A scene from Ibsen's *Enemy of the People*, about a man who tries to make the local council close down a polluted water supply.

TOLSTOY, Leo Nikolaevich

Russian writer 1828-1910

Tolstoy was a generous landowner. He built schools and hospitals for his workers, and introduced modern methods of farming. But he won fame as a writer, and for two great novels in particular, which rank with the finest in all world literature. *War and Peace* is about the invasion of Russia by **Napoléon I**, shown through the lives of three aristocratic families. *Anna Karenina* tells of the doomed love-affair between a young officer, Count Vronsky, and Anna, an unhappy wife whose husband refuses to give her a divorce.

In 1879 Tolstoy gave up his wealth to live like a hermit. He announced that governments and churches should be abolished, which caused the authorities to ban many of his books. But he had become one of Russia's best-loved writers, and after his death his birthplace, Yasnaya Polyana, was established as a place of pilgrimage.

TOLSTOY: Napoléon I 451

Leo Tolstoy.

DICKINSON, Emily

US poet 1830-86

From the age of 30, Dickinson was a "recluse". She never left her home, saw few visitors, and kept up her friendships chiefly by letter. She poured out her feelings in poetry, and her poems are ranked with the finest ever written in English. She wrote about nature, love, sorrow and, above all, religion. She was a mystic: someone who thinks about the nature of God and about how human beings can understand and relate to it. Her poems are short and simple, and many twentieth-century poets have admired and imitated them.

BRAHMS, Johannes

German composer 1833-97

Although Brahms' parents were poor, they managed to pay for their musically talented son to have piano lessons, and were happy for him to practise music for seven or eight hours each day. By the time Brahms was 19 his playing and composing impressed the most important musicians of the day. One of them, **Schumann**, even called Brahms **Beethoven**'s heir, and the genius German music had been waiting for. This reputation later led to a war of words between Brahms' champions and those of the composer **Wagner**, whose supporters regarded *his* music as the greatest of the century.

Brahms spent nine months of each year at home in Vienna, composing, conducting or playing at concerts and meeting friends. Two or three times a year he went on concert tours, and every summer he took a month's holiday in the Austrian Alps, Switzerland or Italy, often working on new pieces while he was away. He composed four symphonies, four concertos, and other large-scale works (for example *A German Requiem*, for soloists, chorus and orchestra), which spread his fame throughout the world. But his favourite music was on a smaller scale. Brahms wrote dozens of songs, piano pieces, short orchestral pieces and, above all, chamber music – often written for himself and his friends to play.

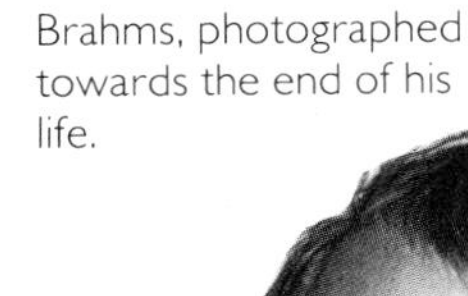

Brahms, photographed towards the end of his life.

BRAHMS: Beethoven 28 Schumann 35 Wagner 36

DEGAS, Hilaire Germain Edgar

French artist 1834–1917

Degas was the son of a banker, and had enough money to do as he liked. He travelled to the Far East, where he studied Japanese prints; he also experimented with the new hobby of photography. In the 1870s he began painting subjects from modern life, similar to the scenes people liked to see in photographs – unlike the works of most artists of his time.

Like the Impressionists with whom Degas exhibited, he focused on the world of entertainment and the leisure activities of ordinary people. He was fascinated by the effect movement has on light and colour. He painted racecourse scenes, concentrating on the crowds as well as on the blurred shapes of horses and jockeys rushing past. He painted acrobats and circus performers working, dressing and bathing. Later, he turned to the theatre. His paintings and pastel sketches showed actors, singers, comedians, the orchestra and, above all, ballet dancers exercising and performing.

When Degas was 60 he began to go blind, and found sculpture easier than painting. One of his first sculptures caused a scandal. It showed a young ballet dancer, modelled in wax, but wearing a real ballet dress, complete with tutu (stiff skirt) and shoes. At the time people thought the mixture of "art" and "reality" shocking, and called Degas a fraud. But tastes in art soon change: nowadays this statue, along with Degas' other sculptures and pastels of ballet dancers, are among his most popular works.

TWAIN, Mark

US writer 1835-1910

Mark Twain was the pen-name used by Samuel Langhorne Clemens, a steamboat pilot on the river Mississippi in the southern USA. He wrote humorous articles for newspapers about the characters he met on his river-trips. "Mark Twain" was what sailors shouted when testing the river depth. (It means two fathoms, or five metres, deep.)

In 1865, at the end of the American Civil War, Twain left the Mississippi and went to look for gold in Nevada, but had no luck. He travelled abroad and published a witty and successful account of his travels, and was soon one of the best-known journalists in the USA. Two favourites among his many books are *Tom Sawyer* and *Huckleberry Finn*, both based on memories of his childhood in the country along the Mississippi. Unlike the brave, keen heroes of most children's books of the time, the main characters in both books were lazy and mischievous, so that when the novels were first published many people thought them unsuitable for children.

An illustration of Tom Sawyer's lazy days on the Mississippi.

CÉZANNE, Paul

French painter 1839-1906

Cézanne specialized in painting landscapes (especially those of his native Provence, in the south of France), still-lifes, and groups of people enjoying their leisure. Other Impressionists, such as Manet, studied the effect of light on their subjects. But Cézanne was more interested in the geometric shapes (circles, cubes and triangles) that give an object or scene its depth and volume, and how this could be shown just by using colour. He was virtually unknown as a painter in his lifetime, but influenced the ideas of **Picasso**, and so helped to begin the Cubist movement.

Cézanne's painting *Still Life With Tureen* uses colour to bring out the geometric shapes in ordinary objects – the kind most people hardly look at twice.

CÉZANNE: Picasso 60

The Battle of Borodino. The *1812 Overture* tries to give a musical picture of scenes like this.

TCHAIKOVSKY, Piotr Ilyich

Russian composer 1840-93

Tchaikovsky forced himself to lead a busy public life. He wrote ballets and operas for the leading theatres in Russia, and went on conducting-tours in Russia, Germany, Italy, France, England and the USA. He was a famous man, giving newspaper interviews, appearing at concerts and parties, writing articles and joining committees. But he seems to have hated every minute of it, preferring a quiet life at home working at his music. He liked to compose in the morning, walk in the afternoon, then relax in the evening by playing cards, or by writing letters (some to his friend, the widow Nadezhda von Meck, who helped him with money, on the unusual condition that they never met).

Tchaikovsky loved reading – and he often wrote music based on the books he read. Two of his orchestral works (*Hamlet* and *Romeo and Juliet*), for example, are based on the plays by **Shakespeare** and his ballets *Swan Lake, The Nutcracker* and *The Sleeping Beauty* are based on fairy tales. He also wrote the *1812 Overture* (a musical picture of a huge battle between the Russians and French at the time of **Napoléon I**), and symphonies and concertos which are among the most famous pieces of classical music ever composed.

Cartoon of Zola, at the end of his life, still working even though exhausted by all the books he has written.

ZOLA, Émile

French novelist 1840-1902

Zola began his writing career as a journalist, and that training taught him how to express ideas in a few well-chosen words. He became famous when his novel *Thérèse Raquin* was published in 1868 – a grim story about a woman and her lover who plot to murder the woman's husband. Zola carefully researched the settings and characters for his

TCHAIKOVSKY: Napoléon I 451 Shakespeare 16

books, to ensure that his stories would be realistic and convincing.

Zola's concern with the social problems of France in the nineteenth-century as it gradually became industrialized shows in the themes of some of his greatest novels: *Nana*, about a girl driven by poverty to become a prostitute; *La terre* ("the earth") about grim peasant life; and *Germinal*, about coal-miners striking for better conditions. He also wrote a celebrated article, *J'Accuse*, in which he attacked the army for falsely imprisoning Alfred Dreyfus, an officer of Jewish blood who had been wrongly convicted of selling secrets to Germany.

Rodin's famous sculpture *The Kiss*.

RODIN, Auguste

French sculptor 1840-1917

Impressed by the statues of such Renaissance masters as **Donatello** and **Michelangelo**, Rodin made up his mind to start a new Renaissance in sculpture, a nineteenth-century "Golden Age".

Rodin was an eccentric (unusual) person, with a quirky, unique way of looking at the world – and he insisted on putting his own ideas into his sculptures, whatever public opinion made of them. For example, instead of showing the writer **Balzac** as a dignified gentleman in formal dress, as most sculptors of the time would have done, Rodin showed him in the huge monk's habit he usually wore to work in. This made Balzac's body into one huge humped shape, perhaps to suggest Rodin's idea of the writer's towering genius. By contrast, Rodin's monument to the novelist and poet **Hugo** showed him naked.

When Rodin was 40, he began a project that was to last for the rest of his life. He was asked to make a special door for a museum in Paris. He never finished it, but he did model 200 human figures, many of them twisted in agony, waiting at the gates of Hell, as in **Dante**'s poem *The Inferno*. Rodin had made full-size versions of only a few of the models before he died, and they are now among his best-known works – and some of the most famous sculptures ever made. *The Kiss* shows a pair of lovers, and *The Thinker* shows a naked man, sitting pondering with his arm raised to support his chin.

RODIN: Balzac 32 Dante 8 Donatello 10 Hugo 32 Michelangelo 12

MONET, Claude

French painter 1840-1926

Monet grew up in the French seaside town of Le Havre. Boudin, Monet's first art teacher, made his pupils go into the port and paint not just boats and lobster-pots but also the reflection of sun on water or the effects of wind on the sky. This gave Monet a fascination for painting light and colour which lasted all his life.

In 1872 Monet painted a picture called *Impression: Sunrise.* His idea was to show not a real scene, but an impression of the different shades and colours as the rising sun lit the sea and sky. A critic, seeing the painting's title, nicknamed Monet and his friends "Impressionist painters". He painted seaside scenes, a set of pictures of Rouen Cathedral in France, many views of cornfields, and scenes of the flowers, especially water lilies, in his garden. When you stand close to his pictures, they seem no more than blurs and streaks of paint. But once you step back, they

FRENCH IMPRESSIONIST PAINTERS

The Impressionist painters took their name from Monet's picture *Impression: Sunrise.* Rather than paint exact likenesses of objects, they showed impressions of the patterns of light and colour their eyes saw. The main Impressionists were Cézanne, Degas, Manet, Monet, Pissarro, Renoir and Sisley. At first, their pictures were hardly popular; they are now among the best-loved paintings of all.

Monet's painting *Impression: Sunrise* – the beginning of a new style in art.

come into focus, and the feeling is less like looking at pictures than at real views in real sunlight.

DVOŘÁK, Antonin

Czech composer 1841-1904

When Dvořák was born, there was no such country as Czechoslovakia. It was known as Bohemia, part of the huge Austro-Hungarian empire. Its people were fanatically patriotic (proud of their country). They dreamed of self-government and kept their own language, customs and folk-music alive.

Dvořák filled his own early compositions with lilting tunes and rhythms taken from Bohemian folk-music. It is as if evening-suited musicians suddenly jump up and begin to dance. His first successful work was an opera, followed by songs and dances (for example the *Slavonic Dances*) written in folk-dance style. His fame spread, and people asked him for longer works. He wrote nine symphonies (including the *New World* symphony), concertos, choral music and many other orchestral works, among them the *Carnival* overture and *Serenade for Strings*.

RENOIR, Pierre-Auguste

French painter 1841-1919°

Born in Limoges, a French town famous for decorated china, Renoir worked as a ceramicist – he painted flowers, trees and abstract patterns onto cups and dishes before they were glazed and fired.

When Renoir was 33 he saw **Monet**'s painting *Impression: Sunrise*, and it changed his whole way of painting. He was soon one of the leading Impressionist painters. He painted country scenes – flowers, trees, and groups of people enjoying themselves (for example the happy crowd at a riverside restaurant called *Le Moulin de la Galette*).

The idea of painting scenes of leisure and entertainment appealed to many Impressionists and their friends – for example **Degas**. But above all, Renoir painted pictures of women. They are either dressed in flowery clothes, or naked, and look relaxed and happy. Few other artists have ever equalled Renoir as a painter of nudes - perhaps because the colours he used for skin and flesh are as varied and beautiful as those of real life.

JAMES, Henry

US writer 1843-1916

James was born in the USA, but spent most of his life in Europe. He wrote travel books, essays, plays, novels and over 200 short stories.

Most of James' books are about people unsure of themselves, who try to settle down by moving to a new country or by forming a relationship with someone else. Many describe Americans visiting European cities, or travelling home to find that the old American ways they remembered have changed while they were away. His best-known books are *The Wings of the Dove*, *Portrait of a Lady*, *The Ambassadors*, *Washington Square*, *The Golden Bowl* and *The Turn of the Screw* (a ghost story about two haunted children, made into an opera by Benjamin **Britten**).

The writer Henry James.

RENOIR: Degas 42; Monet 46 JAMES: Britten 74

ROUSSEAU, Henri

French artist 1844-1910

Rousseau is sometimes nicknamed Douanier Rousseau to distinguish him from the thinker Jean Jacques **Rousseau**. *Douanier* means "customs officer", which is what Rousseau was until he retired and took up painting. He used a style called "primitive" because it was simple and natural.

Rousseau liked bright colours and clear outlines: he wanted the trees in his pictures to look like trees, the flowers like flowers, the animals like animals. But he also often painted forests, or banks of tropical flowers – and lurking among the leaves are butterflies, tigers, apes and enormous bees – exactly as he imagined them.

Rousseau took no notice of the great artistic movements of his time, such as Impressionism, and his work was admired by many other painters who developed his ideas, including **Picasso**, **Toulouse-Lautrec** and **Renoir**.

Father Junier's Cart, a painting by Henri Rousseau. He used bright, simple colours and straightforward lines in all his paintings.

ROUSSEAU: Picasso 60 Renoir 44 Rousseau, J J 348 Toulouse-Lautrec 54

GAUGUIN, Paul

French painter 1848-1903

Gauguin was a stockbroker until, at the age of 35, he decided to give the rest of his life to art. He cut himself off from anything which reminded him of his earlier life – including his wife and five children. He gave up everything which was not essential, and lived in poverty.

Gauguin's paintings outraged art critics because they showed things not as they were, but as his imagination saw them. He liked to combine colours on the canvas to create unusual, dream-like effects. He felt, for example, that if the artist "saw" a yellow sea, or red grass, that was how it should be painted.

In 1891 Gauguin made another unexpected move – in search of the paradise of his dreams. He went to Tahiti in the South Seas, where the air was clear, the colours were bright, and life was simple and childlike. He painted people going about their

PRIMITIVE PAINTERS

While most Primitive painters had art training, they made their pictures simple, as if a child or an untrained adult had painted them. The idea was to make them as unlike the great paintings of the past as possible. Well-known primitive painters include "Douanier" Rousseau in France, L.S. Lowry in Britain and Grandma Moses and Grant Wood in the USA. Other painters, including Cézanne, Gauguin, Klee, Munch and Picasso, used primitive ideas.

ordinary lives, working, playing, bathing – and these are the paintings for which he is still best known.

GAUDÍ, Antoni

Spanish architect 1852-1926

Gaudí's architecture is unlike any other style. Most buildings have straight edges, rectangles and flat surfaces; Gaudí's bulge and twist as if they were alive. He used a style called Art Nouveau ("new art"), popular at the end of the nineteenth century. It uses curling, twisting lines and leaf-like shapes, unlike the straight lines rectangles and squares of other art. Gaudí put the same ideas into architecture. One of his blocks of flats seems to flop and ooze like a cream-filled sponge-cake; another has drainpipes and chimneys that curl like vines. His best-known work is all in his native city, Barcelona.

This block of flats in Barcelona shows the natural, waving curves Gaudí liked to use in his architecture – more like a cream-filled cake than the straight-edged buildings we see in most cities.

VAN GOGH, Vincent

Dutch painter 1853-90

Van Gogh began painting seriously in 1880, when he was 27. At first he painted peasants, working people, miners, tramps and drunks. Then he moved to Paris, where he met French Impressionist painters, and from there to Arles in the south of France. He painted sunny landscapes, orchards, wheatfields, meadows and vases filled with flowers. He used dazzling colours and, for extra impact, he often put on the paint with a knife or his fingers, in thick streaks that jutted from the canvas. Some of Van Gogh's pictures from this time, for example *Sunflowers* or *Bridge at Arles*, are among the most famous works ever made.

All his life, Van Gogh suffered from depression. In 1888, he had a terrible argument with the painter **Gauguin**, who was staying with him at the time. Rather than attack his friend, he turned his anger on himself, and cut off part of his ear. Soon afterwards, convinced that he was a danger to society, he went as a voluntary patient into a lunatic asylum. He spent a year there, painting chairs, his pipe, his straw hat, and above all the trees, flowers and birds of the asylum gardens. But he could find no peace, and in 1890, in a fit of black depression, he shot himself dead.

Van Gogh's painting *Siesta*.

VAN GOGH: Gauguin 48

WILDE, Oscar Fingall O'Flahertie Wills

Irish writer 1854-1900

Wilde delighted in shocking people, in doing exactly the opposite of what polite society approved. In London, where he worked as a writer and magazine editor, he was famous for his wit. Some of his comments were funny, but others were insulting, and Wilde made enemies as well as friends. He was accused of being homosexual, which in those days was a crime in Britain, and after two trials Wilde was sent to prison.

Wilde's writings include a novel in the style of **Poe** – *The Picture of Dorian Gray* – a collection of poems, and several successful plays, including *Lady Windemere's Fan* and, his best-known work, *The Importance of Being Earnest*. This is one of the happiest, funniest plays ever written in English, about a young man who leads a double life – as himself, and as his cleverer, much more adventurous self – and the confusion which results.

This picture, by the English artist Beardsley, shows a scene from Oscar Wilde's play *Salome*, from the Bible story about a girl who demanded the head of John the Baptist as a reward for dancing.

SHAW, George Bernard

Irish writer 1856-1950

Until Shaw was 38 he earned his living as a London critic of music, art and drama. He had ideas on all kinds of subjects, and gave talks on vegetarianism, the evils of drink and tobacco, and, especially, on politics. He was one of the first Socialists, devoted to bringing equal rights to people of all social classes.

Shaw's first play was produced in 1892, and from then on he worked chiefly as a playwright. He admired **Ibsen**, and wanted to write similar "plays of ideas", to make his audiences think as well as be entertained. But whereas Ibsen's plays were serious, Shaw put his message over in a light-hearted and witty way. In *Pygmalion*, for example, a bullying professor sets out to educate a poor flower-girl in polite speech until he can pass her off as a duchess. He trains her as one might train a parrot or a pet monkey, but she rebels. The clash of their characters and the arguments between them are fascinating – yet the audience never loses track of Shaw's basic ideas, that men and women are equal and that no one has the right to interfere in other people's lives.

Other well-known plays by Shaw include, *Caesar and Cleopatra*, the comedies *You Never Can Tell* and *The Doctor's Dilemma*, and the joky *Androcles and the Lion*.

By the time Bernard Shaw was 80, he was so famous that people could write him letters addressed simply to "Shaw", from anywhere in the world, and they would be delivered.

WILDE: Poe 34 SHAW: Ibsen 40

CONRAD, Joseph (Teodor Józef Konrad Korzeniowski)

Polish/British novelist 1857-1924

Conrad ran away to sea at 17, served as a sailor for 20 years, and then retired to become a writer. He settled in England, learned English, and wrote his books in English.

Conrad's novels are adventure stories, involving spies, crooks, sea voyages, wars and revolutions. But he used the adventure-story form to put across serious ideas, such as the way money or power corrupts people, whether there is any need for religious faith, or how a person's personality comes out in the way he or she behaves.

Conrad's best-known books are *Lord Jim, The Nigger of the Narcissus, Nostromo, The Secret Agent, Under Western Eyes* and *Heart of Darkness.*

This scene is from Puccini's fairy-tale opera *Turandot*, about a cruel princess in ancient China and the hero who outwits her.

ELGAR, Edward

English composer 1857-1934

Until Elgar was 42, he lived a quiet life. He taught the violin, conducted local choirs and orchestras and wrote music for anyone who asked. All the time, he sent works to London publishers, and had music performed at various festivals, hoping for fame. In 1899 it came at last, when his *Enigma Variations* (a set of musical "pictures" of his friends) had huge success in England and all over Europe.

From that time to the end of his life, Elgar was one of Britain's leading composers. He wrote symphonies, concertos and oratorios (including *The Dream of Gerontius*). He also wrote a famous march: *Pomp and Circumstance No 1 (Land of Hope and Glory)*, England's unofficial second national anthem.

PUCCINI, Giacomo

Italian composer 1858-1924

Apart from a few songs and a mass, written when he was a student, Puccini composed only operas. There are twelve of them, and they include three of the most popular ever written: *La Bohème, Tosca* and *Madam Butterfly*. They are stories of love, despair and revenge, with passionate orchestral music and glorious tunes. Some of the world's finest opera-singers specialize in Puccini – and few other composers offer them such chances to show off their skills.

This silhouette (black cutout) shows Sherlock Holmes' famous hat (called a "deerstalker" because it was invented for hunters not detectives), and his curly pipe.

DOYLE, Arthur Conan

English writer 1859-1930

Doyle invented the great detective character Sherlock Holmes, and wrote dozens of stories (for example, *The Adventures of Sherlock Holmes*) and novels, such as *The Hound of the Baskervilles*, about him. He modelled Holmes on one of his medical professors at university, and gave Holmes a way of analysing problems and working out solutions, very like the way doctors treat disease. Holmes' character was so convincing that many people took him for a real person, and letters are still sent to the address Doyle gave him – 221B, Baker Street, London.

Doyle also wrote several other kinds of book. *The Lost World*, for example is about explorers who find living dinosaurs and Stone Age people deep in the South American jungle. *The White Company* is set in the time of King Arthur's knights.

CHEKHOV, Anton Pavlovich

Russian writer 1860-1904

Chekhov began writing short, humorous stories when he was a medical student, and by the time he was 30 he had published several hundred. As a hobby he enjoyed watching plays, and began rewriting the stories as sketches (short plays) to begin evenings in the theatre.

Chekhov's first full-length play, *Ivanov*, written in 1887, was not a complete success. He wrote several one-act comedies, but it was his later plays that won him real fame – *The Seagull*, written in 1896, followed by *Uncle Vanya, The Cherry Orchard* and *The Three Sisters*. He concentrated on the lives of ordinary people; it was as if the stage were a living-room with one wall removed to let the audience eavesdrop.

The figure of Barrie's magic character Peter Pan, keeping a watchful eye on Captain Hook and the children in Never-Never Land.

BARRIE, James Matthew

Scottish writer 1860-1937

J M Barrie wrote several novels and plays for adults, but he is best known for the children's play *Peter Pan*. This is the story of a magic boy who takes three children flying through the air to Never-Never-Land, where they battle with a gang of pirates led by evil Captain Hook. Barrie wanted the money he earned from *Peter Pan* to go to the Great Ormond Street Hospital for Sick Children in London – a request which needed a special change to be made in English law, so that his work never goes out of copyright. This means that every time anyone pays to read, hear or see the play, a sick child benefits.

DEBUSSY, Claude

French composer 1862-1918

When Debussy was a student, people talked about two kinds of classical music above all others. "Absolute" music was sound organized to give pleasure by the sound patterns alone without suggesting outside ideas; "programme" music told a story or conjured up pictures in the listener's mind. At the same time, Impressionist painters like **Monet** and **Renoir** were showing that there was no need for art to produce exact likenesses, as with photography: impressions were enough, letting the spectator see things through the painter's eyes.

Debussy was interested in making a blend of "programme" music and impressionism. He wanted his works to suggest moods and feelings to his listeners. The "programme" was sometimes exact – a sound picture of a carnival, stormwinds or goldfish, for example. Usually, it was more vague: his works describe things like clouds moving in the sky or the restless, ever-shifting sea.

Debussy also composed many songs, trying to capture the exact mood of a poem in the music to which he set the words. He wrote Preludes and Images ("pictures") for piano, each a sound-picture of a single scene; He also wrote two of the best-known of all orchestral works, *Prélude à l'après-midi d'un faune* ("Prelude to a faun's afternoon"), suggesting a drowsy, lazy afternoon, and *La mer* ("The sea"), which conjures up the sea in all its moods, and the feelings aroused in people who watch it or sail on it.

DEBUSSY: Monet 46 Renoir 47

The colours and heavy lines in Munch's painting *The Scream* help to make us think of danger and terror.

MUNCH, Edvard

Norwegian painter 1863-1944

Munch was one of this century's best known "Expressionist" painters. Expressionists tried to make pictures not just of things (plants, people, landscapes), but of emotions and states of mind. They tried to suggest ideas such as uncertainty or hope, so that people looking at the picture would understand and share these emotions.

Many of Munch's paintings show sad, shabby people in rainy streets or empty rooms. His best-known work outside Norway is *The Scream*, showing a girl shrieking in terror as she runs across a bridge. He is also known for paintings of quite a different kind: landscapes and pictures of sunrise and sunset, full of the glow of Norwegian life. They are expressionist too, but instead of expressing fear or sorrow they suggest eagerness and hope.

The composer Debussy.

TOULOUSE-LAUTREC, Henri Marie Raymonde de

French artist 1864-1901

Jeanne Avril Dancing, by Henri Toulouse-Lautrec.

As a child, Toulouse-Lautrec was crippled in a riding accident. His bones stopped growing, and all his life he remained the size of an 11-year-old boy.

Toulouse-Lautrec lived in Monmartre in Paris, a district of restaurants, music-halls, bars and cheap lodging-houses. He painted prostitutes, beggars, barmen and waitresses, often trading a painting for a meal or a night's lodging. His works were cheerful and full of colour, and many stage stars of the time asked him to paint them for publicity posters.

Toulouse-Lautrec also painted circus and race-course scenes, like his friend **Degas**. But his best-known works are cartoons and paintings of the singers, audiences and dancing girls at the famous Paris nightclub, the Moulin Rouge.

One of the magnificent animal-pictures used to illustrate Kipling's *Jungle Book.*

STRAUSS, Richard Georg

German composer 1864-1949

Strauss was no relation of the Austrian family of waltz composers. He began writing music at the age of 6. When he was 24 he wrote *Don Juan*, one of his best-known works. He used a huge orchestra to make "sound pictures" of events in the story of Don Juan, a man who has affairs with hundreds of women but can never find true happiness.

Strauss wrote other orchestral works (for example *Don Quixote*, a "sound picture" of **Cervantes**' characters), and is also known for operas such as *Salomé* and *Der Rosenkavalier*, and for songs. He was still composing well into his 80s, after one of the longest and most successful careers in music.

KIPLING, Rudyard

English writer 1865-1936

Kipling was born in India, but went to school in England. He wrote about Indian life and customs in stories and poems. *Barrack-Room Ballads* was a collection of poems about the British Empire, and his single full-length novel, *Kim*, was about an Irish orphan brought up in India and sent to work for the British Secret Service in the Himalayas.

Kipling also wrote many books for children: *The Jungle Book*, about the adventures of Mowgli, the boy brought up by wolves in the Indian jungle; the *Just So Stories*, mock folk-tales with titles like "How The Rhinoceros Got His Skin"; *Puck of Pook's Hill*, a collection of myths; and *Stalky and Co.*, set in an English boarding school.

SIBELIUS, Jean

Finnish composer 1865-1957

When Sibelius was a student, Finland was ruled first by Sweden and then by Russia, and the Finns were struggling for political freedom. They were particularly anxious to keep alive their language and the great books written in it, for example the *Kalevala*, a collection of stories about the gods, giants and heroes of Finnish myth. Sibelius wrote several musical

TOULOUSE-LAUTREC: Degas 42 STRAUSS: Cervantes 16

Sibelius' music makes many listeners think of the quiet lakes and woods of his native country, Finland.

works based on *Kalevala* ideas, which so impressed the government that in 1897 he was given a life pension, enough money to live on so that he could concentrate on composing.

In the years that followed Sibelius wrote many other *Kalevala*-inspired works, including *Finlandia*. He wrote music for plays, songs, piano pieces and a popular violin concerto. But he is best known today for seven majestic symphonies, which critics of the time claimed were the finest orchestral works since those of **Beethoven** or **Brahms**.

NATIONALIST COMPOSERS

In the nineteenth and twentieth centuries, many composers wrote works using ideas from folk music, or making "sound pictures" of the landscapes and people of their native countries. These "Nationalist" composers include Albeniz (Spain), Borodin (Russia), Dvořák and Smetana (Czechoslovakia), Grieg (Norway), and, in the twentieth century, Bartók and Kodaly (Hungary), Vaughan Williams (England) and Takemitsu (Japan).

WELLS, Herbert George

English writer 1866-1946

Wells admired the science fiction written by the French writer, Jules Verne, and wrote on similar themes in English. His science-fiction stories, *The Time Machine, The Invisible Man, The First Men in the Moon* and *The War of the Worlds*, are still among his most popular books. However, Wells was also concerned with social as well as scientific progress, and he began writing novels in the style of **Dickens**, telling the lives of London people of his time. Among the best known of these are *Kipps*, about a shop-assistant who inherits a fortune and moves into "high society", and *The History of Mr Polly*, about a little man who has been a failure all his life but who suddenly and unexpectedly finds happiness.

Cartoon of H. G. Wells sitting comfortably in a great big chair.

SIBELIUS: Beethoven 28 Brahms 42 WELLS: Dickens 36

The Guggenheim Museum of Art in New York, designed by Frank Lloyd Wright. He said that he got the idea for it from a child's spinning top.

MATISSE, Henri

French artist 1869-1954

Matisse was impressed by **Gauguin**'s ideas, and used them in his work. In particular, he thought that the colours and shapes in a painting should be beautiful for their own sake, whether they were realistic or not. This was just about accepted for landscapes or interiors, but when Matisse painted his own wife with a green nose (*Portrait of Mme Matisse* 1905), people were shocked. At one exhibition a critic was so horrified that he called Matisse and his fellow-artists *fauves*, "wild beasts" – and the name stuck.

Matisse himself had no idea of wildness. He said that his paintings should be like armchairs, helping people to relax after a hard day's work. Two of his best-known works are *Dance* and *Music* (1909-10), in which the figures are not meant to be realistic, but are simply eye-pleasing arrangements of colour and lines.

In his 80s Matisse turned to a new art-form: papercuts. He trimmed coloured paper into shapes of dancing people, flying birds, trees and waving plants, and stuck them on to painted backgrounds.

Matisse's painting *The Dance*, suggests the grace and movement of dance by shapes alone.

WRIGHT, Frank Lloyd

US architect 1869-1959

Frank Lloyd Wright is considered one of the greatest US architects of the twentieth century. His career lasted for over 70 years: his last building, the Guggenheim Museum in New York, was finished in the year he died at the age of 90. During his lifetime, many other architects (for example **Le Corbusier**) were interested in the "machine look" – using "modern" shapes (simple cubes, that could be repeated endlessly into tower blocks and sky-scrapers) and in "modern" materials such as reinforced concrete, plastic and mirror-glass hung on rectangular steel frames. Wright preferred "natural" designs, and used wood and stone as well as concrete and steel. He designed homes for rich customers, calling them "prairie houses" because they were modelled on the one-storey log cabins of the early US settlers. For companies he designed factories and work-places –

MATISSE: Gauguin 48 WRIGHT: Le Corbusier 64

planned not as boxes for working in, but as "cathedrals of work". He designed spiral staircases, corridors that wound and twisted and fountains, pools and leafy, plant-filled indoor gardens.

PROUST, Marcel

French writer 1871-1922

Proust was a rich man, and spent his early life going to parties, concerts and art-exhibitions. But when he was 35 his mother died, and Proust was so shattered that he became a kind of hermit. He had his apartment sound-proofed to cut him off from the outside world, and spent his time in bed, writing, and seldom went out.

In the next 15 years Proust produced one book, *A la recherche du temps perdu* ("Remembrance of things past"), an enormous work of over 3,000 printed pages. Its characters are the kind of rich, culture-loving, party-going people Proust had known since boyhood. Their dinner-parties, friendships, gossip and scandals are shown through the eyes of a narrator called Marcel, a sensitive man rather like Proust himself.

Proust set out to describe in words every kind of sensation, from the smell of flowers to grief-feelings at someone's death. He thought that the slightest thing – a breeze on the cheek, the taste of cake dipped in tea, the scent of flowers – can flood our minds with memories, bringing the past vividly back to life. This "total recall" is what he aimed for in every sentence he wrote. He died soon after finishing the last page; his novel had consumed his life.

MONDRIAN, Piet

Dutch painter 1872-1944

Mondrian's early pictures showed landscapes, villages and farms; he was especially fond of trees. In 1911 he went to Paris, and came into contact with the Cubists (for example **Picasso**).

This led him to "abstract" or select from nature (taking only essential ideas of line and colour, and not the rest). Eventually he used shades of four colours only: red, yellow, blue and black. Each painting consists of coloured rectangles surrounded by thick black lines. The pictures are huge, and the colours glow like stained-glass panels with the sun behind them.

Mondrian's ideas impressed many other artists, especially in America, where a whole group of painters (called "abstract impressionists") learned from him. His work also affected the look of posters, linoleum, carpets and wall-decorations. The simple beauty of many modern interiors derives from his work.

The writer Marcel Proust.

Mondrian's painting *Composition with Red, Yellow and Blue* (1939-42) is small here, but in real life it fills the whole wall of a room.

MONDRIAN: Picasso 60

Arnold Schoenberg often gave lectures and radio talks, before concerts of his music, to explain what it meant.

SCHOENBERG, Arnold

Austrian/American composer 1874-1951

Schoenberg is one of the very few people to have invented a new way of composing classical music. He replaced the old system of keys and scales with a new 12-note method, in which no note or chord is more important than another. He was trying to find a musical equivalent of the way our emotions change from moment to moment, blurring into one another – and his music is a continuously shifting web of sound.

Composers everywhere eagerly studied Schoenberg's ideas and used them in their work. This means that although Schoenberg's own works are not widely known, (except for his string-orchestra piece, *Verklärte Nacht*, which is often performed), he is one of the most respected of all twentieth-century musical pioneers.

IVES, Charles

US composer 1874-1954

Although Ives trained as a musician, he worked in the insurance business. He wrote music at weekends and on the train to and from his office. He allowed few works to be performed in his lifetime, and felt free to make his music as unusual as he wanted. If a piano sonata needed a flute-tune, for example; an orchestra needed four brass bands (all playing different tunes); or a symphony needed a few bars of *Yankee Doodle*, that's what they got.

In 1919 Ives gave up composing altogether. He rammed his scores (finished bundles of music) into cupboards, stuffed them behind cushions and stacked them on shelves all over his house. It was not until the 1950s that people began discovering his works, and found them exciting and unique. He is now considered one of the USA's main composers, and most later musicians have learned from him.

RAVEL, Maurice Joseph

French composer 1875-1937

Ravel's main works are songs or piano pieces. But he was also a masterly writer for the orchestra, and nowadays such orchestral works as *Boléro* are popular throughout the world. He wrote two piano concertos (the second is played with the left hand only), a ballet (*Daphnis and Chlöe*), and two short operas. He also composed songs, and many piano pieces. They include *Gaspard de la nuit*, which he deliberately devised as one of the hardest piano works ever written, and the beautiful, short *Pavane pour une infante défunte*.

MANN, Thomas

German writer 1875-1955

Mann was fascinated by genius – why certain people become great writers, painters, actors or composers – and wrote about the way "ordinary" people are affected by geniuses. Mann's best-known books are *The Magic Mountain*, in which people in hospital discuss life, politics and the arts, *Death in Venice*, about a dying writer haunted by the sight of a beautiful boy, and *Dr Faustus*, about a composer who turns to black magic to help his work.

Heel-stamping, castanet-clicking flamenco: the folk-dance which Falla admired.

FALLA, Manuel de

Spanish composer and pianist 1876-1946

In the 1910s Falla worked in Paris, and his musical friends included **Debussy, Ravel, Stravinsky** and **Diaghilev**. His main interest was Spanish folk-music, and especially the rhythms and melodies of flamenco (Spanish gypsy dance music). His best-known works are the opera *La vida breve* ("Life is short"), the ballet *The Three-cornered Hat* and the concert opera *Master Peter's Puppet Show* (starring Don Quixote – see **Cervantes**).

LONDON, Jack

US writer 1879-1916

As a teenager London worked as a docker, seal-hunter and pirate. He took part in the Klondike Gold Rush, and tramped across the USA. At 19 he began to write stories for newspapers, usually about the gold-prospectors, fur-trappers, sailors and fishermen he had met on his travels. Soon he was one of the best-known writers in the USA.

London's stories are collected in many books, but he is also known for novels: *Before Adam* (set in Stone Age times), *The Sea Wolf* (about the struggle between a pirate and the city couple he kidnaps), and two animal stories *The Call of the Wild* (about a pet dog taken to the frozen north to be used as a sledge-dog) and *White Fang* (about a wild dog's brutal life on the fringes of human society).

FALLA: Cervantes 16 Debussy 53 Diaghilev 252 Ravel 58 Stravinsky 62

KLEE, Paul

Swiss artist 1879-1940

As a young man, Klee was interested in children's art, which he thought was of the purest kind, with its strong outlines, basic shapes, and bright, simple colours. Klee worked first as an etcher. He began painting for a living in 1919, when he was 40, and later worked as a painting-teacher.

Klee called his way of making pictures "taking a line for a walk" because he began each picture with a line or dot, and then extended it wherever the fancy took him, as if strolling through the countryside of his imagination. His pictures are simple and brightly coloured – a grown-up's magical version of the children's art he so much admired.

An illustration of Béla Bartók, aged about 50.

BARTÓK, Béla

Hungarian composer 1881-1945

Bartók trained to be a concert pianist, and at first composing was his second interest. But when he was 25 he went on a country holiday, and became fascinated by the folk-music played in the villages he visited. He collected folk-songs for twenty years, and became one of the world's leading experts.

In the 1920s Bartók began to use the rhythms and unusual scales of folk-song in his own compositions, blending them with ideas of his own. The result was unlike any music ever written before, and some people hated it. One critic said that Bartók's works were like the hammering of a lunatic blacksmith, and that listening to them was worse than going to the dentist. But Bartók went on working exactly as he chose, and gradually audiences learned to understand and enjoy his work. Nowadays he is considered a giant of twentieth-century music, and several of his works – *Concerto for Orchestra, Music for Strings, Percussion* and *Celesta, Piano Concerto No 3* – are concert favourites.

PICASSO, Pablo Ruiz y

Spanish artist 1881-1973

Picasso learned to paint by imitating such great masters of the past as **Rembrandt** and **Goya**, and by the age of 14 his pictures were good enough to show in art exhibitions and to sell. When he was 20 he moved to Paris. He admired the music-hall posters and paintings of **Toulouse-Lautrec**, and began to make his own pictures of comedians, singers, circus performers and acrobats. Toulouse-Lautrec's pictures were colourful and lively, showing people performing; Picasso's pictures showed them resting, or standing in silent, solemn groups. The background colour of many paintings was blue – which, added to the sadness in many of them, has led people to call the work of this time his "blue period".

In the mid-1900s Picasso saw an exhibition of native African masks: rectangular, shield- or diamond-shapes carved in wood and decorated with zigzags and streaks of paint. He began using these ideas in his own paintings. With a friend, the painter Braque, he invented a new way of painting, showing the cylinders, rectangles and, above all, cubes that make up the human form. The colours were pink, orange, red and brown, and the geometric shapes were sometimes outlined in darker colours. A critic called the new style Cubism, as it is still called today.

Picasso's invention of Cubism affected more people than almost any artistic discovery of the century; most later painters and sculptors learned from it. He went on using it himself for 20 years, and some of his best paintings are in Cubist style.

In the 1920s Picasso began drawing and painting in a style he called Neo-Classical, using ideas from the painting and sculpture of ancient Greece and Rome. The best known of these works include bull-fight scenes, a set of illustrations for **Cervantes**' novel *Don Quixote*, and dozens of drawings of artists (often Picasso himself) and their models. The climax of this work, and one of Picasso's finest paintings, was *Guernica*, a 7 metre-long scene of sorrow inspired by **Franco**'s bombing of the town of Guernica in the Spanish Civil War.

In his long life – he still worked eight hours a day at the age of 90 – Picasso produced a huge quantity of art. As well as paintings and drawings, he made sculptures, ceramics (decorated pottery), prints and cloth designs. Many people regard him as the twentieth-century equivalent of Rembrandt, Goya, and the other master-painters whose work he had imitated as a boy.

When Picasso made his picture *Women Running on the Beach* (1922), he had been looking at sculpture, and was trying to suggest the same kind of chunkiness and weight in paint.

PICASSO: Cervantes 16 Franco 468 Goya 24 Rembrandt 19 Toulouse-Lautrec 54

WODEHOUSE, Pelham Grenville

English/US writer 1881-1975

P G Wodehouse (as he is always called) is known for light-hearted, comic novels – over 90 of them. They are about the foolish rich English of the 1920s and 1930s, young men with plenty of money, no brains and nothing to do but flirt with girls, dine at their London clubs and stay in the country with ghastly relatives.

There are two main series of novels. The Blandings books are set in Blandings Castle in Shropshire and centre on absent-minded Lord Emsworth and his prize pig, called the Empress of Blandings. The Jeeves books tell of the troubles of wealthy, pea-brained Bertie Wooster and of the schemes of his manservant Jeeves to get him out of trouble.

Wodehouse also wrote plays and the words for several hit musicals of the 1930s and 1940s. After the Second World War he went to America, and became an American citizen in 1955.

JOYCE, James Augustine Aloysius

Irish writer 1882-1941

Joyce's first two books, *Dubliners* (short stories) and *Portrait of the Artist as a Young Man*, are logical and easy to follow, like snapshots of the past. In his two finest works, *Ulysses* and *Finnegans Wake*, he described dreams and memories as well as the details of ordinary life. His style sometimes seems as complex and illogical as our own dreams might be if we wrote them down. *Ulysses*, for example, follows the hero through a single day, 16 June 1904, and tells us not only everything that actually happens but the ideas each event puts in his mind. *Finnegans Wake* recounts the thoughts that run through a man's head as he dreams through a summer night. These two books had enormous influence on other novelists, and earned Joyce the reputation as one of the most fascinating writers of the century.

STRAVINSKY, Igor

Russian composer and conductor 1882-1971

In 1910, when Stravinsky was 28, he wrote his first ballet, *The Firebird*, for **Diaghilev**'s ballet company. It was a huge success, and brought him instant fame. He wrote two others for the company – *Petrushka* and *The Rite of Spring* – which are among his best and most exciting works.

Although Stravinsky's works were well known, not all of them were instantly popular. Some people hated them, and claimed that no other

The Moor and the Dancer, two characters from Stravinsky's ballet *Petrushka*, about puppets which come to life.

STRAVINSKY: Bartók 60 Diaghilev 252 Schoenberg 58

Left: Bertie Wooster goes hunting – with Jeeves behind him to carry the gun.

twentieth-century composer, not even **Bartók** or **Schoenberg**, had created such ugly sounds. But Stravinsky ignored such comments – and as often happens, the more audiences heard his works the more they grew to like them.

As well as ballets, Stravinsky wrote four operas (including *Oedipus Rex* and *The Rake's Progress*), symphonies, concertos and sonatas, and a dozen religious choral works (for example *Symphony of Psalms*). But the three ballets he wrote for Diaghilev remain great favourites, especially *The Firebird*, which he turned into a concert suite. This became so popular that he conducted it himself no less than 1,000 times, on average once every three weeks for 50 years.

Left: the Irish writer James Joyce, and *below:* the Czech writer Franz Kafka.

KAFKA, Franz

Jewish/Czech writer 1883-1924

Kafka wrote as if he were describing dreams. His stories have their own mysterious reality, like nightmares in which individuals are alone, baffled and threatened. In the story *Metamorphosis* Gregor, a salesman, wakes up to find that he has turned into an enormous beetle – and the story describes his struggles, and growing despair, as he tries to live a normal human life despite his insect habits and appearance. In *The Castle* a man goes to take up a job in a strange town, finds that no one is expecting him or knows anything about him, and gradually begins himself to doubt whether he really exists or not.

In Kafka's most famous novel, *The Trial*, the hero is arrested with no explanation, and the rest of the book describes his attempts to discover the charges against him so that he can prove his innocence.

In the 1900s, psychoanalysts like **Freud** began publishing accounts of their patients' dreams, using them to show that our "subconscious" mind is just as crowded with ideas as the "conscious" mind we use everyday. For many people, Kafka's novels and short stories are like explorations of the subconscious mind – sinister and alarming. Others find his stories funny – as did Kafka himself.

GROPIUS, Walter

German architect 1883-1969

Gropius believed that new buildings in the nineteenth century had been far too fancy. Architects had added decorations or made designs to please themselves. A bank, for example, might be given pillars and statues like an ancient Greek temple; a factory might have stained-glass windows like a cathedral. Gropius thought that buildings should suit the purpose they were made for. In 1919 he founded a school of architecture called the Bauhaus ("building-house"), to teach his ideas about architecture and design. Bauhaus buildings were like boxes for living or working in. They used steel frames and reinforced-concrete panels. Doors and windows were always rectangular, roofs were flat and there was no unnecessary ornament.

In 1934 Gropius was expelled from Germany by the Nazis, and he went first to England and from there (in 1938) to America. His ideas spread everywhere, and now buildings in Bauhaus style are so common that we hardly notice them.

KAFKA: Freud 383

LAWRENCE, David Herbert

English writer and poet 1885-1930

Lawrence was born near Nottingham, England, the son of a miner. He was first a teacher, then spent the rest of his life travelling the world and writing books and poetry. He became the centre of a scandal because he wrote frankly about sex, and used four-letter words in his novels. Two of them, *The Rainbow* (1915) and *Lady Chatterley's Lover* (1928) were declared obscene. Attitudes change, however, and Lawrence is now much admired for the vividness of his writing and the depth of feeling it shows.

Le Corbusier designed this "Housing Unit" for the city of Marseille in France. It is a complete village in one single block.

LE CORBUSIER

Swiss architect 1887-1965

Le Corbusier was the pen name of Charles-Édouard Jeanneret. He admired the ideas of **Gropius**. He thought that not only buildings should be functional (designed for their use, not beauty) – but even whole towns. He made plans for

This painting by Rivera is one of 27 panels. Together the panels give a picture of industrial workers in Detroit. These men are working with poisonous chemicals, and are wearing gas-masks.

RIVERA, Diego

Mexican painter 1886-1957

Rivera thought that art should be available for everyone, not just for the rich, and should be in a style ordinary people could understand. He thought that the best way to make this kind of "public art" was to paint murals (wall paintings) in public buildings. He chose everyday life as his theme.

Most of Rivera's murals are enormous, two or three hectares in area. They show farmers ploughing, factory production lines, political meetings and, occasionally, strikes, riots and battles. Nowadays, we are used to seeing scenes of human activity – on advertising hoardings, for example. But when Rivera started, the idea was completely new – and few other painters have ever made such a striking political use of "public art".

LE CORBUSIER: Gropius 63

what he called a "radiating town", where the streets radiate from the centre to the suburbs, and the buildings are grouped according to their uses: living areas, factory areas, leisure areas and so on.

In the Europe of the 1920s and 1930s it was hard to use Le Corbusier's ideas, because existing towns and cities were centuries-old and there was little room for change. But the bombing raids of the Second World War flattened huge areas in many towns, and when rebuilding began, Le Corbusier's ideas were followed everywhere. He has influenced the design of town centres, shopping malls and housing estates all over the world: they are now so familiar that we forget how recent they are.

This stained glass window was designed by Marc Chagall as a memorial to the daughter of the d'Avigdor Goldsmid family, who died in a sailing accident in 1967. The window is one of several by Chagall in the All Saints Church, Tudely, in Kent.

CHAGALL, Marc

Russian painter 1887-1985

When Chagall made pictures it was as if he were painting dreams. He took his ideas from Russian-Jewish folk-tales, and from circuses, which especially fascinated him. He used bright, fuzzy colours which make his pictures look as if they are painted on wool or velvet.

Apart from painting, Chagall created huge works of art for public places in Europe and America. He designed stained glass windows for the synagogue at the medical centre of the Hadassah-Hebrew University in Jerusalem, and the cathedrals at Metz and Reims in France. For the Knesset (the Israeli parliament) he designed mosaics and tapestries, and for the Paris Opera House he painted a ceiling.

O'NEILL, Eugene

US playwright 1888-1953

O'Neill was an actor's son, and one of his best-known plays, *Long Day's Journey Into Night*, about a family headed by a bullying, actor-father and a drug-addicted mother, is based on his own life. The stories of O'Neill's plays are gloomy, and his characters are often sad, despairing failures. *Mourning Becomes Electra* turns **Aeschylus'** *Oresteia* into a three-play saga of corruption and murder in a family living in the American South, 100 years ago. *The Iceman Cometh* shows us a group of tramps and drunks talking and telling stories as they wait for something – anything – to happen. (This play impressed Samuel **Beckett**, who used a similar idea in his *Waiting for Godot*.)

O'NEILL: Aeschylus 4 Beckett 72

An illustration of the American actor Robert Mitchum, starring as the detective Philip Marlowe in a film of *Farewell My Lovely*.

CHANDLER, Raymond

US novelist 1888-1959

Chandler perfected the "private eye" story – where a lone detective undertakes an investigation which everyone else tries to hinder. He created the character Philip Marlowe, one of the toughest heroes in fiction. Marlowe is beaten up, drugged, framed for crimes he has not committed, chased by police and crooks alike – and still solves each case. Marlowe appears in all of Chandler's novels, including *Farewell My Lovely, The Long Goodbye* and *The Lady in the Lake*.

ELIOT, Thomas Stearns

US/English poet 1888-1965

T S Eliot (as he is usually known) was a poet, playwright and critic. He was born in the United States, but settled in London and worked first in a bank, then as a publisher. He wrote several hundred short poems, including the children's collection *Old Possum's book of Practical Cats*.

Eliot is best known for two long poems. *The Waste Land* is about human longing for happiness, in the bleak, half-ruined world after the First World War. *Four Quartets* is also about a search, this time for God and for religious belief. Eliot also wrote plays: the best known is *Murder in the Cathedral*, about the assassination of the English archbishop St Thomas à **Becket**.

"WHODUNNITS"

"Whodunnits" are novels in which detectives solve crimes, usually murder. They were favourite reading in Britain and America in the 1930s and 1940s, and are still popular today. Famous "whodunnit" writers (with the names of their detective characters in brackets) include Chandler (Philip Marlowe), Christie (Hercule Poirot; Miss Marple), Conan Doyle (Sherlock Holmes), P.D. James (Adam Dalgleish), Sayers (Lord Peter Wimsey), Simenon (le Commissaire Maigret) and Stout (Nero Wolfe).

Agatha Christie wrote plays as well as books. One, *The Mousetrap*, has been performed almost every single night in London since 1952.

CHRISTIE, Agatha

English writer 1890-1976

Christie was the biggest-selling detective-story writer of the twentieth century, and well deserving her nickname "The Queen of Crime". In some of her 87 books, the crimes are solved by boastful, fussy Hercule Poirot, the Belgian detective. In other stories the detection is done by Miss Marple, a frail old English lady who listens to all the village gossip and annoys the police by being always one step ahead of their investigations, and always right.

ELIOT: Becket 334

Grant Wood called this picture of two Iowa farmers *American Gothic* (1930). He wanted to suggest what simple lives the people lived, and how strict they were in the 1930s.

WOOD, Grant

US artist 1892-1942

Wood made pictures of the people and landscapes round his home town, Cedar Rapids, Iowa. He was one of the leaders of the "realist" movement in modern American art, aiming to show things in direct, simple detail as they are, not distorted and changed as in some other modern art. When you first see his paintings, you might think that they show models of the communities and landscapes, or that he imagined real hills and fields covered with coloured cloths. But when you see the actual landscapes of Iowa, you find that they do look just like that, exactly as Wood painted them.

TOLKIEN, John Ronald Reuel

English writer 1892-1973

Tolkien felt that if a fairy tale was worth reading, adults as well as children would enjoy it. *The Hobbit* was published in 1937, a fantasy about the adventures of Bilbo Baggins, a hobbit, in the company of dwarfs and a wizard called Gandalf, who rob a dragon of its treasure and find a magic ring.

Bilbo and the magic ring also feature in *The Lord of the Rings*, a much longer story. Tolkien was not only telling an exciting story – he created a fantasy world with its own creatures, history, mythology and languages and he told of the battle between good and evil. Many writers have imitated him in stories, films and adventure games.

FITZGERALD, Francis Scott Key

US writer 1896-1940

In the 1920s Fitzgerald was one of America's most successful writers. After the publication of his first book, *This Side of Paradise*, he married the glamorous Zelda Sayre, and began an extravagant life, mixing with the wealthy young people of the US "jazz age". His stories were about that rich American society, and how drink, drugs and endless party-going destroyed people, making them interested in nothing but their own enjoyment.

In the 1930s tragedy struck. Zelda went mad, and Fitzgerald became an alcoholic. These experiences were the basis of his novel *Tender is the Night*. His most famous novel is *The Great Gatsby*, a story of romance and passion set in the glamour of Long Island and the squalor of New York.

Fitzgerald later wrote film scripts in Hollywood, but died aged 44, without ever finishing his final work, *The Last Tycoon*.

FAULKNER, William Harrison

US writer 1897-1962

Faulkner wrote short stories and novels about the southern states of America. He is most famous for a series of books he wrote about an imaginary place, "Yoknapatawpha County", in Mississippi. The books describe conflicts between rich and poor and black and white people in the American south. Faulkner's best-known books include *The Sound and the Fury* and *Light in August*.

George Gershwin composing – a publicity photo of the 1930s.

GERSHWIN, George

US composer 1898-1937

In 1916, when Gershwin was 18, his song *Swanee* was bought and made famous by Al Jolson, one of the biggest singing-stars of the day. From that time on Gershwin wrote hundreds of songs, and they have been performed by every famous name in show-business, from Frank **Sinatra** to Peggy Lee, from Bing **Crosby** to Nat King Cole. His best-known songs are in stage and film musicals, for example those he wrote for Fred **Astaire**: *Lady Be Good; Funny Face; Shall We Dance?* Many had words by his brother IRA GERSHWIN (1896-1983).

As well as show-songs, Gershwin wrote concert works, putting jazz ideas into classical operas and concertos. This was an unusual idea at the time, but Gershwin made it popular. Two of his best-loved works are: the Black American opera *Porgy and Bess* which uses show-songs (for example *Summertime*), and *Rhapsody in Blue* for piano and orchestra.

BRECHT, Bertholt

German playwright 1898-1956

Brecht wrote plays not just to entertain but to make people think about how the world is run and how it can be improved. When he was 30 his play-with-songs *The Threepenny Opera* was a huge success, and he went to work in Hollywood, partly to write for films and partly to avoid Nazi rule in Germany. He went back to Germany in 1949, and started a theatre-company, the Berlin Ensemble, which soon became world-famous. Brecht's best-known plays, *Mother Courage* and *The Caucasian Chalk Circle*, are about ordinary people triumphing against dictators, generals, politicians, bankers and other leaders whose cruelty and corruption Brecht despised.

The German writer and theatre producer Bertholt Brecht.

MAGRITTE, René

Belgian painter 1898-1967

Magritte was a Surrealist artist. He did not paint the "real" world but the

GERSHWIN: Astaire 266 Crosby 268 Sinatra 280 MAGRITTE: Dalí 71 invisible one of dreams, thoughts and imagination. In his paintings an apple is big enough to fill a room, fried eggs have staring eyes for yolks and a man looking into a mirror sees the reflection not of his face but of the back of his head. Some surrealist paintings, for example those of **Dalí**, can be nightmarish; Magritte's are much calmer. Some are funny, while others are mysterious and strange.

This castle by Escher looks normal, until you try to work out whether the people on the top floor are walking up, or down. Then, when you look at the other parts (for example the cellar steps), you wonder what messages your eyes are sending to your brain.

ESCHER, Maurits

Dutch painter 1898-1972

Escher was fascinated by the difference between what our eyes see and the way our brains interpret it. In particular, certain marks and shapes can work "optical illusions", tricking our eyes into believing that a perfectly flat drawing is covered with bumps and hollows. Escher painted castles filled with staircases and corridors. But every step is a deception: stairs apparently going up actually lead down, and corridors which seem to go left take you to the right of where you start. In other pictures, the whole surface is divided into regular polygons that seem to fold in and out.

MOORE, Henry

English sculptor 1898-1986

When Moore was a student, sculptors learned their craft by drawing and modelling from life, and copying classical (ancient Greek and Roman) and Renaissance statues. But people were showing interest in other traditions, especially the sculptures of Africa, Stone Age Europe and South America. Moore admired this kind of sculpture and based his own style on it. He produced chunky, hefty statues, like huge boulders or lumps of metal come to life. He carved in wood and stone (which generations of sculptors had rejected, preferring to model in clay or wax, then have their works made up by assistants in marble and bronze). He liked to let the nature of the material – the gnarled, grainy surface of wood, or the bumps and roughness of stone – affect the final look of the sculpture.

Many of Moore's works stand in parks and civic centres, and he took enormous trouble to find the right spot for others, placing them on hillsides and mountain-tops where they seem to gaze out, like monarchs, over the surrounding countryside. In the 1930s Moore made hundreds of statues of people, alone or in groups. To make them look less boulder-like, he often carved tunnels and hollows in his figures. He became famous for these "statues with holes in them."

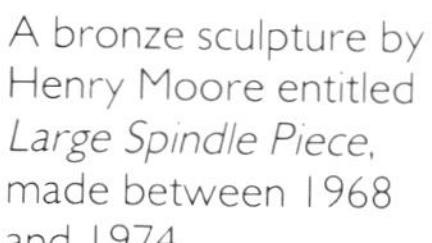

A bronze sculpture by Henry Moore entitled *Large Spindle Piece*, made between 1968 and 1974.

HEMINGWAY, Ernest Miller

US writer 1899-1961

Hemingway was an ambulance driver in the First World War and a newspaper reporter during the Spanish Civil War – and his experiences of the horrors of war gave him inspiration for two of his best-known works, *A Farewell to Arms* and *For Whom the Bell Tolls*. His characters are men of action: soldiers, hunters, fishermen, boxers and bull-fighters. His books are in a clear, descriptive style, and often end sadly, showing that his heroes are not as all-powerful as they think they are.

Hemingway won a **Nobel** prize for his novel *The Old Man and the Sea* (about an aged fisherman fighting to catch a gigantic marlin).

COPLAND, Aaron

US composer born 1900

When Copland was a student he composed in the latest, most up-to-date style, based on jazz and the loud, crashing music of **Stravinsky**'s *The Rite of Spring* – and was horrified to find that audiences hated it. He set out to change his style, to write music which, though still of high quality, would be welcome to the ear. The musical style he devised, with good tunes (some based on American folk songs) and logical, uncomplicated harmonies, has made him one of the most popular of all twentieth-century composers. His best-known works are *El Salón México*, a sound-picture of Mexican dance-hall, *Fanfare for the Common Man* (a pop hit, still often played at sports events), and two ballets, *Billy the Kid*, which uses cowboy tunes, and *Appalachian Spring*, which ranges from variations on the folk-tune *The Gift to be Simple* to a rowdy, cheerful barn-dance.

STEINBECK, John Ernst

US novelist 1902-68

Steinbeck wrote about the lives of the poor and unemployed. His subjects were grim – despair, hunger and the fury that comes from hopelessness. But he wrote about them in powerful language, like that of the Old Testament and the legends of King Arthur, which he admired.

Steinbeck was one of the USA's most respected novelists, some say the finest US writer of this century. Two of his best-known books are *The Grapes of Wrath* (about poor fruit-pickers in California) and *Of Mice and Men* (about the friendship of two farmworkers, simple-minded Lennie and weedy, clever George).

ORWELL, George

English writer 1903-50

Orwell's real name was Eric Blair. He spent some time living with tramps and poor people, and wrote about it in two books, *Down and Out in Paris and London* and *The Road to Wigan* Pier (about unemployed people in the north of England).

Orwell is best known for two political novels. In *Animal Farm* the pigs persuade all the other farm animals to revolt against humans. The story is a satire about the political system in the USSR under **Stalin**. *Nineteen Eighty Four* tells of a

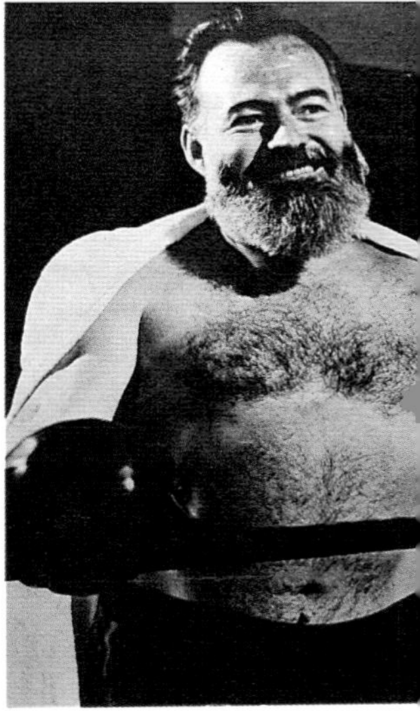

Hemingway liked to keep fit by sparring (pretending to fight) with boxer friends.

HEMINGWAY: Nobel 374 COPLAND: Stravinsky 62 ORWELL: Stalin 462

nightmare future Britain, in which everything people do, say or think is monitored by the State (nicknamed "Big Brother"), and torture is the reward of anyone suspected of disobedience.

HEPWORTH, Barbara

English sculptor 1903–75

Hepworth made many abstract works, shapes created simply for their own beauty. Some of her works are enormous, made to stand in city squares or on hilltops. Others are tiny, intended as ornaments. But in all her work, she was intent on showing the beauty of the material she used: bronze, granite, highly polished woods such as mahogany and ebony, plastic, alabaster, jade and other stones.

DALÍ, Salvador

Spanish artist 1904-89

Dalí was a Surrealist. At the start of his career, dreams – where anything can happen – were especially important to him and that is how he set out to paint. His paintings are as clear and exact as colour photographs – until you look at what they show. Giraffes blaze, watches flop like fried eggs, a woman has a cello for a body, a mountain-range turns out to be a pegged-down giant.

Many of Dalí's paintings were meant to be mysterious or shocking, just as dreams can be. But as he grew older, and more famous, he began making surreal art just for fun – and he earned a lot of money. He branched out into other directions – advertisements, fashion, and movies. Some of his most amusing designs are pieces of jewellery. If you pick up one of his platinum, jewel-studded hearts, for example, it begins beating in your hand.

This painting by Dalí is as unexpected as its title: *Soft Construction With Boiled Beans: Premonition of Civil War.* "Premonition" means "warning" – but what is Dalí's painting warning us about?

SURREALIST PAINTERS

Some twentieth-century painters thought that instead of showing the reality of the world in their pictures, they should show a different kind: the reality of dreams. Their paintings replace ordinary logic with the logic of the artist's imagination, often strange or funny to outsiders. Famous surrealist painters include Chirico, Dalí, Duchamp, Magritte and Miró. Earlier painters, including Bosch and Goya, used surrealist ideas in their work, centuries before the surrealism got its name.

This shadowy scene, from the film of Greene's *The Third Man*, shows hunter and hunted in the tunnels of the Vienna sewers.

GREENE, Henry Graham

English novelist born 1904

Graham Greene, as he is known, has written over thirty novels, stories and plays since his first novel, *The Man Within* was published in 1929. His first novels were thrillers, for example *Brighton Rock*, about a boy gang-leader in the English seaside town of Brighton, or *The Third Man*, from Greene's film about a drugs-dealer in Vienna, Austria, after the Second World War. Greene called these books "entertainments" to show that he considered them quite different from his serious novels.

The settings for Greene's serious books are usually parts of the world far from his native England – Haiti, central Africa, Vietnam, Honduras and Mexico – and he writes of people doing their best in difficult times, for example caught up in revolutions, or struggling against harsh régimes.

Greene's best-known books are *The Power and the Glory* (about a drunken priest in the Mexican revolution), *The Heart of the Matter* (about a weak-willed British police-chief at the end of British imperial rule in central Africa), and the comedy *Our Man in Havana*, about a vacuum-cleaner-salesman in Cuba (before **Castro** came to power), who is recruited by the secret service and who has to pretend to be a master-spy, running a vast network of agents, all imaginary.

BECKETT, Samuel

Irish novelist and playwright 1906-89

In Beckett's early stories and novels, he was particularly interested in tramps, senile old people and the insane – and in the 1950s he began putting the same kind of characters into plays, which brought him international fame. The first, *Waiting for Godot*, shows two tramps by a tree on a country road, waiting for the coming of a man who will bring them happiness. Godot never actually arrives: the whole play consists of the tramps' conversations, squabbles and gossip while they wait. Beckett's other plays include *Endgame*, about a helpless, blind man and his servant after the dropping of the nuclear bomb, and *Krapp's Last Tape*, about an old man who tries to recall the past

GREENE: Castro 475 BECKETT: Laurel and Hardy 258

by playing tapes he recorded in younger, happier days.

Although Beckett's ideas are bleak, his plays are often very funny. He wrote several of them with famous film comedians in mind – **Laurel and Hardy**, for example, were models for the tramps in *Waiting for Godot*.

VASARÉLY, Victor

Hungarian/French artist born 1908

Vasarély invented "Op" (optical) art: pictures that seem to shimmer as you look at them. His pictures consist of row after row of coloured shapes (usually circles or squares), not straight but distorted until they seem to blur or bulge. If you covered spheres, pyramids or other three-dimensional figures with squared paper, you might get a similar result. The colours are dazzling, and some of the pictures are as much as three or four metres high. Vasarély's pictures have influenced many other kinds of art, from computer graphics and posters to the design of such everyday items as fabrics, wrapping paper and carrier-bags.

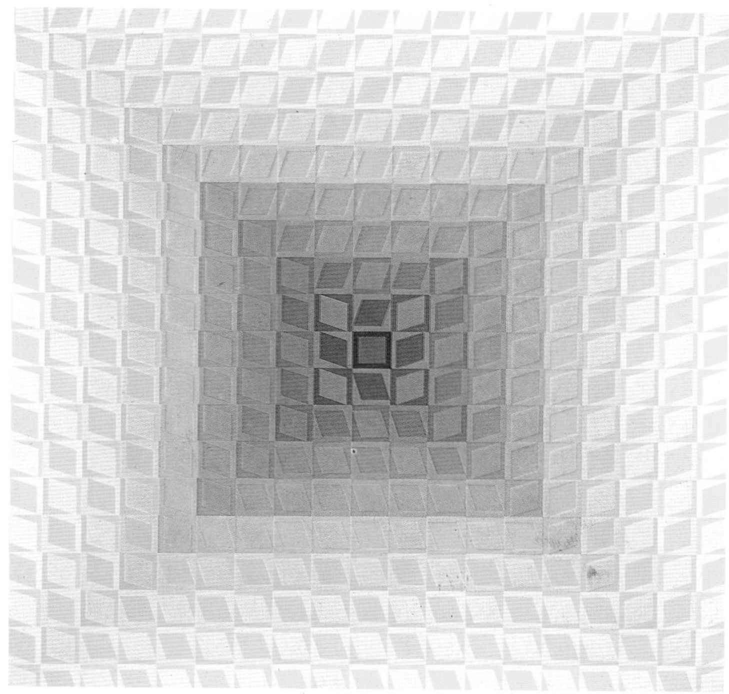

Op art: Vasarély's painting *Composition* c 1960. This kind of art was banned in advertisments in Britain in 1990, because it made some people feel seasick. © DACS 1990

POLLOCK, Jackson

US artist 1912-56

Pollock believed that the act of painting was more important than the finished product. He invented what he called "action painting". He tacked large sheets of canvas to the floor, then dripped and splashed paint all over them. The smears and blobs made patterns, and the patterns made the pictures. At first most art-lovers thought his paintings were the work of a madman, but after a while, as his paintings became more widely known, people began to recognize his genius. His life was cut short by a car accident.

WHITE, Patrick Victor Martindale

Australian novelist born 1912

White worked as a farmer in the Australian outback (remote bush country). His books are about "loners", people whose character or ideas set them apart from everyone else around them. His best-known novels are *Voss* (about an expedition struggling to cross Australia's desert in the 1850s), *Riders in the Chariot* (about discrimination against Jews) and *A Fringe of Leaves* (about a woman shipwrecked off Queensland in the 1840s, who is rescued by a group of aboriginal people and who comes to prefer their ways to those of the white society she has left behind).

Cartoon showing Dylan Thomas with a red nose – associated with drunks as well as clowns.

BRITTEN, Benjamin

English composer 1913-76

Britten's first music successes were for radio plays and films – he later turned the music for one film into a popular concert piece, *Prelude and Fugue on a Theme of Purcell* (or *The Young Person's Guide to the Orchestra*). In 1945 his opera *Peter Grimes* made him internationally famous, and from then on opera-writing was his main musical activity. He wrote 16 operas altogether, ranging from **Shakespeare**-settings (*A Midsummer Night's Dream*) to smaller-scale, cheerful works for children like *Noye's Fludde*. As well as operas, Britten wrote many other vocal works: one well-known work is the *Serenade for Tenor, Horn and Strings*. He wrote instrumental music too, much of it for friends such as the cellist and conductor Rostropovich. But he will chiefly be remembered for his operas, songs, and choral music – particularly the anti-war War Requiem.

A scene from Britten's opera *Peter Grimes*, about a lonely fisherman hounded by local villagers for illtreating his young helper.

THOMAS, Dylan Marlais

Welsh poet 1914-53

Thomas began to write poetry at school, then worked as a reporter before he began to write and produce radio programmes at the age of 25. After the Second World War he became famous for his poetry, and made reading tours, especially in the USA, attracting huge audiences. He was a popular entertainer and made many recordings of his poems. His best known poems are about love, death and the beauties of nature. He is also famous for *Under Milk Wood*, a radio play describing a day in the life of an imaginary Welsh seaside town, and showing us the people's thoughts as they went about their everyday business.

Thomas had a wild life and drank heavily, which led to his early death, aged 39.

MILLER, Arthur

US playwright, born 1915

Miller's plays are about human suffering, and concentrate on tragedy in the lives of ordinary people. His characters are fathers quarrelling with sons, husbands arguing with wives, or people who cannot cope with the strain of life. His best-known plays are *Death of a Salesman*, *A View from the Bridge*, and *The Crucible* – a historical play about witch-hunts in eighteenth-century America, which he compares with the anti-communist "witch hunts" headed by **McCarthy** in the 1950s.

Miller was married to the actress Marilyn **Monroe**.

BRITTEN: Shakespeare 16 MILLER: McCarthy 233 Monroe, M 285

LOWELL, Robert Traill Spence

US poet 1917-77

Lowell was one of the most admired of all twentieth-century US poets. He wrote many autobiographical poems, describing members of his family, places and people he knew, and the landscape and history of America. He also translated foreign poems, and wrote "imitations" (half new, half translation) of poems he admired. He made translations of **Racine**'s play *Phèdre* and of **Aeschylus**' tragedies *Prometheus Bound* and *The Oresteia*. His best-known poetry collections are *Life Studies* and *For the Union Dead*.

SOLZHENITSYN, Alexander Isayevich

Russian writer born 1918

In the years when **Stalin** was dictator in the USSR, people who opposed him were often sent to "labour camps" in remote areas. They were kept in terrible conditions, forced to do hard physical work such as laying railway tracks, kept short of food and medicine, and forbidden to communicate with the outside world. Solzehenitsyn spent 8 years in such a camp, and was only freed when he developed stomach cancer. He wrote books about the camps, *One Day in the Life of Ivan Denisovich*, *First Circle* and *The GULAG Archipelago*. They were banned in the USSR, but have been published throughout the rest of the world.

Solzhenitsyn is one of Russia's most famous "dissidents" (people who oppose the régime). The authorities finally let him leave for the West in 1974. Since then he has lectured and written not only about the evils of the USSR under Stalin, but also about the greed and political humbug of the West.

Solzhenitsyn in 1953, photographed in the Labour Camp, with his prison number painted on his clothes.

BALDWIN, James

US writer 1924-87

Baldwin's writings described the life of black people in the USA, setting out their fury at the way they were treated as second-class citizens in their own country. His main non-fiction books are *Notes of a Native Son*, *The Fire Next Time* and *No Name in the Street*. He also wrote powerful novels (including *Go Tell It on the Mountain* and *Another Country*) and plays (including *The Amen Corner* and *Blues for Mr Charlie*), about blacks in the New York slums. His work helped to change the way people thought; like Martin Luther **King**, he fought for total equality between blacks and whites.

The writer James Baldwin.

LOWELL: Aeschylus 4 Racine 21 SOLZHENITSYN: Stalin 462 BALDWIN: King, M L 236

BOULEZ, Pierre

French composer and conductor born 1925

As a young man, Boulez wrote music of a kind few players had ever met before. It was hard to imagine the sounds, let alone play them. Boulez worked with the performers, helping them to "realize" his works (discover and put over the meaning behind the notes). This work gave him the taste for conducting, and in the 1960s and 1970s he directed orchestras all over the world. He became especially respected for teaching difficult modern music.

In 1977 Boulez went back to the earlier way of music-making, by composing the sounds and then working on them with performers in the studio. He was made head of IRCAM (Institute for the Research and Co-ordination of Acoustics and Music) in Paris. At IRCAM, singers and players work with composers, computer programmers and with engineers to create sounds and sound-combinations not possible before.

MÁRQUEZ, Gabriel García

Colombian writer born 1928

Márquez helped to increase world interest in South American literature when his novel *One Hundred Years of Solitude* was first published in 1967. It takes place in an imaginary South American town, Macondo, a place where real life is mingled with fantasy, as in fairy tales. His characters are housewives, priests, shopkeepers, farmers and soldiers, and seem quite ordinary – except that they have supernatural powers. They understand the secrets of alchemy, live to be over 100, talk of **Cortés** as an "uncle" and befriend ghosts.

Márquez's novel *Love in the Time of Cholera* has a dramatic scene when a gaudy, talking parrot escapes, and taunts its aged doctor owner who climbs up to recapture it, falls and dies.

Márquez's other works include *No One Writes to the Colonel*, *The Autumn of the Patriarch* (the imaginary memoirs of a brutal, none-too-intelligent military dictator), and *Love in the Time of Cholera*.

MAGIC REALISM

Magic realism is a way of writing fiction which first became popular in the 1960s. Realism (likeness to real life) blends with fantasy and magic, as in a fairy tale, so that ordinary people have incredible, dream-like adventures. Famous Magic realist writers include Angela Carter from England, Isabel Allende, Gabriel Garcia Márquéz and Mario Vargas Llosa from South America, and John Irving from the USA.

MÁRQUEZ: Cortés 177

WARHOL, Andy

US artist 1930-87

Warhol began his career as a commercial artist, producing advertisements, labels, designs for tickets, leaflets and other throwaway items. He began to use the same ideas in "fine art", to be shown in exhibitions and hung on walls. He used silk-screen printing and photographs, because he thought brushes and paint made the art too personal. His best-known works in this "pop art" style – as critics called it, linking it with the loud, cheerful style of pop music – are "multi-images": rows of photos of soup-tins, bottles, or film-stars (for example Marilyn **Monroe**).

Left: Multiple (repeated) portrait of Andy Warhol.

Below: One of Hockney's "joiners" – the Desk, created in 1984.

RILEY, Bridget Louise

English artist born 1931

Riley is the leading British painter of "Op Art" (see **Vasarély**). She covers the canvas with parallel lines, sometimes straight, but often curved or zig-zagged. As you look at the picture the shapes seem to move and dazzle the eye. Since the 1960s such designs have become popular in advertising, used on wrapping paper and record sleeves. Riley's work makes you see the beauty of the design for its own sake.

HOCKNEY, David

English artist born 1937

Hockney's early art was mainly portraits, usually pairs of people sitting or standing quietly together without communicating. When he was 25 he went to California, and made a series of paintings of people swimming in pools or the sea, sitting on deck chairs, taking showers or watering plants. The bright, clear colours (especially blues) and simple shapes of these pictures have been widely copied in advertisements, and have made Hockney one of the best-known twentieth-century painters since **Picasso**.

Hockney has designed scenery for operas, made drawings and etchings for books, and invented entirely new art-forms: "joiners", a way of suggesting movement by making a collage of still photographs, and "photocopy art" – making pictures by continually enlarging painted images on a colour photocopier until they are completely transformed.

WARHOL: Monroe, M 285 RILEY: Vasarély 73 HOCKNEY: Picasso 60

GLOSSARY

Alchemist An early scientist, 1,000 years ago, seeking ways to turn ordinary metals into gold and to find the secret of immortality.

Anthem A piece of music for the choir to sing in a Christian church.

Ballad A poem, usually sung, which tells a story.

Cantata A piece of music alternating solo singing with sections for choir.

Chamber music Music for a few players, so called because it was originally meant to be played not in a concert hall but in a "chamber", or ordinary room.

Classical style (in European art) A style using ideas based on those of ancient Greece and Rome.

Concerto A large-scale piece of music for one or more soloists and orchestra.

Etching When you etch, you scratch lines on a metal plate, then use acid to burn away surplus metal. The etching can then be printed, and (if you want) coloured by hand.

Fresco A wall-painting made on wet plaster, which is then allowed to dry.

Hell In the myths of many religions, the place where wicked people go after death.

Knights Rich men in Europe, about 1,000 years ago, who wore armour, fought on horseback and travelled about fighting evil and doing good.

Landscape A picture of countryside.

Literature Poems, novels, biographies and other written works.

Mass The main service in the Roman Catholic Christian church, often set to music by composers.

Masterpiece An outstandingly good piece of work in literature, music, painting, or the other arts: something which only a master could have made.

Medieval Belonging to the "Middle Ages", from about 1,400 to 600 years ago.

Myths Stories (usually from religion) about a country's gods, heroes and supernatural beings. People know that myths are stories, but they use them to help understand our human place in the world, and our relationship with powers which are outside our normal experience.

Novel A book-long story, often in shorter sections called chapters.

Nude (in art) A picture or statue of a naked person.

Opera A play performed in music, by singers with orchestra.

Overture A piece of music which sets the mood at the start of a play or opera, or which exists on its own to paint a sound-picture or tell a story in sound alone.

Panorama A wide picture, usually covering most of a wall, showing a large scene with many people, such as a battle.

Paradise In the myths of many religions, the place where good people go after death, to live forever in happiness with God.

Passion A large-scale piece of music setting the Bible story of Jesus' arrest, trial and death.

Portrait (in art) A picture of a person, suggesting their character as well as showing what they look like.

Prophecy An announcement by a prophet (someone inspired by supernatural powers) of what will happen in the future.

Proverb A wise saying, such as "a fool and his money are soon parted".

Purgatory In Christian myth, the place where sinners go after death until their wickedness is forgiven.

Quest (in stories and legends) A search, usually for something legendary or magical, such as the Golden Fleece.

Renaissance The period in Europe (about 1400-1650) when artists and others were discovering and developing ideas from ancient Greece and Rome. One of the most important times in European artistic history.

Satire Written work or painting criticising something by making fun of it.

Sonata A piece of music for instruments, usually for one, two or three performers only.

Squire The servant of a knight.

Still-life A picture not of people or animals but of fruit, leaves, flowers or other objects.

String quartet A large-scale piece of music for two violins, viola and cello.

Suite A collection of short pieces of music, usually in dance rhythms.

Supernatural Beyond what exists in nature. People often believe in supernatural beings, such as ghosts, spirits and wizards.

Symbol (in art) Something an artist paints to stand for an idea, impossible to represent in paint. A sword, for example, might be a symbol for courage or for war; a placid lake a symbol for peace.

Symphony A large-scale piece of music for orchestra, in several sections (known as movements).

Tapestry A huge, carpet-like woven picture to hang on a wall.

Translation When you make a translation, you turn something (a book, play or poem, say) from another language into your own.

SECTION 2

SCIENTISTS

Science,
Mathematics
Medicine

INTRODUCTION TO *SCIENTISTS*

How did the universe begin? How far are the stars, and why do they shine? Why is the natural world so complex and varied? How does the body work?

For many people throughout the ages such questions could only be explained by one answer: God or the gods made the universe. Curiosity should be replaced with wonder and we should accept the world as the creation of a divine power.

But some people were not content with this answer, and set about tackling such intriguing problems, examining everything, and gathering facts in a logical, ordered sequence to make sense of their surroundings. A number of the new discoveries upset the existing order – usually the religious authorities who wanted to preserve the tradition of the "divine creation" intact.

The first "scientists", in Greece, Mesopotamia and China, 500 years BC, had no clever gadgets, such as lenses, microscopes or calculators. Their science relied on observation, description and measurement. They pondered everything in the universe: light, sky, stars, rocks, water, plants and animals. Their work led to the development of many scientific disciplines still taught and researched today, and they also worked out a scientific method, proceeding by logical steps from idea to investigation to conclusion, and on to the next idea.

The early scientists' ideas were accepted with little change for over 1,500 years. The disciplines of astronomy, geography, mathematics and medicine all relied on books written in ancient times.

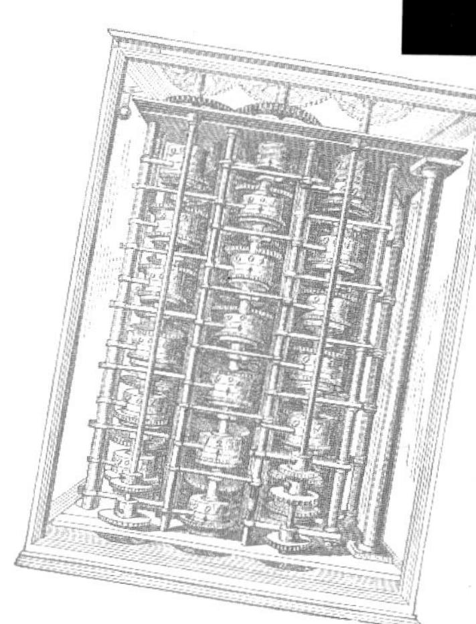

What we call modern science began in Europe in the fourteenth and fifteenth centuries. People began questioning the ancient ideas, and testing them by new observations and experiments. The invention of ever more accurate measuring instruments and mathematical formulas sometimes proved the old ideas right, but just as often showed that they were wrong. Building on these discoveries, later scientists probed into even deeper areas – into the very building-blocks of materials (such as sub-atomic particles and genes) – and developed measuring techniques thousands of times more precise than any human hand or eye.

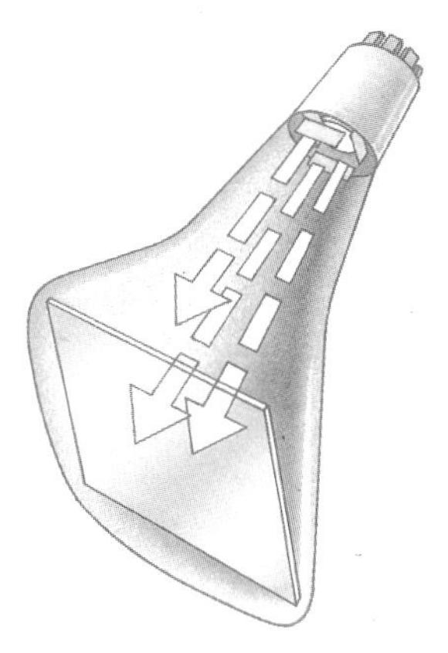

Yet the scientific explanations that are continually being found do not lessen the marvels of the world we have inherited, but add to our respect for it. And the task is endless – for every question to which today's scientists can find the answer, a thousand more appear, each one as mysterious and intriguing as the last.

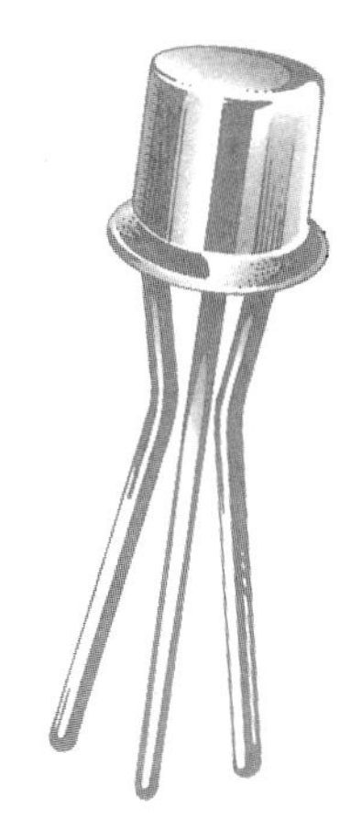

THALES

Greek scholar c 640-546 BC

Thales was a merchant from Miletus, on the Aegean coast of Turkey. He travelled in Arabia, Africa and Babylonia (modern Iraq), and bought back "knowledge" from all these places: views on religion, astronomy and politics. When he retired from business he set up as a teacher, and people flocked to learn from him.

Thales became famous for his wisdom, and is thought to have invented geometry, to have predicted a solar eclipse (a feat which caused a sensation), and to have claimed that water was the element from which everything else in the universe was created.

PYTHAGORAS

Greek mathematician and scholar c 569-506 BC

Pythagoras is remembered nowadays chiefly because of his famous theorem (a provable statement): "In a right-angled triangle, the square on the hypotenuse is equal to the sum of the squares on the other two sides."

In ancient times Pythagoras was known for far more important things. He believed that everything in the universe can be explained by mathematics – a view scientists still hold today. He saw the Earth's shadow on the moon during a lunar eclipse, and its shape led him to work out that the Earth must be spherical, not flat, as was thought at the time. He was also interested in the physics of sound and showed, for example, that if you pluck two lengths of string, one of which is twice the length of the other, the longer string will produce a sound one octave lower than the shorter string.

Pythagoras set up a school in the Sicilian town of Croton. He taught not only maths and astronomy but also about the nature of human beings and gods. He believed that when we die, our true selves, our souls, migrate into new bodies. For this reason, fearing that a slaughtered bird or animal might contain a human soul, he and his disciples were vegetarians. They also tried to keep their souls as perfect as possible by avoiding such "impure" actions as fighting, sex (except for producing children) and breaking an oath.

Pythagoras, working on his theorems. He was the first person to work out that the Earth was a sphere. Pythagoras was killed by a mob, but his disciples, the "Pythagoreans", ruled Croton for 200 years.

DEMOCRITUS (Demokritos)

Greek scholar 5th century BC

Democritus was a teacher who is said to have travelled throughout Greece, Egypt, Persia and even as far as India. His theory of matter was close to very much later ideas of how things are made. According to his theory, the universe consists of just two substances, "is" and "isn't". "Is" is made up of atoms, and "isn't" consists of the empty space between them. The atoms are tiny models of every existing thing – miniature tables, insects, plants and so on – and they wander round "isn't" in random paths. Sometimes they collide, but often they find other atoms of the same kind, stick to them and so produce the objects which we sense. A table is made up of a large number of table-atoms, for example, and a leaf of leaf-atoms. When things "die", their atoms spring apart and begin wandering again in "isn't", looking for new partners.

Cartoon of Democritus, thinking hard about atoms in motion.

HIPPOCRATES (Hippokrates)

Greek doctor c 460-380 BC

Left: Hippocrates, the "father of medicine".

In ancient Greece, doctoring of ten depended less on knowledge than on the supernatural: on spells, potions and magic ceremonies. Hippocrates, a doctor on the island of Cos, began the change to a style of medicine more like today's. He tried to study disease scientifically, working out its causes and listing its symptoms and its cures. He told his patients that their illnesses were caused not by gods or evil spirits but naturally, and were more likely to be cured by proper treatment than by spells.

Hippocrates' fame quickly spread, and Cos became a healing-centre, with sick people flocking for cures and students hurrying to learn his methods. He published over 70 books, with such titles as *Epidemics, Epilepsy* and *A Healthy Environment*.

Until recently, modern doctors used to swear the same oath as Hippocrates taught his students: the "Hippocratic oath". It included such ideas as "I promise to help the sick to the best of my ability and judgement" and "I promise to avoid causing harm, and will not knowingly give or suggest harmful treatment."

EUDOXUS (Eudoxos)

Greek mathematician and scholar 408-353 BC

Eudoxus studied mathematics in Egypt, and then went to teach on the island of Cnidus. He worked out laws of proportion between the sides of geometrical figures (such as triangles and squares), and devised methods for finding lengths on curved lines and the volumes of curved solids. Then he began trying to explain the universe by mathematics. He told his pupils to imagine the universe as a series of spheres, one inside the other, with the Earth at the centre.

Eudoxus' description was meant only as an illustration, not as how the universe actually was. But many people, including **Aristotle**, took him literally, and began to think of the universe as a series of real spheres, humming and vibrating in space to make "the music of the spheres" – a view which lasted for almost 2,000 years, until it was disproved by the discoveries of such people as **Copernicus**, **Galileo** and **Kepler**.

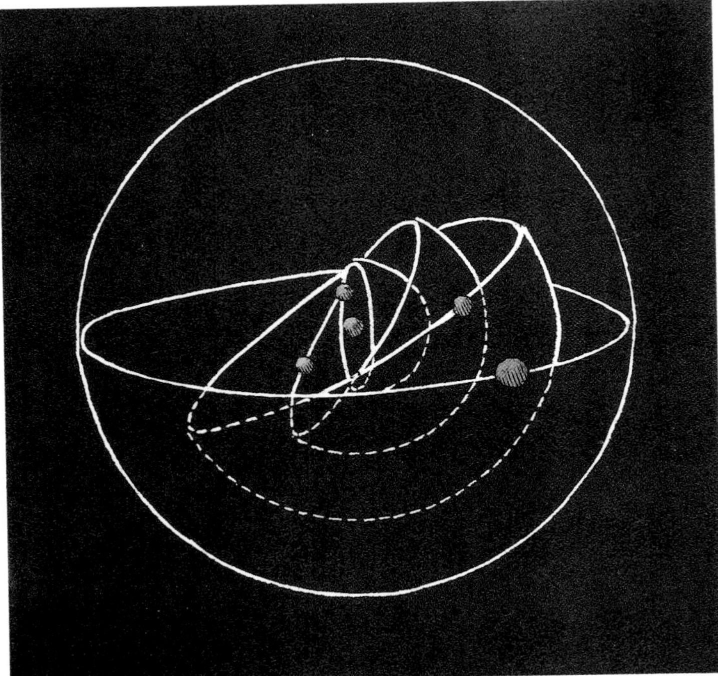

Eudoxus' view of the universe. He thought that the way the spheres are pivoted accounted for the observed movement of the Sun, Moon and planets.

EUCLID (Eukleides)

Greek scientist c 340-270 BC

Euclid worked at the University of Alexandria in Egypt. His job was to collect mathematical knowledge from Greece, Persia, Egypt and Arabia and put it into an ordered, logical form. He was particularly interested in geometry, and stated two "axioms" (self-evident facts): "the shortest distance between two points is a straight line", and "parallel lines can never meet". These axioms led to "theorems" (provable facts, for example: "If the sides of a triangle are equal, so are its angles"), and to "proofs" – and the whole thing was written in clear steps easily learned by heart.

Thirteen books of Euclid's theorems, called *Elements*, survived his death, and have been the basis of geometry ever since.

ARISTARCHUS (Aristarkhos)

Greek scholar 310-230 BC

Aristarchus was born on the island of Samos, and taught mathematics at the University of Alexandria. He is said to have invented the sundial, and to have tried to calculate the sizes of the Sun and Moon, and their distance from Earth. He was one of the first people to suggest that the Earth was round and that it orbited the Sun – a theory ignored or mocked for 1,600 years, until **Copernicus** and others proved it right.

Aristarchus' sundial. As the sun moves across the sky, the shadow moves around the stone to show the hour of the day.

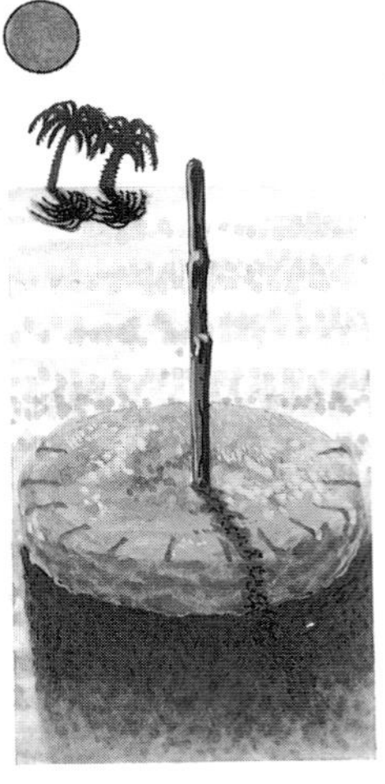

EUDOXUS: Aristotle 328 Copernicus 93 Galileo 96 Kepler 98 ARISTARCHUS: Copernicus 93

HEROPHILUS (Herophilos)

Greek doctor 3rd century BC

Herophilus worked in Alexandria, one of the few places in the civilized world at that time where dissection (cutting up dead bodies) was allowed. He was the first person to give accurate descriptions of the reproductive organs, the eyes and especially the brain, which he (correctly) said was the centre of the nervous system, not the heart as previous thinkers had believed.

ARCHIMEDES (Arkhimedes)

Greek scientist and inventor c 287-212 BC

Archimedes lived in Syracuse in Sicily, and was famous as a mathematics teacher and inventor. He was particularly interested in what scientists now call mechanics: the study of how things move, of mechanisms both natural and artificial. He invented the "Archimedes screw" – a way of raising water from one level to another by turning a person-sized screw inside a hollow tube. It was originally devised for bailing ships, but was – and still is – more often used in irrigation schemes all over the world.

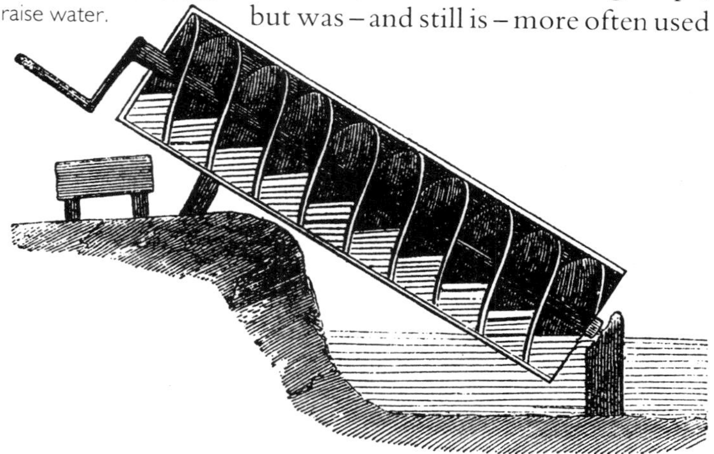

The Archimedes screw – a brilliant invention to raise water.

But Archimedes' most famous discovery, called the "Archimedes principle", is that if an object is immersed in a fluid (a liquid or gas), it appears to lose an amount of weight equal to the weight of fluid displaced. He is said to have worked this out in the public baths, while wondering how to find out if the gold in the king's crown was pure or mixed with cheaper, lighter metals. He also realized that if the crown were pure gold, it would displace the same amount of water as a lump of gold that weighed the same. If it contained a mixture of metals, it would displace more water. He leapt out of the bath shouting "Eureka" ("Got it!"), and ran off naked to tell the king.

When the Romans besieged Syracuse in 212 BC, Archimedes helped his city by inventing defence-machines such as boulder-hurling catapults and even, it is said, by setting fire to the sails of the Roman ships by focusing the sun's rays through a piece of glass. In spite of this, the Romans captured the city – and a soldier saw Archimedes drawing diagrams in the sand of the market-place, trying to work out what had gone wrong. Thinking that the circles and triangles he saw were battle plans, the soldier took Archimedes for a spy and killed him.

ERATOSTHENES

Egyptian/Greek scholar and writer c 280-200 BC

Eratosthenes began his career as a writer. He wrote plays, poems and a chronological history of the world, moving from myths about the gods to such real events as the Persian invasion of Greece and the exploits of **Alexander the Great**.

In 246 BC Eratosthenes was appointed head of the huge Library and University of Alexandria. He turned from writing to mathematics, trying to work out (among other things) the distances between different places on Earth and between Earth and the stars. He was the first person to make an accurate calculation of the circumference of the Earth (see picture).

In Egypt Eratosthenes made observations of the angle of the shadow of the Sun, cast at noon. He was thus able to calculate the Earth's circumference.

HIPPARCHUS (Hipparkhos)

Greek scientist c 180-125 BC

Hipparchus taught astronomy on the island of Rhodes, and built an observatory there. Although, like all ancient astronomers, he was hampered by having no lenses, and so had to make every observation with the naked eye, he charted the positions of no fewer than 1,080 fixed stars and made accurate maps of the Moon's surface. He was the first person to make a scientific analysis of the connection between the movement of heavenly bodies and the Earth's seasons. His work was amazingly accurate and modern scientists have only corrected his calculations by a few centimetres in the kilometre and a few seconds in the year.

The idea of the signs of the Zodiac dates from the time of Hipparchus.

Hipparchus is remembered above all for two inventions: trigonometry and the idea of lines of latitude and longitude. Trigonometry is the branch of mathematics concerned with calculating the angles of triangles or the length of their sides. Lines of latitude and longitude on maps make it possible to locate places with complete accuracy.

ERATOSTHENES: Alexander the Great 412

SOSIGENES

Greek/Egyptian astronomer 1st century BC

Sosigenes taught astronomy in Alexandria. He was asked by **Julius Caesar** to reform the old Roman calendar, which until then had had 355 days in each year, so that a whole 20-day month had to be inserted every two years to bring it back in line with the seasons. Sosigenes divided the year into 365½ days, and made 12 months instead of ten. With a few modifications, his calendar is still used in most of the world today.

PLINY "THE ELDER" (Gaius Plinius Secundus)

Roman scientist 23-79

Pliny had a distinguished career as an army officer and politician. His hobby was science, and he read the work of every available Greek scientist. Wherever he went, he collected strange and unusual facts, which he used to produce an encyclopedia called *Natural History*: 37 volumes on subjects ranging from astronomy, biology and medicine to magic and the history of painting.

In the end, Pliny's scientific curiosity led to his death. In AD 79 he was stationed at Misenum, overlooking the Bay of Naples, when Mount Vesuvius began to erupt. Instead of rushing to safety, Pliny went closer to observe the eruption – and was choked to death by the volcano's poisonous fumes.

Pliny is usually called "the Elder" to distinguish him from his nephew, Gaius Plinius Caecilius Secundus – the writer Pliny "the Younger".

PTOLEMY (Claudius Ptolemaeus)

Egyptian/Roman scientist 90-168

Ptolemy was a university teacher in Alexandria, and wrote books on a many subjects, from geometry to the mathematics of musical sound. He published maps of the world so accurate and complete that they were used virtually unaltered for over 1,000 years.

Ptolemy's main work was astronomy. He published a book called *The Almagest*, based on his own work and that of **Hipparchus**. It contained maps of the stars and planets, and gave mathematical explanations of their paths and orbits.

The Almagest was the standard book on astronomy for 12 centuries, until the time of **Copernicus** and **Kepler**. Although its central idea was wrong – Ptolemy thought that the Sun orbited the Earth, not the other way about – his calculations and observations (made without lenses, which were unknown in his day) were so thorough and so convincing that no one ever thought of challenging them. It was only when Copernicus compared what he read in Ptolemy with what he could see and calculate for himself that he began making new and totally unexpected discoveries.

Ancient astronomers like Ptolemy (above) thought that the Earth was the centre of the universe, and that everything else moved around it on circular orbits (below).

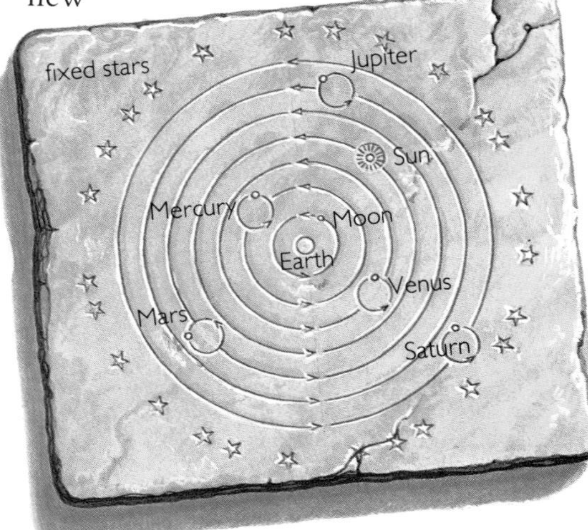

SOSIGENES: Caesar 415 PTOLEMY: Copernicus 93 Hipparchus 88 Kepler 98

The discoveries of Galen, a surgeon of ancient times, about how the human body works were considered to be authoritative for 15 centuries.

GALEN

Greek doctor 130-200

Galen began his career as a doctor in a school for training gladiators. His experience with gladiators' wounds gave him a fascination with the way the body works, and he spent many hours dissecting apes – the nearest thing the law allowed to human beings – and writing books about their muscles, organs and skeletons.

Many of Galen's names for bones are still used today. His writings made him famous, and he was invited to Rome to become physician to the Emperor and the court. He linked certain diseases with certain organs – sometimes correctly, sometimes not – and his ideas stood virtually unchallenged till the sixteenth century, the time of such men as **Harvey**, **Vesalius** and **Paracelsus** (who burned Galen's books in a spectacular public ceremony). Apart from **Hippocrates**, no other ancient surgeon had more influence than Galen on Western medicine.

The astrolabe – a device for measuring the distance of stars, said to be invented by Hypatia. The curved pointers indicate certain stars, and the instrument could be set to show the appearance of the sky for any date or time. Astrolabes were still used by sea navigators up until the end of the eighteenth century.

HYPATIA

Greek scholar 375-415

Although many women in the ancient world were as well-educated as men, it was practically unheard-of for a woman to teach or give lectures in public. Hypatia was an exception. She was a professor at the University of Alexandria, where she taught philosophy (especially the ideas of **Plato**), geometry, astronomy and algebra. She invented an apparatus for distilling water, an astrolabe (an instrument for measuring the distance of stars from Earth) and a planisphere (a three-dimensional model of the Earth and stars, which can be rotated to show how star-positions change with the seasons).

Unfortunately for Hypatia, her teaching was based on ancient Greek or Arabian knowledge and was directly opposed to the views of the Christian church. She made matters worse by giving lectures saying that the Biblical view of the creation of the universe was unscientific and unprovable. In 415, Clement, the Patriarch (leading bishop) of Alexandria, hired a mob to break up one of her lectures, but they went too far and murdered her.

GALEN: Harvey 98 Hippocrates 85 Paracelsus 93 Vesalius 94 HYPATIA: Plato 326

Al-Hasan, an expert on optics, seen here teaching chemistry.

AL-HASAN (Alhazen)

Arab scientist c 956-1038

His full name was Abu-Ali Al-Hasan Ibn Al-Haytham, but he was known to non-Arabic speakers as Al-Hasan. He was an expert on optics, and wrote a book about light, refraction and colour. Until his time, scientists had thought that we see because our eyes send out rays which bounce off objects and carry their images back to us. Al-Hasan showed that the eyes are not transmitters but receivers, accepting light rays from external objects.

Al-Hasan's book on optics was translated into Latin and published in 1572. A century later, **Newton** read it and set out to correct some of its wrong ideas – the beginning of Newton's own work in optics.

AVICENNA (Ibn Sina)

Persian doctor and thinker 980-1037

Avicenna's main work was in medicine. He was the personal physician of many of the sultans (rulers) of Ecbatana (modern Hamadan, in western Iran), and published a book entitled *Qanum* ("Canon") which was used as a medical textbook for centuries, second in importance only to **Galen's** works. His medical research led him to study the doctors and scientists of ancient Greece, and he translated **Euclid** into Arabic. He wrote essays on mathematics, music, astronomy and religion, trying in particular to show how Islamic religious ideas could exist side by side with the teaching of such great non-Islamic thinkers as **Aristotle** and **Plato.**

AL-HASAN: Newton 102 AVICENNA: Aristotle 328 Euclid 86 Galen 90 Plato 326

ALBERTUS MAGNUS (Albert von Böllstadt)

German scientist and saint 1193-1280

Albertus Magnus was a German aristocrat who became a Roman Catholic monk, and rose to high office as Bishop of Regensburg. As one of the leading religious teachers of his time, he published many books on Christian thought.

One of Albertus' interests was in making links between Christian belief and the discoveries of science. He studied such past writers as **Aristotle** and **Pliny the Elder**, and did experiments to test the truth of what they wrote. He also studied alchemy, believing that although the alchemists' main aim (to try to change ordinary substances into gold) was inspired by the Devil and against God's law, many of their experiments and discoveries might nevertheless be useful. He said that religion and science need not be enemies, and that investigating the nature of the universe should increase people's respect for God, rather than lessen it.

Albertus retired from church work in 1262, and gave all his time to research and writing. His aim was to be a Christian equivalent of Aristotle, writing books which would describe all the world's knowledge in Christian terms. He completed 38 volumes before he died; they deal with such subjects as astronomy, chemistry, geography and medicine.

Albertus Magnus was made a saint in 1931. He is the patron saint of students of natural science.

The saint, Albertus Magnus.

BACON, Roger

English monk, scientist and scholar c 1214-92

The people of Bacon's time called him Doctor Mirabilis ("Knowledge wizard"), and some said that the Devil had sold him all the knowledge in the universe in exchange for his soul. He certainly knew a great deal about science, and wrote it down in his *Opus Majus* – a summary of the scientific knowledge of his age. He made several important advances, including demonstrating that air is needed for combustion and being the first to use lenses to correct sight. Bacon has also been credited with inventing gunpowder, the glass mirror and the magnifying glass, but in fact these had been known long before his time, and he probably did no more than improve on existing ideas.

"Doctor Mirabilis" Bacon looking over Oxford from his observatory.

ALBERTUS MAGNUS: Aristotle 328 Pliny the Elder 89

COPERNICUS
(Mikolaj Koperningk)

Polish astronomer 1473-1543

Many people before Copernicus had believed that the Sun and not the Earth was the centre of the solar system: **Aristarchus**, for one, suggested it in the fourth century BC. But Copernicus was able to prove it scientifically, by exact observation of star-movements in the sky.

Copernicus was a Roman Catholic priest, and knew that his book *On the Revolution of the Heavenly Bodies* would cause a scandal, because it contradicted the Church's teaching that God created the Earth as the centre of the universe. He therefore refused to publish the book in his lifetime. When it did come out, soon after his death, it caused a sensation. Astronomers could see that it disproved the ideas of **Ptolemy**, which had lasted unchallenged for 1,400 years. Led by **Galileo** and **Kepler**, they set about making accurate observations and exact calculations to prove that Copernicus was right.

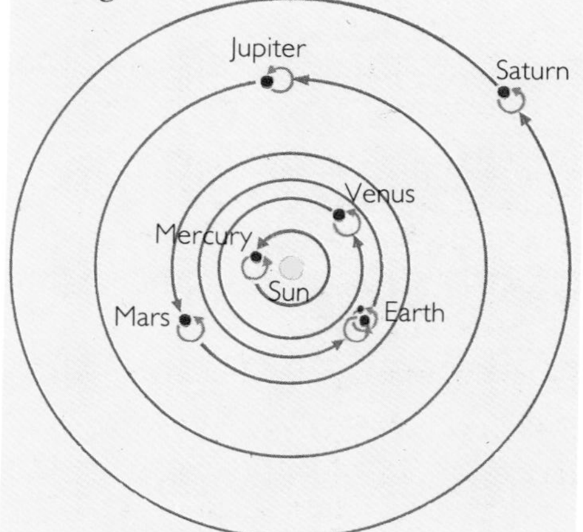

Copernicus proved that the Earth was not the centre of the universe but orbited the Sun, just like other planets.

PARACELSUS
(Theophrastus von Hohenheim)

Swiss doctor 1493-1541

Paracelsus was a fierce-tempered man, determined to make medicine a proper science instead of the mixture of magic, luck and old wives' tales he thought it had been until his time. When he became Professor of Medicine at Basle University, he caused scandal by making a bonfire of all **Galen's** and **Avicenna's** books from the University library, the medical books doctors had relied on for centuries. He infuriated the Church authorities by saying that diseases were not caused by the Devil and could not be cured by miracles. He studied the chemistry of medicines, and carefully updated **Hippocrates'** writings on the symptoms and treatment of disease.

Paracelsus burning library books in the courtyard of Basle University.

COPERNICUS: Aristarchus 86 Galileo 96 Kepler 98 Ptolemy 89 PARACELSUS: Avicenna 91 Galen 90 Hippocrates 85

Maps of the known world were at first drawn assuming the Earth was flat. Once it had been proved to be a sphere, a map was necessary that allowed for the world's curvature yet could be drawn on paper. Mercator's map, published in 1569, meant navigators could plot their courses accurately.

MERCATOR, Gerardus (Gerhard Kremer)

Flemish map-maker 1512-94

Mercator worked for the German Duke of Cleves. He made him a map-book with a picture on the front of Atlas, the giant in Greek mythology who supports the sky. Map-books have been called "atlases" ever since.

In Mercator's day no one had worked out a way of showing the Earth, a sphere, in two-dimensional drawings on flat paper. He was the first to do so, by increasing the east-west scale in the higher latitudes. The "Mercator projection", as it is called, is still used on many maps of the world today.

VESALIUS, Andreas

Flemish doctor and artist 1514-64

Vesalius was Professor of Surgery at Padua University, and wrote many books on anatomy. He is best known today for *The Structure of the Human Body*, a set of detailed drawings of muscles, nerves and bones. He researched his drawings by dissection (cutting up dead bodies), something condemned at the time because people thought that it might prevent the dead rising complete on the Day of Resurrection. His book served as a guide not only to surgeons but also to sculptors and painters wanting to know more about the structure of the body beneath the skin.

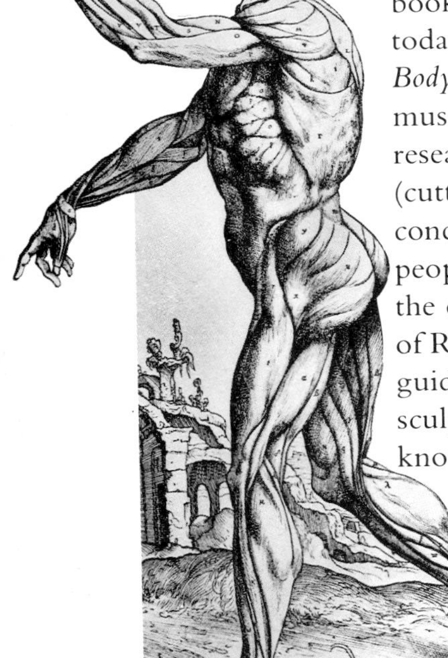

Vesalius' detailed drawings of the corpses he dissected resulted in the first reliable book of human anatomy.

GILBERT, William

English doctor 1544-1603

Gilbert was employed by **Queen Elizabeth I**, who was determined to look and feel young for as long as possible. Gilbert did research into how the body ages. He studied the works of the medieval alchemists, who thought that if you could change the amounts of each of the elements of the human body, you might discover the secret of immortality.

Gilbert found no help for Queen Elizabeth's age problem in alchemy, but he became fascinated with something else: the "lodestone", a lump of iron oxide which alchemists had for centuries thought able to change all other elements. In fact, lodestones were magnetic, although no one used the description until Gilbert – and it was the magnetic properties of iron oxide which he investigated. He also experimented with electricity, but he could see no real use for it, and soon gave it up to concentrate on magnetism.

GILBERT: Elizabeth I 436

BRAHE, Tycho

Danish astronomer 1546-1601

In Brahe's time, astronomy was in ferment. **Copernicus** had upset theories about the Sun and stars which people had believed for 2,000 years, and other scientists were daily finding new evidence to prove his ideas. Brahe was less of an original thinker than Copernicus or **Galileo**, but he was a careful, thorough scientific observer. He made lenses and measuring-instruments far more accurate than any produced before, and used them to chart the position of every visible body in the sky. His charts and tables were so precise that astronomers used them, virtually unchanged, for 300 years.

NAPIER, John

Scottish mathematician 1550-1617

Napier invented logarithms, the decimal point and the "scientific notation" method of expressing very large and very small numbers (see example). He also devised a kind of calculating machine, which his rivals scornfully nicknamed "Napier's bones", as if he were no more than a fortune-teller. It was the ancestor of the slide-rule, a mathematical tool widely used until the invention of the electronic calculator.

Napier worked out a shorthand way of expressing numbers, so that 35×10^6 means 35,000,000.

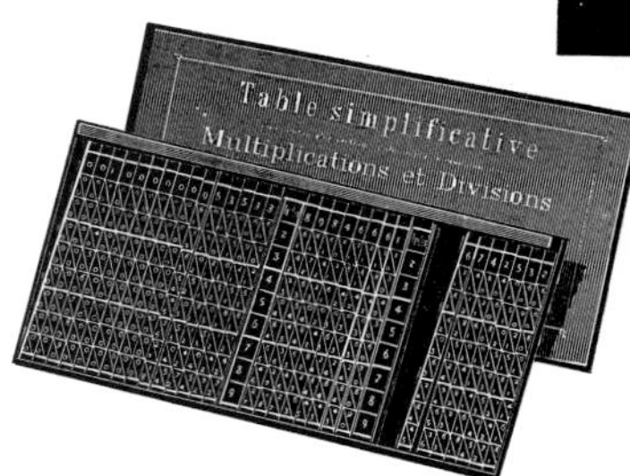

BACON, Francis

English courtier, scientist and philosopher 1561-1626

Bacon was Lord Chancellor – the person in charge of England's laws. In his spare time he wrote essays on all kinds of subjects, from wealth to death, from truth to gardening. Some people claim that he was the real author of **Shakespeare's** plays.

One of Bacon's hobbies was science. He said that research should be a matter not of guesswork and "good ideas" only, but of careful observation and experiment. He collected observations on everything he could see, feel, taste or hear, and published two books, *Advancement of Learning* and *Novum Organum* ("New Arrangement").

Although Bacon's work was thorough and careful, he did not use what people now think of as "scientific method": his fact-collecting was random rather than purposeful. But the idea that observation and experiment are vital processes is crucial to modern science – and Bacon first put it into words.

Francis Bacon's ideas influenced many early scientists. His encyclopedia, *Novum Organum* (below), set out the proper way to carry out scientific research, known as the induction method.

BRAHE: Copernicus 93 Galileo 96 BACON: Shakespeare 16

GALILEI, Galileo

Italian scientist 1564-1642

Galileo, Italy's great scientist of the Renaissance era.

Galileo, like **Leonardo**, is always known by his Christian name. As a student and professor of maths, he came to believe that if an idea could be proved, it was real; if it could not, it was not. This view directly opposed Christian teaching of the time, which said that what the Church taught was inspired by God and was therefore true, whether it could be proved or not.

Galileo's clash of views with the Church brought him trouble in later life. But until he was 40 his career was serene enough. As a young man he studied medicine, maths and physics at Pisa University. He was interested in the physics of movement, and one day, after watching a pendulum in Pisa cathedral and timing its swings with his pulse, he began to do laboratory experiments with pendulums. His discovery brought him instant fame in Italy, and led to his being made Professor of Physics at Pisa University.

In the next few years, Galileo did more research with falling weights. From this, he was able to conclude that if there were no air to slow down the fall of some objects, they would all hit the ground at the same time, no matter what their size or weight.

Galileo's discovery caused an uproar, because it challenged the teaching of **Aristotle**, believed for 2,000 years, that objects fall at different rates according to their weights. He was forced to give up his job, and in 1592 he went to teach in Padua University, where he stayed for 18 years. At Padua, he investigated the expansion and contraction of metals, and his work on mercury led him to invent the thermometer.

One of Galileo's hobbies was model-making, and in 1609 he put it to scientific use. He heard of the recent invention of the telescope by **Lippershey**, and built one of his own. He wanted to check **Copernicus'** theories on the movement of heavenly bodies, and used his new telescope to explore the sky.

At first, astronomy was a leisure interest, but it soon came to occupy all of Galileo's time, and led to his most important scientific work. He made several observations now taken for granted, such as the fact that the

Galileo worked out that a pendulum will always take the same time to swing, no matter what the length of the swing, and he used this knowledge to build accurate clocks.

Moon reflects the Sun's light and has no light of its own, or that the Milky Way is not a single band of light but is composed of millions of individual stars. He discovered sunspots, four of Jupiter's moons, Saturn's rings and the "phases" of Venus. Above all, his study of the sky – always backed up by thousands of hours of observation and page after page of mathematical proofs – led him more and more to share Copernicus' view that the Earth moves round the Sun and not the Sun round the Earth. He began teaching and writing about this theory, and at once the Church authorities stepped in, ordering him to stop or risk punishment.

By this time Galileo was in his 50s, a frail, sick man. He was terrified that if he defied the Church he would die in prison, and he tried to do as he was told and to forget his astronomical research. But his scientist's mind was anything but frail, and in the end he found it impossible to keep silent about things he thought were facts provable beyond doubt. When he was 68 he wrote a book comparing old and new views of the universe, and favouring the new. The Church authorities ordered him to state publicly that he was wrong, or be tortured to death.

Galileo, once again physically terrified, backed down, and soon afterwards retired from public life, living for ten more years as a sick, blind old man. But although the Church had broken his spirit, it could not censor his views out of existence. The theory that the Earth moves round the Sun was an "idea whose time has come": one stated at exactly the moment people were ready to receive it. No one has seriously challenged it since Galileo's time, and even the Church, only a few years after his death, announced that it agreed with him.

Galileo researched into the speed of falling weights by dropping objects from the top of the Leaning Tower of Pisa.

GALILEO: Aristotle 328 Copernicus 93 Leonardo 11 Lippershey 341

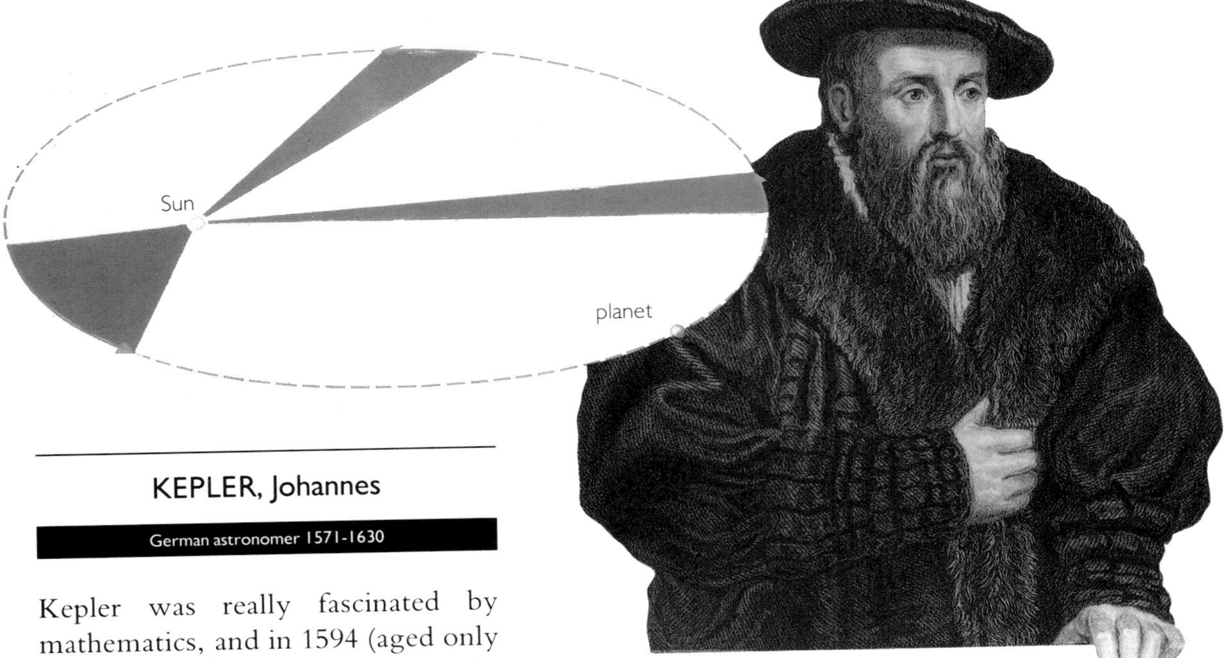

Johannes Kepler, one of the founders of modern astronomy. He discovered that planets orbit the Sun in ellipses, and showed that planets move faster when closer to the Sun.

KEPLER, Johannes

German astronomer 1571-1630

Kepler was really fascinated by mathematics, and in 1594 (aged only 25) he was made Professor of Maths at Graz University in Austria. But Graz was a Roman Catholic city, and at that time Protestants like Kepler were in danger from Catholic gangs in the streets. Kepler was attacked several times, and in 1600 left for the safety of Protestant Denmark, to work with **Brahe**. He succeeded Brahe as royal astronomer.

With the aid of Brahe's detailed observations Kepler was able to formulate the laws of planetary motion named after him, showing that each planet moves around the Sun not in a circle – as had been believed till then – but in an ellipse. He suggested that tides in the sea might be caused by the movement of the Moon – an idea **Newton** took up when he was working on the theory of gravitation.

Kepler was the first person to try to prove **Copernicus'** theories by precise observation and exact calculation, and his work was crucial not only for astronomy but also for the breakthrough in mathematics which came about in the seventeenth century.

HARVEY, William

English doctor 1578-1657

Until Harvey's time, people believed that blood lay in the body's veins and arteries like liquid in a jar: life-giving but stagnant. Harvey, who was the English royal doctor, caring for both King James I and **Charles I**, was fascinated by anatomy, the recently developed skill of learning about the body by dissecting dead people. He discovered that the heart pumps blood round the body in a constant stream, first to the lungs, then to the limbs and internal organs and back to the heart.

William Harvey, the doctor who discovered that blood circulates round the body.

KEPLER: Brahe 95 Copernicus 93 Newton 102 HARVEY: Charles I 442

GUERICKE, Otto von

German scientist 1602-86

Guericke invented the vacuum pump, and demonstrated it by placing two copper hemispheres together, pumping out the air and showing that the air pressure outside held them together so firmly that two teams of 15 horses each could not pull them apart. He also gave some of the earliest demonstrations of electricity. He rotated a sphere of sulphur until it became charged, and then showed how feathers and other objects stuck to it.

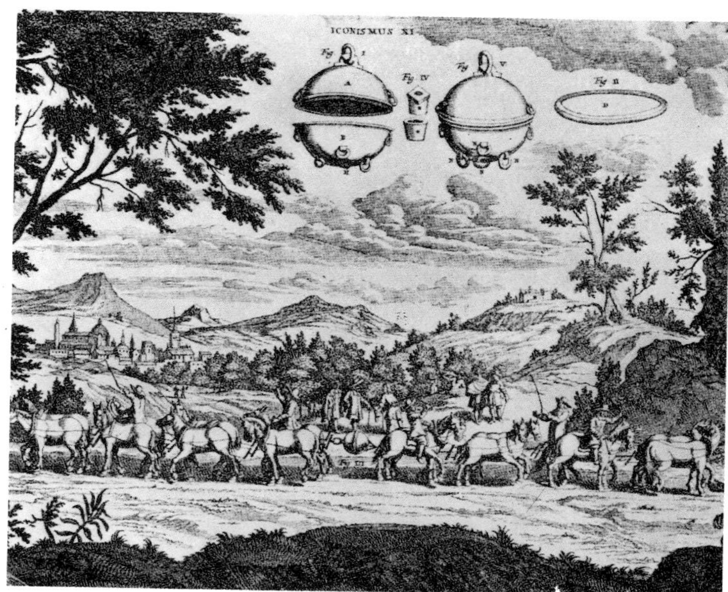

Von Guericke's demonstration of the force of atmospheric pressure.

TORRICELLI, Evangelista

Italian scientist 1608-47

Torricelli was a pupil of **Galileo**, and followed him as Professor of Maths at Florence University. Although he worked on many things, including the development of the microscope and telescope, he is best remembered for inventing the barometer. This came from work on something entirely different: the problem of draining water from flooded mines. "Lift pumps" were used for this work – but no one, not even Galileo, could explain why no lift pump would ever raise the water more than ten metres.

Torricelli decided to try to find out why this happened. Instead of using a ten-metre column of water, he used mercury, which was much denser and therefore took up less space. From his findings he was able to work out that it was air pressure that determined how high the lift pump could raise water. He also noticed that the height of the column varied from day to day: the air pressure changed according to the weather conditions.

Although Torricelli died before completing his work, others used his ideas to produce an instrument – the barometer or pressure gauge – which measures air pressure and from it forecasts the weather.

BORELLI, Giovanni Alfonso

Italian scientist 1608-79

Borelli was a professor of maths, and his hobbies were astronomy and the study of volcanoes, called vulcanology. But he is best remembered today for his medical research. He described the physics of the body, as if it were a collection of pumps, levers, hinges and other mechanisms. He was one of the first people to treat the human body as an object for scientific investigation instead of as something divinely created and almost magical. His work was crucial to the development of medicine as a practical, scientific skill.

TORRICELLI: Galileo 96

PASCAL, Blaise

French scientist and thinker 1623-62

Pascal was a mathematical genius. At eleven he worked out the first 23 propositions of **Euclid**, something even university students in those days found hard. At 16, he wrote a paper on geometry, so brilliant that **Descartes**, a leading thinker of the time, refused to believe that it was the boy's unaided work.

Soon afterwards, Pascal began a series of scientific experiments to prove **Torricelli's** theories about air pressure, and invented a counting machine to help his calculations. It was patented in 1647, and was one of the first-ever "intelligent" machines. It could add and subtract, using cogs and levers. His mathematical research, helped by this machine, inspired **Newton** and **Leibnitz**, and paved the way for the invention of differential calculus.

Pascal was a deeply religious man, and in 1654, after seeing two religious visions, he determined to give the rest of his life to God. He began thinking and writing about Christian belief, and published a book, *Provincial Letters*, on such matters as whether God's existence can be proved by reasoning.

In the next five years Pascal made notes for a book on religious faith. It was published after his death under the title *Pensées* ("Thoughts"). *Pensées* influenced many later thinkers, such as **Rousseau** and **Voltaire**, and is still considered one of the greatest of all writings about why and how the human race should think about God.

BOYLE, Robert

Irish scientist 1627-91

Until Boyle's time, most scientists still agreed with medieval alchemists that everything in existence was made up of four elements: earth, air, fire and water. Boyle's book *The Sceptical Chemist* changed all that. He showed that matter consists of compounds and mixtures not of four basic elements but of many dozens (over 100 are now known). If you change the balance of the elements in a mixture or compound you produce a different substance.

Boyle also did important physics experiments. He researched into sound waves and air pressure, and is remembered today for "Boyle's Law", which says that at constant temperature the pressure of a gas increases as its volume decreases.

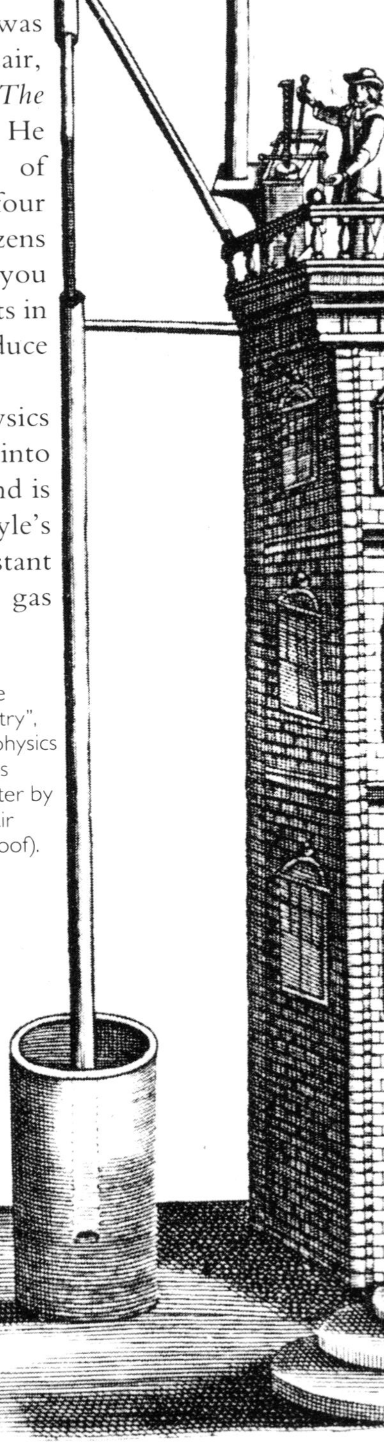

Robert Boyle, the "father of chemistry", also carried out physics experiments. This device raised water by suction (Boyle's air pump is on the roof).

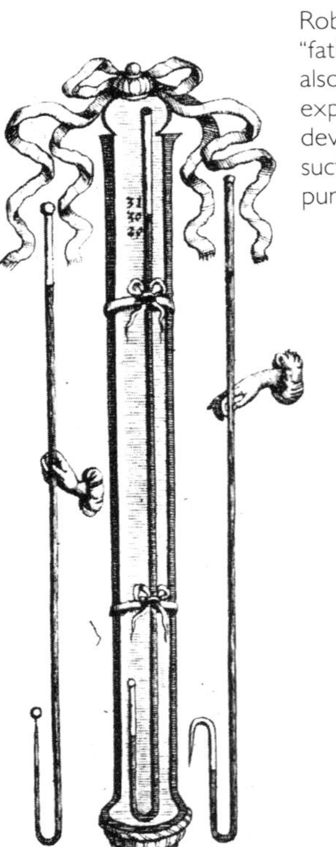

One of Boyle's syphon barometers.

PASCAL: Descartes 342 Euclid 86 Leibnitz 103 Newton 102 Rousseau, J J 348 Torricelli 99 Voltaire 344

Right: Hooke's scientific drawings, such as this one of cork, were real works of art.

HUYGENS, Christian

Dutch scientist 1629-95

Huygens was an expert in grinding and polishing glass, to make lenses for spectacles and telescopes. Using one of his own telescopes, he was the first person to see that the "rings" of Saturn vary in appearance as the planet orbits the Sun. He also experimented with clockwork, and invented an accurate form of pendulum-clock. He was a friend of **Newton**, but did not share his views on gravity and light. He thought that light consisted not of particles, as Newton said, but of waves; later physicists (such as **Einstein**) showed that both men were correct.

Huygens' first telescope gave up to eight times magnification.

LEEUWENHOEK, Anthony van

Dutch scientist 1632-1723

Leeuwenhoek perfected the microscope, and used it to study the body in detail never seen before. He was the first person to see how blood flows through the capillaries (veins as thin as hairs), and to describe blood corpuscles.

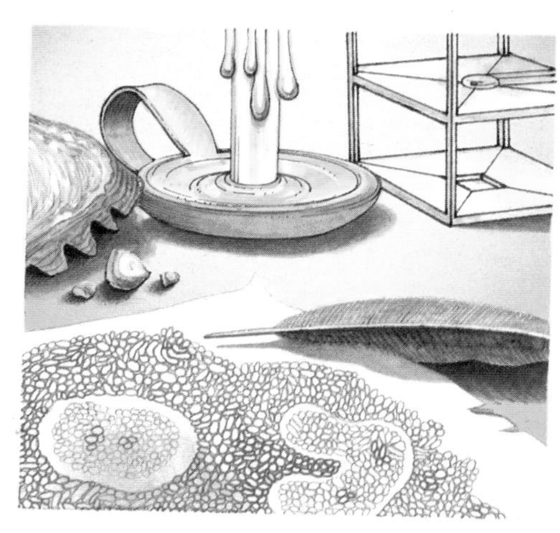

HOOKE, Robert

English scientist 1635-1703

Hooke originally studied for the Church, but took up science instead because he claimed it was "less strenuous". He worked as a surveyor, drawing plans for roads and buildings, and made a fortune. He was said to be so miserly that he refused to trust bankers with his money, keeping all his wealth in gold coins in the cellars and attics of his house.

Hooke's spare time was spent doing scientific experiments and making observations, and he drew beautiful, minutely detailed pictures of the things he saw through his microscope. He was the first person to see that plants have cells; he discovered this while looking through his microscope at a slice of cork (which is made from the bark of a type of oak tree).

It was said that Hooke was a prickly, difficult man, jealous of other scientists' successes. When **Newton** published the laws of gravitation in the 1680s, Hooke commented sourly that he wasn't surprised – he'd known of them for years.

HUYGENS: Einstein 146 Newton 102 HOOKE: Newton 102

Newton's few simple laws explained some of the complex and varied aspects of the natural world. The sight of an apple falling from a tree led to his thoughts about gravity and the movements of planets and the tides.

NEWTON, Isaac

English scientist 1642-1727

Newton spent a lonely childhood. His father, a prosperous farmer, died when he was a baby, and his mother remarried, so he was brought up by his grandmother. Ignored by the village children, who thought him a snob, Newton spent much of his childhood alone, reading books and making scientific models.

The result was that when Newton went to Cambridge University at 17, he already knew more than many of his professors. In 1667 he was made Professor of Mathematics, a job he kept for the next 34 years. He was also a Member of Parliament, and spent 28 years as Master of the Mint, responsible for making Britain's coins and banknotes.

Newton's first scientific work was the study of light, or "optics" as he called it. He brought a prism at a fair, and used it to show that "white" light, for example sunlight, can be split up into the seven colours of the rainbow. If you pass the colours through a second prism they recombine to form "white" light again. He called the range of colours the spectrum.

Newton also studied motion. About 150 years earlier, when

Newton also discovered the colour spectrum of "white" light, and designed and built the first reflecting telescope.

NEWTON: Copernicus 93 Einstein 146 Galileo 96 Leibnitz 103

Copernicus was wondering why planets orbit the Sun, the only answer he could think of was "Because they do." Later, **Galileo** had shown that since all natural movement is in a straight line, a force is needed to keep the planets moving in curved orbits. Newton suggested that this force was the same as that which makes a ripe apple drop from a tree to the ground: bodies such as the Earth pull other objects towards them (making them "gravitate" or move). The bigger the body, the bigger the "gravitational force".

In 1687 Newton published a book, *Principia Mathematica,* developing his ideas on gravity and giving mathematical proofs. He showed that the laws of gravitation mean that the planets must orbit the Sun in ellipses (flattened circles), because they move faster when they travel towards the Sun (pulled by its gravity) and slower when they move away (held back by its gravity).

Newton also formulated three laws of motion, which helped to explain many of the mysteries about how and why things move, on Earth and in space. Later, they were slightly changed by **Einstein's** theory of relativity, but none the less remain Newton's most vital contribution to science.

To help make his calculations simpler, Newton devised a new way of calculation, which he called "fluxions". This was similar to **Leibnitz's** calculus of 1684 – which led to a furious row about whose came first. Calculus, whether Newton's or Leibnitz's, is one of the sources of modern maths – and it has been a vital tool of science ever since it was invented.

Engraving of Gottfried Leibnitz.

LEIBNITZ, Gottfried Wilhelm

German mathematician 1646-1716

Leibnitz, a diplomat, met **Huygens** on a mission to France, and Huygens' work inspired him to develop his own interest in maths. He invented a calculating machine which was operated by cogs and a cylinder turned by hand, and also a calculating system called differential calculus. But he never published his ideas, and in the 1690s had a row with **Newton,** who claimed to have invented calculus first.

Leibnitz believed in logic, the art of thinking in single steps from simple ideas to complex ones. He thought that this process could be applied not just to thinking but to everything in the universe. He believed that the entire universe was built from single, simple units called "monads", as a nation was built from single individuals. At the moment of creation, God put these monads into a graceful, orderly form, and so made the world we know today. Human beings had disturbed the order of the universe by illogical thought and action, but if they worked hard to restore it – for example by using universal, logical laws and a single, simple language – the world would once again recover its tranquillity.

A scene from the Bayeux Tapestry showing Halley's comet.

BERNOULLI FAMILY

Swiss mathematicians 17th and 18th centuries

The Bernoullis were one of the most amazing dynasties in the history of science. For more than three generations, all the men in the family specialized in maths or physics at various European universities. One Bernoulli or another, for example, was Professor of Mathematics or Physics at Basle University for over 80 years.

JACQUES (or JAKOB) BERNOULLI (1654-1705) became Professor of Mathematics at Basle in 1687, and is noted for his work on the calculation system known as calculus and on the theory of probability.

Jacques' brother JEAN (or JOHANN) BERNOULLI (1667-1748) was also a Professor, at Groningen in Holland, until Jacques' death, when he followed him as Professor in Basle. Jean was a jealous man. It is said he stole ideas from the rest of the family and claimed them as his own; he also once expelled his son Daniel from the university for winning a prize he had hoped to win.

DANIEL BERNOULLI (1700-82) was the family's most brilliant scholar. He was made Professor of Physics at St Petersburg University in Russia at the age of 23, and ten years later returned to Basle where he became, in turn, the Professor of Anatomy, Botany and Physics.

Other scientific members of the family include NICHOLAS BERNOULLI (1695-1726), Daniel's elder brother, also JEAN BERNOULLI (1710-1807), his younger brother, and Jean's two sons JEAN BERNOULLI II (1744-1807) and JACQUES BERNOULLI (1759-89).

HALLEY, Edmund

English astronomer 1656-1742

Halley was a friend of **Newton**, and wondered if he could use mathematical equations, based on Newton's work, to predict the movement of stars and planets in the sky. He travelled to the Atlantic island of St Helena, where the skies are particularly clear, built an observatory and began charting star-movements.

Edmund Halley – England's second Astronomer Royal.

Halley was especially interested in comets, and he formed the theory (which has since been confirmed) that

HALLEY: Hutton 109 Lyell 122 Newton 102

each follows its own unique orbit through the universe, and reappears above the Earth at fixed and predictable times.

One comet in particular, nicknamed the "Great Star", attracted Halley's attention. It had last been seen in 1682 and was the brightest comet known. By checking historical reports of sightings and working out its orbit, he calculated that it swept past the Earth every 76 years, and would next appear in 1758. It did, and was given his name. Halley's Comet has appeared regularly ever since, and was last seen in 1986.

Although Halley's main work was in astronomy, he was also interested in other matters. Sixty years before **Hutton** and **Lyell**, he suggested that physical science might be used to calculate the age of the Earth. He also made wind charts for the British navy, and surveyed the currents and sandbanks of the English Channel, going out himself in a small boat to make the measurements.

TOURNEFORT, Pierre de

French scientist 1656-1708

Tournefort travelled all over the world, collecting plants for the Jardin du Roi, the royal collection in Paris (later called the Jardin des Plantes: see **Jussieu**). He studied the plants in their natural habitats, and illustrated his descriptions with beautiful, detailed drawings.

One of Tournefort's expeditions was to Mount Ararat in Turkey. In the Bible story of Noah and the flood, the Ark came to rest on Mount Ararat, and Tournefort wanted to find out what plants grew on the mountain. He thought that if they had survived the flood, they might show the kind of plants which clothed the Earth in the time of the Garden of Eden. He found that the higher he climbed, the fewer plants there were: he was the first scientist to show that where plants grow is affected by altitude as well as by latitude.

Tournefort's studies on Mount Arafat (5,155 metres high) showed that altitude limits where plants can grow.

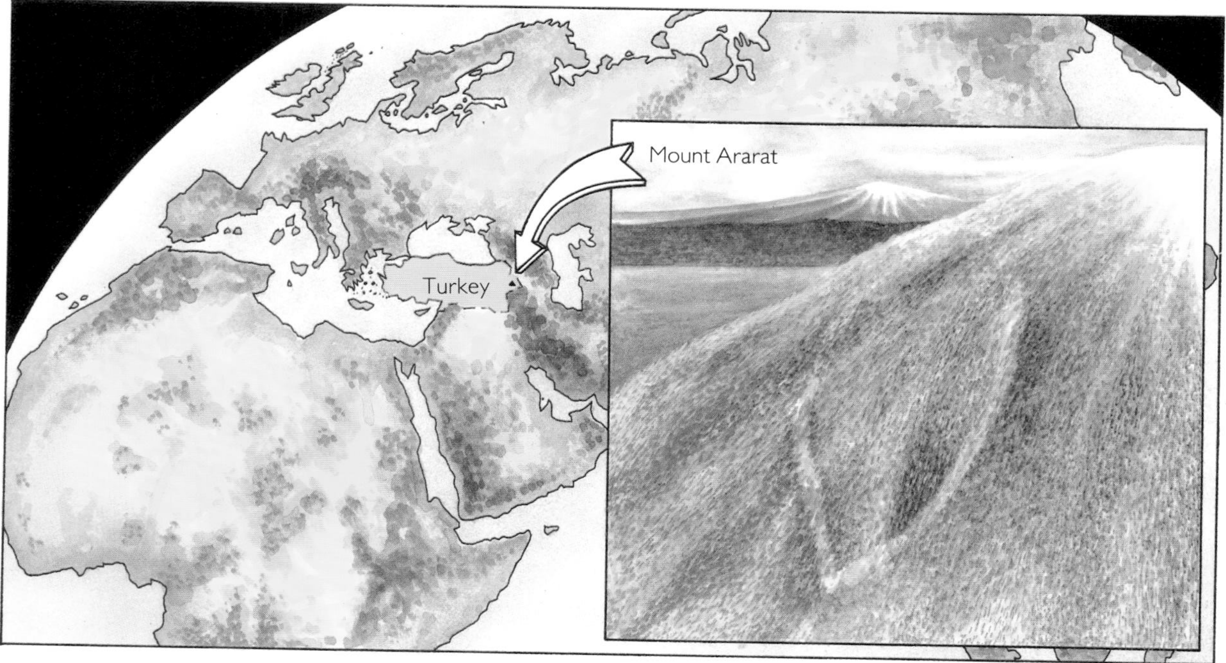

TOURNEFORT: Jussieu family 107

RÉAUMUR, René Antoine Ferchault de

French scientist and writer 1683-1757

Réaumur interested himself with how to assemble knowledge and present it in a logical, scientific way. He believed that if people understood how the universe worked, they would be set free from the superstition and oppression which had imprisoned the human race for centuries.

Réaumur began his first collection of facts, *Description and Perfection of Arts and Crafts*, when he was 12. His idea was to describe every manufacturing process in existence, to show the scientific principles on which it worked and to suggest ways of improving it. At first the work seemed simple enough: listing a stone-mason's tools, for example, or describing forestry, metal-smelting or mining. But the huge number of discoveries made in the early eighteenth century (for example how to harness steam power to drive industrial machines) led to an enormous increase in Réaumur's work, and the encyclopedia took him 50 years to finish and ran to 121 separate sections.

Side by side with his research into technology, Réaumur began a second survey, *Research Notes on Insects*. This, too, took longer than he expected; the last of its six volumes was not published until 1742, when he was 59. The books described every species of insect then known, showing their anatomy and giving an account of their behaviour and their habitats. The complete *Research Notes on Insects* rivalled **Linnaeus'** plant classification as the most thorough scientific encyclopedia of the eighteenth century.

Réaumur is also remembered for the "Réaumur thermometer", whose scale is divided into 80 equal sections (or degrees) between the freezing point of water (0°) and the boiling point of water (80°).

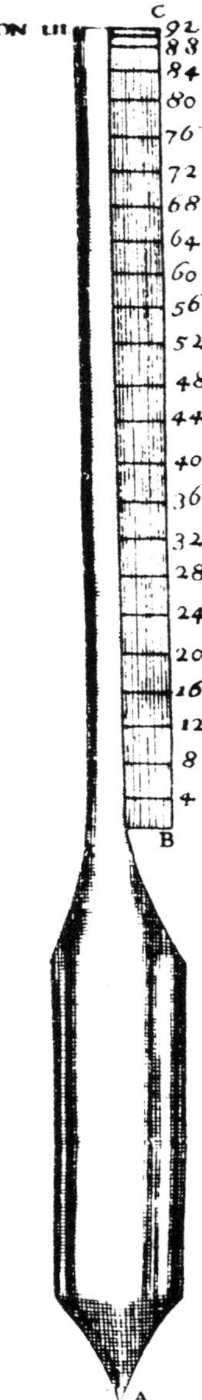

Fahrenheit's thermometers were the first to use mercury.

FAHRENHEIT, Gabriel Daniel

Dutch scientist 1686-1736

Fahrenheit invented a system of measuring temperature. The coldest temperature he could obtain was by mixing ice and salt, and he made this his zero (0° Fahrenheit). On this scale, ice by itself melts at 32° and water boils at 212°.

Left: Réaumur, and friends.

RÉAUMUR: Linnaeus 107

JUSSIEU FAMILY

French scientists 17th-19th centuries

Four members of the Jussieu family played a leading role in the development of the science of botany. Much of their work was connected with the Jardin des Plantes, a plant garden established by King Louis XIII in Paris.

ANTOINE JUSSIEU (1686-1758) was an expert in herbal medicine. He wrote an encyclopedia of medicinal plants.

BERNARD JUSSIEU (c 1699-1777), Antoine's brother, supervised the breeding of exotic plants. He began a catalogue of all plants by species, a task completed by his son ANTOINE LAURENT DE JUSSIEU (1748-1836), who successfully ran the gardens during the French Revolution, stopping the mob from looting them by dispensing plant medicines free of charge. He was allowed to remain curator when the gardens were nationalized after the Revolution, and kept his job for 40 years.

Antoine Laurent's son ADRIEN JUSSIEU (1797-1853) corresponded with **Darwin** on plant evolution, and wrote a book on botany and a history of his family's work with plants.

LINNAEUS, Carolus (Carl von Linné)

Swedish scientist 1707-78

Linnaeus devised the method of classifying plants and animals which is still used today. It is called the "binomial" ("two-name") system, because the name of each species consists of two parts, given in Latin. The first part is the genus ("group"), such as *Canis* (dog) or *Felis* (cat). The second part is the particular type of animal or plant belonging to that genus. For example, the wolf is known as *Canis lupus*, and the European wildcat as *Felis sylvestris*.

Linnaeus named over 4,000 different species, but his system has grown and changed over the years, and now covers millions of animals and plants.

Linnaeus, whose work was commemorated when the English Biological Association changed its name to the Linnaean Society.

EULER, Leonhard

Swiss mathematician 1707-83

Euler was a tireless worker in the fields of maths and science. During his lifetime he published (in Latin) over 500 essays and articles, and another 200 were discovered and published after his death.

Following a long career as Professor at the St Petersburg Academy and the Berlin Academy of Sciences, Euler eventually became blind. Assistants wrote down his calculations and read them back to him – and he claimed that because he could see nothing to distract him, his mind could concentrate even more closely on his work.

Leonhard Euler.

Left: Bernard Jussieu.

JUSSIEU FAMILY: Darwin 124

HALLER, Albrecht von

Swiss/German scientist and thinker 1708-77

Until Haller was 45, he worked as Professor of Anatomy, Botany and Medicine at Göttingen University. He studied the way muscles work, and made the first-ever distinction between "irritability" (involuntary reaction of muscle tissue to electric shocks, heat, pinpricks and so on) and "sensibility" (muscle movement controlled through the nervous system by the brain).

Haller had a restless mind, and by the time he was 45 he was bored. He retired from Göttingen and went back to his birthplace, Berne, to become a writer. He wrote poems, three novels, eight volumes on medicine (with the title *Elements of Human Physiology*) and four huge bibliographies – lists with comments on every available book on botany, anatomy, surgery and medicine. He took opium to soothe the pain of gout, became an addict, and wrote scientific accounts of his own feelings and hallucinations.

CELSIUS, Anders

Swedish scientist 1710-44

Celsius was an astronomer, and particularly interested in the aurora borealis or "northern lights". However, he is remembered today for devising a new temperature scale, using melting ice and boiling water. He gave the freezing point of water the value 100 degrees, and boiling point the value 0 degrees. But it was later turned upside-down to become the system we use today: the Celsius or centigrade ("100 step") scale.

Anders Celsius.

AGNESI, Maria Gaetana

Italian mathematician 1718-99

Agnesi, daughter of the Professor of Mathematics at Bologna University, was a child prodigy. Aged 6 she could speak a dozen languages, and at 7 she knew more maths than scholars many times her age, including her own father. Although women were not allowed to study science, when she was 9 she spoke for an hour, in

Latin, to a university council trying to persuade them that female scholars were as good as male.

Later Agnesi published *Analytical Institutions*, a book which inspired mathematicians all over Europe, and when her father fell ill, the University asked her to be professor in his place. This was the highest honour they could offer, and a reversal of their earlier view that "a woman's place is in the home", but she refused, preferring to teach selected pupils privately.

HUTTON, James

Scottish scientist 1726-97

Hutton was one of the first-ever geologists (people who study rocks and the formation of the Earth). In 1785 he published a book entitled *Theory of the Earth*, about how the Earth's rocks, continents and mountains had been formed. Until then religion had taught that everything was created instantaneously, by supernatural powers. Hutton suggested that they had, rather, grown naturally over millions of years, as the result of processes of erosion and accretion (the addition of extra material). Sand and mud, for example, are washed from the land into the sea by rivers and the rain, and are compressed by their own enormous weight over millions of years to form "sedimentary" rocks.

While Hutton's theory, which he called "uniformitarianism", angered Christians, it excited scientists. In particular, it inspired **Lyell** to try to prove it by scientific investigation, and Lyell's work led **Darwin** to formulate other theories about the origin of species.

CAVENDISH, Henry

English scientist 1731-1810

Cavendish was the youngest son of an aristocratic family, and inherited a fortune which he spent on scientific research. He lived in London, and was said never to leave his house if he could help it, because he believed that women contaminated the planet, and that if he walked about in the streets he might meet one by accident. He went out only once a week, travelling in a carriage with darkened windows to dinner at the Royal Society (where, in those days, he was sure to meet only men).

Locked in his house, Cavendish worked on science for 18 hours each day. He also did research into gases. By treating metal with acids, he succeeded in making hydrogen. He also reacted hydrogen with oxygen to make water, and tried the effect of electric sparks on gases.

Cavendish gave money for scientific research, especially to Cambridge University, which named the Cavendish Laboratory after him. Under **J J Thompson**, it later became one of the most famous research laboratories in the world.

Henry Cavendish – a man who did much for science, if not for the status of women.

Many sedimentary rocks form in seas from material worn from the land, and transported by rivers to the sea.

HUTTON: Darwin 124 Lyell 122 CAVENDISH: Thomson, J J 141

PRIESTLEY, Joseph

English scientist 1733-1804

Until Priestley's time most chemists had believed that there was a gas called phlogiston ("fiery") in every substance, and that it was released when the substance was burned. Phlogiston was thought to have negative weight, so that when the substance burned, it increased in weight.

But no one had ever actually found phlogiston, and Priestley helped to disprove its existence. In his best-known experiment, he heated mercury oxide in the laboratory and produced oxygen. He went on to study the new gas, and showed that a candle burned in it with a bright flame, that plants produce it, and that a mouse could survive in it. He worked on other substances too, and was the first person to isolate ammonia, suphur dioxide and hydrogen chloride in the laboratory.

COULOMB, Charles Augustin de

French scientist 1736-1806

Coulomb was a military engineer, building roads and bridges in the West Indies. He was interested in forces (cohesion, tension, torsion), and in the efficiency and output of machines; this in turn encouraged him to start researching into electricity and magnetism.

As a result, Coulomb made a number of important discoveries and inventions. He invented the torsion balance, and used it to measure two kinds of force: electrostatic and magnetic. He checked **Priestley's** observation that two similar electric charges repel and two opposite charges attract each other, and proved that the force between them decreases as the square of the distance between them increases.

LAGRANGE, Joseph Louis

French scientist 1736-1813

A mathematician, Lagrange devised a calculation system, called the calculus of variations, which made him famous before he was 20. He went on to become one of Europe's leading mathematicians.

In 1787, when the French Revolution began, Lagrange offered his services. He worked out a new money-system for the revolutionary government, replacing the old "louis d'or" (named after King Louis, and with the king's head on it) with the "franc" (named after France). For simplicity's sake, the franc was divided into 100 "centimes" or hundredths. This idea was imitated in later decimal money-systems all over the world.

Joseph Lagrange.

HERSCHEL FAMILY

German/English scientists 18th and 19th century

WILLIAM HERSCHEL (1738-1822) began his career as a musician in Germany, but moved to England in his 30s and took up astronomy. CAROLINE HERSCHEL (1759-1848), his sister, was his housekeeper and shared his business. She made and sold telescopes and lenses, and William used the profits to finance his scientific work. He designed, and Caroline built, the biggest telescope so far made.

COULOMB: Priestley 110

The Herschels worked on star-maps and diagrams of heavenly bodies. William made most of the observations, and Caroline edited the information, did the mathematical calculations and wrote down the results. They charted the positions of over 3,000 stars. They also made the first map of the mountains of the Moon, and in 1781 William was the first person to see the planet Uranus.

JOHN HERSCHEL (1792–1871), William's son and Caroline's nephew, followed in their footsteps, and was a pioneer in the use of photography for astronomical purposes. He also invented a way of "fixing" photographs (removing the unused silver salts so that only the silver image is left). He used sodium thiosulphate, which was then called "Hyposulphate of Soda". He shortened the name to "hypo", and photographers have called it that ever since.

Left: John Herschel, pictured late in his long life.

Above: William Herschel, one of the greatest of observers, holding a chart of the "Georgian Planet" (Uranus).

Herschel had his largest telescope in his garden. Its mirror was 122 cm in diameter and the tube was 12 m long.

GALVANI, Luigi

Italian scientist 1737-98

Galvani taught anatomy at Bologna University, and was famous for his lectures on the workings of muscles, veins and nerves. He discovered that if you separate a dead frog's leg from the body and pass an electric shock through it, it jerks. He believed that there was "animal electricity" leaping through the leg.

The experiment, and the explanation, became world-famous. Even now, people talk of being "galvanized" – that is, being made to jump into action as if by an electric shock – despite Galvani's theory having been later disproved by **Volta** and others.

The botanist Joseph Banks.

BANKS, Joseph

English scientist 1743-1820

Banks travelled with the explorer **James Cook** as scientific officer. He was interested in animals, and especially in the marsupials of Australia, such as kangaroos, which he claimed were more primitive than any other animals in the world. But his main concern was plants. He identified hundreds of previously unrecorded species, and pioneered plant-collecting: taking seeds from one country or continent to another and trying to make them grow. His name is commemorated in the common Australian flower *Banksia*.

Lavoisier, a French chemist who made important contributions to modern chemistry, and introduced metric measurement during the French Revolution.

LAVOISIER, Antoine Laurent

French scientist 1743-94

Lavoisier made a fortune by collecting taxes for the king, and adding a little to each person's taxes to pay for his own "expenses". In this way, by the time he was 35 he had made so much money that he was able to retire.

But Lavoisier was not idle. Inspired by the experiments of **Priestley** and **Cavendish**, he decided to give the rest of his life to science. He was the first person to prove that air is a mixture of two gases (which he named oxygen and nitrogen) and that water is formed from oxygen and hydrogen.

When the French Revolution came, Lavoisier worked for the revolutionaries. He standardized the measurement of distance, making centimetres, metres and kilometres the rule all over France. But because of his early years as a royal tax-collector, the revolutionary leaders were suspicious of him. They arrested him, tried him on the trumped-up charge of cheating the soldiers of their full tobacco ration, and sent him to the guillotine.

LAMARCK, Jean Baptiste

French scientist 1744-1829

Lamarck worked for the French royal family until the Revolution in 1789, and afterwards became a professor at the Paris Natural History Museum. He believed that all plants adapt to suit their environment, and then pass on successful changes to their offspring. This idea, known as the

BANKS: Cook 186 LAVOISIER: Cavendish 109 Priestley 110 LAMARCK: Darwin 124 "theory of the inheritance of acquired characteristics" was the first consistent theory of evolution, but later it was largely superseded by that of **Darwin**.

Lamarck was also responsible for inventing the name "biology" to describe the study of living organisms.

Volta with two "voltaic piles" (the first batteries).

VOLTA, Alessandro

Italian scientist 1745-1827

Volta was a professor at Pavia University. Having seen **Galvani** demonstrate how a dead frog's leg placed between two metal rods will twitch if an electrical charge is passed through it, he tried the same experiment in his own laboratory. He discovered that there is no need for a frog's leg to be used at all: if any moist conductor is placed between two different metals, electricity is produced.

From this discovery, Volta went on to invent the first battery (or "Voltaic pile", as people called it after him). He sandwiched wet pasteboard between alternate discs of copper and zinc to form a column (or pile), and found that when a wire was connected to each end of it, an electric current flowed between. This invention meant that people could produce a steady stream of electricity, instead of the single sparks that had been possible before.

Volta's work led not only to the electromagnetic experiments and discoveries of the nineteenth century, but to the idea that electricity could be harnessed to benefit the human race. The unit of electric potential, the volt, is named after him.

VOLTA: Galvani 111

JENNER, Edward

English doctor 1749-1823

Jenner worked in the farming town of Gloucester, where he heard an "old wives' tale" that anyone who had had cowpox (a mild infection humans caught from working with cows) would be immune to the far worse, often deadly, disease smallpox. He wondered if, by, giving people a small dose of cowpox, he could prevent them catching smallpox. To test the idea, he gave an eight-year-old boy a dose of cowpox followed by a dose of smallpox, and the child survived. Jenner called this treatment "vaccination", after the Latin word vacca (cow), and it has been used to prevent infectious diseases ever since.

Dr Edward Jenner gives the first vaccination.

LAPLACE, Pierre Simon

French scientist and politician 1749-1827

The son of a farm labourer, Laplace attracted attention as a small child by his mathematical genius. At that time, French thinkers were fascinated by the question "are human beings naturally intelligent, or can we learn intelligence?". To find out more, they worked with so-called "savage" children, who had been brought up in backward areas where there was little or no education. Their idea was to see how much the children knew by instinct and what they could be taught. Laplace was one of these children – and he progressed so quickly that at 22 he was appointed Professor of Mathematics at the highest military academy in France.

Laplace had a wide-ranging career. He is best-remembered as an outstanding mathematician, but he also worked with **Lavoisier** on the combustion of gases, correcting some of **Newton's** results, which had stood unchallenged for 100 years. And as an astronomer, he spent 26 years predicting and analysing star-movements throughout the solar system. He believed that as well as the stars we can see, Newton's gravitational theory must mean that there are also stars so small and dense that no light can escape from them – an idea mocked at the time, but which later led to the theory of "black holes" (see **Hawking**).

Werner rightly thought that rocks were formed of layers of different materials. Conglomerates are types of sedimentary rocks containing pebbles; sandstones are grains of sand cemented together. In the Grand Canyon in Arizona the original layers are clearly visible in the eroded landscape.

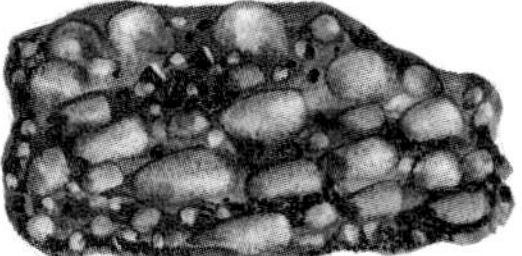

conglomerate

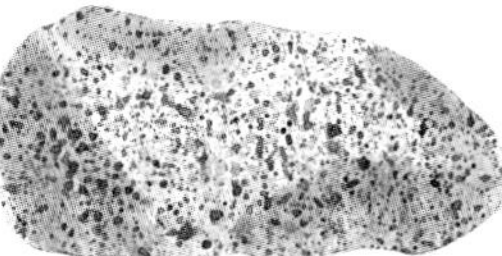

sandstone

WERNER, Abraham Gottlob

German scientist 1749-1817

Werner studied rocks and the minerals which could be extracted from them. This led him to wonder how the rocks could have been formed in the first place, and he came to the same conclusion as **Hutton** – that the Earth was not formed instantaneously by some "vital force" (for example, by God at the moment of creation), but evolved slowly over hundreds of millions of years.

In 1787 Werner published a book classifying rocks by age: Primary (those which were chemically deposited, crystalline and without fossils), Transitional (sedimentary rocks, containing fossils), and Recent (volcanic).

Below: A handful of the thousands of minerals known throughout the world.

quartz

calcite

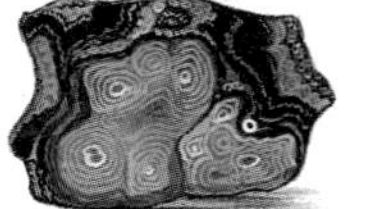

malachite

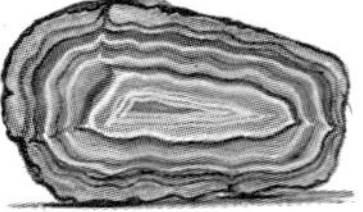

agate

LAPLACE: Hawking 157 Lavoisier 112 Newton 102 WERNER: Hutton 109

BLUMENBACH, Johann Friedrich

German scientist 1752-1840

Blumenbach studied to be a doctor, and became Professor of Medicine at Göttingen University. But his main interest was anthropology, the study of different human types. His stated scientific opinion, that all human beings were the same under the skin, that no race or colour was superior or inferior, earned him considerable unpopularity. It took over a century after his long life for scientists to prove him right, and there are still people, of all skin colours, who refuse to accept his views.

THOMPSON, Benjamin ("Count Rumford")

English scientist 1753-1814

When Thompson was born, in Massachusetts, America was still a British colony. During the American War of Independence, he worked as a British spy. Following the British defeat, he moved first to England and then to Bavaria in Germany, where he worked for the Elector (prince).

"Why do the cannon barrels get so hot?"

Among other things, Thompson introduced the potato to continental Europe, and built the first work-houses (places where poor people were given food and a bed in exchange for work) in Munich. The Elector made him a Count in 1790, and Thompson called himself Count Rumford after the name of his birthplace in America.

Thompson continued his interest in science – and it led him to make a discovery crucial to later physics. Until his time, people thought that heat was a fluid (**Lavoisier** called it "caloric"), which flowed through substances as blood flows through the body. One day, while Thompson was supervising cannon-barrels being bored in the Munich gun-factory, he noticed that the barrels grew hot during the boring process and had to be cooled with water. To try to find out why, he worked with a brass gun barrel in a wooden box filled with water, and found that after two and a half hours' boring the water boiled. He refused to believe that the reason was "caloric" leaking from the metal into the water, and concluded that the movement of the borer must be heating the water. In other words, motion was being converted into heat.

In the 1790s Thompson went back to live in England. There, in 1799, he founded the Royal Institution, a centre for scientific research, in London, and invited **Davy** and **Young** to come and give lectures. In 1804 he settled in Paris, where he married – and later divorced – Lavoisier's widow.

THOMPSON: Davy 119 Lavoisier 112 Young 117

HAHNEMANN, Samuel Christian

German doctor 1755-1843

Hahnemann invented homeopathy, a method of treating illness. It involved giving the patient small doses of substances which caused symptoms of the same illness in a healthy person. He found that this encouraged the body's own defence-mechanisms to build up resistance to the substances – and so combat the disease.

DALTON, John

English scientist 1766-1844

Dalton was interested in all kinds of science. As a boy, he began a nature-diary, recording the things he saw each day. He kept it up throughout his life, and when he died it contained more than 200,000 observations.

One scientific area that attracted Dalton's attention was the physics of light, and in particular what makes people colour-blind (unable to tell the difference between certain colours). Dalton suffered from colour-blindness himself, and it is sometimes called "Daltonism" after him.

Dalton also worked on gases, and studied how their pressure changes when they are heated or cooled. He is also remembered for his theories on atoms. Many centuries earlier, the ancient Greek scholar **Democritus** had stated that every substance in the universe consists of a combination of tiny particles or atoms. Using this idea, Dalton formulated a new definition: that an atom is the smallest particle of a substance which can take part in a chemical reaction.

The atomic theory was old, but no one till Dalton had applied it to modern chemistry. He found it hard to persuade people of his ideas, partly because he was bad-mannered, and partly because he was a clumsy and careless experimenter. But later scientists, notably **Berzelius** and **Avogadro**, took up and developed his ideas, and changed the whole face of science. More advances in experimental science were made in the following century than in the entire span of history until Dalton's time. The unit of Relative Atomic Mass (Atomic Weight) is called the dalton in his honour.

John Dalton.

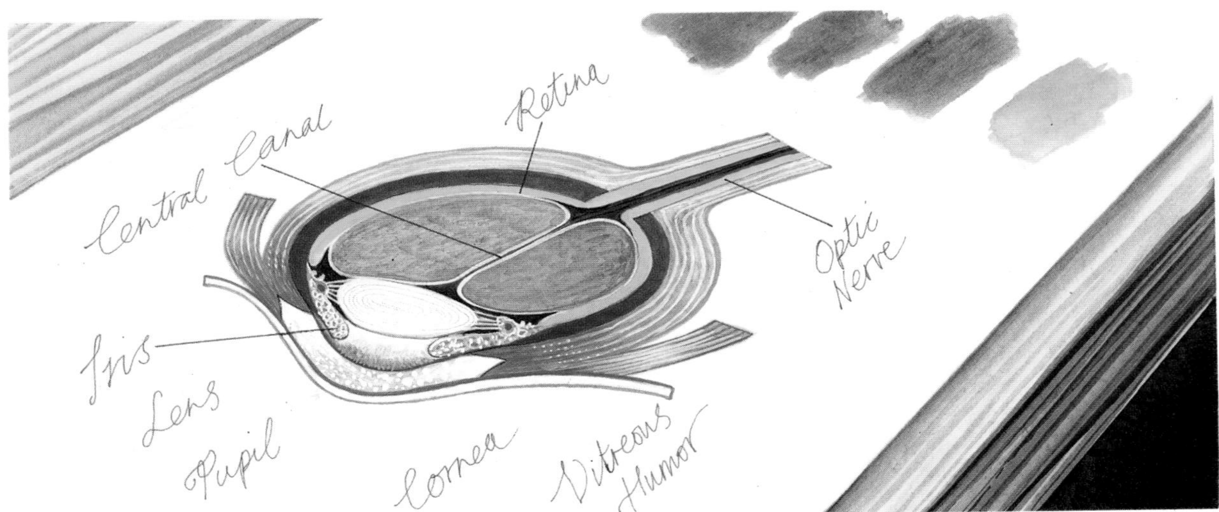

Dalton's detailed research into the eye led him to discover why some people are colour-blind.

DALTON: Avogadro 118 Berzelius 120 Democritus 85

Young developed the idea of primary colours, and showed how white light is formed from the rays of red, blue and green light (above, left). Mixing different coloured paints reduces the amount of light that is reflected, giving almost black (above, right).

YOUNG, Thomas

English scientist 1773-1829

Young's brilliance became obvious at a very early age. He could read at two years old, and had read the Bible twice through before he was four. As a schoolboy, he spent his spare time learning languages (including Polish and Hungarian), and repeating **Newton's** optical experiments to search out flaws. When he went to Cambridge University, admiring fellow-students nicknamed him "phenomenon Young", and said that there was nothing he could not do – he was even supposed to have strung a tightrope from window to window across a college lawn, and danced along it.

Young went to work at the London Royal Institution in 1794, at the same time as **Davy**. He studied the way light strikes the eye and makes us see, and showed how we "focus" our eyes by changing the shape of the lens so that we see clearly objects at varying distances from us. He was sure that light was a wave motion, not rays as Newton had suggested – and showed that just as water-waves undergo diffraction and interference, so do light-waves. He put forward the theory that all the colours we see are mixtures of three basic colours – red, yellow and blue – known as primary colours. Young's discovery later led to the development of colour printing and colour television.

Young also studied elasticity and surface tension, and wrote science articles for the first edition of the *Encyclopedia Britannica*. In 1814, after spending his spare time deciphering the hieroglyphics on the Rosetta Stone (a monument in three languages, only two of which were known), he worked out how ancient Egyptian was written down. Young thought of this work as no more than a way to occupy his mind when he was not doing science – but it was vital to the expanding science of archaeology.

Thomas Young.

YOUNG: Davy 119 Newton 102

AMPÈRE, André Marie

French scientist 1775-1836

Ampère's work confirmed that an electric current creates a magnetic field around itself.

Ampère is best-known for his work on electricity and magnetism. He was inspired by **Oersted's** discovery that a current flowing through a wire produces a magnetic field round the wire, and began investigating to learn more about it. He found that if two parallel wires carry a current, there is a force between them. This effect is now used to define the unit of current, called the ampere (or amp) after him.

AVOGADRO, Amedeo

Italian scientist 1776-1856

Avogadro was the Professor of Mathematical Physics at Turin University. In 1811 he proposed the theory that equal volumes of gases, at the same temperature and pressure, contain the same number of molecules. No one understood the importance of this until 1858, when Cannizzaro used it to help determine the masses of molecules – a vital step in bringing order to chemical classification.

The first electrical device for carrying messages – the telegraph – was invented by Gauss and Weber.

GAUSS, Carl Friedrich

German mathematician and scientist 1777-1855

Gauss had uncanny ability at calculation, and when he was 14 he was summoned before the Duke of Brunswick, who was so impressed by him that he agreed to pay for the boy's high school and university education. By the age of 22, Gauss was a Doctor of Mathematics, and aged 30 he was appointed Professor of Mathematics and Director of the Astronomical Observatory at Göttingen University.

Gauss' first work, completed while he was still a student, was in number theory: he invented a logical way of handling complex numbers. He went on to work in a variety of scientific fields. His study of the movement of planets and other heavenly bodies, called celestial mechanics, led to his devising a new way of calculating planetary orbits.

But he had many other interests, including optics (the study of light), electromagnetism, and also land surveying. And, most important of all, in collaboration with two pupils, he produced the first new system of geometry since **Euclid** 2,000 years before.

Gauss made many discoveries in statistics and probability. The "normal distribution curve", which describes the way that many measurements are spread out, is often called the "Gaussian curve" in his honour. But he is also generally known for something else: with Wilhelm Weber, he invented the electric telegraph, a way of sending messages by varying the electrical signal passing down a wire.

AMPÈRE: Oersted 119 GAUSS: Euclid 86

OERSTED, Hans Christian

Danish scientist 1777-1851

Oersted discovered that electric currents have magnetic effects, and that a magnetic needle turns at right angles to an electric current. His work began the branch of physics known as electromagnetism.

DAVY, Humphrey

English scientist 1778-1829

Davy was fascinated by the possibilities of using gases in medicine. He did experiments into the effects of gases on health, and was the first person to discover that nitrous oxide can be used as an anaesthetic (that is, if you breathe it in it kills pain). Davy went on to try other gases on himself – a risky thing to do, as one of them, water gas (a mixture of hydrogen and carbon monoxide) was poisonous and he nearly died.

In 1799, aged 21, Davy wrote a book about his gas experiments, and his easily-understood, lively accounts of his scientific work so impressed the authorities of the Royal Institution in London that they appointed him lecturer, with the job of explaining science to the general public.

As well as giving lectures, Davy carried on research in both chemistry and physics. He discovered and named several new metals: barium, calcium, magnesium, potassium, sodium and strontium. He investigated the properties of hydrochloric acid and chlorine, wrote a book on the use of chemicals in farming, and studied (for the British Navy) the reasons why rust attacks copper-bottomed ships.

Davy proved the safety of his lamp by going down the mines himself.

Apart from the Royal Institution lectures, Davy is best-remembered for inventing a safety lamp for miners. Methane gas (known then as "firedamp") often seeps into mine-shafts from the surrounding rock, and, when mixed with air, explodes if it touches a naked flame. Until Davy's time, miners had lit their work with candles, and firedamp-accidents had been common. Davy devised a way of shielding the heat of the flame from gas – and for a century afterwards, until the "Davy lamp" was replaced by even safer electric lamps, it saved the lives of thousands of miners.

BERZELIUS, Jöns Jakob

Swedish scientist 1779-1848

Berzelius pioneered two systems vital to modern chemistry. From 1810 to 1820 he analysed and listed 2,000 elements and compounds according to their atomic and molecular weights, comparing the weights of their atoms with those of oxygen. Then he listed all chemical compounds according to the composition of each separate molecule. Each molecule of water, for example, is formed from two hydrogen atoms and one oxygen atom, and Berzelius therefore listed the compound as H_2O. Berzelius' symbols are a kind of shorthand, making calculations and experiments quicker to write down.

HOOKER, William

English scientist 1785-1865

and

HOOKER, Joseph

English scientist 1817-1911

William Hooker and his son Joseph collected, bred and studied plants. William was the first director of Kew Gardens in London, a laboratory for growing and breeding plants from all round the world. Joseph went on plant-collecting expeditions, and brought back to London seeds and shoots of many species previously unknown in Europe. He was a friend of **Darwin**, and many of his finds supported Darwin's theory of evolution by showing how different plants had adapted to suit their surroundings.

HOOKER: Darwin 124

OHM, Georg Simon

German scientist 1789-1854

Ohm worked on electricity, trying to measure the current which flows along a wire. He discovered that its amount depends on the length and thickness of the wire. He is remembered today for Ohm's Law, explained on the right. The unit of electrical resistance, the ohm, is named after him.

Ohm showed that the amount of electricity passing through a conductor (here a carbon rod) depends on its length and thickness. A short fat rod has low resistance and the current is strong (top lamp), but the thinner and longer the rod, the more it resists the current and the lamp can only glow (bottom).

Many Victorian Londoners "took the air" at the Royal Gardens, Kew, and marvelled at the collection of trees and plants from all over the world.

FARADAY, Michael

English scientist 1791-1867

A bookbinder's apprentice, Faraday was determined to educate himself. He went to **Davy's** public lectures at the London Royal Institution, took notes, and sent them to Davy – who was so impressed by their neatness and accuracy that he gave Faraday a job as laboratory assistant.

At first, Faraday helped Davy in his public lectures. But after a while, he started lecturing himself, with even greater success. In 1825 he was put in charge of the Royal Institution laboratory; six years later he was made a professor.

Faraday's first experiments were with gases, and he discovered that they could be turned to liquid by the application of pressure. But his most important work was on electromagnetism, following on from **Ampère**. He found that a moving magnet produces a current in a coil. He also demonstrated that if two coils, insulated from each other, are wound onto the same iron ring, a current flowing in one will cause a current to flow in the other. Faraday's work led to the development of the electric motor, the dynamo and the transformer. The electrical unit of capacitance, the farad, is named in his honour.

Faraday's work explained the connection between magnetism and electricity, and he also invented the dynamo. Together his discoveries formed the basis for the modern electrical industry.

BABBAGE, Charles

English mathematician 1792-1871

Babbage, a maths professor at Cambridge University, spent his free time making barrel-organs. They worked by driving air through holes punched in card, to blow each pipe at exactly the right moment to fit the tune. He thought the same kind of system might work a machine which could make mathematical calculations without the possibility of human error. He drew up plans and made a prototype machine, called the "Difference Engine".

In 1823, Babbage asked the British government to finance research for a new machine. This one was to be programmable: a set of instructions could be fed to it in advance, via punched cards. These instructions (the program) would be stored inside the machine, telling it what to do. But it did not look very convincing – it bristled with cogs, levers, gears and ratchets, was operated by steam and needed a coal-scuttle and a watering-can. The government at first agreed to back the project, but eventually refused to go any further with it.

Babbage had little choice but to go back to barrel-organs. Over a century later, however, his vision of how punched cards could be used proved right after all. In the Second World War, when people started building electronic calculating machines to crack enemy codes, they used the stored program system, and the maths that lay behind it. What Babbage had invented, 120 years before the technology could cope with it, was the computer.

Babbage's Difference Engine – the first "computer".

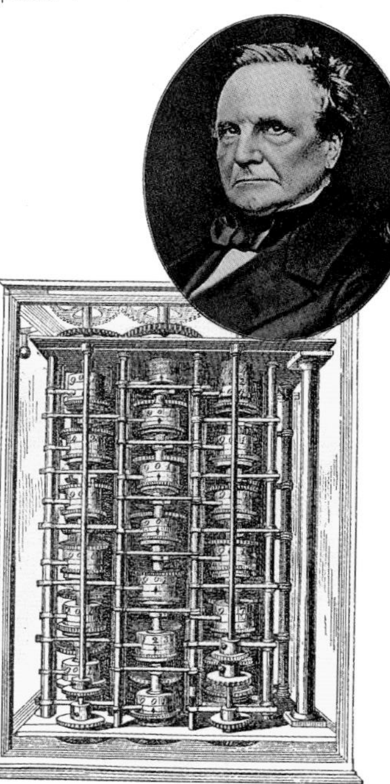

FARADAY: Ampère 118 Davy 119

LYELL, Charles

English scientist 1797-1875

Until Lyell's time, most people had thought that rocks, like everything else, were made by God during Creation, and had not changed since. Only the Scottish scientist **Hutton** had believed differently, suggesting that rocks were more likely to have been made by natural forces such as volcanic activity or erosion, that they must have taken many millions of years to reach their present forms, and that they are still evolving.

Lyell's studies gave scientific backing to Hutton's theory. His work also interested scientists in other areas. One of the first people it influenced was **Darwin**, whose theory of evolution applied it to living creatures as well as rocks.

Mary Anning, reputed to be the first person to discover the fossilized skeleton of an ichthyosaurus.

ANNING, Mary

English scientist 1799-1847

Anning lived in the English seaside town of Lyme Regis, and from the age of five helped her father by gathering seashells and fossils to sell to visitors. She was fascinated by the fossils' shapes, and wondered what sort of creatures and plants they could have come from. She began to teach herself geology and natural history.

According to tradition, in 1811 Anning found the first complete fossil skeleton ever seen in England of an ichthyosaurus (a fish-like reptile). She wrote to the British Museum to ask what it was. The experts there were so impressed by her knowledge that they had no idea she was not a scientist, and wrote back to her as if she were. However, since Anning would have been only 11 at the time, some scholars believe the discovery was actually made by her mother, also called Mary.

At any rate, Anning's ideas, and the fossils she unearthed were soon to catch the interest of scientists all over Europe. Her discoveries contributed to the growth of the science of palaeontology (studying fossils and trying to reconstruct the original creatures and their environment), and she went on to become one of the world's leading experts in the field.

LYELL: Darwin 124 Hutton 109

WÖHLER, Friedrich

German scientist 1800-82

At the beginning of the nineteenth century, chemists separated all matter into two types, "organic" and "inorganic". Organic substances, they said, came from living organisms, and behaved in a different way from inorganic substances, which did not. It was regarded as a basic law of science that the two types of matter were absolutely separate.

In 1828, Wöhler, one of **Berzelius'** research students, proved these theories wrong. He was working with inorganic compounds, breaking them down and isolating their elements. One day, he boiled dry a solution of ammonium cyanate in the laboratory, and found that it produced a white powder. When he analyzed the powder, he discovered that it was chemically identical to urea, a substance produced by the kidneys. In other words, by heating an inorganic compound he had produced an organic substance. It was one of the most important discoveries in nineteenth-century chemistry, clearing the way for all later work on molecules.

DOPPLER, Christian Johann

Austrian scientist 1803-53

Doppler is best-known for the so-called "Doppler effect". He explained why, when an object such as a train is moving towards you, it seems to make sounds at a higher pitch than when it is moving away. He showed that the sound waves from the approaching object are compressed and therefore reach the ear close behind each other – thus raising the frequency and pitch of the sound.

Doppler believed that since light, like sound, travels in waves, a similar effect might be observable in light. He thought that light approaching would be at a higher frequency than light moving away: "bluer" when approaching, and "redder" when departing. Modern physics has proved him right.

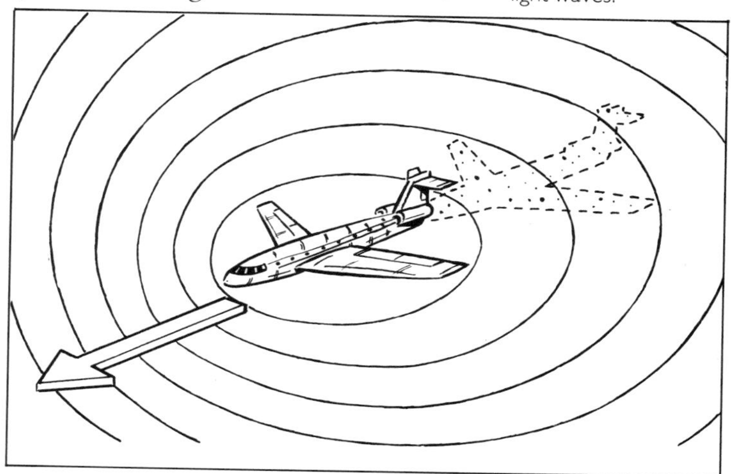

The narrower the bands, the higher the sound frequency. This is known as the Doppler effect, and it equally applies to radio and light waves.

LIEBIG, Justus von

German scientist 1803-73

Liebig was a pioneer of organic chemistry (the branch of science concerned with the compounds of carbon). He divided foodstuffs into carbohydrates, fats and proteins, and experimented to see how each group was formed and what function it performed in the body. He was one of the first people to suggest that artificial fertilizers, made from chemicals, might be more efficient than the animal dung most farmers used.

Nowadays, Liebig is best-remembered in science laboratories for the Liebig condenser, a device commonly used to distil liquids.

WÖHLER: Berzelius 120

DARWIN, Charles Robert

English scientist 1809-82

Until Darwin's time, Christians had believed for nearly 2,000 years that the world and everything in it were created at the same time by God. They thought that all species of plants and animals had existed in exactly the same form ever since the Creation. Anyone who challenged this "creationist" theory was threatened and oppressed by the Church. Only a few scientists, among them **Lamarck**, had been bold enough to suggest that species had not always been the same, and that they would have changed over time.

As a boy, Darwin believed firmly in creationism. He even thought of going into the Church, and studied theology at Cambridge University. But his other passionate interest was Biology, and he spent many hours with John Henslow, the Cambridge Professor of Biology, studying plants. When Darwin left university, he decided to take a few years off before finally deciding his future – and Henslow got him a place as naturalist on the British ship *HMS Beagle*, which was to spend five years exploring the world's southern oceans, making scientific observations.

The *Beagle* visited Tenerife, the Cape Verde Islands, Brazil, Montevideo, Tierra del Fuego, Chile, the Galápagos Islands, Tahiti, New Zealand, Tasmania and the Keeling Islands. During this time, Darwin made notes about every plant and creature he saw, and about how each was adapted to its environment.

When Darwin returned to England, in 1836, he married and settled to a quiet life of studying and writing. He published an account of his travels, *The Voyage of the Beagle*, and scientific books and articles on such various subjects as worms, finches, the expressions of the face, fossils (he was fascinated by the discoveries of **Mary Anning**) and coral reefs. But all the time he was thinking out an entirely new theory

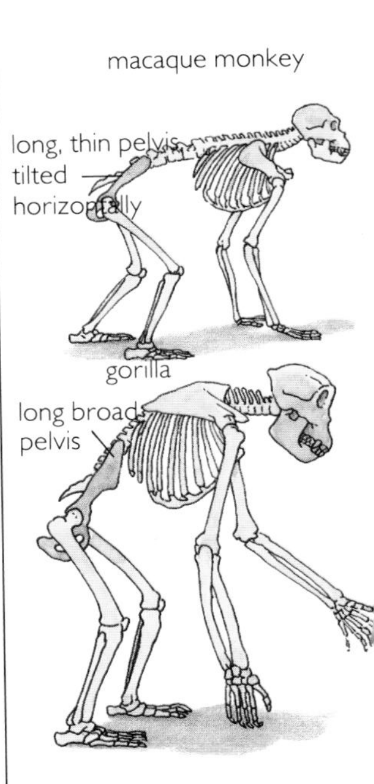

Above right: Evolution explained. The pelvic girdle evolves to support the weight of a creature walking first on four legs, gradually straightening, to just two. Modern humans find four-legged walking uncomfortable – their pelvic bones are wrongly shaped.

The voyage of HMS *Beagle*.

A coral reef, one of Darwin's *Thirty Plates Illustrative of Natural Phenomena, etc*, published in 1849.

DARWIN: Anning 122 Galileo 96 Huxley 134 Lamarck 112

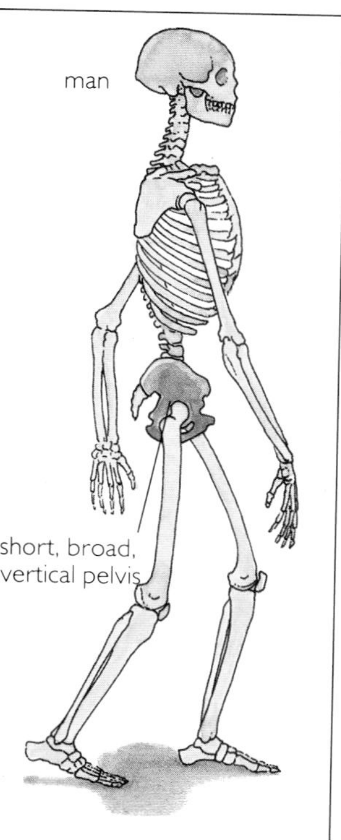

about how the world and its creatures came to be the way they are.

Then Darwin received a letter from Alfred Russel Wallace, another British scientist, putting forward a theory similar to his own. This encouraged Darwin to "go public", and in 1858 he and Wallace presented their ideas to the Linnaean Society in London. This was followed in 1859 by Darwin's book *The Origin of Species by Means of Natural Selection.* (The belief behind it – that plants and animals have not always been the same, but instead evolve over time – is explained on the left).

The Origin of Species caused uproar. The religious authorities denounced Darwin, and newspapers rushed to ridicule his ideas. But many distinguished scientists (for example **Thomas Huxley**) spoke up for him. Unlike the creationist theory, which depends on unquestioning acceptance that the Bible is the true word of God, the theory of evolution by natural selection is based on scientific observation. It begins with facts, and always modifies theory to fit the facts, never facts to fit the theory.

Within ten years, Darwin's ideas were known and were an inspiration to scientists all round the world. Darwin went on writing, adding evidence to support his theory. In 1871, he caused another uproar with *The Descent of Man*, which suggested that the human race, instead of being created (as Adam and Eve) in the Garden of Eden, had evolved over millions of years just like any other species – and that one of our evolutionary ancestors was related to the apes. Once again the Church thundered against him; once again scientists leapt to his support.

For all the complex arguments which back it up, Darwin's theory is easy to understand. Like many of the world's most vital discoveries, it seems perfectly obvious once you see it, as if it has always been part of human thinking. But in the nineteenth century it was news, a matter for frantic argument – and some Christians refuse to accept it still.

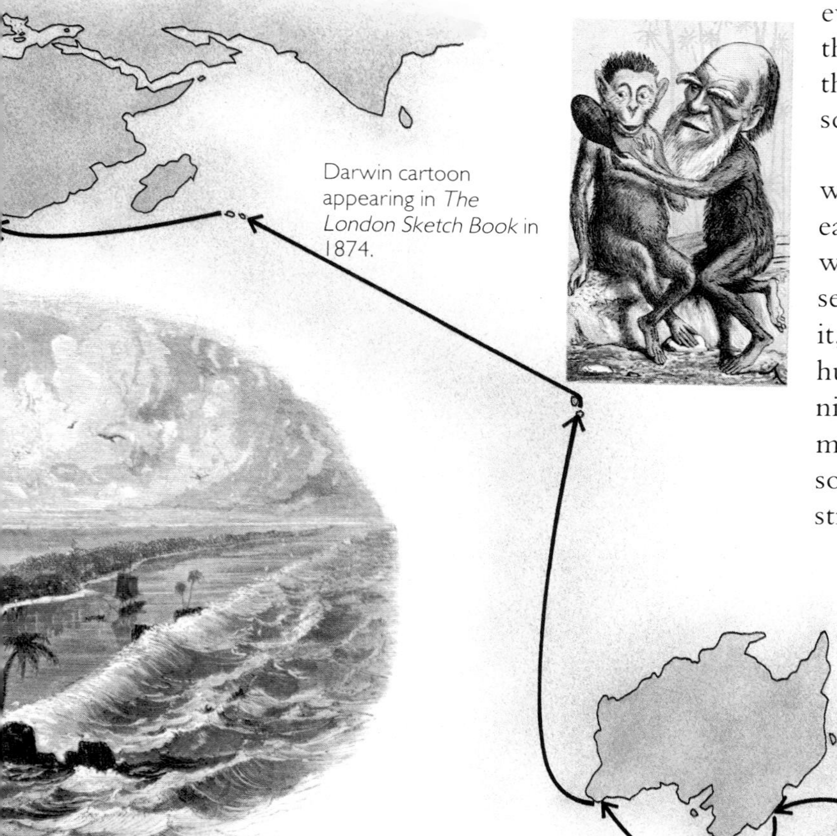

Darwin cartoon appearing in *The London Sketch Book* in 1874.

Theodor Schwann.

SCHWANN, Theodor

German scientist 1810-1882

Ever since **Hooke**, 150 years before Schwann's time, examined cork through a microscope and discovered that it was built up from cells, biologists had been working to find out exactly what cells were, how they were formed and how they worked. In 1839, Schwann, building on an unproven theory of the French biologist Dutrochet, showed that cells are the basic building blocks of all living tissue, plant or animal, that life begins from a single cell, and that large organisms are created by the endless division and co-operation of cells. This discovery was as crucial for biology as the atomic theory was for physics.

BUNSEN, Robert Wilhelm

German scientist 1811-99

Bunsen was a pioneer of spectroscopy: analysing elements by energizing their atoms so that they appear as coloured bands in an instrument called a spectroscope. He and his colleague Kirchhov showed that every element has its own spectrum, as individual as a human fingerprint. In 1861 their work led to the discovery of two new elements, caesium and rubidium.

To provide heat for his work, Bunsen devised a candle-shaped gas burner which produced a clear upward flame. It has been called a "Bunsen burner" after him ever since.

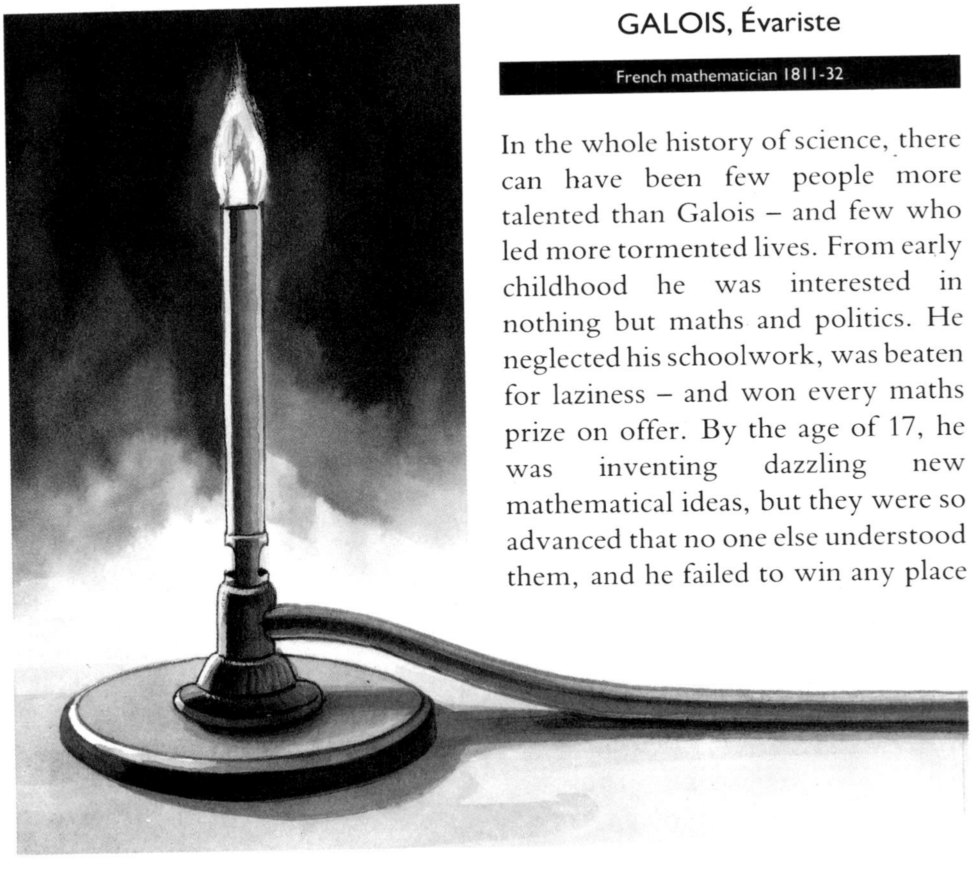

The Bunsen burner gives off great heat but little light, because the gas mixes with air drawn through an intake in the vertical tube before burning at the top of the tube.

GALOIS, Évariste

French mathematician 1811-32

In the whole history of science, there can have been few people more talented than Galois – and few who led more tormented lives. From early childhood he was interested in nothing but maths and politics. He neglected his schoolwork, was beaten for laziness – and won every maths prize on offer. By the age of 17, he was inventing dazzling new mathematical ideas, but they were so advanced that no one else understood them, and he failed to win any place

SCHWANN: Hooke 101 GALOIS: Newton 102

in higher education.

When Galois was 18, his father committed suicide, leaving him with no money to live on. Hoping to win cash and fame at the same time, Galois submitted his mathematical ideas for a prize awarded by the Academy, the leading intellectual group in France – and the Academy secretary lost them. Galois bitterly gave up maths, turned to politics instead, and was thrown into prison as a dangerous revolutionary. When he was released he fell in love – and was at once challenged to a duel, was seriously wounded, and died just before his 21st birthday. Fourteen years later his work was published at last, and people recognized his mathematical genius.

Galois was a pioneer of what is now called "pure maths". Until his time, all maths, even **Newton's**, had started from real things: calculating planetary orbits, for example, or measuring the shifts and bends in light. Galois suggested, by contrast, that figures and calculations have their own independent life and can be studied for their own sakes without worrying about their practical applications.

This new type of maths helped to solve all kinds of problems which had troubled mathematicians up to then. Previously, formulas and solutions had constantly run into difficulties: what happened in real life did not seem to bear out the figures. Now the figures could stand alone, and could lead to new, far more complicated calculations and ideas. Galois' mathematical systems, called "abstract algebra", were one of the most vital stages in the development of scientific thought.

LEVERRIER, Urbain Jean Joseph

French astronomer 1811-77

Leverrier mapped movements of the stars and planets. When he found that Uranus moved in an orbit no one could explain, he decided that it must be affected by the gravitational pull of another planet, so far unknown. He worked out the orbit, size and position of this planet, and in 1846 another astronomer (Galle) used Leverrier's calculations to guide his telescope, and found it: Neptune, the third biggest planet in the solar system.

Urbain Leverrier.

Neptune, seen here from the surface of one of its two moons, is one of the four giant planets of the solar system, which are made almost entirely of gas.

SIMPSON, James Young

Scottish doctor 1811-70

Simpson had heard about **Morton's** US experiments, using ether as an anaesthetic in operations. He wondered if chloroform might not be more effective, and especially if it might help women during childbirth. At first, no one took him seriously, and some bishops even claimed that labour-pains were God-given, a punishment to womankind for Eve's disobedience in the Garden of Eden. But then Queen **Victoria** used chloroform during the birth of her son Leopold, and it instantly became fashionable.

SIMPSON: Morton 129 Victoria 454

James Prescott Joule.

JOULE, James Prescott

English scientist 1818-89

Joule's main scientific interest was the connection between heat and work. He realized that when mechanical work is done an equivalent amount of heat is produced, and did many experiments in friction, converting motion into heat. He concluded that heat is a form of energy.

Joule's researches proved what had been earlier stated by Mayer as the principle of conservation of energy – that energy can neither be made from nothing nor destroyed: it exists, and all our efforts do no more than convert it from one form to another. They also led to the first law of thermodynamics, which states that in a closed system, the total amount of energy remains constant, but it can be converted between its various forms (for example, from mechanical energy to heat).

In honour of Joule's achievements, the basic unit of energy is named after him.

The sparks from the braking wheels of a steam engine show mechanical energy converting to heat.

SEMMELWEISS, Philip Ignaz

Hungarian doctor 1818-65

Semmelweiss was a surgeon at Vienna General Hospital, and began to wonder why so many patients died from infection after operations. The hospital had two labour wards (where women gave birth), one staffed by surgeons and the other by midwives. Semmelweiss calculated that only three per cent of the women in the midwives' ward died of fever after their babies were born, compared with 30 per cent in the surgeons' ward. Then, one day when he was in the hospital dissecting-room, examining the body of someone who had died of fever, he found that the diseased body-tissue was exactly like that of women who died in the surgeons' ward.

Semmelweiss realized that medical students must be carrying the fever as they moved from dissection-room to ward, and insisted from then on that all his students should scrub with disinfectant after each dissection. At once deaths from fever grew fewer in his part of the surgeons' ward. But Semmelweiss was only an assistant professor, and his supervisors refused to accept his ideas. He resigned from his job – and on his last day in the hospital accidentally cut his finger during an operation, causing a wound which became infected and led to his insanity and death.

Foucault was able to demonstrate the Earth's rotation using a pendulum in a lofty church.

FOUCAULT, Jean Bernard Léon

French scientist 1819-68

Foucault devised a way of working out the speed of light by using a rotating mirror, and showed that light travels more slowly in water than in air. He demonstrated, by using a pendulum, that the Earth rotates. He also invented the gyroscope, the lens now called the Foucault prism, and ways to improve the mirrors used in reflecting telescopes.

MORTON, William Thomas Green

US dentist 1819-68

Morton pioneered the use of ether as an anaesthetic in the United States. He used it first on dental patients, and then (in 1846) showed that it could help people in surgery of all kinds.

GALTON, Francis

English scientist 1822-1911

Galton was **Darwin's** cousin, and a restless, inventive man who changed careers and interests several times during his life. He began as an explorer in South Africa, and then gave that up to study meteorology. He invented a kind of weather map which became the basis for those still used today. Next he turned to the study of heredity (the science which investigates whether looks, character and abilities are our own or are passed on to us by our parents). He was one of the founders of the science of quantitative genetics – the study of the inheritance of characteristics such as height. Although his work was done on humans, it has led to important applications in animal and plant breeding.

Included among Galton's other achievements was his pioneering work into ways of treating colour blindness, and the compilation of some of the first ever intelligence tests. But he is perhaps best-remembered for the discovery that everyone's fingerprints are unique. Before long, police forces all over the world were able to solve crimes by taking ink prints of suspects' fingers and comparing them with fingerprints collected at the scene of the incident.

GALTON: Darwin 124

MENDEL, Gregor Johann

Austrian scientist 1822-84

Mendel belonged to a teaching order of monks, the Augustinians, and taught science. In 1857 he began a series of experiments on breeding peas at his monastery. He worked with a variety of peas which had markedly different characteristics: some tall, some short, some green, some yellow.

Until then, people had thought that if you cross-bred two different varieties, you would get a half-way result: so that tall and short, for example, would produce medium-size. Mendel discovered that this was not so. The offspring always retained the characteristics of one parent or the other. Mendel concluded that there were factors, for example those controlling the height of the plant, which kept their individuality from generation to generation. He used the phrase "dominant factors", and where a factor was not always clearly handed on, but could be hidden in some way, he said that it was "recessive".

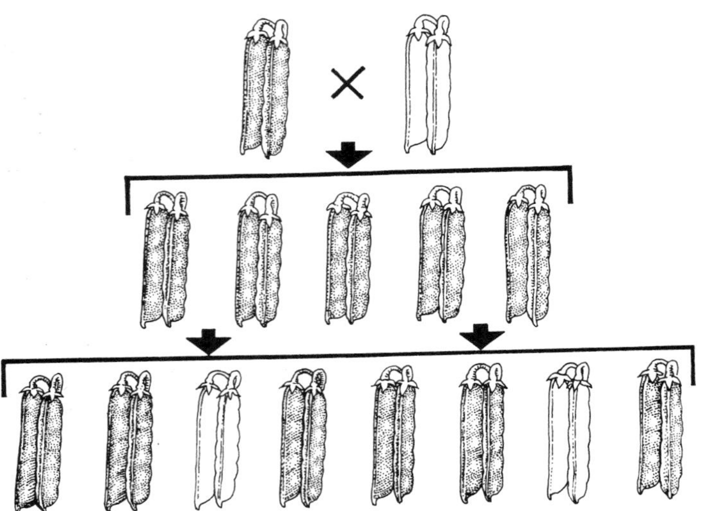

This example of peas illustrates the dominant and recessive factors discovered by Mendel.

Mendel's work was careful and thorough. But he was not a professional scientist, and did not know how to bring his research to the notice of scientists in other countries. He published his results in a small local science paper – and few readers took any notice. Convinced that his research was of no value, Mendel gave up biology to concentrate on his religious work instead, and in 1869 was made abbot (chief monk) of his monastery.

It was not until 20 years after Mendel's death that others realized the importance of his scientific work. He had solved a major remaining problem in evolutionary theory (see **Darwin**). Previously, it had not been clear how living things could become better adapted to their surroundings if useful characteristics would not necessarily be passed down to the next generation. Mendel's pea experiments proved that useful characteristics do pass unchanged from one generation to another.

Mendel's discovery showed how evolution is a logical process. It also laid the foundation for a new branch of science, called "genetics" by the scientist Bateson in 1902.

Left: Gregor Mendel, the monk who laid the foundations of modern genetics.

MENDEL: Darwin 124

PASTEUR, Louis

French biologist 1822-95

The son of an army officer, Pasteur taught science at Strasbourg and Lille Universities and then in Paris. In his spare time he did research, and in 1857 began experiments to see why liquids such as milk, wine and beer ferment (turn sour). He discovered that fermentation is caused by micro-organisms known as bacteria, and that if these are killed by heating the liquid, then fermentation does not occur. This showed that bacteria do not simply appear, seemingly from nowhere, as had been thought until then, but breed like other living things. The process of sterilizing liquids (killing the bacteria in them) by heating became known as "pasteurization" and is still used all over the world.

Louis Pasteur in his Paris laboratory.

Pasteur went on to wonder if diseases in other living things might, like fermentation, be caused by bacteria. He researched first into silkworm diseases, and then into chicken cholera, and found that both are caused by bacteria. He decided to try **Jenner's** idea of vaccination: using a less dangerous substance to inoculate (build up defence) against a more deadly one. He grew cholera bacteria in the laboratory and made from them a vaccine (substance for vaccination) which successfully slowed down or stopped the real disease. He went on to develop vaccines against anthrax and rabies, and had great success: improved versions of these vaccines are still used today.

Not everyone admired Pasteur. Although some doctors (for example **Lister**) welcomed his work, others resented anyone without a medical degree trying to cure disease, and called him a quack. He annoyed fashionable hostesses at dinner-parties by refusing to shake hands (in case of infection), by examining the bread carefully for what he called "foreign bodies" and placing any he found on the tablecloth, and by wiping even the cleanest-looking knives and forks on his napkin before using them. But the newspapers loved him, and carried what they called the "germ theory of disease" all round the world. The French people collected money to build the Pasteur Institute in Paris in his honour. It is now one of the world's main centres of research into micro-organisms and disease.

PASTEUR: Jenner 113 Lister 134

SCHLIEMANN, Heinrich

German archaeologist 1822-90

By the time he was 40, Heinrich Schliemann was a multi-millionaire thanks to his family's successful dye-manufacturing business. His passion, however, was not for business but for archaeology. He believed that **Homer's** *Iliad* and *Odyssey*, which told of the heroes of ancient Greece and Troy, were not mythical but true, and that the places named had actually existed. Schliemann financed archaeological expeditions to look for the site of Homer's Troy, and in the early 1870s he found it at Hissarlik in Turkey.

From Hissarlik, Schliemann went on to Greece, to look for the palace of Agamemnon, the mythical warrior-king who had led the Greeks at Troy. On a hillside in the middle of an empty plain, the only visible remains of Mycenae, Agamemnon's kingdom, Schliemann's team unearthed a castle the size of a small town, and at its heart a ring of graves filled with treasure. He was sure that this was Agamemnon's stronghold and that one of the graves was Agamemnon's own.

Later scholars have proved Schliemann wrong. The remains he found at Hissarlik are too late for the likely date of the Trojan War, and those at Mycenae are several hundred years too early. But few archaeologists have ever gone on more spectacular quests or had more triumphant results. Schliemann's discoveries at Hissarlik, Mycenae and later at Tiryns (the palace of the mythical hero Perseus) showed that the myths may well, as he always claimed, have been based on fact.

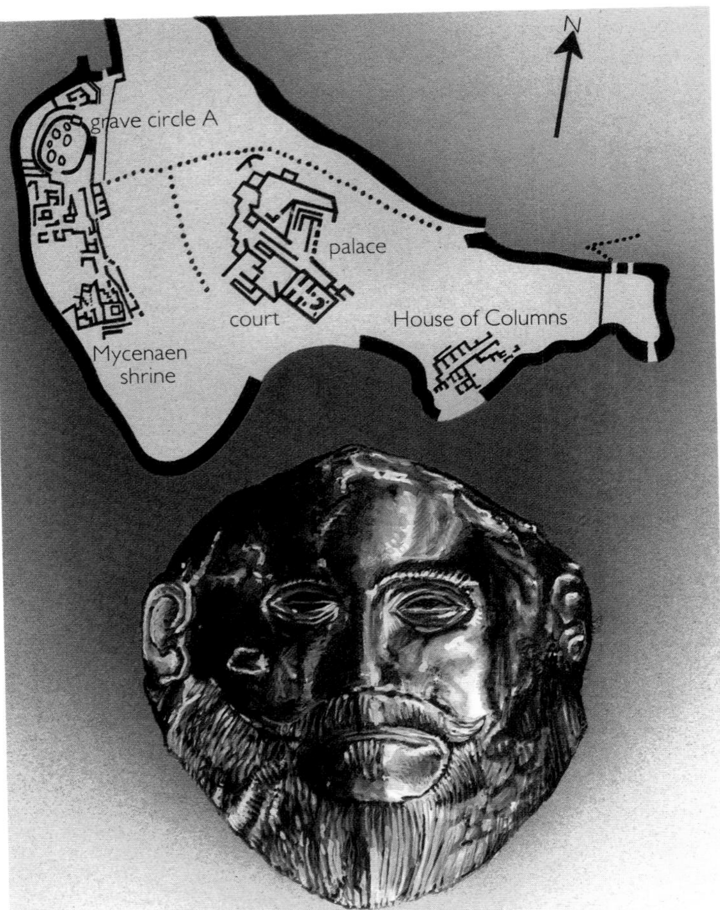

The golden mask, discovered by Schliemann in the remains of Mycenae. The plan of the castle grounds shows the palace and main buildings. The treasure was buried in Grave Circle A.

FABRE, Jean Henri

French teacher and scientific writer 1823-1915

Fabre is best-known for his work on entomology (the study of insects). He wrote about such things as the praying mantis, the mayfly, and especially the social insects: ants, wasps and bees. His books were best-sellers, and were unusual in that, although in every other way he was scientifically accurate, he wrote as if insects behaved and thought like human beings.

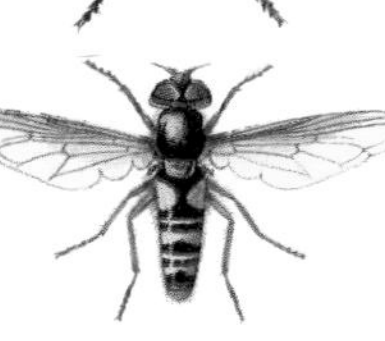

SCHLIEMANN: Homer 4

KELVIN, Lord (William Thomson)

Scottish scientist 1824-1907

Kelvin was a child prodigy in maths, so brilliant that he went to university when he was ten. At 22 he was made Professor of Natural Philosophy at Glasgow University, and stayed there for 53 years until he retired. In his lectures, he was famous for forgetting what he was saying halfway through a sentence – something interesting would occur to him, and he would start discussing it whether it had any connection with his lecture or not.

Kelvin was one of the most eccentric science teachers Britain has ever had. But he was also one of the greatest – one admirer said that nineteenth-century physics without Kelvin would be like **Shakespeare's** *Hamlet* without the prince. He was particularly interested in energy. He showed that a moving body has energy (he called it "kinetic energy"), and said that in any conversion of energy – heat into light, for example – a certain amount of energy is lost into the environment.

Kelvin's best-known invention is a temperature scale, now called the Kelvin scale. The scale starts at absolute zero – which is the coldest temperature possible, equivalent to -273° Celsius. Absolute zero is written as O K – Kelvin temperatures are written without the degree symbol.

Kelvin always wanted scientific discoveries to be put to practical use, and for 20 years he was science adviser to the company which designed and laid the first successful telegraph cables across the Atlantic, an enormous breakthrough in international communication. He was one of the most famous people of his time, a public figure whose name was known by millions who knew little of his scientific work.

In 1902, when Queen **Victoria** wanted to create a special honour (the "Order of Merit") for 24 living Britons who had done most for science and the arts in their lifetimes, Kelvin's name was one of the first on her list.

On board the ship, the *Great Eastern*. Kelvin's galvanometer, a machine to detect small electric currents, is being used to test the 1865 Atlantic telegraph cable.

Lord Kelvin.

KELVIN: Shakespeare 16 Victoria 454

HUXLEY, Thomas Henry

English scientist 1825-95

Huxley supported **Darwin's** theory of evolution. When the Church authorities objected to Darwin's views, because they treated human beings as animals like any others, rather than as creatures especially favoured by God, Huxley made himself Darwin's main supporter. He held public discussions and debates, wrote articles and gave lectures. His work spread Darwin's ideas far more quickly than Darwin's own efforts.

Thomas Huxley was the grandfather of the novelist Aldous Huxley, author of the science fiction novel *Brave New World*.

MARSH, Othniel Charles

US scientist 1831-99

Marsh was a palaeontologist – an expert on fossils. He spent each year working at Yale University, and in the summer went fossil-hunting with his students in the Rocky Mountains. He unearthed the remains of over 1,000 different species of dinosaur, the largest number ever found by a single individual.

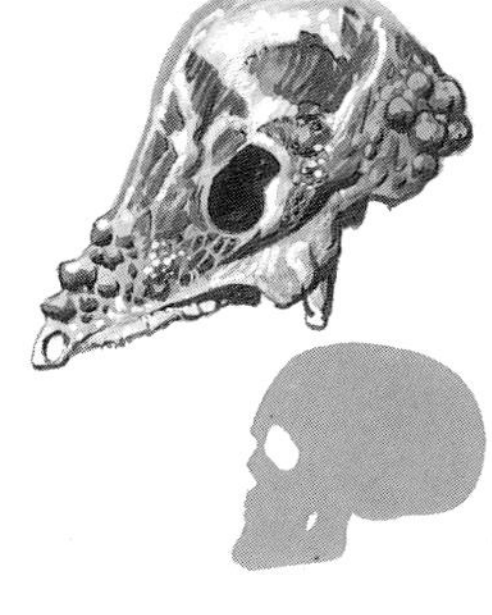

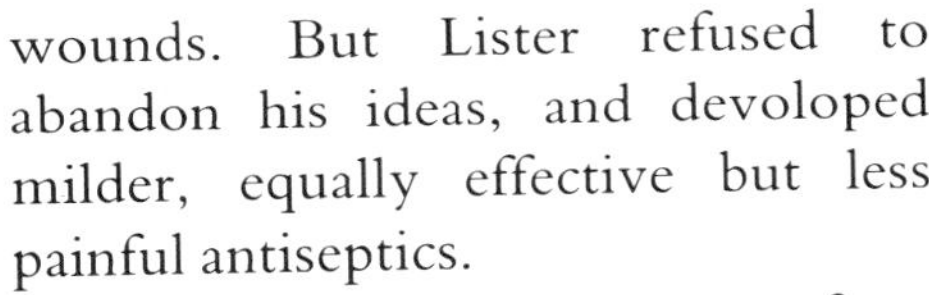

Above: Pachycephalosaurus (thick-headed lizard) was just one of the dinosaurs that roamed North America, using its skull (20 times thicker than a man's) in battle. *Left: Struthiomimus* (ostrich dinosaur) had long legs for sprinting at up to 80 km an hour.

LISTER, Joseph

Scottish doctor 1827-1912

Lister read about **Pasteur's** work, and wondered if bacteria might not also cause septicaemia during surgery: that is, breed in open wounds and cause infection. In those days, although the recent invention of anaesthetics (substances that relieve pain for a while) had made it possible for many more people to be saved by operations, many still died from infection shortly afterwards. Lister looked for a substance which would kill bacteria without killing people – and found carbolic acid. He insisted that it be used to make hospitals and especially all their operating theatres sterile (bacteria-free).

To begin with, the acid was so strong that it caused skin-irritation in the doctors and nurses, and agony when it was poured into the patients' wounds. But Lister refused to abandon his ideas, and devoloped milder, equally effective but less painful antiseptics.

Since Lister's time, every surface, operating tool and person involved in an operation has been scrubbed or steamed clean before it starts. The doctors and nurses wear gowns, gloves and masks, and wounds are covered with antiseptic dressings and sterile bandages. Lister's ideas reduced the death toll from post-operative infection to less than 15 per cent; nowadays the figure is minute.

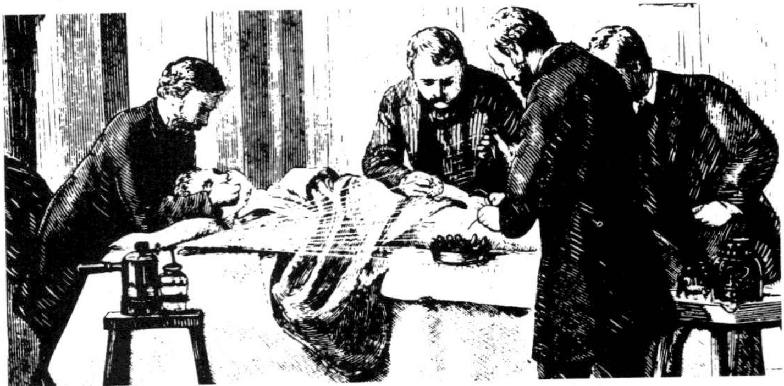

An operation, performed in 1882, using Lister's carbolic acid spray (also called phenol).

HUXLEY: Darwin 124 LISTER: Pasteur 131

MAXWELL, James Clerk

Scottish scientist 1831-79

Maxwell was an outstanding maths student. When he was only 14, he was invited to tell the scientists of the Royal Society of Edinburgh about his work in geometry: he had devised a new formula for drawing a particular kind of oval curve.

Maxwell's main work was in electromagnetism, the study of the magnetism caused by electric currents. He set out first to provide mathematical proofs for **Faraday's** electrical experiments, and then to express all basic laws of electricity and magnetism in mathematical form. The work took 25 years, and gave a proper scientific basis to the whole subject.

Among Maxwell's important discoveries was the idea of the electromagnetic field. He showed that electricity and magnetism are linked, that a changing magnetic field produces a changing electric field and vice versa. His equations predicted, but did not yet prove, the existence of electromagnetic waves moving at the speed of light, and led him to conclude that light itself is an electromagnetic wave. (Following Maxwell's work, **Hertz** was the first to produce electromagnetic waves in the laboratory.)

James Clerk Maxwell.

MENDELEYEV, Dmitri Ivanovich

Russian scientist 1834-1907

Mendeleyev devised the periodic table of chemical elements, grouping them in order of increasing atomic weight. He showed that elements with similar properties (such as the halogens fluorine, chlorine, bromine and iodine) fall into sequences (or periods).

Dmitri Mendeleyev.

The periodic table (showing atomic weights)

Group → / Period ↓	IA	IIA	IIIB	IVB	VB	VIB	VIIB	← VIII		→	IB	IIB	IIIA	IVA	VA	VIA	VIIA	O
	Alkali metals	Alkaline earth metals	← Transition metals							→	Noble metals						Halogens	Inert gases
1	1 H* 1.008																	2 HE 4.003
2	3 Li 6.939	4 Be 9.012											5 B 10.811	6 C 12.011	7 N 14.007	8 O 15.999	9 F 18.998	10 Ne 20.183
3	11 Na 22.990	12 Mg 24.312											13 Al 26.982	14 Si 28.086	15 P 30.974	16 S 32.064	17 Cl 35.453	18 Ar 39.948
4	19 K 39.102	20 Ca 40.08	21 Sc 44.956	22 Ti 47.90	23 V 50.94	24 Cr 52.00	25 Mn 54.94	26 Fe 55.85	27 Co 58.93	28 Ni 58.71	29 Cu 63.54	30 Zn 65.37	31 Ga 69.72	32 Ge 72.59	33 As 74.92	34 Se 78.96	35 Br 79.909	36 Kr 83.80
5	37 Rb 85.47	38 Sr 87.62	39 Y 88.905	40 Zr 91.22	41 Nb 92.906	42 Mo 95.94	43 Tc 99	44 Ru 101.07	45 Rh 102.91	46 Pd 106.4	47 Ag 107.87	48 Cd 112.40	49 In 114.82	50 Sn 118.69	51 Sb 121.75	52 Te 127.60	53 I 126.904	54 Xe 131.30
6	55 Cs 132.905	56 Ba 137.34	57 La** 138.91	72 Hf 178.49	73 Ta 180.95	74 W 183.85	75 Re 186.2	76 Os 190.2	77 Ir 192.2	78 Pt 195.09	79 Au 196.97	80 Hg 200.59	81 Tl 204.37	82 Pb 207.19	83 Bi 208.98	84 Po 210	85 At 211	86 Rn 222
7	87 Fr 223	88 Ra 226.05	89 Ac† 227.05															

*Hydrogen is sometimes placed above fluorine at the head of group VIIA. It is not included in the alkali metals.

** Lanthanides (rare earth metals)

58 Ce 140.12	59 Pr 140.907	60 Nd 144.24	61 Pm 147	62 Sm 150.35	63 Eu 151.96	64 Gd 157.25	65 Tb 158.92	66 Dy 162.50	67 Ho 164.93	68 Er 167.26	69 Tm 168.93	70 Yb 173.04	71 Lu 174.97

† Actinides

90 Th 232.12	91 Pa 231.05	92 U 238.07	93 Np 237	94 Pu 239	95 Am 241	96 Cm 242	97 Bk 247	98 Cf 251	99 Es 254	100 Fm 253	101 Md 256	102 No 254	103 Lr 257

Metals

Semiconductors

Non-metals

Scientists use Mendeleyev's periodic table which groups the 105 elements into related "families". It is arranged in horizontal periods and vertical groups. All the elements in one group have similar physical and chemical properties.

MAXWELL: Faraday 121 Hertz 142

LANGLEY, Samuel Pierpoint

US scientist 1837-1906

Langley was an astronomer, with a special interest in the Sun's radiation. He also studied aerodynamics, the way the flow of air over and under a bird's wings supports it as it flies. This work led him to experiment with flying-machines, and in the early 1900s he made a quarter-sized model plane which flew successfully. But it was powered by steam, and when he tried to make a full-size plane, big enough to carry a human being, the engine was too heavy and the plane failed to fly. However, Langley's work was later used by the **Wright brothers**, the first people to design and fly a powered aircraft.

WAALS, Johannes Diderik van der

Dutch scientist 1837-1923

Van der Waals was a genius, but was too poor to afford proper research facilities or a complete university education. He struggled as a schoolteacher, and did research work (on the forces which turn gases to liquid) in the evenings and at weekends. In 1873, aged 36, he finally sent his research work to Amsterdam University. The authorities were so excited by it that they made him a Doctor of Science on the spot, and four years later appointed him Professor of Physics.

Van der Waals went on to do research into the weak attractive forces between molecules (now called "van der Waals' forces" after him). In 1910 this work won him the Nobel Physics prize, the climax of a lifetime of dedicated and determined work.

MACH, Ernst

Austrian scientist 1838-1916

Mach taught maths and physics at the Universities of Graz, Prague and Vienna. He did research into projectiles moving at high speed, investigating whether their physical properties remain the same or change.

Today, Mach is best-remembered for the "Mach" number, relating the speed of a moving body to the speed of sound. A body travelling at Mach 1 moves at exactly the speed of sound: 331 metres per second or 1,191.6 kilometres per hour. Mach numbers above 1 indicate "supersonic" speeds, above the speed of sound.

Aircraft like the Red Arrows are supersonic – they break the speed of sound. There are aeorodynamic problems with flying at speeds greater than Mach 1. The aircraft are designed with swept back wings and a small wing area, to help overcome these problems.

LANGLEY: Wright 385

Right: Bacilli, micro-organisms invisible to the naked eye, under the microscope.

DEWAR, James

Scottish scientist 1842-1923

Dewar experimented with gases at such low temperatures that they had become liquid, and found that the best way to do this was to place their containers in a vacuum jacket. Heat passed very slowly through the vacuum, and so the gases stayed cold, and therefore liquid, longer. Dewar's "vacuum flasks" were later taken up by the food industry, not for keeping things cold but for keeping them hot – and this is still the main non-scientific use of vacuum (or thermos) flasks today.

Although Dewar is chiefly remembered for the vacuum flask, he did useful work of many other kinds. The government consulted him about the best way to dispose of London's sewage, and he helped to perfect the filter system still used in sewage works. He discovered that charcoal is an efficient absorber of gas molecules – and this led to the development of charcoal gas masks, issued to soldiers in millions during the First World War. As with the vacuum flask, Dewar could have made his fortune from this discovery, if he had bothered to patent it. But he was more interested in science than in money-making, and left others to enrich themselves from his ideas.

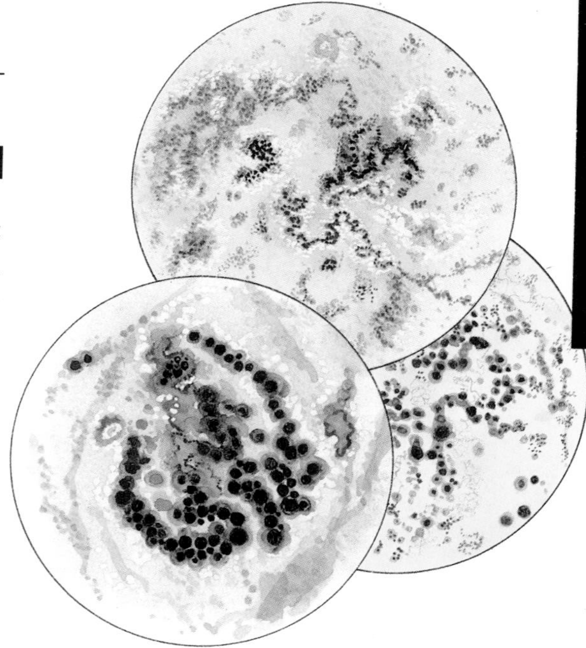

KOCH, Robert

German scientist 1843-1910

Koch began his career as a country doctor. His wife gave him a microscope, and he turned part of his surgery into a laboratory and began studying the micro-organisms, called bacilli, which cause disease. He developed a method of staining the bacilli with coloured dye and photographing them: this is still a main way of studying them today.

After this, Koch took up the science of bacteriology full-time. He moved to Berlin where, although some people called him a yokel because he spoke with a thick country accent, he became a professor at the Institute for Infectious Diseases. From Berlin he travelled all over the world, isolating micro-organisms and finding out ways to combat them. The diseases he worked on included tuberculosis, cholera, anthrax, malaria, sleeping sickness and bubonic plague – and it is partly thanks to his pioneering work that they are controllable today.

Early vacuum flasks, as developed by James Dewar.

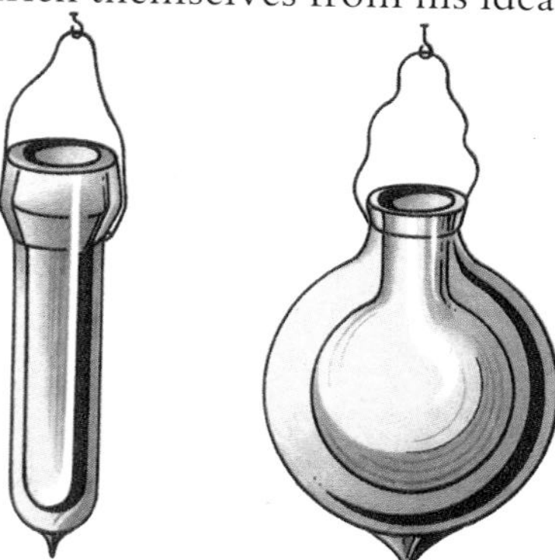

RÖNTGEN, Wilhelm Conrad

German scientist 1845-1923

Röntgen worked on the conduction of electricity through gases. In one experiment, using a cathode ray tube he noticed that a sheet of paper on the other side of the room, coated with barium platinocyanide, began to fluoresce (glow in the dark). It seemed that the tube was sending out rays, invisible to the eye, which made the paper glow. Röntgen called the rays "X-rays", because of the phrase, common in those days, "X marks the unknown". He was quite embarrassed when the newspapers coined the term "Röntgen-rays" instead.

As soon as Röntgen wrote about the rays, other scientists began to do research on them – work which led indirectly to the discovery of radioactivity and of the structure of the atom. Röntgen was given the 1901 Nobel Prize for physics. But even before then, his rays had become famous for a reason he could never have expected. If you pass X-rays through an object (for example a human body), they make an image on specially coated paper, like light rays on photographic film. X-rays pass more easily through soft tissue (like clothes or flesh) than through hard tissue (like bone), and this makes the hard tissues show darker on the "photograph" than the soft tissues, and produces an image of what is inside the person or object being photographed.

Soon after X-rays were discovered, a US doctor used them to "photograph" the inside of someone's leg, and caused a sensation. X-ray machines were quickly developed for hospitals (where they are called radiograph machines), and are now used throughout the world. They have other uses too: they can examine oil pipelines for faults, for example, without stopping the oil-flow; and at airports, they can show if luggage contains guns or bombs.

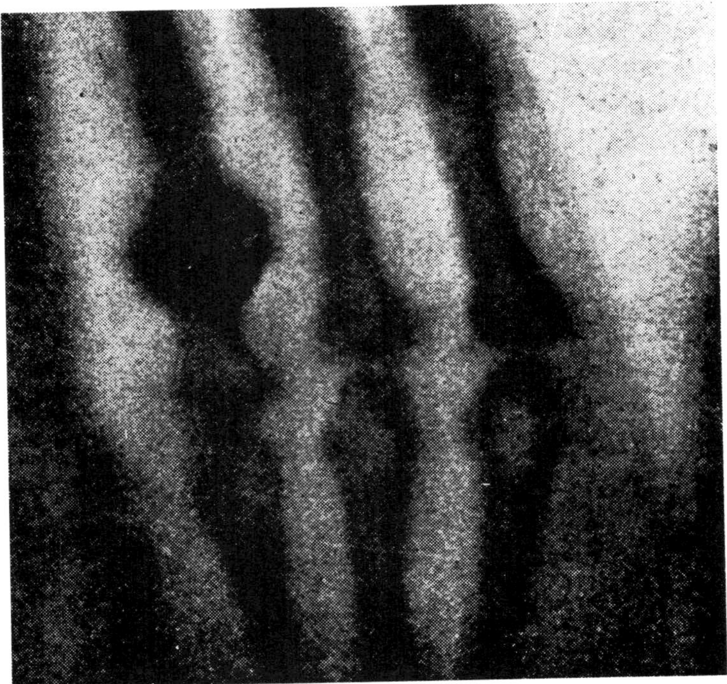

One of the first X-rays of a woman's hand. Her ring is clearly visible.

BURBANK, Luther

US scientist 1849-1926

Burbank was the son of a Californian farmer, and decided to use scientific methods to breed plants that would produce better crops, be more tolerant of bad weather and have greater resistance to disease. His greatest successes were with potatoes, tomatoes and soft fruit such as strawberries, plums and peaches. He developed the nectarine, a variety of smooth-skinned peach. The town of Burbank, north of Los Angeles, is named after him.

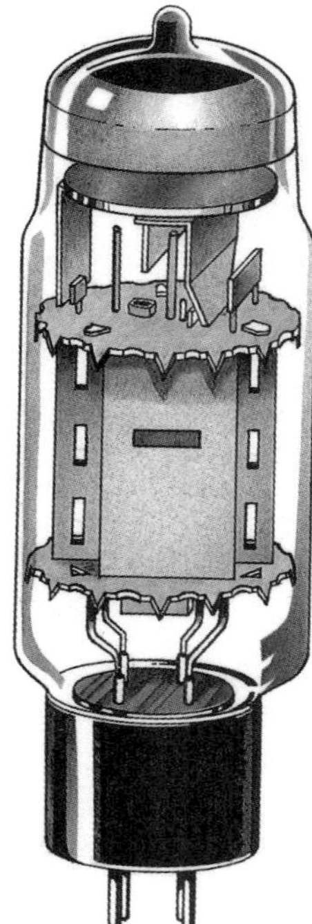

The first radios used valves of this type. Each valve was about 18 cm high – so there were no portable radios.

FLEMING, John Ambrose

English scientist 1849-1945

Fleming was interested in developing practical uses for electricity. He invented the potentiometer, a well-known piece of apparatus in physics laboratories, used to measure potential differences (also called voltages). As scientific adviser to **Edison's** telephone and electric light companies, he worked on ways of distributing electricity to every home in Britain.

During the 1880s, working with **Dewar**, Fleming immersed wires in a Dewar flask which held liquid air at low temperature. He found that the wires became far better electrical conductors – a discovery which led the way to superconductivity.

Fleming's best-known invention, made in 1929, was the diode or rectifying valve. Although valves have now been replaced by transistors, they were a crucial first step in electronics, and it is partly to Fleming that we owe today's vast communication, entertainment and computer industries.

Valve radio sets like these started to appear in family homes from the 1930s.

FLEMING: Dewar 137 Edison 380

PAVLOV, Ivan Petrovich

Russian scientist 1849-1936

Pavlov was interested in what makes animals produce saliva. He knew that animals salivate at the sight or smell of food, and he wondered if this was a physical or psychological response. He began ringing a bell just before feeding the experimental animals (dogs) each time. Then he left out the food – and discovered that simply ringing the bell was enough to make the dogs salivate. The reflex of salivation had been "conditioned" (artifically programmed).

Following this discovery, Pavlov began a series of experiments with live animals to find out where and how this "conditioned reflex" happened in the brain. His work won him a Nobel prize in 1904 – and the anger of animal-lovers throughout the world, who objected to what they thought was cruelty.

BECQUEREL, Antoine Henri

French scientist 1852-1908

In 1896 Becquerel discovered that uranium is radioactive. He had accidentally left a bottle of uranium salts on top of a packet of photographic plates. When the plates were developed, they were fogged (darkened) except for where a key had been, showing that the plates had somehow been affected by rays coming from the uranium.

Becquerel suggested to **Marie** and **Pierre Curie** that they should do research into the radioactivity of the uranium ore pitchblende – work crucial to the development of all later atomic and nuclear physics. In 1903 he shared with the Curies the Nobel prize for physics. One of the standard units of radioactivity is called the bequerel after him.

PETRIE, Flinders

English scientist 1853-1942

Before Petrie, archaeology was more like a hobby than a science. People dug where they liked, and seldom bothered to make notes of their work as it went ahead. Even **Schliemann**, the greatest of all nineteenth-century archaeologists, destroyed layer after layer of remains to reach the particular layer he wanted.

Petrie was the first archaeologist to work scientifically. At his digs – most of them in Egypt – he photographed, drew and mapped each stage of the operation. His accounts were so exact that you could have used them to restore the site precisely as it was before he started.

EHRLICH, Paul

German scientist 1854-1915

A colleague of **Koch's** at the Berlin Institute for Infectious Diseases, Ehrlich was looking for chemical substances which would kill the bacteria responsible for a disease without producing harmful side-effects on the body. One of the worst killer-diseases of the time was syphilis – and Ehrlich set out to find a cure. He experimented with a total of 605 different substances without success before trying salvarsan (an organic arsenic compound), which worked. The discovery won him the 1908 Nobel prize for medicine.

Sir Flinders Petrie, arranging some of the ancient pottery work he found in southern Palestine.

BECQUEREL: Curie 144 PETRIE: Schliemann 132 EHRLICH: Koch 137

LOWELL, Percival

US astronomer 1855-1916

Lowell spent many years observing and mapping Mars. In 1906 he published a book claiming that the lines on Mars' surface were canals, and that the planet was inhabited. The idea boosted science fiction, but did little for true science. Lowell went on to observe Uranus, and worked out the position of another, so far unknown planet: Pluto. However, he was unable to find it, and it was not seen until 1930 (by Clyde Tombaugh). Lowell's observatory at Flagstaff, Arizona, is still one of the USA's main centres of astronomical research.

The "canals" Lowell saw on Mars are craters and areas of darker rock on its desert surface – the planet is lifeless. It appears red because winds blow the fine desert dust into the air.

THOMSON, Joseph John

British scientist 1856-1940

Thomson was elected Professor of Experimental Physics at Cambridge University when he was only 27, and during the next 30 years he turned the Cavendish Laboratory there into one of the finest centres for scientific research in the world. He and seven of his assistants won Nobel prizes for their work.

Thomson's first research was concerned with the ability of gases to conduct electricity. As soon as **Röntgen** discovered X-rays in 1895, Thomson went to work on them, and discovered that they made gases at ordinary pressure conduct electricity (they usually conduct only at low pressure).

Later, Thomson studied so-called "cathode rays" (see picture), and his experiments led him to conclude that they are not rays at all but streams of negatively charged particles, many times smaller than atoms. He concluded that these particles – now called electrons – must be part of all atoms, and proposed that an atom must consist of a positively charged sphere with negatively charged electrons embedded within it, like currants in a bun. The discovery of electrons was one of the most revolutionary advances in physics since **Newton's** time, and paved the way for the work of such later scientists as **Einstein** and **Rutherford**.

Thomson continued his research, winning the Nobel prize for physics in 1906. In 1918 he became Master of Trinity College, Cambridge, and for the next 20 years he was a "grand old man" of science, advising the British government on scientific matters, speaking at international conferences and above all visiting and corresponding with fellow-scientists all over the world.

Thomson found that a beam of cathode rays can be passed through a small hole to illuminate a phosphorescent screen (as in a TV tube). If a magnet is brought near this beam, the beam is deflected sideways – just as it would be if it were a stream of negatively charged particles (as in an electric current).

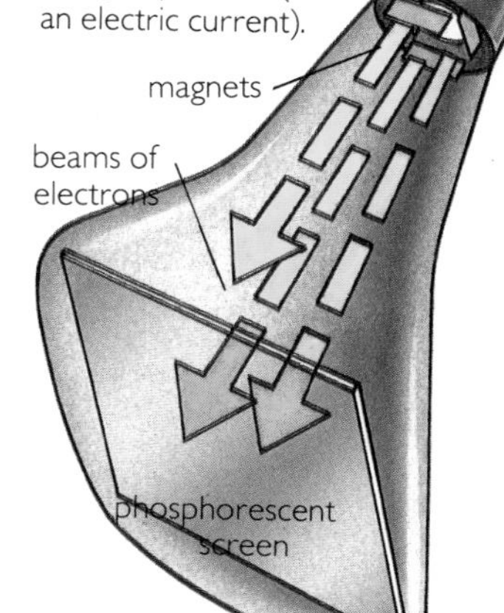

THOMSON: Einstein 146 Newton 102 Röntgen 138 Rutherford 145

Heinrich Hertz, pioneer of radio communication.

HERTZ, Heinrich Rudolf

German physicist 1857-94

A physics professor at Karlsrühe and Bonn Universities, Hertz did research into the relation between light and electricity. **Maxwell** had predicted, on mathematical grounds, the existence of electromagnetic waves, and had said that since they behaved in the same way as light, light itself might be an electro-magnetic wave. Hertz's practical work proved this theory true.

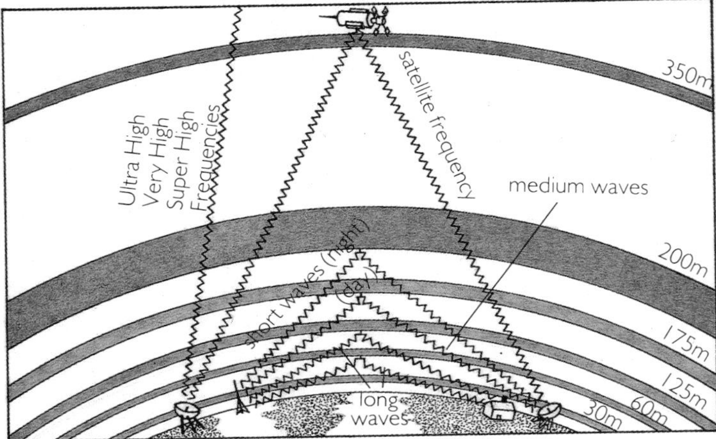

Radio waves are restricted in the range they can travel. Long, medium and short waves remain inside the Earth's atmosphere. Satellite frequency rays and Ultra High Frequency rays travel into space.

The rays Hertz discovered were called "Hertzian waves" after him, and in 1896 **Marconi** used them to send signals through space. Marconi's experiments led to the development of radio, and Hertz's waves are now known as "radio waves". The standard unit of frequency is named the hertz.

Max Planck.

PLANCK, Max Karl Ernst Ludwig

German physicist 1858-1947

Planck studied thermodynamics, the science dealing with the relationship between heat and other forms of energy. His particular concern was with "black-body" radiation: the heat and light emitted by objects which look black at normal temperatures but which glow when heated. Earlier physicists had failed to produce a mathematical formula which explained the range of this radiation – and that is what Planck set out to do.

As often happens in experimental work, Planck's researches led him to something completely unexpected, utterly unknown before. His measurements showed that radiation is not produced continuously, as had been supposed until then, but is emitted in a series of small packets of energy. Planck called these packets "quanta" (plural of the Latin word *quantum*, meaning "an amount"). He showed that the energy of the quantum is related quite simply to the frequency of the radiation (heat or light) produced by the hot body. The relationship linking them involves a number now called the Planck constant.

When Planck published his quantum theory in 1900, it revolutionized work on the physics of energy. **Einstein** used it, for example, to explain photo-electric emission. Planck won the Nobel prize for physics in 1918, and continued as one of Germany's leading scientists until he retired in the mid-1920s.

During the 1930s, then aged over 70, Planck used his reputation as the "grand old man" of German science to speak out against the way **Hitler** and the Nazis were persecuting Jewish scientists. He was too famous for the Nazis to punish personally, but they took their revenge ten years later when they falsely accused Planck's son of taking part in **von Stauffenberg's** plot to assassinate Hitler, and he was executed.

HERTZ: Marconi 388 Maxwell 135 PLANCK: Einstein 146 Hitler 466 Stauffenberg 232

Daniel Hale Williams the black surgeon who pioneered open-heart surgery.

WILLIAMS, Daniel Hale

US doctor 1858-1931

Williams was one of the first US blacks to qualify as a doctor, in 1883. At that time, blacks were banned from working as hospital surgeons, and Williams raised money for a multi-racial hospital (the Provident Hospital, Chicago), which opened in 1891. Two years later, a man was brought in suffering from a knife-wound which had severed one of the arteries to his heart. Instead of leaving him to die (as the custom was then for heart-wounds), Williams opened the man's chest, sewed up the artery and saved his life. It was the first-ever open-heart operation.

SHERRINGTON, Charles

English doctor 1861-1952

Sherrington studied the brain and nervous system. He discovered that both are worked by tiny pulses of electrical energy, triggered by chemical changes. His work formed the basis for a far greater understanding of the brain, and modern methods of brain-surgery.

BRAGG, William

English physicist 1862-1942

and

BRAGG, Lawrence

English physicist 1890-1971

William and Lawrence Bragg were one of the very few father-and-son teams in science. They did much research together, shared their ideas – and in 1915 won a joint Nobel prize. They worked in the field of X-ray crystallography: using an X-ray diffractometer (a device invented by William Bragg for measuring the wavelengths of X-rays) to discover the arrangement of atoms or molecules in crystals.

MORGAN, Thomas Hunt

US biologist 1866-1945

Morgan had a particular interest in heredity (the way creatures inherit from their parents characteristics such as blood type or eye colour). He worked with rats, mice and insects, especially the fruit fly, and showed that messages are transmitted from parent to offspring in the chromosomes – string-like bodies formed in the nuclei of all plant and animal cells.

What **Mendel** called "factors", Morgan termed "genes" after the word "genetics" – the name given to the scientific study of inheritance only a few years before by the English scientist Bateson.

MORGAN: Mendel 130

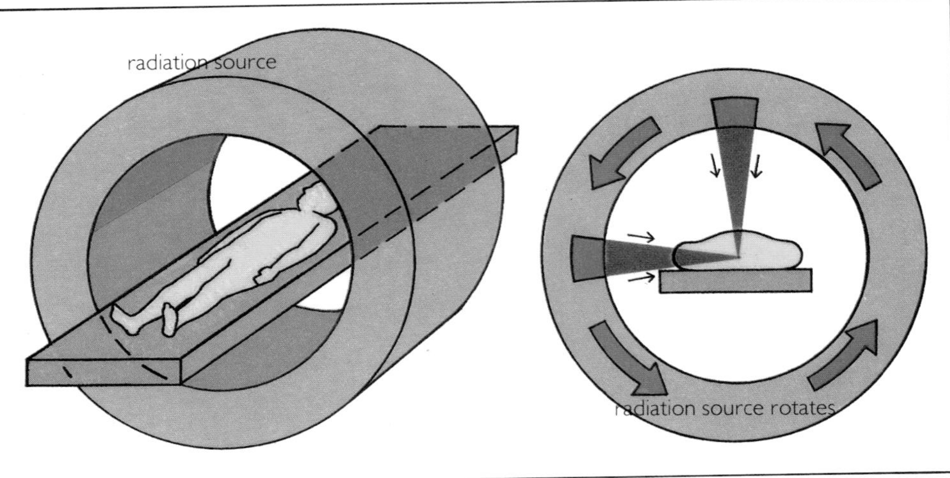

Left: Marie Curie. She and her husband, Pierre, devoted their lives to the study of radioactivity. In a radiation machine, rays can be directed to precise parts of the body to hinder or kill cancer cells.

CURIE, Marie

Polish-French scientist 1867-1934

and

CURIE, Pierre

French scientist 1859-1906

Marie Curie, whose maiden name was Maria Sklodowska, studied science at Sorbonne University in Paris. There, she married one of her professors, Pierre Curie, and together they worked to investigate the rays given off by substances such as thorium and uranium.

As a result of their experiments, the Curies discovered an important substance, which they called radium. This was very difficult to purify – to produce just one gram required no less than eight tonnes of radioactive uranium ore (called pitchblende).

The Curies discovered that the rays given off by radium are dangerous when used carelessly, but ideal for medical treatments such as weakening cancer cells. They thought these uses so important for the human race that they refused to patent their process or to make money from it: instead, they published it openly for all to use.

In 1906, two years after he and Marie won a Nobel prize for their discovery, Pierre Curie was run over in Paris by a horse-drawn cab and killed. Marie Curie became professor in his place, and five years later won a second Nobel prize for her medical research, into what is now called radio-therapy, the use of radio-activity to cure disease. She went back to Poland in 1919, and became the first-ever woman professor at Warsaw University.

LANDSTEINER, Karl

Austrian scientist 1868-1943

Until Landsteiner, people had thought that everyone's blood was the same. No one knew why, after blood transfusions, some patients lived and others died. Landsteiner discovered that there are different kinds of blood (he called them "blood-groups"), and that if people are given blood from a different group, the body rejects it. His system of grouping blood (A, B and 0) is still in use, along with other systems such as the Rhesus system.

RUTHERFORD, Ernest

New Zealand/British scientist 1871-1937

Rutherford followed **J J Thomson** as Professor of Physics at Cambridge University and head of the Cavendish Laboratory. His main work was studying radioactivity (the streams of particles which radiate from certain substances). He found that uranium salts emit two different kinds of radiation, which he named alpha particles and beta particles.

Rutherford showed that alpha particles are very like helium atoms – in fact they are helium atoms which have lost two electrons each – and that beta particles are electrons (which Thomson had recently discovered). He wondered why radioactive substances should behave like this, and in 1902 proposed that it was because some of their atoms had disintegrated. Many scientists scoffed at the idea, but Rutherford maintained that the explanation fitted his experimental results.

In another experiment, Rutherford fired alpha particles at a sheet of gold foil, and was astonished to find that one in 10,000 bounced back. He concluded that each particle which returned had passed very close to the centre of a gold atom and been strongly repelled. He proposed that each atom must consist of a small, positively charged nucleus containing most of the mass and surrounded by negative electrons which orbit it as planets travel round the Sun.

This was a giant step forward in atomic physics. Rutherford went further and tried bombarding gases such as nitrogen with alpha particles, to see what would happen. He found that the bombardment resulted in the first artificial change of one element to another: collision with alpha particles converted some nitrogen atoms into oxygen atoms. At the moment of collision, new, positively charged particles ("protons") were ejected.

Rutherford had shown that the nuclei of various atoms could be broken up, a discovery that led directly to the splitting of the atom by **Fermi**, and from there to today's vast nuclear industry and to atomic and nuclear bombs.

RUTHERFORD: Fermi 152 Thomson, J J 141

Ernest Rutherford. His work with atoms led to the splitting of the atom and the start of the nuclear industry.

Rutherford in his laboratory.

MEITNER, Lise

Austrian/Swedish scientist 1878-1968

Meitner worked with **Hahn**, and in 1917 they announced the discovery of a new radioactive element, called proactinium. At the beginning of the Second World War, Meitner went to live in Sweden, and she was one of a team of scientists who made the breakthrough in discovering the process of nuclear fission. She was horrified when this discovery was used to make bombs, and spent the rest of her long life working for organizations devoted to the harnessing of nuclear power for peace, not war.

MEITNER: Hahn 148

EINSTEIN, Albert

German/US scientist 1879-1955

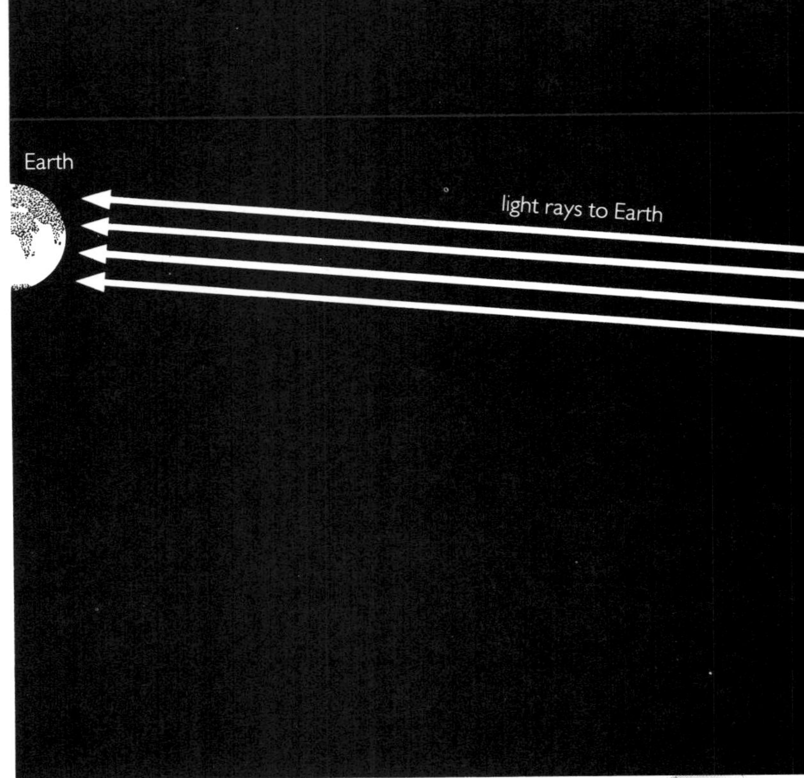

In the 1890s, when Einstein began his work, scientists were still trying to find out exactly what light consisted of. Was it streams of small particles ("corpuscles", as **Newton** had called them two centuries before), or did it move in waves, like sound or water, as **Huygens** and others had suggested? There seemed to be no way to prove either theory beyond doubt. Some experiments favoured one opinion, others the other; in the mid-nineteenth century the wave theory was favourite. However, in the 1880s, a discovery had been made which confused the situation even further. It was found that when light of the right frequency was shone on to various metals, electrons were produced (this is called photo-electric emission). If light were thought of as a wave, the occurrence could not be explained.

The next major advance in understanding light came at the turn of the century. In 1900, **Planck** advanced his quantum theory – and five years later Einstein suggested that light could be thought of in the same way. He called each quantum of light a "photon". With this idea about light he was able to explain photo-electric emission.

Even so, the problem had not yet been fully solved. Einstein's photons were rather like Newton's corpuscles, so the whole argument about the nature of light started up again. It was not till later that physicists began to think of light as neither wave nor particle only, but both at once.

Einstein went on to study light movement even more minutely. Building on recent discoveries that light always moves at the same rate, he provided proof of why this must be the case. He explained that difficulties in measurement are due to the changing point of view of the observer in relation to the source of light. Points of view are constantly varying because everything in the universe is in motion with respect to everything else.

The idea that nothing is absolutely stationary, known as the "theory of relativity", had been suggested by the

Albert Einstein (right) with Nobel prize-winning chemist Fritz Haber, c 1910.

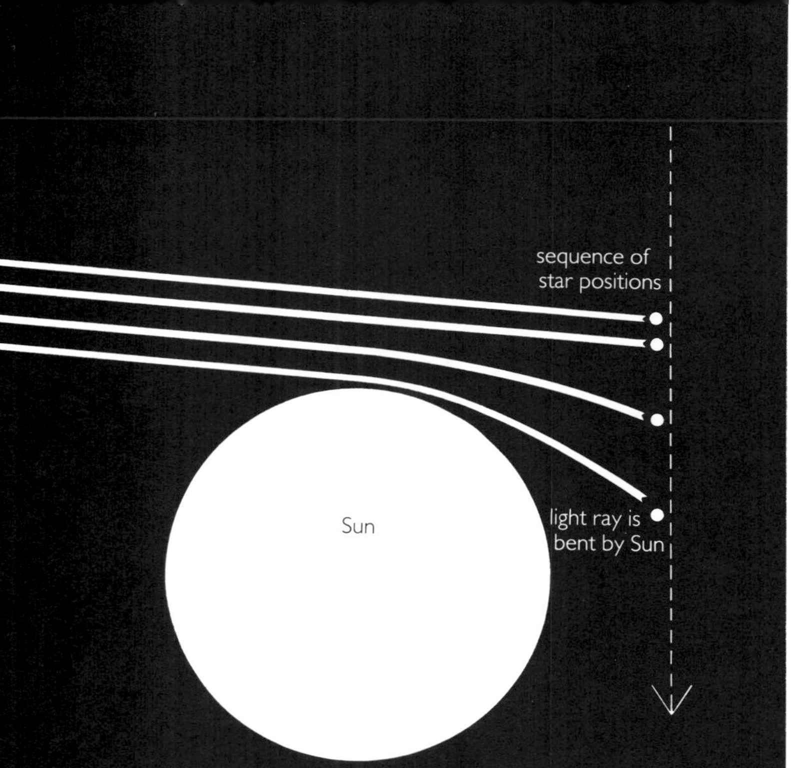

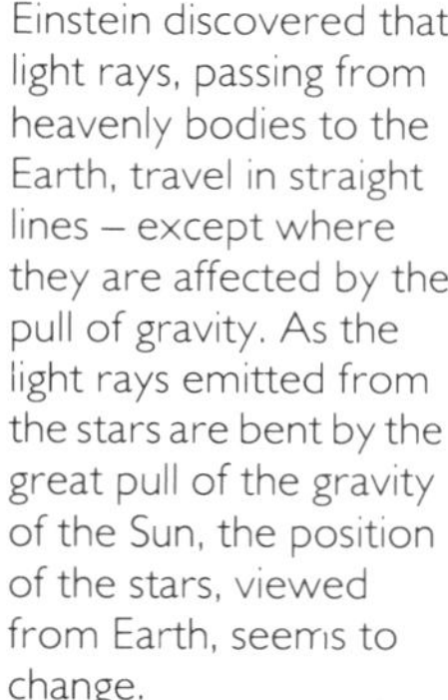
Einstein discovered that light rays, passing from heavenly bodies to the Earth, travel in straight lines – except where they are affected by the pull of gravity. As the light rays emitted from the stars are bent by the great pull of the gravity of the Sun, the position of the stars, viewed from Earth, seems to change.

Einstein's Theory of Relativity, published in 1916, completely changed people's understanding of their world.

French scientist Poincaré in 1904, but Einstein developed it and backed it up with mathematical proof.

Einstein made many other important discoveries. He showed, for example, that the speed of light cannot be exceeded. He also stated – and later experiments proved him correct – that as the velocity of an object increases (that is, as it moves faster), its mass also increases, and that mass and energy are equivalent. This is expressed mathematically as

$$E=mc^2$$

where E is the amount of energy obtained if a mass m is totally converted into energy, and c is the speed of light.

Einstein's discovery explains what happens during the fission and fusion of atoms (see **Fermi**): mass is converted into energy. Fission, on Earth, can lead to nuclear power and to the atomic bomb. Fusion, in the Sun and stars, generates their energy; scientists are still working to harness its energy on Earth.

So far, Einstein had produced what he called the "special theory of relativity", applied only to motion which is constant and does not accelerate. He went on to consider accelerating systems, in what he called the "general theory of relativity". His calculations showed that gravity and acceleration affect objects in exactly the same way. Light passing a heavenly body is bent by its gravitational pull; space itself is curved. All earlier scientists had believed that, as **Euclid** said, "the shortest distance between two points is a straight line". Einstein showed that this was not always the case.

Einstein's ideas completely changed the way scientists thought. Until his time, they had always worked towards such things as exactness and absolute truth. Their explanations had depended on all human beings sharing the same viewpoint: we observe time, space and other phenomena in the same way. Einstein's theory meant that nothing was certain. If you looked at time or space on another planet, or from outer space, they might be totally different from our earthly idea of them. For physics, this was as revolutionary as the ideas of **Copernicus** or **Darwin** had been in other fields.

EINSTEIN: Copernicus 93 Darwin 124 Euclid 86 Fermi 152 Huygens 101 Newton 102 Planck 142

HAHN, Otto

German scientist 1879-1968

Hahn spent his life working with radioactivity, and in the 1930s, following up the work of the **Curies**, he investigated the effects of bombarding uranium atoms with neutrons (which had recently been discovered by **Chadwick**). He and his colleague Strassman discovered that each atom was split into two unequal-sized pieces, with the release of more neutrons. This work won Hahn the Nobel prize for physics in 1944. **Fermi**, who had been working on similar research, went on in the 1940s to harness this process – a feat which eventually led to the building of the first atomic bomb. However, Hahn was horrified by the idea of nuclear power being used for war, and took care not to tell his Nazi employers of the fearful possibilities his discovery had opened up.

In 1946 Hahn was made head of the Max Planck Society in Göttingen, a centre for nuclear research – and in 1960 he and 17 colleagues signed the "Göttingen Declaration", a promise never to use their knowledge to help the West German government develop nuclear weapons. Although Hahn was by then over 80, he devoted the rest of his life to campaigning against nuclear arms.

WEGENER, Alfred

German scientist 1880-1930

In 1915 Wegener published a book saying that the Earth's continents and islands had not always been the same, made by God and forever fixed. Originally there was just one enormous mass of land on Earth – which he called Pangaea ("all Earth") – surrounded by ocean. Over millions of years this land mass split into smaller pieces. The pieces drifted apart very slowly – as little as a centimetre a year – and formed the continents, islands and other fragments of land we know today.

At first, Wegener's theory was not taken seriously. But, over the years, improved methods of charting the position of the continents have shown that he was right – and that in fact the continents are still drifting, moving at a rate of up to ten centimetres per year.

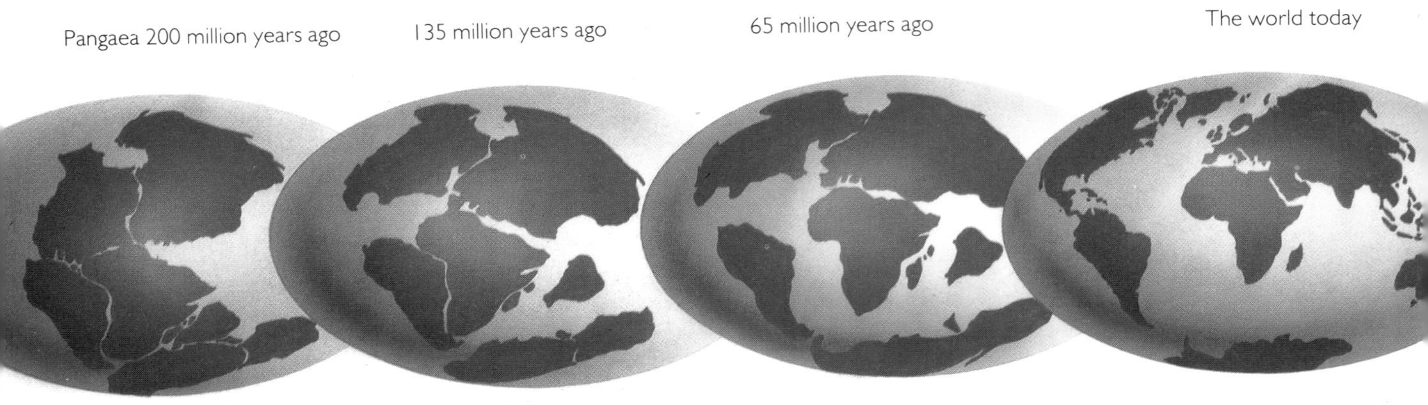

Two hundred million years ago, there was one supercontinent, Pangaea. Gradually the land broke up and the pieces drifted apart. This "continental drift" continues today.

Pangaea 200 million years ago

135 million years ago

65 million years ago

The world today

HAHN: Chadwick 150 Curie 144 Fermi 152

FLEMING, Alexander

Scottish scientist 1881-1955

Fleming was a bacteriologist, who followed up the earlier work of **Pasteur** and **Koch**. He researched into ways of controlling the micro-organisms which cause infection. He grew bacteria for his experiments in a type of jelly smeared in glass dishes. One day he noticed that mould had grown on part of the jelly in one of the dishes, and that there were no bacteria anywhere near it. That meant something in the mould had killed them.

Fleming wrote about his discovery in 1929, but it was not until ten years later that he, together with Howard Florey and Ernest Chain, managed to extract the bacteria-killing substance from the mould and make it into a drug which would prevent or cure infection. The drug is penicillin, and it is still one of the main so-called antibiotics used to save millions of lives every year.

The discovery of penicillin won Fleming, Florey and Chain the Nobel prize for medicine in 1945.

GEIGER, Hans

German scientist 1882-1945

Geiger worked with **Rutherford** on the "gold-leaf" experiment, and he and Rutherford invented the first alpha-particle detector. Later, with Muller, Geiger invented a machine for detecting radioactivity. This is the "Geiger counter" which clicks when passed over a radioactive source. The faster the clicks, the greater the radioactivity.

BOHR, Niels

Danish scientist 1885-1962

Niels Bohr.

As a young man, Bohr worked with **J J Thomson** and **Rutherford** in England, and in 1913 devised a model for the atom which improved on Rutherford's "solar system" model. Bohr's work produced the results which marked a major advance in atomic theory, and led to his being awarded the Nobel prize for physics in 1922.

In the 1930s, when the Nazis began persecuting Jewish scientists in Germany, Bohr found jobs for many refugees at the Copenhagen Institute where he was head. The Germans occupied Denmark at the beginning of the Second World War, and he was forced to flee the country. He fled to Sweden, and was smuggled from there to England in the bomb-bay of a plane. (He nearly died on the journey, for he was not wearing headphones and so missed the pilot's order to put on the oxygen mask.) From England he emigrated to the USA, and worked there with **Oppenheimer** and the team which perfected the atomic bomb.

Checking for radiation using a Geiger counter, and wearing a safety suit.

FLEMING: Pasteur 131 Koch 137 GEIGER: Rutherford 145 BOHR: Oppenheimer, J 154 Rutherford 145 Thomson, JJ 141

HUBBLE, Edwin Powell

US astronomer 1889-1952

Using the huge telescope at Mount Wilson Observatory in the USA, Hubble investigated the theory that distant galaxies are not static but moving away from us. He wanted to find the speed of their movement, and did so by measuring the red shift (see **Doppler**) of light coming from them. His research led him to propose what is now called Hubble's Law: that the velocity of a galaxy is proportional to its distance away from us (for example, a galaxy twice as far away as another is moving twice as fast).

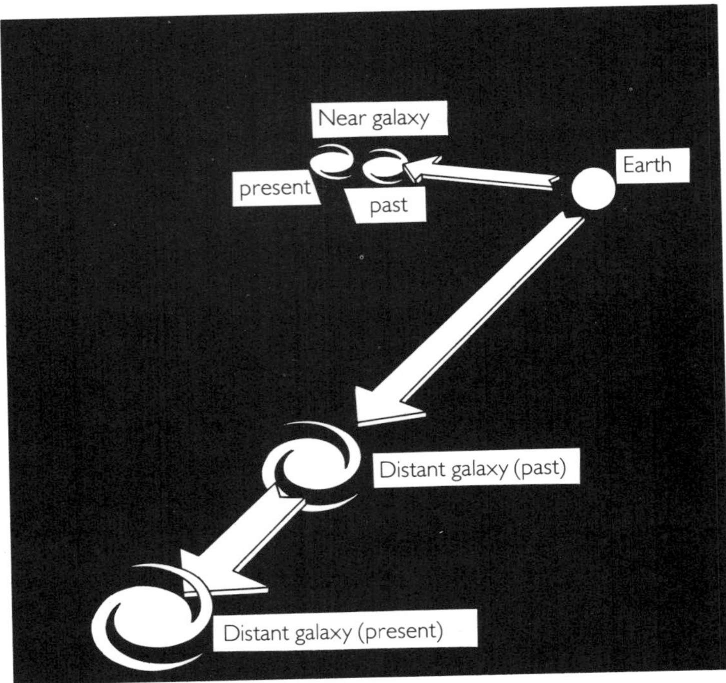

Illustration of Hubble's Law. Hubble observed that fainter (presumably more distant) galaxies were moving away faster than brighter (nearer) ones. In the same time, the distance to the distant galaxy will have increased much more than the distance to the near galaxy.

BANTING, Frederick Grant

Canadian scientist 1891-1941

and

BEST, Charles Herbert

US scientist 1899-1978

Banting and Best discovered insulin, the hormone which keeps us alive by controlling the amount of sugar in our blood. Without a daily dose of insulin, diabetics (people unable to control their own blood-sugar levels) would die.

Left: Frederick Banting, one of the two scientists who discovered insulin.

CHADWICK, James

English scientist 1891-1974

As a young man, Chadwick worked with **Rutherford** on scattering alpha particles and the disintegration of the nucleus. Later, as Professor of Physics at Liverpool University, he continued this work. He bombarded various elements with alpha particles, and observed the effects. In most experiments, protons (positively charged particles) were released. But when Chadwick bombarded beryllium, a new particle was emitted from the nucleus. It had the same mass as a proton, but no charge.

Because the new particle was neutral (with neither negative nor positive charge), Chadwick called it the "neutron". He went on to show that neutrons and protons are the fundamental particles which make up the nucleus of almost all atoms – work which won him the Nobel prize for physics in 1935.

James Chadwick.

HUBBLE: Doppler 123 CHADWICK: Rutherford 145

The Joliot-Curies, They and James Chadwick were joint winners of the Nobel prize for physics in 1935.

JOLIOT-CURIE, Irène

French scientist 1897-1956

and

JOLIOT-CURIE, Jean Frédéric

French scientist 1900-1958

Irène Curie was the daughter of **Pierre** and **Marie Curie**; Jean Frédéric Joliot was a student in Marie Curie's laboratory. When he married Irène, they both took the name Joliot-Curie.

The Joliot-Curies worked at the Radium Institute in Paris, and in 1932 Irène became its head. She and her husband were interested in the effects of bombarding substances with radioactive particles, and in 1933 they discovered that if boron (a non-radioactive substance) is bombarded, radioactivity results. This means that radioactivity has been artificially created.

The Joliot-Curies were committed Communists, and spoke out against Fascism. During the Second World War, when France was occupied by the Nazis, Jean Frédéric worked for the Resistance (hampering Nazi rule and saving Jews and others from persecution). After the war he was appointed High Commissioner for Atomic Energy, but was sacked when he condemned France's decision to use atomic power not for peaceful purposes but to build bombs. He went on working for peace, and was made president of the World Peace Council. At the same time, he and his wife continued with their scientific work, training a new generation of students and doing research.

Like all early workers with radioactivity, the Joliot-Curies had little idea of the health risks involved, and both were fatally contaminated. Irène's health broke down in the 1950s, and in 1956 she died of radiation burns. A few months later Jean Frédéric learned that he, too, had cancer, and he died of it in 1958.

JOLIOT-CURIE: Curie 144

FERMI, Enrico

Italian/US scientist 1901-54

Fermi worked on radioactivity. In 1933 he predicted a new sub-atomic particle that must be released during some of the processes of radioactive decay. It would have virtually no mass and no electrical charge. He called it the "neutrino" – and neutrinos are so hard to catch (they even pass mostly undetected through the Earth) that it was another 22 years before anyone could prove that his theory was correct.

In 1934, soon after **Chadwick** found neutrons, Fermi discovered that some non-radioactive elements can be made radioactive if neutrons are fired at them. These were some of the first-known radioactive isotopes (varieties of an element containing different numbers of neutrons in the nucleus). He also discovered that certain materials can slow down neutrons which pass through them. This work won him the Nobel prize for physics in 1938.

At that time Italy was ruled by the Fascist government of **Benito Mussolini**. The Fascists held the same views about Jews as **Hitler** and the Nazis, and when Fermi and his (Jewish) wife went to Scandinavia to collect the Nobel prize, they took the chance to escape to the USA.

In the USA Fermi went on with his experiments. He and his colleagues fired neutrons at uranium atoms, and found that each atom split into two unequal pieces. This is called "atomic fission" or "splitting the atom". Fermi realized that each time a uranium atom was split, more neutrons were produced which would in their turn split more uranium atoms. It was a "chain reaction" – one which duplicates itself endlessly. If it could be controlled it would provide energy; if not it would cause an explosion.

By then America was at war with Japan and Japan's ally Germany, and there were rumours that the Germans were working to harness atomic energy to make bombs. President **Roosevelt** set up a top-secret team, including Fermi, to make an American bomb. They code-named their experiments "The Manhattan Project", and in 1942 they achieved the first controlled chain reaction: the race for atomic power was won.

Enrico Fermi, the Italian atomic physicist who split the atom, lecturing in 1949.

FERMI: Chadwick 150 Hitler 466 Mussolini 465 Roosevelt 464

HEISENBERG, Werner Karl

German scientist 1901-1976

As a young man Heisenberg did work based on **Planck's** quantum theory, and in 1927 he put forward what is now know as the "theory of indeterminacy" or the "Heisenberg uncertainty principle". Because the sub-atomic particles are so small, it is very difficult to make accurate measurements. The uncertainty principle says that it is impossible to determine exactly where such a particle (for example an electron) will be at a specified time. If you specify a particular moment, you can only say that the electron will be "within" a particular volume; if you specify the exact position, you can only say that the electron will be there within a range of times.

PAULING, Linus Carl

US scientist born 1901

Pauling won two Nobel prizes: for chemistry (1954) and for peace (1962). He won the chemistry prize for working out the structure of complex compounds such as proteins. He found that proteins have a spiral structure – a discovery which influenced the work of **Crick and Watson** on DNA.

When Pauling retired from experimental science he took an interest in science teaching in schools and colleges, advising on what should be taught and writing several textbooks. He also became a world-wide campaigner against nuclear weapons – the work for which he won his second Nobel prize.

GIBBONS, John Heysham

US doctor born 1903

Gibbons perfected the heart-lung machine, which pumps blood round the body and controls the patient's breathing during operations. It is particularly important in heart operations, keeping the patient alive while his or her own heart stops beating.

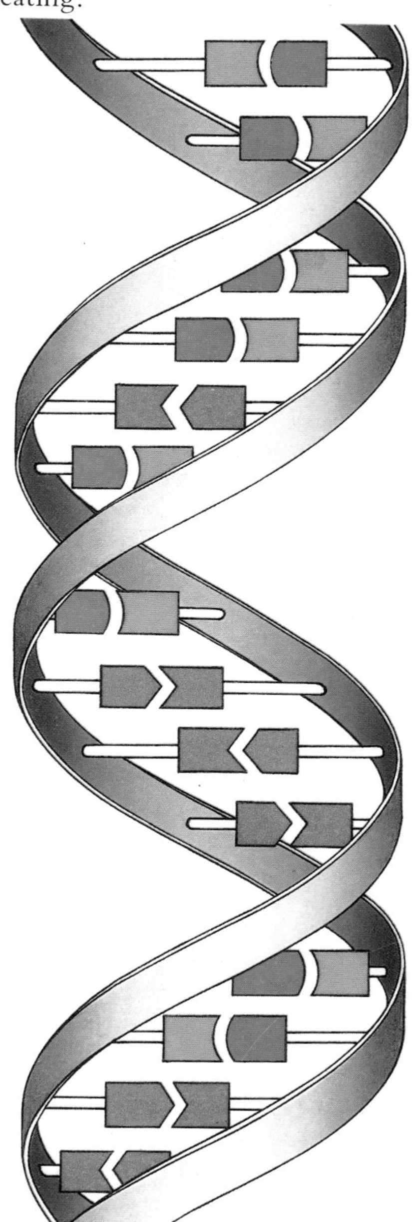

This diagram shows the double helix of DNA, a nucleic acid which is the main component of the chromosomes of almost all organisms. The work of Pauling on chemical bonding led to the discovery of the spiral structure.

HEISENBERG: Planck 142 PAULING: Crick and Watson 157

LEAKEY, Louis Seymour Bazett

English/Kenyan anthropologist 1903-72

Leakey was keenly interested in palaeontology (the study of fossil bones). He worked in Kenya, and he and his wife Mary and sons Jonathan and Richard spent their holidays unearthing the sites of prehistoric human settlements.

The Leakeys were looking for the oldest human bones they could find. Until then, most scientists believed that the human race had existed on Earth for little more than half a million years, and that we have been "civilized" for only about the last 10,000 years. The Leakeys, however, found skulls and other remains which proved that our ancestors lived in Africa around 3.75 million years ago, and that their society was more organized than any apes had ever been. Their best-known find was the skull of a being they called *Homo habilis* ("adaptable human"), because he or she was the first person known to have made and used tools.

So far as these goslings were concerned, Lorenz was Mum.

LORENZ, Konrad Zacharias

Austrian scientist born 1903-89

Lorenz was a pioneer of ethology, the study of animal behaviour. He believed that all actions follow a logical sequence, rather like the steps in a computer program. There are two kinds of sequences (or "fixed action patterns"): instinctive (genetically inherited from the parents) and learned (the animal's response to its environment).

Sequences are triggered by stimuli, and always follow the same logical and predictable pattern. One set of experiments showed this in a particularly dramatic way. Lorenz took creatures such as goslings from their mothers immediately after birth, and gave them alternative mothers (other creatures, including himself, or objects such as lumps of wood). The young creatures accepted the substitute mothers as their own, and a whole behaviour-sequence was triggered – that of learning from one's parent. The baby animal tried to behave like its new mother, even if "she" belonged to a completely different species, or to none at all.

OPPENHEIMER, J Robert

US scientist 1904-67

In 1943 the US government made Oppenheimer head of a team of scientists developing the first atomic bomb. Two years later the bomb was dropped on Hiroshima in Japan. Oppenheimer was shocked at the enormous loss of life, and spent the rest of his life campaigning for peaceful uses of nuclear energy.

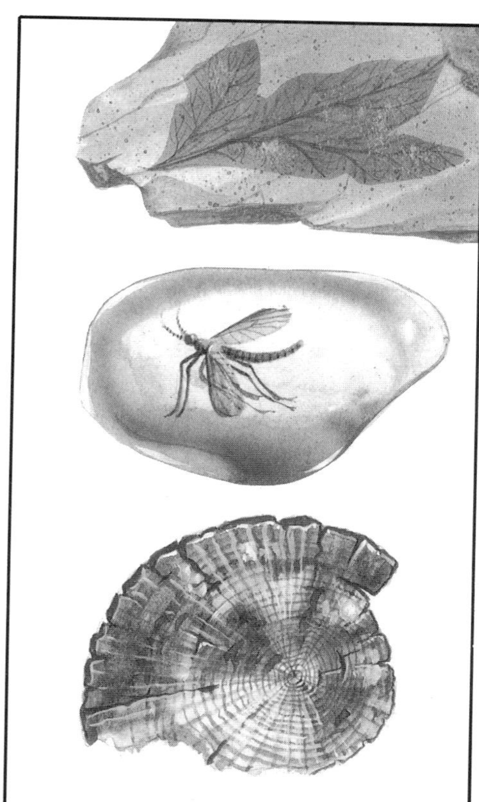

Left: The remains of ancient life are preserved in various ways: leaves can become fossilized as carbon smears on rocks; insects get trapped in tree sap which hardens as amber; buried tree trunks are replaced, molecule by molecule, by minerals – yet each tree ring remains clearly visible.

CARSON, Rachel Louise

US marine biologist 1907-64

In the 1950s Carson worked for the US Fish and Wildlife Services, and became horrified at the way the human race, without realizing it, was polluting and destroying wild life on the planet. The amount of insecticide sprayed each year on Californian farms, for example, if it had been put directly into the water supply, would have been enough to kill four times the world's entire human population.

Carson began writing and lecturing about the dangers of pesticides, artificial fertilizers and other scientific ways of increasing crop production. Her book *Silent Spring* was a world best-seller in the 1960s, making the problems of chemical pollution headline news.

LIBBY, Willard Frank

US scientist born 1908

Libby invented radio-carbon dating, a way to find out the age of fossils and other remains of living things by measuring their radioactivity. He realized that, since the rate at which the radioactivity of carbon decays is known, this means that anything that once lived, and still has some carbon left in it, can be dated. The process is so accurate that things that lived hundreds of thousands of years ago can be dated to within a few centuries.

SHOCKLEY, William Bradfield

US scientist 1910-89

Shockley led the team of scientists who perfected the transistor in 1956. Transistors carry the tiny electrical impulses which power electronic logic circuits. Without them, none of today's hi-fi and computer industries would exist.

Electrical machines like radios and TV sets use transistors. These small devices amplify, or increase, small electric currents, and can also switch currents on and off.

KOLFF, Willem Jan

Dutch doctor born 1911

Kolff invented the "artificial kidney", a machine able to cleanse waste materials from the blood outside the body. At the time, the Nazis were invading Holland, and Kolff hid the secret of his invention from them in case it helped them. After the war, instead of patenting his invention and making a fortune, he gave it to countries which had helped Holland in the war, so spreading its benefits freely to the human race.

BRAUN, Wernher von

German scientist born 1912

Braun was a pioneer in rocket engines, and designed the engines for the V2 rockets which **Hitler** used to attack London during the Second World War. In 1950 he emigrated to the USA, and worked on engines for the rockets which were to put satellites, and eventually human beings, into space. The climax to his career came in 1969, when he was in charge of the US Space Program: the space vehicle Apollo 11, powered by rockets of his design, put the first man (**Neil Armstrong**) on the Moon.

The V2 missile, used by Germany in the Second World War. It stood 14 metres tall and could carry a one-tonne bomb 300 kilometres.

TURING, Alan Mathison

English mathematician 1912-54

In the early part of his career, Turing worked on the theoretical possibilities of electronic computers, even though they had not yet been invented. He showed that a very simple computer – the "Turing machine" – could be programmed to perform most mathematical calculations.

During the Second World War, Turing successfully broke the "Enigma" code used by the Germans to send secret messages.

Left: The Turing machine – the Enigma code breaker.

STEPTOE, Patrick Christopher

English doctor 1913-88

After 12 years' work, Steptoe and his colleague Robert Edwards succeeded in fertilizing a human egg artificially, in the laboratory, and returning it to the mother's womb. Louise Brown, the first "test-tube baby", was born in 1978.

SALK, Jonas Edward

US doctor born 1914

In 1954 Salk discovered the first effective vaccine against the paralysing disease polio.

BRAUN: Armstrong, N 236 Hitler 466

CRICK, Francis Harry Compton

English scientist born 1916

and

WATSON, James Dewey

US scientist born 1928

Crick and Watson met in England, at the University of Cambridge. They worked to find out the shape of the molecules of DNA (dioxyribonucleic acid), the substance in living cells which passes information from one generation to another – so that bees' offspring, for example, are bees, not wasps or ferns. They proved that the structure of DNA is two intertwining spirals, known as a double helix. (Their research depended on work done by two other scientists, Maurice Wilkins and Rosalind Franklin, who used X-rays to analyse the structure of the DNA crystal.)

In 1962 Watson, Crick and Wilkins were awarded the Nobel prize for physiology and medicine.

BARNARD, Christiaan Neethling

South African doctor born 1922

In 1967 Barnard performed the first successful human heart-transplant operation.

BELLAMY, David

English scientist born 1933

Bellamy, a botanist, is concerned about the way human beings are destroying the planet. He has made hundreds of TV programmes to teach people about the environment, and uses his fame to get world-wide publicity and stop further damage. In 1983 he was arrested while protesting with other people against a hydroelectric scheme which would flood a Tasmanian nature reserve – and work was stopped. In 1986 Bellamy was appointed ambassador for Greenpeace, the world-wide group dedicated to warn people about ecological disaster, or to stop it before it happens.

HAWKING, Stephen William

English scientist born 1942

It is possible that our grandchildren will rate Hawking, as a scientific thinker, with **Newton** or **Einstein**. He studies the physics of space, and has proved that black holes not only exist, but emit radiation – something no scientist had ever done before, and which few believed until they saw Hawking's proofs. He has gone on to show that the "Big Bang" theory of the origin of the universe – that everything began with a single vast explosion – is scientifically provable. To non-scientists, one of the most remarkable things about Hawking is that he is almost totally disabled. His phenomenal mind is locked in a wasted body, and he works with the help of assistants, and with a voice synthesizer which lets him "speak" tinny, computer-generated sounds.

HAWKING: Einstein 146 Newton 102

GLOSSARY

Alchemy For 2000 years, until about 1500 AD, people studied alchemy. They thought that by melting, powdering and mixing metals, plants and rocks they could change them into other substances. They hoped to find the "elixir of life" (a drink which would give immortality), the "panacea" (a medicine to cure all diseases), and the "philosopher's stone" (which would turn ordinary metal into gold). These quests failed, but many of the alchemists' discoveries proved useful in later science, especially chemistry.

Antibiotic A drug which kills micro-organisms, or slows down their action.

Astronomy The scientific study of heavenly bodies (for example stars and planets) and the universe of which they are part.

Atmosphere The layer of gases (carbon dioxide, nitrogen, oxygen and others) that surrounds the Earth: the "air".

Atom The smallest particle of a substance that can take part in chemical change.

Aurora borealis (or "Northern lights") Flashes and streams of colour seen in the sky in northern countries, especially near the North Pole. They happen when energy particles from the Sun, trapped in the atmosphere, interact with gases in the atmosphere, making them glow.

Calculus Used in mathematics, a way to calculate tiny changes in continuously varying quantities (for example changes in the position of a moving object).

Chromosome A protein in the cells of living things, make up of units (genes) that are responsible for the transfer of characteristics from parent to offspring.

Combustion In chemistry this is what happens when a substance combines with oxygen to produce heat and light. When you light a fire, for example, combustion happens: heat and light are produced, and gases ("smoke") are given off.

Conductor A substance which allows heat or electricity to pass through it. "Good" conductors (such as metals) let them pass much more freely than "bad" conductors (such as wood). This is why electric wires are usually made of metal, and saucepan handles are often made of wood.

Diffraction The spreading or bending of light rays or sound waves as they strike or pass through an object.

Elements The basic substances in nature, combining to make everything which exists. Over 90 elements occur naturally, and scientists have created a dozen more.

Ellipse A closed, rounded shape, like a flattened circle.

Erosion Wearing away. Over a long period of time, wind and water erode earth and rock. Chemicals in the atmosphere (for example in "acid rain") erode the metal of cars and the stone of buildings. Animals and people can also erode the landscape, by such activities as digging and tunnelling.

Hallucination A wild idea or vision, flashing through the brain. People affected by drugs often "see" colours and shapes inside their heads, without using their eyes. These are called hallucinations.

Hieroglyphics Picture writing, especially from ancient Egypt, Mesopotamia and Pakistan. Instead of using letters of the alphabet, people "write" using tiny pictures or symbols. Road signs are often hieroglyphics: a picture of two children holding hands, for example, means "School ahead".

Hypotenuse In a right-angled triangle, the hypotenuse is the side opposite the right angle.

Interference This term describes what happens when two light waves or two sound waves combine. Each has its own pattern. When they combine, they either form a new, stronger pattern, or cancel each other out.

Latitude and longitude This idea is used in map-making and navigation. You imagine the Earth covered with lines, as if held in a net. The lines go round the globe, north/south and east/west. The distance between each line and the next is the same. Using the grid of lines, you can work out your position exactly, or make an accurate map. Lines of latitude run east/west; lines of longitude run north/south.

Marsupial A mammal (such as a kangaroo or opossum) whose young are born immature, and spend the first weeks or months of life in a pouch on the mother's belly, suckling from her teats.

Meteorology Study of the atmosphere and its effects on the Earth's surface. Weather studies are one of the main branches of meteorology.

Molecule Two or more atoms held together by chemical bonding. The smallest particle of an element or compound that can exist by itself.

Optics The study of light and sight.

Orbit The curved path or route one object takes round another. Planets move in orbits, under the influence of gravity, round the Sun. Electrons travel in orbits round the nucleus (centre) of an atom.

Organ In biology, a distinct part of the body of an animal or a plant with a special function. Each organ helps to keep the plant or animal alive. Hearts pump blood, for example; roots draw nourishment from the soil.

Patent When you invent something, you can "patent" it. This is a way of legally protecting your idea or invention so that no one else can claim it or earn money from it without your permission.

Radioactive As atomic substances decay, their atoms send out streams of radiation as particles. This is radioactivity, and the substances are radio active.

Reflex An action that "replies" to something else, without needing the will to guide it. If someone pricks you with a pin, your flesh recoils. This is a reflex.

Superstition A belief that cannot be proved. Religious believers say that belief in luck or ghosts is superstition. Non-believers say that religion is superstition.

Symptom In medicine, a change in the normal working of the body which tells a doctor that you are suffering from some disease or sickness. A runny nose and a high temperature, for example, are symptoms which suggest that you may have 'flu.

Trigonometry A branch of mathematics and physics based on the measurement of triangles.

SECTION 3

PEOPLE OF ACTION

Pioneers,
Explorers,
Reformers

INTRODUCTION TO *PEOPLE OF ACTION*

Most people find that the ordinary business of living takes every minute of their time. Work and family fill their days. There is room for a little relaxation – talking to friends, perhaps listening to music or dancing – but otherwise everyday life is their whole existence, and hopes, ambitions and dreams must take second place.

Such people are the majority of the human race – and this book mentions not a single one of them. Everyone included here did something out of the ordinary. They fulfilled their ambitions and lived their dreams. Not all of them were honest or kind, though – in fact some were fanatics, whose actions caused other people hardship or misery.

Many "people of action" were explorers. They felt an urge to visit remote places and see rare sights. They paid for their trips themselves, or raised money by offering to find new empires for princes, new converts for religion, or new trade routes for business companies. They brought back riches, not just gold or slaves (nicknamed "black gold" in the days before the trade was abolished), but stories of wondrous places, or exotic plants and animals, to feast the imagination of people who stayed at home. Some explorers spent their time conquering sea, air or outer space, discovering how to survive the hardships of life in the wild, in deserts or on polar ice. They used their restlessness in the name of scientific discovery, not politics or trade.

The second main group of people in this book are reformers and revolutionaries. Instead of just grumbling about life's unfairness, they did something about it. Some made speeches and wrote articles, pestering till they got their way. Others took up arms, to fight for justice. In the history of the world, there have always been men – and some women – whose "work" was going to war. Most found a just cause, something worth killing, and dying, for. But a few went fighting just for the fun of it, and became pirates and adventurers.

This volume also includes a small number of adventurers of a different kind: people whose battles were fought not with swords and guns, but in business. They made killings not on the battlefield but in the stock market. And many of them poured their profits back into doing good. Like most explorers and warriors in this book, they used their love of risk-taking not just to please themselves, but also to benefit the rest of us.

CINCINNATUS, Lucius Quinctius

Roman soldier 5th century BC

Cincinnatus, a Roman consul (head of state), resigned because he was disgusted by the plotting against him by enemies of the Roman republic. He went back to cultivate his farm, but in 485 BC an enemy army almost reached the walls of Rome, and the Senate begged him to take the post of dictator (supreme commander) for six months. He accepted, gathered soldiers, routed the enemy, and resigned again – all within 16 days!

Naturally, Cincinnatus' enemies feared for their lives after his triumph. But he refused to take advantage of his remarkable success and went back to his farm. Ever since, the term "a Cincinnatus" has been used to describe "a truly honourable person", and the name of Cincinnati in Ohio means the "city where everyone is honourable".

HANNIBAL

Carthaginian general 247-183 BC

Throughout the third century BC, Rome was fighting Carthage for control of trade in the countries round the Mediterranean, and especially for rule in Spain, where rich metal ores were to be mined. The Punic Wars as they were known (after the Roman name for the Carthaginians: *Poeni*, meaning "Phoenicians") lasted on and off for a century, and at first the Romans had the upper hand. But as soon as Hannibal took command of the Carthaginians, things changed. In 218 BC the Romans set out to invade Spain and crush the Carthaginians. But Hannibal force-marched his army, including 37 elephants, through Alpine passes into Italy, and beat the Romans at Cannae in 216 BC.

Following this triumph, Hannibal marched on Rome itself, and the Romans only survived by burning the crops ahead of him and killing their animals so that Hannibal's soldiers had to waste their energy foraging for food, while the Romans massacred them in bloody guerrilla raids. Outmanoeuvred, Hannibal had to flee to southern Italy, where Carthage had loyal allies.

Hannibal lived in exile until 203 BC. Then the Romans invaded north Africa and besieged Carthage itself. Hannibal quickly returned to defend his city, but was defeated in 202 BC at the battle of Zama, with which the war ended. Hannibal then turned his

Hannibal, leading one of his daring campaigns against the Romans, enemies of the Carthaginians.

genius to political reforms, which prompted his rivals to demand his execution, and in 195 BC he fled to Greece. But the Romans continued to demand his surrender, and finally he poisoned himself.

Although Hannibal lost more battles than he won, the Romans always considered him the greatest general they had ever faced. He is chiefly remembered nowadays for crossing the Alps with his elephants. But in his own day he was famous as the man who very nearly captured Rome – an event which would have changed the course of history.

The Gracchus brothers – two of the earliest-known reformers – working out how to distribute public land among the peasants.

GRACCHUS, Tiberius Sempronius

Roman politician c 168-32 BC

and

GRACCHUS, Gaius Sempronius

Roman politician 153-21 BC

In the time of the Gracchus brothers (or "Gracchi"), a few hundred rich families ruled Rome. Their wealth came from enormous estates, many of which were farmed by a cruel system using slave labour. The Gracchi proposed new laws, splitting up the estates and giving each rich person's land to hundreds of poorer citizens. The other aristocrats hated the brothers for this, and before the Gracchi could succeed in their plans, TIBERIUS was murdered. GAIUS continued the struggle to give the peasants their own land for another 12 years, until he, too, was mysteriously killed. The Gracchi have been remembered ever since as two of the world's first true democrats, fighting for the rights of ordinary citizens.

POMPEY THE GREAT (Gnaeus Pompeius Magnus)

Roman general 106-48 BC

The Roman Senate (the group of aristocrats who ruled Rome) feared that Julius **Caesar** was trying to take sole power, and asked Pompey to lead the state's armies against him. Pompey had had a dazzling career as general, but he had also once been Caesar's friend, son-in-law and partner. However, because he wanted sole power for himself, he agreed to do as the Senate asked.

Pompey encouraged disorder and unrest, in the hope that he would be promoted. But when civil war broke out Caesar defeated Pompey at the battle of Pharsalia in 48 BC. Pompey fled to Egypt, where he was promptly stabbed to death.

Pompey had been the senators' last hope of bringing down Caesar; after his death the only way they could find to stop Caesar was to murder him.

Pompey the Great.

POMPEY: Caesar 415

SPARTACUS

Greek freedom fighter 1st century BC

Like many other prisoners of the Roman wars, Spartacus was sold to a trainer of gladiators. He was taken to the games in Rome to fight, but he and 70 others escaped. They were joined by runaway slaves and formed a vast army. For three years they remained free, and took control over most of southern Italy, defeating the Roman forces sent to capture them. Finally, in 71 BC, the Roman general Crassus led one of the largest forces ever seen in Italy until that time, and defeated Spartacus. The slaves were returned to their masters; Spartacus and the other leaders were crucified in a line of crosses stretching all the way from Rome to the heel of Italy.

Spartacus and other gladiators, escaping from the coliseum.

ANTONY, Mark (Marcus Antonius)

Roman general 83-30 BC

Antony is chiefly remembered for his love affair with **Cleopatra**, Queen of Egypt. But he was also a brilliant soldier. He served with Julius **Caesar**, who trusted him like a brother. When Caesar was assassinated in 44 BC, Antony at first transferred his loyalty to Caesar's heir, Octavian, (who later become the Emperor **Augustus**). They joined forces to hunt down Caesar's murderers, and then tried to govern the empire together. But Octavian began to suspect Antony of plotting to seize sole power, and the two men quarrelled. Octavian claimed that Antony and Cleopatra were plotting against Rome, and persuaded the Romans to declare them public enemies. He defeated Antony in a fierce sea-battle near Actium in 31 BC, and Cleopatra's fleet retreated. Antony fled to Alexandria, where he was falsely told that Cleopatra had committed suicide, and he killed himself.

Antony and Cleopatra

ABĪ BAKR

Muslim prince 573-634

Abī Bakr was the prophet **Mohammed**'s father-in-law, and one of the first people to be converted to Islam, one of the world's great religions. When Mohammed died in 632, Abī Bakr became ruler of the city of Medina, the holy city of Islam. He began the idea of the *jihad* or "holy war", conquering in Allah's name and creating an empire of people who followed Islam. With his holy war conquests, Islam spread through much of Arabia, North Africa, and the countries north of the Persian Gulf (modern Iraq, Afghanistan and part of Iran).

ANTONY: Augustus 416 Caesar 415 Cleopatra 416 ABĪ-BAKR: Mohammed 332

ALI

Muslim religious leader c 600-67

Ali was **Mohammed**'s cousin and, like **Abī Bakr**, one of the first people in the world to be converted to Islam. He was the fourth Caliph (successor) to rule the Muslim Empire after Mohammed's death.

Shi'ite Muslims say that Ali was Mohammed's first true follower, and that only his descendants have the right to be *imams*, or religious leaders. But according to Sunni Muslims, the other main Muslim group, all Caliphs were Mohammed's true followers, and any of their descendants can be *imams*.

XUAN CANG (Hsuan-tsang)

Chinese traveller and teacher 602-64

Xuan Cang was a Buddhist and, at the age of 19, he set out for India to visit the places where **Buddha** had lived and taught. His party crossed the Gobi Desert and the Tien Shan Mountains, visited the cities of Tashkent and Samarkand, and finally walked through the Hindu Kush and the Khyber Pass to Peshawar and Kashmir in what is now Pakistan. Over the next few years Xuan Cang visited Buddhist sites and temples throughout the whole of the Indian continent.

Xuan Cang returned to China and translated the holy Buddhist writings into Chinese. He also wrote the story of his adventures, which later became the basis of a legend of how three gods, beset at every step by demons and witches, guided the bearer of the Buddhist holy scriptures from India to China – the story known in the west as *Monkey*.

ASHA BINT ABĪ BAKR (Ayeshah)

Islamic leader c 613-78

Asha's father, **Abī Bakr**, was chief advisor to the prophet **Mohammed**, and Asha became the prophet's third and favourite wife when still a child. She was 18 when Mohammed died and, as he had no son, she played an important part in deciding who should succeed him as Islamic leader. Her involvement was remarkable, since few women in her day had any active part in public life.

When **Ali** became leader and gave an interpretation of Islamic laws quite different from Mohammed's teaching, Asha gathered an army against him. The battle of 656 near Basra is called the Battle of the Camel because Asha was seated on a camel at the scene of the fighting. Her army lost, but she was allowed to go free on condition that she took no further part in politics.

Early explorers travelled mainly on foot, using mules or donkeys to carry their supplies.

Left: The dome of a magnificent mosque in Isfahan, Iran. For Muslims the dome is a symbol of the Universe.

XUAN CANG: Buddha 324 'A'ISHAH BINT ABĪ BAKR: Abī-Bakr 166 Ali 167 Mohammed 332 ALI: Abī-Bakr 166 Mohammed 332

ERIKSSON, Leif

Icelandic sailor eleventh century

Eriksson's father, Erik the Red, was the first Icelandic explorer to reach Greenland and had told his son about a fabulous country to the south and west of Greenland, seen from the sea by one previous explorer (Bjárni Herjólfson) but never visited. Leif was determined to see if the land really existed, and set out to prove it. His men were sure that instead of discovering land they would topple over the lip of the waterfall which, according to mythology, poured from the flat Earth down to Hell. None the less, Leif forced them to row, and eventually they did discover the new country. Leif named it Vinland, after the clusters of wild grapes he found growing. Many historians believe it was Nova Scotia or Massachusetts, and that Leif was the first European to set foot in America, nearly four centuries before **Columbus**. Others dismiss the whole story as fiction, because the main evidence for it comes from three adventure stories written by Leif's son nearly 50 years after the explorer's death.

SALADIN

Muslim general c 1137-93

Saladin's Arabic name was Salah-ed-din Yussuf ibn Ayub; his Christian enemies found this too hard to say, and shortened it to Saladin. He was ruler and general of the Muslim forces in the Middle East. Palestine is the Holy Land of Muslims as well as Christians, and under Saladin they declared a *jihad* (holy war) to drive the Christian crusaders from the kingdom of Jerusalem and the coastal towns they had taken by force.

Saladin defeated the Christian king of Jerusalem in a battle near the Sea of Galilee in 1187, and although the English crusader-king **Richard I** overcame Saladin's army in 1191, he failed to recapture Jerusalem. Eventually Richard and Saladin signed a truce and the English king sailed home, leaving Jerusalem and many coastal towns in Muslim hands. Saladin died in Damascus soon afterwards, but his leadership had united much of the Muslim Middle East and dealt a lasting blow to the crusaders' hopes in the Holy Land.

This cartoon shows what early explorers feared would happen if they sailed too far across the sea.

EIRIKSON: Columbus 172 SALADIN: Richard I 426

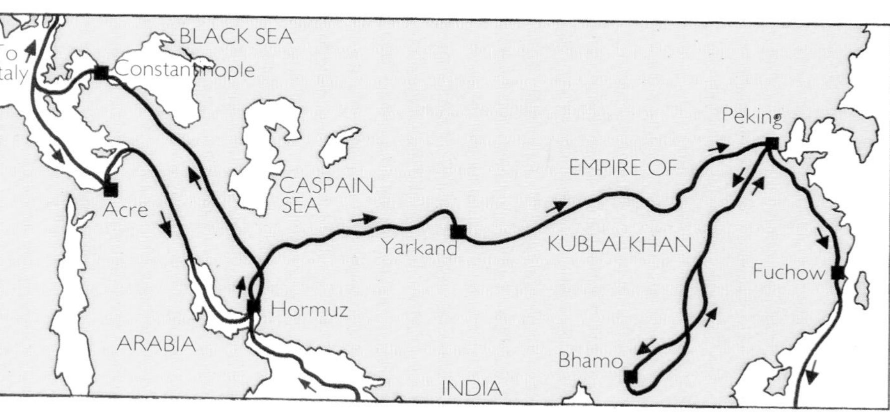

By the end of Marco Polo's travels through the Far East, during the years he spent in the vast empire of Kublai Khan (shown on the map), he had probably travelled further than anyone before him.

Alexander Nevsky.

NEVSKY, Alexander

Russian warrior-prince 1220-63

Nevsky ruled in Novgorod, an independent city-state in the Russian northwest which was repeatedly under attack. He fought invaders from Sweden, on the shores of the Baltic Sea and on the borders between what are now Poland and the western republics of the USSR. He was given the name Nevsky ("Nevaman") to honour his defeat of the Swedish army on the banks of the river Neva. Later, he fought off an attack by the Teutons on the ice of the frozen lake Peipus. (He had his men's horses shod with spikes, to grip the ice.) After his death Nevsky was made a saint of the Russian Orthodox Church, and people in the USSR still regard him as one of the greatest heroes in Russian history.

POLO, Marco

Italian traveller and merchant c 1254-1324

Polo's father and uncle, both merchants, went on a 14-year-long trading trip, travelling overland from Venice to China. **Kublai Khan**, Emperor of China, asked them to bring "one hundred learned men" to teach Western wisdom to the Chinese people. But the only Westerner the Polos could find who was willing to go was Marco. He worked for Kublai Khan for 17 years as a trading and political ambassador, travelling all over China, and even into Tibet and Burma. In 1292 Kublai Khan sent Polo back to Europe, as escort to a princess who was to marry the Persian emperor. The journey lasted three years, and took Polo to Sumatra, India, Persia, and to the cities of Trebizond (Trabzon) and Constantinople (Istanbul) in Turkey.

When Polo reached Venice at last he planned to settle down. But war flared between Venice and a rival city, Genoa, and in the fighting Polo was taken prisoner. During the year he spent in jail, he dictated the story of his adventures to a fellow prisoner, and it became a best-seller. Polo told tales about giants, monsters and magic. But he also told of the peoples and customs of the east, and some of the wonders he described – coal fires, printing-presses and paper money – must have sounded just as fantastic to readers at the time as his tales of giants and monsters.

POLO: Kublai Khan 428

ZHENG-HE (Cheng Ho)

Chinese admiral 1368-1433

In 1368, the year of Zheng-He's birth, the Chinese finally revolted against rule by the Mongols. The new emperor, Ming **Hong Lo**, was anxious to show the rest of the world that China was now peaceful and eager for friendship and trade, not conquest. He sent out expeditions overland to nearby countries, and trading-ships to every coastal town and city they could find.

Zheng-He was the fleet's admiral. His ships were laden with silk and the magnificent china made in the Ming emperor's factories, and his orders were to promise riches to any foreign ruler who agreed to make peace with the Chinese and to trade with them. Zheng's voyages took him first to Thailand and the islands of Indonesia, then west to Sri Lanka and India, and finally to the Persian Gulf, the Red Sea and the coast of East Africa. It would be wrong to think that the Indian Ocean was not "discovered" until Vasco **da Gama** explored it; Zheng-He's trading fleet, journeying from east to west, had already charted the great ocean.

JOAN OF ARC (Jeanne d'Arc)

French soldier and saint 1412-31

Joan of Arc, the daughter of poor French peasants, grew up believing God had chosen her for a special mission. When she was 13, she began hearing voices, which she said were those of the saints Catherine, Margaret and Michael, telling her to free France from the English (who claimed it in the name of their king, Henry VI) and to see that Charles VII, French heir to the throne, was crowned in Rheims Cathedral.

At first Joan was terrified by the voices. But she became more and more convinced by what they said, and in 1429, when the English besieged the town of Orléans, she went to Charles and told him that God had sent her to end the siege. She rode in front of the army, carrying a Christian banner and surrounded by priests singing hymns. Her presence filled the soldiers with great courage, and after only a few hours' fighting they ended the siege. Joan, the "maid of Orléans", and her soldiers then escorted Charles to Rheims, where he was crowned king.

But the English put a price of 10,000 gold pieces on Joan's head. In 1430 she was duly captured,

This portrayal of Joan of Arc at the head of her army is a stained-glass window design, by Lechevallier-Chevignard in 1883.

imprisoned for six months and finally sent to Rouen to be tried by the Inquisition. Her "crime" was not military but religious: by obeying "voices" instead of priests and bishops, she had scorned God's holy church. She endured three weeks of interrogation and torture, but when she was finally declared guilty and condemned to death, terror briefly overcame her and she denied ever having heard voices. A few days later, however, she recovered her courage and cancelled her denial. On 30 May 1431 she was burnt at the stake by the English.

Thirty-four years after Joan's death, another court examined her case and declared her innocent. In 1920, almost 500 years later, she was made a Roman Catholic saint.

The explorers John and Sebastian Cabot. A famous map made by Sebastian Cabot of his and his father's discoveries is kept in Paris.

CABOT, John (Giovanni Caboto)

Italian sailor 1425- c 1500

and

CABOT, Sebastian

Italian sailor 1474-1557

John Cabot, a sailor from Genoa, was probably the first European to reach the mainland of North America. He would work for anyone who provided him with ships and, in 1497, King Henry VII of England sent him "to sail to all parts, countries, and seas of the East, of the West, and of the North" and to find lands no Christian had ever visited before. After several months' sailing west Cabot reached land; probably what is now Cape Breton Island, off the coast of Nova Scotia in Canada. He went on a second westward expedition in 1497, and never returned.

Sebastian Cabot was one of John's sons. He spent many years as a cartographer, making maps, and exploring the coasts of the two Americas for the kings of England and Spain. He followed the routes of previous sailors, checking and revising ancient maps and charts. During one expedition to South America he explored the estuary of the river Plate, looking for the legendary city El Dorado, whose streets, it was said, were paved with gold. In 1544 he published a fanciful account of his and his father's voyages, full of stories of sea-monsters, giants and events as fabulous as those in the *Arabian Nights*. Back in England, four years later (at the age of 74!), he joined his brothers in founding the Muscovy Company, created especially to find a northeast passage to India.

Bartolomeu Dias.

DIAS, Bartolomeu

Portuguese sailor c 1450-1500

From the beginning of the fifteenth century, Portuguese sailors had been exploring and mapping the coasts of Africa. (All the main trading countries of Europe were hoping to find a sea-route to India which could be used for the profitable spice trade). In 1488 Dias' ships were the first Portuguese fleet to round the Cape of Good Hope. Soon afterwards his crew mutinied and forced him to turn home, but he had proved that there *was* a sea-route east round Africa – Westerners had previously wondered if land stretched from the Mediterranean all the way south to Antarctica – and that it was possible to sail to India.

Dias never commanded another fleet, but he accompanied Vasco **Da Gama** for part of an expedition, and later **Cabral**. But on this second voyage his ship sank in a storm and he was drowned.

COLUMBUS, Christopher

Italian sailor 1451-1506

Columbus was christened Cristoforo Colombo; Columbus is the Latin form of his name. He ran away to sea when he was 14, and became a pirate. A few years later he was shipwrecked off the coast of Portugal and settled there, changing his name to Cristobal Colón.

Unlike many people of his time, Columbus believed that the world was a sphere, not flat, and that there was a way to reach the rich trading countries of the East by sailing west across the Atlantic. He spent many years trying to persuade various European kings and queens to pay for an expedition that would prove him right. In the end, his efforts were rewarded: King **Ferdinand** and Queen **Isabella** of Spain agreed to finance a small expedition.

None of Columbus' sailors shared his belief that the world was round. They thought that if they sailed too

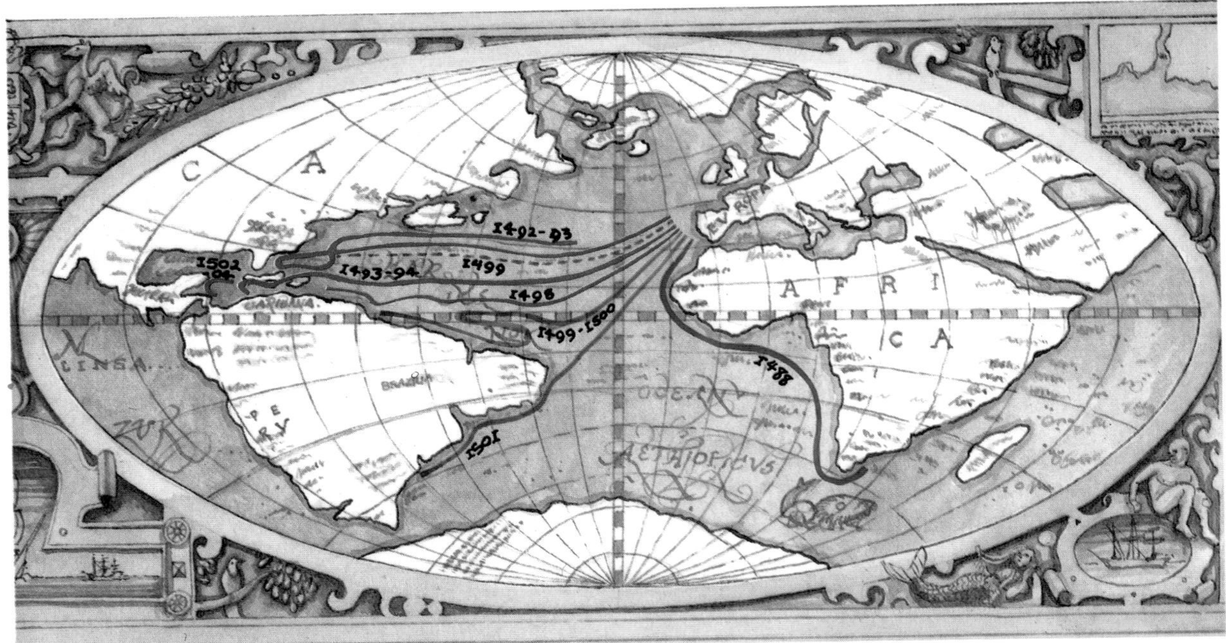

The routes of the three explorers are shown on an early map of the known world in the late fifteenth century. Dias' route is shown in green, Columbus' three voyages are in red and Vespucci's in blue.

DIAS: Cabral 174 Da Gama 174 COLUMBUS: Ferdinand and Isabella 433

Columbus first glimpses the "New World".

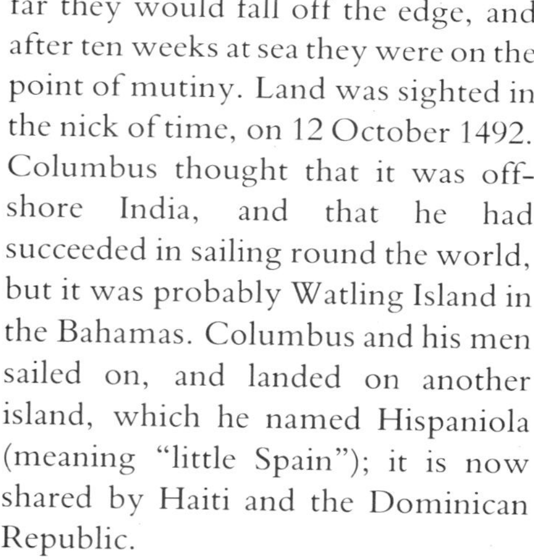

far they would fall off the edge, and after ten weeks at sea they were on the point of mutiny. Land was sighted in the nick of time, on 12 October 1492. Columbus thought that it was off-shore India, and that he had succeeded in sailing round the world, but it was probably Watling Island in the Bahamas. Columbus and his men sailed on, and landed on another island, which he named Hispaniola (meaning "little Spain"); it is now shared by Haiti and the Dominican Republic.

Although Columbus' expedition had failed to find the western sea-route to India as he had promised, the king and queen were encouraged by his discoveries in the Caribbean, and in 1493 sent him to explore further. He visited the islands now called Guadeloupe, Jamaica and Trinidad, but was again threatened with mutiny by his crew, and forced to return to Spain. On his third voyage, in 1498, he landed on the South American mainland. But he never found the wealth he had promised, and Ferdinand and Isabella refused to go on financing his travels. It was not until several years after his death, when full exploration of the New World began, that people realized that Columbus had been the first European on a new continent.

VESPUCCI, Amerigo

Italian explorer 1451-1512

Vespucci had supplied provisions to Christopher Columbus' expeditions, and heard the tales of his explorations. In 1499 Vespucci decided to follow in the wake of Columbus, and joined an expedition to the Caribbean. When he arrived home in Italy he published a letter, dating it two years earlier, claiming he had visited a huge continent, long before Columbus. In two further trips he explored the coasts of Guiana and Brazil. Both continents have been called America (after his first name) ever since.

Vespucci claimed to have made four voyages to the New World. In fact, he probably only sailed on one or two expeditions, and his claim to have discovered the mainland of South America was also false.

VESPUCCI: Columbus 172

The monk Savonarola was against all luxuries, including jewellery and fine clothes. His followers in Florence built huge bonfires, where people publicly burnt their finery.

SAVONAROLA, Girolamo

Italian preacher 1452-98

Savonarola lived in Florence, Italy, during the rule of the **Medicis**. He preached fierce sermons against such great families, saying that they were so concerned with wealth and power that they had forgotten God. He spoke out against all forms of luxury and vanity, which made him very popular with ordinary people.

When Lorenzo de' Medici died in 1492, the Pope made Savonarola leader of Florence. But the preacher's ideas proved too extreme once he was in power. He wanted Florence to be a Christian city, ruled by God's laws and free from such vices as music, literature, painting, rich food and wine. The Pope, fearing that Savonarola had become too powerful, declared him an enemy of the church, and Savonarola's enemies captured and executed him. Florence was restored to its former magnificence as if he had never existed.

CABRAL, Pedro Alvares

Portuguese sailor c 1460-1520

In 1500 the Portuguese government sent Cabral with 13 ships to follow **Da Gama**'s newly established sea-route to India. However, he may have had secret instructions to sail west, not east, and to investigate South America instead. Whether obeying orders or not, he landed in Brazil, and claimed the whole vast country as a Portuguese colony. He took on supplies, and sailed back across the Atlantic, round the coast of Africa, and picked up Da Gama's route east. He landed on Mozambique before sailing on to Calicut in India, where he left a small group of men to set up a spice trade between Portugal and India. In 1501 he finally sailed home, laden with treasure, and retired from the sea.

DA GAMA, Vasco

Portuguese sailor c 1460-1524

Once **Dias** had proved that there was a sea-route round Africa, the Portuguese were determined to sail round the Cape of Good Hope and on to India, where they wanted to take control of the profitable spice trade. In 1497 Da Gama was sent with three ships to explore the route. But instead of hugging the African coastline, he sailed west out into the Atlantic, landing on the tiny island of St Helena, before returning to the route round the southern tip of Africa. He sailed north up the coast to Malindi in Kenya, where he hired a famous Arab navigator, Ahmad ibn Majid, to

SAVONAROLA: Medici family 431 DA GAMA: Dias 172

For many years, people thought that Da Gama ignored his orders by sailing to the island of St Helena in the Atlantic. In fact, he may have shown good sense, because he could use the strong westerly winds to help his fleet sail safely around the Cape of Good Hope.

guide his fleet across the Indian Ocean.

The Portuguese ships landed at Calicut in India in May 1498. But the Indian merchants were reluctant to offend their usual Muslim customers by offering Da Gama spices. He sailed home to Portugal, almost empty-handed, but in 1502 he set out again. En route he founded a new Portuguese colony, Mozambique and on arrival in Calicut, with a bigger, better-armed fleet, he terrorized the Indians into making a trade-agreement. When he sailed home, this time in triumph, he retired from the sea.

Twenty years later, however, Da Gama made one further trip to India, this time as Portuguese viceroy ("king's representative"), to settle a trading dispute in Calicut. It was his last voyage; he died soon afterwards, and his body was taken home in state for burial.

Above right: Many European explorers were lured by stories of fabulous wealth in South America. The Incas used gold in great quantities for jewellery, ceremonial masks and sacred images of their gods. Much of it was plundered by the invaders.

PIZARRO, Francisco

Spanish conqueror c 1470-1541

Pizarro was a Spanish army officer based in Panama. He joined **Balboa**'s expedition across the Isthmus, and was one of the first Europeans to see the Pacific. Later, the Spanish government sent him to South America to investigate stories of a fabulously wealthy country called *El Dorado*, "the golden". This was the empire of the Incas (part of what is now Peru), ruled by the god-king **Atahuallpa**. Pizarro and his men captured and executed Atahuallpa, the Incas surrendered and Peru became ruled by Spain. For a time Pizarro was governor, but he quarrelled with a fellow officer, over which of them owned the town of Cuzco and therefore had a right to plunder its treasures. Pizarro had the man executed, but his own soldiers mutinied and he was hacked to death.

BALBOA, Vasco Nuñez de

Spanish explorer 1475-1519

Balboa was the first European ever to see the Pacific Ocean. In 1513, he led an expedition from east to west across Darien, part of the Isthmus of Panama (the narrow stretch of land joining North and South America), and claimed it as a new Spanish colony. He found huge quantities of gold, which he took back to Spain, and was given a hero's welcome.

However, later it emerged that he had in fact been a stowaway on the expedition, and had taken over command by force. He was tried for this crime, found guilty, and executed.

PIZARRO: Dias 172 Balboa 175 Atahuallpa 436

BERLICHINGEN, Götz von

German soldier and adventurer 1480-1562

Götz von Berlichingen, a German nobleman, travelled all over Europe, fighting for anyone whose cause appealed to him. In 1505 he lost his right hand in a battle, and had it replaced with a metal one, which earned him the nickname "Ironhand". His daring escapes, dazzling swordsmanship and chivalry, and the cunning with which he outwitted his enemies became legendary. In 1525, when German farm-workers revolted against savage taxes, "Ironhand" fought on their side against his fellow aristocrats. He was captured, and sentenced to life imprisonment. But he was freed in 1540, and two years later he was fighting again, this time in Hungary against the Turks. By then, he was 60 years old and had not ridden a horse or held a sword for over 15 years. He was in his 70s before he retired to write his memoirs.

MAGELLAN, Ferdinand (Fernãode Magalhães)

Portuguese explorer c 1480-1521

Magellan sailed with the Portuguese navy to Morocco, India and the Far East. But he was wrongly accused of stealing, and fled to Spain where he offered his services to the king, **Charles V**. At that time the Portuguese controlled the only sea-route, via the Cape of Good Hope, to the East Indies and the lucrative spice trade. King Charles sent Magellan to find an alternative, western, route.

Magellan sailed west with five ships across the Atlantic, and rounded the tip of South America by the dangerous seaway which is now called the Straits of Magellan. He reached a second vast ocean, which he named the Pacific because it seemed so calm after the stormy Atlantic. His fleet successfully crossed the Pacific and landed in the Philippines to buy spices, but Magellan was killed in a dispute with the islanders. None the

There are many seamen's tales about the perils of the narrow straits between the tip of the South American mainland and the island of Tierra del Fuego. The straits came to be known as Magellan's Straits after his ship endured storms and treacherous seas to reach the Pacific.

MAGELLAN: Charles V 436

less, his fleet continued eastwards, round the Cape of Good Hope into the Atlantic, and home to Spain – the first European expedition to sail all round the world.

CORTÉS, Hernán (Hernando Cortez)

Spanish soldier 1485-1547

When Cortés was 19 he sailed to the New World, accompanying Velazquez, the Spanish governor of San Domingo (Dominican Republic) in his expedition to Cuba. The Spanish were anxious to conquer the New World for two reasons: to plunder its wealth and to spread the Christian faith. Velazquez had heard of the riches of mainland America, especially the Aztec kingdom of Yucatán, where gold was said to be as common as wood or stone. In 1518 he suggested to Cortés that he should command an expedition to Mexico and, before permission was granted from Spain, Cortés took 550 Spaniards and a dozen horses, and sailed for the mainland.

The Aztec people believed that one day their god Quetzalcoatl would come down to Earth to rule them. When they heard accounts of Cortés on horseback – the first white man and first horse ever seen in mainland America – they thought that he must be their god. **Montezuma**, the Aztec emperor, sent him gifts of gold and Cortés pressed on, eager to conquer the land where such riches could be found. He came at last to Tenochtitlán, capital of the Aztec Empire, where he was welcomed as a god. Cortés' response was to make Montezuma his prisoner and to demand ever-larger offerings of gold from the people. But Mexican hatred for the Spanish invaders was growing and Velazquez sent ships and soldiers to stop Cortés. The conqueror, though, defeated the forces, and persuaded them to mutiny against Velazquez and join him instead. But, during his absence from Tenochtitlán, the Aztecs had besieged Cortés' followers in the city. Furious, Cortés led a Spanish army to recapture Tenochtitlán. After many months of fighting, during which Montezuma was killed, the Aztecs finally surrendered. Cortés declared their empire Spanish, and the Spanish king made Cortés its governor. But the king had never forgiven Cortés for exploring without permission in the first place. He sent officers from Spain, with secret orders to take over Cortés' power. In 1540 Cortés returned to Spain, a country he had hardly seen in 35 years. He died in poverty in 1547. Almost 20 years later his body was dug up and reburied in his beloved Mexico.

An Aztec drawing of Cortés (on horseback) conquering the people of Mexico.

A highly decorated Aztec sacrificial knife.

CORTÉS: Montezuma 434

ORELLANA, Francisco de

Spanish explorer c 1511-49

Orellana was a lieutenant serving with Gonzalo Pizarro (half-brother of Francisco **Pizarro**). He joined the Spanish expeditions to the centre of South America, but deserted his comrades. He was the first European to follow the entire course of the Amazon, the largest river in the world, from its source in the Andes of Peru to the Atlantic, off the coast of North Brazil. He was made governor of the region, but died before he could take up the post.

HIDEYOSHI, Toyotomi

Japanese military leader 1536-98

Hideyoshi came from a humble family, but he rose quickly to a high position in the army of the *daimyo* ("great lord") Nobunaga. He assisted Nobunaga in his power struggles against other *daimyo*, and when Nobunaga was murdered he took over the leadership of his campaign. One by one, Hideyoshi conquered the *daimyo* of each of the Japanese islands except Hokkaido, which was seen as an uncivilized place, inhabited by barbarians and not worth conquering.

Although Hideyoshi always claimed to be a loyal subject of the emperor, in fact he held all the real power, and he used it to pass laws unifying Japan and to make sure the country remained Japanese by driving out foreigners. His treatment of Christian missionaries and traders was particularly ferocious. He also re-introduced the old, rigid class system which would prevent anyone of poor birth (like himself!) ever rising to challenge those in power. In 1592, having decided to increase Japan's greatness by conquering an empire, he sent a fleet to invade Korea. The Chinese defended Korea, and fighting went on for five years; a truce was only declared after Hideyoshi's death.

Although Hideyoshi was a harsh and arrogant ruler, he was a cultured man, and did much to encourage painters, musicians and, above all, the actors and singers of Noh drama (Japanese plays, full of song and dance, based on stories from myth and legend), to an extent which has never been repeated.

Hideyoshi, shown as an old man.

ORELLANA: Pizarro 175

DRAKE, Francis

English sailor 1540-96

When Drake was a boy he ran away to sea. He worked in the slave trade, shipping captured Africans across the Atlantic to the West Indies to work in the sugar plantations, carrying sugar back to Britain, and then going to Africa to buy more slaves. In his 30s he began attacking Spanish ships in the Gulf of Mexico for their rich cargoes, and making raids on Spanish towns. This amounted to piracy – a crime for which he would have been hanged, had the Spanish been able to catch him. In 1577 he left Plymouth on an expedition round the southernmost tip of South America and into the Pacific. His ship (later called the *Golden Hind*) travelled up the west coast of the American continent at least as far as Oregon (some say he got to Vancouver Island) before he turned southeast, sailed across the Pacific, and round the Cape of Good Hope at the southernmost tip of Africa into the Atlantic. He returned home to England – the first Englishman to sail all round the world – and Queen **Elizabeth I** knighted him for his achievement.

In the next few years the quarrel between the English queen and Philip, King of Spain, grew more fierce, without ever spilling into war. Drake, with his continued attacks against Spanish ships, was partly to blame. Elizabeth encouraged him to make ever more daring raids against Spanish towns in the New World, and finally against the port of Cadiz in Spain itself, where Drake sank 33 ships and escaped without losing a single man. Drake called this adventure "singeing the king of Spain's beard", and it led to war between England and Spain. The Spanish Armada ("armed fleet") sailed to attack England in 1588. Legend says that when the Spaniards' approach was announced, Drake was playing bowls on Plymouth Hoe. He refused to break off the game, saying "There's plenty of time to finish, and thrash the Spaniards too." The battle raged fiercely, made worse by dreadful weather, and eventually storms helped drive the Spanish ships into the North Sea, where many of them were wrecked.

After the successful defeat of the Armada, Drake, by then nearly 50, retired from the sea and went into politics. But his love of adventure never left him. In 1595 he set out again for the New World on a new trading (or raiding) expedition, but he became ill and died.

After fierce fighting, the weather helped the English to defeat the Spanish Armada. Queen Elizabeth gave silver medals bearing her portrait to the English naval officers who had fought in the sea battle.

A portrait of Francis Drake, engraved by Goldar Joulp in 1786.

DRAKE: Elizabeth I 436

RALEIGH, Walter

English adventurer 1552-1618

In his 20s Raleigh was a pirate, robbing Spanish settlers in the New World. In 1580 he helped to quell a rebellion in Ireland, and Queen **Elizabeth I** rewarded him with a knighthood and huge Irish estates. She also fell in love with him, and favoured him above all her other courtiers. He used his new riches to pay for expeditions to the New World where he claimed a district as a new English colony. He called it Virginia after Elizabeth, the "virgin queen". His men brought back plants so far unknown in Europe, including potatoes and tobacco, and Raleigh successfully grew them on his Irish estates, before showing them to the royal court.

In 1587 Elizabeth found a new favourite, the handsome young Earl of Essex. She also discovered that Raleigh was having an affair with one of her maids, Elizabeth Throgmorton, and banished him from court. He went back to sea, and helped **Drake** to plan and carry out raids on Spanish towns in the New World, and later on Cadiz in Spain itself. These triumphs brought Raleigh back into favour, and in 1600 he was made governor of the Channel island of Jersey. But Elizabeth died in 1603, and the new ruler, King James I, accused Raleigh of plotting against him and imprisoned him for 14 years in the Tower of London. Raleigh passed the time by doing scientific experiments and writing accounts of his voyages, poems and an unfinished history of the world.

In 1616 Raleigh was released to lead a gold-hunting expedition to South America, but most of his crew died from disease and Raleigh returned alone. When the Spanish (who were allies of King James, just as they had been enemies of Queen Elizabeth) heard of his latest adventure, they accused Raleigh of piracy, and when he returned to England in 1618 James had him beheaded.

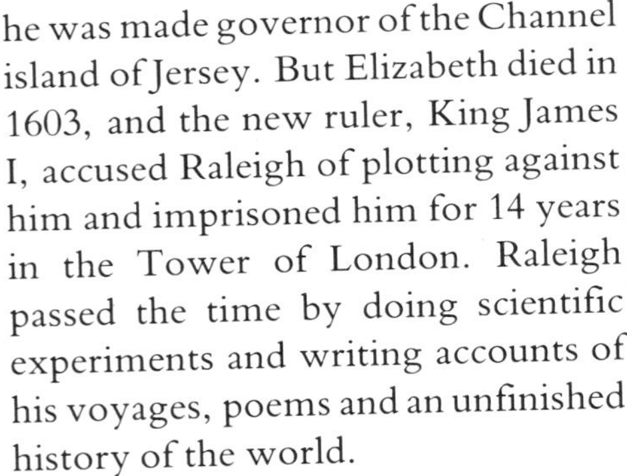

AMINA

Nigerian soldier 1560-1610

As soon as Amina was big enough to ride a horse and throw a spear, she became a warrior. At the age of 15 she was made second-in-command to the chief Karama, and when he died two years later she inherited his position. She spent the next 30 years conquering and plundering all the neighbouring tribes. Wherever her soldiers camped for more than a few days, she made them build a stone fortress. Whenever she conquered a town she forced its chief to make love to her, and then beheaded him. Her people made up songs and myths about her, as if she were a god. So much was she feared that the mention of her name was enough to strike panic into whole tribes and send them scurrying to the hills.

RALEIGH: Drake 179 Elizabeth I 436

Champlain became a friend of the Amerindians in Canada. He learned their way of life, and was able to do what he loved best: explore the vast wilderness of the interior of Canada.

CHAMPLAIN, Samuel de

French explorer c 1567-1635

Champlain began exploring the coasts and interior of Canada in 1603. He was content with a simple life, and learned the ways and languages of the Amerindians. He spent most of his time in the western prairies and the northern hills and plains (of what is now French Canada), where in 1608 he founded Québec – the first European settlement north of Florida. He explored the vast St Lawrence estuary and the Great Lakes, and set up trading posts to buy furs and dried fish from the local people. He discovered an enormous lake, as big as an inland sea. It lies across the boundary between Canada and the states of Vermont and New York State in the USA, and is called Lake Champlain after him.

In 1613 the French king made Champlain governor of New France (as Canada was then called), a post he held for 16 years, but he continued to explore and travel rough at an age when most men of the time would have been glad to retire from active life. In 1629, during fighting between the English and the French, he was taken prisoner and sent to England. But he returned to Canada in 1633 (aged 66), and died there two years later, one of the most honoured men in the country's history.

HUDSON, Henry

English explorer died 1611

Hudson, like many explorers, tried to find the northwest passage, a sea-route through the Arctic which would allow trading-ships to sail between the Atlantic and Pacific oceans. He failed in this, but explored and charted large areas of unknown territory in the frozen wastes off the coasts of northern Norway, Greenland and North America. Hudson Bay, the Hudson Strait and the Hudson River are all named after him – even though he was not the first European to explore them.

The Last Voyage of Henry Hudson, painted by Charles John Collier. When Hudson decided to spend a winter in Hudson Bay his crew mutinied and cast him adrift. The crew returned to England, but Hudson was never seen again.

WALLENSTEIN, Duke of

Bohemian soldier 1583-1634

Albrecht Wenzel Eusebius von Wallenstein was a nobleman from Bohemia (modern Czechoslovakia). From boyhood, he had a thirst for power, and cared little how he won it. He was born a Protestant, but when his father died, his uncle brought him up as a Catholic. This was at the time of the Thirty Years War (1618-48), which began as a tempestuous struggle between Catholics and Protestants in Europe. Wallenstein offered to serve the Holy Roman Emperor Ferdinand II (leader of the Catholics) by recruiting, training and leading an army. In return he was given vast estates which had been seized during the war and many titles of honour (including his dukedom). Historians argue over whether Wallenstein really was a good general, or just lucky. But whatever the reason, he won almost every battle he fought, until he was defeated in the Battle of Lützen in 1632, although not before the Protestant commander (and King of Sweden) **Gustavus Adolphus** was killed. But Wallenstein began to see that there would be more advantages for him if the Protestants and Catholics were not at war. He plotted against Ferdinand, but was killed by one of his own followers.

An engraving of Albrecht, Duke of Wallenstein.

TASMAN, Abel Janszoon

Dutch sailor 1603- c 59

Tasman worked for the Dutch East India Company, traders whose headquarters were in Batavia (now Jakarta, Indonesia). The governor-general of Batavia, Antony Van Diemen, hired Tasman to explore the Pacific ocean, looking for the "Great South Land", which people believed to be there but which no European had ever seen. (Although Dutch navigators had visited Australia, they did not know if it was the huge continent thought to balance Europe.) In 1642 Tasman landed on a huge island, and called it Van Dieman's Land after his employer; it was later renamed Tasmania after him. He also saw (but did not explore) New Zealand. He was the first European to land on the islands of Fiji and Tonga, and to explore Australia's northern and western coasts.

WALLENSTEIN: Gustavus Adolphus 441

MORGAN, (Captain) Henry

Welsh pirate c 1635-88

As a boy, Morgan was kidnapped by pirates, and shipped to Barbados. He too became a pirate, as soon as he was old enough, and robbed Spanish treasure-ships in the Caribbean sea and along the north western shores of South and Central America. In 1681 he led a pirate army across the Isthmus of Panama and attacked the rich Spanish town of Panama. In the battle the Spaniards set bulls loose to terrify Morgan, but he stampeded them and turned them back on the Spaniards. He then looted the town: his own personal share was 250,000 gold pieces.

Morgan was triumphant and unstoppable, in spite of complaints from Spain to the English king, Charles II. The king secretly was in favour of Morgan, just as **Elizabeth I** had approved of **Drake** and **Raleigh**, and when Morgan finally retired from piracy Charles gave him a knighthood and made him lieutenant-governor of Jamaica.

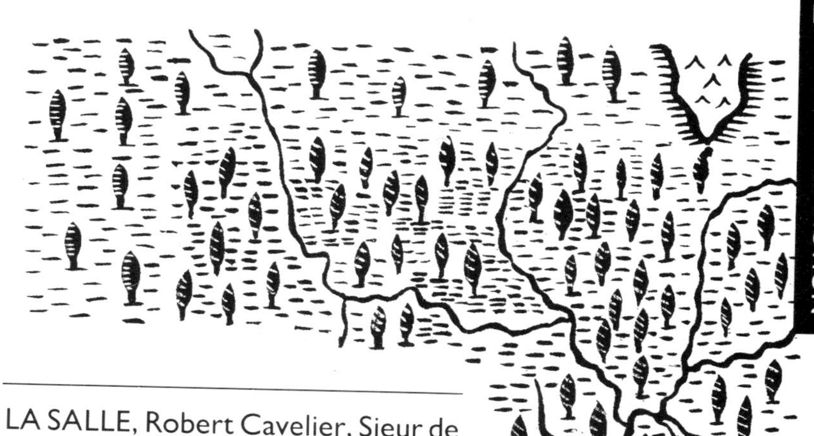

LA SALLE, Robert Cavelier, Sieur de

French explorer 1643-87

La Salle grew up in France, but settled in New France (as Canada was called at the time) when he was 23. He was interested in exploring the entire continent southwards, particularly to find out if the Ohio River flowed all the way to the Gulf of Mexico. He discovered that huge though the Ohio was, it was only a tributary of an even larger river, the Mississippi. He travelled down the Mississippi to the sea, a journey through unknown territory which lasted a dozen years. In 1682 La Salle claimed for France all the land between the Rocky Mountains and the Mississippi, and called it Louisiana after King Louis. (Over a century later, after the American War of Independence, **Jefferson** bought it back from France for 15 million dollars. The "Louisiana Purchase" more than doubled the size of what was to become the United States.)

In 1684 La Salle led an expedition to explore the Mississippi, this time from the sea towards its source. But he started in the wrong place, and spent two years hopelessly trying to find his way up the main channel. His men finally grew so tired of wandering in semi-wilderness that they mutinied and murdered him.

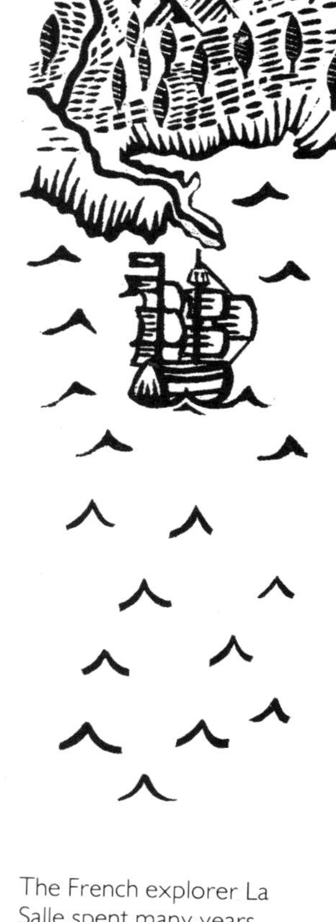

The French explorer La Salle spent many years exploring the territory of the Mississippi and its tributaries, but he never founded the French settlement in Louisiana, as he intended.

MORGAN: Drake 179 Raleigh 180 Elizabeth I 436 LA SALLE: Jefferson 448

Right: An illustration by Howard Pyle of the pirate Captain Kidd.

PENN, William

English settler 1644-1718

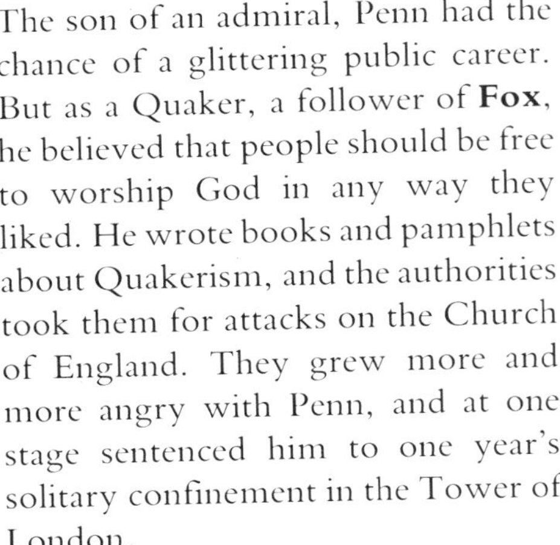

The son of an admiral, Penn had the chance of a glittering public career. But as a Quaker, a follower of **Fox**, he believed that people should be free to worship God in any way they liked. He wrote books and pamphlets about Quakerism, and the authorities took them for attacks on the Church of England. They grew more and more angry with Penn, and at one stage sentenced him to one year's solitary confinement in the Tower of London.

Penn was freed with the help of a friend of his father's – the Duke of York (later King James II). But Penn was still unpopular in England for his beliefs, and in 1681 he went to America to start a Quaker community, with anyone who chose to go with him. Penn and his followers were given a large stretch of land, west of the river Delaware. Here Penn amazed the native Americans by treating them as friends instead of shooting them. Gradually the settlement grew, as Quakers and others moved from Europe to live there. Soon it was a thriving town. Penn called it Philadelphia ("brotherly love"), and after his death the area round it was named Pennsylvania after him.

William Penn, holding the democratic constitution (set of laws and rules) in which he insisted on tolerance of all religions that did not conflict with Christian beliefs.

KIDD, (Captain) William

Scottish pirate c 1645-1701

Kidd was a minister's son who ran away to sea and rose through the ranks from cabin-boy to captain. He became well known for his courage, and in 1696 a group of London merchants, angry that pirates in the Caribbean were hijacking their ships and robbing them, gave Kidd a 30-gun warship and sent him to the Caribbean to clear the pirates out. Kidd, however, decided that since his ship out-gunned every other vessel in the area, he would make a better living as a pirate himself. He started a reign of terror: looting, kidnapping and murdering. Then, after two years' mayhem, he went ashore at the port of Boston in America, where the authorities arrested him and sent him to Britain. He was tried as a criminal, and tortured, as the merchants attempted to learn where his loot (their property) was hidden, but he refused to speak. He was hanged with his secret in 1701, and to this day the bulk of his hoard may still lie buried somewhere in North America.

PENN: Fox 342

BERING (BEHRING), Vitas Jonassen

Danish sailor and explorer 1681-1741

Bering was one of the first foreigners to join **Peter the Great**'s new Russian navy. He rose to the rank of captain and fought in Peter's war with Sweden for control of the Baltic, which won him medals for bravery. In 1728 Peter asked him to lead an expedition to chart the seas north and east of Siberia. Bering spent the rest of his life travelling these waters, in particular those now named after him, the Bering Sea and Bering Strait, between the USSR and North America.

Bering's last voyage was in 1741. He was shipwrecked on a deserted island, caught scurvy and died. His companions buried him on the island, which was later named Bering Island after him.

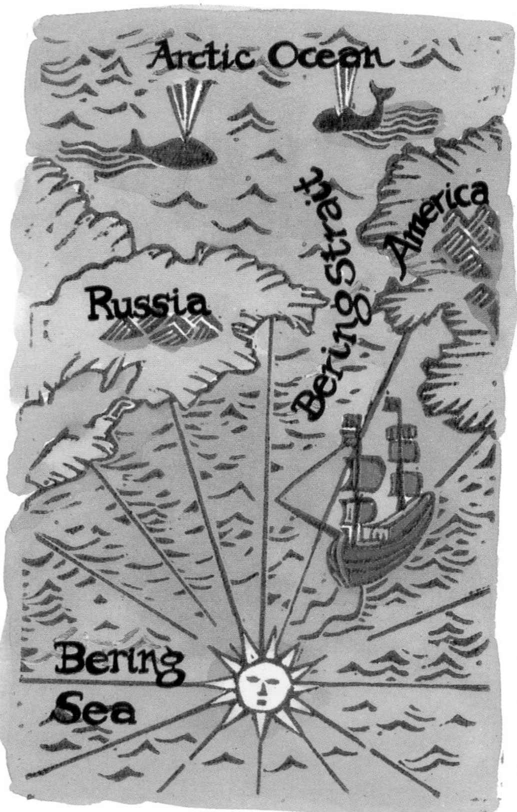

BERING: Peter the Great 444

CASANOVA, Giovanni Jacopo

Italian adventurer and writer 1725-98

When Casanova was a teenager he decided that life was there to be enjoyed, and that he would spend his time doing exactly that. Over the next 45 years he worked, at one time or another, as professional gambler, violinist, spy, journalist, even adviser to the Doge (prince) of Venice, suggesting a lottery as a painless way to raise money. He also dabbled in alchemy (trying to turn ordinary metals into gold), and in black magic. He took Holy Orders (the first step to becoming a priest), and then joined the Freemasons, something outlawed at that time by the church authorities. He was thrown into jail in Venice, and spent five years in a dungeon while the Inquisition tried to make him change his ways.

When Casanova was 60 he settled down as secretary and librarian to Count Waldstein in Bohemia (modern Czechoslovakia), and began writing his memoirs. They ran to 12 volumes, and include much boasting about how, from the age of 13, Casanova had amorous adventures with women. He claimed that no female could resist him, and that he took as his lover every woman he desired, from countesses to chamber-maids, from highwaywomen to nuns. Nowadays "Casanova" is the name given to a seducer whose charms seem irresistible to women.

Casanova's boasting about his seductions of women may well have been exaggerated, but his name lives on because of his claims.

John Howard, who spent many years campaigning for better treatment of prisoners.

HOWARD, John

English prison reformer 1726-90

In Howard's time most people thought that prisoners were subhuman. They were locked away to protect society, and no one cared if they lived or died. Howard had had first-hand experience of the dreadful conditions of hunger, overcrowding, filth and disease in prisons because, in 1756, during a sea voyage to Lisbon, he was captured by a French crew and thrown into jail. Later, he toured jails all over Britain, Europe and the USA, campaigning for better conditions. (He had to travel on horseback as the smell from the prisoners on his clothes made him an unpopular passenger on the stage-coach.) Howard said that if prisoners were treated like human beings, given proper food, light, work and religious instruction, they might end their evil ways and become useful members of society again. He was arguing for what is now known as rehabilitation of offenders – a new idea at the time. As a result of his efforts, two acts of Parliament were passed in 1774 to improve prison conditions.

Ironically, Howard caught a fever in a Russian prison camp he was visiting, and died.

COOK, James

English sailor 1728-79

Cook enlisted as a merchant seaman when he was 16, and 11 years later he volunteered to join the Royal Navy. In those days, when most seamen were victims of the press gang, snatched in the streets of coastal towns and made to go to sea, experienced volunteers were rare and earned quick promotion. Cook spent much time charting the east Canadian coast and the St Lawrence river, work of great value to both trading vessels and warships. In 1768 the navy sent him with his ship *The Endeavour* to the southern hemisphere to chart the path of the planet Venus across the sky and to find out as much as possible about a huge continent, the "Great South Land" which people believed must lie in the southern seas, but which only **Tasman** had seen, over 120 years before. Cook and his crew visited and mapped most of the coasts and seachannels of New Zealand and eastern Australia.

In 1772 he was sent on a second journey, this time to find out the size of Antarctica by sailing all round it, and to investigate the "Great South Land" further. During the winter, when the Antarctic Ocean was too ice-locked for exploration, Cook turned north into the Pacific, where he charted Tahiti, the New Hebrides, and discovered New Caledonia. In 1776 he made his last voyage, this time to the northern Pacific to look for the northwest passage (the sea-route around the coast of North America everyone hoped to find). Cook landed on the island of Hawaii and was killed when recovering a stolen boat from the natives.

Cook's expeditions were peaceful and scientific, unlike those of pirates, and he claimed more territory for Britain than almost any other explorer: Canada, New Zealand and Australia were a main part of the British Empire for 200 years. One reason for his success was that he kept

COOK: Tasman 182

his crew loyal and healthy. He had discovered that without regular vitamin C in the diet, people contract the deadly disease, scurvy. Cook fed his crew oranges, lemons and limes, and tried to find fresh meat whenever possible. Thanks to his discovery, scurvy was unknown on any of his expeditions.

BRUCE, James

Scottish explorer 1730-94

As a young man, Bruce tried several jobs: he was (among other things) a lawyer, a wine-merchant and a diplomat. He married a beautiful girl, whom he adored. But she died soon after their marriage and, heart-broken, he decided to travel. He sailed to Egypt, and in 1768 travelled up the river Nile looking for its source. Two years later, in Abyssinia (Ethiopia), he thought he had found it, but it was just one of the Nile's several sources – the so-called Blue Nile. After this discovery, he became known as the Abyssinian.

When he returned home, he wrote a book about his adventures. It was a best-seller, because people thought some of his stories (for example about Masai tribespeople slicing up animals and eating them raw) were so ridiculous that Bruce had invented them. Later, other travellers confirmed that his accounts were true.

James Cook's ship *The Endeavour*, beached on the coast of south-east Australia in 1770. Cook's explorations greatly increased European knowledge of the southern hemisphere.

A painting by Robert Lindneux of Daniel Boone, pioneer trapper and hunter.

BOONE, Daniel

American frontiersman 1735-1820

In Boone's boyhood, white people knew little about the interior of America. Most settlements were made on the eastern coast, and only a few intrepid adventurers crossed mountain ranges (such as the Appalachians). These people were called "frontiersmen", and Boone was one of the first and most colourful of all. From 1769 he lived in the forested interior, and learned hunting, trapping, tracking and other survival skills. He was twice captured by Amerindians, and even adopted by a Shawnee chief.

In 1784 Boone published an account of his adventures. It made him a national hero, inspiring a legend of the hard-living, hard-fighting frontiersman (similar to the cowboy hero a century later). Boone continued exploring, usually alone, until he was over 70.

A drawing of Thomas Paine, made in 1801.

REVERE, Paul

American patriot 1735-1818

Revere learned the trade of goldsmith from his father, and produced many famous works. He became one of the heroes of the American War of Independence. In 1773 he was one of the Boston citizens who dumped tea into the city's harbour, in protest against the British tax on imported tea. The event became known as the Boston Tea Party, and was one of the incidents which led up to the War of Independence.

Revere belonged to a secret society, formed to spy on the British troops. In 1775 he made two famous rides on horseback, galloping from Charlestown to Lexington, to warn people about the plans of British troops. Helped by this knowledge, the Americans defeated the British at the Battle of Lexington.

PAINE, Thomas

British revolutionary 1737-1809

Paine was a customs officer for the British government, but he was not popular with them because he demanded that all officers be paid more money. He had been impressed by **Franklin**, whom he had once met, and in 1774 he decided to emigrate to America. He wrote newspaper articles, telling the people of America that they would be far better off if they were independent of British rule. Many leaders of the American Revolution, including **Washington**, said later that Paine's writings helped to form their political ideas. After the War of Independence ended in 1776, Paine served Congress (the ruling body of the new republic) as an expert on foreign affairs.

In 1787 Paine heard that the French were planning a revolution, and hurried back to Europe to support them. He wrote a book called *The Rights of Man*, saying that all humans have an equal right to happiness, and that states should be governed not by kings, lords and other unelected leaders, but by the votes of all citizens. These were the views of the American and French revolutionaries, but no one had ever explained "democracy" in such simple words.

Although revolutionaries and democrats in Europe and America admired Paine, he annoyed the French revolutionary leaders by telling them that they had been wrong to execute the king. **Robespierre** threw him into prison, and he was lucky to escape the guillotine.

Paine wrote another book, giving his ideas about God and religion, but it was not welcomed. When he returned to America in 1802, he found himself an outcast in a changed society. However, his political ideas have lived on: *The Rights of Man* is still considered one of the best arguments for democratic government ever written.

MONTGOLFIER, Joseph-Michel

French air pioneer 1740-1810

and

MONTGOLFIER, Jacques-Étienne

French air pioneer 1745-99

The Montgolfier brothers invented the hot-air balloon. Their balloon consisted of a linen holder, lined with paper to make it airtight. The linen bag was filled with air heated by a great fire of paper. In 1783 JOSEPH-MICHEL made the first-ever public flight, and flew nine kilometres. But JACQUES-ÉTIENNE preferred inventing balloons to flying them: all his life, he stayed firmly on the ground.

The eigthteenth-century discoveries made about gases began the new, often dangerous, pastime of ballooning. The first manned Montgolfier hot-air balloon successfully flew across Paris in 1783.

ARNOLD, Benedict

American soldier 1741-1801

Arnold became a soldier at the age of 14, and later fought bravely on the American side in the War of Independence against Britain. In 1775 he was made brigadier-general for his gallantry in battle. But he had many powerful enemies, and several times failed to get the promotion he thought he deserved. This made him bitter, and in 1780 he secretly agreed to surrender the West Point Naval Academy (where he was commander) to the British. The plot was discovered and Arnold fled to join the British. Later, he even led an expedition against the Americans. He spent the rest of his days in England, despised by his new countrymen and hated in the USA.

PAINE: Franklin 346 Robespierre 450 Washington 447

TOUSSAINT-L'OUVERTURE, Pierre Dominique

Haitian leader 1746-1803

Toussaint was a Negro slave on the small Caribbean island of Sainte-Dominique, who taught himself to read and write. He read about Julius **Caesar** and **Alexander the Great**, and their exploits encouraged him to try to help his own people. At the time, France ruled the island, and in 1791 – soon after the French Revolution – the government freed all slaves and made Toussaint commander-in-chief. England and Spain, fearing revolts on other Caribbean islands, sent troops to Sainte-Dominique. After seven years of fighting, Toussaint and his army of ex-slaves, backed by French troops, drove the British and Spanish from the island.

Toussaint then declared Sainte-Dominique a republic, and set about rebuilding plantations ruined in the war, and running a banana business with blacks, not whites, in charge. However, three years later, in 1801, a new French government under **Napoléon** declared that slavery was to be re-established. Toussaint resisted. Napoléon sent troops who arrested him and he died, two years later, in a French prison. In 1804 another ex-slave, General Desallines, led the islanders in a revolt which at last won independence from France. They renamed their country Haiti, and it keeps that name today.

The former slave Toussaint-L'Ouverture showed great military skill in keeping first the British, then the Spanish from conquering Haiti. As governor, he introduced a new constitution, and ruled the island with fairness and good sense.

BLANCHARD, Jean-Pierre

French air pioneer 1753-1809

Blanchard invented the parachute and, with the American John Jeffries (1744-1819), he was also the first man to cross the Channel in a hot-air balloon, in 1785. He later toured the USA and Canada, making balloon ascents. He proved that parachutes were safe by fastening them to cats and dogs, throwing the animals out of the balloon and watching them glide safely to land. He also built one of the first-ever helicopters, following the designs of **Leonardo da Vinci**. It was powered by hand. But even his nerve failed when it came to test-flying it, and it never left the ground. Blanchard was killed during a practice jump from a balloon.

Blanchard was one of several air pioneers to use animals to test the safety aspects of their inventions. Happily, his parachute was proved safe.

TOUSSAINT-L'OUVERTURE: Alexander the Great 412 Julius Caesar 415 Napoléon I 451 BLANCHARD: Leonardo da Vinci 11

BLIGH, William

English naval officer 1753-1817

Bligh sailed with Captain **Cook** on his second voyage around the world (1772-74). In 1789 he was made captain of the *Bounty*, and sent on a voyage to collect breadfruit seeds from Tahiti in the Pacific, take them to the Caribbean islands and start plantations. The crew were happy to spend six months on Tahiti, but when Bligh forced them to set sail they mutinied. The mutineers put Bligh and 18 loyal officers in a small boat and abandoned them. The small boat was at sea for three months but, incredibly, Bligh and his officers sailed almost 6,500 kilometres to the East Indies and safety.

The tale of the "Mutiny on the Bounty" achieved fame everywhere. Bligh's crew had settled on Pitcairn Island in the Pacific, and spread the story that he was a tyrant whose floggings and keel-haulings had left them with no choice but to mutiny.

But Bligh was the official hero, and his courage was rewarded by the government, who made him governor of New South Wales in Australia. He tried to end rum smuggling and was, once again, accused of tyranny. His men mutinied, and he was imprisoned for two years. He retired to England in 1811, aged 57, where the government gave him a pension and the rank of Admiral. Yet it is his reputation for cruelty, deserved or not, that keeps his name alive.

MACKENZIE, Alexander

Scottish/Canadian explorer 1755-1820

Mackenzie was a fur-trader and travelled all over Canada, setting up new trading posts. In 1789 he journeyed 1,600 km along a massive river, from the Great Slave Lake to the Arctic Circle. He nicknamed it the "River of Disappointment", when he found that it led, not to the Pacific Ocean as he had hoped, but to the Atlantic. It is now called the Mackenzie river. On a second, three-year expedition, Mackenzie was the first European to cross the Rockies to reach the Pacific coast.

A painting by Robert Dodd of the *Bounty* mutineers, led by Fletcher Christian, casting Captain Bligh and his officers adrift in 1789.

Lafayette, the French political reformer, who was active in both the American War of Independence and the French Revolution. Over 160 years later, during the Second World War, American troops landing on the Normandy beaches shouted "Lafayette, nous voilà!", in recognition of his part in their independence movement.

LAFAYETTE, Marquis de

French general 1757-1834

Marie Joseph Paul Yves Roch Gilbert Motier, Marquis de Lafayette, fought under **Washington** in the American War of Independence, and persuaded France to help the revolutionaries. After the success of the American Revolution, he began working for the same ideas in France: liberty, equality and fraternity. He formed the National Guard, the force of armed citizens which was to fight for freedom. But when the revolution actually began and extremists seized control, he spoke out against the execution of the royal family, and risked facing the guillotine himself. He fled to Belgium, only returning to France ten years later, when **Napoléon I** guaranteed his safety. He spent a total of 12 years as a Deputy (member of parliament), and was known as a fiery, left-wing speaker. In the 1830 Revolution, Lafayette, then aged 73, led the National Guard once more, to help the Duke of Orléans become King Louis Philippe – a complete change of politics for a man who had been a firm republican all his life.

Action during the sea battle of Trafalgar in 1805. In the moment of victory, Admiral Nelson was wounded and later died.

NELSON, Horatio

English admiral 1758-1805

Nelson joined the Royal Navy when he was 12 and was a captain before he was 30. He won several naval battles by using new, daring manoeuvres, such as sailing round to attack the enemy from behind, instead of facing their guns head-on. He lost an eye and had his right arm amputated, but he remained in command of his fleet. His particular enemies were the French. In 1798 he destroyed **Napoléon**'s fleet off the coast of Egypt, making the British navy supreme in the Mediterranean, and halted the French army in Egypt, which hampered Napoléon's plans to conquer Europe. His most famous victory was as admiral-in-chief, commanding the British ships at the battle of Trafalgar in 1805, a victory which prevented Napoléon's army from crossing the Channel to invade England. Nelson was fatally

NELSON: Napoléon I 451 Washington 447

wounded during the fighting, but his faithful officers followed his plans and won the day.

Nelson was a dazzlingly successful seaman and one of the finest admirals in British history. But his unusual methods were unpopular with older officers, and he also caused a scandal by his love-affair with Emma, the beautiful young wife of elderly Lord Hamilton. None the less, his seamanship saved Britain from French conquest and, after his last victory, a statue of him was put up on a tall column in what became known as Trafalgar Square in London.

WILBERFORCE, William

English politician 1759-1833

In the eighteenth century Europeans practised a particularly vicious form of slavery. They bought black people in Africa, shipped them across the Atlantic to sugar plantations in the New World, and imported the sugar to Europe, taking some of the profits to Africa to buy more slaves. It was a cruel trade, but few people spoke out against it – and those who did faced the fury of individuals and governments, much of whose wealth depended on the slave trade.

Wilberforce was one politician who did speak out for the abolition of slavery. His campaign took 19 years. He proposed law after law in parliament, but was defeated each time, thanks to the power of wealthy slave-owners. At last, in 1807, his determination succeeded. Parliament passed a law forbidding British companies to buy more slaves. It was one of the first anti-slavery laws in Europe, and Wilberforce's success encouraged campaigners in other countries. He then set himself an even harder task: persuading people to free the slaves they already owned. This took the rest of his life: he died one month before this second law was passed.

The Slave Deck at Albanez by Francis Meynell (1821-70). A painting of slaves bound for the New World, made when Meynell was ship's mate on the *Penelope*, c 1845.

GARNERIN, Jacques

French air pioneer 1769-1823

Garnerin was a pioneer balloonist, and in 1797 he made the first-ever parachute jump. **Leonardo da Vinci** had thought of parachutes as long ago as 1485, but until Garnerin jumped, three centuries later, no one had dared to try one. Garnerin had watched **Blanchard**'s experiments with cats and dogs, and knew that parachutes could give a soft landing. But the early jumps were terrifying. His first parachute had no air-holes in it to control the speed of his fall, as modern parachutes do. Garnerin swung on the end of his ropes like the weight on a pendulum, and was so airsick that he was only just able to control his landing, steering beyond trees and houses to open fields.

Garnerin made the first parachute descent in 1797, dropping 610m from his balloon.

GARNERIN: Blanchard 190 Leonardo da Vinci 11

HUMBOLDT, Alexander von

German traveller and scientist 1769-1859

Alexander von Humboldt was born into an aristocratic family; his father was a courtier of the king of Prussia. He studied geology and biology at university, and did research on the nervous system of animals. When he was 30, he began a five-year expedition to South America, travelling in Mexico, Cuba and the basins of the rivers Amazon and Orinoco. Wherever he went he made maps and charts, noted the geography and geology of the area and the atmosphere and planets visible above it, and studied its people, animals and plants. His collection was so vast that when he went back to Germany it took him 20 years to put it in order and publish his findings, in no less than 30 volumes. His work inspired naturalists and other scientists all over Europe, and in 1829 Tsar Nicholas I invited him to make a similar expedition to Russia. Humboldt visited the Steppes and the Ural Mountains, mapping the land and examining its geology. He found valuable minerals – gold, platinum, diamonds – and again made careful notes on the climate, geography, flora and fauna of the area.

When Humboldt returned from Russia, he wrote about his travels, and then began work on his most ambitious book of all: *Cosmos*. It took 17 years to write, and gave a complete account of the then-known universe.

Humboldt's name has been given to many natural features: the Humboldt Current in the South Pacific, the Humboldt Glacier in Greenland, the Humboldt Mountains in New Zealand, the Humboldt Bay and river Humboldt in the USA and there are also towns called Humboldt in Tennessee, Iowa and in Canada.

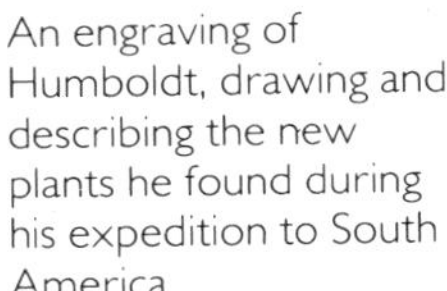

An engraving of Humboldt, drawing and describing the new plants he found during his expedition to South America.

WELLINGTON, Duke of

English general and politician 1769-1852

As a boy Arthur Wellesley, later Duke of Wellington, was a good violinist and wanted a musical career. But his mother insisted on the army. He joined when he was 22, and served as an officer in India. In his 30s he was made governor of the Indian province of Mysore, but returned to Europe in the mid-1800s to fight the French. He was one of the generals who pinned down **Napoléon**'s army in the Peninsular War (1808-14), and in 1815, together with the Prussian troops under General Blücher, commanded the army which defeated

WELLINGTON: Napoléon I 451

Napoléon at the battle of Waterloo. His military courage and fine leadership earned him many awards, including the distinguished foreign honour – the Golden Fleece.

When Wellington retired from the army he went into full-time politics. He was Prime Minister of Britain from 1828-30, and foreign secretary from 1834-35. He was also chosen as Chancellor of the University of Oxford in 1834 and, although he retired from public life aged 75, he served as commander-in-chief of the British army until he was 83.

His name is often remembered today for a frivolous reason. He ordered his army to be equipped with waterproof boots made of rubberized cloth, and they were nicknamed "Wellingtons" after him.

Left: A cartoon of Arthur, Duke of Wellington, made by Paul Pry in 1827.

OWEN, Robert

Welsh socialist 1771-1858

Owen was a cotton-mill manager in northern England, and was horrified by the slum conditions in which factory-people lived and worked. He set out to improve what the English poet Blake called the "dark, satanic mills". He built a new kind of factory in New Lanark in Scotland: a large, airy building where each person worked in comfort and safety at the machinery. He built the workers a village with gardens, a church and a meeting-hall and opened a school – the first school for infants in Britain.

Owen wrote books and articles about his ideas, and villages modelled on New Lanark were built in England, Ireland and the USA (at the aptly named New Harmony, Indiana). Owen went on to work for other rights for workers: minimum wages, shorter hours, sick pay and health care. He organized working-people into groups to look after their own affairs: the first trade unions.

An 1825 engraving of Robert Owen's meeting-hall in New Lanark, Scotland.

The coast-to-coast expedition by Lewis and Clark across America did not lead to the discovery of a water route to the Pacific Ocean, but they gained valuable information on the land and native people, and opened the way from east to west.

LEWIS, Meriwether

American explorer 1774-1809

and

CLARK, William

American explorer 1770-1838

In 1804 the American president, **Jefferson**, sent Lewis and Clark to cross the country from east to west. They had several tasks: to find out if there was a sea-passage between the Atlantic and Pacific oceans; to see if beavers and other fur-bearing animals lived in the west as well as in the east; and, above all, to make contact with native Americans, and to persuade them to accept rule by the "great white chief", Jefferson himself.

Lewis and Clark travelled for months, moving inland along the Missouri River, making maps and collecting rocks, animals and plants. As Jefferson had ordered, they visited as many native tribes as possible, treating them as allies instead of enemies. The Mandans gave them guides and the Shoshone gave them an interpreter and horses, to help them on their way. After 18 months they reached the Pacific coast, in what is now the state of Oregon. They spent the winter there before retracing their steps and reporting to Jefferson. There was no sea-passage between the Atlantic and Pacific. But the tales Lewis and Clark told of the vast, beautiful land they had explored, and of the natural wonders they had seen, inspired Americans with a patriotic passion for the rivers, trees and land of their country – a passion which still survives today.

STANHOPE, Hester Lucy

English aristocrat 1776-1839

At the age of 27 Stanhope went to keep house for her uncle, the Prime Minister William Pitt the Younger. When he died in 1806 the state gave her a pension in thanks for her services. She had planned to marry a soldier, Sir John Moore, but he was killed in battle in 1809 and she left England the following year for the Middle East. She travelled in Palestine, Turkey and Syria, where she took as her lover a younger man, a Syrian. To the horror of her English relatives, she lived the rest of her life in a Lebanese mansion, dressed in Arab clothes, smoking a hookah and spending all day in bed writing her memoirs. She took part in local politics, supporting the Turks against the Egyptians led by **Mehemet Ali**, and gave her money away to anyone who asked for it.

After several years, the English government felt they could no longer turn a blind eye to her behaviour, and stopped her pension. She died in

LEWIS AND CLARK: Jefferson 448 STANHOPE: Mehemet Ali 450

poverty and alone (her lover had long ago deserted her). But although her life ended sadly, she had, as she wrote in her Memoirs, thoroughly enjoyed doing exactly as she pleased, ignoring the stuffy "rules" laid down for early nineteenth-century English gentlewomen.

BELZONI, Giovanni Battista

Italian explorer 1778-1823

Belzoni earned his living as a fairground strongman in England. He was over two metres tall, and able to lift eleven people at a time, but he also amazed people with his models of hydraulic engines. He travelled to Europe and then went to Cairo, where the Egyptian viceroy asked him to build a hydraulic irrigation machine. Belzoni spent his spare time exploring the treasures of ancient Egypt. He even removed the huge stone bust of the pharaoh **Rameses II**, which he sent to the British Museum in London, although he had to fight a rival group of French collectors who also claimed the stone.

Belzoni became so fascinated by the remains of ancient civilization that he stayed in Egypt for four years. He made thorough, detailed drawings of the sites and cleared rubble from the temple ruins at Abu Simbel. He was the first person in modern times to open up the pyramid containing the tomb of Seti I in the Valley of the Kings.

For years people viewed Belzoni only as a vandal or a thief. But his excavations, and the fine objects he sent to London, began an English passion for Egyptology (the study of Egypt's past) – the basis of the new science of archaeology. In fact, "archaeologist" was a word unknown in Belzoni's lifetime, but that is what he was.

BELZONI: Rameses II 407

O'HIGGINS, Bernardo

Chilean soldier and statesman 1778-1842

O'Higgins was the illegitimate son of an Irish diplomat who worked in Chile and Peru. He was educated in Europe at the time of the French Revolution, which may have inspired O'Higgins to lead a Chilean revolt against the Spanish in 1810.

On 2 October 1814, O'Higgins' forces fought bravely against a much larger Spanish army. O'Higgins was defeated (some say because of treachery in his own ranks), and was forced to escape by trekking across the Andes into Argentina. He re-formed his army in 1817, and this time beat the Spaniards. He declared himself the first President of the new republic of Chile.

Once the republic was established, O'Higgins tried to bring in laws reducing the power of the rich and distributing their property among ordinary people – as revolutionaries had done almost 30 years before in France. This made him unpopular, and the rich, not unexpectedly, rebelled. O'Higgins had to choose between resigning as president or ruling by force. Rather than risk civil war, he chose to resign. He went into exile in Peru, where he later died. This last brave choice, and his struggle to free his country from Spanish rule, have meant that his name lives on as one of the noblest heroes in Chile's history.

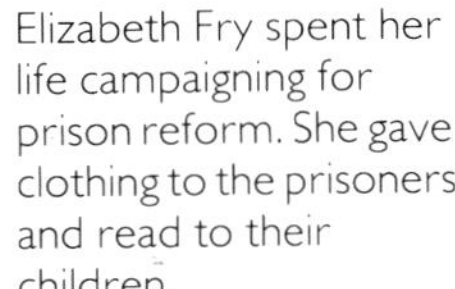

Elizabeth Fry spent her life campaigning for prison reform. She gave clothing to the prisoners and read to their children.

FRY, Elizabeth

English reformer 1780-1845

Elizabeth Fry was a Quaker who devoted her life to prison reform. She used to visit women in jail, imprisoned with their children, and, like **Howard**, was horrified by their conditions. She argued with the authorities that even prisoners were God's creatures, and deserved dignity and fair treatment – whatever their crime. She started schools, run by prisoners, first for children and then for their mothers. In 1817 she founded a prison reform society which campaigned for better conditions in prisons, convict ships (rotting old warships where dangerous criminals were chained), mental hospitals and asylums all over Europe. She also successfully worked to stop British prisoners being transported to Australia.

FRY: Howard 186

RAFFLES, Thomas Stamford

English settler 1781-1826

Raffles was lieutenant-governor of the island of Java, which the British captured from the Dutch in 1811. He was a most unusual governor for his time: he abolished slavery, learned the local language, and treated the people with dignity and respect. He was a friend of the plant scientist Joseph **Banks**, and went on natural history trips into the jungle, sending notes, drawings and specimens back to Banks in London. He also founded the London Zoo.

In 1818 Raffles founded a trading port, Singapore, on an island at the tip of the Malay Peninsula. It became the centre of British trade in southern Asia, and is now one of the busiest, most flourishing cities in the world.

BOLÍVAR, Simón

South American liberator 1783-1830

Bolívar studied law in Europe, and was impressed by the ideas of **Rousseau**, **Voltaire** and the French revolutionaries. He planned to free South America from the Spanish and Portuguese rule it had endured for 300 years, and to made it a single, united country. At first he had just 600 soldiers, and could only attack small Spanish settlements one by one. But guerrilla war soon grew into a massive freedom struggle, and when the Spaniards tried to stop Bolívar in a final, desperate onslaught, he led his followers to safety across the Andes mountains (4,500 metres high), and began the guerrilla war in other parts of South America. By 1824 the Spanish had been forced to surrender Ecuador, Chile, Peru, Colombia and Venezuela, and Bolívar was hailed as "the liberator". His followers put up his statues in many South American cities and named a country (Bolivia) after him.

But although many people idolized Bolívar the man, few agreed with his ideas of a single "Republic of the Andes" – a United States of South America. They preferred to keep their countries separate, and Bolívar realized that this would cause endless political squabbling, and perhaps war, all over South America. To prevent this, he made himself dictator. He took control of the army, and used force to make everyone keep his laws. This was tyranny, not democracy, and when Bolívar died other army leaders, who were less honest and public-spirited, seized control. In the 160 years since Bolívar's death, only a few South American countries have ever successfully replaced dictatorship with long-term democracy.

Simón Bolívar was known as "the liberator" because he led the drive to expel the Spanish and Portuguese from South America and then to create independent republics.

A painting by an unknown artist of Simón Bolívar meeting his lieutenant Antonio José de Sucre in the struggle to free South America from European rule. De Sucre became Bolivia's first president in 1826.

RAFFLES: Banks 112 BOLÍVAR: Rousseau, J J 348 Voltaire 344

Johann Ludwig Burckhardt.

BURCKHARDT, Johann Ludwig

Swiss traveller 1784-1817

The secrets of the Arab world were closely guarded at the beginning of the nineteenth century. Burckhardt had to disguise himself as a Muslim merchant in order to travel in Syria, Jordan and Lebanon – areas forbidden to non-Muslims at that time. In a rocky valley in the south of present-day Jordan, he found the beautiful tomb-city of Petra, carved from solid rock, the capital of the ancient Nabataean kingdom.

The Wild West hero Davy Crockett. It is said he was an expert marksman with his rifle "Betsy".

CROCKETT, David

US politician 1786-1836

Davy Crockett was a lawyer, but he liked to act as a tough-talking, hard-shooting frontiersman – a kind of early cowboy. He was elected to represent the southern state of Tennessee in 1821 in the American parliament (Congress), but during the Texas fight for independence from Mexico, Crockett was killed at the battle of the Alamo. His tough character and bravery were much exaggerated in a song about him, which still keeps his name alive.

FRANKLIN, John

English explorer 1786-1847

As a young man Franklin joined the navy, and in 1805 he was one of **Nelson**'s officers at the battle of Trafalgar. He continued in the navy till 1836, made several expeditions to northern Canada and the Arctic, and became an expert on polar survival. In 1845 the government sent him with two ships to find the northwest passage through the Arctic between the Atlantic and Pacific oceans. He never returned. His disappearance was one of the great unsolved mysteries of the time, and over 40 expeditions set out to look for him. On one of them, a record of the expedition up to 1848 was discovered which proved that Franklin had discovered the passage. It told how Franklin's ships had been crushed in the polar ice, how he himself had died, and how the survivors had set out, on foot, across the icefloes, but all died of disease or frostbite.

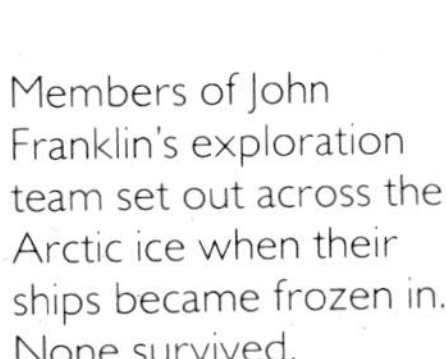

Members of John Franklin's exploration team set out across the Arctic ice when their ships became frozen in. None survived.

FRANKLIN: Nelson 192

STUART, Miranda Barry

Scottish doctor 1795-1865

When Stuart was 15, she dressed as a man, called herself James Barry and trained to be a doctor. Later, still taken to be a man, she joined the British Army. She served all over the world, and had a brilliant medical career, finally serving as Inspector General of Hospitals. She always wore padding to make her look brawny and she was called "the Kapok doctor". She worked to ensure better administration and cleanliness in the medical service, and was one of the few people who dared to criticize Florence **Nightingale** – for low standards. All her life she played the part of a man so successfully that no one she worked with suspected her. Only after her death was it discovered that she was a woman, and that at an early age she had borne a child.

"TRUTH, Sojourner"

US campaigner against slavery 1797-1883

She was born a slave with the name Isabella von Wagener. As a child, she was sold several times, and when she was a mother herself two of her four children were sold, and she had to fight in court to keep her son. In her 30s she was given her freedom at last and settled in New York. She was a fervent Christian, and in 1842 changed her name to Sojourner Truth. She was a spell-binding public speaker, first spreading God's word, and later preaching against the evils of slavery, drink and the unfair way women were treated.

Sojourner Truth, formerly a slave became a famous speaker against slavery.

During the American Civil War (1861-65) Truth raised money for black volunteer regiments to fight on the side of the north, for which she was publicly thanked by **Lincoln**. She was the first black person to win a slander case against white people, and the first woman to go to law to challenge the segregation laws in Washington DC.

BROWN, John

US revolutionary 1800-59

Brown was passionately against slavery in America, and thought that the best way to abolish it was to start a revolution in each of the slave-owning southern states. He gave refuge to runaway slaves and gathered together people in the fight to free slaves. He made a raid on a weapons store at Harper's Ferry in Virginia, to arm his men, but it failed and he was arrested. He was tried for treason and murder, found guilty and hanged. When the civil war began in 1861, the song "John Brown's body lies a-mould'ring in the grave, but his soul goes marchin' on" was used as a marching song by armies of the northern states, and it is one of the American freedom-songs still sung today.

The American revolutionary John Brown.

STUART: Nightingale 208 TRUTH: Lincoln 452

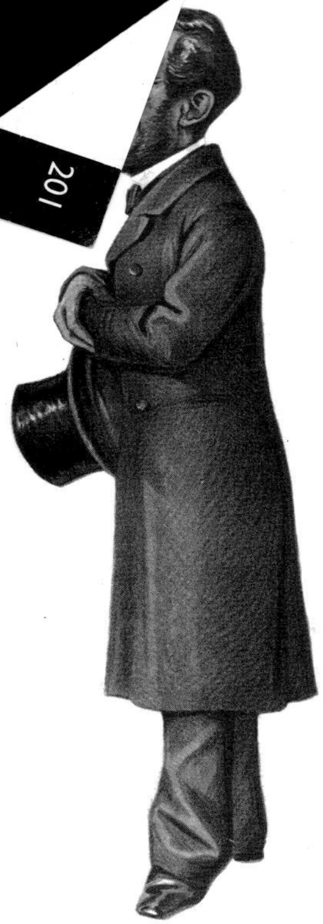

The seventh Earl of Shaftesbury, shown in a 1869 edition of *Vanity Fair*.

SHAFTESBURY, Lord (Anthony Ashley Cooper)

English politician 1801-85

Unlike many aristocrats of his time, Shaftesbury was determined to improve ordinary people's lives. He felt particularly strongly about the harsh conditions endured by workers in Britain's towns and cities since the industrial revolution. Until his time, there had been no limit to the hours people could be forced to work in factories. Shaftesbury persuaded Parliament to pass several laws to improve working conditions. Ten hours a day became the maximum anyone could work. Women and children, some of them as young as three or four, could no longer be employed to work underground in coal-mines, and sweeps could no longer send small boys up chimneys to sweep them. Shaftesbury also had public lodging-houses built for the homeless, and "ragged schools" to provide free elementary education for all city children whose parents could not afford to pay.

Few people in history with as much wealth and power as Shaftesbury ever use their privileges to improve the lives of ordinary people, and his reforms enraged his fellow aristocrats. But when he died thousands of ordinary people lined the streets to watch his funeral procession and pay their respects.

One of the few remaining illustrators of Mary Seacole, from *Punch*, 1857.

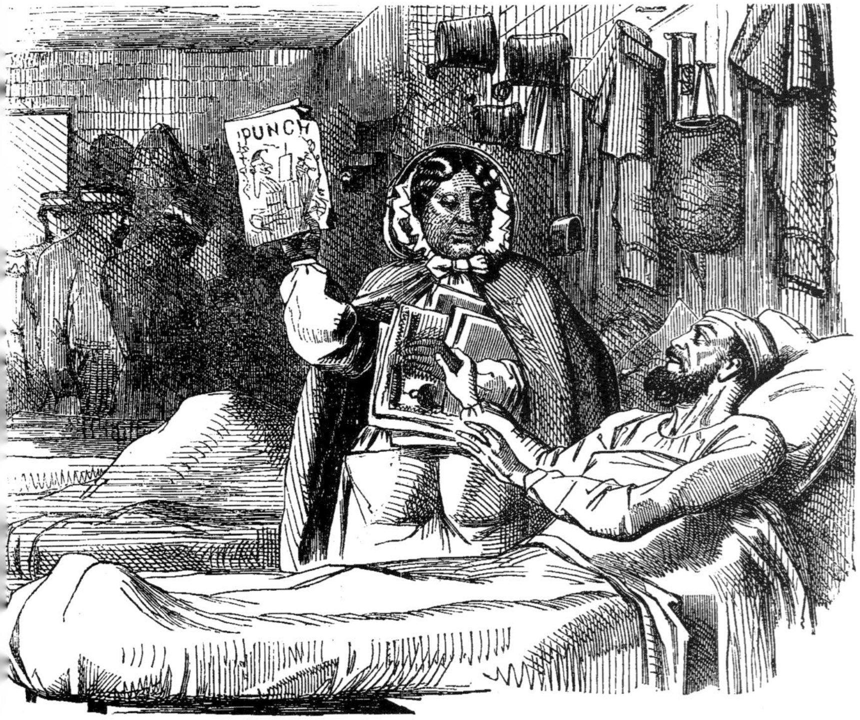

SEACOLE, Mary

Jamaican/Scottish nurse c 1805-81

Seacole's father was a white sailor, and her mother was a black hotel-owner in Kingston, Jamaica. Seacole became interested in nursing during a cholera epidemic in 1850, when she volunteered to help look after the sick. In the next few years she travelled all over the Caribbean and Central America, nursing sick people. In 1853, when war broke out in the Crimea between Britain and Russia, she sailed to London and volunteered as an army nurse. She was refused by the government in London because she was black, but she was determined to help, and travelled to the Crimea at her own expense.

Seacole worked in the Crimea with Florence **Nightingale** throughout the three years of war, and when she went back to London she was given medals for her bravery by the same authorities who had spurned her. She wrote a best-selling autobiography, *The Wonderful Adventures of Mrs Seacole in Many Lands*, and spent the rest of her life in London.

SEACOLE: Nightingale 208

LEE, Robert Edward

US soldier 1807-70

Before the American Civil War, the most important event of Lee's military life was when he commanded the soldiers who quelled John **Brown**'s rebellion. In 1861, when the civil war began, Lee was ordered to lead the government troops. But he put loyalty to his own state (Virginia) before loyalty to the government, resigned from the army and was given command of the Confederate army of the southern states. He managed to hold out against the North for four years – a remarkable achievement as his men were always outnumbered by better trained northern troops – but he finally surrendered in 1865.

After the war Lee was stripped of all his property (one of his estates is now Arlington cemetery, the main US military burial ground). He would have been executed or imprisoned, had he not persuaded his former followers to rejoin the United States. He retired from military and political life and spent his last few years as President of what came to be called the Washington and Lee University at Lexington, Virginia.

Robert E Lee who led the Confederate army in the American Civil War.

GARIBALDI, Giuseppe

Italian soldier 1807-82

Garibaldi is the central figure in the story of Italy's independence. Since the fall of the Roman Empire, Italy had been a divided country. Parts of it were ruled by the powerful cities of Venice, Naples, Milan and Rome; other parts were controlled by Austria and France. Garibaldi, who had fought guerrilla wars in South America, led a liberation movement called the Risorgimento (meaning resurgence), designed to free Italy from foreign rulers and to unite it under a single government. He spent most of his life fighting for this cause, both politically and as leader of the army of men known as "Redshirts" (because of their uniforms) – and he lived long enough to see his dream come true: Italy finally became a unified, self-governing country in 1870.

Garibaldi was the leader of the Italian patriots. With his famous "thousand" Redshirts he fought for the unity of Italy.

LEE: Brown 201

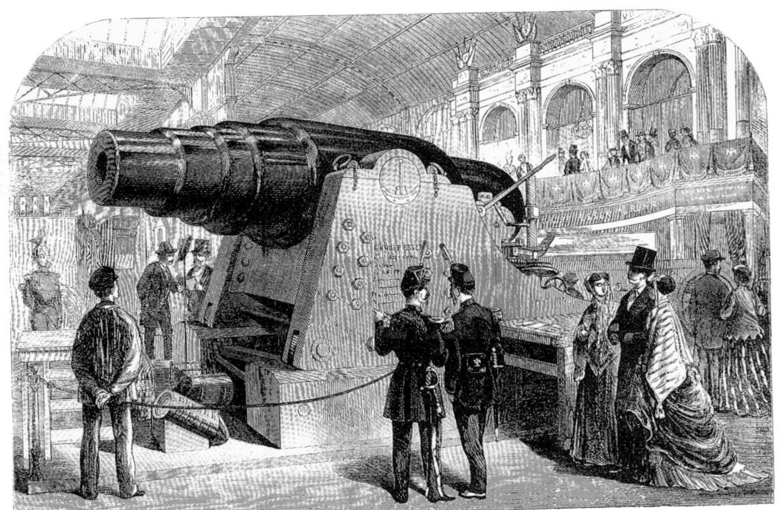

"Big Bertha", the Krupp gun shown at the Paris exhibition of 1867. It was a steel cannon weighing 50 tonnes, and was later presented to the King of Prussia.

KRUPP FAMILY

German businessmen 19th-20th century

In 1810 the Krupp family built an iron works near Essen in Germany which became the basis of a vast industrial empire. The firm made the first steel gun in 1847, and pioneered the **Bessemer** process. Krupps became the leading arms supplier in the world. The Kaiser's forces in the First World War (1914-18) used a giant gun manufactured by Krupps; it was nicknamed "Big Bertha" after one of the Krupp daughters.

Between the two world wars, the Krupps' business concentrated on agricultural machinery and steam engines, but by the Second World War (1939-45) they had become major arms suppliers to the Nazis. Efforts were made after the war to break up the Krupps' empire, but in fact it played an important part in West Germany's recovery. The Krupp family fortune continued to expand until they gave up all claim to the profits by declaring the company public in 1968.

FORTUNE, Robert

Scottish plant-collector 1813-80

In 1843 the London Botanical Society sent Fortune to the Far East to collect seeds and shoots of oriental plants. Over the next three years he sent back many shrubs and plants, including rhododendrons, chrysanthemums and azaleas, which have since become common in European gardens. His trip was such a success that he was sent back to China on a secret government mission. At the time, China was the main country where tea was grown. The Chinese controlled most of the world's tea trade, and the British government feared that the trade would stop if war broke out with China. They therefore decided to try to start tea plantations in India, then under British rule, and Fortune was sent to smuggle out tea-bush seeds and cuttings. He hid them in his clothes and luggage, and carried them undetected to India. This was the start of the enormous tea industry in India, which now exports many varieties of tea to every country in the world – including China.

LIVINGSTONE, David

Scottish traveller 1813-73

Livingstone grew up in the slums, and until he was 24 he worked in the local cotton factory. But he planned to become a doctor and a Christian missionary and each night after work he studied for two hours.

Livingstone was 27 when he completed his studies, and he went to work in Southern Africa. But he

KRUPP: Bessemer 366

faced fierce resistance from white settlers, who objected to black people being converted to the Christian faith. Livingstone was determined to open more trade routes east and west, to enable other missionaries to reach black people, even if their way from South African ports was blocked. He travelled north to find a route from the west coast to the Zambezi river. He saw huge waterfalls on the Zambezi and called them the Victoria Falls after the English queen. He made careful notes on the country and its native peoples, and drew many maps.

However, Livingstone converted only one person to Christianity during his years as a missionary and the church refused to pay for further trips. In any case, Livingstone wanted to concentrate on exploration, and his next trip was financed by the government. He headed an expedition to explore the course of the river Zambezi, and to investigate where British trading settlements might be built. He spent six years exploring the Zambezi, finally returning to England in 1863 to report that it was unsuitable for ships.

In 1866 Livingstone set out on another expedition, to settle the arguments about the source of the river Nile. Many months passed, and it was feared that he was missing, if not dead. There were rumours of a crazy white man, and finally an American newspaper sent its star reporter, H M **Stanley**, on a "quest for Livingstone" in 1871. Stanley found him, by then in very bad health, but Livingstone refused to go home until the disputes over the source of the Nile had been settled. For a time, he and Stanley explored the lakes and mountains together, but in 1873 Livingstone died of fever. His body was taken home to London and buried in Westminster Abbey.

Nothing had been heard of Livingstone for several years before Stanley discovered him near Ujiji, in present-day Tanzania, in 1871.

LIVINGSTONE: Stanley 215

STANTON, Elizabeth Cady

US campaigner for women's rights 1815-1902

Stanton learned from her father (a judge) that wives had no legal protection against their husbands: however badly they were treated, if they left their husbands they would lose all claims to their children and property. Stanton decided to work for women's equality. At her wedding in 1840 she refused to promise obedience to her husband, as the marriage laws of the time required, and she spent part of her honeymoon at an anti-slavery convention in London. But women were not even allowed to sit in the hall. Outraged, Stanton and a Quaker anti-slavery worker, Lucretia Mott, organized the first Women's Rights Convention, at Seneca Falls, USA. From 1842 until 1859, as well as bearing seven children, Stanton gave lectures all over the country on education and family law. In 1850, she met two other women's rights campaigners, **Bloomer** and **Anthony**, with whom she wrote the first three volumes of a huge *History of Women's Suffrage*. Stanton also published the *Women's Bible*, and campaigned for women to be allowed to become priests.

REUTER, Paul Julius, Freiherr von (Israel Beer Josaphat)

German news agency founder 1816-99

Reuter worked as a bank clerk and knew **Gauss**, one of the inventors of the electric telegraph. He realized that European banks would benefit from quick, reliable reports of each other's dealings, and formed an organization for sending commercial news by telegraph. In 1851 he made his headquarters in London, where the newspapers used his service for political news. Gradually, Reuter built up his system to receive and send reports from his correspondents based all over the world.

Reuter began delivering financial information in 1849, using trains, the telegraph and pigeons. In 1883 he used a column printer, an early form of the teleprinter. By 1923, the company was transmitting in Morse code, using long-wave radio. In 1964, Reuters introduced its first desktop terminal. It now communicates all over the world by satellite.

BLOOMER, Amelia

US campaigner 1818-94

Bloomer toured the USA, campaigning for women's rights and for temperance (giving up alcohol).

STANTON: Anthony 207 Bloomer 206 REUTER: Gauss 118

Bloomers really caught on, and gave rise to several music-hall songs, including "I want to be a Bloomer!"

She also pioneered a "bicycling garment" for women, consisting of a loose skirt worn over trousers gathered at the ankles. Elasticated women's trousers worn as underwear have been nicknamed "bloomers" ever since.

LIVERMORE, Mary Ashton

US campaigner 1820-1905

Horrified at the conditions of homeless people and refugees during the American Civil War, Livermore campaigned to improve their lives. She lectured about the need for clean drinking-water, proper sanitation and temperance (giving up alcohol). In the 1880s she fought for women's rights. She and her followers toured the USA, demanding that women be given the vote, and be treated as equals with men.

ANTHONY, Susan Brownell

US campaigner 1820-1906

Susan Anthony, one of the leaders in the campaign for women's rights in nineteenth-century America.

Anthony's father was a pioneer campaigner for the abolition of slavery and, had women been allowed, she might have gone into politics. Instead, Anthony turned to public speaking and campaigning to persuade people to demand reforms. She began by speaking against the evils of alcohol, from which the government was making a fortune in taxes. Her research into alcohol addiction took her to the slave plantations of the southern USA, and she soon joined the campaign to abolish slavery.

In the 1850s Anthony took up a third cause: women's rights. Women were treated as second-class citizens, and for 50 years she fought to give them the right to vote and equality in education, work and marriage. She was over 80 when she founded the International Woman Suffrage Alliance, which greatly encouraged campaigners like the **Pankhursts** in Britain. She died before US women actually got the vote (in 1920), but her tireless work had helped to give women this important right.

BURKE, Robert O'Hara

Australian explorer 1820-61

and

WILLS, William John

Australian explorer 1834-61

In the 1850s the South Australian Government offered $4,000 to the first white travellers to make a successful trip across desert and scrub to the north of Australia, and back. In 1860 Burke and Wills, basing their plans on accounts of earlier desert expeditions in Africa, set out with 28 horses and 26 camels, laden with provisions, guns, ammunition and no less than 60 gallons of rum. Foolishly, Burke scorned the advice of aborigines about the best routes to take and how to live off the land. They covered dozens of kilometres each day through uncharted country, in scorching heat, and often without water. They made rough maps, and organized food-dumps for the return journey. The outward crossing was successfully completed, but on the journey home they lost their way and died of starvation before they could be rescued.

ANTHONY: Pankhursts 218

NIGHTINGALE, Florence

English nurse 1820-1910

Until Nightingale's time, there were few professional nurses. Most sick people were nursed by their own families, or by untrained and sometimes drunken men and women – little better than the gaolers who "looked after" prisoners.

Nightingale was determined to change this system and to improve nursing standards. She trained as a nurse on the Continent, and in 1854 took a team of 38 nurses to tend British soldiers injured in the Crimean War between Russia on the one side and Turkey, France, Sardinia and Britain on the other. Nightingale was known as "the lady with the lamp", because she went round with a lamp each night, making sure each man was as comfortable as possible.

In 1856, Nightingale returned to London, and was given a fund of £50,000 to set up the first-ever training school for nurses, at St Thomas's and at King's College Hospital in London.

BAKER, Samuel White

English traveller 1821-93

Baker was a rich man whose hobby was travelling – what people in those days called "knocking about the world". In his 20s he went to Ceylon (modern Sri Lanka), where he set up a farm and helped to build a railway. When he was 40 he and his wife sailed up the river Nile in Egypt, joining in the search for its source. They learned Arabic in the course of their travels, and met **Speke** and Grant, who told them of a great lake they had discovered and named Lake Victoria. Lured by tales of another vast lake, the Bakers went on to Nyasaland (modern Malawi), and discovered a huge lake, which they named Albert, after Queen **Victoria**'s husband.

Baker was in his 50s when he was put in command of an expedition in Egypt, to end the slave-trade and claim British rule over the equatorial regions of the Nile. The passion for seeing new places never left him, and in his 60s and 70s he visited Cyprus, Syria, India, Japan and the USA.

Portraits of Samuel Baker and his wife.

An artist's view of Florence Nightingale, visiting wounded soldiers in the Crimean War.

BAKER: Speke 210 Victoria 454

BURTON, Richard

English traveller and writer 1821-90

From boyhood, Burton had a remarkable gift for learning foreign languages. By the time he was 20 he had learned Latin, Greek, French, German, Italian and Arabic, and in his lifetime he learned to speak over 30 different-languages.

In 1853 Burton explored Arabia, disguised as a Muslim pilgrim. The holy cities, Medina and Mecca, were barred to non-Muslims, but Burton's disguise and his skill in speaking Arabic were so perfect that he was able to visit them undetected. He was the first Westerner ever to do so, and later he published an account of his adventures.

Burton returned from Arabia and fought in the Crimean War. Then in 1854 he set out with **Speke** to explore Somaliland, a region of East Africa, and specifically to search for the source of the river Nile. They were the first whites to explore Lake Tanganyika, but they argued over whether or not it was the true source of the Nile, and parted company. Travelling alone, Speke discovered Lake Victoria, and he returned to London with the news that this was the source of the Nile. Burton, angry at losing the credit he thought he deserved, demanded a public debate to settle the matter. But Speke accidentally shot himself before it could take place, and the row was left unsettled.

Burton never lost his love of exploration, and spent several years travelling in the USA before working for the British government in Africa and Brazil, and as consul in Syria. He wrote many books about his travels, and translated some of the great books of the East into English, including *The Arabian Nights* and two famous books about sex and love – the Indian *Kama Sutra* and the Arabic *The Perfumed Garden*. Both books were considered shocking in Burton's time, and are still banned in some countries.

When Burton died he was buried in a stone tomb, carved to look like an Arabian tent – complete with tassels, entrance flaps and dangling camel bells.

Burton could easily pass as an Arab when he disguised himself, and was able to explore parts of Arabia that few other Westerners ever saw.

BURTON: Speke 210

An illustration advertising the "Underground Railway" from the *Western Citizen* in 1844. The "railway" was an escape network formed to help runaway slaves escape from the southern states of America to freedom in the north.

The former slave Harriet Tubman became a "conductor" of the Underground Railroad, guiding many slaves to freedom.

TUBMAN, Harriet

US campaigner against slavery c 1825-1913

Tubman was born into slavery in Maryland, but in 1849 escaped to Philadelphia. She went back to rescue her sister and brother and their families, which became the start of her dangerous work smuggling black slaves to freedom. A network system developed, which was nicknamed "the underground railway", and people like Tubman were known as "conductors". She was wanted, dead or alive, in many slave-owning states, but was so skilled at disguises that she was never caught, and led over 300 slaves to freedom. During the civil war she worked as cook and nurse for the northern army, and on one raid guided soldiers so that they could free 700 slaves. After the war she worked to provide schools for freed slaves and campaigned for women's rights. She went on travelling and lecturing until she was well over 80.

SPEKE, John Hanning

English explorer 1827-64

Ever since **Bruce** discovered the source of the Blue Nile, the Royal Geographical Society of London was determined to find the source of its companion stream, the White Nile. In 1857 they paid for an expedition by **Burton** and Speke, two professional explorers. Burton and Speke disliked each other intensely, which didn't bother their employers but caused trouble throughout their expedition.

After a difficult journey Burton and Speke reached Lake Tanganyika in East Africa: the longest freshwater lake in the world. They were the first white people ever to see it, but at once they quarrelled over whether they really had discovered the source of the White Nile. The two explorers parted angrily and Speke, travelling alone, came to a huge inland sea, which he called Lake Victoria after the English queen. He went home in triumph, proclaiming that Lake Victoria was the source of the White Nile. He persuaded the Royal Geographical Society to send him to Africa again, to prove his claim. In 1862, near Lake Victoria, he found a high waterfall ending in a broad, deep river. Certain that this river was the White Nile, he decided that there was no need to follow its entire course to join the sea.

Speke returned to London and published a book about his travels. While many readers believed his claim that Lake Victoria was the White Nile's source, **Livingstone**, Burton and other African explorers did not, because Speke had not proved it by sailing down the river to the sea. Before a public debate could be held Speke accidentally shot himself. After his death, further exploration by Burton, Livingstone and others who had criticized Speke finally proved him right: Lake Victoria is the source of the White Nile.

SPEKE: Bruce 187 Burton 209 Livingstone 204

DUNANT, Jean Henri

Swiss relief-worker 1828-1910

Dunant was a businessman from Switzerland, a neutral nation (one which takes no side in wars). Few civilians had any idea of what battlefield conditions were really like, but in 1859 Dunant was accidentally caught up among the wounded soldiers after the battle of Solférino and saw for himself the pain and suffering. In 1862 Dunant suggested that an international organization should be created to help the medical services on the battlefield. It would be politically neutral, and would give help to all sides equally. Its symbol, a red cross – or, in non-Christian countries, a red star or crescent – would appear on its buildings, vehicles and the clothes of its workers, so that no one would mistake them for enemies.

In 1869 the Red Cross decided to give help not only in war, but also with such disasters as floods, earthquakes, epidemics and famine. It quickly grew into one of the world's main relief organizations, and Dunant's work earned him the first-ever Nobel Peace prize in 1901. The International Red Cross organization itself won the prize in 1917, 1944 and 1963.

Above: Henri Dunant, founder of the Red Cross, suggested that the wounded, and those tending them, should be seen as neutral. *Below:* Members of the International Committee of the Red Cross in 1981, help in the exchange of prisoners taken during the Iran-Iraq war.

The Arctic explorer, Nordenskjöld.

NORDENSKJÖLD, Nils Adolf Erik

Swedish explorer and scientist 1832-1901

Nordenskjöld grew up in Finland, where he studied mineralogy and chemistry. When he was 28 he went to work for the Swedish Museum of Natural History. He made several expeditions to Greenland and Spitsbergen in the Arctic Circle, and in 1868 set a record for the most northerly journey ever made by Europeans until that time. In 1878 he led an expedition, in the Swedish navy ship *Vega*, to try to navigate the northeast passage through the icy northern seas to the Pacific Ocean. Although his ship was trapped in ice for nine months off the Siberian coast, it successfully completed the voyage and returned to Stockholm in 1880, the first ship ever to sail this route. The careful planning and detail of the *Vega*'s voyage is recorded in Nordenskjöld's accounts of the expedition. His methods inspired and guided many other explorers in the world's frozen waters.

Right: Cartoon of Andrew Carnegie holding four of the many libraries he financed.

Below: The *Vega* expedition under Nordenskjöld, 1878-79.

CARNEGIE, Andrew

Scottish/US businessman 1835-1919

Carnegie made millions of dollars from oil, steel and railways. But he believed that rich people should share their wealth with the workers who helped to create it. When he retired from business in 1901 he began giving money away to build universities, libraries, concert-halls and parks in towns, both in Britain and the USA. He also gave scholarships to schools and universities and he founded a yearly prize to encourage people to work for international peace. No one knows the exact total of his gifts, but it would be equivalent today to billions of dollars.

ANDERSON, Elizabeth Garrett

English doctor 1836-1917

When Garrett was a girl, women were barred from many professions: there were no women politicians, lawyers, religious leaders or doctors. But Garrett was determined to become a doctor. Women were not allowed to study at any of the official English medical schools, so she had to learn medicine privately at home, and in 1865 was the first woman to pass the Apothecaries' Hall exam. In 1870 the University of Paris gave her a medical degree, and she became the first qualified woman doctor in Europe. Her success encouraged other women to take up a career in medicine, and in 1884 the London School of Medicine for Women was founded. She also became Mayor of Aldeburgh – the first woman mayor in England.

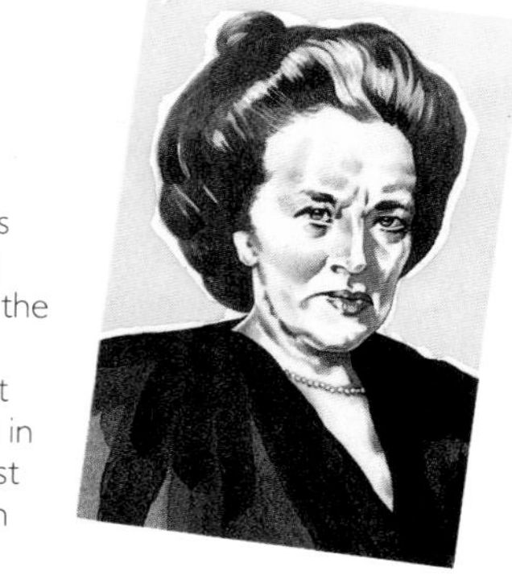

This stained-glass window (above) commemorates the achievement of Elizabeth Garrett Anderson (right) in becoming the first woman doctor in Europe.

MAUCH: Solomon 408

MAUCH, Karl

German explorer 1837-75

Mauch was the first European to see the fabulous ancient city of Great Zimbabwe, the heart of a large African trading nation which had existed 1,500 years earlier. He (wrongly) identified it with Ophir, a region fabled for its gold and precious stones, from where, according to the Old Testament, the Queen of Sheba went to visit King **Solomon** of Israel. The modern state of Zimbabwe is named after the city.

The walled remains of the ancient city of Great Zimbabwe, heart of a powerful nation which flourished between the thirteenth and fifteenth centuries. Many artistic symbols of this lost civilization have been discovered, including the Great Zimbabwe Birds.

Nikolai Przhevalski.

PRZHEVALSKI (Przewalski), Nikolai Mikhailovich

Russian explorer 1839-88

Przhevalski, a Russian army officer, led exploration teams into the remote regions of Mongolia, Turkestan and Tibet, reaching to within 202 km of the "forbidden city" of Lhasa. His surveys of the mountains and rivers of Central Asia are the basis of maps still used today, and he made a valuable collection of unusual plants and animals, including a rare species of wild horse which was named after him. He died in Karakul, near the Chinese-Russian border; the town was later renamed Przhevalsk to honour him.

ROCKEFELLER FAMILY

US industrialists and benefactors 19th-20th centuries

The Rockefellers ran a farm business, dealing in hay, grain, meat and other products. In the 1860s they realized the value of oil – which many people found on their land and regarded as a nuisance – and began buying it in quantity for their oil refinery in Cleveland, Ohio. Six years later they formed the Standard Oil Company, and by the end of the nineteenth century the family owned 98% of the entire US oil industry.

The Rockefellers, like **Carnegie**, felt that rich people ought to share their wealth. JOHN ROCKEFELLER Senior (1839-1937) began a family "trust", a company formed especially to give money to deserving causes. He and his son JOHN D. ROCKEFELLER Junior (1874-1960) gave over five billion dollars to build hospitals, churches and universities and to finance medical research. The Rockefeller Foundation was set up in 1913 to "promote the well-being of mankind" and JOHN Junior 3rd (1906-78) became its chairman. Eager to help bring about world peace, he also gave land to the United Nations for its New York City headquarters. His brother NELSON ROCKEFELLER (1906-79) decided to help people by going into politics. He was particularly interested in welfare: looking after those too poor to help themselves. He was Governor of New York State for 14 years, and was elected US vice-president in 1974.

A man called six times to give Mr. Rockefeller a cure for dyspepsia. But John D. knows what he needs.

A cartoon of the tycoon John Rockefeller, taking his daily dose of oil. The family fortune was built up by quite ruthless means, and Rockefeller was known throughout America as "the father of trusts, the king of monopolists, the tsar of the oil business".

ROCKEFELLER: Carnegie 212

STANLEY, Henry Morton

Welsh journalist and explorer 1841-1904

At the age of 15, Stanley went to sea as a cabin-boy, sailed to America and joined the army. The American Civil War was beginning, and Stanley fought first for one side, then for the other. But his skills as a journalist were becoming clear, and he wrote colourful accounts of his adventures and sent them to several newspapers. In 1867, aged 26, he was a top reporter, working for the *New York Herald.* At first he covered the US interior, reporting on government treatment of the native Americans (see **Geronimo**), but he was soon travelling widely as the paper's special correspondent. He went to Zanzibar to investigate the slave trade and to Egypt in 1869 to describe the opening of **de Lesseps**' Suez Canal. When news came that **Livingstone**, the greatest explorer of the day, was missing in Africa, the paper sent Stanley to find him.

Thanks to his journalist's skill at finding things out, Stanley tracked Livingstone down on the shores of Lake Tanganyika – and greeted him casually enough, after a 1,000-kilometre safari through "darkest" Africa: "Doctor Livingstone, I presume?" The two men spent some time exploring together, before Stanley returned home and published a triumphant account: *How I found Livingstone.* The book brought him international fame, and two other newspapers asked him to complete Livingstone's work. He was sent to cross the African continent, explore the Congo river, and investigate all the theories about the true source of the river Nile.

When Stanley was 54 he gave up exploring and went into politics, becoming a British MP. In his will, he asked to be buried in Westminster Abbey, next to Livingstone. The request was refused – one of the few failures in Stanley's busy, ever-surprising and exciting life.

Henry Stanley, the journalist turned explorer, who found David Livingstone.

STANLEY: Livingstone 204 Geronimo 456 De Lesseps 362

SLOCUM, Joshua

US sailor 1844-c 1910

Slocum was a captain in the merchant navy, carrying trade-goods from country to country across the world. In 1886 he made a private expedition to South America with his wife and children. They were shipwrecked off the coast of Brazil, but managed to build a canoe and paddle 8,000 km back to New York. In 1895 Slocum set off from Boston to be the first person to sail single-handed round the world. Three years later he returned in triumph, and published an account of his journey. In 1909 he set out on another solo voyage, and was never seen again.

NATION, Carry

US campaigner against alcohol 1846-1911

Nation's first husband was an alcoholic, and his behaviour so outraged her that it turned her into a fanatical opponent of drinking. Other anti-alcohol campaigners gave lectures about the evils of drink; Nation and her followers stormed into bars with axes and smashed everything in sight. Nation was a terrifying sight on these expeditions: a tall woman dressed in black and white, wielding a huge axe while her followers sang hymns. Her opponents beat her up, knifed her, shot at her, and took her to court – she paid her fines by selling souvenir axes. She also campaigned against "pin-up" photos, smoking and foreign food.

Left: The formidable figure of Carry Nation. A tiny axe worn as a brooch was the symbol of her anti-alcohol campaign. She was nicknamed the "bar-room smasher".

WOOLWORTH, Frank Winfield

US businessman 1852-1919

Woolworth worked as a farm labourer before becoming a shop-assistant. He had the idea of starting a shop where everything would cost exactly the same low price. The first shop failed, but the second, called a "five-and-dime" store because everything cost either five cents or ten cents (a dime) was a triumph. The company soon had a chain of stores and, at the time of Woolworth's death, there were over 1,000 in America, with others being built in Britain and elsewhere around the world.

The Woolworth headquarters in New York was, for a time, the tallest building in the world, over 240 m high. It is now dwarfed by modern skyscrapers.

RHODES, Cecil

English settler 1853-1902

Many Europeans in Rhodes' day believed that unless white people took control in Africa, the black Africans would never take their place in the modern world. By taking over the industrial development of

A portrait of Cecil Rhodes.

Southern Africa, many white settlers made their fortunes. Rhodes, for one, managed gold-mines and diamond-mines in South Africa, and quickly became a multi-millionaire. He treated his workers as if the mining company were a kingdom and he were its prince.

In 1887 the British government, keen to gain new territory in Africa, asked Rhodes to settle the area north of South Africa. He established a new colony, Cape Colony, and was its prime minister from 1890-6. It was called Rhodesia after him (now the Republic of Zimbabwe). Rhodes believed in white supremacy – a belief that continues to dominate politics in Southern Africa. However, for the black people, rule by Rhodes was not all bad. His factories provided employment, and a higher living-standard than most people could earn as farmers. He also paid for nearly 200 "colonials" to study in British universities each year, hoping that they would return to rule their own countries and spread Western ways. His dream was to make Africa British from "Cairo to Cape Town", convinced that he had the best interests of Africa, as well as of the British Empire, at heart.

Robert E Peary, leader of the first expedition to reach the North Pole.

PEARY, Robert Edwin

US explorer 1856-1920

Peary, an American navy admiral, had read **Nordenskjöld**'s book *Exploration of Interior Greenland*, and was inspired to take up polar exploration himself. He hoped to be the first explorer to cross Greenland, and was disappointed when **Nansen** did so before he had time to organize a US expedition. However, Nansen was sure that if carefully made advance camps were set up, a team of explorers carrying only light packs could make a quick dash to the North Pole – and he recommended Peary as leader of that expedition. In 1909, after two failed attempts, Peary, his assistant Matthew Henson, and four Inuit Eskimos were the first men to reach the Pole.

Even then, the story was not over. Another American, Frederick Alfred Cook, contested Peary's claims, saying that he had reached the Pole months before Peary – and he certainly arrived home first. For months his story was believed. But then Peary produced photographs and other convincing evidence – and Cook had none. Everyone accepted Peary's claim, and Cook was jailed for defrauding the companies who had invested money in his expedition.

PEARY: Nansen 219 Nordenskjöld 212

Baden-Powell, in scout uniform.

BADEN-POWELL, Robert Stephenson Smyth

English soldier and Chief Scout 1857-1941

As a small boy, Baden-Powell was fascinated by stories of **Crockett**, **Boone** and other US frontiersmen, especially by their skills – stalking prey, making bivouacs, lighting fires – developed for survival in the wild. This interest served him well in later life, when he joined the army as an officer. By 1899, when the British were fighting the Boers in South Africa, he was a general and won fame defending the town of Mafeking. He noticed how useful locally recruited "scouts" were: young boys trained in stalking, camping skills, carrying messages and generally doing everything the adult soldiers did except fight.

When Baden-Powell returned to England, he founded the Boy Scouts, a youth movement giving boys a taste of soldierly activities, but for fun instead of for battle. He took groups of boys camping, and in 1908 published *Scouting for Boys*, setting out his ideas. The scout movement quickly spread, and in 1910 Baden-Powell and his sister founded the Girl Guides, to give the same chances to girls. (In those days, when equality between the sexes was rare, this was a revolutionary idea.)

The Pankhursts protested publicly to win women the right to vote.

PANKHURST FAMILY

English feminists 19th-20th century

EMMELINE PANKHURST (1858-1928) was a friend of **Stanton**, and they agreed that if men would not give women the vote by choice, they should be forced to. With her daughters CHRISTABEL 1880-1958) and SYLVIA (1882-1960), she formed the Women's Social and Political Union, and toured Britain making speeches about women's rights. They would chain themselves to railings, in public protest at women's unfair treatment. All three Pankhursts were imprisoned, but they continued to demand fair treatment of women by going on hunger strike.

In the First World War women did the work of men who had gone to fight. And, when the war ended, British women finally won the vote. Emmeline and Christabel planned to continue their campaign for women's rights but Emmeline was in poor health, and she died. Christabel gave up politics and turned to preaching. In the 1930s Sylvia joined the communist party and, when **Mussolini**'s army invaded Ethiopia, she went to live there and to work for the poor.

BADEN-POWELL: Boone 188 Crockett 200 PANKHURST FAMILY: Stanton 206 Mussolini 465

ADDAMS, Jane

US social reformer 1860-1935

Addams was lucky: she was rich, educated and beautiful. So she was horrified to see for herself how the poor lived, and, with a friend, Ellen Starr, bought Hull House in a poverty-stricken area of Chicago. At first, it was run as a private charity, providing leisure facilities, a nursery, a dispensary and classes in the arts and physical fitness. But Addams decided that poverty needed tackling at the state level. Armed with statistics, she successfully campaigned for an act that insisted on safe conditions in factories, provided the first juvenile court, gave recognition to trade unions, and set a maximum eight-hour day for women working in factories.

Gradually Addams moved into national politics. She worked for women's right to vote and racial equality, and spoke out against US involvement in the First World War. She was awarded the Nobel Peace prize in 1936.

NANSEN, Fridtjof

Norwegian explorer and statesman 1861-1930

Nansen first visited the Arctic when he was 21. Amazed at the size of Greenland, he determined to be the first person ever to cross it from east to west – a feat he achieved in 1888, on skis. He then formed a plan to reach the North Pole by letting the drifting ice-cap carry his ship. He allowed his specially designed ship, *Fram* ("Onward"), to get frozen into an ice-floe and drift with the current. The "hitch-hike" journey lasted for three years, and although Nansen and his crew never reached the Pole – which lay out of the path of the ocean currents moving the ice – his expedition went further north than any previous exploration.

For a time after this expedition Nansen worked as a scientist in Oslo. But he also turned his attention to politics. After Norway won its independence from Sweden in 1905, he was sent as the Norwegian ambassador to Britain. During the First World War, and the Russian Revolution which followed it, he organized food aid for starving refugees, for which he won the Nobel Peace prize in 1922. He did much for international peace by helping to set up the League of Nations, a forerunner of the United Nations.

The Norwegian explorer Nansen, who used skis to cross Greenland, the largest island in the world.

The Ford Model T, or "tin Lizzie", the first "people's car", built in 1908.

FORD, Henry

US businessman 1863-1947

When Ford was in his teens, cars were built by teams of craftsmen, and only the very rich could afford to buy one. Ford dreamed of making cheap cars for ordinary people. To do this, he invented the "production line", now used in factories worldwide. On a production line, each person (or, today, a robot) does one job, time and time again. The goods are moved along a conveyer belt, very slowly, and as they pass each worker a new part is added, or a new process takes place. At the end of the line the goods are complete.

Ford's production-line factories made hundreds of cars each day, and by 1928 28 million had been sold in the USA alone. Ford's best-known car was the "Model T", nicknamed "tin Lizzie". This is the kind of car used in the old **Laurel** and **Hardy** films. When other manufacturers started making even cheaper cars, Ford brought out a new model – which started the idea that a car has a limited life. Today millions of people will buy the latest model every three or four years.

FORD: Laurel and Hardy 258

HEARST, William Randolph

US newspaper owner 1863-1951

When Hearst was 22 he was thrown out of university for writing mocking articles about his professors. He took over his father's newspaper, the *San Francisco Examiner*, and his career began. Hearst thought that what people wanted from papers was entertainment, not information, and that meant news had to be fun. His reporters wrote sensational stories about enemy spies, UFOs, sex scandals and horrific murders. Hearst pioneered the use of comic strips, huge photographs, and what the modern press calls "screamers" – sensational headlines filling most of a page and meant to grab attention. When Hearst took over the *New York Journal* in 1895 its sales trebled. Jealous rivals (such as **Pulitzer**) called Hearst's papers "the yellow press" or "the gutter press", claiming that his reporters intruded on

Portrait of Henry Ford, American engineer and founder of the Ford Motor Company.

The luxurious swimming pool of the newspaper tycoon William Hearst. His home at San Simeon, California, was filled with whatever money could buy, and wild animals roamed the grounds of the mansion.

people's privacy and were happy to invent smears and lies. Many people were alarmed at the way Hearst's papers formed opinion in the USA. People believed what they read in their papers, whether it was the truth, or biased or false.

Whatever the critics thought, the public loved Hearst's ideas, and there was soon a "gutter press" in all countries. Hearst became one of the richest people in the world. He owned land and property in many towns, financed films starring the women he loved, and tried to use his influence to enter politics. He built himself a fairy-tale castle in California, stuffed with treasures from all round the world.

SCOTT, Robert Falcon

English naval officer and explorer 1868-1912

Scott spent the two summers of 1899-1901 in the Antarctic, making maps and scientific notes. His expedition got closer to the South Pole than any previous team. In 1909 **Shackleton**, one of Scott's junior officers, led a separate expedition and nearly reached the Pole. Scott was determined to get there first and gathered backers to fund a private expedition of his own.

Unlike other Antarctic explorers, Scott thought dog-sledges were inefficient. Instead, he equipped his 1910 expedition with motor-sledges and ponies. But the sledge engines broke down and the ponies sank in the snow. Dragging the sledges themselves, Scott and four companions began to trudge towards the Pole. But when they reached it they discovered that **Amundsen**'s Norwegian expedition, using dogs, had beaten them by a month.

Disheartened, Scott and his men turned back. They were weak from hunger and frostbite. One man, Evans, died of hypothermia, and another, Oates, knowing that he too was dying, bravely told the others that he was leaving the tent for a short time, and disappeared into a blizzard. Scott and his remaining companions struggled on, but finally all three died, only 16 km from safety.

For years after his expedition, Scott was honoured as a national hero. Recently, however, people have questioned his leadership and the methods he chose. If he had used Eskimo ways of travelling and keeping warm, as others did, he might have reached the Pole before Amundsen – and more importantly, he and his companions might have come back alive.

Scott's final expedition to the Antarctic ended in disaster. He reached the South Pole to find that his trek had been beaten by a Norwegian expedition. On the return journey he and his companions died of hypothermia.

SCOTT: Amundsen 222 Shackleton 224

LUXEMBURG, Rosa

Polish/German revolutionary 1870-1919

Luxemburg shared **Marx**'s ideas, and made speeches saying that capitalism should be overthrown and that a workers' state should be set up in Germany, giving a share in national wealth to the people whose hard work created it. During the First World War she was imprisoned for saying that the struggle had nothing to do with ordinary people, and that the soldiers should refuse to fight.

In 1917, after the Russian Revolution, Luxemburg (nicknamed "Red Rosa") and Karl Liebknecht founded the Spartacists, a militant group whose aim was to create a Russian-style revolution in Germany. They organized strikes, sit-ins and street protests. In 1919, they were murdered in Berlin (some say by the police, others by a right-wing mob). In the next few years, with the rise of **Hitler** and the Nazis, Marxism was banned in Germany. None the less, Luxemburg has never been forgotten as a founder, and martyr, of European communism.

MONTESSORI, Maria

Italian teacher 1870-1952

Until Montessori's time, all school-children, including infants, were taught in a strict, disciplined way. They sat up straight, learned what they were told, and dared not ask questions or move freely from their seats. Montessori felt that pupils would learn more, and be happier, if they were given the conditions to find out for themselves. The room should be organized not with straight rows of desks, but into "corners" and "areas", each allowing a new discovery or activity. Children should be encouraged to move about as they wanted. Other teachers of the time predicted a total collapse of classroom control. But Montessori tried her methods in slum schools and with backward children, and was triumphantly successful. In Western schools most infants' classrooms, and many for older children, are still organized using her ideas.

Maria Montessori founded a new approach to education, which allowed children to move freely from task to task in the classroom. Her methods are still used in Western schools: this photograph was taken in 1988 at the Montessori Children's House, part of the Maria Montessori Training Organization in Hampstead, London.

AMUNDSEN, Roald Engelbregt Gravning

Norwegian explorer 1872-1928

Amundsen had always wanted to be an explorer. He was fascinated by accounts of **Franklin**'s search for the "northwest passage", the route round the icy wastes of North America to the Pacific Ocean – and in 1903-6 he was captain of the first ship ever to make the journey. Fired by the success of this trip, he made plans to be the first person to reach both the North and the South Poles. He made careful preparations, studying the

Amundsen, the Norwegian explorer who reached the South Pole in 1911.

LUXEMBERG: Hitler 466 Marx 369 AMUNDSEN: Franklin 200 Peary 217 Scott, J 221 methods native Arctic dwellers used to keep warm and dry, and ways of reducing the weight of his dog-sleds by more than two-thirds. In 1909 he was beaten to the North Pole by **Peary**, but two years later, in a race against **Scott**'s expedition, he was first to reach the South Pole.

In later life, Amundsen interested himself in airships and aeroplanes. In 1926, with Lincoln Ellsworth and Umberto Nobile, he flew across the Arctic – the first time this had ever been done. In 1928 Nobile set out to reach the North Pole by airship, and crashed. Amundsen led the search party for Nobile, but was killed when his plane also crashed.

RUBINSTEIN, Helena

Polish/American businesswoman c 1872-1965

In the 1900s, there were very few women in business. Rubinstein opened a London beauty salon in 1908 – the start to her worldwide cosmetics empire.

Helena Rubinstein's beauty products are world-famous. She introduced one of the first cosmetics ranges for men and also the health-farm idea as an aid to beauty.

BLÉRIOT, Louis

French aircraft pioneer 1872-1936

In 1909 Blériot was the first person to fly a plane across the Channel from France to England. He had scalded his foot the day before, and was on crutches. The morning was so misty that he had to ask bystanders in which direction the Channel, and Dover, lay. His flight was the longest over water anyone had made, and lasted 38 minutes. Blériot went on to found a plane-making company, which built many of the aircraft used by France in the First World War.

Right: Louis Blériot was the first person to cross the Channel in a heavier-than-air aircraft. The crossing from Calais to Dover won him a £1,000 prize offered by the *Daily Mail* newspaper.

McCLUNG, Nellie Letitia

Canadian feminist and writer 1873-1951

McClung taught herself to read and write. One of her favourite authors was **Dickens**, and she grew up horrified to think that the grim conditions he described could still exist for the poorest of people. When she was older she campaigned for equal justice for everyone – rich or poor – for women's right to vote, and for a ban on alcohol. In 1916 Canada's Western Provinces finally allowed women to vote.

McClung was also a writer. One of her books is the famous children's story *Sowing Seeds in Danny*. Many libraries and colleges in Canada are named after her.

McCLUNG: Dickens 36

A cartoon of the Irish explorer, Ernest Shackleton, which appeared in 1909, after Shackleton's expedition reached the South Magnetic Pole.

SHACKLETON, Ernest Henry

Irish explorer 1874-1922

As a naval officer, Shackleton joined **Scott**'s Antarctic expedition of 1899. He led a party further south on the polar ice than anyone had been before, and might have reached the South Pole itself, but he fell ill with scurvy and had to be sent home. In 1909, commanding a second expedition, Shackleton set a new record: he and his men reached the South Magnetic Pole, and came within 150 km of the true South Pole.

But it was **Amundsen** who reached the South Pole first, in 1911, and Shackleton's ambition changed. In 1914 his party set out to be the first to cross the vast continent of Antarctica. But ice crushed their ship, the *Endeavour*, and they were marooned on Elephant Island. Shackleton and five companions made an heroic journey of over 1,200 km in a small boat across the stormy South Atlantic to fetch help. Thanks to this brave act, and to Shackleton's leadership, not one life was lost.

BINGHAM, Hiram

US professor and explorer 1878-1956

Bingham, a history professor at Yale University, was fascinated by the Inca ruins of Peru. In 1911 he led the expedition which discovered the fabulous ruined city, Machu Picchu.

TROTSKY, Leon

Russian revolutionary 1879-1940

Leon Trotsky was the pseudonym of Lev Davidovich Bronstein. Aged 19, he was sent to Siberia for belonging to a Marxist group. But he escaped, and befriended **Lenin**, whom he helped to organize the 1917 Russian Revolution. In the civil war which followed, he took charge of the Red Army, and in four years built it up from 7,000 to five million men.

When Lenin died in 1924, the two most powerful men in Russia were Trotsky and **Stalin**. But Stalin wanted complete control and plotted against Trotsky – who accused him of

SHACKLETON: Amundsen 222 Scott, J 221 TROTSKY: Lenin 460 Stalin 462

dictatorship. The struggle ended with Trotsky being imprisoned, and finally banished from Russia in 1929. He spent the 1930s touring Europe, giving his own version of what had happened. Stalin sentenced Trotsky to death in his absence in 1937. He was murdered in 1940, stabbed with an ice-pick by an assassin in Mexico City.

Trotsky believed that communism – equality for all in the creation and enjoyment of wealth – was the way to organize civilized society. But he thought that since most countries were run by capitalists and other rich people they would never accept a system which meant that their share would have to dwindle as other people's grew. His answer was "world revolution". Workers everywhere should revolt against the rich and replace all other systems of government with a communist state. For a time in the early 1920s this was Russian policy, and there are still "Trotskyites" in many countries who believe in working to destroy old forms of government so that communism can take their place.

Leon Trotsky, one of the leading figures in the Russian Revolution of 1917. He became the minister responsible for war and foreign affairs in the first Russian Soviet government.

KELLER, Helen Adams

US writer 1880-1968

As a baby Keller had scarlet fever so badly that it left her blind and totally deaf. The only contact she had with the outside world was by touch. She was too young ever to have learned to read or to speak properly. But her parents refused to believe that this "wild creature" had no abilities, and hired a dedicated teacher, Annie Sullivan, to train their daughter. She taught the child to communicate; Keller learned to "hear" by touching people's throats as they spoke, and to talk by touching her own throat and experimenting until she made the same sounds. She went on to learn French and German, and was one of the first people to master braille (the system invented by **Braille**, allowing blind people to read by touching raised letter shapes).

Thanks to Sullivan's hard work, and her own enormous efforts, Keller was finally able to go to high school. She passed her exams and went on to university. She spent her life lecturing and writing about her fight to overcome her disabilities, and gave hope to thousands of handicapped people. She never allowed people to treat her differently because of her disadvantages – an attitude which made many people change the way they behaved towards all handicapped people. She raised over two million dollars for charities which helped the blind.

Helen Keller, the blind and deaf author and teacher who became an inspiration to handicapped people everywhere.

KELLER: Braille 364

George Marshall.

MARSHALL, George Catlett

US soldier and politician 1880-1959

After the Second World War Marshall organized American aid for the countries of Europe. Under the "Marshall Aid" plan, the USA sent billions of dollars to help rebuild Europe and to clothe and feed its people. Marshall won the Nobel Peace prize in 1953 – the first professional soldier ever to receive it.

OPPENHEIMER, Ernest

South African businessman and politician 1880-1957

Oppenheimer owned a large mining company in South Africa and, by the time of his death, his company controlled 95% of the world's supply of diamonds. Oppenheimer was also a philanthropist, interested in improving the lives of his fellow-citizens. He used his wealth to found libraries, schools and universities. He devised slum clearance schemes, and built good homes for his workers. After his death he left one third of his fortune to charity.

SHAARAWY, Hoda

Egyptian feminist 1882-1947

Shaarawy's family were devout followers of Islam, and wives were seen as their husbands' possessions. But she was a passionate believer in women's rights. She founded a girl's school – the first in Egypt – and became leader of the first women's rights association in the Arab world. She successfully campaigned to allow women to remove their veils in public (something thought shocking at the time). Later, she led the All-Arab Federation of Women, and after 1945 she spoke out against nuclear weapons.

PICCARD FAMILY

Swiss scientists and explorers 19th-20th century

Above, right: August Piccard, the Swiss scientist, inside the bathyscaphe he designed for exploring the ocean depths, preparing to make a dive.

AUGUSTE (1884-1962) and JEAN-FELIX (1884-1963) PICCARD were twin brothers; JACQUES (born 1922) is Auguste's son. Auguste took up ballooning as a way of collecting information about the stratosphere – and became fascinated by the idea of exploring the extremes of both sky and sea. In 1932 he made the highest-ever manned flight, 16,900 metres into the stratosphere – a record broken a few years later by Jean-Félix, who reached 17,672 metres. In 1953 Auguste and Jacques set another record – this time sinking 3,150 metres under the sea in a diving vessel called a bathyscaphe, and in 1960 Jacques descended 11 kilometres into the Mariana Trench in the Pacific Ocean.

ARDEN, Elizabeth

Canadian businesswoman 1884-1966

Arden trained as a nurse and then worked in a cosmetics shop. At the time, make-up often used impure ingredients – sometimes even dangerous chemicals. With her medical knowledge Arden prepared safer, cleaner beauty products, which were an instant success. Her first salon, opened in 1912, became the basis of a worldwide cosmetics empire.

GARVEY, Marcus Mosiah

Jamaican social reformer 1887-1940

Garvey was sacked from his foreman's job for organizing a strike in protest at the (white) owners' ill-treatment of the (black) workers. He went to work in Central America, and was horrified by the conditions he found among poor people, black and native Indian alike. He decided to spend his life trying to reform the system that made such miserable lives possible.

In 1914 Garvey founded UNIA, the Universal Negro Improvement Association, and the African Communities League (ACL). He travelled all over America and the Caribbean, giving talks on black history, black pride and black culture. He began a newspaper, *Negro World*, and founded schools and colleges for black education.

One of Garvey's ambitions was to set up black-owned businesses and banks in the USA, so that blacks would equal whites in power as well as in law. One of the businesses was a steamship company, and Garvey raised money for it by selling shares. But the company went bankrupt, and Garvey's white enemies had him arrested, tried for fraud (stealing people's money by making false promises), and sent to prison. President Coolidge pardoned him, on condition that he never again set foot in the USA. He spent the next seven years working as a politician in Jamaica, and then, in 1935, moved to London to restart UNIA. But no one showed any interest, and five years later Garvey died in poverty.

Although Garvey's personal career was tragic, his ideas lived on. He was the first person ever to teach that blacks and whites were equal, and in the 1960s US national laws on racial equality gave black people the chance of social and political respect which had been Garvey's lifelong dream.

The Jamaican Marcus Garvey, who campaigned throughout his life for racial equality.

MONTGOMERY, Bernard Law

English soldier 1887-1976

In 1942-43 Montgomery led the British army which defeated the Axis forces (made up of German Nazis, Italian Fascists and Japanese) in Egypt, chasing them from El Alamein at the mouth of the Nile across the desert to Tunisia, where they surrendered. He then led invasions of Sicily and Italy, and in 1944 helped to supervise the liberation of France from Nazi rule. After the war he was made deputy supreme commander of the NATO troops in Europe. He was a proud, peppery man, and stood no nonsense. Superior officers disliked his impertinence, but his soldiers loved him. Unlike many generals in history, who treated their men as "cannon-fodder", to be moved about like pawns on a chessboard, Montgomery never forgot that they were human beings. On his death-bed, he told a friend that he was embarrassed to think that in the after-life he would meet the thousands of men he had killed in his career. "Sir", said the friend, "They'll be overjoyed to see you".

BYRD, Richard Evelyn

US explorer and aviator 1888-1957

Byrd learned to fly with the Fleet Air Arm of the US Air Force. He was put in charge of the fuelling station for flying-boats trying to make the first Atlantic crossing and designed several navigation aids which helped them make the crossing in 1919. He later joined a small expedition to Greenland and decided to attempt the first flight over the North Pole. He succeeded in 1926, beating **Amundsen**, Ellsworth and Nobile. Three years later he set out to be first to fly over the South Pole too. He succeeded, although he had to throw out his emergency supplies to make the plane light enough to cross the Queen Maud Mountains.

In 1933 Byrd survived an entire winter alone in the Antarctic, but he was no longer interested in personal success. His attention was turned to scientific discovery, and he was made head of the US polar scientific programmes, supervising highly technological, government-funded expeditions.

Richard Byrd, the American explorer who lived by himself for five months on Ross Island in the Antarctic. He described his experience in a book, *Alone*.

LAWRENCE, Thomas Edward

English soldier 1888-1935

In his early 20s Lawrence was an archaeologist, excavating crusader castles in Syria and Palestine, and he got to know many of the nomadic desert tribes. When the First World War began he joined the British

The battle of El Alamein was fought by two of the greatest generals in history. Montgomery (left) inspired his men by his self-confidence, and he never lost a single battle.

BYRD: Amundsen 222

T E Lawrence led a small force of Arabs in their fight for freedom from Turkey.

Secret Service. Because he could speak Arabic and had travelled all over the Middle East, he was given the job of organizing a resistance movement, leading the Arabs (allies of Britain) against the Turks (allies of Germany). He spent the war as a desert freedom-fighter, and later wrote a book about it, *The Seven Pillars of Wisdom*, which made him famous. Both British and Arabs honoured him as a hero, and he was nicknamed Lawrence of Arabia.

In the 1920s Lawrence completely changed his life. He made no secret of his homosexuality, but he hated being mocked for it by his upper-class fellow army officers. He was also plagued by journalists hungry for stories. He joined the RAF, thinking that it would be more tolerant than the army. He enlisted as Aircraftsman Ross, and not as an officer. When the press discovered his trick he enlisted again, this time under the name of Shaw, and served peacefully for ten years. He was killed when his motorbike crashed in 1935.

ROMMEL, Erwin

German general 1891-1944

Rommel fought bravely in the First World War, and was quickly promoted. After the war he joined the Nazi party, and in the Second World War commanded the Afrika Korps in North Africa. He was famous for leading his soldiers from the front, showing little concern for his own safety. In 1942, however, the British, led by **Montgomery**, forced Rommel to retreat from El Alamein and he was recalled to Europe. **Hitler** put him in charge of defending the Channel coast of occupied France against an allied invasion from Britain. But, by this time, Rommel was convinced that Hitler was a madman and that, unless he was removed from power, Germany would lose the war. Rommel supported **von Stauffenberg**'s plot to kill Hitler in 1944 and, when the plot was discovered, knowing he would be shot, he committed suicide.

The military skills and daring of Rommel (right) were admired even by his opponents, and he was nicknamed Desert Fox.

ALCOCK, John William

British aviator 1892-1919

and

BROWN, Arthur Whitten

British aviator 1886-1948

In 1919 Alcock and Brown attempted the most ambitious flight ever made at that time – a 3,000 km non-stop journey across the Atlantic, from Newfoundland to Ireland. The flight lasted 16 hours, 27 minutes – a record which stood for eight years, till **Lindbergh** flew the same distance single-handed.

ROMMEL: Montgomery 228 Stauffenberg 232 Hitler 466 ALCOCK AND BROWN: Lindbergh 231

SANDINO, Augusto César

Nicaraguan soldier 1893-1934

In 1926-27 there was civil war in Nicaragua, between supporters of two political groups: the liberals and the conservatives. The USA came up with a peace settlement, but Sandino (a liberal) refused to accept it . The USA sent "military advisers" to train the Nicaraguan National Guard – and also sent the Marines to fight Sandino's followers, forcing them to retreat to the mountains. Sandino was supported by the local people and by many other Latin-American countries, alarmed by what they thought was American interference in the internal affairs of a foreign nation. In 1933, unable to defeat the guerrillas, the US Marines left Nicaragua, and the Nicaraguan president began to negotiate a treaty with Sandino. But Somoza, the conservative leader of the National Guard, had Sandino and his fellow guerrilla leaders murdered. Somoza seized power, but Sandino's fame as a patriot spread over a large part of Latin America. Later Nicaraguan politicians have called themselves the Sandinistas after him.

HEATH, Sophia

US/British air pioneer and feminist 1896-1939

Heath was a keen sportswoman, and a founder of the British Women's Amateur Athletic Association in 1922. She was the only woman allowed to give evidence to the International Olympic Committee when they were deciding if women could take part in the Olympic Games. She learned to fly planes and fought the ban on women becoming commercial air pilots. She took and passed all the tests for pilots and the ban was lifted. She broke several air records and became the first woman pilot for KLM (Royal Dutch Airlines). She spent the last years of her life working for safety in the air. In 1936 she was severely injured in an air crash, and eventually died from her wounds.

EARHART, Amelia

US air pioneer 1898-c 1937

In 1928 Earhart became the first woman to fly a plane solo across the Atlantic, and in 1935 she made an even longer solo flight across the Pacific. Two years later, attempting to be the first person to fly all the way round the world, she vanished and no one has ever found out what became of her.

Woman air pioneers Amelia Earhart (below) and Amy Johnson (right).

"Scarface"

CAPONE, Al

American gangster 1899-1947

At the turn of the twentieth century, immigrants from Europe poured into America. Many were extremely poor people, others were criminals, some of whom were from southern Italy and Sicily – home of the Mafia. They settled in the big cities, such as New York and Chicago, and organized gambling, prostitution, burglary and other crimes. Al Capone was one of the Chicago gang leaders.

In 1919 the US government banned the sale and drinking of alcohol. The Prohibition, as it was called, lasted until 1933. Big-city criminals made fortunes by buying cheap whisky and selling it at a great profit. They bribed their way out of trouble or, if bribery failed, they used guns. During the 24 years of Prohibition Capone's profits were calculated at over a billion dollars.

In 1931 Capone was arrested. But people were too frightened to give evidence against him, and the authorities could only charge him with not paying his income tax. He was sent to prison for 10 years. But when the USA entered the Second World War there was less scope for organized crime. Capone died a lonely, bitter man – a sorry end for the one-time king of crime.

Charles Lindbergh (right) made history with his solo non-stop flight from New York to Paris. He was greeted by enormous crowds, and became a hero internationally. But his fame also brought tragedy and pain, when his young son was kidnapped and killed.

LINDBERGH, Charles Augustus

US air pioneer 1902-74

In 1927 Lindbergh became the first person to fly the Atlantic single-handed – from New York to Paris – a record attempt which had already claimed six lives. His plane was named *Spirit of St Louis*, and he later wrote a book about his trip with the same title.

JOHNSON, Amy

English air pioneer 1903-41

Johnson specialized in breaking records in long-distance flying, a dangerous but exciting sport in the flimsy planes of her time. She flew solo from Britain to Australia in 1930, to Japan via Siberia in 1931 and in 1936 she broke the record for the fastest flight between London and Cape Town. In the Second World War she became a delivery pilot, flying new planes from factories to the airfields. Flying over London in 1941 she had engine trouble, and is thought to have bailed out and drowned in the river Thames.

The tycoon Howard Hughes designed and flew some amazing aircraft. His *Spruce Goose* was an enormous wooden seaplane, which only once flew successfully. It is now on display in Florida in the USA.

SPOCK, Benjamin McLane

US doctor and writer 1903-87

Spock was a child-care expert, and in 1946 he wrote *A Common Sense Book of Baby and Child Care*. It sold in millions throughout the world. Spock thought that if parents learned to communicate with their children, even as tiny babies, trying to understand their individual needs and feelings, both children and parents would be happier. It sounds obvious today, but in the 1940s it was a revolutionary idea, and was angrily opposed by other child-doctors, who thought that the old ways were best.

Spock's views affected the upbringing of a whole generation born in the 1940s and early 1950s. Children of the "Spock generation" were thought to be healthier and happier than any group before them. But in the USA they also grew up to fight in the 1960s Vietnam War, and thousands were killed or maimed. Spock, horrified that "his babies" were being slaughtered, spoke out against the war. He wrote a book, *Dr Spock on Vietnam*, went on marches, gave lectures and appeared on television attacking the government. He stood for the US presidency in 1972 and the vice-presidency in 1976. His rivals called him a crank and a fool, and his political chances were ruined. But, more importantly, his ideas had changed the way children were brought up throughout the Western world.

Dr Spock, with one of the generation which was brought up on the advice of Spock's *Book of Baby and Child Care*. When his book was published, it outsold the Bible.

HUGHES, Howard Robard

US businessman 1905-76

Hughes inherited a fortune from his father, and used it to finance films and design aircraft. He built and flew some of the fastest planes then known. In 1946 Hughes survived a plane-crash, but his character changed. He hated meeting people, and although he controlled the US airline TWA, he would only do business over the telephone. People claimed that he never washed, shaved or cut his hair or nails. Nowadays people still remember him for his weird lifestyle – and forget that he was once one of the USA's most successful film producers and aircraft designers.

STAUFFENBERG, Berthold von

German army officer 1907-44

Von Stauffenberg worked with **Hitler** in the small room from which German army movements were controlled in the Second World War. He, along with other officers, became convinced that Hitler was mad, and that he was leading Germany into disaster. A plan was made to assassinate Hitler, and von Stauffenberg had to leave a bomb hidden in a briefcase at a meeting with Hitler. Just before the bomb was due to explode, von Stauffenburg left the meeting – and, by chance, someone moved the briefcase to the other side of the table from Hitler, thus lessening the force of the blast. Hitler survived the explosion, and ordered his soldiers to strangle von Stauffenberg with piano wire.

STAUFFENBERG: Hitler 466

McCARTHY, Joseph Raymond

US politician 1909-57

McCarthy was an extreme right-winger – he was fanatically against communists, homosexuals, blacks, and anyone else he suspected of "polluting" the American way of life – an alarming set of prejudices for a man who was a state judge. He was elected to the Senate in 1950, but his real reign of terror began in 1953 when he was made chairman of a spy-hunting committee to investigate whether there were communists within the US government. In a series of unofficial trials, often on television, he interrogated anyone he suspected of having left-wing views of any kind. A number of mostly innocent citizens and officials were victimized by McCarthy. He would shout at and insult them, make up evidence, and would even demand that they proved their loyalty to the USA by handing over lists of any friends or colleagues who might have communist sympathies. Dozens of people committed suicide; thousands lost their jobs; and only a few dared answer McCarthy back.

Finally, McCarthy went too far. He made a verbal attack on J Robert **Oppenheimer**, leader of the team which had developed the atomic bomb in the 1940s. There was public outcry: "McCarthyism" was at last discredited and the "witch hunts" were over.

In the seven years of his power, McCarthy was one of the most feared men in the USA and he probably did more than anyone else to damage the USA's reputation for free speech and political openness.

Senator McCarthy, exhibiting "evidence" which he claimed proved there were spies within the US government. Little he did or said seems to have been true, but he succeeded in making headline news and terrorizing many people.

COUSTEAU, Jacques-Yves

French underwater explorer born 1910

Cousteau invented the aqualung while he was a naval officer, but kept it secret during the Second World War, to prevent the Nazis from using it. He also developed underwater television cameras and, after the war, he retired from the navy and became a pioneer of underwater filming and research, explaining the sea's mysteries and wonders to huge TV audiences.

McCARTHY: Oppenheimer, E 154

Mother Teresa, the Roman Catholic missionary, famous throughout the world for her work with the poor in India.

MOTHER TERESA OF CALCUTTA

Yugoslavian/Indian missionary born 1910

She was christened Agnes Gonxha Bojaxhiu, but took the name Teresa at the age of 15, when she became a nun. She went to India aged 18, to teach in a convent school. She was horrified by the lives of poor people in the Calcutta slums, and determined to spend her life helping them. She went to Paris to train as a nurse, and then returned to India to open her first school for poor children in Calcutta. She founded a sisterhood (a community run by nuns), the Missionaries of Charity. The sisters run schools, orphanages and hospices (hospitals for the dying). In 1957 Mother Teresa widened her work to look after lepers and other outcasts from ordinary society. Her influence has spread round the world, and Missions of Charity have been opened in the slums of many cities. Mother Teresa won the Pope John XXIII Peace prize in 1971, and the Nobel Peace prize in 1979 – and each time gave all the money to the Missionaries of Charity to help the poor.

HEYERDAHL, Thor

Norwegian anthropologist born 1914

Heyerdahl is an anthropologist (someone who studies the different tribes, peoples and nations of the world). He was fascinated to find that the customs of some Polynesian peoples, from remote islands in the Pacific, were very like those of the ancient people of Peru in South America. He wondered if the Peruvians could have sailed all the way to Polynesia on balsa-wood rafts. To test whether such a voyage was possible, he built a raft (called *Kon-Tiki*) in 1947, and floated with the prevailing winds and ocean currents from Peru to Polynesia. His success brought him world-wide fame. In 1970 and 1977 he made similar journeys, to show possible sea-links between prehistoric peoples now geographically remote from one another: in a papyrus boat from Morocco to the West Indies, and in a reed-boat from Iraq to Djibouti in the Horn of Africa. His books about his expeditions were very popular, and made people more interested in the work of anthropologists.

Thor Heyerdahl's *Kon-Tiki* voyage of 1947 proved that Peruvian natives might have crossed the Pacific to settle in the islands of Polynesia long ago.

TENZING, Norgay

Nepalese mountaineer 1914-86

Tenzing was a Sherpa (a people living on the slopes of the Himalayas, known for their mountaineering skills). He went on his first climbing trip when he was 21. Between 1935 and 1953 he acted as porter and guide for 19 expeditions – and on the last of them, in 1953, he and **Hillary** were the first people to climb Everest.

TENZING: Hillary 235

MANDELA, Nelson Rolihlahla

South African civil rights leader born 1918

Mandela trained as a lawyer, but he has become one of South Africa's most important leaders in the struggle for the rights of black people. After the Second World War the white government introduced the policy of apartheid – "separate development" – in South Africa for blacks and whites.

In 1944 Mandela joined the African National Congress (ANC), a political party working to win blacks equality with whites in South Africa. He later became its president. In his youth he had known **Gandhi**, and he encouraged his followers to use Gandhi's idea of "passive resistance" and other non-violent ways of protest. For the next twenty years he organized campaigns against the white South African government and its racist policies.

In 1964 Mandela was arrested, charged with several "political offences," and sentenced to life imprisonment. He stayed in prison for 26 years but remained leader of the ANC. He had little contact with the outside world – and other leaders, notably his wife Winnie Mandela, took up the struggle to win justice and equal rights for the black citizens of South Africa. The white authorities said they would not free Mandela, or discuss black rights, whilst he refused to order his followers to give up violence. But, in 1990, after an international campaign for his release, Mandela was finally set free – and serious discussions on the democratic future of South Africa could begin.

Nelson Mandela and his wife Winnie on their wedding day in 1958.

HILLARY, Edmund

New Zealand mountaineer born 1919

In 1953, Hillary and **Tenzing** were the first people ever to reach the summit of Mount Everest, the world's highest peak, and return safely. Five years later Hillary was in a party of explorers which reached the South Pole overland, following **Scott**'s 1911 route. When he retired from exploring he went to Tibet, to work on educational, medical and social projects for the Sherpa people.

Edmund Hillary and Tenzing Norgay on their way to the summit of Mt Everest.

MANDELA: Gandhi, M 459 HILLARY: Scott, J 221 Tenzing 234

Che Guevara, who became a hero of young revolutionaries throughout the world.

GUEVARA, Che Ernesto

Argentinian revolutionary leader 1928-67

Guevara was convinced that revolution was the only way to improve the harsh social conditions in Latin America. He met Fidel **Castro** and with him played an important part in the Cuban revolution. Guevara served for six years in the new revolutionary Cuban government. He then led a guerrilla group in an attempt to overthrow the Bolivian government. His revolutionary ideals made a great impression on the youth of the 1960s, and his violent death at the hands of the Bolivian army made him a hero of the people.

People sometimes say "Lincoln freed the slaves in America, Luther King gave them their self-respect".

KING, Martin Luther

Black US civil rights leader 1929-68

King grew up at a time when blacks and whites were treated very differently in parts of the southern USA. Many whites felt that blacks were inferior beings, and kept them apart or "segregated". Blacks had to live in separate areas from whites – they even had separate seats in public places. Some states denied blacks the right to vote, and gave them no chance of a good education.

Throughout King's boyhood, the black people of the south fought for equal rights. Many of their leaders were pastors of the Baptist church, like King's father. King decided to become a preacher and to join the struggle for equal rights.

King used **Gandhi**'s methods of non-violent protest, such as sit-ins and boycotts. He led marches and spoke at public meetings of his dream that one day all human beings would be treated equally. Even when white extremists fire-bombed his house, with his wife and baby inside it, he continued to preach non-violence. In 1964 he received both the Kennedy Peace prize and the Nobel Peace prize.

In 1968, speaking at a rally in Memphis, Tennessee, King was assassinated. His murder shocked America, but it also finally triggered the change he had dreamed of all his life. Action was speeded up to "desegregate" the south, and to change the way blacks and whites thought about each other.

Right: The footprint of the first man on the Moon: Neil Armstrong. The US astronauts left on the Moon one of the medals of the Russian cosmonaut, Gagarin, who died in 1968.

ARMSTRONG, Neil

US astronaut born 1930

On 21 July, 1969 Armstrong became the first man to set foot on the surface of the moon. His words as he stepped from the ladder of the landing craft *Eagle*, "That's one small step for a man, one great leap for mankind", have passed into history.

GUEVARA: Castro 475 KING: Gandhi, M 459

GAGARIN, Yuri

Russian cosmonaut 1934-68

Gagarin began the history of manned space flight in 1961 when he became the first man to make a successful orbit of the Earth in his tiny *Vostok 1* space capsule. In 1968 he was killed during training.

TERESHKOVA, Valentina

Russian woman cosmonaut born 1937

Tereshkova, an engineer, was inspired by **Gagarin**'s historic space flight, and wrote to the Soviet Space Agency asking if she could become a cosmonaut – and, amazingly, she was accepted for training. Three years later, in 1963, she became the first woman ever to travel in space. She piloted *Vostok 5* for 49 Earth orbits – over 2.2 million kilometres.

UEMURA, Naomi

Japanese mountaineer 1941-84

Uemura set a record by climbing the highest peaks in five continents: Mont Blanc in Europe, Kilimanjaro in Africa, Aconcagua in South America, Mount Everest in Asia, Mount McKinley in North America. In 1984 she went on a second expedition to Mount McKinley, and never returned.

WALESA, Lech

Polish trade union leader born 1943

In 1980, during massive factory unrest, Walesa became leader of the independent trade union Solidarity.

He won worldwide fame for getting workers' rights recognized in Poland, and was given the Nobel Peace prize in 1983.

Lech Walesa is a central figure in Polish politics and his Solidarity union has been successful in forming the first coalition government in Poland for 45 years without a Communist majority.

GELDOF, Bob

Irish pop singer and fund raiser born 1954

Geldof first made the music headlines as a rock singer. In the mid-1980s he began an entirely different career, as a famine fund raiser. He organized music marathons with international pop bands playing to raise money for Africa. The world-wide response to his work astonished politicians and professional fund raisers alike. Geldof became famous for his outspoken way of getting the message across – either on TV shows or at meetings with prime ministers and presidents.

In 1987 Bob Geldof was knighted for his part in organizing funds for famine relief. However, he cannot call himself "Sir Bob" as he was not born in the United Kingdom.

FOX, Terry

Canadian fund raiser 1958-81

Fox had one leg amputated when he was 18, because of cancer. Using an artificial leg, he began a sponsored coast-to-coast crossing of Canada. He had raised over a million dollars when he learned he had lung cancer. He died ten months later. But his bravery inspired others, who finished his marathon. Their joint efforts raised over 23 million Canadian dollars for cancer research.

TERESHKOVA: Gagarin 237

GLOSSARY

Aborigine Native inhabitant of a country, especially Australia.

Aristocrats Lords, ladies and other people whose families have been noble and wealthy for generations.

Assassinate To murder a ruler or other important person.

Boycott When you boycott something, you refuse to have anything to do with it, as a form of protest. Black people, for example, often boycott parliaments filled with white racists: they refuse to join.

Cartographer Someone who surveys the landscape and makes maps of it.

Civil war War between groups of people belonging to the same country.

Colony One country ruled by another.

Crucify To kill someone by nailing him or her to a wooden cross.

Crusader Christian soldier, 800 years ago, fighting to win control of the Holy Land (Palestine) from the Muslims.

Democracy A form of rule where every citizen has a vote, and therefore a share in political decisions.

Dictator Someone who has sole rule of a country, often by force.

Epidemic An outbreak of disease (often fatal) which attacks most of the people in a district or country.

Expedition (1) a journey of exploration; (2) the explorers who make the journey.

Flora and fauna Flora are all the plants native to a country. Fauna are all the animals.

Frontiersman In eighteenth- and nineteenth-century America, someone who explored the country beyond the frontiers of European settlement.

Gladiator In ancient Rome, a slave forced to fight other gladiators or wild animals to the death, to entertain crowds in the Circus.

Hookah A tobacco pipe popular in Muslim countries. The tobacco burns in a bowl above a jar of scented water. You suck the smoke through the water, using a flexible tube.

Hydraulic engine The early nineteenth-century name for a machine worked by water power, or for a device such as a water wheel, to lift water from one level to another.

Hypothermia When your body temperature drops too low, you suffer from hypothermia, and it is often fatal.

Illegitimate A child born to two people who are not married.

Inherit To receive goods, money or power from your parent after he or she dies.

Kapok A tree-fibre, like thick cotton-wool, often used in the nineteenth century for stuffing clothes and furniture.

Keel-haul A punishment on ships, used from the sixteenth to the nineteenth century. You passed a rope under the ship, fastened the person to be punished to one end, and hauled him right round the ship's keel underwater. The haul might take as much as five minutes, and was often fatal.

Martyr Someone cruelly killed because of his or her beliefs.

Mayhem Riot, noise and vandalism.

Missionary Someone who tries to convert other people to his or her religious belief.

Mutiny Refusal to obey orders – used especially when sailors or soldiers defy their officers.

Navigator (1) in former times, someone who travels, especially by ship; (2) nowadays, the person who works out the course of a journey, especially on a ship or plane.

Pamphlet A short booklet, or single sheet of paper, explaining something (for example the layout of a famous building) or putting a political or religious point of view.

Plantation A farm, often in the tropics, where a single crop is grown: bananas, pineapples or sugar cane, for example. In former times, the workers on plantations were often slaves.

Press gang A gang of sailors who roamed the streets of seaside towns at night, kidnapping able-bodied men and forcing them to serve at sea.

Protestant Christian who does not agree with the beliefs of the Roman Catholic church.

Republic A state headed by a president rather than by a king or queen.

Roman Catholic Christian ruled by the Pope, from Rome.

Scurvy A malnutrition disease (often fatal) caused by lack of Vitamin C.

Sermon A talk by a priest or minister about religion or morals.

Sit-in When workers occupy a factory, or students occupy the offices of a university or school, refusing to let the management run things until they agree to the workers' or students' requests.

Smear A false story about someone, deliberately spread to embarrass them. Common in politics and in tabloid newspapers.

Stratosphere The outermost layer of the Earth's atmosphere.

Transportation An eighteenth-century legal punishment in England: sending guilty people to the "colonies" (especially Australia) to live in convict settlements.

Truce When fighters agree to stop fighting while peace terms are discussed.

Tyranny Cruel rule.

SECTION 4

SPORT AND ENTERTAINMENT

Athletes,

Actors,

Musicians ...

INTRODUCTION TO *SPORT AND ENTERTAINMENT*

Unlike other creatures, which spend every waking moment grazing or hunting for food, avoiding predators or rearing offspring, most human beings have time to spare. Our big brains and clever hands guarantee survival with (if we are lucky) only a few hours' work each day. We can use the rest of our time for relaxation. We play more than any other animals; leisure activities are vital to our peace of mind.

Some humans pastimes are passive Talking to friends and listening to music, for example, are favourite relaxations for people of every age, all over the world. But we also enjoy more energetic activities, which test our mental and physical skills. Hobbies stretch our minds and bodies. We play sports and games of every kind, from chess to handball, from jacks (the most popular game in history) to football (the most widespread of modern sports), we tell stories, play instruments, sing, act and dance.

Taking part is one kind of fun. Another, just as great, is seeing other people – experts – perform. We enjoy watching their skills, and at the same time we feel challenged, if we tried, perhaps we could do just as well. If you asked most ordinary people who their heroes were, a few might name explorers, rulers or thinkers. But most would probably talk of "stars": singers, actors or sportspeople, whose performance is dazzling.

One of the sad things about stars is that passing time dims their glory. Who can remember, now, the sports heroes or popular singers of 100, 50 or even 20 years ago? New records are set, new hits are made, the standard constantly changes, and we forget many of our favourites of only a few years before. In sport and entertainment, fashion rules – so the achievements of the entrants in this volume will change of course, and we hope to update the entries as new stars come along and new records are made.

This section is crammed with stars. Each of them was, or is, supreme in what he or she did. Some – Houdini, Chaplin, Piaf – have endured, and their fame remains undimmed. Others have faded, and a few are now hardly known. But in his or her time, each gave pleasure to millions – and it is fascinating to compare today's admired actors, singers and sports heroes with those who enthralled our grandparents.

Note In this section, pop groups are placed by the dates when they were founded. This gives some idea of what else was happening when each group was born. The Beatles' "birthdate", for example, is 1960 (see page 312).

PHEIDIPPIDES

Greek athlete c 510-490 BC

There are several versions of the legend of Pheidippides. The most famous says that when the Persian army landed at Marathon to attack Greece in 490 BC, Pheidippides was sent to warn the citizens of Athens and Sparta. He began by running 42 km from Marathon to Athens, and then covered the 150 km to Sparta. The whole run took two days, and the exertion killed him. Whether this story is true or not, Pheidippides' name lives on as the originator of the "marathon", a long-distance race over a similar distance to that between Marathon and Athens.

GWYN(NE), Nell

English actress and royal mistress 1650-87

As a teenager, Gwyn sold oranges in London, for people to eat during theatre shows. Later she became an actress, famous for both wit and beauty. King Charles II saw her in a play, fell in love with her and made her his main mistress. He was married already, and could not make Gwyn queen. But he treated her exactly as a wife. She was his favourite companion to the end of his life, and his dying words are said to have been "Let not poor Nellie starve".

The beautiful Nell Gwyn.

KEMBLE FAMILY

English actors 18th and 19th centuries

Only one other family in the history of the arts – the **Bachs** – has ever rivalled the Kembles. For 200 years, something like 25 family members worked in drama: acting, directing, singing, writing plays and running theatres.

Despite their busyness, many of the family were little known, even in their own day. But five, at least, were famous. SARAH SIDDONS (1755-1831) (born Kemble) was a powerful tragic actress: in such parts as Lady Macbeth, she is said to have made audiences shriek and faint with emotion. Her three brothers, JOHN PHILIP KEMBLE (1757-1823), STEPHEN KEMBLE (1758-1822) and CHARLES KEMBLE (1775-1854) were also stars. John Philip specialized in playing generals and statesmen. Stephen was fat, famous as the only actor able to play **Shakespeare**'s Falstaff without padding. Charles played Hamlet, and later became an actor-manager. His daughter FANNY KEMBLE (1809-93) began as an actress, but later became famous for touring Britain and the USA giving readings of Shakespeare. She went on performing until she was over 80.

John Philip Kemble, as the Roman general Coriolanus in Shakespeare's play.

KEMBLE: Bach 22 Shakespeare 16

PAGANINI, Niccolò

Italian violinist and composer 1782-1840

As a teenager Paganini went on his first violin-playing tour, and was hailed as a virtuoso. Everywhere he went, he was mobbed by fans, and people whispered that his playing was helped by the Devil himself, Paganini usually played his own compositions, which were designed to show off his skills – for example bouncing the bow over the strings and playing left-hand pizzicato.

Towards the end of his life Paganini suffered from ill-health, and lost most of his vast fortune by buying and running a gambling house in Paris. When he died, the French church authorities refused to bury him because of his rumoured connection with the Devil. His coffin lay in a cellar for five years before it was finally accepted for burial in his home town, Parma, in Italy.

KEAN, Edmund

English actor c 1787-1833

Kean's private life was a scandal: he drank, gambled and seduced women. But his acting was magnificent: the poet Coleridge said that watching him was "like reading **Shakespeare** by flashes of lightning". He specialized in larger-than-life characters, such as **Richard III**, Shylock and Othello. He was electrifying to watch, and apparently could make an audience shiver or weep just by the way he said a line. Seeing him act was disturbing but exciting: if what is written about him is true, few other actors can ever have had such skill.

DEBURAU, Jean-Gaspard

French actor 1796-1846

Deburau's parents were acrobats, and he started his career as a tumbler in the family act. In his mid-20s he became a mime artist, expert at expressing emotion and action by graceful body-movement without speech or stage-props. He used the famous character of Pierrot, a sad-faced clown in a white silk costume sewn with pompoms. Pierrot longed for wealth, power and love – and always failed to win them. People enjoyed Deburau's slapstick act, especially his fights with comic

policemen. But they also enjoyed his blend of sadness with hilarity, and the beauty of his movements. He is the ancestor not only of later mime-artists like **Marceau**, but of such sad–funny film comedians as **Chaplin**, **Keaton** and Stan **Laurel**.

Edmund Kean, as the wicked king in Shakespeare's play Richard III.

KEAN: Richard III 434 Shakespeare 16 DEBURAU: Chaplin 257 Keaton 261 Laurel and Hardy 258 Marceau 284

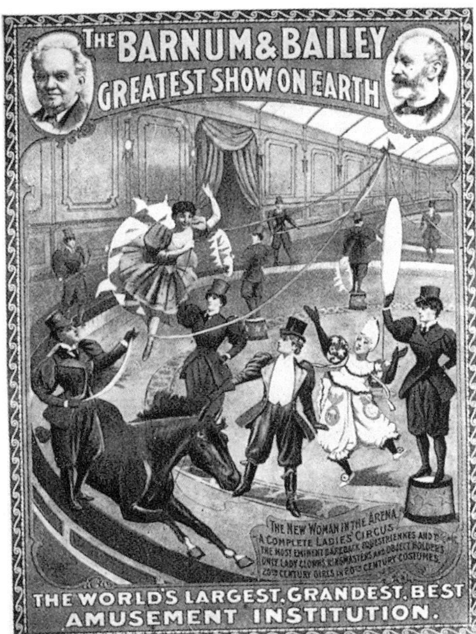

Left: A poster for Barnum and Bailey's "Greatest Show on Earth".

BARNUM, Phineas Taylor

US showman 1810-91

Barnum organized exhibitions, shows and theatre performances. Wherever he could find an audience, he put on a show – and if no hall or theatre was available, he set up a tent. He began in fairgrounds, showing freaks such as the famous dwarf General Tom Thumb, "mermaids" (probably walruses or seals) and talking dogs. He became known throughout America in 1850 when he organized a tour for the popular opera-singer Jenny **Lind**. His worldwide fame began in 1871 when he started a touring circus modestly advertized as "The Greatest Show on Earth". In 1881 the show merged with James Bailey's circus, to make the famous "Barnum and Bailey Circus". In its "big top" (the tent where performances took place) it had three rings where clowns, acrobats and animals performed at the same time – hence the nickname for a large, impressive show: "three-ring circus". For many years, its most popular act was Jumbo the Elephant.

PETIPA, Marius

French dancer and choreographer c 1818-1910

By the time Petipa was 23, he was well known in France, Spain and the USA. In 1848 he was invited to St Petersburg (modern Leningrad) to become leading dancer of the Imperial Ballet – and spent the rest of his life in Russia.

In the 1850s, ballet consisted mainly of "divertissements": spectacular exhibitions of dancing without story. Petipa began making ballets which did tell stories, like plays in dance. Nowadays he is best known for his work with **Tchaikovsky** on *Swan Lake, The Nutcracker* and especially *The Sleeping Beauty*, for which he invented the choreography (dance-steps). The picture many people have of ballet – girls in white tutus and men in tights performing fairy-tale stories in mime and athletic dance – comes mainly from the work of Petipa. He perfected the style, and his training-methods are still used by many ballet companies in the world today.

A scene from Tchaikovsky's ballet *Swan Lake*, danced at the Maryinsky theatre in Leningrad in 1929. The performance used the choreography first invented for the ballet by Petipa and Leo Ivanov in 1895. Here, the swans are gathering by the lakeside to perform the "Dance of the Little Swans".

BARNUM: Lind 247 PETIPA: Tchaikovsky 44

An illustration of Jenny Lind in her 20s, when she sang before the Swedish court at Stockholm.

LIND, Johanna Maria

Swedish opera singer 1820-87

Jenny Lind trained at the Royal Opera School in Stockholm, and became well known in Scandinavia. She had many admirers, and several men asked her to marry them – including, at one stage, Hans Christian **Andersen**. She began to star in the opera houses of Paris, Berlin and London. Her fans nicknamed her "the Swedish nightingale". In 1850 **Barnum** invited her to make a concert tour in the USA, and from then on she no longer appeared in opera, preferring solo concerts and oratorio. She died in England, and was buried in Westminster Abbey.

BLONDIN, Charles

French stuntman 1824-97

Blondin made his first appearance as an acrobat when he was 6 years old, billed as "The Little Wonder". In 1859 he became world-famous by walking across the Niagara Falls on a tightrope. Later, when other people started challenging this feat, he repeated it in even more hair-raising ways, for example blindfold, backwards, on stilts, on a one-wheeled bike or pushing an assistant in a wheelbarrow.

GILBERT, William Schwenk

English librettist 1836-1911

and

SULLIVAN, Arthur Seymour

English playwright and composer 1842-1900

In the 1870s Gilbert and Sullivan wrote a comic opera, *Trial by Jury*. Its success began a partnership which lasted for 18 years, until it ended because of a business argument. The partners' operas were the London stage-hits of the 1880s and 1890s, and the combination of Gilbert's witty words and Sullivan's catchy tunes have kept them popular ever since. The 13 "Savoy Operas" (after the Savoy Theatre, where they were first performed) include *The Pirates of Penzance, The Mikado, The Gondoliers* and Sullivan's own favourite, *The Yeomen of the Guard*.

PATTI, Adelina (Adela Juana Maria)

Italian opera singer 1843-1919

A year after Patti's birth her parents, who were both professional singers, emigrated to New York. Patti first sang in public at the age of 7, starting a remarkable career which lasted nearly 60 years. She took in most of the world's first-ranked opera houses and ended after 9 years of "farewell" performances. Patti's beautiful sound and perfect voice control can still be heard on the early gramophone records she made when she was over 60. She was also famous for her acting, and the press eagerly reported the huge sums she was paid, her enormous jewels, and the way she refused ever to attend rehearsals.

LIND: Andersen 33 Barnum 246

The actress Sarah Bernhardt in stage costume. She was nicknamed the "Divine Sarah".

BERNHARDT, Sarah

French actress 1844-1923

When Bernhardt was 18 she joined the Comédie-Française, the Paris theatre company which specialized in putting on plays by such great writers as **Racine** and **Molière**. By 1869, at the age of 25, she was a star, famous for her beautiful, clear voice, and the emotion she put into playing tragic parts. (She was also famous for a less important reason: whenever she felt like it, she could cry convincing tears.)

For over 50 years Bernhardt was one of the best-loved actresses in the world. People fought for tickets at her performances, and critics and writers (for example the great novelist **Proust**) wrote glowing accounts of the way she played each part. Outside the theatre, she lived a glittering social life. Her friends included many of the best-known people in Europe, and her beauty brought her many admirers. Newspapers reported her parties, and published accounts of her tantrums, her fury when actors and stagehands refused to do as she wanted, and her rows with rival stars.

In the 1880s Bernhardt began to make foreign tours. She played her parts in French, and the other actors spoke the language of the country they were in: Bernhardt said that people were paying to see her act, not struggle with a foreign language. She travelled in her own private train, the "Sarah Bernhardt Special". She took up ballooning and sculpture as hobbies, and tried acting in silent films and singing in the music-hall. In 1915 her right leg was amputated after an accident, but not even this stopped her working. She went on touring, and when people objected that she was too old to play young heroines, she dressed in male costume and played Hamlet or Faust instead.

CODY, William ("Buffalo Bill")

US showman 1846-1917

As a young man Cody worked for the Pony Express, delivering mail on horseback. He earned his nickname "Buffalo Bill" when he promised to provide meat for workers building a railway, and killed 5,000 buffalo for them, single-handed, in 17 months. He served in the US army during the Sioux Indian Wars as a "scout". In 1883 he started what he called a Wild West show, and toured with it throughout the USA. Its stars included Annie **Oakley** and the Sioux chief Sitting Bull; there were bucking broncos, lariat-whirling cowgirls, sharpshooters, trick riders

BERNHARDT: Molière 20 Proust 57 Racine 21 CODY: Oakley 250

and stuntmen – and the show always included Cody himself, firing at a target while galloping on horseback.

GRACE, William Gilbert

British cricketer 1848-1915

Grace's mother was a keen cricket watcher and trained her five sons to play the game. All five did well, but "W.G." became one of the most famous cricketers who have ever lived. He set many records: he was the first player to make more than 2,000 runs (in fact 2,739) in a single season, and he scored 1,000 runs and took 100 wickets each year from 1874 to 1878. He is still the only cricketer ever to have scored 100 runs and taken 10 wickets in a single test match.

An engraving of W G Grace at the wicket. Posters outside cricket grounds used to announce: "Admission 6d. If Dr Grace is playing, admission 1 shilling." (Sixpence was 2½p; 1 shilling was twice as much).

ARCHER, Fred

English jockey 1857-86

Archer took part in his first public race at the age of 8 and rode his first winning horse when he was 12. He was British champion jockey from 1874-85, winning all of the five most important flat horse-races, including the St Leger six times and the Derby five times. He rode in 8,084 races and had 2,748 winners.

In 1884 Archer's wife died in childbirth, and he became severely depressed. The effort of trying to keep his weight down – all jockeys must be light – broke his health, both mental and physical, and he lost most of his money by betting. In the end, he shot himself. His record number of wins in a single season (246 in 1885) was not surpassed until 48 years later, by Gordon Richards.

DUSE, Eleonora

Italian actress 1858-1924

Duse rivalled **Bernhardt** as the finest actress of her time. Her private life was stormy. Newspapers were full of her parties, her love-affairs and her quarrels with jealous rivals. Onstage, by contrast, she was restrained and calm, able to make even the most melodramatic characters seem real. She had huge success, for example, as Tosca, the woman whose betrayal by a wicked police chief drives her to murder and suicide. In later life she played many of **Ibsen**'s heroines, people whose outward calm masks hysteria and despair.

A cartoon of Eleanor Duse, from the French magazine *Le Rire*, in 1905.

DUSE: Bernhardt 248 Ibsen 40

OAKLEY, Annie

US markswoman and entertainer 1860-1926

Oakley was born in a log cabin to a Quaker family, whose Christian ideals she followed all her life. Her father died when she was 10 and she helped the family income by shooting and selling birds and rabbits. In 1879 she won a shooting match against Frank Butler, a well-known marksman and vaudeville performer. They married, and toured the country giving demonstrations of marksmanship. Butler soon retired to become his wife's manager, and she developed a solo act, joining circuses such as **Cody**'s Wild West Show. She ended her act by shooting cigarettes from her husband's mouth – and once did the same for Kaiser Wilhelm II of Germany (at his request). She could slice playing cards held with the edge towards her, or shoot them full of holes as they fell to the ground. (Punched tickets were once nicknamed "Annie Oakleys" because of this.) In 1918 she was hired to give shooting demonstrations to the US army.

MELBA, Nellie

Australian opera singer 1861-1931

Melba's real name was Helen Porter Mitchell. She took her stage name from her home town of Melbourne. Her 1887 debut in Brussels took the operatic world by storm, and she was recognized as the foremost soprano of her time. She sang high, hard music, especially at the beginning of her career, and she was noted for keeping absolutely in time and for the constant quality of her voice. Melba made 150 records (although only one with **Caruso**, her famous stage partner). Many of them had a special mauve label, the "Melba" label, and were the highest-priced records of their time. Two famous foods, Peach Melba and Melba toast, were invented in her honour.

MÉLIÈS, Georges

French film-maker 1861-1938

Méliès began his career as a stage conjurer, and he was always on the lookout for new ideas to put in his act. In 1895 he saw the "moving pictures" made by the **Lumière** brothers, and decided that he might be able to use film to show tricks impossible in real life. He quickly taught himself how to use a camera, and went on to make more than 500 short films. Most were 2-3 minutes long, and showed single tricks: a man with a rubber head which he could pull into any shape he chose, cheeses

Melba used to wear strings of pearls and a huge silken cloak when she sang in concerts.

OAKLEY: Cody 248 MELBA: Caruso 253 MÉLIÈS: Lumière 384

"Moon landing", from one of Méliès' fantasy films – the next frame in the film says "Ouch!"

Above, right: Baron Pierre de Coubertin, founder of the modern Olympics.

skipping, a magician pulling dancers from his mouth like flags. A few films were longer, and showed fantasy journeys: to the Moon, to the North Pole, under the sea, to the centre of the Earth.

Nowadays camera tricks are normal. Every TV advertisement uses them, people can do them with their own home video cameras, and nothing seems impossible. But in Méliès' day, his film "illusions" made audiences gape – and as with all the best conjuring tricks, it is still hard to see how some were done.

COUBERTIN, Pierre de

French Olympics pioneer 1863-1937

Coubertin had the idea of restarting the Olympic Games. These athletics contests, held in friendship and peace, began in ancient Greece over 2,700 years ago, but were abolished 1,000 years later by Christian Roman emperors because they were held in honour of Zeus, a pagan (non-Christian) god. Coubertin hoped that the modern Olympics would reduce tensions between nations. The first modern Games were held in Athens in 1896, and there have been Games in different cities round the world every four years since then, except during the two world wars.

TOSCANINI, Arturo

Italian conductor 1867-1957

At 19 Toscanini was a cellist on a Brazilian tour when a conductor was booed by the audience, and fled from the theatre. Toscanini took over, conducting **Verdi**'s opera *Aida* from memory, without rehearsal – a feat which gave his career a triumphant start. Twelve years later he was made conductor of Italy's leading opera house, La Scala in Milan. He spent most of his life conducting there or at the Metropolitan Opera in New York. He demanded concentration from both players and audiences, using his fiery temper to get his way. He was intensely patriotic, resisting fascism in Italy and supporting Jewish victims of Nazism. He had poor eyesight, so learned all the music by heart, rehearsing and conducting from memory. He was one of the first conductors to record most of his performances.

TOSCANINI: Verdi 37

skills from all the arts: painting (scenery and costumes), literature (story), music and theatre. In 1908 he founded a company especially for touring: the Ballets Russes ("Russian ballet"). It began in Paris, and was a huge success.

When Diaghilev was planning new shows, he called on the finest talents he could find. He hired painters (for example **Picasso**), writers, choreographers and composers (for example **Stravinsky**). It was hard then – and still is – for creative people to find sponsors in order to get their work heard or seen. For the creators he supported, Diaghilev provided cash, limelight and almost sure success.

After Diaghilev's death his dancers and choreographers went on to work in other companies, carrying the brilliance and dazzle of the Ballets Russes throughout the world.

Left: Sergei Diaghilev, founder of the *Ballets Russes*, the man who presented Russian ballet to the rest of the world at the beginning of the twentieth century.

DIAGHILEV, Sergei

Russian impresario 1872-1929

The word *impresario* means "showman", and describes Diaghilev exactly. All his life, he wanted to show people things, to impress them with beautiful and amazing sights. He became director of the Maryinsky Theatre in St Petersburg (modern Leningrad), and brought European and American stars to Russia to perform plays, ballets and operas.

As well as importing foreign talent, Diaghilev exported Russian skills abroad. He took the stars of the Maryinsky Theatre on tour, performing opera and ballet in many European towns and cities. He chose opera and ballet because they used

LOUIS, Spiridon (Spyros)

Greek athlete 1872-1940

Twice a day Louis ran beside his mule which carried water to Athens, about 14 km from his village. In 1896, when the Greek organizers of the first modern Olympic Games announced a marathon race to commemorate **Pheidippides**' run, Louis took part. There were 16 runners, and several had never run such a distance before. The marathon was the last event, and until then Greece had not had a single victory in the Games. When Louis was first past the finishing line there was pandemonium. As the winner he was offered a farm, and free meals and shaves for life. But when he was asked what he would

DIAGHILEV: Picasso 60 Stravinsky 62 LOUIS: Pheidippides 244

really like, he answered "A new horse and water-cart". He retired from athletics and never ran another race.

CARUSO, Enrico

Italian opera singer 1873-1921

Caruso was the eighteenth child of poor parents in Naples, Italy, and the first to survive. He was encouraged to take up singing by his friends at work. At first he sang small parts in small theatres. But the beauty of his voice made such an impression that he soon became an international star. He sang in opera houses throughout the world, sometimes with **Melba**, but the peak of his career was the 17 years he spent with the Metropolitan Opera Company of New York. His success came at the same time as the birth of the recording industry, and he made 154 records. His 1902 recording of "On with the Motley" from the opera *I Pagliacci* was the first record to sell over one million copies.

MISTINGUETT

French entertainer 1873-1956

Mistinguett's real name was Jeanne-Marie Bourgeois. She was a dancer and comic actress, one of the most famous French stage stars of her time. Her legs were insured for a fortune, in case she broke them dancing. She starred as a dancer at the Casino de Paris and the Folies Bergères until she was 50. She was also a popular actress in comedies, farces, and later in serious plays, for example a stage version of Victor **Hugo**'s novel *Les misérables*.

HOUDINI, Harry

Hungarian/US stuntman 1874-1926

"Harry Houdini" was a stage-name; Houdini's real name was Erich Weiss. At first he was a trapeze artist, then a magician and finally he began to specialize in daring escapes. His assistants would handcuff him, chain him, lock him in a box and hang it high in the air or sink it underwater – and Houdini would escape in seconds, making the crowds gasp. To this day, no one knows how some of his tricks were done.

EWRY, Ray

US athlete 1874-1937

Ewry caught polio when a boy, but recovered the use of his legs and strengthened them by exercise. He competed in four Olympic Games (1900, 1904, 1906, 1908) in every jumping event – long, high and triple jumps. He is the only person ever to have won 10 Olympic gold medals.

CARUSO: Melba 250 MISTINGUETT: Hugo 32

CASALS, Pablo (Pau)

Spanish cellist and conductor 1876-1973

Pablo Casals, playing the instrument that made him famous throughout the music world.

At 11 years old, Casals was already learning piano, violin and organ when he heard a cello and insisted on studying that as well. He first played in public three years later, and decided to make his career in music. He became one of the most famous cello soloists ever, and also played chamber music and conducted.

Casals opposed fascism, and in the mid-1930s, when **Franco** came to power in Spain, he went into exile. He refused to play in Germany or Italy while **Hitler** and **Mussolini** were in power. He went on playing well into his 80s, and conducted his last concert when he was 94.

Anna Pavlova on "points" in the beautiful costume from her famous solo dance "The Dying Swan".

LANDOWSKA, Wanda

Polish harpsichord player 1877-1959

Until the mid-eighteenth century, the favourite keyboard instrument was the harpsichord, not the piano. But then harpsichords began to fall out of fashion, and by the end of the nineteenth century they were almost forgotten. Landowska, a pianist who specialized in **Bach**'s music, decided to play his work on the harpsichord – the instrument for which it was written.

Landowska's concerts astounded audiences. It was the first time people had heard the sounds earlier composers had meant. Nowadays "authentic" performances are standard in classical music; Landowska was one of the pioneers.

PAVLOVA, Anna Pavlovna

Russian ballet dancer 1881-1931

When Pavlova was a child she saw *The Sleeping Beauty* in St Petersburg (now Leningrad), and decided at once to become a dancer. By the age of 18 she was one of Russia's leading stars. She went on tours where she danced in *Giselle* and *The Dying Swan*. Audiences were ecstatic; in Sweden a crowd of fans pulled her to the theatre in a carriage. She toured the world, dancing in theatres and music-halls, bringing ballet to more people than any dancer before or since. In 1931, on her way to dance in Holland, she caught a cold which turned to pneumonia and killed her.

CASALS: Franco 468 Hitler 466 Mussolini 465 LANDOWSKA: Bach 22

DE MILLE, Cecil Blount

US film director 1881-1959

Cecil B. de Mille, as he was always known, acted on the stage and wrote several plays before he decided to make his career in films. He went to Hollywood in the 1910s, soon after the film industry started there, and made hundreds of short comedies, dramas and cowboy films. In the 1920s he decided that some of the best stories for film were in the Bible. He made a dozen enormous Bible "epics" (adventure films), often – as the posters rightly said – with "casts of thousands". The best known are *The Ten Commandments* (about **Moses**), *Samson and Delilah* and *King of Kings* (about **Jesus**).

FAIRBANKS, Douglas

US film actor 1883-1939

Fairbanks' real name was Douglas Ullman. He was one of the biggest stars of silent films, but retired in 1927 when sound films began. He made fast-action adventure films, and was famous for acrobatic stunts. He always played the same kind of hero: a thin-moustached, handsome man in a white shirt, who duelled with villains, foiled dastardly plots and saved damsels in distress. His best known parts include Robin Hood, Sinbad the Sailor, d'Artagnan (in *The Three Musketeers*) and Zorro. His son DOUGLAS FAIRBANKS JUNIOR (born 1909) also acted in adventure films (his best-known part was the villain in *The Prisoner of Zenda*) until the 1950s, when he became a TV producer and director.

A scene from the film *The Bride of Frankenstein* with Boris Karloff and Elsa Lanchester.

KARLOFF, Boris

English actor 1885-1969

In 1919 polite, soft-spoken George Pratt went to Hollywood to seek his fortune as a film actor. He played all kinds of parts: lords, butlers, surgeons, an African explorer. But his greatest success came when he changed his name to Boris Karloff and began to play mad scientists, crooks and villains. In 1931 he was asked to play the monster, made from human spare parts, in the story of *Frankenstein*. His performance was just as gentle and friendly as ever. But the contrast between Karloff's soft voice and the monster's uncontrollable, murderous strength made the film a world-wide hit. A year later, in *The Mummy*, Karloff played an Egyptian mummy which awakes in a pyramid after 4,000 years – and his career as a horror-film star was fixed for good. He starred in over 200 films. In real life, he often made charity appearances, putting on his most ghoulish act to raise money for good causes.

DE MILLE: Jesus 329 Moses 406

RUBINSTEIN, Artur

Polish/US pianist 1887-1982

Rubinstein was coached by famous piano teachers, and played his first solo concert at 5 years old. All through his career, he alternated performing with long periods of "retirement", during which he spent his time practising and thinking about music. He was renowned as one of the world's best players of **Chopin**'s music (just a small part of his enormous repertory). He often played two or three concertos in one evening – a feat equalled only by **Liszt** a century before.

FONTANNE, Lynn

English/US actress 1887-1983

and

LUNT, Alfred

US actor 1893-1977

Fontanne was born in England, but settled in the USA after she married Lunt in 1913. They acted separately in plays, but were best known for starring together. Double-acts are usually comedians, but the Lunts' act was theatrical. Their most famous performances were in such light-hearted plays as **Shaw**'s *Arms and the Man*, Giraudoux's *Amphitryon 38* and **Shakespeare**'s *The Taming of the Shrew*. But they were also successful in serious plays, for example Maxwell Anderson's history-play *Elizabeth the Queen* and Dürrenmatt's savage comedy *The Visit of the Old Lady*, which they starred in when Lunt was 67 and Fontanne was 73.

LEHMANN, Lotte

German/US singer 1888-1976

Lehmann started as a professional singer in 1910, and later won fame by starring in operas by Richard **Strauss**, who composed several operas with her in mind. She was based in Vienna until 1938, when she left after the Nazi takeover. She continued her career in Britain and the USA and also became famous as a singer of *lieder* (songs by composers such as **Brahms** and **Schubert**). She gave her last public performance in 1951, aged 63, but went on making records until she was over 70.

Lynn Fontanne and Alfred Lunt, playing a scene from Shakespeare's comedy *The Taming of the Shrew*.

BERLIN, Irving

US composer 1888-1989

Berlin was born in Russia, with the Russian name Israel Balin. His family emigrated to New York when he was 4. He was working as a singing waiter when he first began setting words to other people's music. Soon he began to write the music too. In 1911 he

RUBINSTEIN: Chopin 34 Liszt 35 FONTANNE AND LUNT: Shakespeare 16 Shaw 50 LEHMANN: Brahms 42 Schubert 32 Strauss 54 wrote *Alexander's Ragtime Band*, which became the biggest hit of its day. Berlin wrote over 1,000 songs, many of them worldwide hits. Remarkably, Berlin never needed, in his long career, to learn how to read or write music, nor to play the piano in any key except G flat (using mainly black notes). He once had a special piano built, with a mechanism which would shift the hammers to left or right. That way, he could play in G flat, and the hammers would hit the strings in whatever key singers asked for.

Berlin's hits include "standards" (songs everyone sings) such as *Easter Parade* and *There's No Business Like Show Business* – and two of the best-known songs composed this century, *White Christmas* and *God Bless America*, which is almost an unofficial US national anthem.

CHAPLIN, Charles Spencer

English comedian and film-maker 1889-1977

Chaplin had a grim childhood. His father was a drunk and his mother was mentally unstable. The family lived in the London slums, and there was little money even for essentials like food and clothes. By the age of 8 Chaplin had begun performing on the music-hall stage, and before he was 18 he was a leading comedian.

Chaplin went to the USA in 1913, and almost at once began writing, directing and performing in silent comedy films. He played the same character in most of them – a tramp with a bowler hat, tiny moustache, trousers far too big for him, floppy cane and feet facing outwards at 180 degrees so that instead of walking he waddled like a duck. By the time he was 35 he was world-famous. He specialized in slapstick: chases, fights, falls and comic acrobatics.

Once his fame was secure, Chaplin put serious ideas into his films as well as funny ones. In *Modern Times* he is a meek factory-worker who leads a protest-march by mistake. In *The Great Dictator* he is a poor Jewish tailor mistaken for **Hitler**.

Chaplin was proud of the political ideas in his films, which show deep sympathy for the suffering of the poor, and hatred for the cruelty of war. But they now seem less important than the genius of his comic ideas and the grace and dazzle of his performances.

There are serious ideas behind the humour of Chaplin's films. In *The Kid*, for example, the tramp (Chaplin) tries to save a 4-year-old orphan from being put in a children's home.

CHAPLIN: Hitler 466

NIJINSKY, Vaslav

Russian dancer 1890-1950

Few dancers in history have been more talented than Nijinsky. By the time he was 17 he was a star at the Maryinsky Theatre in St Petersburg (modern Leningrad). In 1909 the theatre manager, **Diaghilev**, took his dancers to Europe, and Nijinsky's dancing enthralled audiences. He was the most athletic dancer anyone had ever seen. Until his time, male dancers had generally been less important than female. Their main jobs were to support the women while they twirled, and to lift them into the air. Nijinsky's energetic, sexy dancing changed all that. One after another, old ballets were revised to show off his skills, and new ballets were created for him. Other male dancers learned from him, and soon male and female dancers were equal in ballets everywhere. He affected the ballet world as a meteorite lights up the sky, dazzling everyone.

Nijinsky's dancing career was tragically short. In 1916 he began to show signs of mental illness, and from the early 1920s until his death he spent his life in asylums.

LAUREL, Stan

US film comedian 1890-1956

and

HARDY, Oliver

US film comedian 1892-1957

Laurel (whose real name was Arthur Stanley Jefferson) and Hardy began their careers as solo comedians. They were first teamed in 1926, and went on to become one of the best-loved double-acts in film history. In fact Laurel claimed to dislike the acting part of his job. He preferred to direct, and worked on the stories and direction of most Laurel and Hardy films, while Hardy spent his spare time playing golf.

Laurel's screen character is "Stan" (the thin one); Hardy's is "Ollie" (the fat, pompous one). Between them, they have not enough brains to outwit a sparrow. In some films they are down on their luck, in others they have jobs (as piano-movers, policemen, shopkeepers, carpenters). Sometimes they are married, to fierce, snapping wives; in one film they join the Foreign Legion. They visit the Wild West, sell Christmas trees, travel to Scotland to pick up an inheritance. In one film (*A Chump at Oxford*) Stan is knocked on the head and becomes a brainy, brilliant

In the film *Early to Bed* (1928) Stan becomes Ollie's butler, and finds the job more painful than he expected.

Right: The bandleader Paul Whiteman, who was known affectionately as the "rajah of rhythm". He was an expert on the violin as well as on the piano.

NIJINSKY: Diaghilev 252

scholar at Oxford University, with Ollie as his long-suffering butler.

Laurel and Hardy made over 100 films. The funniest include *The Music Box* (in which they heave a piano up a huge flight of steps), *The Battle of the Century* (which contains the biggest pie-throwing fight in history) and *Way Out West*, in which they also dance and sing.

WHITEMAN, Paul

US band leader 1890-1967

Whiteman was a famous band leader many years before big bands became fashionable. He used his popularity to promote jazz and invented the band show. Although his band was not a true jazz band (because its music was all written down, not improvised) he employed many famous jazz players of the time (for example Bix **Beiderbecke**). Many stars owe their first taste of fame to Whiteman; one of the best known in later years was Bing **Crosby**. The Whiteman band gave the first performance of **Gershwin**'s *Rhapsody in Blue*, a piece blending classical ideas and jazz.

WHITEMAN: Beiderbecke 270 Crosby 268 Gershwin 68

MARX BROTHERS

US comedians 19th-20th century

There were five Marx brothers, born into a poor Jewish family. All were known by boyhood nicknames. GUMMO (Milton Marx, 1897-1977) gave up performing early, to become an agent. ZEPPO (Herbert Marx, 1901-79) played the handsome, un-comic hero in the brothers' stage shows and early films, but retired in the 1930s. CHICO (Arthur Marx, 1891-1961) wore a hat shaped like an upside-down ice-cream cone, played the piano and talked in a fake Italian accent. HARPO (Adolph Marx, 1893-1964) wore a baggy raincoat and a wig the size of an ostrich's nest; he played a mute (someone who cannot speak), who rolled his eyes, grinned and hooted a motor-horn instead of speaking. He played the harp and chased women. GROUCHO (Julius Marx, 1895-1977) wore a tail-coat, wire-rimmed glasses and a wide painted moustache. He loped like an ape, while smoking a cigar and making jokes.

The Marx brothers in stage shows were comic mayhem. They pelted the other actors with flour, climbed into the audience to chase pretty women and insult ugly ones, broke off the story to sing songs, play music or do conjuring tricks. Above all, they had zany conversations with each other.

After huge stage success in the 1920s, the Marxes went into films, and made some of the funniest movies in the business, including *Animal Crackers, Duck Soup, A Night at the Opera, A Day at the Races* and *A Night in Casablanca.*

Four of the Marx brothers: Zeppo (the smoothie), Chico (with the hat), Harpo (with the great big smile) and Groucho (with the great big cigar).

SEGOVIA, Andrés

Spanish guitarist 1893-1987

Until Segovia's time, the guitar had been considered chiefly a folk instrument, unsuited to classical music. His dazzling playing, his arrangements of hundreds of pieces of music, his pupils, and the many sonatas and concertos written for him by famous composers changed all that. The guitar is now one of the most respectable, and popular, of all classical solo instruments.

GRAHAM, Martha

US dancer born 1894

As a young dancer, Graham became interested in using movement to express mood and emotion. In 1929 she started her own ballet company, and for many years she devised new ballets, designed costumes and danced leading roles. Many of her ballets were protests, commenting on the position of women, and several were influenced by Greek myths, and by her ideas on how ancient Greek dancers moved. She retired from dancing in 1973, aged 79, but went on teaching and writing for many years after that.

SMITH, Bessie

US jazz singer 1895-1937

Smith's first success came from her tours of the American South, singing the blues in "tent shows" (literally shows given in tents, not concert halls). Then, in 1923, a talent scout heard her and asked her to record for Columbia Records. Her *Down Hearted Blues* was an overnight success. She became the most famous jazz singer in the world, and was known as "Empress of the Blues". Six years later, when talking films took over from jazz as the main entertainment fashion, her career began to fade. She went on singing, however, and was just making a comeback in 1937 when she was killed in a car accident.

RUTH, George Herman

US baseball player 1895-1948

"Babe" Ruth was not only gifted as a pitcher, but was magnificent at the bat. His frequent home runs (his record was 60 in one season, in 1927) changed people's ideas about how baseball should be played and so made the game more exciting. He attracted huge crowds, and set many records, including leading the home-runs in the American League for twelve seasons, and getting 457 total bases in 1921 (the most ever scored in a single season).

FLAGSTAD, Kirsten Malfrid

Norwegian opera singer 1895-1962

Flagstad, born into a musical family, learned the part of Elsa (the heroine of **Wagner**'s opera *Lohengrin*) at the age of 10. She went on to become a professional singer and sang in Scandinavia until she was 38. Then she was invited to sing at Bayreuth, Wagner's own opera-house in Germany. Because Wagner's music needs great physical stamina, fine Wagner-singers are rare – and

"Babe" Ruth, one of the finest players in the history of baseball.

Bessie Smith.

FLAGSTAD: Wagner 36

Flagstad is remembered as one of the greatest of them all.

Although Flagstad's husband supported the Nazi rulers of Norway in the Second World War, she herself refused to sing in Norway at this time. But even a distant connection with Nazis damaged her reputation, and in her later years she was faced by angry demonstrators, especially in the USA. She retired in 1953.

KEATON, Joseph Francis ("Buster")

US comedian and film-maker 1895-1966

Keaton began work as a comedian when he was 3 years old, in his parents' slapstick act. His father pretended to punch him, kick him, hit him with broom-handles and hurl him about the stage – and baby Buster escaped each "attack" in the nick of time. His parents often had to leave town in a hurry, to avoid arrest for supposed cruelty for children. Buster continued in stage slapstick until he went into films at 22. In his first silent comedies he starred with the comedian Fatty Arbuckle, but from 1920 he wrote, co-directed and starred in his own solo films.

In his comedies, Keaton played a handsome, stony-faced young man. Whatever disasters loomed, his face never flickered. He packed the films with stunts: diving from upstairs windows, swinging on ropes to rescue girls from raging rapids, cartwheeling and tumbling in a hurricane, standing still while buildings fell all round him. His short films include *Cops* (in which he accidentally blows up a police parade and is chased by every cop in town) and *The Boat* (in which he builds, and tries to sail, a leaky homemade boat). His feature films include *The Navigator* (in which he and his girlfriend are marooned on an empty ocean liner) and *The General*, in which he is a train-driver who defeats the enemy single-handed in the American Civil War.

In the 1930s Keaton became an alcoholic, and his work suffered. It took him 20 years to recover, and to rebuild his career. But in the 1950s his films began to be reissued, and people everywhere discovered what his fans had claimed for years – that he was one of the funniest of all the silent film comedians.

Buster Keaton, playing the part of a lonely millionaire in his comedy film *The Navigator*.

FORD, John

US film director 1895-1974

Ford began working in Hollywood in the early days of film, and by 1915 was a busy actor. In 1916 he turned to directing, and in the next 54 years made 120 films of all kinds: comedy, history (for example *Young Mr Lincoln*), detection and war (for example *Vietnam, Vietnam*). He is best known for westerns. Many of them star his friend John **Wayne**, and include several of the most famous ever made: *Stagecoach, My Darling Clementine, The Man Who Shot Liberty Valance, She Wore a Yellow Ribbon.*

Busby Berkeley, surrounded by film from *The Gold Diggers of 1935.*

BERKELEY, Busby William Enos

US film director 1895-1976

Berkeley began as a stage dancer and choreographer, but moved to Hollywood in the 1930s to direct film musicals. He favoured huge spectaculars, filling the screen with hundreds of dancers: girls in long, sequinned dresses and men in top hats and tails. Often, he filmed the dancers from high above, so that they looked like flower-petals or sea-anemones opening and closing in time to the music. The best-known musicals Berkeley worked on are *Forty-Second Street, Dames, Gold Diggers of 1935, Babes in Arms* (starring Judy Garland and Mickey Rooney), *Strike Up the Band* and *For Me and My Gal* (starring Judy Garland and Gene **Kelly**).

NURMI, Paavo Johannes

Finnish athlete 1897-1973

As a boy of 12 Nurmi invented his own training programme. He ran not against other athletes but against the clock, using a stop watch to time each lap exactly and adjusting his pace to increase or slow down his speed – an idea followed by long- and middle-distance runners ever since. In the 1920 Olympics he won the 10,000 m, and took an individual and a team medal in the cross-country race.

In the 1924 Olympics Nurmi won 5 gold medals – a record which still stands – for the 1,500 m, 5,000 m, cross-country (individual and team) and steeplechase. In the 1928 Olympics he won the 10,000 m. He was hoping to enter the marathon in

FORD: Wayne 272 BERKELEY: Kelly, Gene 277

the 1932 Games, but was banned for professionalism – the Olympic Games are officially only for amateurs. At the Helsinki Games of 1952, then aged 55, he carried the torch into the arena, the only holder of 12 Olympic medals for athletics – 9 gold and 3 silver.

The Finn Nurmi, winner of 12 Olympic golds.

EISENSTEIN, Sergei

Russian film director 1898-1948

In the early days of film, directors simply pointed the camera at actors and left them to perform. There was no "montage": using cuts, close-ups and other editing skills to control the speed and viewpoint of a story. If, for example, early film-makers wanted to show someone making a phone call, they showed just that: an actor picking up a phone, getting the number and talking. A modern director might cut between close-ups of dialling fingers, the phone ringing at the other end, people's faces as they talked and so on: unreal and unnatural, but giving an impression of fast-moving reality. Eisenstein perfected this kind of montage, and all later film-makers learned from him.

Eisenstein's films were all on historical subjects, and about groups of people. They include *Battleship Potemkin* (about a strike and riot just before the Russian Revolution, and their savage repression by the authorities), *October* (about the storming of the Winter Palace in Leningrad during the Russian Revolution), *Alexander Nevsky* (about **Nevsky** the medieval warrior-prince) and *Ivan The Terrible*, set in the court of a tyrannical emperor from Russia's past.

ROBESON, Paul Le Roy

US actor and singer 1898-1976

In his youth Robeson was successful as both scholar and athlete. In 1921 he had his first stage success, and spent his 20s and 30s playing serious, leading parts in days when blacks were usually confined to acting slaves or comic, eye-rolling servants. He was also a singer, famous for his deep bass voice. He specialized in negro spirituals and in such songs as "Ol' Man River" from the musical *Showboat*. Robeson was also interested in politics. He supported **Roosevelt**'s New Deal in the 1930s, and in the 1940s and 1950s campaigned against **McCarthy**'s anti-left "witch-hunts". Because of his politics he was exiled from the USA from 1958 until 1963; he settled in England, and starred in many stage-shows, including a season of plays at Stratford-on-Avon, **Shakespeare**'s birthplace. He went back to the USA in 1963, in the heyday of **Kennedy**'s presidency, and supported the equal-rights movement led by Martin Luther **King**.

The talented Paul Robeson. Before he took up acting and singing, Robeson graduated from Rutgers University in New York State with a law degree.

EISENSTEIN: Nevsky 169 ROBESON: Kennedy 472 King, M L 236 McCarthy 233 Roosevelt 464 Shakespeare 16

LENGLEN, Suzanne Rachel Flore

French tennis player 1899-1938

Lenglen's father watched English women play tennis in Nice and realized that his daughter could beat them if she trained and played in the more aggressive men's style. She did – combining it with speed, grace and accuracy. She was admired for her fashionable – if then rather shocking – clothes, and other female tennis players imitated her. She won 15 Wimbledon titles, 6 French and 2 Olympic medals, and lost only one singles match (because of an asthma attack). Many people consider Lenglen the best-ever female tennis player. After she retired from tournaments in 1927, she spent her time coaching children and writing books. She died of leukaemia in 1938.

The energetic leaps made by Lenglen were much admired by the crowds. Here, she is playing at Wimbledon, in the summer of 1922.

Bogart at his best, playing the part of Rick in *Casablanca*, who helped his former lover to escape from the Nazis. Bogart became famous for playing the part of tough guys with soft hearts.

BOGART, Humphrey

US film star 1899-1957

Bogart started his acting career on the stage, but had no great success until he went into films. At first he specialized in playing gangsters and thugs, with a cigarette dangling from his mouth, a sneer on his face and a lisping, rasping voice. In the 1940s he changed his screen image, still playing the tough guy but this time with a heart of gold. His best-known parts of this kind include Sam Spade, detective hero of *The Maltese Falcon*, Rick the innkeeper fighting Nazis in *Casablanca*, and the grumpy fisherman of *To Have and Have Not* whose boat is hijacked by gun-smugglers. Bogart's other famous films include *The African Queen* and *The Caine Mutiny*. He died of cancer, brought on by the thousands of cigarettes he smoked.

ELLINGTON, "Duke" Edward Kennedy

US jazz musician 1899-1974

Ellington was nicknamed "Duke" at school, and kept the name ever afterwards. He played the piano, but soon began composing for and leading large groups of jazz players – big bands. Many of the best jazz musicians played in his band, and

Ellington used their different ways of making music in his works. He is considered one of the pioneers of jazz, and many of his compositions, for example *Mood Indigo* and *Sophisticated Lady*, are still known worldwide. He was the first jazz musician whose works were played in Westminster Abbey, London.

ABRAHAMS, Harold

English athlete 1899-1978

When Abrahams was an undergraduate at Cambridge University, he just failed to reach the final of the 100 m race at the 1920 Olympic Games. He spent the next four years working single-mindedly to improve his running technique, and went to the 1924 Paris Olympics as British national record holder of the long-jump, and champion of the 100 yards dash at his university. At the Paris Olympics he won the 100 m: the first European to win an Olympic sprint. At the time, many athletes thought that the way he trained was unsporting – because he took it seriously, as if he were a professional and not an amateur. There was particular rivalry between him and Eric **Liddell** (a story later told with many exaggerations, in the film *Chariots of Fire*). In 1925 Abrahams gave up racing because of injury and began two new careers: as an administrator and as one of the first-ever sports broadcasters.

The sprinter Harold Abrahams reaches the finishing line.

HITCHCOCK, Alfred

English film director 1899-1980

"Hitch" (as he was nicknamed) made thriller films. His heroes and heroines are innocent people who witness crimes, or are wrongly suspected; they find themselves on the run from crooks, the police or both. Hitchcock filled his films with jokes and unlikely happenings. In *North by Northwest*, for example, the hero is attacked by a crop-spraying aircraft; in *The Birds* birds turn on human beings and try to exterminate them. The chases which end the films take place in unlikely places: on the torch of the Statue of Liberty, for example, or across the eyebrows and down the noses of the giant stone faces carved on Mount Rushmore in America. Hitchcock himself made a fleeting appearance in every film, and set his fans the riddle of spotting him. His best-known films include *Dial M for Murder, Strangers on a Train, The 39 Steps* and the creepy *Psycho*. He also made a TV series called "Alfred Hitchcock presents...", and edited many books of stories in each of which, to use his favourite phrase, "Something h-h-horrible" is sure to happen.

Hitchcock's thriller *The Birds* is based on a story by novelist Daphne du Maurier. It tells of birds massing to attack human beings. It took months to train the birds.

ABRAHAMS: Liddell 268

Fred Astaire, dancing with Ginger Rogers in the 1935 film *Top Hat*.

ASTAIRE, Fred (Frederick Austerlitz)

US dancer, singer and actor 1899-1988

In his 20s Astaire had huge success as a stage star, dancing and singing with his sister Adèle. When Adèle retired to get married, Astaire continued for a time on his own, and then went into films. He starred in some of the best-loved film musicals of the 1930s and 1940s, including *Top Hat, Shall We Dance?* and *Easter Parade*. Leading composers of the time, including **Gershwin**, Kern and **Berlin**, wrote songs for him, and Frank **Sinatra** once said that "Fred introduced more hit tunes than all the rest of us put together". Astaire's specialities were ballroom-dancing (often with Ginger Rogers), whirlwind tap-dancing, and comedy dance-routines (for example in *Easter Parade*, where he and Judy Garland danced as tramps).

Louis Armstrong, who was nicknamed "Satchmo" or "Satch", because of his large "satchel" mouth.

ARMSTRONG, (Daniel) Louis

US jazz musician 1900-71

Armstrong was brought up in a children's home, where he learned to play cornet and trumpet. At this time, jazz was the most popular music in New Orleans (Armstrong's home town), and after a few years he began playing with bands. In 1925 he formed his own bands, the Hot Five and Hot Seven, to make records. These records took the sound of jazz round the world.

Armstrong played with great wit and style, and used higher notes than most trumpeters were willing to risk. He also sang, in a unique, gravelly voice. He invented "scat" singing: putting nonsense syllables ("ba doo ba doo ba") to the notes of a jazz solo, "playing" his voice like an instrument. In 1947 he formed the All Stars, a band which lasted for the next 38 years. He had a warm-hearted, "larger-than-life" personality, and made many successful appearances in films. In 1964 his recording of *Hello Dolly* knocked even the **Beatles** from first place in the pop-music charts.

BUÑUEL, Luis

Spanish writer and film-director 1900-83

Buñuel's parents wanted him to be a priest, but he preferred writing and film-making. He was a friend of the

ASTAIRE: Berlin 256 Gershwin 68 Sinatra 280 ARMSTRONG: Beatles 312 painter **Dalí**, and like him was a "surrealist", believing that the dream world was as important, and as fascinating, as the real world. In Buñuel's films, nothing is quite what it seems. People eating at a dinner-party suddenly find that they are in a play on a stage, and have forgotten the words; priests turn out to be criminals; torture brings people not suffering, but ecstasy.

Buñuel was anxious to show how false the values of ordinary, polite society seemed to him. He satirized big business, aristocrats, politics and religion. Many Christians find the ideas in his films blasphemous: beggars washing each other's feet, for example, or parodying **Christ**'s Last Supper. In some Roman Catholic countries (including his native Spain) Buñuel's films were banned for years. But they are now available, and many people think him one of the finest directors in cinema history.

Buñuel's best-known films include *Los Olvidados* (about a gang of beggar-children in Mexico City), *Robinson Crusoe, The Exterminating Angel, The Discreet Charm of the Bourgeoisie* and *That Obscure Object of Desire*.

DISNEY, Walt

US artist and film-maker 1901-66

Disney was a pioneer of cartoon films, which use drawings instead of live actors. His character Mickey Mouse, invented in 1928, became so popular that Disney was able to build his own studio to make cartoons (the first in the world). Disney drew the initial ideas for each cartoon himself, then handed his sketches over to a team of artists, who made thousands of drawings for every film. Their short comedy cartoons "starred" animated characters such as Goofy, Pluto and Donald Duck – and in 1938 they made the first full-length cartoon film, *Snow White and the Seven Dwarfs*.

In the 1950s, as well as cartoons, Disney Studios began to make family adventure films (for example *Twenty Thousand Leagues Under The Sea* and *Treasure Island*). They also made films (such as *Mary Poppins*) blending real actors and cartoon characters. Nowadays they make and finance films of every kind. Disney was also one of the first people to begin "character merchandising": letting people use his characters on clothes, and selling them as toys. In the 1960s he opened Disneyland, a huge park and funfair, where people could go and meet all the characters from his films, played by dressed-up actors. It was the first theme park ever built.

Disney's character Mickey Mouse was not just seen on the screen. All sorts of novelties – toys, watches and clothing – began to appear. The first were these toys, pictured with Walt Disney in 1929.

BUÑUEL: Jesus Christ 329 Dalí 71

CROSBY, Harry Lillis ("Bing")

US singer and film actor 1901-77

Crosby began his career as a singer with Paul **Whiteman**'s band. He sang solos, and in a group called the Rhythm Boys. After some months, he was unexpectedly offered a daily radio show and shot to stardom. He specialized in "crooning" (singing softly, close to the microphone), as well as singing jazzy, comic songs. He recorded 2,500 songs, and had hundreds of hits. His version of *White Christmas* is one of the best-selling records ever made.

From 1930 onwards, Crosby made films, chiefly musicals (for example *Going My Way*, in which he plays a singing priest), and comedies. His best-known films are *Sing You Sinners, High Society* and a series of "Road" comedies (*Road to Singapore, Road to Rio, Road to Bali* and so on), which he made in a wisecracking double act with Bob Hope (born 1903). In the "Road" films Crosby and Hope play a couple of conmen, down on their luck, each competing with the other to make his fortune and to win the girl. In private life Crosby and Hope were good friends, who often played golf together in charity matches. Crosby died on the golf course in mid-shot – the end he always said he wanted.

Bing Crosby (right) with Bob Hope in *The Road to Bali.*

HEIFETZ, Jascha

Russian/US violinist 1901-87

Heifetz was a child prodigy, playing **Mendelssohn**'s Violin Concerto at the age of 6. His public career began when he was 11, and continued until 1972. He was not a showy performer, but his technical and musical mastery were awesome, earning him the nickname of the "fiddle-players' fiddler" and a reputation as the greatest violinist of his time.

LIDDELL, Eric

Scottish athlete 1902-45

Liddell was a strict Christian. At the 1924 Olympics he was entered for the 100 m sprint and for the relays, but withdrew when he found that they all had heats or finals on a Sunday. To run on the Sabbath day would have been against his religious ideas. Many people in Britain had hoped to see a showdown between Liddell and his rival **Abrahams**. Liddell did not believe in training, apart from playing rugby, while Abrahams did. Both entered the 200 m sprint, but neither won. Liddell then ran in the individual 400 m, and won it by the huge margin of 5 m, an Olympic record and an astonishing feat. Not long after these Olympics, he retired from athletics and went to China as a missionary. He died as a prisoner of war during the Second World War.

The violinist Jascha Heifetz, for whom many composers wrote music, including the American Samuel Barber and the Englishman William Walton.

CROSBY: Whiteman 259 HEIFETZ: Mendelssohn 34 LIDDELL: Abrahams 265

JONES, Robert Tyre

US golfer 1902-71

"Bobby" Jones learned to play golf by watching his parents. He won his club's tournament at 9 years old, and at 14 entered the US amateur championship. He went on to win this five times. As well as playing amateur golf, he entered professional championships, and won the US Open four times and the British Open three times. He is remembered as the world's finest golfer of the 1920s and 1930s.

RODGERS, Richard

US composer 1902-79

When Rodgers was a music student, he wrote songs for university shows, and this kindled his interest in the stage. He was 25 when he composed his first hit musical, *Connecticut Yankee*, to words by Lorenz Hart (1895-1943). The two men went on to write many more successes, including *On Your Toes* and *Babes in Arms*. After Hart's death Rodgers teamed up with Oscar Hammerstein II (1895-1960) to write some of the best-loved musicals of the century: *Oklahoma!*, *Carousel*, *South Pacific*, *The King and I*, and *The Sound of Music*.

RIEFENSTAHL, Leni

German film director 1902-88

Riefenstahl began her career as a ballet dancer, and also enjoyed skiing and mountaineering. In 1929 she acted in a film about climbing, which gave her the taste for cinema. She took up directing – a rare thing for a woman at that time – and began making films about the Nazi party. **Hitler** asked her to film the 1934 Nuremberg Rally, the biggest gathering of Nazi supporters ever seen. Riefenstahl filmed the rally like an epic, showing Hitler idolized by millions of cheering followers. The film, *Triumph of the Will*, earned Riefenstahl high honour in the Nazi party. She then made another propaganda masterpiece, *1936 Olympic Games*. It showed athletes preparing for and competing in the games – and its commentary boasted that white athletes were superior to all others. Riefenstahl avoided showing Hitler's fury at the extraordinary victories of the black US athlete Jesse **Owens**.

During the 1940s Riefenstahl made other Nazi films, and after the war no one would employ her. She published books of photographs, and experimented with underwater photography. But politics had engulfed her talent; when the Nazi dream died she made no more films.

A close-up shot of one of the white athletes performing in the 1936 Olympic Games, from the film with the same title, directed by Leni Riefenstahl.

RIEFENSTAHL: Hitler 466 Owens, J 278

The bandleader and trombonist Glen Miller.

BEIDERBECKE, Leon ("Bix")

US jazz musician 1903-31

As a child, Beiderbecke taught himself to play both piano and cornet. He heard jazz musicians (including Louis **Armstrong**) play on Mississippi river-boats, and later joined a band called the Wolverines. Eventually he became a featured player in Paul **Whiteman**'s band, though he was often missing because of excessive drinking. Eventually he died of alcohol-related diseases.

All jazz cornet players envy Beiderbecke's dazzling rhythm and perfect sense of pitch. He was one of the first white jazz players to be admired by black musicians. His style is "cooler" than the "hot" jazz of such people as Armstrong.

FERNANDEL (Fernand Joseph Désiré Contandin)

French film comedian 1903-71

Fernandel began as an acrobatic dancer in music-hall. He was famous for his long, horsy face with its toothy grin. In the 1940s he began making films, and specialized in lunatic comedies. His greatest success was as Don Camillo, a Catholic priest forever squabbling with the communist mayor of his small Italian town. In the 1950s and 1960s Fernandel's half dozen Camillo films, especially *The Little World of Don Camillo*, were worldwide hits.

Fernandel as the Catholic priest in *The Little World of Don Camillo*, in 1952.

MILLER, Glen

US jazz bandleader 1904-(?)44

Miller began his career as a band arranger and trombone player, and began founding bands of his own in the 1930s. He experimented with different instrumental sounds and combinations of players, and in 1939 the "Glen Miller sound" caught on. His band had two enormous hits, *Moonlight Serenade* and *In the Mood*. In 1942 Miller and several of his players joined the US army to play for the troops. Two years later, after a tour in Britain, Miller set out by plane for Paris – and was never seen again.

WEISSMULLER, Johnny (Peter John)

Romanian/US swimmer and film star 1904-84

In the 1920s swimming was not a scientific sport. Training was non-existent, and there were none of today's official, exactly described styles (such as butterfly or backstroke). Weissmuller changed all that. He trained every day and developed a fast, "freestyle" stroke which brought him over 50 US titles and over 60 world records. In the Olympics of 1924 and 1928 he won five gold medals, plus a bronze for water polo.

BEIDERBECKE: Armstrong, L 266 Whiteman 259

In 1932 Weissmuller was invited to Hollywood to star as Tarzan the ape-man. In the film, he dived and swam, swung on rope-like creepers from tree to tree, and used a long yodelling shout which became his trademark. He starred in half a dozen films, and made Tarzan a world-famous name. In 1942 he gave up films, and began a third career as a swimming coach, going back to Hollywood briefly in 1975 to act in the spoof adventure film *Won Ton Ton, the Dog that Saved Hollywood*.

FONDA FAMILY

US actors 20th century

Jane Fonda with her father Henry, in a happy scene from *On Golden Pond*, when father and daughter are reconciled at last.

HENRY FONDA (1905-82) was one of the best known of all Hollywood film stars. He specialized in "strong, silent" characters, forced to take action to right terrible wrongs. In the film based on **Steinbeck**'s novel *The Grapes of Wrath*, for example, he played a man driven to murder by poverty and injustice. In other films he played such heroes as Abraham **Lincoln** and Wyatt Earp. He also made comedies (for example *Yours, Mine and Ours*, where he played the harrassed father of a large teenage family), and a moving film about an old man realizing that he still loves the daughter (played by his own daughter, Jane) he has refused to speak to for years: *On Golden Pond*.

JANE FONDA (born 1937), Henry's daughter, began as a model and stage actress, and in her 20s moved into films. In the 1960s she made comedies (for example, the spoof western *Cat Ballou*), science fiction (for example *Barbarella*) and serious films (for example *Klute*). In 1968 she began to involve herself in politics, speaking out against US involvement in Vietnam. She began to pick and choose her parts, and made more serious films than earlier in her career: **Ibsen**'s *A Doll's House, Coming Home* (about a woman who falls in love with a crippled Vietnam veteran), and *The China Syndrome*, a thriller about the cover-up after a near-catastrophe at a nuclear power station.

In the 1980s she spent much time publicizing the Jane Fonda way to health: a system of diet, yoga and aerobic exercises, now practised around the world.

PETER FONDA (born 1939), Jane's brother, won stardom in *Easy Rider* in 1969. He has since produced, directed and acted in over a dozen films, including a western (*The Hired Hand*) and the comedy *The Hostage Tower*, about a gang of crooks who steal the Eiffel Tower.

FONDA FAMILY: Ibsen 40 Steinbeck 70 Lincoln 452

GARBO, Greta

Swedish film star 1905-90

Garbo's real name was Greta Gustafsson. She began in Swedish films, but moved to Hollywood when she was 19 and became one of the most famous stars in history. She always played beautiful women who were mysterious, who had a "secret". The press claimed that this was her character in real life too: it was headline news when Garbo smiled for the first time on screen (in *Ninotchka*, her 26th film).

Garbo enjoyed being mysterious. She never gave interviews and never spoke to fans. In 1941 she retired from acting and has hardly been seen or photographed since. One of her catch phrases was "I want to be alone" – and she has made it as true in life as in her films.

Actors John Wayne (right) and James Stewart (left) take a break from shooting the film *The Man Who Shot Liberty Valance*, directed by John Ford (seated in the centre) in 1962.

WAYNE, John

US film star 1907-79

Wayne's real name was Marion Michael Morrison. He was an athlete and a skilled horseman. He began his film career as a stuntman in westerns and adventure serials. Gradually he was given larger parts, and by his 70th film, *Stagecoach*, he was a star. *Stagecoach*, like many of Wayne's later films, was directed by his friend John **Ford.**

Wayne specialized in action films. Some (*The Sands of Iwo Jima* and *The Green Berets*) were set in modern wars, and showed the courage and heroism of US fighting men. But most were westerns – and they include some of the most popular ever made: *Red River, She Wore a Yellow Ribbon, Rio Bravo, The Alamo* and the comedy *True Grit*.

In his last years Wayne suffered from cancer, and insisted that his condition should be openly reported. His fight against the disease gave hope to many other sufferers. His last film, made when he was already ill, is *The Shootist*, about an ageing gun-fighter, dying of cancer, who decides to rid the world of as many bad guys as he can before he dies. It is not only Wayne's bravest performance, but his best.

Right: Laurence Olivier, playing Hamlet in his 1947 film version of Shakespeare's play.

WAYNE: Ford 262

Um Kalthum, Egypt's superstar singer of the twentieth century.

OLIVIER, Laurence

English actor and director 1907-89

Olivier spent some years as a Hollywood star (in such films as *Wuthering Heights* and *Rebecca*), but his main interest was the stage. He acted in everything from comedy to Greek tragedy, and in the course of his life played most of the star roles in **Shakespeare**'s plays.

Olivier was interested in management as well as acting. He formed several companies, in London and to tour the world. He worked long and hard for the creation of the British National Theatre, and became its first artistic director in 1963. He was made a knight in 1947 and a lord in 1970 – the first actor ever to be so honoured.

As an actor, Olivier was superb in such grand, heroic parts as Oedipus (in the play by **Sophocles**) or Shakespeare's Coriolanus. He also excelled as shifty, villainous characters, rolling his eyes and flicking his tongue like a viper. His performances, on stage and screen, as Shakespeare's **Richard III** and as a seedy, failed comedian in John Osborne's *The Entertainer* made other actors avoid those parts for years, afraid that they could never equal him. He directed himself in *Richard III*, and in two other Shakespeare films, *Hamlet* and *Henry V*. In his 60s and 70s, plagued by bad health, he took up TV acting, and played guest parts in many films: a sinister dentist in *Marathon Man* (torturing Dustin Hoffman with a dentist's drill), a Jewish rabbi in *The Jazz Singer*, and Van Helsing, the scientist who helps to combat the evil count in *Dracula*.

KALTHUM, Ibrahim Um

Egyptian singer 1908-75

When Kalthum was 6 she began singing in public at weddings. Her parents had her educated in the Islamic musical tradition. She intended to become a professional singer from the age of 14, but did not give her first successful concert until 1926, aged 22. After this, however, her fame quickly grew. She used to sing solo for several hours to huge crowds at open air venues, and she made many musical films in the 1930s and 1940s. She retired in 1973, aged 65, and when she died, two years later, millions of people, ordinary and famous, attended her funeral.

OLIVIER: Richard III 434 Shakespeare 16 Sophocles 5

TATI, Jacques

French comedian and film-director 1908-82

In the 1930s Tati performed comic mimes in music-halls. He imitated tennis-players, fishermen and other sports performers. In his most famous mime, he played both horse and rider, prancing round an imaginary circus ring. In the 1940s he started making comedy films. In *Jour de Fête* he plays a country postman whose eagerness to learn the latest efficient methods causes chaos. In *Monsieur Hulot's Holiday*, tall, clumsy Mr Hulot (Tati) goes to the seaside, and creates havoc. His canoe folds in two as he paddles it, looks like a shark and causes panic. He gets lost in the dark, strikes a match, and finds that he is inside a shed full of fireworks. In *My Uncle* Mr Hulot's attempts to entertain his nephew totally destroy the tidy, well-organized world of the boy's parents and their snooty friends.

Vanessa Redgrave as Madame Arkadina in Chekhov's play *The Seagull*, in the London performance in 1985.

REDGRAVE FAMILY

English actors 20th century

The Redgraves are one of the main twentieth-century families in English theatre. MICHAEL REDGRAVE (1908-85) was famous both for playing in **Shakespeare** and as the decent, ordinary hero in such war films as *The Dam Busters*. His wife RACHEL KEMPSON (born 1910) gave up full-time acting to bring up their family, but played small parts on stage or in films. Their daughter VANESSA REDGRAVE (born 1937) was famous both for her stage-performances (in such plays as **Chekhov**'s *The Seagull*) and for her revolutionary politics. Her brother CORIN REDGRAVE (born 1939), sister LYNN REDGRAVE (born 1943), daughter JOELY RICHARDSON (born 1966), and Corin's daughter JEMMA REDGRAVE (born 1965), also followed the family tradition, appearing in films, TV and on the stage.

KARAJAN, Herbert von

Austrian conductor 1908-89

In 1923 Karajan saw **Toscanini** conduct and decided to become a conductor. His first professional post was at the opera house in Ulm, where he learned all aspects of opera production, including direction, costume design and lighting. In 1937, after guest-conducting operas in

Herbert von Karajan, one of the best classical conductors of the century.

REDGRAVE FAMILY: Chekhov 52 Shakespeare 16 KARAJAN: Mozart 26 Toscanini 251

Vienna and Berlin, he was hailed as a star, and in 1955, despite doubts about his support for the Nazis during the Second World War, he was made director-for-life of the Berlin Philharmonic, one of the finest orchestras in the world. He was also artistic director of the **Mozart** Festival at Salzburg, his own as well as Mozart's birthplace. He made more records, CDs and video discs than any other classical conductor.

BRADMAN, Donald George

Australian cricketer born 1908

Bradman played in his first international match at 20 and became captain of Australia in 1936. During the 12 years of his captaincy, his team never lost. His batting skill was tremendous, and many of his records still stand. Almost 40% of his innings ended in centuries, and his career average in Test matches of 99.94 runs per innings is unsurpassed. When he retired from cricket he became a successful businessman and golfer.

Fast action frozen by the camera. Don Bradman at the wicket in a Test match.

GRAPPELLI, Stephane

French jazz violinist born 1908

Grappelli studied violin at the Paris Conservatoire. For a time he lived from hand to mouth in Paris, busking and accompanying silent films. In his early 20s he met Django **Reinhardt**. They played jazz together and formed a group which quickly became famous as the Quintette du Hot Club de France. Although this broke up at the beginning of the Second World War (when Grappelli went briefly to live in London), Grappelli continued as one of the few jazz violinists. In the 1970s he was persuaded to play in a new version of the Hot Club Quintet, and unexpectedly became an international star in his 70s. His old records were reissued and he made many new ones, some with the classical violinist Yehudi **Menuhin**.

TATUM, Arthur ("Art")

US jazz piano player 1909-56

Although almost blind from birth, Tatum began to play piano jazz when a young child. His playing was phenomenal: both jazz and classical musicians then and now speak of him with awe. Over a bouncy left-hand beat he varied the tune in showers and cascades of right-hand notes, with obvious enjoyment.

GRAPPELLI: Menuhin 281 Reinhardt 276

"Hot and cool": *Above* the jazz musician Benny Goodman and...

GOODMAN, Benny

US jazz musician 1909-86

When Goodman was 11 years old, he began to learn the clarinet, and by 13 he was good enough to play jazz in bands. Six years later his father died, and Goodman supported his mother and 11 brothers and sisters by working as a session musician, playing in recording studios. Throughout his life he formed big and small groups, using many well-known jazz musicians. In his early days his music was so "hot" that it made audiences riot with joy, and in 1938 he was one of the first jazz musicians to appear at Carnegie Hall, the main New York concert hall. In the 1940s he began to record pieces of classical music (for example **Mozart**'s Clarinet Concerto), and leading composers of the time, including **Bartók** and **Copland**, wrote works for him.

REINHARDT, Jean Baptiste

Belgian jazz guitarist 1910-53

"Django" Reinhardt was a gypsy, and played the violin and guitar. When he was 18 two fingers of his left hand were paralysed after a fire in his caravan, and he had to develop a new, unique way of playing the guitar. He played for a while in night clubs, then in 1934 he and Stephane **Grappelli** formed the Quintette du Hot Club de France, the first European jazz band to win real fame. After the Second World War Reinhardt tried to compose but found the writing of music difficult. (It was the same with words: he only ever learned to write his name). Jazz players (especially guitarists) idolized Reinhardt, but in his final years, despite regular recording and club work, he began to prefer fishing to playing jazz. He died suddenly of a stroke at 43.

HENJE, Sonja

Norwegian skater and actress 1910-69

Henje was Norway's women's ice skating champion at 11, and took part in her first winter Olympics at 15, winning a gold medal for skating *The Dying Swan*. Her performance changed people's ideas about women's ice skating, making it an artistic sport as well as an athletic one. Henje went on to win 10 world championships from 1927 to 1936, and is still considered one of the finest figure-skaters there has ever been.

After 1936 Henje began a second career, as a Hollywood film-actress. She made musicals, many with

Right: Norway's ice-skating champion and Hollywood star Sonja Henje.

GOODMAN: Bartók 60 Copland 70 Mozart 26 REINHARDT: Grappelli 275 skating stories. She retired in 1952 and with her husband founded a modern art museum in Oslo.

KUROSAWA, Akiro

Japanese film director born 1910

Kurosawa began as an artist and an assistant director, and made his first film as director in 1943. His best-known films are historical, and many take place in the time of the samurai, Japanese warriors in the Middle Ages. *The Seven Samurai* is about a group of heroes who protect a peasant village against bandits. (It was remade as a Hollywood western, *The Magnificent Seven*.) *Kagemusha* ("The Shadow Warrior") is about a warlord trying to hold the nation together against plots, invasions and treachery. *Rashomon* shows the investigation into murder in an eerie forest. *Throne of Blood* resets the story of **Shakespeare**'s *Macbeth* in Japan, making Macbeth a warlord, and *Ran* does the same with the story of *King Lear*.

FANGIO, Juan Manuel

Argentinian racing driver born 1911

Fangio began circuit racing in Europe when he was 37 years old, in a car he built himself. His career until then had been hindered by lack of money and by military service in the Second World War. He won his first world title in 1951, and was champion again from 1954 to 1957 – a record. He was a calm driver who always went for the slowest times at which he could win and who could patiently nurse a failing car to the finishing point.

KUROSAWA: Shakespeare 16

The Argentinian driver Fangio, aged 76, taking part in the veteran car rally, prior to the 1987 Grand Prix in Brazil, in his Mercedes 154.

KELLY, Gene

US dancer, actor and director born 1912

Kelly began as a stage dancer, but moved into films when he was 30. He starred in some of the best-loved of all film musicals (*On the Town; An American in Paris; Singin' in the Rain*), and helped with the choreography and direction as well as dancing. He sang and acted in a cheerful, light-comedy style. In later years he turned to directing and his films include the musical *Hello Dolly* and the drama *Marjorie Morningstar*. Apart from his dancing, he was best known for his happy-go-lucky charm; as one critic said, "His grin could melt a stone".

The energetic dancer and film star Gene Kelly.

OWENS, Jesse

US athlete 1913-80

Owens came from a poor family – his grandparents had been slaves. His school coached him in sprinting and long jump, and he was so talented that 28 universities offered him athletics scholarships. In 1935, while at university, he broke six world records in one afternoon.

When **Hitler** staged the 1936 Olympic Games in Germany, he was determined to show that white people were superior to black. He made a speech at the opening ceremony, saying that black people were sub-human. Unfortunately for Hitler, Owens (who was black) won gold medals in no fewer than four events, 100 m, 200 m, long jump and 4×100 m relay, and equalled or broke 12 Olympic records. He was one of several black athletes to gain the crowd's support. After the Games, Owens turned professional, running against greyhounds and horses. Later, he was a supporter of Martin Luther **King**. His granddaughter carried the Olympic flame into the Los Angeles stadium in 1984.

Jesse Owens, the black American athlete of the 1936 Olympics who embarrassed the Nazis by his outstanding success.

Di MAGGIO, Joe

US baseball player born 1914

Di Maggio played for the New York Yankees between 1936-42 and 1946-51, and was one of the best centre fielders and hitters ever known. He was voted Most Valuable Player for three years, 1939, 1941 and 1947. For a short time in the 1950s he was married to Marilyn **Monroe**.

DIDRIKSON, Mildred ("Babe")

US athlete 1914-56

Didrikson was one of the most talented athletes of all time. At 16 years old she broke the world javelin record. She played basketball and baseball to national standard. At 17 she was both long-jump and 80 m hurdles champion, and the following year she represented her club at national level, competing in 8 events in two and a half hours, and winning five firsts.

At the 1932 Olympics, Didrikson won gold medals in the javelin and 80 m hurdles, and a silver in the high jump. She is the only person ever to have won Olympic medals in running, jumping and throwing.

Throughout her life, Didrikson showed talent at every sport from boxing to fencing, billiards to tennis, and after the 1932 Olympics she turned professional, giving athletics exhibitions. She then learned golf and won 17 international championships between 1934 and 1950.

OWENS: Hitler 466 King, M L 236 DI MAGGIO: Monroe, M 285

LOUIS, Joe

US boxer 1914-81

Louis was the world heavyweight champion for 12 years (1937-49) and successfully defended the title 25 times. In his whole career he fought 71 professional fights, and lost only two of them.

Joe Louis, the heavyweight champion who dominated the world of boxing in the 1940s.

HOLIDAY, Billie ("Lady Day")

US jazz singer 1915-59

Holiday had a poverty-stricken, loveless childhood and became a teenage prostitute. She realized that singing could save her from such a life, and in 1933 she joined Benny **Goodman**'s band. She went on to sing in other great jazz bands, such as Count Basie's, and began a solo career in 1939. She is remembered as one of the greatest jazz singers of the century.

All through her life, Holiday was insecure, and eventually she became a heroin addict. She always wore long gloves at performances, to hide the needle-scars in her arms. She died of an overdose in 1959.

Billie Holiday, one of the most popular of all jazz singers, who also wrote many of the songs she sang.

PIAF, Édith

French singer 1915-63

Piaf's life was filled with tragedy. Her only child died, her lovers betrayed her, and she was often ill. Her songs, too, are filled with sadness. She began singing in the streets as a child, and then in music-hall. The name "Piaf" means "little sparrow", and Piaf was indeed tiny (1.45 m tall) and waiflike. But her voice was large, powerful and moving. Her best-known songs are *Je ne regrette rien* ("No Regrets") and *La vie en rose* ("The Good Life"), which she also wrote.

HOLIDAY: Goodman 276

Left: Orson Welles, playing Harry Lime in the film of Graham Greene's thriller *The Third Man.*

WELLES, Orson

US film director, actor and writer 1915-85

When Welles was 23, he wrote and starred in a radio version of H. G. **Wells**' novel *The War of the Worlds,* about a Martian invasion of Earth. Welles filled the play with spoof newscasts, announcing the approach of invading space-ships – and people all over the USA took them for real, and panicked. Welles became famous overnight. He was invited to Hollywood to make any film he liked. He directed and starred in *Citizen Kane,* the story of a multi-millionaire newspaper owner who goes insane with power. The film was a masterpiece; many people ever since have put it head of their list of the ten best films ever made.

Welles never had such success again. He continued to work as an actor, and over the next 40 years appeared in nearly 100 films, and on the stage in such plays as *Othello*, *Macbeth* and *King Lear*. He used the money he earned to finance films of his own: thrillers, versions of **Shakespeare**, comedies and documentaries. He also financed his films by acting in TV commercials: a huge, bearded man advertising sherry and cigars. His hobby was conjuring: he was one of the most skilful magicians in the USA.

WELLES: Shakespeare 16 Wells 55

Stanley Matthews, showing a favourite dribbling technique used by many great footballers.

MATTHEWS, Stanley

UK footballer born 1915

When Matthews left school, at 14 years old, he went to work as an office boy for Stoke City Football Club. He played in the reserves and then, at 17, in the first team. He first played for England at 19. His professional career lasted 33 years, and included 886 matches. He was the first footballer to be given a British knighthood, becoming Sir Stanley Matthews in 1965.

SINATRA, Frank (Francis) Albert

US singer and actor born 1915

Sinatra showed little interest in singing until he was 18, when he heard Bing **Crosby**. At once he began entering talent contests and sang whenever he could. Sinatra noticed how Crosby's career had taken off when he had a radio show, and offered to sing free for a local radio station. The band leader Harry James heard him and signed him up. Sinatra made his first recording in 1939, and six months later joined the Dorsey band, in which many jazz players and singers won their first fame.

In the early 1940s Sinatra was one of the most popular singers in the USA, attracting hordes of fans. In 1944 there was a riot, the "Columbus Day Riot", when 30,000 fans mobbed a New York cinema where he was due to perform. In the 1940s, too, he began making films. He starred in such musicals as *Anchors Aweigh, Take Me Out to the Ball Game* and *On the Town,* and also acted in serious films, winning an Oscar in *From Here to Eternity*.

The ever-popular entertainer, Frank Sinatra.

The coming of rock 'n' roll in the 1950s ended Sinatra's popularity with teenagers. He began to tour night-clubs and cabarets, and made many hit records, including *My Way*, which was in the British pop charts for a record 122 weeks, from 1969 to 1971. He starred in another musical, *High Society* (with Louis **Armstrong** and Bing Crosby), and acted in a score more films. He officially retired from singing in 1971, but has since made many more records, TV appearances and stage comebacks, enthralling a whole new generation.

MENUHIN, Yehudi

US/English violinist and conductor born 1916

Menuhin played **Beethoven**'s Violin Concerto at a concert in New York when he was 11 years old, and recorded **Elgar**'s Concerto when he was 16, with the composer conducting. In the 1940s and 1950s he was one of the world's leading soloists, and was famed for the huge number of concerts (over 100 a year, or two a week) he gave for US troops during the Second World War.

In the 1960s Menuhin broadened his career. He began conducting, and toured Asia, developing his interest in Eastern philosophy and music. He also acted as unofficial ambassador for the United Nations, speaking on behalf of world peace, making links between otherwise hostile countries. In 1963 he began a school for musical children in Britain, and many leading players are among its graduates.

BERGMAN, Ingmar

Swedish film writer and director born 1918

Bergman wrote the scripts for all his films, and also controlled the sound, direction, lighting and camera-angles. Apart from a few comedies (for example *Smiles of a Summer Night)*, he specialized in films about people whose loneliness is made worse by their own grim, harsh personalities. The characters in some of his films are married couples unable to find happiness with each other; others are priests, actors or doctors whose lives have been ruined because they have not been able to love, or to be loved, as they might have wished.

Bergman's best-known films include *The Seventh Seal, Wild Strawberries, Through a Glass Darkly* and *Fanny and Alexander,* the latter based on Bergman's own childhood in 1920s Sweden.

SINATRA: Armstrong, L 266 Crosby 268 MENUHIN: Beethoven 28 Elgar 51

BERNSTEIN, Leonard

US conductor and composer born 1918

Bernstein learned the piano from the age of 10, but only began specialist music training at 21. Four years later, he was asked at short notice to conduct the New York Philharmonic Orchestra because the conductor had fallen ill. The concert was a success, and Bernstein became famous overnight. He has since made music with every important symphony orchestra in the world. From the start, he combined conducting with a second career, as composer. Many of his works blend classical ideas and jazz: Symphony No. 2, the ballet *Fancy Free, Prelude Fugue and Riffs,* written for Benny **Goodman**. Bernstein's best-known works include two musicals, *On the Town* and *West Side Story,* updating the story of **Shakespeare**'s *Romeo and Juliet.*

BLANKERS-KOEN, Francina

Dutch athlete born 1918

Fanny Koen took up athletics at 16, training for the 800 metres. But this event was not then available to women at the Olympics, as it was considered too long and stressful. Koen turned to other events instead, and between 1942 and 1951 set world records in the high jump, long jump and pentathlon.

In 1940 Koen married her coach, Jan Blankers. He encouraged her to specialize in sprinting and hurdling. In the 1948 Olympics, then aged 30, she won four events: 100 m and 4 × 100 m relay, and 200 m and 80 m hurdles. She had been stung by press comment on her age, and her husband used this to needle her to victory, saying "You're too old, Fanny!", just before the hurdles – her hardest race. Until then, no other woman had ever won four gold medals at the same Olympic Games.

Fanny Blankers-Koen, winning the 80 metres hurdles at the 1948 Olympics.

FITZGERALD, Ella

US jazz singer born 1918

In 1934 Fitzgerald won a talent competition, and decided to become a professional singer. She joined Chick Webb's band, and was soon his lead singer. She had huge success with a jazz version of "A tisket, a tasket", and her career was launched. Since then she has sung every kind of song in every jazz style from scat to ballad, from blues to bossa nova. She has made famous versions of songs by **Berlin**, **Gershwin** and Cole Porter. Her *Lady be Good, Manhattan* and *Every Time We Say Goodbye* are known worldwide. Many people consider her to be the greatest female singer in the history of jazz.

Ella Fitzgerald – known to her fans as the "Queen of Jazz".

BERNSTEIN: Goodman 276 Shakespeare 16 FITZGERALD: Berlin 256 Gershwin 68

Right: The ballerina Margot Fonteyn.

FONTEYN, Margot (Margaret Hookham)

English ballet dancer born 1919

Fonteyn studied at the Sadler's Wells ballet school in London, and first performed in **Tchaikovsky**'s *The Nutcracker*. She was soon dancing leading roles to great acclaim, and many modern parts were created for her. She danced all over the world, and became world-famous for her partnerships with Robert Helpmann in the 1940s and Rudolf **Nureyev** in the 1960s. She continued dancing until 1979, after one of the longest careers as a ballet soloist.

PARKER, Charlie ("Bird")

US jazz musician 1920-55

Charlie "Bird" Parker, one of the greatest saxophone players in the history of jazz.

Parker dropped out of school to play the saxophone in local jazz bands. With another musician, Dizzy Gillespie, he helped to develop a new jazz craze, "bebop". Bebop is New York teenage slang for a knife fight, and the music is rhythmic and aggressive. Parker spent most of his life playing with small jazz groups. His solos were so complex that few other musicians could compete with them, and his playing has influenced most later saxophone players. He died of drug addiction and alcoholism.

SHANKAR, Ravi

Indian musician born 1920

Shankar plays the sitar. When he began his career, the kind of music he plays was little known outside India; its worldwide fame today is largely due to him. He has composed music for films (especially by his friend Satyajit Ray), ballets and dance-plays. But he is best known for music making in traditional (or "classical") Indian style, using *ragas* (note-patterns) which have been known for centuries. People in the West know his music partly because of famous admirers who learned from him and made music with him: the **Beatles** and Yehudi **Menuhin**.

FONTEYN: Nureyev 293 Tchaikovsky 44 SHANKAR: Beatles 312 Menuhin 281

CALLAS, Maria Meneghini

Greek opera singer 1922-77

Callas showed talent at an early age for a singer: her first professional performance was when she was 16, at the Athens Royal Opera. By the mid-1940s she was a star. She became legendary not only for her superb voice but for her powerful, emotional acting. She was also famous for the scenes she made off-stage, arguing with managers, quarrelling with conductors, suing newspapers. For many years she was the lover of the Greek shipping millionaire Aristotle Onassis, and their lives were daily news. She retired from the stage in 1965 but continued to make records, especially of the rare nineteenth-century operas at which she excelled.

ZATOPEK, Emil

Czech athlete born 1922

Zatopek was the first runner to train to improve both stamina and speed. Even in the winter, he would run for hours, with spells of leaping strides and jogging. He won the 10,000 m race at the 1948 Olympics, and in the 1952 Olympics he achieved more than any other athlete that year: gold medals in the 5,000 m, 10,000 m and marathon (a distance he was running for the first time). In 1954 Zatopek held the world record for all nine distances between 5,000 m and 30,000 m.

MARCIANO, Rocky

US boxer 1923-69

Marciano took up boxing as a soldier during the Second World War, and became world heavyweight champion in 1952. He retired four years later, having fought 49 professional fights without a single defeat.

MARCEAU, Marcel

French mime artist born 1923

Marceau's most famous character is the clown Bip, and he has played the part all over the world, introducing mime to millions of people. Bip is tall, thin and gawky, like a scarecrow. His face is deathly white, with a sad, red mouth. His clothes are too big, and are covered in gaudy patches. His battered top hat has a flower in it. Marceau shows us Bip cleaning windows, climbing ladders, drinking, walking in a high wind, sailing, fighting, being thrown into jail – all by the skill of his movements alone. In his best-known mime of all, he shows us Bip's whole life, from birth through childhood and maturity to old age and death.

SELLERS, Peter

English actor 1925-80

Sellers began as an impressionist, "the man of a thousand voices". In the 1950s he was one of the stars of radio's *The Goon Show*, and appeared in dozens of other comedy shows. He began making films in 1951, and starred in some of the funniest English comedies of the time; *The Lady Killers, I'm All Right Jack, The Smallest Show on Earth*. He specialized in character-parts, playing a completely different kind of person in every film. In *Doctor Strangelove* he

Peter Sellers, as the accident-prone Inspector Clouseau in the film *The Pink Panther Strikes Again*.

Paul Newman and Robert **Redford** prepare for the final shootout in the film *Butch Cassidy and the Sundance Kid.*

played three parts: a US president, a big-moustached RAF officer and a mad scientist.

In 1963, in *The Pink Panther*, Sellers created the part of clumsy, dim-witted Inspector Clouseau, and went on to make half a dozen other Pink Panther films, which brought him international fame.

FISCHER-DIESKAU, Dietrich

German singer born 1925

Fischer-Dieskau is known for his warm, expressive voice, particularly in *lieder* (German songs by such composers as **Schubert**, **Schumann** and **Brahms**), at which he is one of this century's leading masters. He also appears in opera and oratorio.

The screen goddess Marilyn Monroe.

NEWMAN, Paul

US film star and director born 1925

Newman studied drama at university, then served as a radio operator in the Second World War. After the war he began acting on TV, before turning to films during the 1950s. In many of his best-known films, he plays "thinking" cowboys: *Hud, Hombre, Cool Hand Luke, Judge Roy Bean, Butch Cassidy and the Sundance Kid.* His other films include *Harper, The Sting, The Hustler, The Color Purple* and the comedy *Slap Shot*, in which he is the coach of a dim-witted ice-hockey team, who teaches his men to win by cheating. He also has directed films, including *Rachel, Rachel* and *Harry and Son.*

MONROE, Marilyn

US film star 1926-62

Monroe's real name was Norma Jean Baker. She was one of the sexiest actresses ever to appear in films, and was usually given the part of a brainless beauty who made every man she met buckle at the knees. This casting made Monroe rich and famous, but she hated it. She was a serious actress, and felt trapped by her beauty and her fame. Her private life grew ever more tormented. She took drugs to send her to sleep, to wake her up, to keep her alert – and finally died, lonely and miserable, from an overdose which may or may not have been accidental. Her personal life was tragic, but her work was magnificent. She is at her best in four sparkling comedies: *How to Marry a Millionaire, Gentlemen Prefer Blondes, The Seven-Year Itch* and *Some Like it Hot.*

FISCHER-DIESKAU: Brahms 42 Schubert 32 Schumann 35 NEWMAN: Redford 292

BERRY, Charles Edward ("Chuck")

US singer, guitarist and songwriter born 1926

Berry was a founder of rock 'n' roll, and is still one of its legendary performers. He is famous for the witty, sexy lyrics of his songs.

Berry's first hit was *Maybellene* in 1955, and his biggest hit was *My Ding-a-Ling* in 1972, still a huge favourite at his concerts. Unlike many rock artists, Berry never tries to give his records a "studio" sound: he is eager that they should be in the same unfussy style as his stage performances, as if he were at a private party, playing and singing to entertain his friends.

DAVIS, Miles

US jazz musician born 1926

Like Louis **Armstrong,** Davis began a completely new style of jazz trumpet playing, but "cool" instead of "hot". He also introduced other instruments to jazz: French horn, tuba, flugel horn, electronic and Indian instruments. For over 40 years he has been a main influence on jazz musicians of every kind.

Jazz trumpeter Miles Davis.

SUTHERLAND, Joan

Australian opera singer born 1926

Sutherland's mother encouraged her to sing and gave her lessons. Later, Sutherland took part in singing competitions to earn enough money to move to London and continue training there. In 1951 she succeeded and the following year started to sing at Covent Garden Opera House. Her accompanist was Richard Bonynge (born 1930), who later became her husband, manager and chief conductor of the operas in which she sang. He encouraged her to extend her singing voice upwards, where she kept full control, even while singing the incredibly demanding star parts in operas by the two great nineteenth-century composers, Bellini and Donizetti.

Joan Sutherland, singing in the role of Anna Bolena at the Royal Opera House, Covent Garden, in London, 1988. She was nicknamed *La Stupenda* ("the Incredible").

WINKLER, Hans Günter

German show-jumper born 1926

Winkler has won five Olympic Gold medals, one individual (1956), and four team medals (1956, 1960, 1964 and 1972). He won the World Championship twice (1954-55) and the European Championship in 1957.

HALEY, Bill

US singer 1927-81

Haley was the first truly international pop star. In 1954 he and his group, The Comets, recorded two songs, *Shake, Rattle and Roll* and *Rock Around the Clock*. They were the first pop hits, and made the new music famous throughout the world. *Rock Around the Clock* was recorded in 35 different languages, and sold more than 22 million copies.

Bill Haley, and the famous kiss-curl.

DAVIS: Armstrong, L 266

Right: Dirty Harry. As well as acting, Eastwood has directed films, including *Play Misty for Me* and *"Bird"* – about Charlie **Parker**.

KELLY, Grace

US film star; princess of Monaco 1928-82

Kelly went to drama school when she was 18, and then began working as a professional actress. In the 1950s she starred in several successful films, including a western *(High Noon)*, mysteries *(Dial M for Murder; Rear Window)* and a musical *(High Society)*. In 1956 she married Prince Rainier III of Monaco. She spent much of the rest of her life working for charity, until she died in a car crash in 1982.

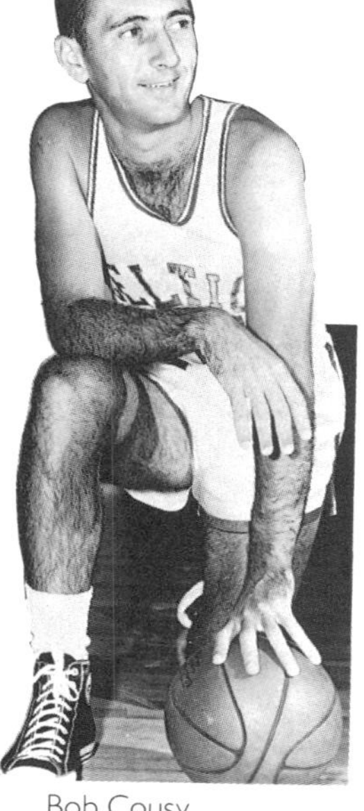

Bob Cousy.

Roger Bannister, finishing the mile in under four minutes in 1954.

COUSY, Robert

US basketball player born 1928

Bob Cousy played as guard and helped his team mates to score goals (a record 715 times in one season; 1959-60). With him, the Boston Celtics won the national championships six times running. Many people consider him to be the finest basketball player in the history of the game.

BANNISTER, Roger

English athlete and doctor born 1929

Bannister trained to be a doctor at Oxford University. But he was also a talented athlete, and in May 1954 he became the first person ever to run the mile in less than 4 minutes. His world record time was 3 minutes, 59.4 seconds. Later the same year he won the 1500 m at the European Championships, then retired to take up his medical career.

EASTWOOD, Clint

US film star born 1930

Before Eastwood became an actor, he was a lumberjack, an army swimming-instructor and a student of business administration. From 1958 to 1965 he appeared in the TV cowboy series *Rawhide*, and in the 1960s he starred in three film westerns which brought him international fame: *A Fistful of Dollars*, *For a Few Dollars More* and *The Good, the Bad and the Ugly*. Since then he has specialized in action films. In westerns he plays a mysterious stranger who rides into town and single-handedly drives out the bad guys and rights every wrong. In detective films he plays another kind of "loner": a cop who hunts down villains without asking help from anyone. He has also starred in two war-thrillers, *Where Eagles Dare* and *The Eiger Sanction*. He was elected mayor of Carmel (1986-88), a small Californian seaside town, and now works in local politics as well as films.

EASTWOOD: Parker 283

Patricia McCormick.

McCORMICK, Patricia

US diver born 1930

McCormick took two gold medals, for springboard and platform diving, at both the 1952 and 1956 Olympic Games. Until the Australian Greg Louganis equalled her record at the 1988 Olympics, she was the only person to win both titles at consecutive Olympic Games.

"Willy the Shoe", riding to another victory in the Santa Anita Handicap.

SHOEMAKER, Bill

US jockey born 1931

Shoemaker is the most successful jockey in history. In his 40-year career, he has ridden almost 10,000 winners. He has won all three races of the US Triple Crown, the Kentucky Derby (4 times), the Preakness Stakes (twice), the Belmont Stakes (5 times), the Hollywood Gold Cup (8 times) and the Santa Anita Handicap (11 times). His prize money totals more than US$80 million.

Bikila, after winning the 1964 Olympic marathon.

BIKILA, Abebe

Ethiopian athlete 1932-73

In 1960 Bikila, a member of the Ethiopian Emperor Heile Selassie's bodyguard, won the Rome Olympic marathon, running barefoot. This was only the third time he had run the distance, and he was the first person from Africa to win an athletics gold medal. In 1964 he won the marathon again, this time in shoes, and only six weeks after having his appendix out. In the next five years he competed in 11 more marathons, winning all but one. In 1969 a car accident confined him to a wheelchair. Undefeated, he took up archery instead.

TRUFFAUT, François

French film director and actor 1932-84

In the 1950s Truffaut led what was called the "New Wave" in France: a group of directors trying to create a European way of making films, full of new ideas about editing, sound and camera work, very different from the production-line movies made in Hollywood at the time. Truffaut directed films of all kinds, from love stories to murder mysteries, from SF to comedies about film-making itself. His best-known films are a series about the same young man growing up: his schooldays *(Les quatre cents coups)*, his first jobs *(Stolen Kisses)* and his first love affairs *(Bed and Board)*.

Truffaut acted in several of his own films, and played the French scientist in **Spielberg**'s *Close Encounters of the Third Kind*.

MAKEBA, Miriam Zenzi

South African singer born 1932

During the 1950s and 60s Makeba (nicknamed "Mama Africa") was a

TRUFFAUT: Spielberg 302

hit singer in South Africa. She then toured the USA, singing and speaking out about racism. She became involved in the civil rights movement led by Martin Luther **King**. In 1963 she gave evidence to the United Nations about apartheid, and as a result was exiled from South Africa. She now lives in Guinea, still working to end racism in South Africa.

TAYLOR, Elizabeth

English/US actress born 1932

and

BURTON, Richard

Welsh actor 1925-84

ELIZABETH TAYLOR left Britain for Hollywood when she was 10 years old. She went into films and became a star almost at once with two films about a girl and her pet dog Lassie, and with *National Velvet*, about teenagers who train a horse to win the Grand National (an important British steeplechase). In the 1940s she played teenagers in several "family" films including *Little Women* – and then, in the 1950s, she startled her fans by starring as the seductive heroine of several films, including **Cleopatra**.

Taylor's co-star in *Cleopatra* was RICHARD BURTON. He had had stage successes in **Shakespeare**, and had moved to Hollywood to make films (mainly adventure or history). Taylor and Burton were one of the most glamorous couples in the world, famous for their quarrels, the jewels they gave each other, their marriages, divorces and remarriages. They made many films together, including *Who's Afraid of Virginia Woolf*, for which Taylor won an Oscar.

Elizabeth Taylor and Richard Burton in the film *Dr Faustus* – based on the story of the alchemist who sells his soul to the devil for one glimpse of Helen of Troy, the most beautiful woman in history.

CONNOLLY, Maureen ("Little Mo")

US tennis player 1934-69

Connolly took up tennis against her parents' wishes, and won the US singles title at 16. Throughout her career she only ever lost four matches. At 17 she made her first appearance at Wimbledon, and took the singles title. In 1953 she was the first woman to win the "Grand Slam": the singles title of all four major tennis tournaments (Wimbledon, US Open, French Open, Australian Open). She looked set to remain the world's top tennis player for many years, but after winning her third Wimbledon title in 1954 she damaged her leg in a riding accident and had to retire. She worked in broadcasting and as a coach until she died of cancer.

MAKEBA: King, M L 236 TAYLOR AND BURTON: Cleopatra 416 Shakespeare 16

PRESLEY, Elvis Aaron

US singer and film star 1935-77

Presley made his first record for his mother's birthday in 1953. A record company heard it and signed him up. His first hit, in 1956, was *Heartbreak Hotel*, and in the following year he made *All Shook Up*, his biggest-selling single.

Presley was an unforgettable stage performer: only Tina **Turner** and Michael **Jackson**, 25 years later, have ever rivalled him. He wore dazzling white suits with tight trousers and huge, jewelled jacket-lapels; he caressed his guitar and wriggled his hips in a sexy way which earned him the nickname "Elvis the Pelvis". Some older people were scandalized, but teenagers loved him. When he began making films in the late 1950s *(Jailhouse Rock, GI Blues, Blue Hawaii)* he won fans among the older generation too. He went on singing and performing throughout the 1960s, and no fewer than 56 of his singles were hits.

Presley's life ended tragically. His marriage broke up in 1973, and his health collapsed. He became a drug addict, and nearly trebled in weight. In the end he retired to his beautiful house Graceland (famous for its guitar-shaped swimming pool), where he died of a heart attack in 1977.

ALLEN, Woody

US comedian and film maker born 1935

Allen's real name is Allen Stewart Konigsberg. When he was 17, he began appearing as a comedian: a short, weedy-looking man who wore big spectacles and talked about how he failed at everything he did, especially sex. He became one of the USA's favourite comedians, and in 1965 he was asked to write the script for a Peter **Sellers** film, *What's New, Pussycat?* It was an enormous hit, and the start of Allen's film career. He wrote, directed and starred in comedies such as *Bananas* (about a coward who gets caught up in a South American revolution), *Sleeper* (about someone transported 200 years into the future by mistake) and *Annie Hall* (about a sad-funny love affair). His other films (for example *Manhattan* and *Hannah and Her Sisters*) are more serious, about the way our lives never quite match our hopes.

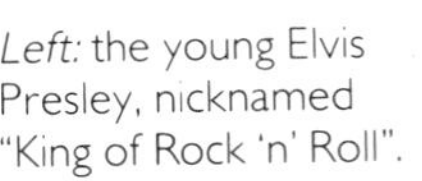

Left: the young Elvis Presley, nicknamed "King of Rock 'n' Roll".

PRESLEY: Jackson 310 Turner, T 293 ALLEN: Sellers 284

PAVAROTTI, Luciano

Italian opera singer born 1935

Pavarotti had his first success in 1961, and went on to become one of the world's best-known and best-paid singers. He is admired especially for his clear, thrilling high notes; at his peak, few tenors in the world could match him.

Pavarotti, the Italian tenor, as Radames in **Verdi**'s opera *Aida*, in 1984.

HOLLY, Charles Hardin ("Buddy")

US singer and songwriter 1936-59

Holly was one of the first-ever pop stars. In 1957 he and his group, The Crickets, had a hit with *That'll Be the Day*, and he became internationally famous. He made other hit records, including *Peggy Sue* and *Maybe Baby*, and went on tours, playing to huge, adoring audiences. On his last tour, in 1959, his plane crashed in a snowstorm and he was killed. His music inspired many later pop musicians, including such stars as Bob **Dylan** and Paul McCartney of the **Beatles**. McCartney was so impressed by Holly's songs that he bought the rights to publish them.

CLARK, Jim

Scottish racing driver 1936-68

In the 1960s Clark was twice world champion, admired for the way he could handle any car in any conditions, and for his inspired starts on the Hockenheim circuit in Germany. He won 25 Grand Prix. His skill deserted him only once – and the crash was fatal.

CHAMBERLAIN, Wilton Norman

US basketball player born 1936

Nicknamed "Wilt the Stilt" because of his height (2.2m), Chamberlain scored a record number of points for his college team. He turned professional after graduation, and from 1960 to 1967 scored most points in every season, including an as-yet unbroken record of 100 points in a single game. He has a career-best total of 31,419 points.

OERTER, Alfred

US athlete born 1936

Al Oerter won four successive gold medals in discus throwing at the Olympic Games held from 1956 to 1968, breaking the world record each time. He retired in 1968, but came back in 1976, and was still ranked second in the world at the time of the Moscow Olympics in 1980. However, he had no chance to prove his skill at these Olympics, as the USA boycotted them for political reasons.

PAVAROTTI: Verdi 37 HOLLY: Beatles 312 Dylan 295

REDFORD, Robert

US film star born 1936

After trying his hand at painting, Redford took up acting, first on the stage, and then on film. He starred in films of all kinds, from comedies to westerns, from spy stories to sports sagas. His best-known films are *Butch Cassidy and the Sundance Kid* (in which he played a wisecracking train-robber in cowboy times), *The Candidate* (in which he played an eager politician), *The Sting* (in which he played a conman) and *All the President's Men* (in which he played one of the reporters who uncovered a scandal during Nixon's presidency).

The American singer Grace Bumbry, playing the captive Ethiopian princess in **Verdi**'s opera *Aida* in 1972.

SOBERS, Garfield St Aubrun

Barbadian cricketer born 1936

Sobers was a magnificent all-round cricketer, and created many records in batting and in bowling. He was able to bowl slow or fast, often changing styles in the course of an innings. He was a superb fielder, especially close to the bat, and the shrewd captain of the famous West Indian cricketing eleven. He is the only man ever to have made 1,000 runs and taken 50 wickets in the ten Sheffield Shield matches in Australia, and has done so twice.

Garfield Sobers, going for the boundary.

BUMBRY, Grace Melzia Ann

US opera singer born 1937

Bumbry was taught by Lotte **Lehmann**, and began her career in Europe as a mezzo-soprano. In 1961 she was the first black singer to appear at the Bayreuth Festival in Germany. In 1970 she began to sing soprano parts too, adding upper notes to a voice that already had a very wide range. She is also a fine actress, particularly famous for performing in dramatic operas like *Carmen*.

BURTON, Beryl

British cyclist born 1937

Burton was the British all-round cycling champion from 1959 to 1973, and won seven gold medals in world championships. She often beat male riders in open events – the only woman ever to do so – and in 1967 broke the male-held record by cycling 446.19 km in 12 hours.

FRASER, Dawn

Australian swimmer born 1937

Although Fraser suffered from asthma throughout her career, she

BUMBRY: Lehmann 256 Verdi 37

was one of the world's outstanding swimmers. She set 39 world freestyle records, and is the only swimmer to have won a gold medal in three successive Olympic Games (1956, 1960, 1964). Her last gold medal was won at the age of 27 – extremely old for a swimmer – and her total of four gold and four silver medals has yet to be surpassed.

LAVER, Rod

Australian tennis player born 1938

Laver was a master at serving the ball with top spin so that other players could not return it as they wanted. He won the amateur Grand Slam in 1962, and then played on the professional circuit until 1969, when he won the first professional Grand Slam. (The Grand Slam is all 4 major singles titles: Wimbledon, the French, US and Australian championships.)

NUREYEV, Rudolf Hametovich

Russian ballet dancer born 1938

Nureyev began dancing in folk groups, and did not start ballet training in Leningrad until 1955. He became a solo dancer with the Kirov Ballet and was a star by the time the company went on a European tour in 1961. They were in Paris about to board the plane for London when Nureyev suddenly ran to an airport building and asked for political asylum. In London he became **Fonteyn**'s main partner in the Royal Ballet, and has since danced and choreographed with most ballet companies in the world.

Nureyev appears in all kinds of ballet, from forgotten works by **Petipa** to modern works created specially for him. Many of his best performances have been filmed, and he is known as a choreographer and teacher of ballet. Many critics think him the finest, and most important, male ballet dancer this century – after **Nijinsky**.

Australia's swimming superstar Dawn Fraser.

TURNER, Tina

US singer born 1938

Turner was christened Annie Mae Bullock. She married Ike Turner, and in 1966 they recorded *River Deep Mountain High*, a soul song which became a massive hit. Ike and Tina Turner had other successes, but then their marriage broke up. In 1982 Tina went to work with the UK group Heaven 17, and this led in 1983 to her first solo success, *Let's Stay Together*. Her next big hit came in 1984: *What's Love Got to Do With It*.

Turner is famous not only for singing, but for her outrageous, witty stage act. She rivals **Madonna** and Michael **Jackson** as one of the most stunning solo acts of the 1980s. In 1985 she played a magnificently evil villainess in the adventure film *Mad Max Beyond Thunderdome*.

Tina Turner. She once said, after a performance, "Not bad for 50, huh?"

NUREYEV: Fonteyn 283 Nijinsky 258 Petipa 246 TURNER: Jackson 310 Madonna 314

PELÉ, Edson Arantes do Nascimento

Brazilian footballer born 1940

Pelé combined the skills of every type of footballer: he could control the ball equally well with his feet, head or body. He began playing for his country at the age of 16, the first of 111 appearances (a world record). He was the most gifted member of a brilliant national team, and during his career Brazil was considered one of the toughest teams to beat, and the best to watch. Pelé scored more goals in his career than any other player: 1,271. He retired in 1977, and began appearing in films and teaching slum children to play football. In 1980 he was given the title "Athlete of the Century".

RICHARD, Cliff

English pop singer born 1940

Richard's real name is Harry Roger Webb. He began singing with school skiffle groups (early pop bands). In 1958, after his first hit record, *Move It*, people called him the English Elvis **Presley**. He was one of the first UK singers to make a success with rock 'n' roll. He and his then backing group, The Shadows, had several other hits, including *Bachelor Boy*, and made pop films including *Summer Holiday*, about a group of teenagers who tour Europe in a double-decker bus. Richard represented Britain three times in the Eurovision Song Contest, winning in 1968 with *Congratulations*.

In 1966, Richard became a born-again Christian, and has often spoken and written about his faith. Instead of his career fading as he grew older (and as many people said it might), it has gone from strength to strength. Over 30 years after his first success, he has made more than 70 hit records, and is still a star.

DOMINGO, Placido

Spanish opera singer born 1941

Domingo's family moved from Spain to Mexico while he was still a boy. He showed early musical talent, eventually deciding on a singing career. He made his debut at 16 (as a baritone), but three years later changed to tenor. He is considered one of today's finest singers, and in 1985-86 used his huge earning power to raise money for the victims of the Mexico City earthquake.

Cliff Richard in 1960, at the start of his long career.

Left: Pelé in action during the World Cup final Brazil (4), Italy (1) in Mexico, 1970.

RICHARD: Presley 290 DYLAN: Presley 290 Thomas 74

DYLAN, Bob

US singer, poet and composer born 1941

Dylan's real name is Robert Allen Zimmerman; he called himself Dylan after the poet Dylan **Thomas**. He began playing the guitar at 12, and formed groups while he was still at school. In 1960 he dropped out of college to become a folk singer. He wrote all his own songs, a blend of blues and country and western. The words of many of his songs have a political message. In 1961 he was signed by Columbia Records, and in 1964 his album *The Times They are a-Changin'* won him worldwide fame.

Dylan was the biggest star of the 1960s protest movement. Young people were protesting against war, racism and lack of freedom in US universities – and Dylan's songs exactly caught their mood. Unlike many songs of the time, Dylan's had poetry and meaning: the words were as important as the music.

In the 1970s Dylan's popularity began to fade, and he has never repeated his 1960s triumphs. But, like **Presley**, he is one of the founders of rock music, and many 1980s artists have imitated both his way of singing and his idea that rock is not just dance music for teenagers, but can have serious and important things to say.

McKAY, Heather

Australian squash player born 1941

From the start of her squash-playing career in 1959 until she retired in 1979, McKay lost only two games – the last in 1962. She also played hockey for her country, and after moving to Canada in 1975, took up racketball. In 1976 she was the best female player in Canada, and she was US Women's Professional Racketball Champion (equivalent to being world champion) from 1980 to 1981 and again in 1984.

HENDRIX, Jimi

US rock musician 1942-70

Hendrix began his career playing the guitar for such stars as B. B. King, Ike and Tina **Turner**, Little Richard and Wilson Pickett. In the mid-1960s he formed The Jimi Hendrix Experience, and recorded his first hits: *Hey Joe, All Along the Watchtower* and *Purple Haze*. He was one of the first rock guitarists to use electronic effects such as feedback and the wah-wah pedal, and was famous for tricks like playing the guitar with his teeth or behind his back. In the last years of the 1960s, he was one of rock music's best-known performers, and is acclaimed as the finest guitarist of his time. But he became addicted to drugs and alchohol, and in 1970 died in an ambulance after choking on his own vomit.

Bob Dylan.

Jimi Hendrix liked to wear psychedelic clothes – as colourful as his music.

HENDRIX: Turner, T 293

AGOSTINI, Giacomo

Italian motorcyclist born 1942

Agostini began his professional racing career at 19, and finished fourth in his first Grand Prix in 1965. From then until his retirement in 1977 he won 122 races in both the 350cc and 500cc classes. He took the world title seven times in the first class and eight in the second, twice more than his nearest rival.

ALI, Muhammed (Cassius Clay)

US boxer born 1942

When Cassius Clay was 12 he went to a policeman to report the loss of his bicycle. The policeman was supervising a boxing match and invited the boy to join him. From that moment on, Clay determined to become the greatest boxer in the world.

In 1960, at the end of his amateur career, Clay won a gold medal at the Olympic Games. In 1964, he took the professional world heavyweight title from Sonny Liston. His movements were lighter and faster than any other heavyweight boxer of the time – as his second put it, he could "float like a butterfly, sting like a bee!" Soon after this match Clay joined the Black Muslims, and changed his name to Muhammed Ali. His religious beliefs meant that he had to refuse army service in the Vietnam War, and as a result in 1967 the boxing authorities took away his world title and his licence to box. Already known as a showman in sport, he now also became a symbol for oppressed people everywhere.

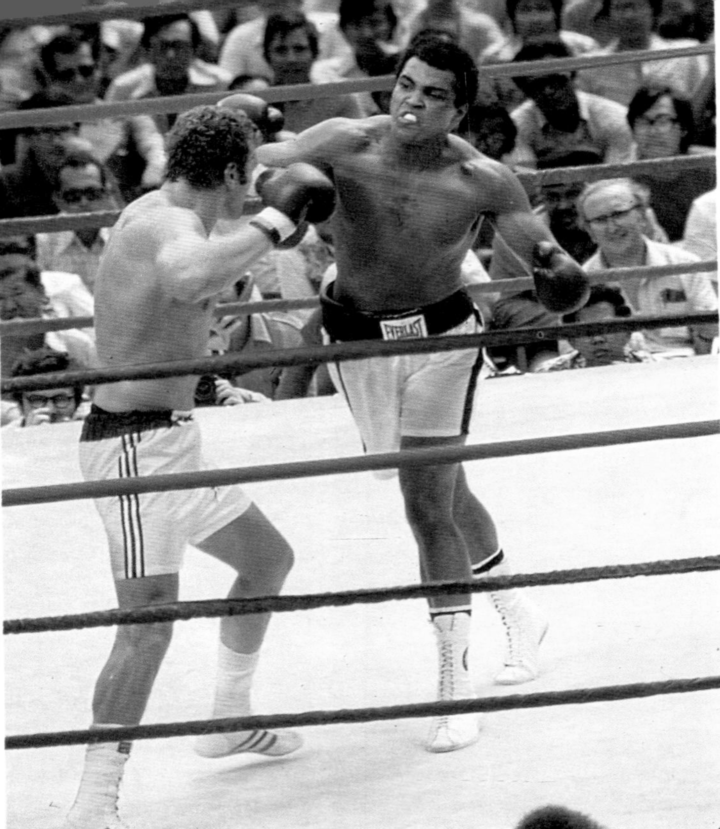

Muhammed Ali knocks out Joe Bugner in Kuala Lumpur in 1975.

In 1970 the decision was reversed, Ali won back his title from George Foreman in 1974. In 1978 he lost it to Leon Spinks, but 7 months later won it back again – the only man to win the world heavyweight title three times. Soon afterwards he retired from boxing and now works with young people, especially the deprived.

CÁSLAVSKÁ, Vera

Czech gymnast born 1942

Cáslavská first trained as an ice skater, but took up gymnastics at the very late age of 15. Three years later, in 1960, she won her first Olympic medal (a team silver), and at the 1964 Olympics she won two individual gold medals. In 1968 Soviet troops entered Czechoslovakia eight weeks before the Olympics. Cáslavská found that the tense political situation affected her training, but still she led her team's challenge against the Russian team. Her efforts won huge applause from the audience, who thought that what she was doing had political parallels: a small nation standing up to the might of a then unbeaten rival. She won four gold medals, and her floor exercise (to the music of "Mexican Hat Dance") will always be remembered. She gave her medals to her country and took up a career coaching young gymnasts.

STREISAND, Barbra Joan

US singer and actress born 1942

Streisand was 19 when she began singing in New York night clubs, and acting in musicals. She signed her first recording contract when she was 21, and the following year appeared in *Funny Girl*, a stage musical about the 1930s comedy actress Fanny Brice. This made her a star, and when it was made into a film in 1968 she won an Oscar, and became famous throughout the world.

Streisand continued making films throughout the 1970s: musicals (*Hello Dolly*), comedies (*The Owl and the Pussycat*; *What's Up Doc?*), and tragedies (*A Star is Born*). In 1983 she directed herself in *Yentl*, based on I. B. Singer's story about a girl in a poor 1920s Jewish village who has to dress as a boy to get an education – and then falls in love. As well as making films, Streisand has continued to appear on TV and in night clubs, and has made many records. She is particularly known for singing ballads, in a style halfway between the "big-band singer" sound of Ella **Fitzgerald** or Frank **Sinatra** and modern pop.

Barbra Streisand, in her film *Yentl* in 1983.

FISCHER, Bobby

US chess player born 1943

Fischer was the youngest-ever US chess champion at junior and national level, as well as the youngest Grand Master – aged 15. In 1972 he won the world title from the Russian champion Spassky. People were fascinated by the match, not just because of the chess, but because there seemed to be such a contrast between the characters of Spassky (tidy and precise) and Fischer (eccentric and awkward). The Russians wanted a return match, with Fischer playing their new champion Karpov, but Fischer refused. In 1975 he gave up chess for a life dominated by religion.

STREISAND: Fitzgerald, E 282 Sinatra 280

Skiing ace Jean-Claude Killy, tackling the slopes of the Val d'Isère in his native France.

KILLY, Jean-Claude

French ski champion born 1943

Killy could ski at the age of 3. He first represented France when he was 16, and in 1966 he won the downhill race and the combined world championship title. He did not specialize in downhill, slalom or giant slalom, but won all three events in the first World Cup in 1967. He also took gold medals in each of the three events at the 1968 Winter Olympics, and then retired from amateur skiing. Five years later he won the Grand Prix professional title.

Joe Namath in action in 1975. Namath loved publicity, and once appeared in an advertising campaign wearing tights, and saying: "If they look this good on me, imagine what they'll do for you!"

KING, Billie Jean

US tennis player born 1943

Between 1961 and 1979, King (or Billie Jean Moffitt as she was known until her marriage in 1965) won 20 Wimbledon titles and 19 other major championships. In 1973 her winning match against Bobby Riggs (the 1939 Wimbledon men's champion – who had boasted that men could beat women any time, anywhere) helped her successful campaign to show that women's tennis deserved the same rewards as men's.

NAMATH, Joe Willie

US American football player born 1943

Namath played for the University of Alabama American football team in 1964 when they won every match. He went on to play professionally, spending most of his career with the New York Jets. He became the top quarterback of his time, in spite of being handicapped by the deforming effects of knee operations. He was a superb "reader" of the game, able to foresee in an instant what the opponents' "plays" were going to be, and to beat them before they could develop.

ROSS, Diana

US singer and film star born 1944

For ten years, 1959-69, Ross was lead singer with the Supremes, making such hits with them as *Baby Love*. In 1969 she began a solo career, and has had dozens of hits, including *I'm Still Waiting, Touch Me in the Morning* and *Work That Body*. She has also acted in films, notably *Lady Sings the Blues*, a biographical film about Billie **Holiday**.

Right: Diana Ross, from one of her solo performances.

ROSS: Holiday, B 279

MARLEY, Robert Nesta (Bob)

Jamaican singer and composer 1945-80

Bob Marley formed his band, The Wailers, in 1964. He made reggae music popular throughout the world, singing songs about love, politics and religion. He and many of his fans were Rastafarian Christians, and also followed the teaching of the black leader Marcus **Garvey**.. Most people in Jamaica revered him, but he was unpopular with right-wing political bosses, and was forced to live for a time in exile in the USA. He made many of what have become reggae classics: *Jammin', No Woman No Cry* and *I Shot the Sheriff* (later recorded by Eric **Clapton**). Marley died of cancer in 1980, and his biggest hit came three years after his death with *Buffalo Soldier*.

Reggae star Bob Marley in concert. In the background sits Jamaica's prime minister Michael Manley.

DU PRÉ, Jacqueline

English cellist 1945-87

Du Pré began learning the cello when she was 5 years old, and studied with some of the best teachers and players of the time. A mystery benefactor, who refused to give his or her name, gave her a **Stradivarius** cello, which she used for her first professional recital in 1961. She recorded all the major cello concertos, often working with her husband Daniel Barenboim, the pianist and conductor. She will be remembered most of all for her interpretation of **Elgar**'s wistful, haunting Cello Concerto. In the early 1970s she developed the disease MS (multiple sclerosis). It stopped her own playing, but she went on teaching for several years.

CLAPTON, Eric

English guitarist and composer born 1945

Clapton bought his first guitar when he was 17, and taught himself to play along with records by blues stars such as Muddy Waters, Chuck **Berry** and Big Bill Broonzy. In 1967 he formed the rock band Cream, and by 1970 he was a star. His first solo hit in the USA was *After Midnight*, and his biggest success was *I Shot the Sheriff* in 1974.

In the 1970s, at the height of his fame, Clapton had to retire because of drug addiction, and it was several painful years before he recovered and could return to music. He began writing songs as well as playing, and his most recent hit album was *August*, produced by his friend Phil Collins. Fellow-musicians admire him as one of the finest of all rock guitarists – they nickname him "God" – and young players learn from him in the same way as he studied the old blues masters at the start of his career.

MARLEY: Clapton 299 Garvey 227 DU PRÉ: Elgar 51 Stradivari 342 CLAPTON: Berry 286

Cycling champion Eddy Merckx in action in 1977.

BEAMON, Bob

US athlete born 1946

In 1968 at the Olympic Games held in Mexico City, Bob Beamon, whose best previous long-jump had been 8.33 m, jumped 8.90 m. He added 55 cm to the world record, which has never been bettered, not even by Beamon himself.

MERCKX, Eddy

Belgian cyclist born 1945

Merckx won the Tour de France, the most famous cycle road-race, five times – 1969-72 and 1974. He holds 39 classic road-racing titles, 17 more than his nearest rival.

Bob Beamon, caught in mid-jump at the 1968 Olympics.

PARTON, Dolly

US singer and film star born 1946

Parton first sang professionally when she was 12, and later appeared in the country-music stage show of Porter Wagoner, playing a big-busted, spangle-costumed, good-time girl whose hair looked like a blonde-sprayed bird's nest. She played the same cheerful, golden-hearted person in several comedy films, including *The Best Little Whorehouse in Texas*. As a solo artist, she spends half the time sending herself up and the rest singing soulful country ballads like *Jolene*, her biggest hit. She runs a chain of US restaurants called Aunt Granny's, and sends money to her home town to help young people.

SZEWINSKA, Irena

Polish athlete born 1946

From 1964 to 1976 Szewinska won Olympic and European medals in the 100, 200 and 400 m, the 4 × 100 m sprint relay and the long-jump. She was the first woman in the world to run 400 metres in under 50 seconds, and at various times she held ten world records.

BOWIE, David

English singer and actor born 1947

Bowie's real name is David Robert Jones. He played saxophone at school, and when he left he worked as a session musician (playing in backing groups and bands) and as an actor with a mime company. In 1972 his pop record *Space Oddity* was a worldwide hit.

After the success of *Space Oddity*, Bowie invented different characters for his stage acts: Ziggy Stardust, the pop megastar destroyed by his own success, a sexless being, half-male half-female, and "The Thin White Duke". He has also had a successful acting career, in such films as *The Man Who Fell to Earth, Absolute Beginners* and *Merry Christmas, Mr Lawrence.* He acted on stage as the Elephant Man. He has had over 60 hit singles and albums, including *Let's Dance* in 1983.

David Bowie, giving one of his dramatic stage acts as Ziggy Stardust.

CRUYFF, Johan

Dutch footballer born 1947

When Cruyff was 10, he was selected to play for the Ajax juniors. He was very small for his age and learned how to survive by skill rather than strength. In 1965 he became a professional player for the club, and in the next nine years they won many tournaments and titles, including three consecutive European championships. In 1974 Cruyff captained the Netherlands team who were runners-up to West Germany in the World Cup. In 1973 he joined Barcelona, for a record transfer fee (at the time) equal to £400,000. In the 1970s he was considered one of the world's finest footballers, equal to **Pelé** in his heyday.

JOHN, Elton

English pop star born 1947

John's real name is Reginald Dwight. He learned the piano as a child, and joined many groups as a teenager. His early professional career was in the soul band Bluesology, which played as backup for visiting US stars. In 1967 John began to compose songs with the lyric-writer Bernie Taupin, which he (John) sang with huge success. He accompanied himself on the piano, and became famous for wearing outrageous costumes – metre-high boots, vast floppy hats and plastic spectacles shaped like pianos, butterflies, birds and the letters of his name. His first success was *Your Song* in 1970, and his biggest hits were *Daniel* in 1973 and *Don't Go Breaking My Heart*, with Kiki Dee in 1976. In 1975 he played "Pinball Wizard" in the film *Tommy*, inspired by The **Who**.

CRUYFF: Pelé 294 JOHN: Who 317

Director Spielberg and friend, ET.

SPIELBERG, Steven

US film director born 1947

Spielberg worked first as a TV director, but moved into films at the age of 26. His hits include several of the most successful and popular films ever made: *Jaws* (about a giant shark which terrorizes a small US seaside town), *Close Encounters of the Third Kind* (about people making contact with UFOs – spaceships from other galaxies), *E.T.* (about a boy who befriends a being from outer space), *The Color Purple* (about black life in the US Deep South), and three fast-action adventures starring Harrison Ford as archaeologist Indiana Jones.

The masked figure from *The Phantom of the Opera*, the story of a disfigured man who kidnaps the star of the Paris Opera House, and takes her to his hideout in the sewers below. Lloyd Webber's music for the stage version of the legend became another of his string of successes.

BARYSHNIKOV, Mikhail Nicolayevich

Russian ballet dancer born 1948

Baryshnikov went to a special school for promising singers and ballet dancers, and by the time he was 20 he was a star dancer with the Leningrad Kirov Ballet. In those days Russian dancers were given fewer roles and performances than Western dancers, and Baryshnikov wanted to extend his range. In 1974, on a Canadian tour, he asked for political asylum, and has lived and worked in the West ever since.

Baryshnikov's brilliant, athletic dancing amazed Western audiences. On his first appearance in New York he was applauded for 27 minutes. Many critics think him the equal of **Nureyev** or **Nijinsky**, the finest male dancers of the century. Since 1980, as well as dancing ballet, he has choreographed, danced ballroom and tap on TV (in a tribute to Fred **Astaire**), and made his debut as a singer and actor.

LLOYD WEBBER, Andrew

English composer born 1948

Lloyd Webber wrote his first hit musical, *Joseph and the Amazing Technicolor Dreamcoat*, when he was 19. He and his partner Tim Rice, who wrote the words, were two of the first people to use pop and rock in musicals. Lloyd Webber's successes include *Jesus Christ Superstar* (treating **Jesus** as if he were a pop star), *Evita* based on the life of Eva **Perón**), *Cats, Starlight Express* (in which dancers play the parts of trains, rushing round the theatre on roller-skates), *The Phantom of the Opera* and *Aspects of Love*. Apart from musicals, his works include *Requiem* and Variations for Cello and Orchestra (written for his brother, the cellist Julian Lloyd Webber), and music for the films *Gumshoe* and *The Odessa File*.

CURRY, John

English ice skater born 1949

As a boy, Curry wanted to become a ballet dancer, but his father told him to take up skating because it was a sport, and likely to give him a more reliable career than dancing. Curry, however, began ballet classes again

BARYSHNIKOV: Astaire 266 Nijinsky 258 Nureyev 293 LLOYD WEBBER: Jesus 329 Perón 474 after his father's death, and his unique, artistic skating style is based on dance. He won the British National Championships in 1970, and in 1976 won the European, Olympic and World Championships. He has since run his own ice-show, completely different from any other. It is ice-ballet, and many world-famous choreographers have created works for him.

LAUDA, Niki

Austrian racing driver born 1949

When Lauda was 17, he saw the German Grand Prix, and was so determined on a racing career that he managed to persuade his bank to sponsor him for several seasons. In 1974 he joined Ferrari, and won the world championship the following year. In 1976 the Ferrari and McLaren teams were locked in rivalry, and in the German Grand Prix Lauda almost died in a horrific accident. Six weeks later he was back, driving in the Italian Grand Prix, but he lost the drivers' championship to McLaren's James Hunt by one point. However, Lauda went on to win two more championships, in 1977 and 1984.

MATTHES, Roland

German swimmer born 1949

Matthes won both the 100 m and 200 m backstroke at the 1968 and 1972 Olympic Games, the 1970 European Championships and the first swimming World Championships in 1973. At the second World Championships in 1975 he won the 100 m. Altogether, he broke the world record for the 100 m eight times, and the 200 m record nine times. He used 8–10 fewer armpulls for each length than most of his rivals. At European and national level he also held records for butterfly, medley and freestyle.

SPRINGSTEEN, Bruce

US singer and songwriter born 1949

As a teenager Springsteen admired the **Beatles**, and determined to make rock music his career. His first hit was *Hungry Heart* in 1980, and his biggest hits are *Dancing in the Dark* (1984) and *Born in the USA* (1985). He was one of the biggest world stars of the 1980s, famous for his guitar playing, the power and energy of his singing, and his spoken comments and recitations, influenced by Bob **Dylan**. Other musicians, and his fans, know him by the nickname "the Boss".

Bruce Springsteen, the "Boss", in action, before a huge American flag.

SPRINGSTEEN: Beatles 312 Dylan 295

VIREN, Lasse

Finnish athlete born 1949

After **Nurmi**, Finnish runners had little success, a disappointment to a nation that revered the sport. This situation changed dramatically at the 1972 Olympic Games. The Finnish runner Viren was bumped and fell in the final of the 10,000 m race, but quickly made up ground, winning in a world record time of 27 minutes 38.4 seconds. Viren had previously excelled at the 5,000 m (rather than the 10,000 m), and a week later he won that too. Only three other runners had achieved this "double". Despite injury and many indifferent races in the next few years, Viren repeated his double success at the 1976 Olympics – the only person ever to do so. He also tried to win the marathon, and so equal **Zatopek**'s 1952 feat of winning over all three distances, but came in fifth. (His time, however, was 10 minutes better than Zatopek's had been.)

WENDEN, Michael Vincent

Australian swimmer born 1949

Wenden was a world class freestyle swimmer from 1960 to 1974, breaking six world records. His training was phenomenal, and used an unusual amount of dry land work (isometric exercises), first tried by Wenden as building exercises for a broken leg.

Left: Swimming star Mark Spitz, one of the legendary names in the history of the sport.

WILLIAMS, John Peter Rhys

Welsh Rugby Union player born 1949

"J.P.R.", as he is known, was capped a record 55 times for Wales, and 10 times for the British Lions. At 17 he won the junior lawn tennis title at Wimbledon, and is now a consultant in orthopaedic surgery, specializing in sports injuries.

SHEENE, Barry

English motorcyclist born 1950

In 1970, aged 20, Sheene won the British 125cc championship. He only missed the World Championship in the same class in 1971 by a narrow margin: eight points. Four years later, after a horrific crash, he returned to racing with metal pins in his legs, and went on to win the first 750cc Championship in 1973 and the 500cc World Championship in 1976 and 1977. He crashed again, and the X-rays showing the large amount of metal in his legs became famous. He retired in 1985, and began a second career as a TV sports presenter.

SPITZ, Mark Andrew

US swimmer born 1950

Although Spitz set a world record in the 400 m freestyle, he specialized in shorter distances, breaking or

Viren, leading the field at the 1976 Olympics.

VIREN: Nurmi 262 Zatopek 284 SPITZ: Ewry 253 Nurmi 262

equalling another 32 world records. At the 1968 Olympics he won one solo silver and one solo bronze medal, as well as two golds in relay races. At the 1972 Olympics he swam 13 races, broke seven world records and won seven gold medals. The events were 100 m and 200 m free-style, 100 m and 200 m butterfly, 4 × 100 m and 4 × 200 m freestyle relays and 4 × 100 m medley relay. Spitz, along with **Nurmi** and the Russian gymnast Latynina, comes second only to **Ewry** in the total number of gold medals won.

Stevie Wonder. The song says: "and I mean it from the bottom of my heart."

WONDER, Stevie

US singer, musician and songwriter born 1950

Born Steveland Morris, Stevie Wonder was a musical prodigy. Although blind from birth, he learned to play a dozen instruments by the time he was 8, and at 12 he had his first hit record, *Fingertips*. His style is based on soul music, but he uses ideas of all kinds, from classical to country and western, from blues to pop. He has written rock songs, love songs, and songs about politics and religion. His hits include *Blowin' in the Wind, For Once in My Life, You are the Sunshine of My Life* and in 1984 he had his biggest success of all, with *I Just Called to Say I Love You.*

CONNORS, James Scott

US tennis player born 1952

Jimmy Connors won the US junior singles tennis title seven times, and reached the Wimbledon singles finals in 1972, when he was 19. He used both hands to play both forehand and backhand and, in spite of arguments on the court with referees and other officials, he soon began winning international championships. His main titles were Wimbledon (1974, 1982), the US Open (1974, 1976, 1978, 1982-83), and the Australian Open (1974, 1977). He teamed up with the Czech player Ilie Nastase (born 1953), winning the doubles at Wimbledon in 1973 and the US Open in 1975.

PIQUET (Soutomaior), Nelson

Brazilian racing driver born 1952

Soutomaior's parents opposed the idea of a motor-racing career for their son, so he had to use a false name, Piquet, which he has kept ever since. He was hampered by lack of money, but still managed to be runner-up in the World Championship in 1980, his second season. Since then he has won the championship three times – in 1981, 1983 and 1987. He is considered one of the most skilful drivers ever to take up the sport.

Chris Evert at the baseline, poised to return service.

GREEN, Lucinda (Prior-Palmer)

English horsewoman born 1953

Green has won the European individual gold medal for 3-day eventing (also known as "horse trials": dressage, showjumping and speed and endurance tests) twice (1975 and 1977); she was world champion in 1982, and won an Olympic team silver medal in 1984. She is the only person to have won the Badminton Horse Trials six times, and on six different horses.

MOSER-PRÖLL, Annemarie

Austrian skier born 1953

From 1972 to 1975 women skiers competed in 28 World Cup downhill races, and Pröll won 19. In 1976 she briefly retired when she married Herbert Moser, but soon returned to racing. Altogether, she has won 16 World Cups, was women's overall world champion from 1971 to 1975, and won a gold medal at the 1980 Winter Olympics.

How to bend for a slalom "gate": Annemarie Moser-Pröll in action.

EVERT, Christine Marie

US tennis player born 1954

Chris Evert had already been playing for ten years when, at 16, she was part of the winning USA team in the Wightman Cup. She went on to become one of the most technically skilled tennis players of the 1970s to 80s, with her precise ball-placing, her two-handed backhand, and her calm, steady concentration. After her marriage in 1979 she was known for some years as Chris Evert-Lloyd, but later divorced and went back to her former name. She won the US Open Championship six times, both Wimbledon and the French Open three times, and the Italian Open twice. Until her retirement in 1989, she worked to get her fellow women professionals equal prize money with men.

PAYTON, Walter

US American football player born 1954

Payton played American football at Jackson State University, and when he left he was offered a contract with the Chicago Bears. He rushes (runs with the ball) with great force, and opposing teams often need several men to mark him, instead of the usual one. In 1977 he made a record-breaking rush of 275 yards – the record still stands – and in 1988 he rushed a total of 16,726 yards, another record. In his spare time he runs an investment business, and works for charities which help people with hearing handicaps.

KORBUT, Olga

Russian gymnast born 1955

Korbut was a reserve for the USSR ladies Olympic gymnastic team, and only took part in the 1972 Olympics because another team member was injured. Her child-like appearance, brilliant floor exercises and her bravery and skill on the bars caught the imagination of audiences, inspiring a worldwide surge of interest in gymnastics. She won two individual gold medals at these games, and an individual silver and a team gold at the 1976 Olympics – where she competed against a new young star, Nadia **Comaneci**, who had been inspired by Korbut to take up gymnastics in the first place.

Grace and balance as Olga Korbut ends her floor exercises.

PROST, Alain

French racing driver born 1955

No-one has won more Grand Prix racing titles than Prost (32 by 1988). In 1984 he equalled **Clark**'s record for Grand Prix victories in a single season: seven. He has also won the World Championship three times.

MOSES, Edwin

US athlete born 1955

In the 1976 Olympics Ed Moses won the gold medal in the 400 m hurdles with a world record. The US stayed away from the 1980 Games, but in 1984 Moses again won gold. He also came first in the World Cups of 1977, 1979, and 1981. He broke the world record for this gruelling and technically demanding race four times, and until 1988 was unbeaten for 122 consecutive races – another record. Although he came third at the 1988 Olympic Games, his world record time still stands.

RATTLE, Simon

English conductor born 1955

Rattle came from a musical family and at 9 years old he was arranging percussion parts for his family to play records at his own Sunday afternoon concerts. He was playing percussion for the Merseyside Youth Orchestra at 11, and also joined the National Youth Orchestra. He soon realized, however, that his main interest was conducting. He conducted his first professional concert at 19 and has been particularly successful with twentieth-century music. So far, he has refused to become an international star, jetting about the world to "guest" with famous orchestras. Instead, he has settled in the English Midlands to train and build up public support for the City of Birmingham Symphony Orchestra.

Simon Rattle.

KORBUT: Comaneci 314 PROST: Clark, J 291

COE, Sebastian Newbold

English athlete born 1956

Coe, trained by his father, was a talented junior athlete, and had his first adult success in 1977, beating Bayi, who was at that time the world record holder over the mile. In 1979, in less than two months, he set new world records for the 800 m, mile and 1500 m, and became the first person to hold all these records at once. In the 1980 and 1984 Olympics he won gold medals at 1500 m – the only athlete to do so in this event in two successive Olympic Games. He has also set several indoor world records and was a member of the relay team which set a new world record for 4 × 800 m in 1982.

Until Coe's time the 800 m race had not been considered a sprint, but an endurance race. Coe was one of a group of athletes who introduced sprinting techniques to the race and to training, completely changing its character. He retired from racing in 1989, to begin a new career in politics.

Mel Gibson, starring in *Mad Max 3*.

GIBSON, Mel

Australian film star born 1956

The muscular Gibson stars in adventure films. Best known are the "Mad Max" series of films involving a fast-riding motorcycle warrior in a nightmare future world, and the "Lethal Weapon" series, tough police stories set in the USA.

NAVRATILOVA, Martina

Czech/US tennis player born 1956

In 1975 Navratilova left her native Czechoslovakia to live in the USA. Over the next ten years she became one of the world's greatest women tennis players. She has dominated the game, winning Wimbledon eight times (an unbeaten record), the US Open four times, the French twice and the Australian three times. She has also won 29 major doubles titles. In 1984, as well as winning the Grand Slam in singles, she and Pam Shriver also won it in doubles.

Left: Coe, winning the 1500 metres at the 1984 Olympics in Los Angeles. Just behind him is another British runner, Steve Cram.

Right: Severiano Ballesteros.

STENMARK, Ingemar

Swedish skier born 1956

Stenmark learned to ski at the age of 5, trained by his father, and when he was 13 he was selected to train for the Swedish junior team. He soon rose to leading positions in World Cup rankings, and won the World Cup three times in a row (1976-78). Then the scoring rules were changed so that competitors had to gain points from all three events: slalom, giant slalom and downhill. Since Stenmark had never been a downhill racer, people thought that this change had been made to handicap him. He did begin downhill training, but after a fall returned to concentrate on slalom events. He won both slalom events three years running (1979-81), and the slalom only, in 1983. He retired in 1989.

Stenmark in full flight in the giant slalom, in 1987.

BALLESTEROS, Severiano

Spanish golfer born 1957

"Seve" Ballesteros was the leading European golfer of the 1980s. His major tournament wins include the British Open in 1979, 1980, 1984 and 1988, and the US Masters in 1980 and 1983.

DAVIS, Steve

English snooker player born 1957

Davis dominated snooker in the 1980s, and was World Professional Champion five times. He was the first player ever to become a snooker millionaire.

KOCH, Marita

German athlete born 1957

Koch has held world records for most distances from 60 m to 400 m, and also for the 4 × 100 m, 4 × 200 m and 4 × 400 m relay. She was unbeaten at 400 m from 1977 to 1981, and in 1985 in Canberra she set a world record of 47.60 seconds, matching **Liddell**'s time of 1924.

KOCH: Liddell 268

Torvill and Dean. In this part of their programme they are skating to build up speed before a jump.

TORVILL, Jayne

English ice-dancer born 1957

and

DEAN, Christopher

English ice-dancer born 1958

Like John **Curry**, Torvill and Dean brought artistry to their sport. At first their routines were based on ideas from plays or films, even a circus act (in "Barnum"), but they later developed them into individual interpretations of the music (for example **Ravel**'s *Bolero*). They won three World Championships (in 1981, 1982 and 1984) and the 1984 Olympic gold medal in Sarajevo.

DECKER-SLANEY, Mary

US athlete born 1958

At 14, Mary Decker was the youngest person ever to run for her country. She set her first world indoor record for the 800 m race the next year, and has gone on to set records at every recognized outdoor distance from 800 m to 10,000 m, and broken six world records. Indoors, she has had equally distinguished victories from 800 m to 2 miles, but has so far failed to win an Olympic gold medal.

JACKSON, Michael

US singer and dancer born 1958

When Jackson was 8 he toured the world with The Jackson Five (later known as The Jacksons), a group formed with his brothers. They stayed together for 14 years, and had 25 hits. Jackson also began a solo career, and had a hit with *Got to be There* when he was 13. His biggest hits are *Billie Jean* and the album *Thriller* – one of the best-selling LPs and videos ever made.

Jackson sings in disco-pop style, in a way many have imitated but no one has surpassed. But the main excitement of his performances is his dancing. He surrounds himself with fine fellow-dancers, and uses wildly unusual dance-steps and fantasy stories to accompany the music. (The video *Thriller*, for example, takes

TORVILL AND DEAN: Curry 302 Ravel 58

place in a graveyard and gives dance-routines to the living dead.) Some critics rate Jackson as the finest song-and-dance-man of his time, a 1980s Fred **Astaire**.

Michael Jackson.

THOMPSON, Daley (Francis Morgan)

English decathlete born 1958

As a child, Thompson was hyperactive (hard for his mother to control), and was sent to a state-run boarding school at 7 years old. It was here that he discovered his athletic talents. At first, he wanted to be a sprinter, but in 1975 his coach persuaded him to try the decathlon, a collection of ten events, spread over two days, in which the competitors are awarded points. Although Thompson was offically under age, he scored 6,685 points, beating the previous junior record by 2,000 – and went on to win more points as British junior champion than the senior champion had taken.

At the 1976 Olympic Games, Thompson competed against many more experienced athletes, including Bruce Jenner (who eventually won the gold). Although Thompson was finally placed 18th, he learned much from watching the other competitors, and over the next four years he trained hard, concentrating on the throwing events which he finds harder than the others. He won the gold medal at the 1980 Moscow Games – and repeated the feat in 1984, only the second decathlete to do this. He came fourth in the decathlon at the 1988 Olympics. His record points score of 8,847, set in 1984, has yet to be beaten.

Daley Thompson, over the bar, in the high jump.

JACKSON: Astaire 266

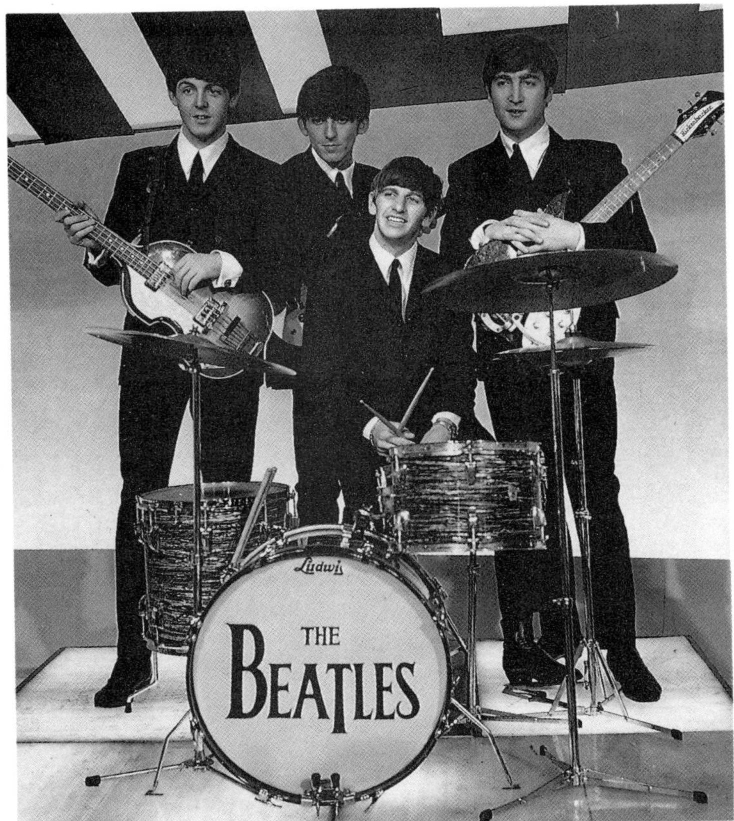

The Beatles – Paul, George and John, with Ringo on the drums.

BEATLES, The

English pop group formed 1960

The Beatles were JOHN LENNON (1940–80), PAUL McCARTNEY (born 1942), GEORGE HARRISON (born 1943) and RINGO STARR (born Richard Starkey, 1940). The group began as The Quarrymen in 1956, changed its name to The Silver Beatles in 1959, and to The Beatles in 1960 (with Pete Best as drummer instead of Ringo Starr). Their first hit was *Love Me Do* in 1962. Helped by the publicity genius of their manager Brian Epstein and the skills of their arranger George Martin, they quickly became the world's best-known pop group – and many people still regard them as the finest band in the whole history of pop. Lennon and McCartney wrote most of the group's songs, and became a hit song-writing team. Harrison also wrote songs, often using ideas from Indian music. Starr contented himself with drumming and occasional singing.

For six years the Beatles had one hit after another. Twenty-eight of their songs went into the top twenty (17 reaching Number One), including *She Loves You, I Want to Hold Your Hand, A Hard Day's Night, Paperback Writer* and *Hey Jude*. In 1964 and 1965 they made two joky films, *A Hard Day's Night* (about a rich band on the run from fans) and *Help!* They also provided voices and music for a fantasy cartoon film, *Yellow Submarine*, in 1968.

In 1968 Lennon set up home with the Japanese artist Yoko Ono, and a few months afterwards, in 1970, the band broke up. Lennon and Ono continued Lennon's interest in Eastern mysticism, and began making appearances in the cause of world peace. This was the height of the hippie movement, "flower power", and the couple were two of its leaders. In 1971 McCartney and his wife Linda formed another group, Wings, whose many hits include the album *Band on the Run*. Harrison made a few solo records but then went into film production, working among other things on *The Life of Brian, The Long Good Friday* and *Time Bandits*. Starr made one hit solo album, *Ringo*, and then concentrated on film acting. For years there were rumours that the Beatles would one day record again, but the only work they did was the sad song *All Those Years Ago*, made by McCartney, Harrison and Starr after Lennon was shot dead in 1980.

BRISCO, Valerie Ann

US athlete born 1960

At the 1984 Olympic Games, Brisco won two individual gold medals in the 200 m and 400 m sprints, the first person ever to do this at the same Olympic meeting. She was also part of the USA gold-winning 4 ×400 m relay team. All of these performances set new US and Olympic records. In 1988 Brisco-Hooks (as she became known after her marriage) won a silver team medal in the US 4 × 400 m relay.

CAUTHEN, Steve

US jockey born 1960

Cauthen was US champion jockey in 1977, won the US Triple Crown in 1978, and became British champion in 1984, 1985 and 1987. He is the only jockey to have achieved this.

GRIFFITH-JOYNER, Florence

US athlete born 1960

"Flo-Jo" (as she is nicknamed) won the silver medal in the 200 m at the 1984 Olympics. Four years later she won a silver medal in the US 4 × 400 m relay team, and three golds, at 100 m, 200 m and in the 4 × 100 m relay. In the 200 m she set a new world record of 21.34 seconds.

LENDL, Ivan

Czech tennis player born 1960

Lendl dominated men's singles tennis in the 1980s. He won the US title three times (1985-87), the French three times (1984, 1986-87), and the Australian once (in 1989). He was World Champion for 3 years, 1986-88, and earned more money from the game than any other player except Martina **Navratilova**.

Eddie Murphy stars as the cop with an answer for everything.

MURPHY, Eddie

US comedian born 1960

Murphy began to work as a stand-up comedian when he was just 16, and by the age of 19 he was a TV star. In 1982 he went into films, and had international success with *Trading Places* (in which he played a tramp who changed places with a white millionaire) and *Beverly Hills Cop*, in which he played a fast-talking policeman, firing wisecracks like bullets and thinking so fast that not even his partners can keep up with him, let alone the crooks.

"Flo-Jo", going for the line in the 200 metres at the 1988 Olympics in Seoul.

LENDL: Navratilova 308

BEACH BOYS, The

US pop band formed 1961

The Beach Boys were the Wilson brothers: BRIAN (born 1942), DENNIS (1944-83) and CARL (born 1946), their cousin MIKE LOVE (born 1941) and schoolfriend AL JARDINE (born 1942). Brian Wilson formed the group, composed most of its songs, and invented its unique sound: high, close-harmony singing, Hawaiian-style guitar chords, with catchy tunes and lyrics about the good things of life. The Beach Boys' songs were popular on the sound-track of "surfin' movies" or "bikini movies" in the 1960s. In nearly 20 years the Beach Boys had over 30 hit singles. Their first international success was *Surfin' USA* (1963); their biggest-ever hits were *Do It Again* and *Good Vibrations*.

The Beach Boys.

Pop star Madonna.

COMANECI, Nadia

Romanian gymnast born 1961

Olga **Korbut**'s triumphs in the 1972 Olympics meant that few people paid much attention to Comaneci, even when she won 4 out of 5 European gymnastic gold medals at the age of 13. But on the first day of the 1976 Olympics, Comaneci scored the maximum mark of 10, the first of 6 such "perfect" scores, and went on to win one team and three individual gold medals. At the Moscow Olympics, in 1980, she won two more golds, but found it hard to keep up her 1976 record of perfection.

MADONNA (Madonna Caccione)

US pop star born 1961

Madonna is famous not only for her music (which is bright, cheerful disco-pop) but also for the way she performs it. She wears revealing, sexy costumes, and dances to the accompaniment of strobe lights and lasers. Her first success was *Holiday* in 1983-84, and her biggest hits were *Into the Groove* and the name-track from the album *Like a Virgin*. She has also acted in films, including *Desperately Seeking Susan* and *Shanghai Surprise*, in which she co-starred with her then-husband, the actor Sean Penn.

GRETZKY, Wayne

Canadian ice-hockey player born 1961

Each winter Gretzky's father flooded the backyard of his home, and from the age of 3 Wayne was skating on the

COMANECI: Korbut 307

family "icerink". At 6 he was playing with a team of 10 to 11-year-olds, and at 16 he was the youngest player and the top scorer of the Canadian team playing at the junior Ice Hockey World Cup. He turned professional in 1978 and soon joined the Edmonton Oilers. Since 1978 he has broken many ice-hockey records: he has won the most points in a season (215 in 1985-86), the most goals in a season (92 in 1981-82) and was the first person to reach 300 points in the fewest games (159). He is sometimes known as "The Great One" and is the most publicly recognized sportsperson in Canada.

Ice hockey superstar Wayne Gretzky.

LEWIS, Frederick Carlton

US athlete born 1961

Carl Lewis was born in Alabama, like Jesse **Owens**, and competes in the same events. He equalled Owen's long-jump record in 1979, and would have taken part in the 1980 Moscow Olympics, had his country not boycotted them. In 1983 he came second to **Beamon**'s legendary long-jump at 8.79 m. (Beamon's distance was 8.9 m, 11 cm further.) In the 1984 Olympics, Lewis won four gold medals in the individual 100 m and 200 m sprints (setting a world record in the 200 m), the long-jump, and as part of the US 4 × 100 m relay team – another world record. In 1988 he fulfilled his hopes of becoming the second man (after Archie Hahn in 1904-06) to win a second gold medal in the 100 m sprint, but only after his rival Ben Johnson had been disqualified for drug-taking. Lewis won another gold in the long-jump and a silver in 200 m sprint.

LEWIS: Beamon 300 Owens 278 PRINCE: Keaton 261

MARADONA, Diego Armando

Argentinian footballer born 1961

Born into a poor family, Maradona showed footballing talent as a young child, and first played for Argentina at the age of 16. In 1986 he was the hero of Argentina's World Cup winning side, and is one of football's present-day world superstars.

PRINCE

US pop star born 1961

Prince's full name is Prince Rogers Nelson. He formed his first band when he was 12, and had his first hit with *I Wanna Be Your Lover* in 1979. He is multi-talented: he wrote, produced, sang and played all the instruments on this record and on his first album in 1980. In his stage-shows he dances, sings and plays, and he is famous for his colourful, costumes and his unsmiling, Buster **Keaton**-like expression. His biggest hit was *When Doves Cry* in 1984, and his *Purple Rain* became one of the best known of all songs in the 1980s. In 1989 he wrote and recorded the music for the film *Batman*.

Carl Lewis.

JOYNER-KERSEE, Jacqueline

US heptathlete born 1962

Joyner began competing in athletics at 9 years old, and at 14 was a US national junior champion. She won a basketball scholarship to university and at first concentrated on this sport and on the long-jump, but was persuaded by the assistant coach, Bob Kersee, to train for the heptathlon. Kersee made her work on her weaker events (hurdles, javelin and shot), and in 1984, in spite of injury, she won a silver medal in the heptathlon at the Los Angeles Olympics. Later, she also gained the US long-jump record, and in 1986 married Kersee (and added Kersee to her surname). She was the first US woman since **Didrikson** to hold a world record in a multi-event. At the 1988 Olympics she won gold medals in the long-jump and heptathlon.

Ronnie Wood (left) and Mick Jagger, two of the Rolling Stones.

KASPAROV, Gary

Russian chess player born 1963

Kasparov's parents hoped that he would become a musician, but he chose instead to concentrate on chess, a game he had played since he was 6 years old. At 15 he beat a Grand Master, and continued through regional and international matches until at 22 he was acknowledged as the challenger to the then-world champion, Anatoly Karpov. In February 1985 the championship began, but arguing among the chess authorities postponed it until September, when Kasparov, playing his high-risk, spectacular game, won. He was the youngest person ever to win a world title, and he has kept it ever since.

ROLLING STONES, The

English pop band formed 1963

The original Rolling Stones were BILL WYMAN (born William Perks, 1936), CHARLIE WATTS (born 1941), BRIAN JONES (1942-69), MICK JAGGER (born 1943) and KEITH RICHARD (born 1943). After Jones drowned in his swimming pool (perhaps after a drugs overdose), MICK TAYLOR replaced him, and Taylor in turn was replaced in 1975 by RON WOOD.

One of the Stones' first hits was *I Wanna Be Your Man*, written by Lennon and McCartney, but soon afterwards they began recording songs written by Jagger and Richard, including (in 1965) their biggest-selling record, *I Can't Get No Satisfaction*. In the mid-1960s they were second only to the **Beatles** in

JOYNER-KERSEE: Didrikson 278 ROLLING STONES: Beatles 312

fame, and were nicknamed the "bad boys of rock" because the words of their songs were about sex, drugs and violence, because of the way they behaved onstage, and because of countless newspaper stories of drugs and orgies offstage.

For all the bad publicity, or perhaps because of it, the Rolling Stones had huge success in the 1960s and 1970s, making over 30 hit singles. They made less music in the 1980s, joining up for the occasional concert or recording, but generally living quieter lives. Jagger, in particular, followed his own career, making records and acting in films (notably *Ned Kelly*, about the famous Australian outlaw).

WHO, The

English rock band formed 1964

The band's original members were ROGER DALTREY (born 1945), JOHN ENTWHISTLE (born 1945), PETE TOWNSHEND (born 1945) and KEITH MOON (1947-78). KENNY JONES (born 1948) took over as drummer after Keith Moon died in 1978, from an overdose of sleeping pills.

In the 1960s The Who had a reputation as the "wild men" of pop. Their music (which inspired later punk and Heavy Metal styles) used loud, crashing chords and driving rhythm, their lyrics were violent and foul-mouthed, and they were famous for drug-taking and for smashing guitars onstage and hotel rooms and lobbies offstage. (Later, Townshend became a powerful anti-drugs campaigner.)

The Who's first success was *I Can't Explain* in 1965, and their greatest hits were *My Generation* and *Pinball Wizard*, from the 1969 rock opera *Tommy*, which began as an album and was later turned into a musical and then a film. Another of The Who's albums, *Quadrophenia*, was also used as the basis for a film.

The Who, in action. Daltrey is at the front, while Townshend makes one of his famous leaps in time to the music.

BECKER, Boris

German tennis player born 1967

Becker became a professional player in 1984 (when he was 17), and went on to win the men's singles championships at Wimbledon in 1985, 1986 and 1989.

GRAF, Steffi

German tennis player born 1969

In 1988 Graf became the first woman player since Margaret Court (in 1970) to win the Grand Slam: the four major world tournaments. In 1988 she won the gold medal at Seoul, the first Olympic tennis competition held for 64 years. In 1989 she repeated her victories of the year before in the Australian and US Open Championships and at Wimbledon, but failed to win the US Open – and hence the Grand Slam – by just one game.

Steffi Graf and Boris Becker, winners of the 1989 Wimbledon tournament.

GLOSSARY

Amateur Someone who does an activity (especially sport), for its own sake, rather than for payment: the opposite of professional.

Asthma A lung disease which makes it difficult or painful to breathe.

Athlete Refers to any sports person. **Athletics** usually means track and field events.

Blasphemy Insulting God or the gods, by saying things about them which offend believers, or using their names to swear by. In some religions (for example Islam), blasphemy is a crime punishable by death.

Blues Slow, dragging songs, usually about the sadness of life. They were invented by slaves in the US South about 100 years ago, and became a main kind of jazz music.

Capped (in sport) When you play for your country's team, you are "capped". The name comes from the old days in Britain, where team members were given real caps to wear.

Choreographer The person who makes up the dance steps and sequences for ballet and stage dancing. **Choreography** refers to the steps and sequences of the dance.

Director (in films) The person who organizes day-by-day filming, telling the actors where to move, arranging sound, light, camera angles and effects.

Documentary A film, TV programme or piece of writing which is not fiction (made up) but shows some part of actual life as it happens.

Fascism A political system involving total state control, often helped by secret police and severe punishment for those who disagree. Begun in Italy by Mussolini about 70 years ago, and also found in 1930s Spain, Germany and several countries in Africa and South America.

Feature film Full-length film, the main "feature" of a programme (hence the name).

Flat race Horse race without jumps: the opposite of steeplechase.

Harpsichord Keyboard instrument where pressing the keys causes the strings to be plucked instead of hammered (as on the piano).

Improvise (in music) To make up what you sing or play as you go along. Most music in the world is improvised. In jazz, Indian music and pop, people improvise according to prearranged rules and patterns.

Librettist The person who writes the words to set to the music of an opera. The **libretto** is the complete text written for the music of an opera.

Lyric (in music) Words of a song.

Melodrama Kind of drama where action is clear and emotions are strong. Soap operas, for example, are melodrama. "Melodramatic" can also mean overdoing your words or actions: going over the top.

Mime A performance which uses movement and gesture only, without speech or any other sound.

Mistress A woman who lives with a man as his partner, like a wife in every way except that they are not married.

Music-hall (UK) or **Vaudeville** (USA) A theatre show which uses "acts": comedians, singers, dancers and jugglers.

Nazis Members of the National Socialist Party in Germany from 1923-45 – the party led by Hitler.

Oscar (in films) An award given to the best actors, directors, scriptwriters and other filmmakers each year. "Oscar" is the name of the statue, of a gold-plated, naked man.

Overdose (in medicine, and especially of drugs) A dose is a precisely measured amount, exactly what you need. An overdose is too much, and can be fatal.

Pizzicato (in music) Plucking the strings of a violin, viola, cello or double bass instead of stroking them with the bow.

Political asylum If your country refuses to let you leave, you can try to get political asylum in another country. It offers you shelter; freedom from pursuit by the authorities in your own country.

Prodigy Someone (often a child) who is astonishingly gifted at some skill or art. The commonest prodigies are in music, maths, chess and sport.

Professional Someone who does an activity (especially sport) for money: the opposite of amateur.

Propaganda False information told to the public as if it were true, to influence the way people think (often in time of war).

Slapstick Physical clowning: fighting, falling, pie-throwing, tumbling. So called from the "slapstick" used in circuses, to make a slapping noise offstage when the clowns pretended to hit each other.

Sponsor A person or business firm who pays to support a sporting or artistic event.

Stand-up comedian Unlike comedians who play parts in comedy plays (for example TV sit-coms), stand-up comedians stand up, as themselves, and tell jokes.

Steeplechase Race where the contestants must jump over obstacles. In horse-racing, the opposite of a "flat-race".

Tumbler An acrobat who somersaults, does handstands and other gymnastic tricks.

Vaudeville *see* **Music-hall**.

Virtuoso Someone amazingly skilled at what they do. The name was first used for outstanding musical performers, but is now used for anyone with unusual skill.

SECTION 5
THINKERS AND INVENTORS

Religious Leaders,
Thinkers,
Inventors and Engineers

INTRODUCTION TO *THINKERS AND INVENTORS*

Human beings are the most ingenious creatures on Earth. In physical skills, other animals easily outstrip us. Size for size, minnows swim faster. Fleas leap higher. Bats hear better. But our brains are the most complex – which is why we control the planet. Curiosity leads us not just to accept the world, but to tinker with it. Inventors devise new machines and ways to do things. Philosophers think about everything we feel, experience or know, and try to give clear explanations.

The processes of invention and thinking begin, each time, with a problem – how to grow more crops, light a dark room, say what the gods are like or discover how we can live happy lives. Already, simply by asking questions, we are using our brains in a way no other creature can. In the second stage, too – finding answers – we behave quite differently. Most creatures move by instinct or by trial and error. We ponder, examine and analyse.

Many pioneering inventions now seem obvious. No one knows who first made a wheel, worked metal, harnessed water power, made glass. Canals, pottery, writing – all were invented long before recorded history, and their inventors' names are lost. We may wonder why it took the human race so long to work out other things we now take for granted: electricity, for example, zips or telephones. Almost anyone could have invented morse code, or braille. But they didn't. There almost seems to be a right time and place for each invention – and when people discover something at the wrong moment, they have no idea how to use it, and must leave it for others to develop later. Development, building on earlier ideas, is vital to invention.

Philosophy, too, is a kind of invention, using ideas to change human life. Philosophers (thinkers) work to improve not gadgets but ideas. Many of the world's religions began with one person's dazzling new vision of the gods or how humans should live. New systems of government arose when people thought about the way states should be run.

Human inventiveness will never end. However well things seem to work, we will always try to better them – and this applies to complex inventions like politics as well as to quite simple ones like radios. To the human mind, nothing ever seems final. There are always new things to discover or fresh approaches to try. Inventing and thinking keep us happy. In fact, that if every machine and every idea in the world were perfect, we might be bored to death.

ISAIAH

Jewish prophet 8th century BC

Isaiah was a prophet, statesman and counsellor of the kings of Judah in Jerusalem at a time when the nation was threatened by the powerful Assyrian empire. He said that their troubles arose because they had stopped believing in the one true God, worshipping instead many false gods and spirits, as their enemies did. Isaiah predicted the defeat of the Jews, but they took no notice of him. Later, when the Jews had been taken to Babylon as prisoners of war, he prophesied that a saviour-king would save them and bring them peace and a true knowledge of God.

Christians have applied this prophecy to **Jesus**, and think that Isaiah will be proved right – that all believers will be rewarded with everlasting life when Jesus comes again to judge the world.

ZOROASTER (Zarathushtra)

Persian religious leader c 628-551 BC

Zoroaster was a priest of the ancient Persian (Iranian) religion, which had many gods and goddesses. He had a vision in which Ahura Mazda, god of light and truth, appeared and said that he was the only god in the universe, and that Persians should worship him alone. Zoroaster began preaching this new faith. He set out his teachings in the 21 books of the *Ayesta*, which describe the battle between Ahura Mazda and Ahriman, god of darkness. Eventually goodness will triumph, and Ahura Mazda will give his loyal followers everlasting life.

ISAIAH: Jesus 329

The ruins of a Zoroastrian temple in Iran (Persia). Zoroastrianism was Persia's state religion for over 1,200 years, until the conquering Arabs replaced it with Islam in the seventh century AD.

LAO ZI

Chinese thinker c 604-531 BC

Lao Zi worked for a time in the emperor's library in Honan, China. But he turned to teaching religion and philosophy, and was soon travelling all over China to explain his ideas. He thought that everything in the universe should exist in a state of perfect peace and harmony, and that we should lead our lives trying to make that possible. This idea, known as Taoism, became the basis for a religion which was followed in China for 2,500 years, and which is still important today.

BUDDHA (Gautama Siddhartha)

Indian thinker c 560-480 BC

Gautama Siddhartha was the son of a rich Nepalese king and was pampered in every way. His parents made sure that all unpleasant sights were kept from him. But when he was 29, he saw for the first time an old person, a sick person, and a dead person – all on the same day. The discovery that there was suffering in the world changed Gautama's life. He went to live among the poor, determined to find out why such misery existed. For six years he wandered as a beggar, but found that this brought him no nearer

an answer than his life of luxury had done. He decided that the way to find the answer was through meditation: sitting quietly, cut off from the world and its distractions, disciplining his mind and his thoughts.

Legend says that Gautama sat under a wild fig tree until he solved his problem. His answer was that human misery was caused by craving. People were so eager for wealth, power, love or success that their minds were in constant turmoil. The way to find peace, he decided, was to give up worldly desires, to wipe everyday worry from the mind.

Gautama's followers called him Buddha ("the enlightened one"), and he is still known by that name today. Buddhist monks and priests lead people not in religious worship but in meditation, which helps them to reach a state of *nirvana*, or total peace of mind and body. Buddhism is followed by over 500 million people, chiefly in Tibet, Nepal, Sri Lanka, South East Asia and Japan.

CONFUCIUS (K'ung Fu Tsu)

Chinese thinker c 551-479 BC

K'ung Fu Tsu means "master K'ung". When his works were published in the West, centuries after his death, people used the Latin form of his name, Confucius. Like many thinkers of his time, for example **Buddha** or **Socrates**, he was interested in what "goodness" was, whether it could be taught and learned, and what sort of life a "good" person ought to lead. He travelled from town to town, studying and teaching, and wrote books explaining his ideas. The most famous is *Analects*, a collection of conversations, lectures and sayings.

By the time Confucius died, he was considered one of the greatest thinkers China had ever known. His followers expanded his ideas into a way of life, called Confucianism, which was used in China almost like a state religion for over 2,500 years, until it was abolished by the communist government in 1966. (It is still the state religion of Taiwan.) Confucianism taught that we are all born good, and that our aim in life is to keep to that goodness, avoiding anything which might lessen it. We have a duty to our fellow human beings, either as superiors, equals or inferiors. Confucianism sets that duty down, giving precise laws about how people ought to behave.

Left: Buddha taught of the need to break away from attachment to worldly things, such as possessions or cares in life. To do this, Buddhists meditate, often sitting in a crosslegged position.

Confucius was renowned for his many sayings. Two of the most famous are: "Never do to others what you would not like them to do to you" and "People control principles; principles do not control people."

CONFUCIUS: Buddha 324 Socrates 326

SOCRATES (Sokrates)

Greek thinker c 469-399 BC

When Socrates was a young man he asked Apollo's oracle "Who is the wisest person in the world?", and the oracle answered "Socrates". After asking everyone who seemed wise what they knew, Socrates decided that he was the wisest because he was the only one who realized how little he really knew. He developed a system of investigation by questioning. To find out about anything – from what the gods are like, to how the memory works – question after question has to be asked. As wrong ideas are eliminated, the questioner ends with a clearer idea of the problem than at the start.

Socrates' main interest was human nature. He wanted to know why we behave as we do, and how we can be better. He believed that philosophy (the search for wisdom and the study of beliefs) should be applied to life, and that to be good we must know what "good" means, and he often enquired into such questions as "What is truth?" His ideas were mocked by some people, including **Aristophanes**, who, in his comedy play *Clouds*, showed Socrates as a kind of lunatic professor who understood nothing about day-to-day existence. But others, especially the young, found Socrates' ideas exciting, and flocked to learn from him. The authorities feared him as a revolutionary, and condemned him to death for denying the existence of the gods and for "corrupting the young". Socrates drank poison and, while it took effect, spent his last hours with his friends discussing whether the soul lives on after the body dies.

Socrates, who, the sacred oracle at Delphi declared, was the wisest person in the world.

Socrates left no writings. His teaching survives mainly in the works of two of his followers, **Plato** and Xenophon. His ideas inspired many later thinkers, including **Aristotle**, and he was respected by Christians because much of his teaching was close to their own ideas.

PLATO (Platon)

Greek thinker 429-347 BC

Plato was an Athenian aristocrat, and at first planned a career in politics. But he disliked the squabbles and lies of those in power, and went to learn from **Socrates**, whom he thought to be the most honest man in Athens. Plato later became a teacher himself, and people gathered from all over Greece to learn from him.

Plato believed that everything there is – from mice to tables, from memory to love – has a perfect form. What we see, feel or know is a blurred

Plato, who was a pupil of Socrates, taught in the grove of Academus, which gave rise to the word academy, meaning "place of learning".

SOCRATES: Aristophanes 6 Aristotle 328 Plato 326 PLATO: Socrates 326

version of that perfect form, because it is affected by our other feelings and senses. If we concentrate hard, if we clear our minds of irrelevant thoughts, we will gradually work out the simple truth about everything. He thought that human inventions such as law and politics also had perfect forms, and if we discover them our lives will be made better. He tried to turn the Sicilian town of Syracuse into a perfect state with an ideal king, but the experiment failed because the king, Dionysius II, was mentally unstable.

Plato wrote dozens of books. They take the form of conversations, written like plays and many of them feature his teacher Socrates. One of the best known is *The Republic*, in which Plato sets out his views on the ideal state. His teaching and his methods have been admired throughout the centuries; many of his views are still taught today.

DIOGENES

Greek thinker c 412-323 BC

When Diogenes was a boy his father was sent to prison for selling metal cut from coins. Diogenes became a tramp and beggar. He would stand in streets and squares telling people how useless wealth was, and how one's true self is corrupted by possessions. He slept rough (legend says in a barrel), and was short-tempered and rude.

Later, Diogenes' way of life, and his hoarse, barking voice, earned him the nickname *cynikos*, meaning "dog-like", and since then the name "cynic" has been given to people who announce that they despise everyone else's ways of life and thoughts. Diogenes died, so the story goes, from eating raw cuttlefish: he was trying to prove to the world that cooking is unnecessary.

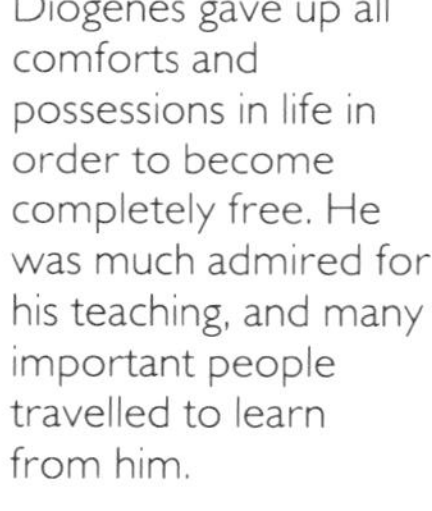

Diogenes gave up all comforts and possessions in life in order to become completely free. He was much admired for his teaching, and many important people travelled to learn from him.

ARISTOTLE (Aristoteles)

Greek thinker 384-322 BC

Aristotle was only 17 when his parents died. He went to study with **Plato** in Athens and stayed there until he was nearly 40. After some years as a travelling professor (one of his pupils was the young Prince Alexander of Macedon – later **Alexander the Great**) he went back to Athens in 335 BC, to set up the school known as the Lyceum.

From boyhood, Aristotle studied everything in nature, making notes about subjects as varied as plants, marine creatures, and the diseases of bees. When he grew up, he was inspired by the theories of **Eudoxus**, and studied the nature of the universe. This led him to lecture and write about rocks, weather, and the "elements" (earth, air, fire, water) from which he said everything was made. He developed a way of studying similar to what we now call "scientific method" – going from one step to the next, considering each new fact in turn and omitting nothing until a whole pattern of ideas is logically built up.

Later, Aristotle used the same logical method to study humans and their activities. He was particularly interested in "ethics": the way we organize our daily lives and deal with our fellow-mortals. He wrote books on law, politics, religion and human nature. His lectures became world-famous, and many rulers, statesmen and aristocrats sent their sons to learn from him. His ideas were rediscovered during the Middle Ages and affected later thinkers and scholars in Arabia, India and Europe.

Below, left: Aristotle's ideas affected thinking in Europe for many centuries. As well as philosophy, he studied science, suggested an ideal system of government, and set out rules for writing good drama.

EPICURUS (Epikouros)

Greek thinker 342-260 BC

Epicurus' main aim was to discover how people could free themselves from worry and care. He taught that the gods are not interested in the affairs of mortals, so that we have no need to fear them or to try to please them. Instead we should try to find happiness and peace, taking each day as it comes and ignoring the bustle of the world. Epicurus' ideas ("Epicureanism") won him many followers, especially among the rich aristocrats of ancient Greece and Rome. The idea that happiness was a right of everyone is written into the American Declaration of Independence (see **Jefferson**).

Epicurus' motto was: live for today – that is, don't let fears or hopes about the future disturb your peace of mind.

ARISTOTLE: Alexander the Great 412 Eudoxus 86 Plato 326 EPICURUS: Jefferson 448

JESUS

Founder of Christianity 1st century AD

Jesus is the central figure of the Christian faith, seen by his followers as God come down to Earth to live as a human being. The name Jesus is the Greek form of Yeshu (or Joshua), which means "God saves". The exact date of Jesus' birth is uncertain, but it is known to have been in the reign of Herod the Great, who died in 4 BC. Accounts of his birth stress its miraculous nature, saying that his mother, Mary, was a virgin, that a mysterious star guided three wise men to the stable where he was born, and that angels brought ordinary shepherds to worship him.

We know little of Jesus' early life. At the age of about 30, he was baptized in the river Jordan. This marked the beginning of his life's work, which was to tell people in Jerusalem and the surrounding area about God's love and that they must believe in God and turn away from sin. Huge crowds listened to his preaching and saw him perform "miracles": healing the sick, giving sight to the blind, walking on water and bringing dead people back to life. They came to see him as the Messiah ("saviour" or "liberator"), who, since the prophesies of **Isaiah**, had been expected to come and save Israel. Although many of his followers thought that he would create God's kingdom on Earth by driving out the Romans, his closest friends (or disciples) thought that he had a much greater mission: as God's son he had come to save the whole world from sin.

Although Jesus never spoke against Jewish religious law, he put such qualities as love, justice and trust in God before full obedience to all the regulations. His popularity and the challenge he posed to the Jewish religious leaders made them hate him. Although he had done no wrong, they persuaded the Roman governor, Pontius Pilate, to have him executed as a criminal by crucifixion (being nailed to a wooden cross to die). Three days after his death, the disciples claimed that Jesus rose from the dead and taught them further, before being carried up to Heaven to sit at God's right hand.

In the century after his life on earth, belief in Jesus as the Son of God spread widely. Matthew, Mark, Luke and John wrote accounts of his life (the "gospels"). The original disciples and **Paul** converted thousands of people in the lands of the Mediterranean and the Middle East. The Roman emperor **Constantine** was converted in 312 AD and by the end of the fourth century Christianity was the official religion of the Roman Empire. Today it is the largest of the world religions, with over 1,000 million followers.

Jesus preached love, trust and forgiveness for wrongdoers, and is the central figure of the Christian faith. The supposed year of his birth is used as the basis for the Western calendar: BC indicates the centuries Before Christ; AD (Anno Domini – year of the Lord) is used for dates after his birth.

Jesus' acts and teaching were written down in the Gospels. This page comes from a copy made by monks at Lindisfarne (also known as Holy Island), off the coast of England, during the late 600s.

JESUS: Constantine 419 Isaiah 324 Paul 330

Early Christians were often persecuted by the Romans because they did not worship the Roman emperor as a god. Some of the Christians were rounded up and sent to the arena to be killed by lions, watched by thousands of eager spectators.

PAUL, Saint

Christian teacher c 3 BC-AD 64

Paul's original name was Saul; he changed it to its Roman form, Paul, when he became a Christian. He was an educated man, expert both in Jewish religious law and the teaching of such Greek thinkers as **Epicurus** and **Aristotle**. He trained as a rabbi and thought that he was serving God by hunting down Jews who had become Christians. When a crowd of people stoned to death the Christian preacher Stephen, Saul stood and watched.

Riding one day from Jerusalem to Damascus, Saul suddenly had a vision. He seemed to see a dazzling light and to hear **Jesus**' voice asking, "Saul, Saul, why do you persecute me?" Saul was blinded by the vision but his sight returned when a Christian in Damascus called Ananias laid hands on him. He was baptized and devoted his life to preaching Christianity as single-mindedly as he had once denounced it.

At the time of Paul's conversion, only a few years after Jesus' death, Christianity was confined mainly to Jewish people; they thought that Jesus was the Jewish Messiah, and some said that a person must become a Jew first before becoming a Christian. Paul, by contrast, said that Jesus had come into the world to save the entire human race from sin, and that all who believed in him – non-Jews as well as Jews – would be granted everlasting life. He travelled around the eastern Mediterranean lands, preaching and setting up Christian groups in every town.

The Romans saw Christians as troublemakers because riots sometimes occurred when they clashed with Jews, and so Christian leaders were often arrested. As a Roman citizen, Paul had the right to be tried before the Emperor **Nero** himself – and when he was arrested he seized this chance of going to Rome to preach. He spent two years in prison in Rome, writing letters to Christians all over the empire and converting anyone who came to him. Many of his letters survive in the New Testament of the Bible and act as an important guide to the Christian belief and way of life.

No one knows what happened to Paul after his imprisonment,

PAUL: Aristotle 328 Epicurus 328 Jesus 329 Nero 418

although tradition says that he was beheaded. He was probably executed during the persecution of Christians ordered by Nero, who blamed them for starting the Great Fire of Rome.

HERO (Heron)

Greek scientist and inventor 1st century AD

Hero taught engineering in Alexandria. He discovered a formula for calculating the area of an equilateral triangle in relation to its sides, and another for the calculation of square roots which is still used in pocket calculators. He also invented things: lifting devices for building sites, a distance-gauge for chariots (using the number of times the wheels rotated to calculate the distance travelled), and a theodolite (an instrument used by surveyors to measure angles). He drew, but never made, a calculating-machine using pins, cogs and dials; 1,600 years later, **Pascal** and **Leibnitz** used the diagram as a basis for calculating-machines of their own.

So far as anyone knows, Hero was the first person to realize the power of steam and to suggest practical ways of using it. His book *Pneumatics* is full of ingenious inventions. They include a steam-powered organ, a fountain worked by steam, a drinks-dispenser worked by a coin placed in a slot, a water-pump suitable for putting out fires, and dozens of mechanical toys.

Hero's most famous invention is the "aeolipile", a metal sphere suspended above a cauldron of boiling water. Steam rises through narrow tubes and makes the sphere rotate. Hero could think of no practical use for this invention, and made models of it just for fun. Sixteen centuries went by before the British inventors Savery and **Watt** realized that Hero had discovered the principle of the steam-engine.

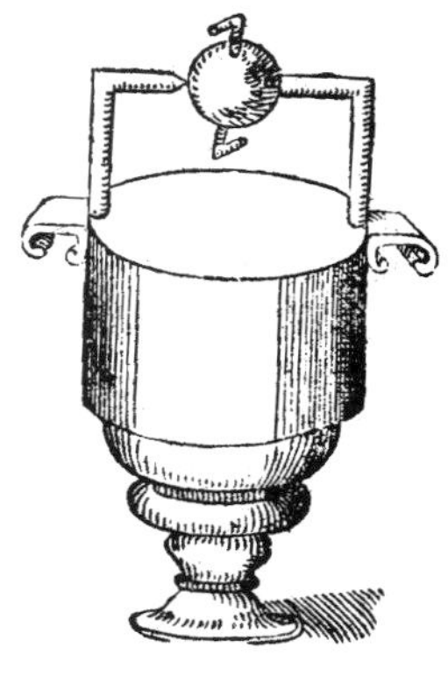

A drawing of Hero's aeliopile from the first century AD. He had discovered the principle of steam power, but without realizing how it could be used.

TS'AI LUN

Chinese inventor c 50-130

Paper is taken for granted these days – it is one of the most common items made in the world. But in ancient times, people had to use other materials for writing on: bone, animal skin, wax, clay, bark, cloth and even a criss-cross lattice of papyrus (a reed which gave "paper" its name). In 105 Ts'ai Lun took rubbish – old ropes, rags and fishing nets – and recycled it by unpicking the fibres, pulping them and wetting them. Then he poured the mixture into wooden trays and let it dry. The result was paper, exactly as we know it today.

The Chinese kept Ts'ai Lun's invention to themselves for 650 years. It was not till an Islamic army invaded China in 751 that the secret was out, spreading first to the Middle East and then throughout the world.

This early illustration shows Chinese paper-makers spreading out large sheets to dry.

HERO: Leibnitz 103 Pascal 100 Watt 350

This stained glass window was designed in the twentieth century for Norwich Cathedral in Norfolk, England. It shows ten saints, including St Benedict, together with the English king Henry I.

BENEDICT, Saint

Italian religious teacher c 480-550

In his 20s, Benedict lived as a hermit – quite alone for months on end, praying to God and thinking about religion. He then set up monasteries: places where people could retreat from the concerns of everyday living and give their lives and minds to God. St Benedict is known as the "father" of western monks, because he was the first one to write down rules for life in a monastery. Benedict's rule instructed monks to teach, learn and carry out tasks such as growing their own food, as well as to pray. The Benedictines (as they were called) were some of the first Christian monks and nuns.

SISSA

Indian thinker 6th century

A Hindu named Sissa invented chess as an alternative to backgammon. He devised it as a war-game, and the pieces were originally modelled on fighters of the time. What Westerners call rooks (or castles) were charioteers, able to leap over enemies and veer from side to side. The queen was modelled on the Hindu death-goddess Kali, able to swoop in any direction and carry destruction over the whole battlefield.

The angel Gabriel is shown in this thirteenth-century painting from Baghdad. In the religion of Islam, Gabriel is the messenger of Allah.

MOHAMMED (Muhammad)

Founder of Islam c 570-632

Mohammed was born in Mecca (in what is now Saudi Arabia) which, during his youth, was a religious centre. The heart of its shrine, called the Kaaba, had altars to dozens of gods, and the priests and townspeople grew rich from tourism and the visits of pilgrims. When Mohammed was 40, he claimed that the Angel Gabriel had visited him in a cave, and told him that there was only one God, Allah, and that people should give up idol-worship and serve Allah alone.

Mohammed's religion is called Islam, which means "surrender to God"; its followers are known as Muslims. At first it spread slowly. Most of the people of Mecca, afraid that it would destroy their tourist trade, persecuted Mohammed and his followers, and in 622 Mohammed moved to another town (now called Medina), where he was made religious leader and ruler. The Muslim calender dates from the "hegira", the journey of Mohammed to Medina, on 16 July 622.

A series of wars followed between the people of Mecca and Medina. In 630 Mohammed captured Mecca, cleared the Kaaba of idols and declared it a shrine to Allah, the one true God. From that time on, Mecca has been the most holy place in the Islamic world. Followers of Islam face in its direction five times a day to pray, and everyone who can afford to tries to make a pilgrimage there once in a lifetime. Devout Muslims are also obliged to confess their faith, make charitable gifts to the poor and fast (do without food) during each day in Ramadan (a religious festival lasting one month).

Although Mohammed had only a few thousand followers in his own lifetime, Islam grew quickly after his death. It is now one of the world's

main religions, with over 500 million followers. Its holy book, the Qur'ān (Koran), is a collection of sayings and teachings which Mohammed claimed the Angel Gabriel brought him direct from God.

CALLINICUS (Kallinikos)

Greek engineer 7th century

Callinicus worked in Constantinople (modern Istanbul, the capital of Turkey). The city lay at the narrow southern entrance to the Black Sea, and was under regular attack from enemy ships. There was no way to keep them away until Callinicus invented what became known as "Greek fire". He filled clay jars with oil and saltpetre (potassium nitrate), and lobbed them at the enemy using giant siege-catapults. The jars exploded on impact, and blazing oil set the ships on fire. Explosives had never been used before, and Constantinople's superstitious enemies were terrified: they took the fire-jars for thunderbolts, hurled at them by angry gods.

ALCUIN

Anglo-Saxon thinker and teacher c 735-804

Alcuin was master of the cathedral school in York for a time, and he was the most famous scholar in England. In 781 Emperor **Charlemagne** asked him to leave England to become his chief adviser on religious and educational matters. Alcuin's royal academy at the palace of Aachen attracted scholars from all over Charlemagne's empire and led to a rebirth of learning in Europe. He established an educational system for use in every abbey and school in the empire. It was based on religious education, Latin and mathematics, and was the form of education in Europe for over a thousand years.

Alcuin revised **Saint Jerome**'s Vulgate translation of the Bible, wrote explanatory commentaries on the Bible, and standardized spelling and handwriting. In 796 he was made Abbot of the monastery at Tours in France, and he made it one of the main educational centres in Europe.

Right: A map of the Holy Roman Empire in the eighth century. The scholar Alcuin planned the educational system which came to be used throughout the empire.

ALCUIN: Charlemagne 422 St Jerome 7

A pen and ink illustration showing how river locks act as a series of steps to transport boats and cargo from one level to another.

CHIAO WEI-YO

Chinese inventor 10th century

In 983, on the Chinese Grand Canal, Chiao built the first river-lock: an enormous water tank which could be filled or emptied to raise or lower boats and so let them sail from one level to another.

BECKET, Thomas à

English archbishop 1118-70

This panel in Canterbury Cathedral in Kent marks the spot where Thomas à Becket was murdered.

Thomas à Becket was lord chancellor of England, and a friend of King Henry II. Henry made him Archbishop of Canterbury (head of the church in England), hoping he would reconcile the rivalry for power that had divided the church and the state. As archbishop, Becket became very popular with ordinary people, because he resisted the wishes of the king and the rich nobles. Henry said that the state had power over every citizen, including priests. Becket said that only the church authorities had power over priests: they were immune from state law. The quarrel was fierce, and Henry was heard to mutter "Will nobody rid me of this turbulent priest?" Four knights took this as an order rather than a question, and murdered Becket in Canterbury Cathedral. In 1173, only three years after Becket's death, Pope Alexander III declared him a Roman Catholic saint.

MAIMONIDES, Moses (Mosheh ben Maymun)

Spanish/Jewish thinker 1135-1204

Maimonides worked as a doctor in Cairo, Egypt (where one of his patients was the Sultan, **Saladin**), and was also a rabbi (Jewish religious teacher). He put the teachings of **Moses** and other Jewish leaders into language that ordinary people could understand. Until his time, Jewish teachers had preached faith alone, saying that all we have to do is believe, and that God will guide us and help us. Maimonides said that people should use intelligence as well as faith. His books (for example, *Guide for the Perplexed*) contain some of the most important of all Jewish teaching about religion. Maimonides was one of the most influential Jewish thinkers for several centuries, and his writings were as important in the Jewish religion as St **Paul**'s were in Christianity.

AL-JAZARI, Ismail Ibn Al-Razzaz

Arab engineer c 1150-1220

Al-Jazari was court architect to the rulers of Amid (modern Diyarbakir, in Turkey). In 1206, in his *Book of Ingenious Mechanical Devices*, he described all kinds of gadgets,

MAIMONIDES: Moses 406 Paul 330 Saladin 168

including cranes, pulleys, drills and cogs. He was the first person to describe a crank-shaft, and may have invented it. He also invented a ratchet-mechanism for opening and closing sluice-gates, and the ox-powered water-scoop still used in irrigation-systems in many parts of the world.

HONNECOURT, Villard de

Flemish architect and engineer c 1180-1250

Honnecourt was a monk who specialized in designing churches: his finest surviving building is Cambrai Cathedral in France. But he is also remembered for a notebook of sketches and designs. Some were practical devices: a screw-jack for lifting heavy weights (similar to the jack people now use when changing car wheels), a mechanical saw worked by water-power, a trebuchet (siege-catapult). Others were more fanciful. Honnecourt designed automata (clockwork models for bell-towers and clock-towers): a clockwork angel which raised its hands in blessing, an eagle which rotated its head and opened its beak, and an execution scene with kneeling prisoner, headsman lifting his axe and priest folding his hands to pray for the prisoner's soul.

FRANCIS OF ASSISI, Saint

Italian preacher c 1181-1226

Giovanni di Bernardone was a rich man, the son of a merchant. When he was 23, he gave up all his wealth and announced that he would live a life of poverty and prayer. He and his followers spent their lives travelling around Italy, preaching Christianity and looking after poor, sick and helpless people.

In 1209 the simple life that Francis (as he was now called) and his followers led was accepted by the Pope and the new "order" (group) of monks called Franciscans was established. Like their founder, the Franciscans believed that human beings share the planet equally with all God's other creatures – that all of us, whether human, animal, bird, insect or fish, are brothers and sisters. In 1212 his ideas were used by St Clare, who founded a similar community for women. Francis was declared a saint two years after his death.

Francis of Assisi, the Italian monk, giving a sermon to the birds.

WILLIAM OF OCCAM

English thinker c 1290-1349

In William's day, thinkers were fond of taking a seemingly simple question, such as "How big is an angel?", and examining it from every possible point of view. (For example, "If angels are huge, why do they not fill the sky?" or "If angels are tiny, how many can dance on the head of a pin?".) The discussions were enjoyable, and people were more interested in talking than in answering the question. William taught exactly the opposite kind of enquiry. He said that answers were as important as questions, and that they could be discovered logically. If there were several possible answers, the simplest should be believed and the others given up. Because this idea sliced away unnecessary discussion, it was nicknamed "Occam's razor". It is now basic to maths and science: Occam's razor trims scholars' thinking and keeps it sensible.

GUTENBERG, Johann

German inventor 1398-1468

Before Gutenberg, there were no printed books. The Chinese inventor Pi Sheng had devised a way of printing in the eleventh century, but it was only used for playing-cards. Every single copy of a book was written by hand, so books were expensive and rare. Gutenberg had the idea that if each letter of the alphabet were carved on wood-blocks, they could be used and re-used to make words and lines of type. The wooden blocks provided the pattern, or mould, needed to cast the type in metal. Every letter had to be carved backwards, so that when the metal type was inked and pressed onto paper, the words read the right way round.

Gutenberg spent several years making blocks and letters small enough, but in 1448 he was ready to print a full-length book using his moveable type method. He set up in business with a man called Fust, who provided money for a factory, but they quarrelled and Gutenberg set up on his own. It took him seven years to produce 300 copies of the Bible, each containing 1,282 pages, as well as copies of a Latin grammar – the first printed books.

Printers with moveable type produced books of great beauty. The letters of Gutenberg's alphabet were carved in wood which was used as the pattern for making moulds to cast more type in metal. Below is a page from Gutenberg's Bible.

ERASMUS, Desiderius

Dutch thinker and writer c 1466-1536

The Renaissance began in Italy in the fourteenth century with a group of scholars who taught the subjects known as humanities (grammar, history, poetry and moral philosophy). They were interested in the works and ideas from the ancient Greek and Roman civilizations and classical Latin and Hebrew texts. At first, their studies were meant to give better understanding of the Bible, but soon became the basis for a new approach to education. People began eagerly discussing the religion, art, literature and everyday life of the ancient Romans and Greeks. With the fall of the Byzantine empire in 1453, hundreds of Greek-speaking scholars made their way to Europe and enriched the "New Learning".

Erasmus was one of the leaders of this work. He began with the Bible, comparing the Latin translation used in his day with older Greek versions and correcting mistakes. He collected and published the works of many early Greek and Latin writers, both Christian and non-Christian, and wrote books of his own in imitation of their style. He travelled all over Europe, giving lectures (in Latin) and spreading his ideas wherever he went.

Erasmus, at work on one of his translations. The Latin and Greek says: Image of Erasmus, by Albrecht **Durer**, drawn from life, 1526.

MACHIAVELLI, Niccolò

Italian thinker 1469-1527

Machiavelli worked as a diplomat for the Council of Ten, which ruled the affairs of Florence at the end of the fifteenth century. He was often sent abroad as the Council's representative, and during his travels he wrote about politics. One of his books, *The Prince*, was a success throughout Europe. In it he described how rulers could be successful and survive. He said that all that mattered was the safety of the state, and that a ruler could do anything he or she liked to keep the state secure. Machiavelli's book was based on his observations of existing Italian rulers, especially Cesare **Borgia**, after he was sent to Borgia's court in 1502. *The Prince* was not published until after Machiavelli's death, and for a long time people thought that he meant his book as good advice to ambitious princes. This earned him the reputation of one who favoured evil deeds and treachery in the interest of the state. To describe someone as "machiavellian" still means he or she is a cunning, selfish person.

Niccolò Machiavelli.

ERASMUS: Durer 12 MACHIAVELLI: Borgia 432

NANAK

Indian founder of Sikhism 1469- c1538

In Nanak's time, there were two main religions in India: Islam, whose followers worshipped one god, Allah, and Hinduism, whose followers worshipped many gods. There was rivalry between them, often spilling into war. Nanak preached a new faith, using ideas from both Islam and Hinduism. He said that there was only one god, and that the most blessed state for humans was total unity with God. People would reach this by meditation, praying, singing hymns and above all by following the advice of a *guru* (spiritual guide). The guru's teaching would help us to ignore our own selfish needs and feelings.

Nanak also said that all human beings were equal in God's eyes. This conflicted with the teachings of both Islam and Hinduism, and led to Nanak's followers being persecuted by people from both religions. His followers declared themselves warriors, ready to fight for their beliefs. They called themselves Sikhs ("disciples"), and vowed to show their faith by five signs: uncut hair (men cover their long hair with a turban), a comb (often in miniature form, as a brooch), a steel bracelet, shorts (usually worn under warmer clothes, at least in cold countries) and a sword (often replaced nowadays by a sword-shaped brooch).

There are over ten million Sikhs in the world. Most live in the Punjab region of India, where there was a Sikh kingdom set up by Ranjit Singh (1780-1839), until it was taken over by the British in 1849. All Sikh men add Singh ("lion") to their names; all Sikh women add Kaur ("princess"). The Sikhs' book of religious guidance is the Adi Granth, compiled in 1604.

A passage from the Sikh holy book is being read to a Sikh family. Sikhs treat their book with great respect, bowing to it, and never touching it with unwashed hands. It is kept in a special room of its own. Few Sikhs have their own copy of the holy book.

LUTHER, Martin

German religious reformer c 1483-1546

Luther became the most important of the founders of the Protestant Church. He studied law, then joined a monastery, becoming a Catholic priest in 1507. He visited the Pope's court in 1511 and was shocked by the luxury he saw. He was also worried by the corruption and false teaching in the church. At that time, a favourite way for the Pope to raise money was by selling "indulgences", which were rolls of paper, each signed by the Pope and granting freedom from punishment in Hell. You could buy a minute's freedom, a day's, a year's or more, depending on how much you paid. Luther said that this was wrong. Only God could free people from punishment, and God's forgiveness was to be earned by faith, not bought with cash. In 1517 he wrote a list of 95 theses (arguments) why indulgences were wrong, and

Luther, nailing his theses to the church door in Wittenberg in 1517.

nailed it to the cathedral door in the city of Wittenberg.

The church authorities acted quickly. Pope Leo X summoned Luther to Rome to explain himself; Luther refused to go. The Pope's officials wrote a book denouncing Luther; Luther burnt it. In 1520 the Pope excommunicated Luther (barred him from membership of the Roman Catholic Church). The next year, Luther was outlawed by the Emperor **Charles V** at a special conference, or "Diet", in the city of Worms. Luther continued to preach freedom of conscience: that people should be allowed to worship God in their hearts and minds, and should not be bound by church rules and rituals. He said that the only thing needed for salvation was faith in **Jesus** and obedience to his word, as revealed in the Bible, not to church rules and regulations. He translated the Bible into German, from the Latin which only priests understood, and wrote prayers and religious poems to help ordinary people put their faith into words. He composed hymn-tunes ("chorales"), basing many of them on folk-tunes everyone would know.

Luther had the support of several German princes and, despite the fury of the Church, his ideas spread quickly. He never intended to split the Church, but to reform it. However, in 1530 a new kind of Christian worship was begun, based on his ideas. It was called Protestantism, because its followers were "protesting" (declaring) that their obedience was to God first of all, and not to any church. By the time of Luther's death, 16 years later, Protestant ideas had swept through Northern Europe, and they are still alive today.

LUTHER: Jesus 329 Charles V 436

LOYOLA, Inigo de Oñez (Saint Ignatius)

Spanish religious leader 1491-1556

Loyola was the son of a Spanish nobleman and became a soldier. He was wounded in battle in 1521, and while he was recovering he read the story of **Jesus**' life. He decided to spend the rest of his life working for Christianity. He became a monk, and wrote the *Spiritual Exercises*, a book of essays containing his thoughts on how good Christians ought to live. In 1540 he set up the Society of Jesus, or "Jesuits", a group of Roman Catholic monks, organized on military lines, who followed the way of life suggested in the *Exercises.*

The Jesuits believed in the importance of education and opened schools and universities. They sent missionaries to non-Christian countries, especially China, Japan and to the Americas, whose existence Europeans were just discovering. Loyola was made a saint in 1622 under the Latin version of his name, Ignatius, and the Jesuits remain an important Roman Catholic teaching "order" (group of monks).

Below, left: Loyola, founder of the Jesuits, a strict Roman Catholic order whose followers set out to convert "heathens" to the Catholic faith.

CALVIN, John

French religious leader 1509-64

Calvin's real name was Jean Cauvin. He signed his books with the Latin form, Calvinus, and has been known as Calvin to most of the world ever since. He trained to be a Roman Catholic priest, but **Luther**'s teaching converted him to Protestantism and he left France to live in Switzerland. At the time, Protestant Christians had no unified set of beliefs: the only idea they shared was rejection both of Roman Catholic teaching and the authority of the Pope. Calvin wrote two books, *Institutes of the Christian Religion* and *Ecclesiastical Ordinances*, setting out what Protestants should believe and how they should behave.

Calvin taught that every word in the Bible is true, dictated by God. He said that all human beings were sinners, and that our only hopes of salvation were to be "born again" in faith, and to live a strict, God-fearing life. Food should be plain, drink should be restricted to milk or water, clothing should be worn for decency and warmth, not for show, money-lending was forbidden, and there should be no swearing, dancing or theatre-visiting. For Calvin, the only "proper" reading material was the Bible; the only music was hymns; life was not there to be enjoyed, but

John Calvin.

LOYOLA: Jesus 329

Right: Harington's water closet. A is the cistern, holding water for flushing; B is the overflow pipe; C is the pipe emptying the water from the cistern; D is the sluice through which the water is flushed; and E is the channel into which the lavatory drained. The fish swimming in the cistern were probably drawn by the original artist as a joke.

Hans Lippershey, who invented the telescope. The story is that two children were playing with the spectacle lenses he made. They noticed that by looking through two lenses at once, things were magnified – which gave Lippershey the idea for his telescope.

meant as a serious preparation for Heaven, in case one was lucky enough to be saved.

This unsmiling approach to human existence – called Puritanism because its aim was to "purify" us, to give the Devil no chance to snatch our souls – was too strict for many people. Geneva in Switzerland was run for a time on Calvin's principles, but the citizens grew tired of them and threw him out. But for many other people, especially in Northern Europe in the mid-seventeenth century, the life Calvin preached seemed right. There were Puritans in Germany, France, England and the Netherlands, and the Pilgrim Fathers who sailed to America lived God-fearing, Puritan lives. Many Christians (for example Methodists, Baptists, Presbyterians and Mormons) still share some of Calvin's ideas.

HARINGTON, John

English courtier 1561-1612

In 1596 Harington published the first-ever designs for the water-closet or flushing lavatory, and installed a prototype in his country house. Water-closets did not become standard, however, until city and town sewerage systems were built three centuries later.

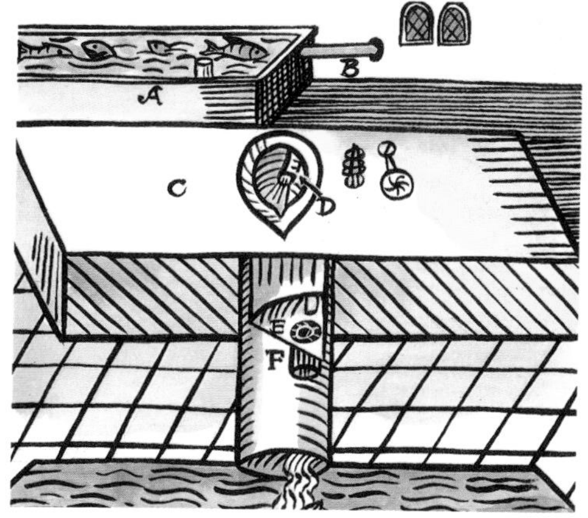

LIPPERSHEY, Hans

Dutch spectacle-maker died c 1619

In 1608 Lippershey invented the telescope. He was looking, by chance, through two lenses at a weather-vane, and realized that the vane appeared magnified. He devised a way of fixing the lenses in a tube, so that they would give maximum clarity and magnification. The Dutch government, thinking that his "far-seer" might be usable for military purposes, tried to keep it secret. But **Galileo** heard about it, built a telescope of his own, and began using it for astronomical observation. Galileo is often credited with inventing the telescope, but in fact Lippershey beat him by about two months.

CALVIN: Luther 338 LIPPERSHEY: Galileo 96

DESCARTES, René

French thinker 1596-1650

Like many of the thinkers of ancient Greece, Descartes believed that understanding mathematics was the key to all knowledge. If you work at algebra and geometry, you learn ways of thought which can be used to examine everything else in the universe. He worked out a way of studying very like **Socrates**' method: you question everything, logically and in order, and take nothing for granted. When every possible doubt has been considered, you will (with luck) reach clear understanding. According to Descartes, everything in the world is made of two quite separate substances: mind and matter. Human beings are unique because they alone have a mind *and* a material body, whereas all other things, both living and non-living, are made only of matter. Because the mind can think, it can control both matter (which can't think) and emotion.

Putting intelligent thought above everything else led Descartes to sum up his view of life in a single short sentence. He asked himself "What do I know, and how do I know it?", and answered in three Latin words, *cogito ergo sum* ("I think – and because I think, I exist").

FOX, George

English religious leader 1624-91

In Fox's time Christianity was a noisy, turbulent affair. There were bitter arguments between Protestants and Catholics, and the Protestants themselves were divided, some favouring one way of worshipping, others another. People went to church expecting sermons on the wickedness of humanity and how much we need to be saved from Hell. Every preacher was certain that his was the only way to salvation, and that anyone who disagreed had to be shouted down.

In this frantic world Fox devised a different kind of Christian worship altogether. He said that we are not all evil. However hard it is to find, there is good in everyone, and if we let it develop peacefully and quietly, it will shine through. He thought that the Holy Spirit is our guide in this development, and that God will come to us in stillness and help us to discover, and show, the goodness inside ourselves.

An etching of George Fox by Robert Spence (1870-1964).

Fox and his followers used no sermons or hymns in their worship. Instead, they sat silently in quiet rooms, waiting for the Holy Spirit. They called themselves the Society of Friends; later, because Fox once told someone to "quake at the word of the Lord", the Friends were nick-named Quakers, and the name has stuck.

STRADIVARI, Antonio

Italian instrument-maker c 1644-1737

Stradivari was the best known of a family of instrument makers. He specialized in violas, cellos and, above all, violins. His violins are now among the most expensive of all, because their sound is said to be the finest in the world. They are known as "Stradivarius" violins, after the Latin version of Stradivari's name.

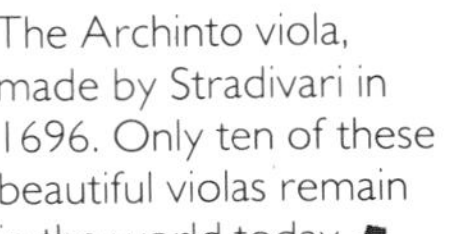

The Archinto viola, made by Stradivari in 1696. Only ten of these beautiful violas remain in the world today.

DESCARTES: Socrates 326

PAPIN, Denis

French scientist 1647- c 1712

Papin researched into steam-power. In 1679 he invented the pressure cooker, and in 1707 he built the first boat ever to be powered by a steam-driven paddle-wheel.

NEWCOMEN, Thomas

English blacksmith 1663-1729

Newcomen invented a steam-driven water-pump. It was first used to pump water from a flooded coal-mine, but the idea was later developed in the steam-engines used to drive factory machinery.

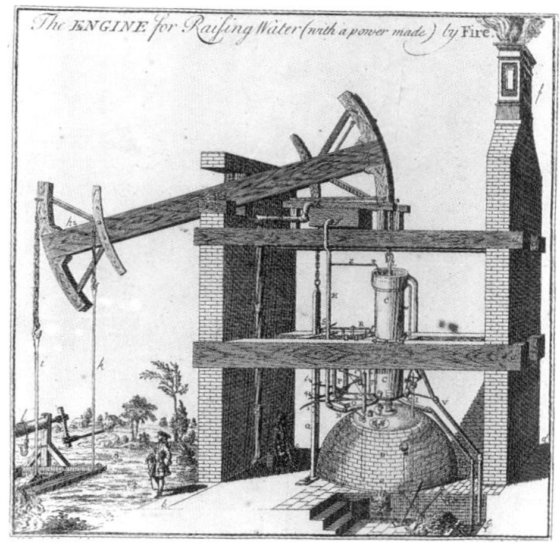

Left: An illustration made in 1717 of Newcomen's water pump. The engine was powered by steam, which rose from the bottom cylinder and was condensed (made liquid) by an injection of cold water. This created a vacuum, which forced a piston, attached to a heavy swinging beam, down into the cylinder. In this way, the beam could be swung as many as 12 times a minute, lifting with every stroke 45 litres of water through a series of pumps.

CRISTOFORI, Bartolomeo

Italian instrument-maker 1665-1731

Cristofori invented the piano in 1709. Unlike the earlier harpsichord and clavichord, his instrument used hammers to hit two or three strings for each note. He called it pianoforte ("soft-loud") because the player's touch on the keys affected the dynamics of the sound.

A 1950s mural, showing Jethro Tull with his seed drill.

TULL, Jethro

English inventor 1674-1741

Tull invented several machines to speed up farm-work. Each was pulled by horses, and did the work of many people. The best known (still used today) was the seed-drill. This scratches straight "drills" (lines a few centimetres deep), drops seeds into them and brushes soil on top to cover them.

DARBY, Abraham

English inventor 1677-1717

A pioneer of the iron-trade, Darby suggested heating blast-furnaces with coke instead of charcoal. This allowed bigger, hotter furnaces to be used, and produced better-quality iron. Darby's factory in the English Midlands became the centre of the British iron-smelting industry, which for nearly 200 years was the largest and most profitable in the world.

HARRISON, John

English inventor 1693-1776

Navigation at sea depends on working out precisely how far you have travelled since you last checked your position. To do this, you need a chronometer (clock) which keeps exact time. A chronometer running only a few minutes fast or slow can produce navigational errors of many degrees, and send a ship into uncharted waters or on to dangerous rocks. In 1714, faulty navigation caused a disastrous shipwreck in the English Channel, and the British government announced a prize of £20,000 (a fortune at the time) for the first person to invent a chronometer which would lose or gain no more than two minutes on a voyage from England to the Caribbean and back.

John Harrison was a carpenter; he had little experience of metalwork and no education in the maths needed to work out the distortions different weather conditions might cause in clock-springs. But he laboriously taught himself all he needed, and in 1735, after 21 years' work, sent a prototype chronometer to the authorities. It was too heavy (30 kilos), too big (the size of a bread-bin), and too inaccurate to win the prize. Undaunted, Harrison began working on a second prototype, more compact and more reliable. He produced four designs altogether, and in 1761, after a total of 37 years' effort, he had built a chronometer which worked. His son took the chronometer (the size of a fat pocket-watch) on an 81-day voyage from Bristol to the West Indies and back, and when he returned the chronometer was only five seconds slow.

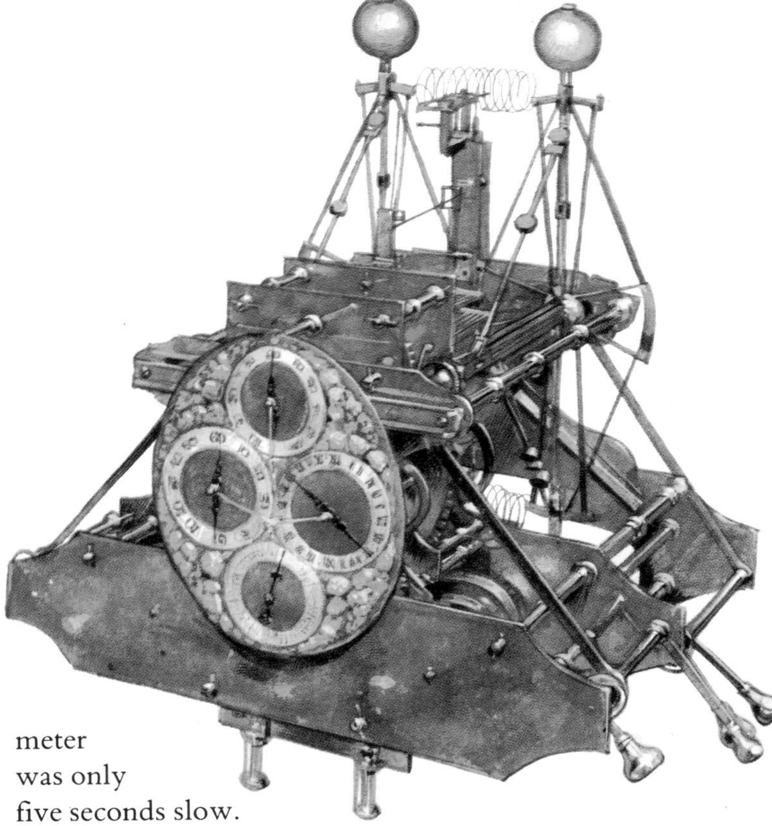

Harrison won the competition, and his chronometer became a standard navigational tool in British naval and merchant ships. But the government refused to hand over the prize. It was not until Harrison, at the age of 80, appealed to King George III (a man fascinated by clockwork) that he was paid at last.

Harrison's first chronometer (top) was far too big for practical use by navigators. His fourth attempt (bottom), however, was a success.

VOLTAIRE (François Marie Arouet)

French writer and thinker 1694-1778

Many eighteenth-century thinkers regarded their time as an Age of Enlightenment – a time of reason and scientific progress, with thinkers questioning tradition, and especially the teachings of the Christian Church. Science was the true road to human happiness, Enlightenment-thinkers said, and, unlike Christian salvation, which was open only to those who accepted the church's teaching, it was available to all.

François Marie Arouet, who wrote under the name Voltaire, was one of the Age of Enlightenment's leading thinkers. He made his name writing historical plays. One of them was so outspoken about the need for political and religious freedom that the French king imprisoned Voltaire as a traitor. On his release Voltaire studied science, and wrote articles on all kinds of subjects – from botany to astronomy, from physics to the essentials of a good diet. He gave lectures on religion and politics, saying that people had a right to think as they liked, providing that they didn't force their views on others.

Voltaire thought England was the most "enlightened" country in Europe. It had religious freedom; science was studied freely; the arts (drama, painting, music and literature) flourished. He wrote a book, *Letters on the English*, comparing British freedom with the censorship in France. The *Letters* caused a storm in France, where many people were already challenging the power of king and church. Voltaire fled to Switzerland, and stayed there to the end of his life.

Only one of Voltaire's books is still widely read: *Candide*. It tells about a man who goes on believing that the human race is good and kind, even though everyone he meets is a cheat, tyrant or criminal. But although Voltaire's other books are largely forgotten, his ideas live on. Democracy, religious freedom, the right to think what we like are things that most of us take for granted, so it is hard to believe that once they had to be taught, and that people like Voltaire were persecuted for teaching them.

Voltaire, the French thinker, believed people should have the freedom to think as they liked. As he once said, to someone who took a different point of view, "I don't agree with what you say, but I'll defend to the death your right to say it".

HARGREAVES, James

English inventor died 1788

Hargreaves invented the "spinning jenny", a machine which allowed one person to spin eight separate threads at once, from which cloth could be woven. He named it either after his daughter Jenny or as a joking form of "spinning engine" (engine was the eighteenth-century English word for machine). His idea was later mechanized by **Arkwright** and further improved by **Crompton**.

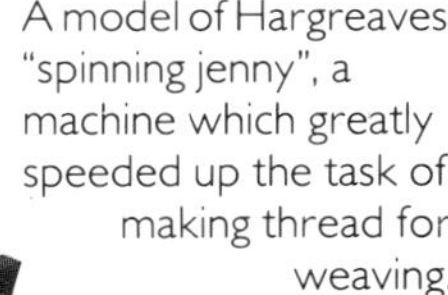

A model of Hargreaves' "spinning jenny", a machine which greatly speeded up the task of making thread for weaving.

HARGREAVES: Arkwright 350 Crompton 353

WESLEY, John

English religious reformer 1703-91

and

WESLEY, Charles

English religious reformer 1707-88

At Oxford University, where he was a "don" or teacher, JOHN WESLEY began to be dissatisfied with the kind of Christian worship used by the Church of England. He thought that the Church had lost much of the simple faith of earlier times and was too concerned with ritual (patterns of prayers and chants which had to be exactly followed). He founded a group at Oxford called the Holy Club, whose members followed a disciplined "method" of worship. The group was given many nick-names by scornful undergraduates, but "Methodists" was the one which stuck. Soon there were Methodist societies throughout England, and in 1743 Wesley drew up a set of rules for them all to follow. At this stage he had no intention of starting a new church; he expected Methodists to attend Anglican services in the usual way. It was not until after his death that the Methodist Church began.

Wesley began touring Britain, preaching and converting at huge open-air services. By the end of his life someone calculated that he had ridden about 100 kilometres each day for 50 years, and had preached over 40,000 sermons. Methodism was important in a great revival of Christian belief which swept Britain in the eighteenth century, and it inspired social reformers including William **Wilberforce** and John **Howard**.

John Wesley's brother CHARLES was a poet. He helped the Methodist movement by writing over 7,000 hymns, dozens of which, including *Hark, the Herald Angels Sing, O for a Thousand Tongues to Sing, Rejoice, the Lord is King*, are still well known.

This statue of John Wesley stands in front of the first Wesleyan chapel, in the City of London.

FRANKLIN, Benjamin

US writer, thinker and inventor 1706-90

Franklin hated chaos, delay and untidiness; if something needed to be done, he did it as quickly and unfussily as possible. Every morning he wrote down in his diary one or two good qualities – for instance kindness, patience, honesty – and tried to live up to them all day. He wrote and edited a newspaper, *Poor Richard's Almanac*. It contained political news and comment, advice on how to live a healthy and happy life and, above all, proverbs and wise

WESLEY: Howard 186 Wilberforce 193

remarks such as "those who hesitate are lost" or "fools babble; wise people listen".

In Franklin's spare time he studied the works of thinkers and scientists of the past; in 1743 he founded the American Philosophical Society to discuss their ideas. He was also an inventor, although he had no scientific training. When he found that he could see perfectly well at a distance, but had blurred sight close-to, he invented bifocal lenses for his spectacles. In 1752 he invented the lighting conductor to attract the massive electrical discharge and carry it harmlessly into the Earth. His experiments also proved the existence of static (natural) electricity.

Above all, Franklin believed – quoting the English poet John Donne – that "no man is an island". We all live in a community with other human beings, and we should try to understand and help them. Like everything else in Franklin's life, this belief led him to action. He became a town councillor, and organized post deliveries, a fire-fighting service, the first free public library and the first street lighting in America. He spent 25 years as deputy postmaster for the American Colonies (which were still under British rule).

In 1776, at the age of 70, Franklin decided to help the American Revolution, and joined **Jefferson** and the other leaders who prepared the Declaration of Independence. When the war was won, he was a member of the committee which wrote the Constitution, the rules by which the new American state was to be governed, and by which the United States still live today.

This illustration shows Benjamin Franklin, thinker and inventor, drawing electricity from a thunder cloud.

HUME, David

Scottish thinker 1711-76

As a young man, Hume worked in France, and became friendly with **Rousseau**. He then worked in London and in Edinburgh (where he was librarian of a law library). Oddly, for someone working with lawyers, he believed that nothing at all can be proved. What we call "proof" he felt was really just lucky chance. We can see that things happen in a particular way, but can never show that it must be the same way every time. **Kant** read Hume's writings, and they affected his thinking.

David Hume wrote the *Treatise of Human Nature*, which is still one of the most important works written by a British philosopher.

FRANKLIN: Jefferson 448 HUME: Kant 349 Rousseau, J J 348

ROUSSEAU, Jean Jacques

French writer and thinker 1712-72

Rousseau began his career writing plays, operas and encyclopedia articles. His work for the encyclopedia increased his interest in primitive, so-called "uncivilized" people, and he began to wonder whether civilization was quite the blessing everyone imagined. Finally, he decided it was not. He thought that the most important things about people were their emotions and feelings (unlike **Descartes**, who chose the ability of humans to reason and think). People are naturally good, he believed, but the need to compete for survival in "civilized" society makes us selfish and corrupt. One of his books, *The Social Contract*, begins "People are born free but are everywhere in chains". He goes on to say that we will win freedom and happiness only if we relearn the ways of the "noble savage", who lives by what he or she naturally needs, without trying to get more possessions or power than everyone else.

Part of Rousseau's teaching was like the revolutionary ideas of Thomas **Paine**. He said that states consist of all the people in them, and that power in a state therefore belongs to everyone. No one person – king, dictator or emperor – has any right to rule over the people. Decisions about laws, wars, taxes and so on can only be made by the people themselves. This idea is called democracy, and it suited the anti-aristocratic French politics of the time – the mood which was to lead, 20 years later, to the French Revolution.

Rousseau wrote other books, setting out his views on education, family life and religion. But it is for his revolutionary ideas, his writings on democracy, that his name lives on.

An engraving of Jean Jacques Rousseau, who thought that the life and ways of the "noble savage" were the only means for people to find freedom and real happiness.

BRINDLEY, James

English engineer 1716-72

In the eighteenth century, before there were railways or major roads, carting heavy loads from town to town was slow, difficult work. The English Duke of Bridgewater owned a coalmine, and wanted a way of transporting coal to his customers in

In the eighteenth century, canals were the most important way of transporting goods in bulk to the growing industrial towns in Britain. James Brindley's canal for the Duke of Bridgewater in Lancashire included the first canal aqueduct, carrying the waterway over the river Irwell.

ROUSSEAU: Descartes 342 Paine 188

nearby Manchester. He thought that barges were the answer, and since there was no suitable river nearby, he asked the engineer Brindley to design and build a canal. This was such a success that Brindley went on to build a network of over 580 kilometres of canals, all over the English Midlands.

Brindley never learned to read and could barely write. He worked out all his calculations in his head – and if they were especially difficult, he went to bed to do it.

SMITH, Adam

Scottish thinker 1723-90

Smith taught theology and politics at Glasgow University, and spent much time travelling in Europe and studying the way different countries were governed. Unlike most political thinkers of his time, who thought that it was the law that controlled a state, Smith said that the controlling force was economics. The way a country earns and spends money makes that country what it is.

In 1776 Smith wrote a book, *The Wealth of Nations*, setting out his ideas. He thought that the state had a duty to use its riches to help its people, and should create wealth with this in mind. On the other hand, he thought that the state should not interfere with the way money was earned. People should be encouraged to use their individual skills to create wealth; state control of industrial methods and markets was bad for business. Later thinkers simplified these ideas into a system called *laissez-faire* ("let people get on with it"), which has been followed by many governments since. It is directly opposed to socialism, which says that *laissez-faire* favours those who are already strong and rich, to the disadvantage of the poor, old or weak, and that the way to help everyone equally is by state control.

KANT, Immanuel

German thinker 1724-1804

A university professor, Kant began his career teaching science, in particular the physics of space. He was influenced by the writings of **Rousseau** and Isaac **Newton** and believed that just as there are laws of physical nature, so there are laws of human nature. Unlike Rousseau, however, he thought that the special characteristic of human beings was not their ability to feel emotions, but to think and reason.

Kant set out to show that God's existence can be proved by logic. He also argued that the only way we can know anything about the world around us is through our senses – we can never prove that anything exists independently of us. He decided that the only "real" things are ideas, and called his theories "Idealism". Kant's best-known book is *Critique of Pure Reason*. He later wrote other books, on metaphysics (the study of ideas not based on the information of our senses, including religion and the supernatural), and about ethics (the science of human morality and behaviour). Kant is famous for his "Golden Rule" for living a good life: we should behave as though every action we take will in the future be made a general rule for everyone to obey. This is roughly the same as "do as you would be done by".

The German thinker, Immanuel Kant. Kant was interested in mathematics, science and politics, as well as philosophy. He supported both the American and French revolutions.

KANT: Newton 102 Rousseau, J J 348

ARKWRIGHT, Richard

English inventor 1732-92

In 1768 Arkwright devised a way to drive **Hargreaves**' "spinning-jenny" with a belt and wheel turned by water-power. The "water-frame", as he called it, could be left to do the spinning by itself; one operator could manage half a dozen frames and so spin dozens of threads at once. Arkwright's invention made him very unpopular, because it put many hand-spinners out of work.

WATT, James

Scottish inventor 1736-1819

Although other people (for example **Papin** and **Newcomen**) were experimenting with steam-power in the first half of the eighteenth century, Watt was the first person to make a cheap, efficient steam-engine. It was used to drive machinery, and soon took over from the water-wheel as the main power-source in factories. Watt designed his engines so that, apart from the cylinder and piston (which his firm supplied), they could be built anywhere by local blacksmiths and carpenters. He came up with the word "horsepower" to describe an engine's efficiency. A "20-horsepower" engine is supposed to have the power of twenty horses.

In his spare time, Watt experimented with gases (trying to find out which, if any, turned into water in their liquid form), and also with electricity. The "watt", used to measure electrical power, is named after him.

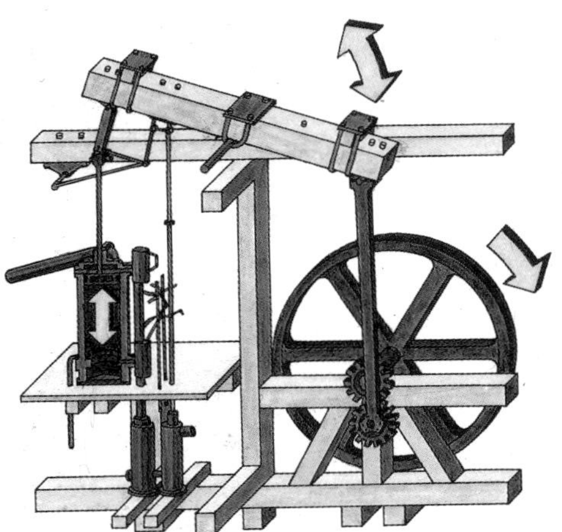

Left: Watt's steam engine developed the ideas of Newcomen. However, it had a separate condenser (for converting the steam back to liquid). Watt had to invent a new type of gear to turn the up/down movement of the piston into a circular motion.

GUILLOTIN, Joseph Ignace

French doctor 1738-1814

Guillotin invented a machine for executing people by chopping off their heads. It was quicker and more reliable than a man with an axe, and was used to kill thousands of people during the French Revolution. The French nicknamed it *Madame la Guillotine*, "Guillotin's wife", and the name "guillotine" has stuck.

The famous guillotine.

EDGEWORTH, Richard Lovell

Irish inventor 1744-1817

Edgeworth was a rich man with estates at Edgeworthstown (named after his family) in Ireland. He was fascinated by gadgets, and invented all kinds of useful devices including a pedometer (a machine you attach to your foot, to tell you how far you have walked) and a velocipede (an early bicycle, without pedals, pushed along by the rider's feet).

One of the problems Edgeworth found on his estates was moving massive objects over soft, boggy ground: carts were no use, because the wheels stuck. Heavy things like

ARKWRIGHT: Hargreaves 345 WATT: Newcomen 343 Papin 343

treetrunks and barrels were impossible for his workmen to lift, so he tried putting them on sledges – with some success. He built a primitive railway and then had the idea of putting the tracks not on the ground but on the vehicle, in the form of a continuously moving belt. It would have dozens of wheels, the way a caterpillar has legs, and would move in the same way, touching the ground with only a few at once and so avoiding being bogged down. The first "caterpillar tracks", as Edgeworth called them, were made of wood attached to chains, and the vehicles were pulled by horses. It was 150 years before caterpillar tracks were perfected, for battle tanks in the First World War. They are now used on vehicles wherever the ground is difficult: from bulldozers to moon-buggies.

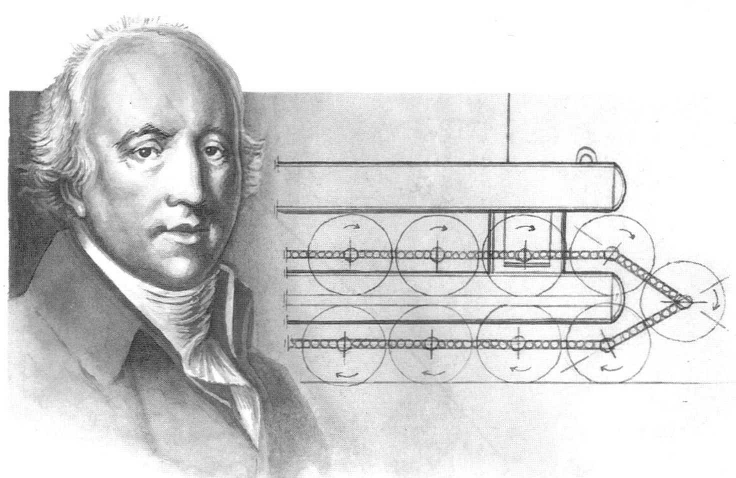

No drawings exist for Richard Edgeworth's "caterpillar track" system, but this diagram shows how the wooden tracks were rolled over one another with a team of horses pulling the chains forward. The idea was later used when battle tanks were built for warfare; moving walkways or elevators use the same basic principle.

BRAMAH, Joseph

British inventor 1748-1814

Bramah invented all kinds of useful devices: the beer-pump used in bars and pubs, the mechanism which flushes a lavatory, a machine for printing bank-notes, and a particularly large and complex lock. He offered a price of £200 (equivalent to about £50,000 today) to anyone who could pick his lock. The winner took 51 hours, non-stop, to do it.

BENTHAM, Jeremy

English thinker 1748-1832

Bentham was a brilliant scholar who went to Oxford University at 13 and began studying law when he was 16. But he never seriously worked as a lawyer. He found the legal system of his time biased and illogical, and decided to spend his life working out a better one, which he hoped to persuade the British parliament to accept. Bentham said that laws should protect everyone equally and do no one harm. He wrote that the purpose of laws and states was to ensure "the greatest happiness for the greatest number of people", and that no laws should be passed except those which made this possible.

Bentham's "utilitarianism" idea attracted many British people of the time. They felt that they should make Britain a fairer and happier place not by fighting each other (as was happening at the time in France during the French Revolution) but by discussion and reason. Lawyers, Members of Parliament, writers and thinkers flocked to talk to Bentham and discuss his ideas. He began to outline the things a state could do to benefit all its citizens. He suggested free education for all children, work for every adult who wanted it, state benefits for sick people and an old age pension. None of these things happened in his lifetime, but they are now common in democratic countries everywhere.

The scholar Jeremy Bentham made an unusual request: that when he died his skeleton, dressed in his clothes, be kept at University College in London. It was, and can still be seen at the university.

Right: A portrait of Jacquard woven on silk on a loom using his process. He is shown pricking out holes in card which allowed his loom to weave automatically.

APPERT, Nicolas François

French cook and inventor c 1750-1836

Until the time of the French leader **Napoléon I**, armies used to forage for food as they travelled, or to rely on supply-wagons lumbering after them with fresh meat and vegetables. Napoléon thought that if a way could be found to store fresh food, it would help his army to become the fastest-moving, most powerful in the world. He held a competition to find such a way, and Appert won it.

Appert was a pastry cook in Paris and often used jam in his cakes and pastries. He wondered if other foods would keep if boiled and stored in glass jars, like jam. He experimented, and found that if he boiled the food directly in the jars to cook it, and then stoppered the jars with large corks, it kept fresh for weeks or even months.

Appert used the prize money to build a factory for making preserved foods. His first contract was to provide food for Napoléon's armies, but he soon began selling his jars to shops as well. His was the first factory-made preserved food ever sold.

A few years later, another inventor, Peter Durand, devised a way to store the food in metal tins instead of glass jars. Since then, tinned food, using Appert's and Durand's basic ideas, has been sold throughout the world.

JACQUARD, Joseph Marie

French inventor 1752-1834

Jacquard invented a mechanical loom which made automatic weaving possible. It was a vital development in the mass-production of textiles. The loom worked by steam-power, and a strip of cardboard punched with holes controlled the movement of threads across the loom, in order to weave the pattern. The loom became known as a jacquard, and so are jumpers with complicated designs on them.

Jacquard's loom did the job of dozens of people, and when it was first used there were riots from the weavers it put out of work. But it was popular with factory-owners, and its punched-card control-system was

APPERT: Napoleon 451 JACQUARD: Babbage 121

copied to drive other machines, and even to play fairground steam-organs. When **Babbage** began to make computing machines, he adapted Jacquard's punched-card system.

CROMPTON, Samuel

English inventor 1753-1827

Until the eighteenth century spinning was a "cottage industry", because it was mainly done in cottages. One person would spin a single thread; making enough yarn to keep a family clothed took a large part of every day.

One major improvement in the spinner's life had been the invention of the spinning wheel, which replaced the older distaff and spindle. Then in the 1730s **Hargreaves**' "spinning-jenny" let one person spin eight separate threads at once, and **Arkwright** devised a way to drive half a dozen "jennies" at the same time by water-power.

Crompton was a theatre violinist; inventing was only a pastime. He combined the ideas of Hargreaves and Arkwright, calling his machine a "mule", because it was a cross between the two inventions as a mule is a cross between horse and donkey. It spun faster than anything known before, and produced thread finer and cheaper than any made by hand.

Crompton's "mule" completely revolutionized the spinning trade. One water-wheel could drive dozens, even hundreds of spindles, and a handful of workers could control them all. The change from cottage industry to production lines, factories and large manufacturing towns is known as the industrial revolution. It began in the spinning trade, made possible by the inventions of first Hargreaves, then Arkwright and Crompton.

McADAM, John Loudon

Scottish engineer 1756-1836

When McAdam was 14 he emigrated to America, and by the time he was 30 he had made his fortune in business. He went home to Scotland to live the life of a prosperous country gentlemen. But he was too active-minded to retire. He improved road-building methods (which had hardly changed since Roman times) by replacing the usual cobbled or earth surface with a layer of granite chippings, pounded flat. This is now called "macadaming" after him. The surface was cambered (sloped) to let rain-water drain to the sides to keep the road dry. Two improvements – pouring tar over the stone-chips (an idea of **Telford**'s) and using a steam-roller to flatten them (an idea of Aveling's, 30 years after McAdam's death) – led to the kind of road surfaces we call "tarmac" today.

A cartoon by H Heath of the engineer John McAdam, entitled "Mock-Adamizing – the Colossus of Roads".

CROMPTON: Arkwright 350 Hargreaves 345 MCADAM: Telford 354

TELFORD, Thomas

Scottish engineer 1757-1834

Telford began work as a stonemason, but became one of Britain's leading civil engineers. He designed and built roads, canals and bridges. His workmen built a road all the way from London to Holyhead (on the Isle of Anglesey, off North Wales), including the suspension bridge built in 1826 over the Menai Straits which is still in use. He devised a road system for the county of Shropshire, and a canal system to connect the rivers Severn, Dee and Mersey. He designed ditches and canals to drain the Fens (marshes) of East Anglia, opening up thousands of hectares of land for farming. In 1801 the government asked him to provide "public works" for Scotland, to make it more attractive to live in and so stop the constant emigration south into England. Over the next 30 years his workmen built more than 1,650 kilometres of roads, bridges and viaducts, and the 100-kilometre Caledonian Canal which crosses Scotland and links the North and Irish Seas. These works were so well built that they have lasted for over 150 years.

Telford's suspension bridge, which spans the Menai Straits between Wales and the island of Anglesey.

WOLLSTONECRAFT, Mary

English writer 1759-97

Wollstonecraft was a teacher, writer, publisher and translator. She believed that girls should be as well educated as boys and was interested in social reform, particularly in the stirrings in France which led to the French Revolution. When the politician Burke published an attack on the revolutionaries, saying that by rebelling against their king they were offending against God's laws as well as human laws, she wrote a savage book in reply, *Vindication of the Rights of Man*, asking what else the revolutionaries could do when their "betters" treated them so badly. The book scandalized "polite" society. In 1792 she caused more outrage with another book, *Vindication of the Rights of Woman*, claiming that women were equal to men.

Wollstonecraft ignored the fury her ideas aroused. She went to France to research a history of the Revolution, and later lived with a man and bore his child without getting married. In 1795 she took another lover, the writer William Godwin, and married him in 1797. She died soon afterwards, having given birth to his child, Mary.

The daughter Mary later married the poet Shelley and became famous for her books, including the novel *Frankenstein*. But campaigners for women's rights never forgot her mother, and *Vindication of the Rights of Woman* is now recognized as one of the first and best books to argue the feminist point of view.

The writer and feminist, Mary Wollstonecraft.

CHAPPE, Claude

French inventor 1763-1805

In the years after the French Revolution (1789), many European nations attacked France all at once. French armies had to fight in several different areas, and there was a need to pass messages quickly between them, in code. Chappe invented a way to do this. He suggested setting up towers every ten kilometres across France. Inside each tower was an operator with a telescope, and on top of it was a long wooden arm which could swing up and down. When a message was to be sent, the first operator would swing the wooden arm into different positions, each of which had a coded meaning. The operator in the next tower would "read" the signal by telescope, and pass it on by swinging the wooden arm on his tower.

In 1793 Chappe's method was tried, and in the next ten years over 4,500 kilometres of lines were built in France, and there were similar systems in Germany and England (where, it was found, a message could travel 100 kilometres in one minute). But the system was inefficient, depending on the operators all keeping awake and alert. Other systems of telegraph ("far writing") were invented, using electricity, and Chappe, in a bout of depression, killed himself.

FULTON, Robert

US inventor 1765-1815

The paddle-steamer had been invented by a Scotsman, William Symington, but the wash from the huge paddles caused damage to the banks, and the idea was dropped. Fulton designed the first successful steam-powered boat, which he demonstrated on the river Seine in France. He then returned to his native America, and in 1807 a steam boat he designed made the 240-kilometre trip up the Hudson River from New York to Albany. This marked the end of sailing ships as the best way to travel by water.

Fulton also built one of the first submarines. It held four people, and used water-tanks for ballast, filled to make the craft submerge and pumped empty to make it rise to the surface. It was powered by hand: the passengers turned handles to crank the propeller-shaft. Fulton took his invention to France, hoping that the government would use submarines in their war against the English. But the French thought underwater warfare was unsporting, and Fulton went back to the USA, leaving his plans in Paris. Sixty years later the writer Jules Verne developed the idea in his novel *Twenty Thousand Leagues under the Sea*. He even called his ship *Nautilus*, after Fulton's submarine.

Robert Fulton's first steamboat, the *Clermont*, built in 1807.

WHITNEY, Eli

US inventor 1765-1825

Whitney invented the cotton-gin, a machine for separating the fluffy fibres of the cotton flower from the seeds and other waste. The fibres could then be spun and woven into cloth. Each Whitney machine did the work of a dozen slaves, and made it possible for thousands of farms to take up cotton production in the southern states of America. But the idea behind the gin was so simple that planters could steal it without paying Whitney anything for his invention. Desperate for cash, Whitney turned his hand to gun-making. In 1798 the American government asked him for 10,000 rifles for the army. It would have taken years to make all the guns individually, so Whitney divided up the work. One group of people made all the wooden parts, another the metal parts, and a third group assembled the finished guns. This "assembly-line" production method was revolutionary. Whitney was able to deliver all 10,000 guns in months instead of years.

Eli Whitney's cotton-gin.

NIEPCE, Joseph Nicéphore

French scientist 1765-1833

In 1801 Niepce invented a way to produce light-images on metal plates, and in 1826 he took the world's first-ever photograph. It took 8 hours to expose the image. Later, with his friend **Daguerre** he developed the kind of early photograph which has ever since been known as a "daguerreotype".

NIEPCE: Daguerre 360

MALTHUS, Thomas Robert

English teacher 1766-1834

Malthus taught maths at a boarding school, and was a Church of England clergyman. In 1798 he published a book predicting a gloomy future for the human race. He wrote that the number of people was growing faster than the plants and animals needed to feed them. Unless the human birth-rate slowed down, the results would be starvation, disease and death. Malthus himself suggested no solution, except that people should

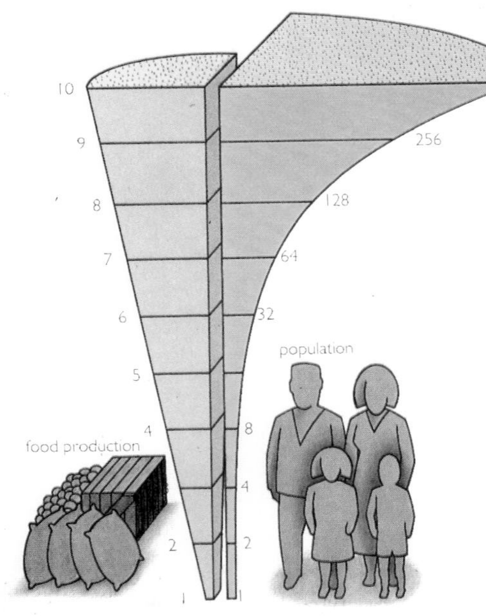

Thomas Malthus realized that the human race was increasing geometrically (1, 2, 4, 8, 16), whereas food production could only increase arithmetically (1, 2, 3, 4, 5). The curves on this graph show how, without checks, the human population increases much faster than the food needed to feed everyone.

give up sex or marry late: he disapproved of birth control. His prophecies have come true – the world population has continued to grow, and still no-one has found a way to prevent the human race overwhelming its environment.

PERKINS, Jacob

US inventor 1766-1849

Perkins invented some of the most useful small items ever devised. They included a nail-making machine, a printing-machine to make bank-notes and stamps which would be hard to forge, and one of the first refrigerators.

TREVITHICK, Richard

English engineer 1771-1833

Until Trevithick's time, steam-engines had been huge and heavy. They were fixed to the ground and were used to drive machinery. Trevithick made the first engine light enough to pull a vehicle. He built a carriage with a steam-engine to replace the horses. His "horseless carriage" gave its first trial ride in 1801. Three years later he made the first steam-engine to pull carriages along rails. In 1808 he demonstrated a steam-carriage in London. He called it "Catch Me Who Can", and charged customers a penny a ride. One of his passengers was George **Stephenson**, who made notes on the way Trevithick's engine worked and how it might be improved. Another passenger was the ambassador from Peru in South America. He invited Trevithick to Peru in 1816, to make steam-engines for pulling trucks in mines. While Trevithick was abroad, Stephenson and others developed his ideas, so that when he returned to England steam-transport was established and his pioneering work was out of date.

TREVITHICK: Stephenson 358

CAYLEY, George

English inventor and air pioneer 1773-1857

Cayley experimented with a variety of ideas: new ways of draining land, the rotation of crops, caterpillar tracks for farm vehicles, telescope lenses and the design of artificial limbs. But his main passion was flying. He studied birds' wings in flight, and decided that human beings could never equal them – fixed wings were essential if a person was ever to fly. In 1808 he built a glider large enough to carry a dog: it was the first heavier-than-air flying-machine, and earns Cayley credit as inventor of the aeroplane. In 1810 he published the first book on aerodynamics (the science of how objects move through air).

In 1849 Cayley built a glider large enough to carry a human being: a 10-year-old boy. It flew for a few metres – terrifying the boy but delighting Cayley. He set to work to design a machine which would carry a full-grown man, and in 1853 launched it from a hillside with one of his coachmen trembling on board. The glider safely reached the other side of the valley – the first manned flight in history. The story is that the coachman clambered out, shook his fist at Cayley and resigned his job, shouting that he had been hired to drive, not fly.

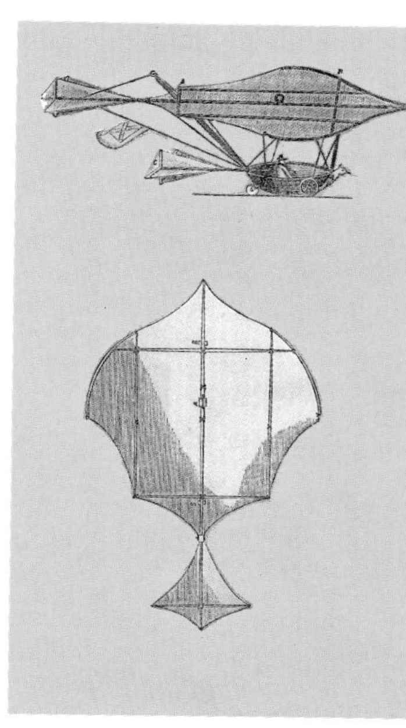

These sketches from an 1852 edition of *Mechanics' Magazine* show the air pioneer George Caley's ideas for what he called a "governable parachute" – an early form of glider.

BEAUFORT, Francis

Irish sailor and scientist 1774-1857

In 1787 Beaufort joined the navy and was quickly promoted, becoming a captain in his 20s and an admiral before he was 40. He was interested in map-making, and in the 1820s led an expedition to make a chart of the shores of Asia Minor (Turkey) and stamp out pirates. In 1829 he left the sea and became a hydrographer (scientist who studies the movement of water in lakes, rivers, seas and clouds).

Beaufort is remembered today chiefly for the Beaufort Scale, a way of measuring wind-speed. It replaces inaccurate description (for example "fierce" or "summery") with a scale of numbers from 0 (calm) to 12 (hurricane) which is understood all over the world.

wind force	speed (kph)	description	effects
0	0-2	calm	smoke rises vertically
1	3-5	light air	smoke drifts gently
2	6-10	light breeze	breeze is felt on face
3	11-20	gentle breeze	leaves shake on trees
4	21-30	moderate breeze	dust blows about
5	31-40	fresh breeze	small trees sway
6	41-50	strong breeze	large branches sway
7	51-60	near gale	large trees sway
8	61-75	gale	people are blown over
9	76-90	strong gale	buildings are damaged
10	91-105	storm	trees are uprooted
11	106-120	violent storm	widespread damage
12	over 120	hurricane	severe damage

Beaufort's wind scale.

LAËNNEC, René Théophile

French doctor 1781-1826

Laënnec invented the stethoscope in 1816. Doctors still use stethoscopes to listen to people's breathing and heartbeat. Laënnec's stethoscope had a wooden tube like a pea-shooter and only one earpiece; rubber tubes came into use over seventy years later.

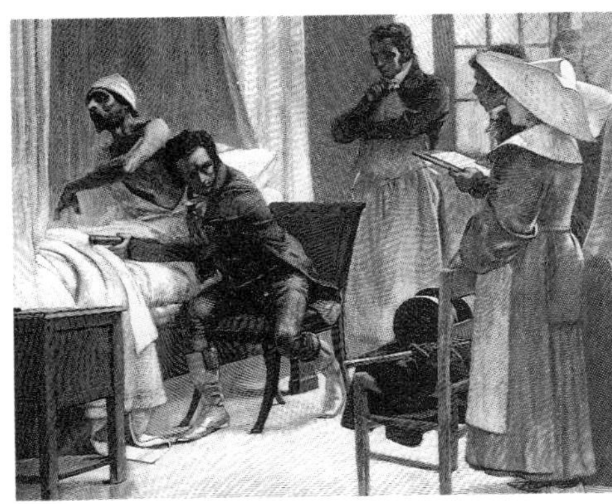

Left: Laënnec, the inventor of the stethoscope, examining a patient at the Necker Hospital in Paris.

STEPHENSON, George

English engineer 1781-1848

and

STEPHENSON, Robert

English engineer 1803-59

The Stephensons, father and son, designed some of the first steam-engines to pull passenger trains. George Stephenson's *Locomotion No 1* ran from Stockton to Darlington in northern England – the first public railway line in the world. The Stephensons' most powerful engine, *The Rocket*, reached a maximum speed of 60km/h. In 1829 they entered it in a competition to haul weights up the 1:100 gradient which would be needed if a station was to be built at Rainhill in Liverpool. *The Rocket* won the competition, and the Stephensons were asked to build a passenger railway from Manchester to Liverpool. They also built a

The excavation of Olive Mount, four miles from Liverpool in England, was part of the Stephenson's engineering project to build a passenger railway between Manchester and Liverpool.

railway north from London to Birmingham; parts of it remain in use, over 150 years later.

WALKER, John

English shopkeeper c 1781-1859

Walker invented matches in 1827. Up until then, people had had to make fire by lighting "tinder" (quick-burning material) from sparks made by scraping metal against flint. Walker's matches were nicknamed "lucifers" after the Devil, who was thought to be able to create fire by snapping his fingers.

STURGEON, William

English scientist 1783-1850

Sturgeon, a shoemaker's son, never went to school: he learned science from books and from attending **Davy**'s and **Faraday**'s lectures at the London Royal Institution. He was fascinated by Faraday's work on electromagnetism, and made experiments of his own. He found that an iron bar surrounded by a coil of wire acts like a magnet when electricity is passed through it: he had invented the electromagnet. Later, using some of Faraday's ideas, he built the first practical electric motor.

SCHOPENHAUER, Artur

German thinker 1788-1860

Schopenhauer believed that he was the greatest thinker since **Socrates**, but he failed to interest many people in his ideas. His books, including *The World as Will and Idea*, written in 1819, were hardly noticed while he was alive; it was only years later, through the work of his supporters, that they began to have influence, on such writers as **Nietszche**, **Freud** and **Mann**.

Unlike **Kant**, who thought that the only "reality" was ideas and thoughts, Schopenhauer thought that the only real thing was Will – desires and wants. He said that the entire universe is governed by Will, an unthinking, blind force which creates everything in existence, from gravity to human emotion. Idea, he said, is only the picture our brains form of existing things; it creates nothing. Even the world we know is no more than an "idea".

Schopenhauer's teaching is gloomy: he believed that there is no end to desire and want. Unsatisfied wishes cause us pain, but satisfying our desires is usually disappointing. He found a solution in the teachings of **Buddha**, who said that the less we desire, the less we suffer. Schopenhauer did not follow his own philosophy: he was said to be heartless, greedy, and fond of good living.

STURGEON: Davy 119 Faraday 121 SCHOPENHAUER: Buddha 324 Freud 383 Kant 349 Mann 59 Nietzsche 378 Socrates 326

DAGUERRE, Louis Jacques Mandé

French inventor 1789-1851

Daguerre began his career as a landscape-painter and stage designer, but is better known for his pioneering work in photography. The first actual photograph had been taken by his friend Joseph **Niepce**. Together, they developed the first practical form of photography, known as the "daguerreotype" process. They covered thin copper sheets with salts of silver to make a light-sensitive surface, and then focused light on them to make a picture.

Daguerreotypes were popular until the 1860s, when quicker and better photographic methods took their place, using gelatine-covered glass or paper, instead of Daguerre's metal plates.

Above: An engraving of Louis Daguerre taken from a daguerreotype. *Left:* A photograph made using the Daguerre process. The image is produced on a metal plate, and is very sharp but the process meant that no duplicate or print could be made. The portrait is of Fox Talbot's daughters.

MORSE, Samuel Finley Breeze

US inventor 1791-1872

Morse perfected the telegraph, a way of sending messages by electrical pulses along a wire. He devised a code for the alphabet, turning each letter into a pattern of long and short pulses, easy to learn and quick to send, as a combination of dashes and dots or long and short light flashes. "Morse code" is still used and understood throughout the world.

Left: An engraving showing Philadelphia in 1890, bristling with telegraph and telephone wires. Modern tele-communications systems carry the wires underground.

COMTE, Auguste

French thinker 1798-1857

Comte thought that the way we organize society is one of the most important of all human activities, and should be studied in a scientific way. He said that knowledge and understanding could only be reached by experience of the real world, and that there was no point in studying questions about God and the meaning of life because such questions could not be answered.

Comte called this new human science "Positivism". He said that it should be used to examine society and that the information gathered should be used for the good of everybody. His ideas encouraged researchers to study the causes of unemployment and poverty, and began the new subject "sociology". Now, most governments use statistics and sociological research to help them make their policies, and sociology is studied in colleges and universities throughout the world.

Auguste Comte.

DAGUERRE: Niepce 356

A photograph of the siting of Nelson's Column in London's Trafalgar Square taken by Fox Talbot in 1843. Talbot's system, known as a "talbotype" or "calotype" (from the Greek word *kalos*, meaning beautiful), allowed a negative to be made. The image was not as sharp as that of his rival Daguerre, but the Talbot system had the advantage that more than one print could be made.

As the industrial revolution progressed, countries wanted to display their new inventions, to show off their achievements, and to attract new markets abroad. To do so, major exhibitions were held, often in giant, purpose-built, halls. *Right:* The southern entrance to the Crystal Palace, which was the main hall for Britain's Great Exhibition of 1851. The palace was erected at an amazing speed, and was one of the first fully prefabricated buildings.

TALBOT, William Henry Fox

English photographic pioneer 1800-77

At the same time that **Daguerre** was working on **Niepce**'s idea of making photographic likenesses on metal plates, Talbot was trying to do the same thing on sheets of paper coated with silver oxide. For a time there was much rivalry between them. Daguerre's system showed more detail, but Talbot's was quicker and cheaper. In the end, Daguerre's process was abandoned, and Talbot's became the basis for all later photography.

Talbot's interests were not limited to photography. He collected and studied new plant-species, he was a Member of Parliament, and he was also a mathematician, fascinated by codes and ciphers. When a hoard of 3,000-year-old tablets from King **Assurbanipal**'s library was found at Nineveh in the 1840s, he was one of the team of ten people who worked out how to read the cuneiform letters in which they were written.

PAXTON, Joseph

English builder 1801-65

Paxton specialized in making steel-frame buildings hung with glass. He began with greenhouses to protect the tropical plants which Victorian explorers were bringing from hot countries to chilly England. As he became more skilled he made larger greenhouses for parks and country houses all over Britain. His biggest steel-and-glass building of all was the aptly named Crystal Palace built in Hyde Park, London. It contained exhibition rooms, a dance hall, a concert hall complete with pipe-organ, and a huge area of covered gardens with full-grown trees. The palace was built for the Great Exhibition of 1851, and was meant to be pulled down afterwards. But it was so impressive, and so strongly built, that it was moved to a permanent site at Sydenham in South London, and was used continuously until it burnt down in 1936.

When the first skyscrapers were being planned in the 1890s, architects adapted Paxton's idea of the steel-frame building, but using concrete panels instead of glass.

TALBOT: Assurbanipal 409 Daguerre 360 Niepce 356

SMITH, Joseph

US religious leader 1805-44

When Smith was 22 he claimed that he had discovered a golden book, written by God's prophet Mormon, which told how God's "chosen people" had moved, centuries before, from the Holy Land to America. Smith published his translation of the Book of Mormon, and founded the Church of Jesus Christ of Latter-day Saints. Although many people were converted, the church was unpopular, partly because Smith preached that a Mormon man ought to have several wives – something which other American people regarded as barbaric. He announced that he was going to stand for election as President, to bring his beliefs into politics. His enemies had him arrested, and stirred up a mob which broke into his cell and killed him.

DE LESSEPS, Ferdinand Marie

French engineer 1805-94

When De Lesseps was a young man, the only way for European trading ships to visit the Arabian Gulf, Australasia and Asia was to sail all the way round Africa. The journey took months, and was filled with every kind of danger, from storms and treacherous currents to pirates. De Lesseps, a diplomat serving in Egypt, realized that if a canal could be dug between the Mediterranean Sea and the northwesterly tip of the Red Sea, ships could journey from Europe to Arabia and Asia in days, not months.

In 1849 De Lesseps resigned from the diplomatic service and began to collect sponsors for his canal. It was to be 165 kilometres long, using the Bitter Lakes, across which **Moses** is said to have led the Israelites from exile in Egypt. Work started in 1860 and in 1869 the Suez Canal (as it was called, after the port at its Red Sea end) was officially opened, to international acclaim. De Lesseps used his diplomatic skills to persuade people to sign an international treaty forbidding warships to use it. The agreement has been broken in every major war since.

After Suez, De Lesseps planned an even grander canal project, linking the Atlantic and Pacific oceans by cutting through the Isthmus of Panama in Central America. But the building conditions (swamps, fever, jungles) were too difficult for De Lesseps' workmen. Tens of thousands died from malaria, and De Lesseps went bankrupt, ending his career in disgrace. It was not until the USA bought the land in 1903, and a cure for malaria was discovered, that the Panama Canal could be finished.

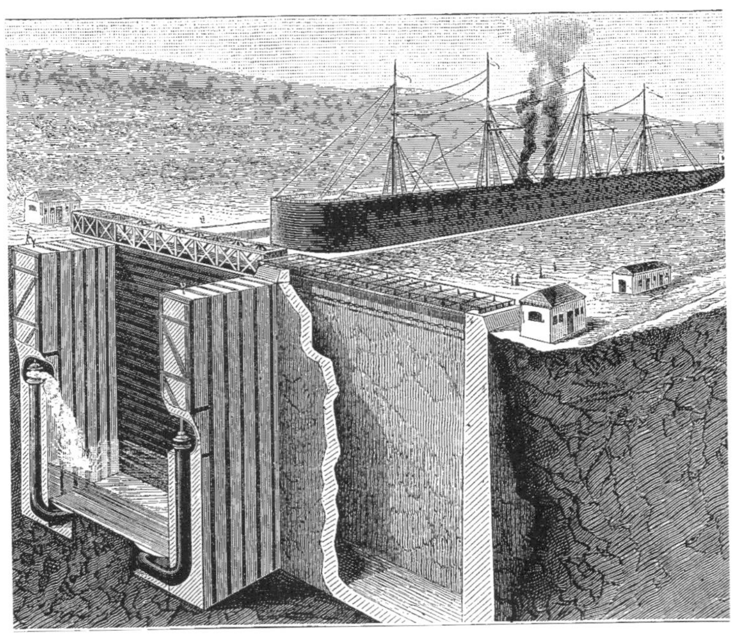

This cutaway diagram of De Lesseps' proposed lock with a sliding gate for the Panama Canal appeared in a French journal, *La Nature*. He never achieved his ambitious project, and died before the canal could be finished – by an American company.

DE LESSEPS: Moses 406

BRUNEL, Isambard Kingdom

English engineer 1806-59

A statue of Brunel, put up in honour of his engineering achievements.

Brunel's father, Marc, was an expert in underwater tunnelling, and Brunel learned his engineering skill working on his father's tunnel under the river Thames in London. Soon afterwards, he went to live in Bristol, a busy river port in southwest England. The Bristol merchants hired him to deepen the city docks, so that bigger ships could use them. In 1833 the same merchants held a competition for a new railway between Bristol and London, and Brunel won. He said his railway would be "not the cheapest, but the best", and planned to make it the safest, quickest and most luxurious in the country. His workmen spent ten years laying track, building bridges and digging tunnels. Brunel supervised the work, and also designed engines, carriages and stations. The Great Western Railway was triumphantly opened in 1846. Queen **Victoria** rode in one of the trains, with Brunel acting as fireman, stoking the engine with coal.

Brunel's other great engineering interest was steamships. He built three of what were then the largest and fastest ships ever seen, crossing the Atlantic in a third of the time taken by sailing ships. *Great Western* was an enormous wooden vessel, driven by paddle-power; *Great Eastern* was at the time the biggest iron ship ever built; *Great Britain* was the first large ocean-going vessel to be driven by propeller.

Nowadays Brunel is remembered for the beauty as well as the originality of the things he made. A good example is the Clifton Suspension Bridge over the deep Avon gorge in Bristol. Other engineers wanted to build 70-metre brick towers from the river-bed, with a road laid on top; Brunel designed a suspension bridge, slung on a web of cables and steel wires. It did – and does – exactly the job it was planned for. But it is also beautiful, an ideal counterpart to the breathtaking Avon gorge.

Brunel's famous Clifton Suspension Bridge in Bristol.

BRUNEL: Victoria 454

ROEBLING, John Augustus

German inventor and engineer 1806-69

Roebling invented a way to twist steel wires into cable, as strands of fibre are twisted into rope. His cables were light, extremely strong, and flexible: they bent without snapping. Until then, suspension bridges had been held up by rigid metal strips, which often snapped in high winds. Roebling suggested that the cables would bend in the wind, and so prevent disaster.

Roebling built bridges in Europe, and his cables were used by other European manufacturers. But his major successes came after he emigrated to the USA in the 1850s. In 1855 he built the Niagara Falls suspension bridge, and in 1869 he began work on the Brooklyn Bridge linking Long Island and Manhattan Island in the city of New York.

The Brooklyn Bridge, New York City. Roebling was killed soon after it was built, but it is considered as one of the most beautiful, as well as practical, bridges in the world.

MILL, John Stuart

Scottish thinker 1806-73

Mill's father realized that his son was brilliant almost as soon as the child could speak. He taught him at home from a very young age and when Mill, aged 17, went to work for the London East India Company, he was as well educated as if he had been to university. During the day he worked as a clerk; in the evenings he read books, wrote articles and went to meetings and philosophical discussions.

Mill's books and articles deal with such subjects as what happiness is and how we should try to find it, how countries should be governed and how wealth should be organized to benefit everyone. He believed that all human beings have equal rights, but that the way we run our society creates inequality. In particular, he shared **Marx**'s disapproval of capitalism, which enriches owners and managers but impoverishes the workers who actually produce the wealth. Mill believed all wealth-producing activities should be owned by the state, and should be used to benefit everyone. On the other hand, he distrusted democracy, because when people elect representatives to speak for them they hand over individual rights. He thought that this could easily lead to "state tyranny", in which the government took less and less notice of each individual's wishes. He became a Member of Parliament in 1865, and spoke out for women's rights, and for education for all. But his ideas were too revolutionary for the times, and in the 1868 election he was defeated because he had announced publicly that he didn't believe in God.

The brilliant John Stuart Mill who, at the age of 3, learnt Greek.

BRAILLE, Louis

French schoolteacher 1809-52

Braille, himself blind, was the headmaster of the National Institute for Blind Children in Paris. He is remembered today for inventing the Braille alphabet. He adapted a system

MILL: Marx 369

used in the French army called "night-writing". This used 12 raised dots in various patterns which could be "written" and "read" in the dark by feeling them. Braille reduced the number of dots to six and worked out an alphabet, to enable blind people to read with their fingertips.

McCORMICK, Cyrus Hall

US inventor 1809-84

McCormick invented the harvesting machine. Until his time, all harvesting of crops had been done by hand, using reaping-hooks; his machine could replace dozens of labourers. Today's huge combine-harvesters are modern versions of McCormick's original vehicle.

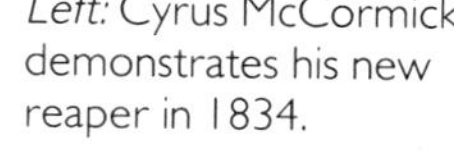

Left: Cyrus McCormick demonstrates his new reaper in 1834.

MACMILLAN, Kirkpatrick

Scottish inventor 1810-78

Macmillan invented pedals and brakes for bikes. Until then, you rode a bike (called a "dandyhorse" or "hobbyhorse" because it had a carved horse's head instead of handlebars) by digging your heels in the ground to push the bike along. The only way to brake was to stand up (while the bike carried on), to jump off or to make yourself fall over.

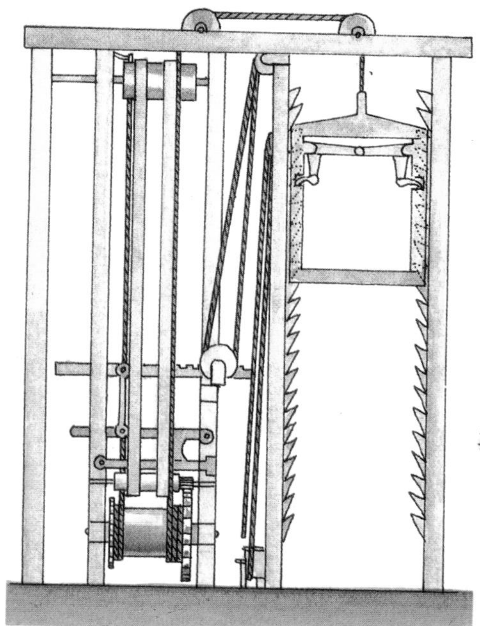

The mechanism for Otis' elevator. Otis gave a public demonstration of his safety elevator in New York in 1854.

OTIS, Elisha Graves

US inventor 1811-61

Otis made the first passenger lift; earlier lifts had been for lifting goods, not people. Everyone was terrified that it would crash to the ground if the cable broke. To show how safe it was, thanks to his newly invented emergency brakes, Otis got into the lift during an exhibition in New York, and arranged for one of his assistants to chop through the cable with an axe. He survived.

SINGER, Isaac

US inventor 1811-75

Singer invented the first successful sewing machine.

Early models of Singer sewing machines. Singer's success was partly due to his love of the stage. He ran a theatre company, and never tired of getting up to demonstrate his machines before the captive audiences.

KIERKEGÅRD, Søren Åbye

Danish thinker 1813-55

After studying theology and philosophy at university, Kierkegård withdrew from public life to write. He was against all abstract theories of human life that other thinkers, for example **Kant**, were developing. He said that people could not lead a good life until they had accepted the necessity for it, and this could not be by logic but only through a "blind leap of faith". His most important book is called *Either/Or* and in it Kierkegård develops his idea that you have to make a choice to lead a good life – or not to – and that once you have made the choice it will influence all your actions. He believed that people's lives were not determined by their character or personality, but by their own free will. This idea was later developed by **Sartre**. Kierkegård also believed that the stress of making the "either/or" decision causes great anguish, or "angst". His ideas have influenced many twentieth-century thinkers and writers including **Beckett**, **Kafka** and **Mann**.

BESSEMER, Henry

English inventor 1813-98

When people imagine inventors as eccentric geniuses, Bessemer is the kind of person they have in mind. He spent all his life inventing, and patented no fewer than 114 different gadgets and ideas, including artificial gold-dust (made from brass) for gold paint, and the first typesetting machine used in printing. He is best-remembered for the "Bessemer process", a way of turning iron to steel by removing impurities such as carbon.

The Bessemer process involved "boiling" molten iron with a strong blast of air which oxidized (burned off) any impurities and released more heat to keep the metal molten. In 1860 Bessemer invented a tilting converter which allowed molten steel to be poured out. This photograph shows the tilting converters in a Bessemer steel plant in 1860. Bessemer's invention made Britain one of the world's steel-making centres for the rest of the nineteenth century.

PITMAN, Isaac

English publisher 1813-79

Scribes of ancient Greece, Rome and Egypt were probably the first people to use "shorthand": ways of shortening words or replacing them with signs so that they can be written down quickly. In 1837 Pitman, a schoolmaster from Gloucester, invented a new and rapid way of recording speech, word for word, which has become one of the most widely used forms of shorthand. Pitman's "phonography" was the first fully phonetic system – able to

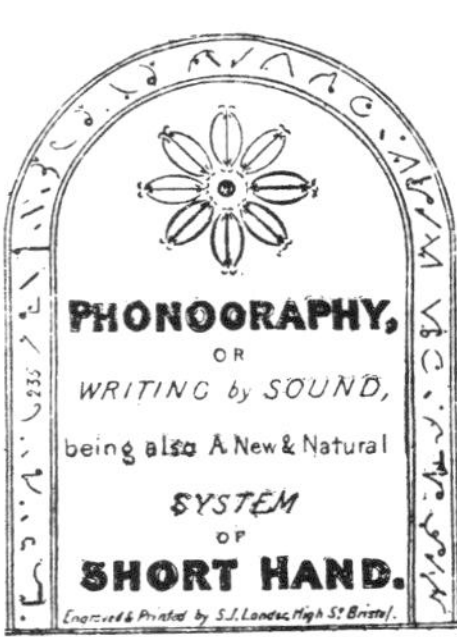

Left: Part of the original "Penny Plate", as it was called, written by Pitman in 1840. Pitman's "Plate" offered the first-ever correspondence course – learning shorthand through the mail. He began on 10 January 1840, the first day of the "penny post" in Britain. Since then, Pitman's name has always been associated with shorthand and business education.

KIERKEGÅRD: Beckett 72 Kafka 63 Kant 349 Mann 59 Sartre 395

reproduce all spoken words as dots and strokes of a pen. By using shorthand, secretaries and reporters can record words at the speed they are spoken, and later translate them into ordinary writing.

GLIDDEN, Joseph Farwell

US inventor 1813-1906

Glidden invented a machine which made barbed wire. It was used to prevent cattle from straying when cowboys were driving huge herds from America's Wild West to the Chicago meat-processing factories. But barbed wire (nicknamed "Devil's rope") soon began also to be used against people, to protect buildings and wartime battle-lines. Glidden made a fortune from his wire machine, but he bitterly regretted inventing it.

COLT, Samuel

US inventor 1814-62

Colt invented the revolver, a hand-held gun which could fire six bullets without being reloaded. It was nicknamed the "Colt" or "six-shooter", and was the favourite weapon of Buffalo Bill **Cody** in his Wild West show. The cowboys' hand-guns you see in western films are Colts.

SAX, Antoine-Joseph Adolphe

Belgian musician and inventor 1814-94

Sax was the son of a musical-instrument maker. He studied the clarinet, and might have been a concert soloist. But he preferred tinkering with instruments to playing them, and took a job in his father's firm. He invented a family of brass instruments called "saxhorns".

Sax's most famous invention was the saxophone, made of brass, but with keys and a reed like a clarinet. Many people hated it, saying that it sounded like a whining child or a howling dog. But the saxophone family became popular in military bands, and later in jazz, where it is most often heard today.

A tenor saxophone, one of the main instruments heard in jazz music today.

SIEMENS FAMILY

German inventors and businessmen 19th-20th centuries

WERNER VON SIEMENS (1816-92) began his career as a soldier, specializing in artillery and communications. In 1847 he founded one of the first businesses to make telegraphic and electrical apparatus. In 1879, at the Berlin Exhibition, he showed the first practical electric railway. He also built the Prussian telegraphic system. The siemens unit named after him, is a measurement of electrical conductance.

Werner's brothers, FRIEDRICH (1812-1904) and KARL WILHELM (1823-83) went to England and opened a branch of the family business. They were interested in metallurgy and invented many processes still used in steel- and glass-making. The firm made telegraph systems, electric lighting, under-water cable, and developed the first trams to be driven by electricity.

Werner's son WILHELM (1855-1919) raced **Edison** and **Swan** to invent the light bulb. Although Edison and Swan were the first to take out patents, Siemen's invention probably came first.

This illustration appeared in an 1883 edition of *City*, a London Journal, and was intended to show the great power and influence of the Siemens family. The three brothers were key figures in major industries – including telecommunications, railways, electricity, as well as cable, steel and glass-making. The Siemens company is a major force in the field of communi-cation today.

COLT: Cody 248 SIEMENS: Edison 380 Swan 372

HARRISON, James

Australian inventor 1816-93

Harrison invented the refrigerator in 1851. The first ones were not for the kitchen, but for meat-processing factories. Harrison went on to design refrigerator-ships, used for exporting deep-frozen Australian beef and lamb all over the world.

Henry David Thoreau.

THOREAU, Henry David

US thinker and writer 1817-62

When Thoreau left Harvard University, he worked as a teacher and as an assistant in his father's pencil-making business. His favourite pastimes were walking and canoeing: he liked to be alone with nature and his own thoughts. In 1841 he made friends with Ralph Waldo Emerson (1803-82), who believed that God was in everything, especially in nature, and was to be found not by joining churches and societies but by living according to one's own true nature and conscience. This impressed Thoreau, who became one of Emerson's most devoted followers.

In 1845 Thoreau went to live alone for two years in a cabin in the woods beside Walden Pond in Concord, Massachusetts. He wrote a book, describing himself as "a refugee from the machine age", and writing about his daily walks, his growing skill in carpentry and stonemasonry, and above all his thoughts about human society, solitude and God's presence all round him. The book, *Walden*, was enormously popular, and many people today take holidays in the "wilderness", hoping to "discover themselves" as Thoreau did.

When Thoreau left Walden, he supported the Amerindians' struggle against the government, and spoke out against slavery and the war being waged against Mexico. When the government imposed a poll tax to raise money for that war, he refused to pay it, and gladly went to prison. In his 40s he often went on long, solitary journeys, and later wrote about them. On one trip he caught a chill, which turned into tuberculosis and killed him.

MEGE-MOURIÈZ, Hippolyte

French scientist 1817-80

In 1869 Mège-Mourièz invented artificial butter, and called it margarine ("pearl-like") because it was white, not dyed yellow as butter-substitutes are today. His original recipe sounds disgusting: a mixture of beef fat, milk, water, minced cow's udder and pig's stomach. In the 1910s whale oil replaced the animal fats. Since the 1960s vegetable oils have been used instead.

BAHÁ'U'LLAH

Persian religious leader 1817-92

Bahá'u'llah ("Glory of God") was the name taken by Mirza Hossein Ali, founder of the Baha'i branch of Islam. His followers believe that he was the Promised One, sent to reveal the true nature of God to human beings. He preached that God wants everyone on Earth to be equal: there should be one faith, one language, and no discrimination on the grounds of race or sex, nor any class-systems based on inherited power or wealth. Although the faith was (and still is) persecuted by orthodox Muslims in Iran (formerly Persia), it has spread to other countries, and has over 500,000 followers throughout the world.

MARX, Karl

German thinker and writer 1818-83

Of all nineteenth-century thinkers, perhaps only **Darwin** and **Freud** have influenced modern life as much as Marx. Modern politics, philosophy, economics and sociology are all affected by his ideas. He thought that the way most countries organized their industry, trade and farming was wrong, because it gave wealth to only a few people, and he suggested a new system of equal shares and rights for all. His ideas, now known as Marxism, have been taken up and adapted by communist (or Marxist) countries in more than half the world.

Marx said that in most countries, all through history, there have been two main groups of people. The first group, "capitalists", own farms and businesses. The second group, the "proletariat", work for the capitalists. Workers have nothing but their ability to work, and however hard they struggle they still end up with nothing else. Capitalists, on the other hand, make profits and grow richer every year. Marx said that the only way to create a fairer system was by revolution. The workers should take all businesses and property into their own hands and run a "workers' state", in which everyone is equal. For a time this state would be a "dictatorship of the proletariat", in which people must forget their own interests and put state interest first. But gradually the state would "wither away", as Marx put it. Fairness and equality would rule; there would be no need for parliaments, civil servants, police forces or managers.

Marx was a quiet man, an invalid. He never took an active part in revolutions, spoke at meetings, organized strikes or went on demonstrations. He stayed at home writing, and when his books caused riots and he was expelled from one country after another, he showed no surprise. He settled at last in London, where he spent the last 34 years of his life. His friend **Engels** gave him enough money to live on, and helped him with his books, especially *Capital* and *The Communist Manifesto*, which set out his revolutionary ideas.

Karl Marx, the founder of modern communism, explaining his ideas to Paris workers in 1844.

MARX: Darwin 124 Engels 370 Freud 383

PINKERTON, Allan

Scottish/US detective 1819-84

Pinkerton emigrated to America in 1842, and after four years as a deputy sheriff in Illinois started the first private detective agency. One of his greatest successes was in 1861, when he heard of a plot to assassinate **Lincoln**, and persuaded the president to take a different route to his inauguration.

Pinkerton's detectives (nicknamed "private eyes") were not police officers, and had other jobs, for example protecting people or looking for lost relatives, as well as solving crimes.

SHOLES, Christopher Latham

US inventor 1819-90

Sholes invented the first practical typewriter. All other inventors had failed because they put the letters on the keys in alphabetical order: this made it slower to type words than to write them by hand. Sholes put the commonest letters together, in the centre of the typewriter. This speeded up typing and made it far more efficient than handwriting. His letter-arrangement (the "qwerty" keyboard) is still used in English-speaking countries around the world.

Friedrich Engels (standing) with Karl Marx, working on their book *Capital* in London, 1867.

ENGELS, Friedrich

German writer and thinker 1820-95

When Engels was 22 he went to Manchester to run his father's English cloth factories. He was appalled at the contrast between the miserable lives of the mill-workers and the wealth and happiness of the people who owned the mills. He wrote a horrifying account of the effects of the industrial revolution in *The Condition of the Working Classes in England*. He became a revolutionary, and in 1848 he worked with **Marx** on another book, *The Communist Manifesto*. This described the struggle between two classes of people, the "proletariat" whose hard work created the wealth and the "capitalists" who spent it. It urged the workers of the world to unite in revolution, to take over the societies they lived in and make better lives for everyone.

For a time Engels gave up the family business to work with Marx.

Left: The watchful eye symbol used by Pinkerton's detective agency.

PINKERTON: Lincoln 452 ENGELS: Marx 369

But funds ran low, and he went back into partnership with his father, using wealth from the business to support Marx and finance his work for revolution. Some people think that he should not have made profits from his workers in the way he despised when other people did it. Others say that Engels was simply using the wealth earned to benefit the whole working class. In 1870 he went to work full-time with Marx in London. He helped him with his book *Capital*, and finished it after Marx's death in 1883.

Nowadays, people think of Marx as the father of communism, whose ideas changed the lives of millions of people in the world, and few remember Engels. Yet, without him, Marx would probably not have been able to work at all.

THOMSON, Robert

Scottish inventor 1822-73

As a young man, Thomson devised a way to detonate dynamite from a safe distance, by using electricity; it was taken up and developed by **Faraday**. He worked for Robert **Stephenson**, and pioneered the building of steam-tractors for hauling goods by road.

Thomson invented many things. Annoyed at the way he had to keep dipping his pen in ink when he was drawing, he invented a pen with its own ink-reservoir: an early fountain pen. He is best known today for the pneumatic tyre. He placed a leather casing round an inner tube of canvas filled with air. Until then, tyres had been solid wood, rubber or metal, and had given a bone-shaking, goods-shattering ride.

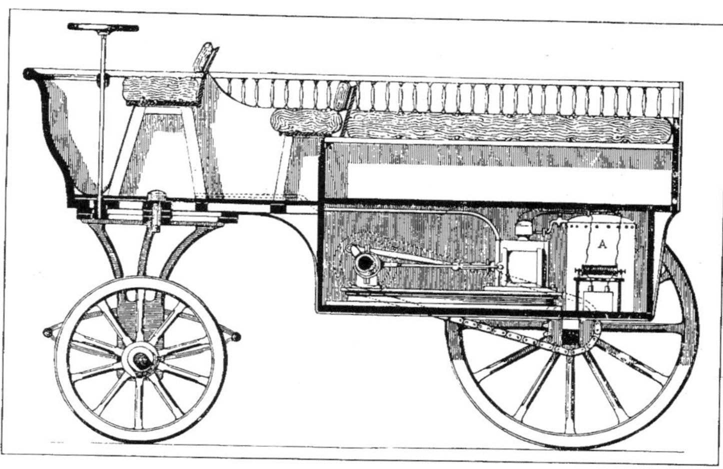

Lenoir's 1862 design for a vehicle with an internal combustion engine, showing the shaft drive to the rear wheel. It was the first practical engine of its kind

LENOIR, Jean-Joseph Étienne

French inventor 1822-1900

In 1860 Lenoir designed the first internal combustion engine. Until then engines had always been steam-powered, and too much energy was lost in the furnace, boiler and pipes which were separate from the cylinder driving the piston. Lenoir's idea was to burn fuel inside, not outside the cylinder – hence the term "internal combustion" – and so to use all the engine's energy to drive the piston. Fuel (coal-gas) was sucked into the cylinder and then ignited by a spark. The resulting explosion pushed a piston up the cylinder, drove the shaft to the wheels and at the same time created a vacuum which sucked in more fuel.

Lenoir's engine was terrifying. Using it was like driving a vehicle by firing a cannon. It was also inefficient, delivering no more than one horsepower (see **Watt**). But it was the beginning of car-engine technology, and when **Otto**, **Benz** and others improved the design, it replaced steam as a way of driving motor vehicles. The Lenoir system of spark ignition is still used today.

One of the earliest pneumatic tyres (filled with compressed air), the invention of Robert Thomson. This one dates from 1845.

THOMSON: Faraday 121 Stephenson 358 LENOIR: Benz 378 Otto 373 Watt 350

BUTTERICK, Ebenezer

US tailor 1826-1903

In 1863 Butterick invented a way of mass-producing paper patterns for home-dressmaking.

At first, Butterick specialized in patterns for men's and boys' clothing. After three years of operation, in 1866, women's dress patterns were produced, and were received with great enthusiasm.

Left: Butterick's paper patterns meant that high fashion was no longer only for the wealthy. Women everywhere could make clothes in the latest styles in their homes.

SWAN, Joseph Wilson

English inventor 1828-1914

Swan invented a form of light bulb, at the same time as **Edison** in the USA. Edison had already patented his idea, and Swan had not, so it looked as if Edison would reap the rewards. But Swan quickly developed and patented several improvements to the original idea, moving far ahead of Edison. The two men went into partnership, and for a long time the "Ediswan" company was the world's main maker of light bulbs and fittings.

BOOTH, William

English preacher 1829-1912

Booth began his career as a Methodist preacher in Nottingham. At that time, many British Christians went abroad to "take Christianity to the natives", as they put it. Booth thought that missionaries were needed just as much in Britain itself, particularly among deprived people in the city slums. He founded what he called an "army of salvation", sending missionaries to fight poverty and despair. The Salvation Army still looks after sick and homeless people all over the world, as well as teaching Christianity.

William Booth, founder of the Salvation Army.

MAREY, Étienne-Jules

French scientist 1830-1904

Marey invented a photo "gun": a camera worked by a trigger which could take up to 12 pictures a second. Although Marey was more interested in the science of movement than in photography, he had invented one of the first practical moving-picture cameras, and his work influenced such later film-pioneers as **Edison** and the **Lumières**.

SWAN: Edison 380 MAREY: Edison 380 Lumière 384

Muybridge became famous for photographing movement. His pictures helped many artists to show motion accurately in their work, and were a trigger for the birth of the film industry.

MUYBRIDGE, Eadweard

English photographer 1830-1904

Quite independently of **Marey**, Muybridge devised a way of photographing movement. He set out rows of cameras along a marked track, and laid strings over the track to trigger them. Then he made people and animals crawl, walk and run along the track. Each camera took one picture, of a different stage in the movement. In Muybridge's time these photo-sequences were revolutionary. No one, for example, had ever shown before that a galloping horse lifts all four legs from the ground at the same time. At first the photographs chiefly interested scientists. But then **Edison** and others began wondering if it might be possible to make real "moving pictures", and films were born.

BLAVATSKY, Helena Petrovna

Russian mystic leader 1831-81

Blavatsky was a princess and a "medium" – someone who claims to be able to communicate with people in the spirit-world. She moved from Russia to France, and then had huge success touring Europe and the USA. She gave seances (sittings) in private houses and public halls. People paid her to contact relatives or famous individuals who had "passed over to the other side" that is ceased to exist in the mortal world.

Although many people regarded Blavatsky as a fraud, she had thousands of devoted followers. She travelled in Nepal and India, and studied the Buddhist and Hindu religions. She began to think that spiritualism (contacting spirits by going into a deep trance) might be a way of learning about God, and developed this into a branch of religion she called Theosophy. It soon became fashionable, especially in the early 1900s, when people linked its investigations with **Freud**'s researches into the unconscious mind. Few people nowadays still believe – as Blavatsky and her followers did – that she worked miracles. But her other ideas, and the theosophical religion she began, still survive.

OTTO, Nikolaus August

German inventor 1832-91

Otto improved **Lenoir**'s design for the internal combustion engine, controlling the mixture of fuel and air which entered the cylinder. This made the engine less noisy and more powerful. He also invented the four-stroke system, in which the engine-cylinder contains not one piston but four, working in sequence. The "Otto cycle", as it was called, gave smoother, more regular power than the jerky explosions of Lenoir's engines. From 1876 it was standard in motor-vehicle engines, and later it was also used in aeroplane engines.

MUYBRIDGE: Edison 380 Marey 372 BLAVATSKY: Freud 383 OTTO: Lenoir 371

The Eiffel Tower, France's monument to technological achievement, and to the genius of its engineer, Eiffel.

EIFFEL, Alexandre Gustave

French engineer 1832-1923

Eiffel worked as a railway engineer, and pioneered a way of making towers and bridges from frameworks of iron girders. He built 42 bridges in France, many of which are still used today. In 1885 he was asked to design the iron structure which holds up the arm and torch of Bartholdi's Statue of Liberty, in New York Harbor.

Soon after his work on the Statue of Liberty, Eiffel won a competition to build a monument to celebrate France's industrial and engineering achievements in the 100 years since the Revolution. He built a 300-metre tower on the banks of the river Seine in Paris. The Eiffel Tower was made from 15,000 iron sections, took 26 months to bolt together, and was opened in 1889. Eiffel meant it to be pulled down after a few years, but it became such a tourist attraction that it was left standing. It is now one of the most famous buildings on Earth.

The tower was Eiffel's last engineering achievement. When it was finished, he built a weather station at the top, to monitor climate in a still atmosphere – something which had until then been possible only on the tops of high mountains. He studied wind power and dynamics, and in 1912 invented the wind tunnel. This work was vital to **Blériot** and other aircraft pioneers, and helped to make France one of the leading countries building light aircraft during the First World War.

EIFFEL: Blériot 223

NOBEL, Alfred

Swedish inventor 1833-1896

Before Nobel's work, explosives were awkward and dangerous to handle. Gunpowder was hard to measure out without spilling, and was so full of impurities that it was dangerously unreliable. The other main explosive, nitroglycerin, was a liquid so eager to explode that the slightest knock would set it off. Nobel mixed nitroglycerin with an inert (inactive) material, making it safe to carry. He called the new explosive *dynamite* ("the powerful one"), and it made him a multi-millionaire.

Nobel always claimed that he had only expected dynamite and its even more efficient successor, gelignite, to be used for peaceful purposes such as blasting rock in quarries, and he was horrified when people began using them for war. When he died, he did

The pacifist Alfred Nobel.

not leave his fortune to his children (who would have spent it making more explosives), but to give prizes each year to the five men or women who had done most to benefit humanity. Nobel prizes are given for advances made in physics, chemistry, medicine and literature, and to the person who has worked hardest for peace throughout the year. (A sixth prize, for economics, was added after Nobel's death.)

MORRIS, William

English thinker, artist and writer 1834-96

Morris hated the factory-made goods of nineteenth-century Britain. He thought that large factories were inhuman places in which to work, and that the products reflected this: however useful, the goods were ugly and poorly made. He pioneered a return to the methods of craftsmen of the Middle Ages, producing hand-made furniture of high quality and beauty. He designed and printed wallpaper and fabrics, using hand-carved wooden blocks in the old way. His bright patterns of flowers and birds were meant to bring cheerfulness into even the poorest of homes. He set up a printing-press to make books by hand. He designed the books himself, wrote the words and drew and painted all the illustrations.

Morris' "arts and crafts movement" failed to brighten ordinary people's lives in the way he hoped. His goods were never cheap enough for them to afford. But his ideas impressed other manufacturers, who began improving the quality and beauty of their goods, and his influence is still felt today. His ideas also had a political effect. His concern for ordinary people's lives inspired many later thinkers, including the founders of socialism and the European Labour movement.

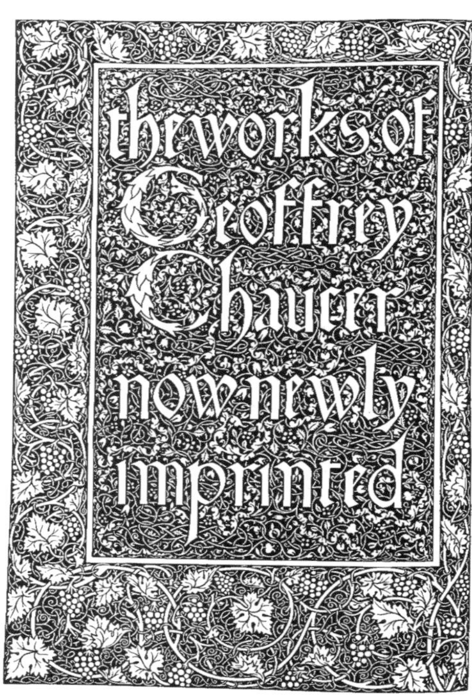

The title page from a 1896 edition of *The Works of Geoffrey Chaucer*, designed by William Morris, and printed by the Kelmscott Press which Morris founded.

DAIMLER, Gottlieb

German inventor 1834-1900

Daimler raced against another German inventor, **Benz**, to be the first to build a road vehicle powered by an internal combustion engine. Benz built the first successful engine, but it was gas-driven and heavy. In 1885 Daimler fitted a lighter, petrol-driven version to a bicycle and so invented the motor-cycle. In 1890 he turned to car-making, and founded his own firm, which he named Mercedes, after his daughter. Mercedes and Benz were rival companies until 1926, when they joined forces as Mercedes-Benz.

Gottlieb Daimler, who launched the motor age with the first petrol-driven car.

DAIMLER: Benz 378

This postcard was issued to commemorate the zeppelin's first trip around the world.

PERKIN, William Henry

English scientist 1838-1907

Scientific research often leads to unexpected discoveries. Perkin was a chemist, interested in making an artificial form of the drug quinine, which is used against malaria and had previously been extracted from tree-bark. In his research, quite by accident, he came across a deep purple compound which dyed everything it touched. Until this time, purple dye had been extracted from flower-heads or the shells of sea-snails. It was rare and expensive – in Roman times it had been so prized that only the emperor was allowed to wear it – and it also faded in use. Perkin's dye, made from coal tar, was lasting, dazzlingly bright and could be made for a few pence a barrel. He gave up research into quinine, set up a dye-factory, and very soon purple (or "mauve" as he called it) was the most fashionable colour in Europe. People wore mauve clothes, had mauve curtains and tablecloths, even dyed their cats and poodles mauve. Perkin's chance discovery made him a millionaire.

Perkin's synthetic dye created a new fashion in the 1890s, which was nicknamed the "mauve decade".

ZEPPELIN, Ferdinand von

German soldier and inventor 1838-1917

Zeppelin invented the first rigid-frame airship: an aluminium framework covered with canvas, which was filled with helium (a gas lighter than air). The gas-bag supported a cabin full of goods or people, and the craft was propeller-driven, like any other aircraft of the time. At first "zeppelins" were used to carry passengers, but in the First World War they dropped bombs. In the 1930s airships were a roomy and luxurious way to travel, and the most famous, the *Graf Zeppelin*, covered over 1.5 million kilometres. But in 1937, after the huge *Hindenburg* crashed in New Jersey, USA, all airships were grounded and the fashion changed to planes.

CHARDONNET, Hilaire

French scientist 1839-1924

Chardonnet was a biologist, and interested in silkworm-diseases. He wondered if cloth could be made from artificial silk, developed from chemicals instead of thread spun by caterpillars. **Swan** had recently patented a way of making artificial threads for the filaments (the parts that glow) in light bulbs. Chardonnet developed the process to make much longer, stronger threads of a new material, which he called "rayon". Thus he began the vast man-made fibre industry we have today.

Rayon, or "Chardonnet silk", was the first man-made fibre to be commercially produced. Filaments or threads of a nitro-cellulose solution were formed by being pushed through small holes and dried in warm air.

HOLLAND, John

Irish inventor 1840-1914

For centuries, inventors had dreamed of the submarine, a boat which would travel underwater. The problem was not the air supply, but how the boat was to be moved. Early submarines were one-person glass bubbles, dragged along by ropes from the surface or rowed awkwardly through leather-protected holes which were seldom as waterproof as they were supposed to be. Holland invented a submarine powered by an engine. It used gasoline when it was on the surface and the exhaust gases could escape; underwater, it used electric power from enormous batteries.

Left: A cutaway view of the electrically powered submarine built by Holland. The craft was 16m long, and was accepted by the US Navy in 1900.

MAXIM, Hiram

US inventor 1840-1916

Maxim is best known for inventing a machine-gun which fired 666 bullets per minute and was used by armies on both sides during the First World War. He also designed mousetraps, fire-extinguishers and steam-powered rides for fairgrounds.

Maxim's oddest, most useless invention was a steam-powered plane. He began experimenting with powered flight in the early 1890s, when only steam-engines were available. To lift the engine, complete with boiler, fire and funnel, Maxim had to build a plane as high as a three-storey house, with a wing-span of 32 metres and a weight of 3.5 tonnes. To launch it, he built not a runway but a railway track. But on the trial flight, the rails ended just as the plane reached its take-off speed of 69km/h. The monster toppled over and crashed, with a hiss of steam which the local newspaper later described as "exactly like a dying man's last gasp".

Maxim with his machine gun.

CHARDONNET: Swan 372

NIETZSCHE, Friedrich Wilhelm

German thinker 1844-1900

Supporters of Nietzsche thought that his ideas on art, religion and human nature were some of the grandest thoughts anyone had ever had; his enemies thought him a lunatic. He believed that humans were the supreme beings in the universe, and that human will-power and energy could achieve anything at all if they were sensibly channelled and organized. He thought that the stronger a person's will is, the better the person.

Nietzsche taught that religion was false, that God did not exist, and that dreams and daydreams gave reliable prophecies if only people understood them properly. He said that the existence of a great man, such as **Alexander the Great** or **Napoléon I** (and there were no great women, in Nietzsche's opinion), was worth any amount of suffering in ordinary people. Among Nietzsche's heroes – "supermen", as he called them – were creative geniuses (or "supreme beings of the mind") like **Wagner** and **Shakespeare**; among "supreme beings of the will" he counted politicians, dictators and, above all, thinkers such as himself.

Nietzsche's ideas were immensely popular in his own time. Other people, such as **Freud**, were roused by his teachings to begin their own researches, and his words inspired generations of psychologists, politicians, religious thinkers and mystics (people who believe in paranormal forces). **Hitler** distorted Nietzsche's ideas about a race of supermen, ruling all creation. Unfortunately for Nietzsche himself, he had little chance to see his ideas take root. In 1889 he went genuinely mad, and spent his last eleven years in lunatic asylums.

The German thinker, Friedrich Nietzsche.

BENZ, Karl

German inventor 1844-1929

Like his great rival **Daimler**, Benz was determined to be the first person to use an internal-combustion engine to drive a road-vehicle. Benz invented an engine powered by coal-gas, and in 1885 put it in a three-wheeled vehicle which was nicknamed the *automobile* ("self-propeller") or "horseless carriage". It was a cumbersome, heavy machine, and could only travel at a maximum of 25km/h. It took another ten years, and development of a petrol-driven engine, for Benz to produce a more practical car. Had he and Daimler joined forces they could have made faster progress. But they remained rivals almost all their lives, and it was not till 1926 that the two car-making companies merged at last.

The Benz tricycle of 1886, with Karl Benz at the controls.

NIETZSCHE: Alexander the Great 412 Freud 383 Hitler 466 Napoléon I 451 Shakespeare 16 Wagner 36 BENZ: Daimler 375

WESTINGHOUSE, George

US inventor 1846-1914

As a young man Westinghouse was appalled by the primitive braking system on trains, worked by a man in every second carriage pulling a separate brake. He wondered how this method would cope with an emergency stop. He invented brakes worked by air pressure. They were connected to a tube of compressed air that ran the whole length of the train, and one man could operate all of them at once.

Westinghouse gathered the heads of the railway company on a train to demonstrate his invention. Before the train reached the pre-arranged obstacle that was to test the brakes, a horse and cart suddenly appeared on the line. The engine-driver applied the brakes, and the train stopped so suddenly that the railway officials were thrown all over their carriage. Westinghouse was given the contract to supply brakes for all steam-trains, and his invention made him a multi-millionaire.

Westinghouse was a businessman as well as an inventor. He set up the Westinghouse Corporation, which provided the first gas and electricity networks in many US cities. This illustration shows his natural gas illumination for the Pittsburgh area.

BELL, Alexander Graham

Scottish/Canadian inventor 1847-1922

Bell came from a family of well-known speech therapists in Edinburgh, Scotland, and was trained to continue the profession. He researched into the way the ears receive sound, and devised all kinds of hearing aids. The family moved to Canada in 1870, and two years later, Bell opened a school near Boston, in the United States, to teach speech to deaf people, using his father's system.

One day, while testing microphones and receivers, one of his assistants, an electrical engineer, twanged a wire by mistake – and the sound travelled down the wire so that Bell could hear it clearly in the next room. Bell wondered if speech could be sent down wires in the same way, and began experimenting. The result was the telephone ("far-voice"), which Bell, then aged 29, patented in 1876. The Bell Telephone Company was for many years the largest phone company in the world.

Bell made other inventions: kites big enough to carry people; a hydrofoil boat which set the world water speed record in 1918; and the "graphophone" – an early machine for recording sound.

Bell demonstrating his telephone system at Salem, Massachussets, in 1877.

When this photograph was taken, in 1888, an exhausted Edison had spent five days and nights at work improving the phonograph.

PULITZER, Joseph

Hungarian/US newspaper owner 1847-1911

In the two centuries of newspapers before Pulitzer's time, editors had concentrated on text: thousands of words in long columns, giving facts and opinions without illustrations. People thought of newspapers more as daily or weekly news-books than as entertainment. Pulitzer saw no reason why news should not be as entertainingly and colourfully presented as the stories in fiction magazines. He cut down the size of papers to make them easier to hold, and began using the new ways of printing illustrations (see **Ives**). He sent cameramen to photograph news events, and told his reporters to match vivid pictures with lively, easily read prose.

The new newspapers caught the eye of people who had never before wanted to read about the news, and have been the most popular kind of newspapers ever since. Pulitzer made a fortune, and when he died he left it to pay for Pulitzer prizes. They are given for the best newspaper reporting, photography, fiction, music and drama produced in the USA each year.

Joseph Pulitzer, founder of the Pulitzer prize.

PULITZER: Ives 382

EDISON, Thomas Alva

US inventor 1847-1931

From his childhood Edison was fascinated by the way things worked. He spent only three months at school in his entire life: his education was all practical – doing and thinking about things for himself. He worked as a newsboy and later as a clerk in the US telegraph office, sending morse-code messages from town to town. Here, as everywhere, he took things apart to see how they worked. Soon he was patenting improvements in telegraph equipment which made him a millionaire.

In 1876 Edison built a laboratory (he called it an "invention-factory") to try out new ideas, and hired a staff of scientists. He would sketch out ideas and give them to his employees to make. In the years that followed the Edison company patented over 1,300 new inventions, including the phonograph (ancestor of the record-player), the film-projector, the carbon microphone (the one inside a telephone) and – perhaps most useful of all – the electric light bulb. Edison grew fabulously rich: he was one of the best-known and most successful inventors in history.

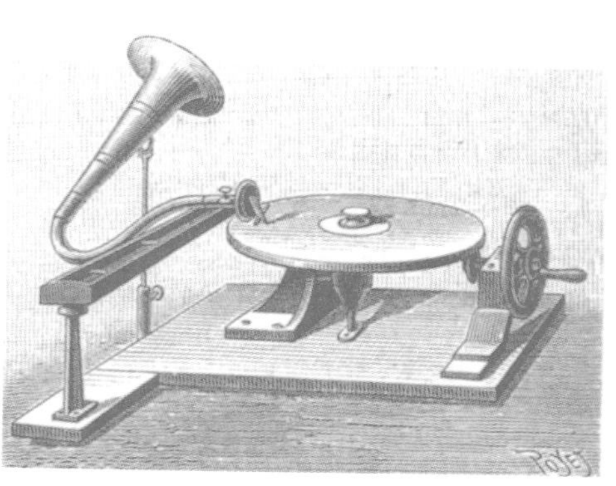

Berliner's gramophone. On the left is the recording stylus and mouthpiece; on the right a disc is being played.

BERLINER, Emil

German/US inventor 1851-1929

Berliner invented the disc-shaped record. Until his time, all records had been cylinders, and Berliner's discs allowed more music to be recorded on one record, and produced a better sound.

LILIENTHAL, Otto

German air pioneer 1848-96

Lilienthal thought that if human beings could be given wings and tails of the right shape and size, they would be able to fly like birds. He made enormous, kite-like structures from paper and cloth stretched over wooden frames, and built an artificial hill near Berlin from which he could take off.

Lilienthal's first flying machine flapped its wings, but he realized that he could make better use of the wind with fixed wings. He hung from the machine, swinging his body from side to side to change direction. He found that if he launched himself into the wind when the conditions were right, he could glide for several hundred metres. Lilienthal made over 2,000 flights, but finally crashed in an unexpected gust of wind, and was killed.

In the years after Lilienthal's death flight experiments moved away from human-sized wings to the idea of making flying-machines large enough to sit in. The **Wright brothers** learned much from Lilienthal's experimental work on flight, and, 60 years later his idea of the person-carrying kite was perfected – the hang-glider.

LILIENTHAL: Wright 385

BERTILLON, Alphonse

French police clerk 1853-1914

Bertillon devised a system of proving someone guilty or innocent now known as *bertillonage*, after his name. He suggested using photographs as a means of identification, and perfected a way of measuring someone accurately and scientifically to show, for example, if an accused person was too short to have stabbed a victim, too heavy to have made a footprint or too fat to have broken in through a window. It seems common sense nowadays, but in the 1870s this kind of evidence was so new that many people considered Bertillon a lunatic. It was many years before scientific evidence was allowed as proof in court – and Bertillon is remembered as one of its most important pioneers.

Right: A 1911 Gillette safety razor. The holder was plated in either silver or gold, and the set cost one guinea (about £1) – a very expensive present in those days.

George Eastman, the inventor of the roll of film for photography. He also designed Kodak cameras, and founded the Eastman-Kodak company.

PARSONS, Charles Algernon

English inventor 1854-1931

Parsons invented the steam turbine engine. His engines were used to power steamships, and are still installed in many power stations to drive the generators.

EASTMAN, George

US inventor 1854-1932

Until Eastman's time, photographs were made using sheets of glass or copper. They were large, awkward to handle and expensive. Eastman experimented by putting a layer of gelatine on a paper strip, and found that this produced photos just as clearly and far more easily. He called his invention "film strip" or "film". It was cheap, and the cameras Eastman made for it were small and easy to carry, unlike the heavy wooden ones people had used before. His inventions made photography a popular hobby. In 1899 he improved film still further, by using celluloid as the base instead of paper.

GILLETTE, King Camp

US inventor 1855-1932

Until Gillette's time razors were simply long, sharp knives, sometimes with folding blades but still highly dangerous. They were rightly nicknamed "cut-throats". Gillette worked as a salesman. His employer had invented the disposable bottle-cap, and advised Gillette, if he wanted to make money, to invent something else that would be thrown away. Gillette realized that the only part of a cut-throat razor that actually did any work was the cutting edge. All he had

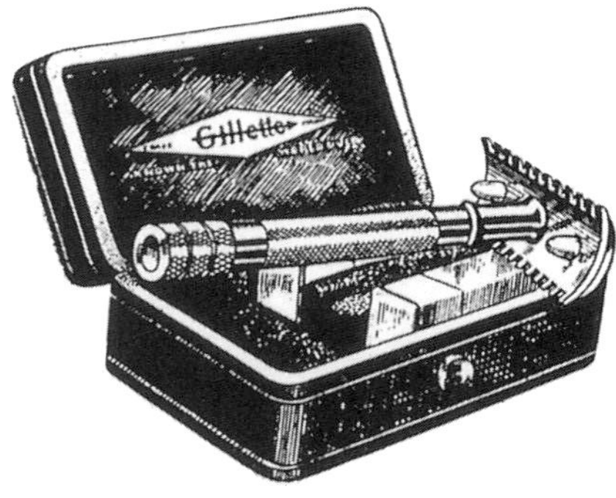

to do was to invent a holder for a throw-away blade, and his fortune would be made. He did: his razor held less than 5 centimetres of blade in a metal safety-guard which made it cut sideways into the hairs of the beard, not downwards into the flesh. Gillette patented it under the name "safety razor" – the forerunner of razors used today.

IVES, Frederick

US inventor 1856-1937

Ives invented halftone printing. This technique turns the light and dark parts of a picture into black dots: many, close together, for dark, and few, widely spaced, for light. The dots are then transferred to a metal block and put in the printing press. Until electronic printing was perfected in the 1970s, halftone blocks were used to print all newspaper photos – and if you look at old newspapers with a magnifying-glass, you can see each separate dot.

Sigmund Freud, photographed in about 1931. Freud's ideas about the unconscious mind have been used by many people, including writers and painters, such as **Joyce**, **Proust** and **Picasso**.

FREUD, Sigmund

Austrian neurologist and founder of psychoanalysis 1856-1939

Freud was a neurologist (a specialist in nerve disorders). He thought that if you could guide the minds of mentally disturbed people into channels of thought and memory otherwise "inhibited" (blocked off) by normal thinking, that might help to cure them. Freud believed that the minds of unconscious people are free, whereas conscious people "inhibit" (control) their thinking with ideas of law, religion, good manners and so on. Although this is no problem to a healthy person, it hampers a sick mind.

For thousands of years people thought that character depended on the balance between four "elements" (earth, air, fire and water), or between good and evil, God and the Devil battling for each human soul. By the late nineteenth century, however, thanks to the discoveries of scientists like **Darwin**, people began to believe that humans were the result of evolution – thousands of minute developments over millions of years – and that we are still evolving, with or without God's help. Freud applied this idea to the mind. He said that our characters begin to evolve from the moment of birth, and that tiny happenings and feelings, even in the earliest moments of babyhood, affect people in later life.

Freud believed that he could get his patients to "unlock" their subconscious minds, by careful questioning and a technique called "free association", in which the patient responds spontaneously to words spoken by the therapist. In this way, childhood experiences are revealed, which Freud believed would help people to understand themselves. He called this work psychoanalysis ("logical study of the mind"), and used it to treat not just mentally ill people but anyone who felt distressed by the tensions of life. He had – and has – fanatical followers, who believe that his methods brought one of the greatest medical advances in human history. His opponents are equally fanatical. They say that he took his obsession with childhood experiences to absurd lengths, and that people are so ready to turn to psychoanalysis when life gets difficult that it has became a fashion, and is valueless.

Despite such arguments about the value of his work, Freud's ideas have completely changed the way we regard the mind. Psychoanalytical methods have become standard in treating mental illness.

FREUD: Darwin 124 Joyce 62 Picasso 60 Proust 57

DIESEL, Rudolf

German inventor 1858-1913

Diesel invented a compression-ignition engine which burns heavy oil instead of the more refined (and therefore more expensive) petrol. Diesel engines are more efficient than petrol engines, because no sparking plug system is needed to ignite the fuel. They are ideal for heavy vehicles such as buses, trucks and trains. At the time, however, Diesel had no idea of this use. He thought that his work had been overtaken by the development of the petrol engine, and committed suicide. His engine, none the less, continues to be used today.

KELLOGG, William Keith

US food manufacturer 1860-1951

Will Kellogg was the business manager of the Battle Creek Sanitarium in Michigan, USA which was run by his brother John, a physician. To assist the recovery of their patients, they developed many kinds of foods suitable for a healthy diet. One of the most popular was a breakfast cereal made from crisp, thin flakes of malted corn. In 1906 Will left his brother to manage the sanitarium, and set up a business to manufacture cornflakes for the general public – the beginning of today's multi-billion-dollar breakfast cereal industry.

Right: The packaging for Kellogg's cornflakes from 1920.

ZAMENHOF, Ludwig Lazarus

Polish optician 1859-1917

Zamenhof wanted all the nations of the world to live in peace together, and he thought that one way to make this happen was to invent an international language. Everyone would speak it, and there would be no more misunderstandings caused by language. He devised a new language, based on Spanish, called Esperanto ("hope"), and in 1887 published a dictionary and a textbook. Esperanto never really swept across the world. But there are still several million Esperanto-speakers, and it is the simplest and most successful artificial language ever invented.

Ludwig Zamenhof, inventor of Esperanto. The green and gold star-shaped badge is worn by speakers of the Esperanto language.

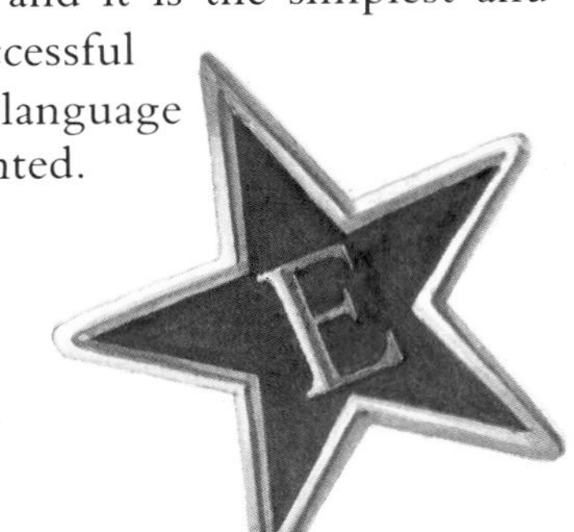

LUMIÈRE, Auguste

French film pioneer 1862-1954

and

LUMIÈRE, Louis

French film pioneer 1864-1948

The Lumière brothers began their career as photographers, taking portraits and wedding-pictures. In the 1890s they began experimenting

Louis Lumière, one of the pioneers of French cinema, photographed in 1937.

with moving pictures, and in 1895 they invented the cinematograph ("movement-painter"). It was a camera able to take moving pictures, and then to project them onto a screen. The Lumières made a two-minute film, *Workers Leaving a Factory*, and showed it at fairs and in music halls. It was a huge success, and they began to make and show films full time. They specialized in two kinds of film: documentaries (scenes from real life, such as firemen fighting a blaze) and comedies, such as *The Hoser Hosed*, in which a boy stands on a hose until the gardener peers down the nozzle to see why the water has stopped flowing.

BAEKELAND, Leo Hendrik

Belgian/US inventor 1863-1944

In the early years of the twentieth century, many items around the home were made from Bakelite. Combs, clock cases, bracelets, telephone receivers and later radio cases were made from this early plastic.

Baekeland studied chemistry in Belgium before emigrating to the USA at the age of 26. He was interested in man-made materials, and in 1904 he discovered that by heating together the resins from formaldehyde and phenol he could make an easily moulded material that would harden as it cooled. It was called Bakelite after him, and its invention marks the beginning of the plastics industry.

WRIGHT, Wilbur

US air pioneer 1867-1912

and

WRIGHT, Orville

US air pioneer 1871-1948

In the 1890s the Wright brothers ran a bicycle shop. But their hobby was designing aircraft. They were determined to be the first people in the world to fly in a powered "heavier-than-air" machine. They studied reports of earlier pioneers, including **Cayley** and **Lilienthal**. Then they designed machines of their own, using bicycle tubes and pipes to build air-frames, and covering them with cloth or paper, to make the fuselage and wings.

In 1903 the brothers made the first-ever powered flight. It lasted for 59 seconds and covered 261 metres. Two years later they were able to stay airborne for over half an hour, and flew 45 kilometres. They patented their flying-machine in 1906, and toured the USA showing people that flying was safe, and fun. In 1909 the US Army began to use planes for reconnaissance (flying over land or sea to see what the enemy was doing). The Wrights founded an aircraft-manufacturing company, and the age of twentieth-century transport had begun.

The Wright brothers Orville (left) and Wilbur (right) in front of one of their early flying-machines.

WRIGHT: Cayley 357 Lilienthal 381

HABER, Fritz

German scientist 1868-1934

Until Haber's time, nitrates (which are essential ingredients of explosives and fertilizers) had to be mined from the ground, and the supply was running out. He discovered a way – now called the "Haber process" – of making nitrates from nitrogen and hydrogen. It is still vital for making artificial fertilizers.

The nitrogen cycle is a natural process, to which humans add artificial nitrates by fertilizing crops. Starved of nitrates, crops are weak and sickly, although too much of the nutrient causes pollution problems when it leaks into rivers and streams.

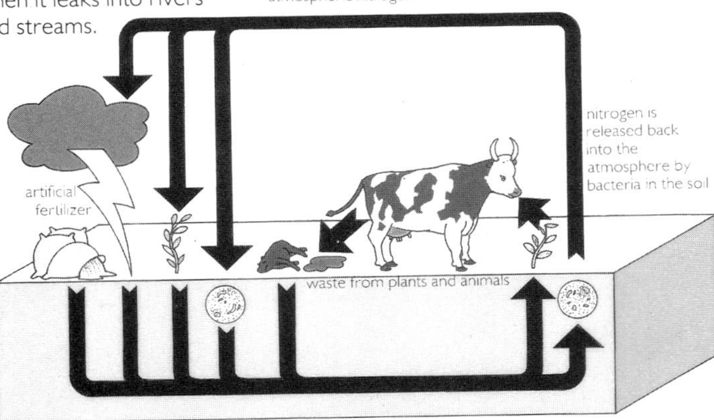

ADLER, Alfred

Austrian psychologist 1870-1937

Alfred Adler.

As a student, Adler was interested in **Freud**'s ideas, and changed from ophthalmology (eye-doctoring) to psychiatry. At first he followed Freud, but in 1911 he began teaching and practising his own ideas. He thought that psychological disturbance, or "neurosis", is often a reaction to shock. If the psychiatrist can discover what the shock was he or she can end the neurosis.

Adler taught that human behaviour is affected by feelings of inferiority and the desire for power. He said that people are of two kinds: those who dominate others and those who are dominated. The domination is usually harmless and unnoticed, but in some people the need to be dominated is extreme, causing mental illness. Adler was describing what became known as the "inferiority complex".

RASPUTIN, Grigori Efimovich

Russian preacher 1871-1916

Rasputin was a peasant with no education, but he discovered that he had a gift for preaching. His words filled people with religious ecstasy, and they did whatever he suggested, almost as if hypnotized. He used this power to make huge sums of money, and also to persuade girls and women to make love with him. He toured Russia, preaching and holding sexual orgies. At first his "converts", as he called them, were ordinary people, then members of the aristocracy, and finally he was discovered by a lady-in-waiting of Alexandra, the Russian tsarina (empress), who took him to court. At that time, the Russian court was fascinated by magic and mysticism, and they soon came to believe that Rasputin had magic powers. The heir to the throne was a haemophiliac (someone whose blood never clots,

Right: A cartoon of Grigori Rasputin, the Russian priest and mystic.

ADLER: Freud 383

who can bleed to death from the slightest cut). Rasputin prayed over him and seemed to help him. From that day on he was the tsarina's favourite, and she did everything he said. He used his power over her for 15 years. It was said that nothing was decided at court unless Rasputin authorized it, and once he ordered the dismissal of a prime minister who argued with him. Not surprisingly, the nobles hated him, and in 1916, after many unsuccessful attempts, they murdered him.

RUSSELL, Bertrand Arthur William

English thinker 1872-1970

Russell worked at Cambridge University. He was particularly interested in "logic": the organizing of complex ideas into short, single steps, each one simple and obvious. He first applied the rules of logic to mathematics, and wrote a book, *Principia Mathematica*, to explain and show his theories. Then he began exploring logic as a possible way in which people build up language, and published books about the thought-processes by which we describe things in words.

Outside his university work, Russell was interested in a huge range of ideas. Many of them went against what most other people thought, and he was often in the news. He was an atheist, and wrote articles to say that God did not exist. He believed that the usual ways of education were wrong, and that children should be free to learn as they chose, guided but not "programmed" by teachers; he and his wife Dora set up an experimental school to test this idea. Above all, he was a pacifist, and went to prison for his belief that war, for any reason and against any enemy, is wrong. He wrote books and made speeches and broadcasts putting this point of view. He was the first president of CND, the British campaign to abolish nuclear weapons.

SANTOS-DUMONT, Alberto

Brazilian air pioneer 1873-1932

Santos-Dumont built and perfected a small, engine-powered airship. In 1901 he won a prize for being the first person to fly from St Cloud to central Paris, once round the Eiffel Tower and back again – all in half an hour. He built himself an airship as small as a private car, which he was able to land and park in an ordinary street. He dreamed of making it the personal transport of the future and used one himself to land at cafés to drink coffee and read the paper, but it never became popular enough to be mass-produced. After further experiments, in 1909 he built a light monoplane – a forerunner of modern light aircraft.

A cartoon of Santos-Dumont, testing his airship built for one person. He flew from a Paris suburb, St Cloud, round the Eiffel Tower, and back.

DE FOREST, Lee

US inventor 1873-1961

De Forest perfected the thermionic valve, which was used to amplify radio signals. This made it possible to transmit radio waves over enormous areas, and without it today's world-wide broadcasting systems would not exist. De Forest was a tireless worker, and took out patents for over 300 new inventions, among them film soundtrack and a way of transmitting photographs by radio waves to produce pictures on television screens.

MARCONI, Guglielmo

Italian inventor 1874-1937

In 1894 Marconi read a newspaper story about the electromagnetic waves whose existence had been described by **Maxwell** and proved by **Hertz** (after whom they were called, in those days, "Hertzian waves"). He was particularly struck to read that the waves travelled through space at the speed of 300,000 kilometres per second, and wondered if they could be used to send messages. (At the time, unless semaphore was used, or two places were connected by telegraph wires, all messages were restricted to the speed at which a messenger could run or ride.)

To make Hertzian waves carry messages, two things were needed: a way to alter them and a way to perceive that alteration (in plain words, a transmitter and a receiver). Marconi began his experiments on a table in his attic. He generated an electric spark at one end of the table, so causing interference with the electromagnetic waves, and tried to "catch" or receive that interference on a metal ring at the other end. After months of trying he succeeded, and in 1895 found that he could transmit the interference all the way across the room, then down through the floors of the house to ring an electric bell (much to the servants' alarm, as this happened in the middle of the night), through the window to a receiving ring in the garden, and finally across fields and woods to a ring on the opposite side of a nearby hill. His brother fired a gun to show that the message had been received.

Once it was clear that the basic principle worked, Marconi had to devise ways of controlling the interference so that he could send precise messages over longer and longer distances. A year later, having had his ideas rejected by the Italian government, he went to London and demonstrated to the officials of the British Post Office that "wireless" messages (literally: messages using no wires) could be sent as far as 300 metres. The Post Office financed his work, and in the next few years he gradually increased the range of his transmissions: first across the Bristol Channel from England to Wales, then across the English Channel from England to France, and finally, in 1901, across the Atlantic from Cornwall in England to Newfoundland in Canada – a distance of almost 5,150 kilometres.

Marconi founded the Marconi Telegraph and Signal Company to perfect "wireless telegraphy", as it was called. His work won him (and Karl Braun) the Nobel physics prize in 1909, and led to today's vast radio-communication systems. Marconi himself moved on to other work. In 1915 he went into politics, and served as a senator in the Italian parliament for 22 years. He represented Italy at the 1919 Peace Conference after the First World War, and in 1929 the Italian dictator **Mussolini** made him a Marchese, or marquis, for his work in science and in politics.

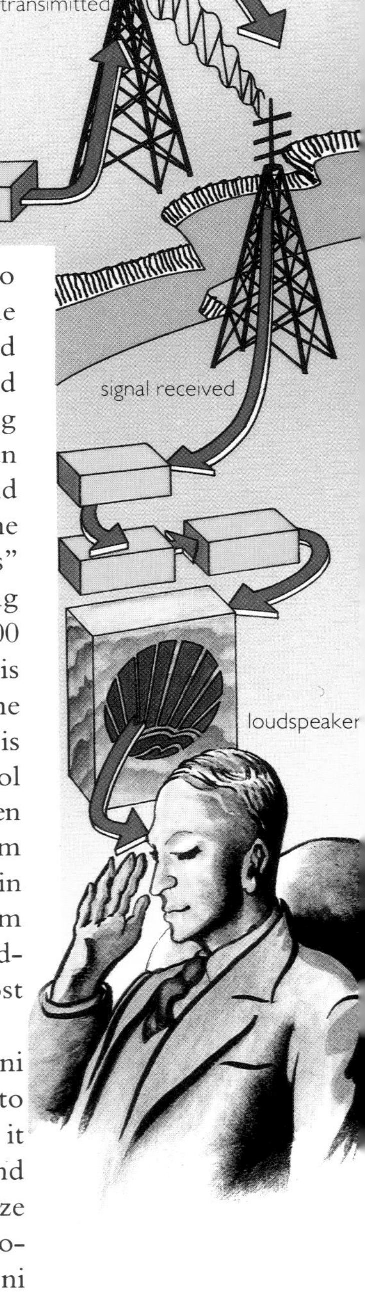

Marconi's experiments with broadcasting were the start of modern electrical communication.

MARCONI: Hertz 142 Maxwell 135 Mussolini 465

Ferdinand Porsche with his son and one of the first sports cars built by the Porsche company.

PORSCHE, Ferdinand

Austrian car designer 1875-1951

Porsche worked for **Daimler**, first in Austria and then in Germany. Inspired by **Hitler**'s vision of a car that ordinary people could afford, he designed the Beetle in 1934 for the Volkswagen company. It was small, beetle-shaped (for low wind resistance), and was the first car to have its engine (in the back) cooled by air, not water. The Beetle was outstandingly successful, and was made in factories all over the world for over 40 years.

Because of Porsche's association with Hitler, he was imprisoned after the Second World War. Later, with his son, he designed the first Porsche sports car, using a rear-mounted, air-cooled Volkswagen engine. Its successors are now among the world's top-selling luxury cars.

JUNG, Carl Gustav

Swiss psychiatrist 1875-1961

Jung began his career as a doctor, and then specialized in mental illness. Like **Freud**, Jung believed that everyone's unconscious mind is a storehouse of memories and feelings, and that these affect our conscious selves and make us the kind of people we are. But he also thought, unlike Freud, that our minds are part of a "collective unconscious": that is, each of us keeps, stored in our unconscious mind, something of the memories and feelings of the whole past human race. This "species memory" affects the way we think and act. Jung also believed that human creativity, resulting in great works of art, poetry and music, arose from the unconscious. He worked with Freud for five years, but in 1912 they disagreed and separated. Each began working on his own theory.

Jung thought that the unconscious mind is built up, as it were, in layers. Psychoanalysis can penetrate the layers one by one, and each layer explains a different part of each person's character. Jung was particularly interested in religious faith and in dreams. In both of them, he thought, the unconscious mind rules the conscious mind, and the "irrational" (that is, any idea or feeling which cannot be proved) is just as important as the "rational".

Right: Carl Jung.

PORSCHE: Daimler 375 Hitler 466 JUNG: Freud 383

CITROËN, André Gustave

French inventor 1878-1935

Citroën was a pioneer car-maker, improving the design of gears, brakes and cooling systems. In the First World War he turned his car-factory over to making guns and tanks, but after the war went back to cars. His ambition was to make a small, light car, cheap enough for anyone to afford but built to last. Although he died before succeeding, it was only a few months after his death that his company produced the first Citroën 2CV, using many of his designs. It has been one of the world's best-selling small cars ever since, for over 50 years.

The Citroën *traction avant* (front-wheel drive).

KEYNES, John Maynard

English economist 1883-1946

Keynes taught economics (the way nations manage money) at the University of Cambridge. Until his time, economists had thought that national finances were a matter of supply and demand. To earn money, you supplied things people needed or demanded; if you failed, you went out of business. Keynes said that this was not the way to solve such problems as mass employment (a new problem at the time, created by the ruin brought by the First World War). He suggested that the government should raise money (if necessary by borrowing) to create new work, for example the building of roads, cities and houses. This work could provide jobs, the jobs would give people money, the people would spend their money buying goods, and still more people would be employed to make those goods. In this way unemployment would be reduced, and the nation's wealth rebuilt. Keynes' theory was the basis for the economic policies of many different governments after the Second World War.

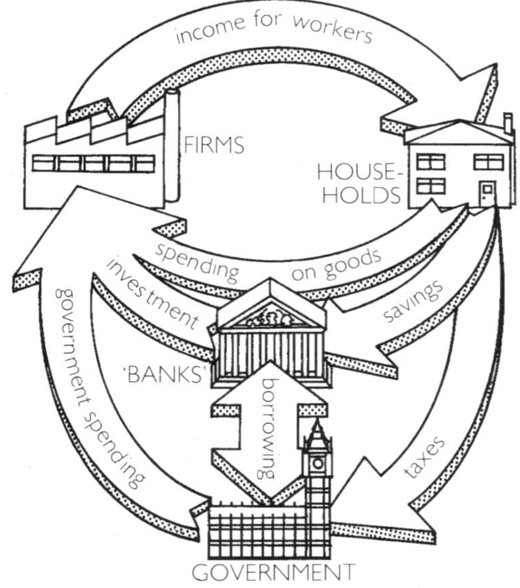

An illustration of the Keynes theory of economics. Keynes believed that governments should borrow money to invest in industry and create jobs. Monetarist thinking, by contrast, is that a government's job is to control inflation (keep prices down) so that people will buy things and more people will be employed in factories and shops.

SUNDBACK, Gideon

Swedish inventor died 1954

Sundback perfected the zip fastener. Zips had been invented by an American, Whitcomb L. Judson, in 1893, but they were unreliable and tended, embarrassingly, to spring apart without warning. Sundback, who had worked for Judson, solved the problem by anchoring the zip's twin rows of teeth to cloth.

STOPES, Marie Carmichael

Scottish scientist/social reformer 1880-1958

Stopes studied science in London and Munich, and in 1904 became the first woman lecturer at Manchester University. Her subject was palaeobotany – the study of fossil plants. She lectured all over the world, at a time when female scientists were still regarded as freaks.

Stopes' first marriage was a disaster. Her husband expected her to give up her career to start a family, which she refused to do, and the marriage ended in divorce. Stopes began working for a better understanding between husbands and wives, and for marriage with women and men as equal partners. She gave lectures, wrote articles and published books on marriage, sex and child-rearing. Her most revolutionary idea, which outraged many people, was that women have a right to enjoy sex without fear of pregnancy, and that birth control is therefore an essential part of a happy marriage. Marie Stopes clinics all over the world still counsel young people on marriage, sex and birth control.

Marie Stopes, whose pioneering work did much to make birth control acceptable.

GODDARD, Robert Hutchings

US inventor 1882-1945

The first rockets used gunpowder, a heavy and unstable fuel. It was fine in fireworks, but useless for larger rockets intended to lift objects or people into space. Goddard invented a new kind of rocket, powered by liquid gas. He hoped that it might be used to launch space vehicles. But the US government ignored his ideas. It was not until after the Second World War, when **von Braun** and his fellow German scientists joined NASA (the US National Aeronautics and Space Administration), that Goddard's rockets were developed – and they are still used today.

Goddard also devised a way of steering rockets in space by changing the direction of the engine jets, and he invented the "multi-stage" rocket, which jettisons each engine-section as its job is done.

GODDARD: von Braun 156

CHANEL, Coco

French fashion designer 1883-1971

Until the First World War women had used corsets to press their bodies into fashionable shapes. Afterwards, they led far more active lives. Chanel designed comfortable clothes for women based on working clothes (sailors' bell bottom trousers, for example, became "yachting pants"). She dominated women's fashions for years. Her flat-chested look, often worn with strings of pearls and with short hair was regarded as the height of elegance. She pioneered braiding on women's suits and sling-back sandals. In 1939 she closed her salon, and spent the next 25 years working in Hollywood films. She re-opened her salon in 1954 and worked on until she died.

Left: Coco Chanel, shown with some of her designs from the 1930s.

BIRDSEYE, Clarence

US inventor 1886-1956

Birdseye devised a way of preserving food by fast-freezing it. "Birdseye" frozen foods were first sold in Massachusetts, USA, and are now common in shops and supermarkets throughout the world.

One of the first packs of frozen peas.

BAIRD, John Logie

Scottish inventor 1888-1946

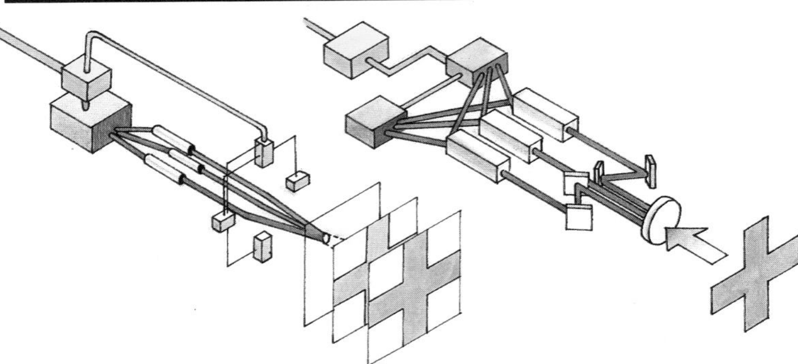

How a colour television works. The picture you see is in fact three superimposed images – red, green and blue. Inside the camera, mirrors separate the three images, which are then transmitted to the receiver. Three electron beams activate red, green and blue phosphors (things which emit light) in the screen, to give a full-colour picture.

Baird spent his early life trying to earn money from inventions like inflatable soles for shoes (which burst). In the 1920s he had the idea of sending pictures, as well as sounds, by radio waves (see **Marconi**). He rigged up a makeshift apparatus using radio valves, cardboard tubes, a tea-chest and some knitting needles. It worked. He demonstrated black-and-white television in public in 1926, and two years later he was able to transmit in colour. But in 1937, when the BBC was choosing a system for TV broadcasting, Baird's was rejected in favour of an American system similar to the one **Zworykin** had devised – and Baird gave up his experiments. During the Second World War he worked on radar with **Watson-Watt**, and on fibre-optics (passing light down wires).

BAIRD: Marconi 388 Watson-Watt 393 Zworykin 393

Igor Sikorsky, at the controls of the first flight of the helicopter, Sikorsky VS-300, on 14 September 1939.

SIKORSKI, Igor

Russian/US inventor 1889-1972

Sikorski saw **Leonardo da Vinci**'s designs for an imaginary flying machine, an "ornithopter", and wondered if he could turn them into a practical machine. He had no trouble devising a way of keeping the machine in the air (with a pair of rotor-blades circling above the roof). But it was not until he invented the correct shape of tail, with a smaller rotor to prevent the whole machine whirling round, that the new flying-machine was perfected. Sikorski called it the helicopter, and it is now, after the passenger jet, the world's commonest flying-machine.

ZWORYKIN, Vladimir Kosma

Russian/US inventor 1889-1982

Zworykin studied physics in Russia, and was interested in the properties of cathode-ray tubes (see **Thomson**). In 1917, at the time of the Russian Revolution, he emigrated to the USA and went to work for the Radio Corporation of America. He experimented with ways of transmitting pictures by radio waves, using cathode-ray tubes to receive them. In 1923 he demonstrated a television system at almost the same time as **Baird** in Britain. Although Baird's system actually came first, it was not based on electronics like Zworykin's, and was therefore harder to develop. The Zworykin method was the basis for all later television systems.

WATSON-WATT, Robert

Scottish scientist 1892-1973

Watson-Watt invented radar (RAdio Detecting And Ranging). A sound is transmitted, bounces off objects and returns to a receiver. Watson-Watt's equipment uses the sound to build up a picture of what lies around the transmitting vessel, and its accuracy is not hampered by fog or darkness. Watson-Watt persuaded the British government that his radar could be used to detect enemy aircraft before they launched an attack. It was crucial for revealing the position of aircraft during the Second World War, and is now standard navigational equipment throughout the world. It is also used for weather forecasting.

Right: Radar works when a radio beam is pulsed from a dish, either on the ground or fitted into a plane, ship or other craft. The signals are reflected from objects such as aircraft. The range of the object can be calculated from the time it takes for the signal to bounce back to the reflecting dish.

SIKORSKI: Leonardo da Vinci 11 ZWORYKIN: Baird 392 Thomson J J 141

CAROTHERS, Wallace Hume

US scientist 1896-1937

Carothers discovered how to make nylon – a plastic material which can be rolled into large sheets or drawn out into long threads. It is immensely strong, and has the property of "shape memory": however you bend or twist it, it springs back to its original shape. The first nylon objects were toothbrush bristles. But Carother's employer, the Du Pont company, began to make nylon stockings in 1936, and by 1939 were selling over 60 million pairs each year. Nylon is nowadays used to make articles of every imaginable kind, from anoraks to the "skin" of planes, from coal-scuttles to fishing-lines.

Right: The strength and qualities of Nylon mean it has countless uses – from stockings the girl is wearing to the tyre she is sitting on.

BIRO, Laszlo

Hungarian inventor 1900-85

Biro invented the ball-point pen. It uses printer's ink, which dries instantly, unlike the water-based ink used by dip-pens and fountain pens. Biro devised the ball-mechanism which controls the ink-flow. His pens were first used by aircraft-navigators during the Second World War, because (unlike ordinary pens) they did not leak at high altitude.

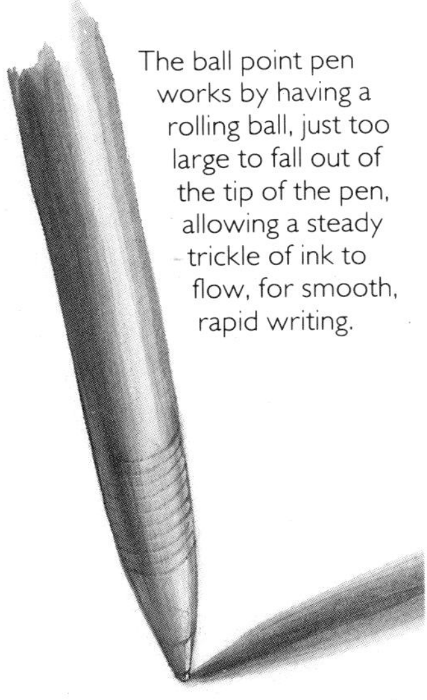

The ball point pen works by having a rolling ball, just too large to fall out of the tip of the pen, allowing a steady trickle of ink to flow, for smooth, rapid writing.

BOOTH, Hubert

US inventor early 20th century

Booth began his career designing fairground rides, especially the enormous wheels known as "Ferris wheels". He was also interested in carpet-sweeping machines. There were primitive machines available, but they all used bellows worked by foot or hand, and scattered as much dust as they collected. Booth planned to use electric suction-power instead. In 1901 he patented an office-cleaning machine – a dust-tank pulled by two horses. It stopped in the street outside the building, and an enormous hosepipe was passed through the office window. Then the motor was started and the dust was sucked out. Unfortunately the motor roared and the vacuum-pump whined; passers-by were terrified and the horses bolted, causing accidents. Booth scaled down his invention to something the size of a desk or a chest-of-drawers, and advertised it for use in houses. At first it was awkward to manoeuvre through doorways and hard to use – and would sometimes blow instead of suck, with alarming results. But Booth gradually improved the

It's easy to see why Booth's first vacuum cleaner was nicknamed the "noisy serpent".

design, and his machine is the ancestor of every vacuum cleaner in use today.

SARTRE, Jean-Paul

French thinker and writer 1905-80

Up to and during the Second World War Sartre was a schoolteacher; during the war he worked for the French Resistance against the Nazis; afterwards he made his living as a writer and as co-editor of the French magazine *Modern Times*. His best-remembered teaching is about the philosopy of Existentialism, an idea he developed with his long-time lover, the writer Simone de Beauvoir. According to Sartre, there is no such thing as an inherited character or personality which determines our lives and how we behave. We are nothing but a reflection of the attitudes and beliefs of the world around us . We have no real identity, but exist in a state of Nothingness, like particles in a vacuum. We can escape from this by choosing the life we want to lead or the kind of people we want to be. That choice carries us from Nothingness to Being, and means that everyone is entirely responsible for his or her actions. This teaching was especially powerful during the war, when people in France had to choose whether to collaborate with the Nazis or oppose them.

Existentialism – which Sartre wrote about in a massive book, *Being and Nothingness* – has affected many later thinkers and writers. Sartre's own novels and plays all deal with it.

During the Second World War, Jean-Paul Sartre and other intellectuals, including his companion Simone de Beauvoir, would meet in the cafes and bars of Paris to discuss politics and ideas.

CARLSON, Chester

US inventor 1906-68

Carlson worked in the patent office of the **Bell** Telephone Company in New York. The office clerks wrote out applications for new patents, and because each application was a legal document, it could have no mistakes. Every time a mistake was made, the whole document had to be retyped. Carlson set out to invent a machine which would make copies, as exact as photos but without the wait while photos were developed and printed. In 1938 he succeeded. His "dry photocopier" was able to produce instant photographic copies on ordinary paper – and one of the first documents it copied was Carlson's application for a patent.

CARLSON: Bell 379

Right: Honda's 1990 model – the VFR 750F.

GOLDMARK, Peter Carl

Hungarian/US inventor and businessman 1906-77

Goldmark studied physics in Vienna, and in 1926 made the first television receiver ever seen in the city. In the 1930s he emigrated to the USA, where he took a job in the laboratories of CBS (the Columbia Broadcasting System). He worked there for 40 years, and invented no fewer than 160 new communications devices, ranging from circuits and filters to the first-ever colour-television system. His best-known invention was the LP (long-playing), "microgroove" gramophone record.

The Mini was first produced in 1959, and was an immediate success. Issigonis designed the car to use very little petrol, with a space-saving engine layout (sideways on) which has since been copied worldwide.

ISSIGONIS, Alec Arnold

Greek/British car designer 1906-88

Issigonis began work with a friend, designing racing cars. When he was 30 he joined Morris Motors. He went on to design some of the best-known Morris cars, such as the Minor of 1948. But he is most famous for the Mini, the best-selling British car ever made. "Mini" became a new word in the English language.

HONDA, Soichiro

Japanese businessman born 1906

Honda founded the motorcycle company that bears his name. His first machines were reconditioned army vehicles from the Second World War. He went on to build up the biggest motorcycle businesses ever known, selling elegant, reliable bikes to people all over the world who had previously thought of motorcycles as noisy machines only for enthusiasts. Honda then turned to cars, and his company is now one of Japan's largest manufacturers.

WHITTLE, Frank

English inventor born 1907

Whittle was an officer cadet in the British Royal Air Force when he had the idea for the jet engine: a light gas turbine which would work more efficiently and at greater speeds than the piston engine which drove the propellers in planes built up till then. He worked on his idea for years in his spare time; it was not till the Second World War that the government gave him money to develop it. Jet engines made possible both the supersonic fighter-planes and the enormous passenger planes in use today.

LAND, Edwin Herbert

US inventor born 1909

Land experimented with the effects of light on glass. He invented a thin coating for glass that would polarize (scatter) light instead of focusing it in lenses. Polaroid glass cuts down glare and is often used in sunglasses, car and plane windows, and anywhere else where unscattered light might harm the eyes. During the Second World War, Land turned to photography, trying to discover a way of taking pictures on film which could be developed instantly, without the need for darkrooms, developing tanks and jars of chemicals. In 1947 he patented the Polaroid camera, which uses specially coated film to give finished pictures almost as soon as they are taken.

The aircushioned hovercraft rides across the surface of water or land, yet it is regarded as an aircraft, which means that the captain must hold a pilot's licence. Cross-Channel hovercraft like this one can carry 400 passengers and up to 50 cars. Similar vehicles can be used in flat areas where no roads exist – such as desert land or mud-flats.

COCKERELL, Christopher

English inventor born 1910

Cockerell wanted to invent a boat which would slide over the surface of water, rather than cutting its way through the waves. It would be more stable, safer and quicker than conventional boats. In his trial models, Cockerell used a vacuum-cleaner mechanism to blow instead of suck, and experimented with different-sized holes in tin cans to see how many holes, and of what size, were needed to create the best "aircushion" to lift the can. When his experiments were complete, he built a vehicle which would ride on an aircushion over water, land or any other surface – the hovercraft.

PLUNKETT, Roy Joseph

US scientist born 1910

Plunkett invented teflon, a waxy-textured plastic with a low coefficient of friction (which means that few things stick to it or erode it). It is also unaffected by heat or cold, except at extreme temperatures. It is used in all kinds of industries, and is painted on space-vehicles to protect them from radiation. It also appears in most people's homes as the "non-stick" coating on pots and pans.

FRIEDAN, Betty

US thinker and writer born 1921

Friedan was a leader of the "women's movement", first in the USA and then throughout the world. She said that, for thousands of years, women had accepted the roles in life invented for them by men, and that it was time for women to understand and fulfil their own needs, to be individuals in the same way that men were. In her book *The Feminine Mystique*, published in 1963, Friedan urged women to break free, to go out into society and live on equal terms with men. In 1981 she wrote another book, *The Second Stage*, in which she looked back on how the feminist movement has changed society and women's lives. She reminded women of their unique, feminine qualities, and said that women and men, instead of trying to outdo one another, should co-operate, using their individual skills and qualities to make the best possible life for everyone.

Right: The work of Betty Friedan (right) has spurred many people into action for equality for women and men.

GLOSSARY

Artificial Not natural; made by human beings.

Ballast Heavy material (such as gravel or logs) put in a ship to keep it stable in the water.

Baptize Sprinkling someone with water, or dipping them in water, to make them a member of the Christian Church.

Bifocal lenses Spectacle lenses divided into two parts, each helping eyesight in a different way.

Capitalism A business system where people lend money to businesses to help their work, and then take a share of any profits.

Censorship Deciding for other people what they should see, hear, or think.

Characteristic Something that gives people or things their "character". Tallness, for example, is a characteristic of skyscrapers; jumpiness is a characteristic of timid people.

Civil engineer Someone who designs or builds roads, bridges, tunnels and other large "works".

Dynamics (in music) Loudness or softness.

Electrical conductance (in science) The ability of a substance to channel electric current. Metal wire is a good conductor; a wooden plank is a bad conductor.

Equilateral triangle A triangle in which all three sides are the same length.

Faith belief in something which cannot be proved, such as the existence of God or the gods.

Feminist Someone who believes that women should work for absolute equality with men.

Hydrofoil A boat with a V-shaped hull, which rises from the water as it travels at speed, "planing" (skimming the surface) instead of cutting through the water.

Inauguration (in US politics) The ceremony in which the new President swears to be loyal and true to the country.

Investigation A process of step-by-step research.

Literature Written poems, plays, stories and other material (such as history or biography).

Messiah Hebrew word meaning saviour-king. Jews believed that he would come at the end of time to save the world. Christians believe that Jesus is the Messiah.

Microfiche A small sheet of plastic with minute printing on it. To read a microfiche, you put it in a machine which magnifies it on a screen. Storing information on a mircofiche takes up a fraction of the space an ordinary book would require.

Miracle An event or happening which cannot be explained by the ordinary laws of nature. Jesus performed miracles in the Bible story when he healed blind people by touching their eyes, and walked on water.

Missionary Someone who goes to persuade strangers (often in other countries) to accept his or her religion.

Monastery A place where religious people live, making the worship of God or the gods their main task in life.

Monks and nuns Monks (men) and nuns (women) give their lives to God or the gods. Although many do ordinary jobs (such as teaching or nursing), they also spend much time praying and thinking about religion, and may live in monasteries (for monks) or nunneries (for nuns).

Nervous breakdown A mental illness where a person is unable to cope with the strain of life.

Pacifist Someone who believes that war, for any reason, is wrong.

Patent When you invent something or have an idea, you can patent it: that is you tell the patent authorities who then protect your discovery. They put information about it on file, and the discovery is your property. No one can use it or benefit from it without your permission.

Persecute To treat someone cruelly because you dislike them or disagree with their beliefs.

Philosophy Thinking about the nature and purpose of human beings, and the meaning of life: the study of ideas, and of how we think about them.

Politics The task of managing countries or (in "local politics") towns, villages and counties. Governments are groups of politicians who run a country.

Proletariat The workers, either in factories and on farms.

Prototype The first version of a new machine or idea, made to be tested and, if necessary, improved.

Psychiatry A branch of healing concerned with mental disorder.

Psychoanalysis A way of finding out (mainly by asking the right questions) what lies in someone's subconscious mind, and then using that information to help the person.

Psychologist Someone who studies behaviour: what we do and why we do it.

Qwerty keyboard The keyboard of an English-language typewriter. It is so-called because the keys on the keys on the top line of letters begin QWERTY.

Ritual A set of actions or words which are repeated time and time again in the same way (for example in religious worship).

Sermon A public talk about religion or morals, usually by a priest in church, mosque or other holy building.

Therapist A person skilled in a type of healing. A speech therapist, for example, works to help people with speech problems.

Tradition An idea or custom which has been handed down to us by our parents, grandparents and the generations before them.

Wind tunnel A tunnel built for testing how wind-power affects vehicles. The vehicle (or a model) is fastened in place, a fan at one end of the tunnel blows wind along at fixed rates, and the effects are measured and photographed.

SECTION 6

LEADERS

Rulers,
Revolutionaries,
Politicians

INTRODUCTION TO LEADERS

If you lived alone on a desert island, you would need no leader: you could organize your life to suit yourself. Leaders are only really useful to communities (large groups of people). Leaders decide what should happen, and how it should be done. They make laws and see that everyone in the community obeys them. They talk with leaders of other states, making agreements for such things as trade and friendship. Their skills are in politics (running state affairs), and decision-making.

Different communities have different kinds of leaders. The decision-makers in some societies are elders (senior people whose experience helps them to understand life's problems. In certain countries the elders are also spiritual leaders. In wartime, elders either lead the fighting themselves – some people included here were still commanding soldiers when they were over 60 – or choose younger people to fight for them.

In other societies small groups take power, and rule. This system is known as oligarchy ("rule by the few"). The rulers' power may be based on wealth or on political experience, or, for a time, on violent protest – as in a revolution. If military officers run an oligarchy, the state is ruled by "martial law".

Often, a single person rules. He or she may be a dictator ruling by force, or a monarch: a member of a family in which power passes by inheritance, from one generation to the next. Some people believe their emperors, kings and queens to be superhuman, almost gods – and many leaders in history have shared this opinion, with disastrous results.

In other states, people change their leaders every few years. Those who want power explain how they mean to rule, and the people vote. Whichever group wins most votes will rule until the electors choose another. This system is called "democracy".

The leaders in this book are as wise, foolish, honest or crooked as anyone else. Some improved the lives of the people they ruled, others made them worse. They were conquerors, law-givers, protectors and reformers. But however the different leaders came to office, and however well or badly they used their power, they are among the most influential individuals in history. They made society what it is today.

CHEOPS (Khufu)

Egyptian pharaoh 26th century BC

Cheops was one of the pharaohs, or kings, of ancient Egypt. Little is known about him except for his one surviving monument, the Great Pyramid at Giza in Egypt. It was built not just as a tomb for his body but as a palace for his spirit in the life after death. At the time the Great Pyramid was built, it was the largest human structure ever made on Earth: a hill 150 metres high, faced with smooth stone blocks the size of carts.

About 2,000 years after Cheops' time, the Greeks listed his pyramid as one of the Seven Wonders of the world. It is the only one of the Wonders that survives.

Cheops' Great Pyramid. The area it covers would give ample parking space for nine jumbo jets.

SARGON I

(ruled c 2310-2279 BC)

Sumerian king 2334-2279 BC

Legend says that when Sargon was born, his mother disowned him. She put him in a basket and let it float away on the river Euphrates. Sargon was rescued by a gardener, and later entered the king's service as a cup-bearer. When he was in his mid-20s he took a group of followers and founded a new city at Akkad in ancient Babylonia. In the next few years he conquered and ruled a huge arch of land extending from the fertile Mediterranean to the Persian Gulf, the first empire ever known.

Sargon's dynasty continued for 200 years after his death. Then, legend says, his descendant Naram-Sin offended the gods by claiming that he should be addressed and treated as divine. Invaders destroyed his kingdom and pulled down Akkad. Whatever the truth of this legend, the city of Akkad has vanished: no one knows exactly where it was.

ABRAHAM

Aramean leader 22nd century BC

Historians believe that the Aramean people migrated, in prehistoric times, from Mesopotamia (in south-west

Abraham was prepared to obey God and to sacrifice his son, Issac. Convinced of Abraham's faith and obedience, God provided him with a ram to kill instead.

The remains of Ur-Nammu's ziggurat which dominated the whole of the city of Ur. At the top was a temple dedicated to the moon-god, Nanna.

The Code of Hammurabi is engraved in over 3,600 lines of tiny cuneiform writing around the pillar. The carving at the top is of Hammurabi (left), receiving the symbols of justice from the Babylonian sun-god.

Asia) to the eastern shores of the Mediterranean Sea. The book of Genesis in the Bible says that their leader was Abraham. He led his people from the city of Ur, first to Egypt, and then to Canaan on the Mediterranean coast, where they settled.

In the Genesis story, Abraham had two sons, each of whom grew up to found a vast people. The first was Ishmael, Abraham's son by the Egyptian servant Hagar. When Sarah, Abraham's wife, discovered that Hagar was pregnant, she banished her. God's angels led Hagar to Egypt, where Ishmael was born. Ishmael grew up, married and had 12 sons, who travelled south and settled in east Africa and Arabia. Through them, legend says, Ishmael was the founder of the Arab nation.

Abraham's second son, according to Genesis, was Isaac, born miraculously when his parents were over 90 years old. When Isaac was 12, God tested Abraham's obedience by ordering him to sacrifice the child. Abraham was about to lift the knife when an angel appeared and gave him a ram to kill instead of the boy. After that, God made a "covenant" (an agreement) with Abraham, promising that his descendants would be as countless as the sand on the seashore or the stars in the sky. So, through Isaac, according to legend, Abraham was the ancestor of the Jewish nation.

UR-NAMMU

(took power c 2113 BC)

Sumerian king 22nd century BC

Ur-Nammu ruled the fertile land between the rivers Tigris and Euphrates (the southern part of present-day Iraq). Like **Cheops** in Egypt, he is remembered mainly for a building: the ziggurat or "mountain of God" constructed in his capital city, Ur. The ziggurat was improved and embellished by many later rulers, including **Nebuchadnezzar**. Its remains are among the best-preserved of all temples dedicated to Mesopotamia's ancient gods.

HAMMURABI

(ruled 1792-1750 BC)

Babylonian king died 1750 BC

The conqueror Hammurabi was known for the savagery of his soldiers and the huge walls he built to keep out enemies. He is also remembered for the "code of Hammurabi", a list of 282 laws inscribed on stone pillars and set up throughout his kingdom. One pillar has survived intact, and gives a clear idea of the way Hammurabi governed his people. Many of the laws concern marriage, inheritance and property – and give women equal rights with men, one of the first times in history this is known to have happened. Others establish a strict class-system, carefully setting out the privileges and duties of each group of citizens. Further laws lay down punishments for every kind of crime, from breaking down a neighbour's fence to murder.

UR-NAMMU: Cheops 404 Nebuchadnezzar 410

Of the few surviving images of Hatshepsut, most show her wearing a false beard – as all pharoahs did (female and male), to show authority.

HATSHEPSUT

Egyptian queen and pharaoh c 1540-1481 BC

Hatshepsut was married to her half-brother, the pharaoh Tutmose (Thothmes) II, and after his death acted as regent for her 6-year-old stepson Tutmose III. Unlike male pharaohs of the time, she was peaceful and gentle. Instead of making war on Egypt's neighbours, she arranged peace treaties and made trading agreements. She also sent explorers south, by land into Africa and by sea to southern Arabia and even, some say, as far as India.

When Hatshepsut died, Tutmose III (by now grown-up) accused her of weakness, saying that although her new trade-routes had made the country wealthy, her dislike of war had also encouraged foreigners to think Egypt easy prey. He declared Hatshepsut a non-person, and ordered his soldiers to smash down her statues and scratch out her name from as many documents and wall-inscriptions as could be found.

The beautiful Nefertiti with the bearded pharoah Akhenaton. He spent much time worshipping the sun-god Aten, neglecting the practical duties of a ruler.

AKHENATON (Amenhotep IV)

(ruled 1379-62 BC)

Egyptian pharaoh 14th century BC

Unlike other ancient Egyptians, who worshipped over 700 different gods, the pharaoh Amenhotep IV believed that there was only one god, powerful but gentle, the creator of the human race. God's symbol was the sun, and just as the sun rose unfailingly each day, so God's goodness was constantly renewed.

The pharaoh built temples and appointed priests to worship the one God, and changed his own name from Amenhotep to Akhenaton ("Glory of the Sun"). His ideas led to civil war between the supporters of the old gods and the new, and in the end Akhenaton was overthrown, his son-in-law Tutankhamen became pharaoh, and the sun-religion was abolished.

The tomb of Akhenaton's chief wife Nefertiti (died c 1346 BC) is one of the most magnificent archaeological discoveries ever made in Egypt. Unlike most Egyptian tombs, which are filled with paintings of war, and tributes and offerings to the grim gods of the Underworld, Nefertiti's tomb is decorated with scenes of happy family life: fishing, children playing, a husband and wife smiling at each other, people gathering flowers and picnicking. A gold-covered statue of her head and shoulders also survives, showing her not as a haughty queen but as a young and beautiful woman.

MOSES (Moshe)

Jewish leader c 14th century BC

The Bible says that the pharaoh of Egypt ordered all new-born Hebrew (Jewish) sons to be killed. Moses' mother wanted to spare him, and floated him in a basket down the river Nile. He was rescued by a princess and brought up in the Egyptian royal household.

When Moses was a grown man, he killed an Egyptian who was ill-treating a Jewish slave, and fled into exile. In the desert, he said, God spoke from a burning bush and told him to lead his people out of Egypt to the Promised Land. This land was

Canaan, now part of modern Israel, the homeland God had promised to **Abraham** generations before.

At first the Egyptian pharaoh, **Rameses II**, refused to let Moses' people go. He relented only when, as Moses predicted, God sent ten plagues to torment the people. Even then, when the Jews began their march, Rameses sent his soldiers to kill them. The book of Exodus says that God saved the Jews by a miracle – he parted the Red Sea to let them pass, and then closed it over the heads of the pursuing Egyptians – and that he guided them through the desert on the other side. Moses led the people as far as the borders of the Promised Land, where he died at the age of 120.

Moses spent much time giving his people laws and instructions. These laws included the Ten Commandments, which he said God dictated to him on the peak of Mount Sinai, and concerned daily life. Others gave instructions on how to build a shrine for God and worship him.

Later religious teachers added to Moses' words, and the resulting books (Genesis, Exodus, Leviticus, Numbers, Deuteronomy – known together as the "Pentateuch") have been the basis of the Jewish faith and way of life, and of religions based on them (such as Christianity) ever since.

Moses, alone on Mount Sinai, receives the law from God. The Ten Commandments are engraved on two stone tablets.

RAMESES II (Ramses II)

(ruled 1304-1237)

Egyptian pharaoh c 1330-1237 BC

In his youth Rameses II was a warrior. He led an Egyptian army across what are today Sinai, Israel, Lebanon and Syria, to challenge the powerful Hittite empire. The Hittites ambushed the Egyptians, and only an act of great personal bravery by Rameses, holding off the enemy until reinforcements arrived, saved his army from disaster. Although neither side won, Rameses built many magnificent monuments in Egypt to celebrate his "triumph". Included among these were four statues, over 20 metres high, at Abu Simbel, which were moved to higher ground in the 1960s, when the Aswan Dam was built to control the river Nile.

Rameses ruled Egypt for 66 years, until he was well over 90. He outlived many of his own children, and was on the throne for so long that most of his subjects could not remember a time before him. For centuries after his death, the word Rameses meant the same as "king".

Rameses II, probably the longest-ruling pharaoh.

MOSES: Abraham 404 Rameses II 407

DAVID

(ruled c 1000-969 BC)

King of Israel died 969 BC

During a war between Israelites and Philistines, David won the favour of Saul, king of Israel, by killing the gigantic Philistine Goliath. Saul made David his servant. But when David became a court favourite, Saul began to fear that the people would one day make him king instead of Saul's son Jonathan. He turned against David and tried to kill him. David lived in hiding in the mountains until both Saul and Jonathan died in battle against the Philistines. After that, the people crowned him king.

David had many successes in battles against Israel's enemies. But in private he was arrogant and self-indulgent. He fell in love with a woman called Bathsheba, and sent her husband Uriah to fight in the front line against the enemy. Uriah was killed, David married Bathsheba, and many of his people never forgave him. When David and Bathsheba's son Absalom was grown-up, the people stirred him to rebel against his father. The rebellion was defeated and Absalom was killed, leaving David heartbroken.

David's relaxation was music. He composed songs and poems of all kinds: hymns in praise of God, marches to be sung during royal processions, love-songs and a magnificent lament for the deaths of Saul and Jonathan. Many of the Psalms in the Bible's Old Testament are said to be his work.

Solomon's Temple in Jerusalem was destroyed and another one built on the same site by King Herod. The only part of his temple that remains is a wall, called the Wailing Wall, which is held sacred by Jews as a place of prayer and pilgrimage.

SOLOMON (Shlomoh)

(ruled c 969-922 BC)

King of Israel died 922 BC

Solomon was the son of **David** and Bathsheba, and inherited his father's throne. Compared to other warrior-princes of the time, he was a peaceful king, using his large army mainly to patrol Israel's borders, to gather taxes and to keep the trade-routes open.

Solomon's merchants travelled to what were then thought to be the ends of the world: the Atlantic Ocean in the west and the Indian Ocean in the south. These merchants imported metal ore, and exported finished metal goods. They also brought back, so the Bible says, such fabulous items from foreign lands as ivory, apes and peacocks, which made Solomon's court one of the wonders of the age.

Solomon kept much wealth for his

SOLOMON: David 408

own personal use. He built a magnificent royal palace, and a harem for his 700 wives, 300 concubines (royal mistresses) and their slaves and guards. The palace stables held 12,000 horses. He also beautified Jerusalem, his capital city, giving it paved streets, stone buildings, aqueducts and water-cisterns. Apart from his palace, the main building in the city was Solomon's Temple, built to honour God. It was the richest and most powerful shrine of the Jewish religion, a centre of worship to rival those of any other ancient gods.

In Solomon's lifetime, many people thought him not only the richest person in the world, but also the wisest. After his death, lists were compiled of sayings he was supposed to have made: they include the books of Proverbs and Ecclesiastes in the Bible. He is also thought to have written, or ordered to be written, the Song of Solomon, a love-poem to God's beloved city (Jerusalem) and church (the Temple).

SARGON II

(ruled 721-705 BC)

Assyrian king died 705 BC

Historians think that Sargon II snatched power after a military coup, and deliberately changed his name to Sargon ("true king") so that people would compare him with the legendary **Sargon I**. A tireless warrior, he spent no more than a few months of his 17-year reign in his capital city, Nineveh. His conquests included much of what are now Iraq, Syria, Lebanon, Israel, Jordan and northern Egypt.

A restored wall of Nineveh (modern Kuyunjok in Iraq). Its mud bricks crumbled long ago, but when it was rebuilt by Assurbanipal, it was said to be the most beautiful city in the ancient world.

ASSURBANIPAL (Asshurbanapli)

(ruled 668-627 BC)

Assyrian king died 626 BC

Assurbanipal was the last king of the empire amassed by **Sargon I** 50 years before. Soon after his death the Medes conquered his people, only to be themselves absorbed into the vast Persian empire of **Cyrus the Great**.

Assurbanipal is remembered mainly for his capital city, Nineveh. He made it one of the most sumptuous cities in the ancient world, with wide, paved streets, walls of brick faced with magnificent carvings, and temples, palaces and public buildings in the grandest style.

Under Assurbanipal, Nineveh became a centre for learning and culture, welcoming scholars and thinkers from Greece, Persia and Egypt. To preserve their thoughts, the king ordered that they should be set down in writing. In those days, the writing was "cuneiform" - wedge-shaped signs cut into clay tablets which were then baked hard in ovens. Some of these clay tablets have lasted 2,600 years.

The rebuilding of Nineveh is recorded on a tablet of baked clay. Assurbanipal's library was filled with such tablets, giving details of science, language, and history of the time. The wedge-shaped signs are still as readable as when they were first cut.

SARGON II: Sargon I 404 ASSURBANIPAL: Cyrus the Great 411 Sargon I 404

NEBUCHADNEZZAR II (Nebuchadrezzar)

(ruled 605-562 BC)

Babylonian king c 630-562 BC

Nebuchadnezzar built up his empire by conquest. He swept west to the Mediterranean, north into the hills of what is now Turkey, and south to the Persian Gulf and the Red Sea. He defeated the Egyptian army in these areas, but thought Egypt itself too far away to invade. Later, he raided Jerusalem, and took almost the whole Jewish nation back to Babylon as slaves. The Bible claims that God punished Nebuchadnezzar for this by driving him mad, so that the king ended up crouched on all fours like a beast in the fields, eating grass.

Nebuchadnezzar spent a fortune on fortifications, roads, bridges and other buildings in Babylon. Of the few which still survive, the most magnificent is the Ishtar Gate, ornamented with blue-glazed bricks and with 575 figures of animals picked out in yellow and white.

An artist's idea of what the Hanging Gardens may have been like. Irrigation was done by slaves, hauling water in a bucket-chain from the river outside the city walls.

His most sumptuous creation, the Hanging Gardens of Babylon, has been famous ever since as one of the Seven Wonders of the World. (See **Cheops**.) The story is that he married a princess from the north, and that she pined in flat Babylon for the green, flower-covered hills of her mountain home. Nebuchadnezzar ordered gardens to be created for her, built on a ziggurat – a series of terraces like an enormous flight of steps. The Gardens lasted for 300 years, until Babylon itself was destroyed.

SOLON

Athenian politician 6th century BC

Solon served as an *archon* or public official, and standardized Athenian weights, measures and money-values. He also rewrote the city constitution (its system of laws). One important change was to abolish an

The Ishtar Gate stood at the main approach to Babylon, the capital of Nebuchadnezzar.

NEBUCHADNEZZAR: Cheops 404

old law which said that anyone who failed to pay back a loan should be sold into slavery. Another was to reorganize the citizens into four groups, or "classes", each with privileges and responsibilities.

Solon's reforms, which he wrote in verse, were the basis for the Athenian system of voting and government called *demokratia* ("rule by the consent of all citizens"). For this reason, Solon is sometimes nicknamed the "father of democracy".

CYRUS THE GREAT (Kurush)

(ruled 539-529 BC)

Persian king c 580-529 BC

Cyrus ("shepherd") was the grandson of Astyages, king of Media (a mountainous kingdom in what is now northern Iran). In 550 BC he dethroned his grandfather, made himself king and plundered the glittering royal capital Ekbatana. In 547 BC his armies conquered the neighbouring state of Lydia, and in 539 BC he captured Babylon, heart of the Babylonian empire.

By then, Cyrus controlled all the land from the Caspian Sea in the north to Egypt in the south, from the Hellespont (the narrow sea channel between Greece and Turkey, now called the Dardanelles) in the west to India in the east. He had won power not by force but by strategy. For example, his soldiers were armed with longbows, able to shoot further and more accurately than the shorter bows of their adversaries, and he often attacked in winter, when traditionally armies disbanded and the soldiers went back to tend their farms.

Cyrus ruled by a mixture of strict laws against which there was no appeal, ruthless cruelty to anyone who broke them, and religious tolerance - letting people keep their own native gods and customs. Once his system of administration had been set up, he travelled the length and breadth of his vast empire, listening to grievances, punishing wrongdoers and rewarding faithful service. On one of these journeys, in 529 BC, he tried to win a tribe of nomads to his empire by marrying their queen, but the tribesmen rioted and killed him.

Cyrus is less well-remembered in modern times than his successors Darius and **Xerxes**, who attacked the Greeks. But his conquests created the Persian Empire, the largest and most powerful known in the world until then. He also founded a glittering new capital city, Persepolis.

The tomb of King Cyrus was built in the desert at Pasargadae in northern Persia (Iran).

CYRUS: Xerxes 412

XERXES (Khshayarsha)

(ruled 486-465 BC)

Persian king c 510-465 BC

Xerxes ("king of kings") was heir to the Persian Empire created 50 years before by **Cyrus the Great**. His father, Darius (Darayvaush), had added Egypt to the empire, but when he tried to conquer Greece his army was defeated at the battle of Marathon in 490 BC. As soon as Xerxes succeeded to the throne, he gathered an army of thousands and a huge back-up fleet, and set out to punish the Greeks.

Xerxes seemed unstoppable. Legend says that when his army's path was blocked by the Hellespont (the narrow sea channel between Asia and Greece now known as the Dardanelles) he ordered his men to lash boats side by side across the channel, and build a road across them. Another story says that when the sea grew stormy he accused it of impertinence and had it flogged with chains.

Xerxes may have tamed the sea, but his forces were no match for the determined Greeks. In 480 BC, 400 Spartans held them back at the mountain pass of Thermopylae, and in the same year the Athenians trapped their fleet near the island of Salamis, and smashed its power. In 479 BC, most surprising of all, the Greek army beat the Persians at Plataea. Legend has it that the fields were red with blood. Unused to such treatment, the Persian army retreated, and never again invaded Greece in force.

Xerxes ruled for 20 more years. He lived in great luxury in Persepolis, his capital city, believing himself secure; but his nobles plotted against him. In 465 BC, led by his own son, they assassinated him.

Persepolis, founded by Cyrus, which Xerxes inherited as his capital city.

XERXES: Cyrus the Great 411

ALEXANDER THE GREAT (Alexandros)

Macedonian conqueror 356-323 BC

Alexander was the prince of Macedonia, a small, mountainous state now divided among Greece, Bulgaria and Yugoslavia. His father, Philip, was a warrior who had spent years invading and conquering Greece. When Alexander became King of Macedonia in 336 BC, he made an even more ambitious plan of conquest: to overrun the huge Persian Empire. At that time the empire was over 3,500 kilometres at its widest – stretching eastwards from the Mediterranean coast as far as the river Ganges in what is now northern India.

Alexander began by advancing down the eastern Mediterranean coast as far as Egypt; then he moved east into Mesopotamia, Babylonia, Parthia and on towards India (see map). He always led his troops

Historians of Alexander's time called him Megistos ("the greatest"), hence his modern title.

personally into battle, winning against overwhelming odds. His soldiers compared him to a god, believing him to be immune from human harm. Throughout his empire, he set up new towns, run by Greek-speaking commanders and with Greek laws and customs. He called many of these towns Alexandria after himself, and Egypt's chief port, at the mouth of the river Nile, still bears his name.

Alexander's conquests took 11 years, and gave him control over huge areas of the known world. He would have pushed on into Asia, but his troops, who had followed him loyally through deserts, over mountains and into lands said to be the home of giants and cannibals, suddenly mutinied. Alexander had little choice but to return to Babylon, the capital of his empire. Before he could reorganize and re-inspire his men, he fell ill (perhaps of malaria) and died.

CHANDRAGUPTA MAURYA (Sandracottos)

(ruled 321-297 BC)

Indian emperor died 297 BC

Chandragupta was a soldier, and possibly a freed slave, who rose through the ranks to become a general and a friend of **Alexander the Great**. In 325 BC he overthrew the rulers of Magadha in the fertile Ganges valley, and made himself king.

Two years later, with the death of Alexander, Chandragupta began to expand his empire north into what is now Afghanistan. This drove him into war with Seleucus, Alexander's former general, who controlled that area. It took 20 years of hill-fighting before Chandragupta won, forcing Seleucus to hand over the new territory in exchange for a dozen elephants.

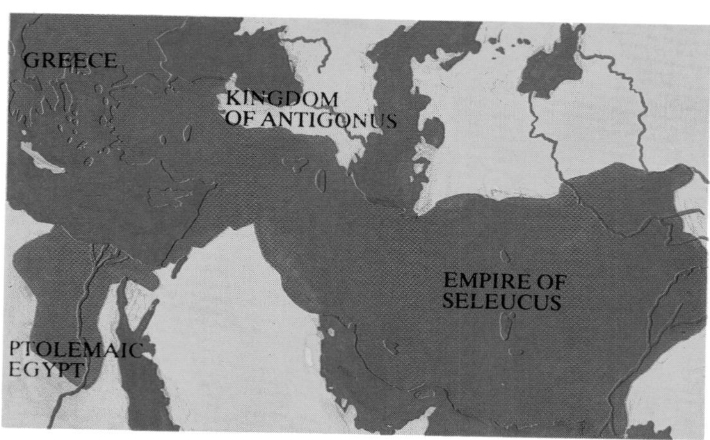

The extent of the empire – an area as large as the modern USA – conquered by Alexander the Great.

Chandragupta also expanded his empire east, into what is now West Bengal, and south to the Vindhya Mountains. He ruled three-quarters of the whole Indian sub-continent, and built a gold-decorated capital city at Pataliputra (modern Patna).

Chandragupta was a ruthless warrior. His power depended on his army: 600,000 foot-soldiers, 30,000 horsemen, 8,000 charioteers and no fewer than 9,000 elephants. But when he had ruled for some 20 years, he was converted to Jainism, a religion which forbids the harming of any living thing. A Jain priest told him that famine would devastate his people, and that he could do nothing to prevent it. Chandragupta, so the story goes, was so horrified that he abdicated from the throne, retired to a monastery and starved himself to death. None the less, the empire he had created lasted for another 100 years, keeping most of the Indian subcontinent united.

A carving of a pontiff (high priest), used by the Jains to guard their temples.

CHANDRAGUPTA: Alexander the Great 412

Asoka made Buddhism a state religion and erected many statues in India to commemorate sacred events in the Buddha's life.

ASOKA (Ashoka)

(ruled c 270-232 BC)

Indian emperor died c 232 BC

Asoka was the last of the Mauryan dynasty of emperors, who ruled over much of the Indian subcontinent. His father, Bindusara, and grandfather, **Chandragupta**, had been warriors, butchering anyone who opposed them – and Asoka began his reign with the same bloodthirstiness. But around 250 BC he was converted to Buddhism, a religion of peace and contemplation, just as his grandfather had earlier accepted Jainism.

A changed man, Asoka now sent priests to convert his people, as eagerly as he had once ordered soldiers to oppress them. He had Buddha's teachings carved on standing stones throughout the empire, and added accounts of his own conversion and pious deeds. These included building hospitals, making drinking-places for people and animals, and planting shade-trees beside each road. He also sent missionaries, including his own son, to Ceylon and China, from where Buddhism quickly spread to Korea, Indonesia and Japan.

For all the spiritual blessings they brought, Asoka's reforms also caused political disaster. Tribesmen from the north and east took advantage of the king who disbanded his armies in the name of peace. They fell on his empire, looted its cities and enslaved its people. India was not united again for 600 years.

The Great Wall of China: 4 m high, as wide as a motorway, with a guard-fort every 700 m.

SHIH HANGDI (Shih Huang-Ti)

Chinese emperor c 259-210 BC

The ruler of Qin (or Ch'in), a small kingdom beside the Yellow River, was determined to make himself the most powerful monarch in the area. He ruled by force, enslaving anyone who broke his laws, using the slaves to build roads, forts and castles. He sent conquering armies south, killed the rulers of the neighbouring states and added their people to his empire. Soon he ruled an area ten times the size of Qin – and gave himself the honorary name Shih Hangdi ("First Emperor").

To help unify his vast empire, Shih Hangdi made everyone learn the same language, replacing local dialects with a single, "purified" form of Chinese. He standardized money, weights and measures, burned all books, except accounts of his own glorious conquests, and executed priests, teachers and anyone else he

ASOKA: Chandragupta Maurya 413

The Terracotta Army "guarding" the emperor's tomb. Each statue was different, representing one of Shih Hangdi's real soldiers, and stood about 60 cm high.

thought might argue with his ideas. To protect his empire from hostile tribes, he ordered the building of a fortified wall – now known as The Great Wall of China – all along the northern frontier. It was built by slaves, and cost over 50,000 lives.

When Shih Hangdi died, he was buried in a vast underground tomb-city, guarded by thousands of life-sized statues of spearmen, archers and horsemen: the "terracotta army". Almost as soon as the funeral ceremonies were over, Shih Hangdi's subjects revolted and dethroned his heirs. His dynasty outlasted him not by the ten thousand years he had boasted, but by four years only. But during his lifetime, Qin was one of the most powerful empires on Earth, and ever since Westerners have called the country after it: "China".

Caesar's own memoirs tell of the seven years he spent fighting in Gaul. He describes events and people clearly and vividly. His account shows that he was a skilful but ruthless general.

CAESAR, Gaius Julius

Roman general 100-44 BC

When Caesar was 23 he was kidnapped by pirates and held to ransom. As soon as the ransom money was paid he gathered an army, rounded up the pirates and killed them; then he used the money to pay his troops. By this one daring feat he made himself a general with a private army loyal to him rather than to the people of Rome. For the rest of his life, although Caesar was officially a state servant, his soldiers' fanatical loyalty let him do much as he pleased.

Caesar fought Rome's enemies brilliantly: he was especially successful in Gaul (a large part of Western Europe) and Spain. But his main interest was political power in Rome. He formed an alliance with two other leading Romans – the banker Crassus and **Pompey**, another general – to bypass the Senate (the governing body in Rome) and run state affairs.

At first the triumvirate ("three-man alliance"), as it was called, worked well, but each member was ambitious and they soon quarrelled. Crassus faded from power, and Pompey and Caesar were at each other's throats. Their quarrel led to bitter civil war.

After a dozen years of fighting, Caesar defeated Pompey at the battle of Pharsalus in 48 BC, and the panic-striken Senate made him *dictator* (chief army commander), hoping that this would keep him under their orders. But Caesar's supporters began saying that the name he really deserved was "king", and it was obvious that he had the power to take that title any time he chose. A group of senators, led by Brutus and Cassius, plotted to murder Caesar, and on the Ides (15th) of March, 44 BC, they stabbed him dead at the feet of Pompey's statue in the Senate House.

CAESAR: Pompey 165

A statue of Cleopatra, which was presented to Juba II, king of Algeria during her lifetime. It was a true likeness of the queen, unlike many images made of her.

CLEOPATRA

(ruled 51-30 BC)

Egyptian queen 69-30 BC

Admirers of Cleopatra said that she was the most beautiful woman in the world. Enemies added that she was politically ruthless, and used her beauty to snare important men and snatch their power. She had a love-affair with **Julius Caesar**, and lived for a time with him in Rome.

When Caesar was assassinated in 44 BC, Cleopatra began another love-affair, with Caesar's old friend **Antony**. She flattered him and treated him like a royal prince instead of a blunt soldier. Antony's enemies said that she was using him: she meant to make him commander of the Egyptian army, beat the Roman generals and rule in Rome. The ambitious Octavianus (**Augustus**), Caesar's heir, spent many years fighting Antony's and Cleopatra's forces, and finally defeated them at the battle of Actium in 31 BC.

After the battle Antony fled to Alexandria. He was tricked into believing that Cleopatra had committed suicide, and killed himself by falling upon his sword. Overcome by grief, Cleopatra let an asp (a poisonous snake) bite her breast and lay down to die beside his corpse.

AUGUSTUS (Gaius Julius Caesar Octavianus)

(ruled 27 BC-AD 14)

Roman emperor 63 BC-AD 14

Octavianus was **Julius Caesar's** great-nephew, and was eventually adopted by Caesar as his son and heir in 44 BC. He supported Caesar against **Pompey** in the Roman civil war, and in the 17 years after Caesar's assassination he fought for power with other leading Romans, for example **Antony**, and beat them all.

Until this time, the Romans had been ruled by a council of leading citizens, the Senate, and hated the idea of any one person's unhindered power. For this reason, Octavianus called himself *Princeps* ("Principal Senator"), not "President" or "King", and adopted the title Augustus ("Serene Highness").

Augustus had become Rome's first emperor – and although he claimed to bow to the Senate's will, he kept two powers which gave him sole rule. One allowed him to propose new laws and to forbid any laws he disapproved of; another gave him supreme command of the army in peace and war.

If Augustus had been a tyrant, no one would have supported him for long. But his rule was efficient, generous and fair, a welcome contrast to nearly 50 years of civil war. He reorganized the government, the army, the lawcourts and the tax system. He rebuilt Rome's main buildings in marble, and paid authors

The Romans often made animal sacrifices to the gods in the hope of winning their favour. Augustus took the old forms of religion very seriously, and encouraged others to do the same.

CLEOPATRA: Antony 166 Augustus 416 Caesar 415 AUGUSTUS: Antony 166 Caesar 415 Livy 7 Pompey 165 Virgil 6

such as **Virgil** and **Livy** to write works glorifying the Roman people. He gave Rome back the dignity and pride it had had in the days before the civil war, and people loved him for it. During his life they called him "father of his country", and after his death they declared that he had gone from Earth to heaven to live with the gods.

BOUDICCA (Boadicea)

British warrior-queen 1st century AD

Boudicca was queen of the Iceni, a tribe in eastern England. When the Romans conquered, she stirred the people to revolt. She led them personally, fixing swords to the axles of her chariot to cut her enemies' legs. She captured two Roman strongholds, London and St Albans, but the Romans finally defeated her in a huge pitched battle, and she killed herself. Her revolt was said to have cost over 70,000 Roman lives.

Boudicca, riding into battle. The story of swordblades attached to the axles of her chariot was probably a myth, made up by frightened Romans.

KANISKA (Kanishka)

(ruled from c 78)

Kushan king 1st century

From his capital city, Peshawar, Kaniska ruled the Kushan Empire (modern Pakistan). He was a Buddhist, and wherever his soldiers went, they took Buddhist beliefs – south across the river Indus, and north into Asia. Kaniska's sculptors made statues of Lord **Buddha**, imitating the style of Greek god-statues left from the time of **Alexander the Great**, 400 years before. The idea of Buddha as a seated, smiling figure dates from this time.

WANG MANG

(ruled from 9-23)

Chinese emperor 1st century

Wang Mang was a member of a corrupt court, in which a dozen powerful families struggled for political control. He acted as regent to two child emperors, and then became emperor in his own right. At once he started to reform the government. He made laws reducing the power of rich and noble families, freed all slaves except those owned by the state and gave peasants loans to buy land of their own to farm.

Wang Mang claimed that his reforms were intended to help the poor, something the Chinese thinker **Confucius** had ordered centuries before. But his enemies said that his real purpose was to lessen the power of every other noble family so that he and his successors could rule unchallenged. His rivals organized revolts in every part of the kingdom, until at last Wang Mang was assassinated and the old ways were restored.

A plump, smiling Buddha, drawn as Kaniska's sculptors liked to show him.

KANISKA: Alexander the Great 412 Buddha 324 WANG MANG: Confucius 325

NERO
(Lucius Domitius Ahenobarbus)

(ruled 54-68)

Roman emperor 3-68

The Emperor Nero was far more interested in his stage talents than in ruling the Roman Empire.

According to tradition, Nero was a monster. He is said to have been a madman who murdered his own mother and his two wives, claimed that he was an immortal god, and set fire to Rome (to make a good backdrop while he sang about the burning of Troy). In addition, he cruelly persecuted anyone he disapproved of, including the Christians whom he burned alive or fed to wild beasts in the arena.

In truth Nero seems to have been a rather different character – spineless, unintelligent and more interested in his own pleasures (sex, singing and acting) than in ruling. It seems that it was his officials who terrorized Rome in his name.

It took 14 years to topple Nero, and his reported last words as he committed suicide are as crazy as any other legend about him: *Qualis artifex pereo!*, "I die – what a loss to the world of art!"

Some of the carved detail from Trajan's Column, one of the many monuments Trajan erected in Rome.

TRAJAN
(Marcus Ulpius Traianus)

(ruled 98-117)

Roman emperor 53-117

In the 50 years or so before Trajan became emperor, Rome had had a series of disastrous rulers including **Nero**, a tyrant (Domitian) and a senile old man (Nerva). Trajan had spent most of his adult life as a general, well away from Rome. In the year he was chosen as emperor he was in Dacia (parts of modern Hungary and Romania), subduing some of the most savage tribes the Romans ever faced. When he came to the throne, the Roman Empire was the largest it had ever been.

As soon as Trajan became emperor, he stopped the bribery and bloodshed that earlier, corrupt, rulers had encouraged. He set out to rule fairly, wisely and well. He founded a state fund to help widows and orphans, and refused to persecute religious minorities (for example Christians). Above all, Trajan reorganized the army, making it smaller and more efficient.

Like many rulers before and since, Trajan spent lavishly on building work. Some of ancient Rome's most impressive monuments date from his reign. The best known of all, and the one which keeps his name alive, is Trajan's Column. This is a pillar of stone, 38 metres high, put up to celebrate the emperor's victories in Dacia. It is covered with a spiral of carvings, showing Trajan and his soldiers. Much of what is known today about Roman army uniforms, weapons, ways of fighting and life in camp comes from this stone.

TRAJAN: Nero 418

Zenobia.

ZENOBIA, Septimia (Bat Zabbai)

(ruled c 268-73)

Syrian queen died c 214

Zenobia was a priestess who married Odaenathus, king of Palmyra (called Tadmour in the Bible) on the borders of Syria and Babylonia. Palmyra was then under Roman protection, and Odaenathus was a puppet-king. In 268 Odaenathus and his son died mysteriously, possibly from poison. At once Zenobia declared herself sole ruler. She gathered an army, drove out the Roman garrison and began making war on neighbouring states.

Zenobia's soldiers swept south and west, and in two years added Egypt and Asia Minor (the coastal region of modern Turkey) to the Syrian Empire. The Romans hastily sent a huge army against Zenobia. They captured her, and led her in golden chains through the streets of Rome. She knelt and swore humble obedience to the emperor, who let her marry a Roman nobleman and gave her a beautiful country house at Tivoli.

Constantine's army had to fight the troops of a rival emperor on the Milvian bridge, near the city of Rome. He won the battle, and many of the opposing troops were drowned.

CONSTANTINE (Flavius Valerius Constantinus)

(ruled 306-37)

Roman emperor c 285-337

A prince of the Roman royal family, Constantine grew up in Britain as a soldier, and became a dazzling, popular general. In Rome, various members of Constantine's family were squabbling for power, and Constantine set out with his followers to claim the throne himself. At the end of his march, facing a hostile army, he saw a vision of Christ's cross shining in the sky, and heard a voice saying "In this, conquer."

Constantine did conquer, and he became Emperor of Rome in 306. He declared the Roman Empire Christian, and banned worship of the old gods. He held a council of bishops to decide on how Christ should be worshipped, and its decisions have formed the basis of much Christian worship ever since.

After a few years of rule, Constantine moved the capital of the empire from Rome to the city of Byzantium (modern Istanbul) at the southern entrance to the Black Sea. He rebuilt the city in marble, glittering with gold and bronze, and renamed it Constantinople after himself. The empire he founded there, the "Byzantine Empire", lasted for 1,000 years.

CHANDRA GUPTA II

(ruled c 380-415)

Indian emperor c 375-415

His grandfather, Chandra Gupta I (ruled 320–c 330), founded the Gupta dynasty, whose imperial city was Pataliputra (modern Patna) in northern India.

Chandra Gupta II extended the empire, making it the main Hindu power in northern India. He helped artists and writers, and some of the earliest surviving Hindu sculpture, and holy writings – the *Puranas* and *Vedantas* – date from his time.

The Guptas were no relation of **Chandragupta Maurya**, founder of the earlier Mauryan dynasty, and scholars think that they took his name to suggest that his ancient glory had been reborn.

ATTILA

(ruled 433-53)

King of the Huns c 406-53

Until Attila was 18, he and his brother Bleda were joint rulers of the vast kingdom of the Huns (a huge wheel of land centred on what is now Hungary). Then, in 434, Attila murdered Bleda and made himself sole king.

At this time the Roman Empire, which had dominated Europe for six centuries, was beginning to crumble, and Attila led his soldiers against one Roman colony after another, pillaging and destroying them. In 447 he besieged Constantinople, home of the Eastern Roman emperor Theodosius, and forced him to sign a humiliating peace-treaty. He then swept west into Gaul (a large part of Western Europe), and was held back solely by the skill of the Roman general Aetius, the only person who ever beat the Huns in battle.

Attila gathered a new army and invaded Italy, intending to destroy the city of Rome itself. His invasion terrified the Romans because it reminded them of **Hannibal's** near-fatal advance of 600 years before. In the end the Pope went to Attila in person and begged him, on bended knees, to spare God's holy city. Attila agreed – for a price – and took his armies home.

Back in Hungary, Attila began organizing what was to be his biggest invasion so far, that of the Balkans (modern-day Yugoslavia, Albania, Bulgaria, Romania and Greece). He saw himself as a second **Alexander the Great**, and he planned to marry and found a dynasty to rule the world. But on his wedding night – which some say was an orgy of drink, food and sex, outdoing anything ever seen before or since – he died of a sudden heart attack. His generals fell on the empire and divided it among themselves.

Attila, the supreme warlord, led his army of Huns into ferocious battles, dominating most of Europe, north of the Roman frontier. He was finally defeated in Gaul in 451 AD.

CHANDRA GUPTA: Chandragupta Maurya 413 ATILLA: Alexander the Great 412 Hannibal 164

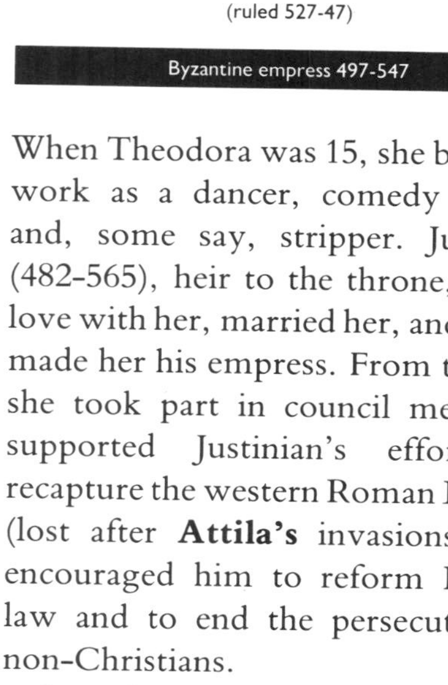

The Byzantine Empress Theodora.

THEODORA

(ruled 527-47)

Byzantine empress 497-547

When Theodora was 15, she began to work as a dancer, comedy actress and, some say, stripper. Justinian (482-565), heir to the throne, fell in love with her, married her, and in 527 made her his empress. From then on she took part in council meetings, supported Justinian's efforts to recapture the western Roman Empire (lost after **Attila's** invasions), and encouraged him to reform Roman law and to end the persecution of non-Christians.

Some historians say that Theodora devised many laws improving the lives of women. Women were allowed to own property and to keep their dowries when they married, and daughters as well as sons were allowed to inherit. Another law made it a crime to sell girl children as slaves.

The great mosque of Cordoba in Spain, built in the reign of Abd er-Rahman as part of his aim to spread Muslim rule throughout the country.

ABD ER-RAHMAN I

(ruled 757-88)

Syrian/Spanish prince 731-88

Abd Er-Rahman I belonged to the Omayyad dynasty in Syria. When he was 18 the Omayyads were overthrown by their rivals the Abbasids, and Abd Er-Rahman was forced into exile, never to return. He travelled through Palestine into Egypt, and then along the African coast to Morocco. He gathered a band of fierce desert fighters, who followed him with fanatical loyalty.

Abd Er-Rahman knew that every country in north Africa was afraid of the Abbasids. So long as he stayed in Africa, his life was in danger. In 756 he led his army into Spain, where there had been civil war since the collapse of the Visigoth empire 45 years before. Spain's defenders were no match for Abd Er-Rahman's desert-trained fighters, and he won a fierce battle on the banks of the river Guadalquivir, between Seville and Cordoba. The following year, he was declared Emir (ruler) of Spain.

In the years that followed, Abd Er-Rahman had a magnificent capital city built at Cordoba, and spread Muslim rule throughout southern and central Spain. He was Emir for 32 years, surviving assassination attempts, political plots and even war with **Charlemagne**. His enemies, Christian and Muslim alike, described him as a tyrant. But by the time of his death, central and southern Spain were secure and well-governed, and Moors (North African Muslims) lived peacefully there for seven centuries, until the time of **Ferdinand and Isabella**.

THEODORA: Attila 420 ABD ER-RAHMAN: Charlemagne 422 Ferdinand and Isabella 433

CHARLEMAGNE

(ruled 800-14)

Emperor of the West 742-814

The name Charlemagne is made from three medieval French words run together: *Charl le magne* ("Charles the Great"). Charlemagne became king of the Franks (a people inhabiting most of modern France and Belgium) in 771 when he was 29, and at once he began conquering neighbouring peoples to east, west and south. In nine years he practically doubled his empire, adding most of what are now East and West Germany, Austria, the Netherlands, Switzerland and northern Italy.

In 800 the Pope crowned Charlemagne "Emperor of the West" – an ancient Roman title which declared him the equal of such men as the Roman Emperor **Constantine**.

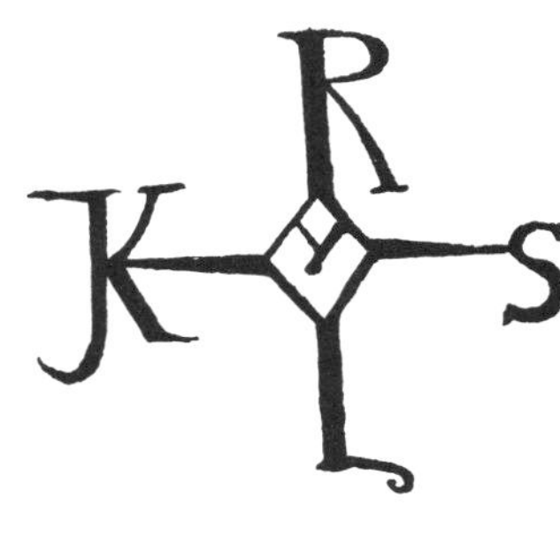

Charlemagne used his power to create an education system, and encouraged people to learn to read and write. *Above, left:* a richly decorated book cover from France. *Above:* The Emperor's cypher, used to sign documents. *Below:* Charlemagne's jewelled talisman was buried with him in 814, but was recovered from his tomb in 1000 AD.

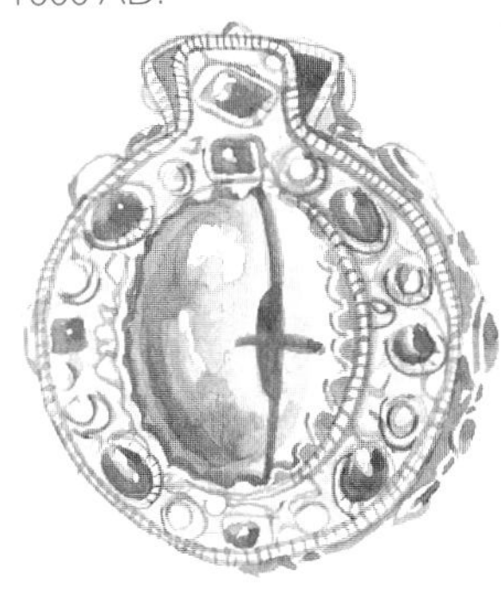

Charlemagne wanted to create one single, united empire, not a collection of different states. He proclaimed the whole empire Christian, and built new churches and monasteries everywhere. In addition, he standardized the laws, and sent imperial officials and soldiers to ensure that they were obeyed. He encouraged his nobles to learn to read and write – and himself set an example by learning to read (though not to write) and to speak Latin and Greek. Furthermore, he asked the scholar **Alcuin** to devise an education system gathering the best ideas of both his own time and the past. He also built roads and aqueducts throughout the empire, and encouraged friendly relations with outsiders such as Arabs and North African Moors.

Charlemagne's ambition was to restore the glory of the ancient Roman Empire – and while he lived, he succeeded. His chroniclers tell of a noble, powerful prince surrounded by a glittering court and devoted to Christian glory, honesty and truth. Unfortunately for Europe, however, Charlemagne's successors could not match him. They fought over the empire and divided it – and Europe has remained a collection of separate, often quarrelsome, countries ever since.

Left: The Holy Roman Emperor Charlemagne. He wanted to create a united Europe, devoted to the Christian faith.

CHARLEMAGNE: Alcuin 333 Constantine 419

HARUN AL-RASHID

(ruled 786-809)

Caliph of Baghdad c 763-809

Harun was the fifth Caliph (religious and political leader) of the Muslim Abbasid dynasty. His capital city was Baghdad in Persia (modern Iran). As a young man, he was supported by a powerful family, the Barmecides, and when he came to power he let them rule in his name, while he lived the life of a spoiled, pleasure-loving prince. He filled his court with artists, musicians and scholars; kept a huge harem of wives and concubines; and spent a fortune on entertaining foreign visitors, including ambassadors from **Charlemagne**.

For 17 years Harun's reign was untroubled. But in 803, for no known reason, he seems to have suffered a fit of sudden insanity, and ordered the execution of the entire Barmecide family. From that time on things went from bad to worse. Harun had none of the Barmecides' political or military skills, and his rule was harsh and cruel. Finally, riding out at the head of his army to pacify a rebel province, he had a stroke and died.

Harun al-Rashid is particularly famous as the hero of a number of stories in *The Arabian Nights*: a kindly prince who disguises himself as an ordinary citizen, wanders the streets at night listening to the troubles of his people, and rides out next morning (still disguised) to put things right by outwitting or fighting the evildoers.

Right: A sixteenth-century engraving of Alfred, who was so wrapped up in the problems of his kingdom that he failed to see a batch of cakes, burning by his side.

Below: Harun al-Rashid, as he was portrayed in *The Arabian Nights*.

ALFRED THE GREAT

(ruled 871-99)

King of England c 849-99

Alfred the Great ruled the ancient kingdom of southern England called Wessex. Unlike many kings of his time, he was interested in books and learning. He filled his court at Winchester with scholars and made his courtiers learn to read and write. He himself learned Latin, and translated Latin books into English. He ordered his scribes to make a year-by-year account of everything important that happened. It was called the *Anglo-Saxon Chronicle*, and still survives.

Following a series of battles against the Danes, Alfred became ruler of all England in 886. He ordered the laws of England to be written down, and made sure they applied equally everywhere in his kingdom. His law-system lasted, unchanged, until Norman invaders, led by **William I**, conquered the country in 1066.

HARUN: Charlemagne 422 ALFRED: William I 424

OLGA

(ruled 945-64)

Russian empress 890-969

Olga's husband, Tsar Igor I, was assassinated in 945, and she was appointed regent until her baby son Sviatoslav was old enough to rule. She rounded up Igor's assassins and boiled them; after that there were no more revolts. In 957 she became a Christian, and hundreds of thousands of people followed her example. After her death she was proclaimed the first-ever Russian Orthodox Christian saint.

BRIAN BORU

(ruled 1001-14)

Irish king 926-1014

When Brian was a boy Ireland was divided into five separate kingdoms. His ambition was to make it one. At the age of 50 he became King of Munster, one of the five kingdoms, and promptly set out with his armies to take over the whole of Ireland. One by one, he conquered the peoples of Leinster, Meath, Connaught and Ulster, and in 1001 he was crowned King of all Ireland. His people nicknamed him Bóroimhe or Boru, "Tribute-taker".

Once Ireland was united, Brian Boru began to defend it against invaders. He fought off Vikings and other raiders, and is said to have been still personally leading his army at the age of 88. The Irish finally defeated the Vikings at the battle of Clontarf in 1014. But victory was no sooner hailed, and Brian was on his knees thanking God, than a traitor crept up behind him and killed him. Ireland has never again been united under a native ruler; Irish people regard Brian Boru as one of the greatest leaders their country has ever had.

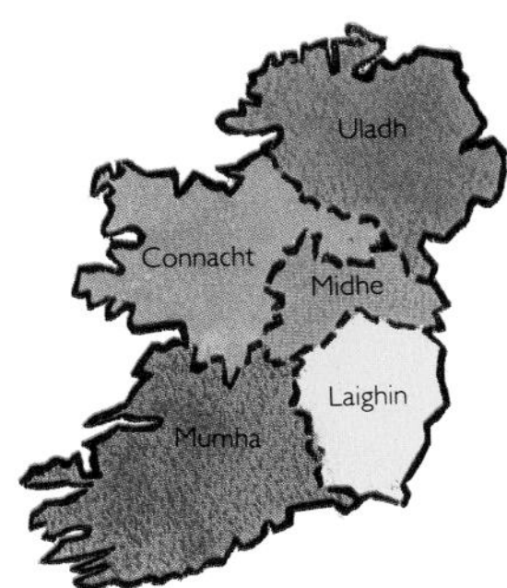

The five kingdoms of Ireland in the time of Brian Boru.

WILLIAM I ("the Conqueror")

(ruled 1066-87)

Norman/English king 1027-87

When childless King Edward the Confessor of England was staying in Normandy in northern France, he declared William heir to the English throne. But when Edward died and William claimed the throne, a number of English lords resisted, and made Harold Godwinson their king.

William invaded England in 1066, defeated and killed Harold at the battle of Hastings, and was crowned king in Westminster Abbey. These events are shown on the famous Bayeux Tapestry.

It took William another dozen years to stamp out those who opposed him (for example Hereward the Wake in the English Fen-country and Malcolm, King of Scotland). But by 1072 he was the undisputed king, and Norman-French laws and ways were imposed on English life.

In 1086 William ordered that every

The Bayeux tapestry shows scenes from William's life before, during and after his conquest of England. Here, he is shown preparing to cross the Channel to reach England.

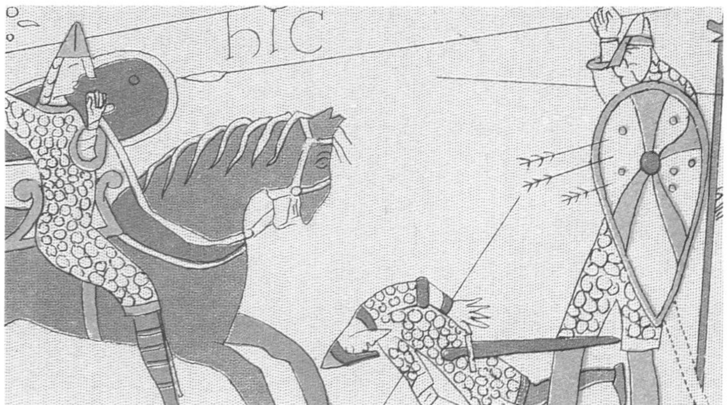

This scene shows the death of Harold at Hastings in 1066.

church, field, village and town in his kingdom should be described and recorded in a book for tax purposes. The result was the "Domesday Book", a unique catalogue of land and wealth in medieval England.

FREDERICK I

(ruled 1155-90)

Holy Roman Emperor c 1122-90

Three centuries after **Charlemagne**, the Holy Roman Empire was falling apart. Its minor rulers were squabbling for power, and there was particularly violent disagreement between the Princes Temporal (monarchs of individual states) and the Princes Spiritual (rulers of the Church, led by the Pope).

Frederick, nicknamed Barbarossa ("Redbeard"), was crowned King of Germany in 1152. First of all he worked to end the feuding in his country, and then he set out to bring the entire Holy Roman Empire under German rule. The task took three years, and he was crowned Holy Roman Emperor by Pope Adrian IV in 1155.

Even after the Empire was conquered, it was difficult to hold it together. When Pope Alexander III, hostile to Frederick, seized control of northern Italy, it took Frederick six years to win back the captured towns. He marched on Rome, but his army was devastated by plague, which his enemies called a judgement from God. As a result, he was forced to make peace with Alexander, and to mark it in a humiliating public ceremony by kneeling beside the Pope's horse, taking a stirrup in his hand and kissing the Pope's foot.

Once Frederick and the Pope were working together, there was only one remaining hostile prince – Henry of Bavaria, Frederick's cousin. Apart from him, the empire was at peace.

For nine years, from 1180–89, Frederick ruled a united, prosperous Europe. He had only one more duty to perform. As part of his punishment for rebelling against the Pope, he joined a crusade in 1190 to defeat **Saladin** and free the cities of Palestine from Arab rule. Saladin was defeated in 1191, and the crusaders returned, victorious. But on the way home Frederick was drowned in the River Selef, and buried in Antioch in Syria. There is still a legend that he is not dead but sleeping, and that when Germany needs him most, he will ride out again with his knights to save the state.

Christians fight Muslims in one of the unsuccessful crusades to try and gain control of the Holy Land.

FREDERICK I: Charlemagne 422 Saladin 168

The most colourful figures of medieval Japan were the samurai, some of the finest professional soldiers the world has ever seen. They guarded their employer and his land, rewarded only with food and shelter and the privilege of carrying arms. Once drawn from its scabbard, the samurai's sword had to be used before it could be put aside again.

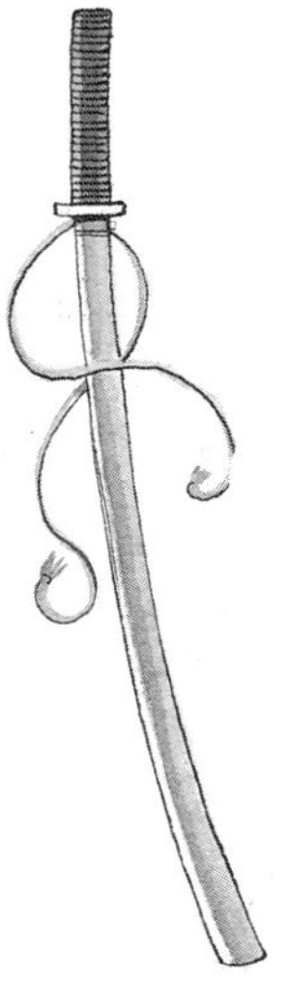

MINAMOTO, Yoritomo

Japanese military leader 1147-99

and

MINAMOTO, Yoshitsuni

Japanese military leader 1159-89

The brothers belonged to one of two aristocratic families, struggling for power in Japan. Towards the end of the twelfth century, the Taira family, rivals of the Minamoto, had intermarried with the Japanese emperor's family, and expected that in due course one of their descendants would inherit the throne. But Yoritomo and Yoshitsuni gathered a Minamoto army, marched against the Taira and ransacked their stronghold. During the fighting the emperor (a child) was drowned.

The Minamoto were now in command. For a time they ruled amicably. But the two brothers quarrelled, and Yoshitsuni went into exile. He became a bandit chief, and was eventually hunted down and killed by his brother's forces. Japanese legends say that he was a favourite of the gods, able to work magic, and that when he died he was taken up to live in heaven.

After his brother's death, Yoritomo Minamoto was sole ruler. He took the title shōgun, or military dictator, and passed the name, and the power that went with it, to his descendants. But he – and they – always claimed to be no more than servants of the emperor. They called their government *bakufu*, "tent rule", as though it were something temporary which they would fold up and put away any time the emperor asked.

RICHARD I

(ruled 1189-99)

English king 1157-99

Richard the Lionheart's arms, the first known in the history of the British Royal Arms.

In the ten years of Richard's reign, he actually spent only six months in England. He was a warrior, and spent his life fighting in foreign countries, for example against the Saracens (Muslims) who challenged the Christians' control of Palestine, the Holy Land. He was a brave soldier, nicknamed "Lionheart" by his soldiers. But people in England complained that he was a bad king, forever fighting foreigners while his own country struggled under the selfish rule of his brother John.

GENGHIS KHAN (Tamujin)

(ruled 1175-1227)

Mongol emperor c 1162-1227

When Tamujin was 13 he became chief of a warrior tribe in Mongolia, part of the borderland between modern China and the USSR. He set about conquering all the neighbouring tribes, and finally ruled so many people that he renamed himself Genghis Khan ("universal ruler").

Genghis Khan's army consisted of a quarter of a million ferocious and merciless horsemen. They swarmed over the Great Wall of China, overran northern China and Korea and streamed into the countries now known as Russia, Iran and Pakistan. Wherever a town or city opposed him, Genghis Khan ransacked it, slaughtered its people and left a pyramid of skulls to remind passers-by of the dangers of resistance.

When Genghis Khan died, his empire was over 6,000 kilometres wide – covering most of the Asian continent. His soldiers carried his body in state to his capital city, Karakoram in Mongolia – and they murdered everyone who saw the procession, so that no word of his death would spread and lead to political unrest. Even so, his sons squabbled over who should succeed him, and it was not until 1259, 32 years later, that Genghis Khan's grandson **Kublai** restored firm rule.

Genghis Khan.

FREDERICK II

(ruled 1220-50)

Holy Roman Emperor 1194-1250

Frederick II was the grandson of **Frederick I**, and was born in Italy. When he was 19 the Pope crowned him King of Germany, a country he had never seen. Seven years later, aged 26, he was crowned Holy Roman Emperor. But for all his titles, Frederick had no interest in ruling. He seldom visited Germany, and left the local princes to govern their own states, and to make peace or fight one another, as they chose.

As part of his Italian upbringing, Frederick learned half a dozen languages including Arabic. His study of history convinced him that war was useless. When the Pope sent him on a crusade, therefore, instead of capturing the cities of Palestine (the Holy Land), by force, he spent many hours negotiating in Arabic with the Sultan of Egypt, and persuaded him to surrender Jerusalem and to declare peace for ten years.

At his Italian court, Frederick lived more as a patron of the arts than as a medieval warlord. He encouraged writers, musicians and artists, and himself sang, played instruments and wrote poetry. He was one of the first European monarchs to use taxes not for his own enrichment but to benefit his people. He threw open his court to Arab merchants and scholars, and introduced Eastern ideas (for example Arabic numerals) to the West. He reigned in such splendour that one visiting English writer nicknamed him *Stupor mundi*, "the wonder of the world".

The Emperor Frederick II with a hunting falcon.

Frederick was no idle ruler and welcomed scholars and artists from East and West to his court.

GENGHIS KHAN: Kublai Khan 428 FREDERICK II: Frederick I 425

KUBLAI KHAN

(ruled 1259-94)

Mongol emperor 1215-94

Kublai Khan was the grandson of **Genghis Khan**, and his empire stretched from the Black Sea to the Pacific Ocean, from the Himalayas to the edge of the Arctic Circle. His first capital city was Karakorum in Mongolia. But he ordered that a magnificent new capital city should be built at Cambaluk (modern Beijing in China), and ruled his great empire from there.

Kublai Khan spent much of his reign conquering or pacifying the southern fringes of his empire – modern Afghanistan, Tibet and Burma. The only place he failed to conquer was Japan: his invasion force of 140,000 men was destroyed in a storm at sea.

Although Kublai Khan's power depended on his ferocious soldiers, among the most terrifying in all world history, once people accepted his rule they found it generous and fair. He ordered roads to be built throughout the empire, and a massive system of waterways to transport grain over 1,800 kilometres from the corn-growing area of China around Hangchow all the way to Cambaluk.

Unlike previous rulers, Kublai Khan allowed freedom of religion, and also encouraged trade with foreigners. The Venetian merchant **Marco Polo** spent 17 years in his service, and wrote an awed account of the magnificence of Kublai Khan's empire and his court.

Kublai Khan died when he was over 80 – and the tolerance of his reign was forgotten in an orgy of barbaric grief. All his wives and concubines (some historians say as many as 3,000 women) were buried alive, and anyone who so much as glimpsed his funeral procession was executed on the spot, because, as the soldiers put it, "Your master needs you in the other world."

Kublai Khan's vast empire was conquered by his armies of ferocious soldiers.

KUBLAI KHAN: Genghis Khan 426 Polo 169

RAMA GAMHEN

(ruled c 1279-1316)

Thai king c 1250-1316

Rama Gamhen ("Rama the brave") was a warrior-prince. He freed the Thai people from the Khmer Empire, and became the first king of independent Thailand. He was a devout Buddhist, and ruled his kingdom by Buddhist principles: the aim of life was enlightenment, and all people were equal. There were no armies, no taxes, no slaves and no laws. If people chose to start businesses, build towns or contribute money for the upkeep of the royal household, that was up to them.

Rama was popular, and his rule was peaceful and secure. He ordered the building of a beautiful new city,

One of the many *stupas* (shrines) in Thailand. Each covers a statue or relic of Buddha.

Si Satchanalai, near the Buddhist shrine of Wat Maha Tat. Its remains, and the magnificent Sawankalok pottery which was its chief source of trade, are still known throughout the world.

ROBERT THE BRUCE

(ruled 1306-29)

Scottish king 1274-1329

In Bruce's boyhood the English ruled Scotland, and he spent many years as a freedom-fighter, until in 1306 he seized the Scottish throne and declared his country free. The English tried to win Scotland back, and Bruce fought many battles against them, including one at Bannockburn, the bloodiest victory ever won by Scots over the English. In 1328, a few months before Bruce's death, the English finally agreed to accept Scottish independence.

A famous folk-legend tells of Bruce's despair during the long years of fighting. He was hiding in a cave from his enemies, wondering whether to surrender or to struggle on. He saw a spider trying to climb the wall, endlessly slipping back, gathering itself and trying again. The sight inspired him with the courage he needed, and he went out with new heart to fight his enemies.

CHU YUAN-ZHANG (Chu Yüan-Chang)

(ruled 1368-98)

Chinese emperor 1328-98

The son of a peasant, Chu Yuan-Zhang joined a band of outlaws. At first they merely robbed people, but after Chu became their leader in 1355 they began to fight for Chinese freedom from the Mongols. More and more people joined them, and in 1368, after Chu's men captured Beijing, the Mongol dynasty was finally overthrown and Chu became Emperor. He took the name Ming Hong-Wu, and founded a dynasty which ruled for 300 years.

Chu was a tyrant, merciless with rivals, greedy for taxes and over-fond of torture and execution. But his successors, the Ming Emperors, gave China a golden age of culture, prosperity and security – which might never have happened without Chu's military genius, and the strict discipline he imposed.

The Mongol Tamerlane held a reign of terror, from 1369 to 1405, in seeking to become ruler of the whole of the Asian continent.

TAMERLANE (Tamburlaine)

Mongol conqueror 1336-1405

Tamerlane became ruler of the central Asian city of Samarkand (in what is now the southernmost part of the USSR) in 1369. Tamerlane and Tamburlaine are Westernized forms of Timur-i-leng ("Timur the Lame"), a nickname he earned because he had a limp. From his capital, Tamerlane began a campaign of conquest, hoping to become sole ruler of the continent as his ancestor **Genghis Khan** had been. He used the same vicious methods, sending armies of bloodthirsty horsemen sweeping across the plains – slaughtering everyone who opposed him and piling their heads in heaps. He conquered the whole of central Asia (modern Iran, Afghanistan and the southern USSR). In 1398 he invaded India, looting the wealth of centuries and carting it back to Samarkand. Then he began expanding his empire westwards, defeating the Syrians and Turks. In 1405 he planned the conquest of China, but he died before the invasion could begin.

After Tamerlane's death, his empire was split among squabbling successors. The Mongols, who had ruled half the known world, never again held such power or wealth. But in Tamerlane's heyday his soldiers were feared wherever they went, and Samarkand was considered one of the most fabulous cities ever built.

HONG LO (Hung Lo)

(ruled 1403-24)

Chinese emperor 1359-1424

Hong Lo was one of the most dazzling emperors of the Ming dynasty, founded 50 years before by **Chu Yuan-Zhang**. He ordered the building of a magnificent new palace in his capital city Beijing: the gold, scarlet and purple "Forbidden City", which is still one of the most glittering reminders of China's past.

Hong Lo sent seafarers to explore the world, one of the best-remembered being **Zheng-He**, who travelled westwards to India and the Persian Gulf. The explorers took goods for trading, including fine pottery; the blue-and-white Ming "china" is still treasured throughout the world.

Ming vases shaped for holding oil (top) and wine (bottom), but chiefly used for show.

TAMERLANE: Genghis Khan 426 HONG LO: Chu Yuan-Zhang 429 Zheng-He 170

MEDICI FAMILY

Italian aristocrats 14th-18th centuries

The Medici were a family of merchants and bankers in Florence, Italy. They were never outright kings or queens, and officially their influence extended only over Florence and its surrounding area. But for nearly 400 years their authority was passed down the family just as rule is in a royal dynasty.

The most powerful of the Medici were COSIMO (1389-1464), who grandly called himself *pater patriae*, "father of his native land", like an ancient Roman emperor, and his great-grandson LORENZO (1449-92), nicknamed "the Magnificent".

Two members of the family became popes. LEO X (1475-1521), who was made a cardinal at 13, poured money into beautifying the Sistine Chapel in Rome. But he was a greedy, corrupt man, and his selling of "indulgences" – religious pardons for sins – finally caused **Luther's** revolt against the Roman Catholic Church. Pope CLEMENT VII (1478-1534) refused to give the English king **Henry VIII** a divorce from Catherine of Aragon, so causing the Church of England to split from the Church of Rome.

CATHARINE (1519-89), daughter of Lorenzo, became Queen of France, and skilfully ran the country through the reigns of her sons François I, Charles IX and Henri III.

For three centuries the Medici were determined to make Florence the most beautiful city in the world, and employed the best architects, sculptors and painters money could buy: not only **Leonardo da Vinci**, but also **Donatello**, **Botticelli** and **Michelangelo**. The whole city is a dazzling memorial to the Medici, and has remained one of the world's main centres of art to this day.

The aristocratic Medici family used much of its great wealth to make Florence one of the most beautiful cities in the world. Statues of the Medici, like this one of Cosimo, Grand Duke of Tuscany, were made by the best sculptors in the land.

MOHAMMED II

(ruled 1451-81)

Ottoman sultan 1430-81

In 1453 Mohammed conquered the city of Constantinople (now called Istanbul), which had been the heart of the Christian Roman Empire since it was founded over 1,000 years before by **Constantine**. Mohammed went on to create a larger Islamic power – the Ottoman Empire – which covered much of what is now Turkey, Greece, Albania, Yugoslavia, Bulgaria and southern Romania.

Soon after the capture of Constantinople, vast numbers of Christian scholars fled to the West. Many settled in Italy, and the ancient Greek and Roman books they took with them gave thinkers, artists and politicians a new interest in the past – the movement now known as the Renaissance.

MEDICI: Botticelli 10 Donatello 10 Henry VIII 435 Leonardo da Vinci 11 Luther 338 Michelangelo 12 MOHAMMED: Constantine 419

BORGIA FAMILY

Italian aristocrats 15th century

The Borgias rivalled the **Medici** as the richest and most powerful family in Italy. Their enemies said that they were ruthless and wicked – and this reputation has stuck to them ever afterwards, true or false.

ALEXANDER BORGIA (1431-1503) almost certainly was as evil as people claimed. His aims were wealth and power, and he seems to have decided that the best way to get them was through the Roman Catholic Church. He became a priest, and in 1476 his uncle Pope Calixtus III made him a cardinal. He spent the next 16 years working to be elected Pope – but instead of following the usual path of devotion to God, he used blackmail, bribery and murder. In 1492 he succeeded, and spent the rest of his life in an orgy of luxury, cruelty and greed. He outdid even the most barbarous Roman emperors, and anyone who dared to oppose him (as **Savonarola** did) died soon afterwards.

At that time Italy was divided, each region being ruled by a different lord, prince or king. One of Alexander's ambitions was to make Italy a single country, a "papal state", ruled from Rome. Because popes were not expected to lead their armies in person, he made one of his 14 illegitimate sons, CESARE BORGIA (c 1475-1507), commander-in-chief. Cesare was a brilliant soldier, but he was just as happy to murder, bribe or cheat to get his way. He brought vast areas of Italy under papal rule, but in 1503, when Alexander died and a new pope (Julius II) was elected, Cesare was driven into exile, and four years later he was killed in battle.

The third famous member of the family, LUCREZIA BORGIA (1480-1519), had for a time the worst reputation of all. She was reputed to be a witch and a poisoner: people believed that she had rings fitted with hinged gems which could be lifted to reveal poison capsules. In 1501 she bore a son, and gossip said that the child's father was either Lucrezia's brother Cesare or her father Pope Alexander.

In 1503, when Alexander Borgia died, Lucrezia married the Duke of Ferrara, and lived contentedly with him for the rest of her life. The gentleness of these years suggests that the scandals of her earlier days were lies, made up by her father's or brother's enemies to discredit the Borgia family. Certainly there were no further stories of orgies or poisonings. Instead, Lucrezia's court was a centre for painting, music and poetry, and her palace, the Villa d'Este, is one of the most beautiful buildings from that time.

Lucrezia Borgia.

Cesare Borgia.

Rumours of the wicked ways of Lucrezia abounded.

BORGIA: Medici family 431 Savonarola 174

FERDINAND ("the Catholic")

Spanish ruler 1452-1516

and

ISABELLA ("the Catholic")

Spanish ruler 1451-1504

Ferdinand and Isabella married when he was 17 and she was 18. They each succeeded to a throne: he became King of Aragon (the north-east of Spain), and she became Queen of Castile (the rest of Spain except for Granada, which had been under Muslim control by the North African Moors for 700 years). Their marriage unified the country for the first time in its history.

Ferdinand's main achievements were military. He drove the Moors from Granada and conquered the ancient kingdoms of Naples and Navarre.

Isabella, by contrast, was a politician. She unified the laws of the two former kingdoms, abolished the feudal powers of the Spanish aristocracy, and appointed local governors responsible directly to Ferdinand and herself. Her great shrewdness and Ferdinand's skill as a general made a combination which their enemies, both in and out of Spain, found unbeatable.

Like many Roman Catholics of the time, Ferdinand and Isabella considered Jews and Moors enemies of Christianity. They set up the Spanish Inquisition, under the monk Torquemada, either to convert or exterminate them. The Inquisition arrested, tortured, killed or banished more than half a million people. The Pope rewarded Ferdinand and Isabella for this work by giving each of them the title "the Catholic".

During the 1490s Ferdinand and Isabella sponsored many voyages of exploration and conquest to the Americas (known as the "New World"), including **Columbus'** expedition of 1492. These voyages led to Spain gaining a vast empire in South America which lasted for three centuries.

In 1504, when Isabella died, her daughter Juana succeeded to the throne of Castile. But Juana was insane, and Ferdinand acted as regent until his own death in 1516, when rule over Spain and its empire passed to Juana's son Charles (later the Holy Roman Emperor **Charles V**). Catherine of Aragon, Ferdinand and Isabella's fourth daughter, became the first wife of the English king **Henry VIII.**

The Inquisition, a special court organized by the Catholic church, had ways of dealing with people they believed were enemies of Christianity.

Ferdinand and Isabella, rulers of Aragon and Castile.

FERDINAND AND ISABELLA: Charles V 436 Colombus 172 Henry VIII 435

RICHARD III

(ruled 1483-5)

English king 1452-85

During the English Wars of the Roses, when two aristocratic families (Lancaster and York) were fighting for the throne, Richard and his brothers led the Yorkists. Richard's elder brother was King Edward IV, and until Edward's death in 1483 Richard was a good and loyal general, seemingly devoted to his brother's family and happy to see them rule.

In 1483, when Edward's 13-year-old son became king, Richard was appointed "Protector", to rule the kingdom till the boy grew up. But almost immediately Richard declared publicly that the boy was illegitimate, not the true heir. He took the throne for himself, and soon afterwards the young prince disappeared. Richard ruled for two years. But the Lancastrians were still determined to take the throne, and in 1485, under Henry Tudor, they defeated Richard's army at the Battle of Bosworth, and Richard was killed in the fighting.

The victorious Lancastrian leader became King Henry VII. Soon after the coronation, his court historians began spreading accounts of Richard's crimes. They said that Richard was a deformed monster, a hunchback in league with the Devil. He (Richard) had plotted all through Edward's reign to snatch the throne, and when Edward died had ordered the young prince and his brother to be murdered in the Tower of London.

Many modern historians think that this account of Richard's villainy was fiction from start to finish, but people in the time of the Tudor rulers (Henry VII and his descendants) certainly believed it. **Shakespeare** used the story in his play *Richard III*, and it has affected the way most people think of the king today.

Richard III, carrying the sceptre of state. British monarchs still use the sceptre on formal occasions.

MONTEZUMA II (Moctezuma)

(ruled 1503-20)

Aztec king 1466-1520

Montezuma II was the last ruler of the Aztec people of Mexico. Only the details of the tragic final months of his reign are known. He ruled his vast empire peacefully, trusting in the gods. But he believed a story that Quetzalcoatl, god of storms, would one day visit the earth in person – and when the Spanish soldier **Cortés** arrived on horseback at the head of a column of men, Montezuma (who had never seen either a white man or a horse before) took him for Quetzalcoatl and offered him gifts. The result was tragedy. The Spaniards, greedy for gold, took Montezuma prisoner, and began to

Amerindians saw white men, horses and guns for the first time when the Spanish invaded their lands, and the natives were quickly conquered.

RICHARD III: Shakespeare 16 MONTEZUMA: Cortés 177

massacre his people. They were finally besieged, with their prisoner, in Montezuma's own capital city. Montezuma climbed on to the walls to reason with his subjects; but he was hit by a stone and killed.

HENRY VIII

(ruled 1509-47)

English king 1491-1547

Henry followed his father Henry VII on the throne, and married Catherine of Aragon, daughter of the Spanish monarchs **Ferdinand and Isabella**.

Throughout Henry's boyhood, the Tudor royal family had been working to secure its power, and Henry hoped to continue the dynasty by becoming father of a male heir. Unfortunately, although Catherine bore him six children, all but one died, and the survivor was a girl, Mary. In the 1520s, therefore, Henry decided to divorce Catherine and to take a new queen, Anne Boleyn, a court lady with whom he was already having a love affair.

Because he was a Roman Catholic, Henry was forbidden to divorce unless the Pope agreed. He tried for years to persuade the Pope to let him divorce Catherine, without success. Finally, in 1533, he announced that in future the Church of England would be entirely separate from the Roman Catholic Church, and that he, not the Pope, would be its head. He divorced Catherine and married Anne.

To Henry's fury, Anne Boleyn produced no sons: her only surviving child was a daughter (who later became Queen **Elizabeth I**). Not only that, but she began having love affairs with Henry's courtiers, and in the end Henry had her beheaded.

Henry VIII, the king of England who had six different queens. On the right is Catherine of Aragon, Henry's first wife, whom he divorced by changing the laws of England.

He married four more times. Jane Seymour did provide him with a son and heir (later King Edward VI), but died in childbirth. Anne of Cleves was ugly, and Henry divorced her after a few months. Catherine Howard was a flirt and was executed for adultery. Catherine Parr, who married Henry when he was old and sick, survived him.

Henry was a charming, witty man, popular both with his courtiers and his people. But he was also ruthless, imprisoning or murdering everyone who opposed him. His political and military successes laid the foundation for England's greatness under his daughter, Elizabeth I. They were exactly what one might have expected from the man shown in his portraits: he behaved as he looked, "every inch a king".

Below: Ann Boleyn, Henry's second wife, mother of Elizabeth I.

HENRY VIII: Elizabeth I 436 Ferdinand and Isabella 433

ATAHUALLPA

Inca of Peru 1500-33

Like all Incas (rulers) of the huge Empire of Peru, Atahuallpa thought that he was an immortal god, the Sun come down to Earth. He won his throne by killing another "god" – his own brother.

At this time, a group of Spaniards, led by **Pizarro**, were treasure-hunting in Peru. The Spaniards captured Atahuallpa, tried him for murder and strangled him. With the god-king dead, his terrified people submitted to Pizarro, and Peru and all its gold were in Spanish hands.

CHARLES V

(ruled) 1519-56)

Holy Roman Emperor 1500-58

Charles' grandfather was the Holy Roman Emperor Maximilian I and his mother was Juana, the insane daughter of **Ferdinand and Isabella**. From his Spanish relatives he inherited the thrones of Spain, the Netherlands, much of northern Italy, Burgundy, and the Spanish South American empire, and in 1519 – when he succeeded his grandfather as Holy Roman Emperor – much of Austria and Hungary as well.

Other European monarchs, and notably François I of France, disputed Charles' claim to all this land, and Europe was at war for 25 years. In the end, finding it impossible for any single nation to win the war, the combatants made peace and left things more or less as they had been when the fighting began.

Charles' position as champion of all European Catholics made him a leader in the struggle against **Luther's** religious reforms and the German princes who supported them. He tried both diplomacy and war, and failed in both. Disheartened by what he considered his failure to defend the faith, he gave up his throne and retired to a monastery in northern Spain, where he spent his last years, sad and in poor health, praying to God to forgive him and save his soul from Hell.

The coat of arms of the Holy Roman Emperor Charles V.

ELIZABETH I

(ruled 1558-1603)

English queen 1533-1603

Elizabeth was the youngest surviving daughter of **Henry VIII**. During the reign of Mary, her elder sister, the country was close to financial and political ruin, partly because of wars against the French and partly because England itself was near to civil war – between Protestants and Catholics (Mary's supporters).

Elizabeth I, after a painting by Marc Gheeraerts in 1588.

ATAHUALLPA: Pizarro 175 CHARLES V: Ferdinand and Isabella 433 Luther 338

In 1558, when Elizabeth succeeded Mary as Queen, she quickly made peace with France. But she refused to keep England Catholic, as it had been under Mary. This infuriated the Catholic kings of Spain, who were also angered by the way Elizabeth had refused to punish **Raleigh**, **Drake** and other English captains for attacking Spanish ships and settlements in the New World (the Americas). Finally, in 1588, King Philip of Spain sent a huge *armada* (armed fleet) to attack Britain – but it was defeated in battle, blown off-course by storms and sunk.

Elizabeth never married. She was proud of her nickname "the Virgin Queen". Her long, peaceful reign restored the prosperity England had lost in Mary's time, and gave it back the glory it had known under Henry VIII. She favoured writers and musicians more than any British ruler before or since, and encouraged explorers and adventurers. British people still look back on her reign, the time of writers and poets such as **Shakespeare** and Spenser, and composers such as Byrd, as one of the richest episodes in their artistic history.

The courtyard and pavilions of Fatehpur Sikri, the magnificent capital city which Akbar the Great ordered to be built. It was eventually completed by his grandson, Shah Jahan.

AKBAR THE GREAT

(ruled 1556-1605)

Mogul emperor 1542-1605

The Mogul emperors, descendants of the Mongolian mountain people of the Himalayas, ruled northern India. Akbar (Abu-ul-Fath Jalad-ud-din Muhammad Akbar) was the third emperor, a distant descendant of **Genghis Khan**. He conquered each of the surrounding states – Bengal, Gujarat, Kashmir, Punjab, Rajput and Sind – and later moved south and added the Deccan to his empire.

Following his successes in battle, Akbar ordered his workmen to build a new capital city at Fatehpur Sikri, which he intended to be the most magnificent city in the world. But after 18 years the water supply dried up, and the emperor moved back to the former capital city, Lahore. Five centuries later his beautiful, abandoned city can still be seen.

Akbar was famous for religious tolerance (allowing other people to worship as they chose). He was a Muslim, but refused to outlaw or persecute the followers of other religions. He passed laws forbidding Muslims to provoke Hindus (for example by killing cows, the Hindus' sacred beasts). He even tolerated Christianity, a religion Muslims elsewhere fiercely opposed.

Some of the finest Indian art and architecture dates from Akbar's reign. Mogul art is treasured around the world, and two feats of Mogul architecture, the city of Fatehpur Sikri and the Taj Mahal mausoleum, built on the orders of Akbar's grandson **Shah Jahan**, are ranked among the finest ever created.

ELIZABETH I: Drake 179 Henry VIII 435 Raleigh 180 Shakespeare 16 AKBAR: Genghis Khan 426 Shah Jahan 441

MARY

(ruled 1542-67)

Queen of Scotland 1542-87

Although Mary became Queen of Scotland when she was one week old, she was brought up in France and lived there until 1561. When she settled in Scotland, she was a weak queen, at the mercy of bullying and quarrelsome nobles. People spread stories about her which increased her unpopularity: they said that she had love affairs, and that she helped one of her lovers to murder her husband. After six unhappy years she gave up the throne and fled for safety to England. At first she lived in peace, protected by Queen **Elizabeth I**. But then she was shown to be involved in Catholic plots to dethrone Elizabeth, who was Protestant. Elizabeth imprisoned her for 20 years, and then, when another plot was discovered, had her tried for treason and beheaded.

MARY: Elizabeth I 436

TOKUGAWA, Ieyasu

(ruled 1603-16)

Japanese shōgun 1542-1616

The head of an aristocratic family, Ieyasu spent his first 58 years leading armies and fighting rivals. In 1600, after the battle of Sekighara, the Tokugawa became Japan's second family (after the emperor and his relatives), and three years later the emperor made Ieyasu Shōgun or military dictator.

Ieyasu was now Japan's true ruler, and he governed the country from a magnificent palace in Tokyo. He thought that the best way to keep the country peaceful – and truly Japanese – was to ban all foreigners, and he and his descendants kept Japan separate from the rest of the world for over 200 years; the last Shōgun did not step down from power until 1868.

Japanese Shōgun in fighting gear.

HENRI IV

(ruled 1589-1610)

French king 1553-1610

King Henri IV of France, who emerged as the leading Protestant in the French wars of religion.

Henri was ruler of Navarre, a small Huguenot (Protestant) kingdom on the borders of two Catholic countries, Spain and France. It was a time of religious fanaticism, and Henri hoped to make peace between Protestants and Catholics by marrying a Catholic princess, the sister of the French king, Charles IX. The marriage took place in 1572, but a few days before it the French army (some say acting on royal instructions) massacred 4,000 Huguenots who had gone to Paris to celebrate the wedding. (This event is known as the

"St Bartholomew's Day Massacre", after the day on which it happened.) Henri was taken prisoner, and forced to convert to Catholicism. It was three years before he was set free and able to return to his Protestant beliefs.

In the 1580s, French religious quarrels were set aside to fight a more serious war, against the Spanish, and Henri, as Huguenot commander-in-chief, made an alliance with the Catholic French king, Henri III. Even so, when Henri III was assassinated in 1589, and Henri IV officially succeeded him, there was fierce opposition from French Catholics, and it was not until 1593, when Henri once again converted (saying, so the story goes, "Paris is worth a mass"), that he was finally able to enter his capital city and live in peace.

Official peace between France and Spain was declared in 1598, and in the same year Henri passed a law called the Edict of Nantes. This gave French Protestants the same rights as Catholics; until then, they had not been allowed to worship freely, lend or borrow money, own property or build churches. For the first time in the Christian West a religious minority, the Protestants, had a place in the national community. The Edict of Nantes finally made both Catholics and Protestants feel that they were not separate groups but men and women of a single country: France.

Henri further benefited his country by reforming the laws and the system of justice, building roads and canals and, above all, simplifying the tax system. In ten years he reduced the national debt from 330 million gold pieces to 50 million, a staggering achievement.

NUR JAHAN: Shah Jahan 441

An engraving of the Massacre of the Huguenots in 1572. After Henri IV signed the Edict of Nantes in 1598, the Huguenots (Protestants) were tolerated in France.

NUR JAHAN

(ruled 1611-28)

Indian empress 1571-1634

Mihr-ur-Nisa, widow of a Persian diplomat in Bengal, went to the court of the emperor Jahangir as lady-in-waiting to his mother. Jahangir took her as his chief wife in 1611, and she became known as Nur Jahan.

Jahangir was an alcoholic and a drug addict, incapable of ruling, and Nur Jahan governed in his name. She passed laws, presided over state occasions, and issued coins with her own name on them (the first woman ruler in India to do so). Her hobbies were tiger hunting and playing polo. She ruled for 16 years, until Jahangir's death, when Khurram (**Shah Jahan**), Jahangir's third son and her nephew-in-law, seized power, and murdered all relatives who challenged him. Wisely – or perhaps by arrangement with Khurram, whose claim to power she supported – Nur Jahan retired from politics, and lived the rest of her life in peaceful obscurity.

Ndongo, a former kingdom in Angola, was a rich source of slaves for Portugese traders.

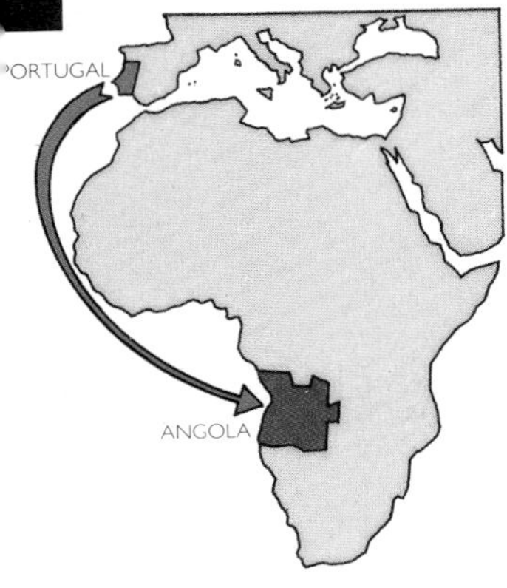

NZINGA, Mbande

Angolan queen c 1582-1663

Nzinga was sister to the king of Ndongo in southwest Africa (part of what is now Angola). In the 1620s, when Europeans began raiding Africa for slaves, she persuaded the Portugese to sign a treaty: if Portugal agreed not to attack her people, she would sell them slaves.

The arrangement worked well for two years, until Mbande Nzinga's brother died and she became queen. Then the Portuguese, thinking the country defenceless, sent an invasion force. They found Mbande Nzinga more than a match for them: she was as skilful a general as she had been a negotiator. She held them at bay for 30 years, until in 1654 they signed a peace-treaty and left her to rule undisturbed until she died.

Cardinal Richelieu – a key figure in the French wars of religion and in the Thirty Years War in Germany.

RICHELIEU: Gustavus Adolphus 441 Louis XIV 443 Medici 43

RICHELIEU, Armand Jean Duplessis

French cardinal and politician 1585-1642

By the age of 21 Richelieu was a bishop, and in 1616, aged 31, he began to work for Marie de Médicis (also known as Maria de' **Medici**), mother of the boy king Louis XIII. Eight years later he was made chief minister of the royal household, and from then until his death he was ruler of France in all but name.

Richelieu laid many foundations of the greatness that was to come to France under **Louis XIV**. He centralized political power in the hands of the king and his ministers, cutting down the power of judges, local magistrates and the nobility.

At that time, France needed a huge amount of money to fight in foreign wars, which Richelieu raised by devising new taxes. The wars were centred on the 30-year struggle in Germany between Catholic and Protestant powers. Richelieu claimed openly to be supporting the Catholic Holy Roman Emperor, but he also sent money and men in secret to help the Protestant king, **Gustavus Adolphus**, the ruler most likely to win the war. When peace came, France had become one of the most powerful states in Europe.

Richelieu's lifelong passion was the glory of France: he was ruthless in its support. His secret police gave him a reputation for bloodthirstiness, and he was feared and hated by the people he devoted his life to serve. In his spare time he wrote plays, and founded the Académie Française, a society (which still exists today) to encourage the finest writers and dramatists in France.

SHAH JAHAN

(ruled 1628-58)

Indian emperor 1592-1666

Khurram was the son of Jahangir and nephew by marriage of **Nur Jahan**. In 1628, when he succeeded to the throne, he took the name Shah Jahan.

The emperor made his rule secure by murdering all his close relatives; only Nur Jahan, who supported his claim to power, was spared. He ruled securely for 30 years, until his son Aurungzebe forced him to give up the throne and retire to private life.

Outside India, Shah Jahan is best-remembered for two magnificent buildings erected during his reign: the Red Fort in Delhi and the Taj Mahal, the mausoleum (palace-tomb) built for himself and his beloved wife Mumtaz-i-Mahal.

The Taj Mahal – a magnificient tomb built by Shah Jahan in memory of his favourite wife Mumtaz-i-Mahal.

GUSTAVUS ADOLPHUS II

(ruled 1611-32)

Swedish king 1594-1632

When Gustavus Adolphus became king, Sweden was fighting Denmark, Poland and Russia over the Baltic Sea and the lucrative trade routes between Russia and Western Europe. Advised by the wily politician Oxenstjerna, Gustavus Adolphus made peace with the Danes, and then spent six years fighting the Russians, before signing a highly favourable truce with them in 1617. He next turned on the Poles, and finally defeated them in 1629.

In his 30s, Gustavus Adolphus took on the most ambitious of all his wars. He saw himself as the "lion of the north", Protestant champion against the Holy Roman Empire in southern Europe. In 1618 the various German princes, Protestant and Catholic, had begun a bitter war (later known as the Thirty Years' War) among themselves. In 1630 one of the princes, the Holy Roman Emperor Ferdinand II, passed a law stripping German Protestants of all political rights. At once Gustavus Adolphus led his armies south.

For two years Gustavus Adolphus won every battle he fought, and in 1631 he prepared to march against Vienna, Ferdinand's capital city. This was his undoing. Ferdinand sent a brilliant Catholic general, Count **Wallenstein**, to attack Swedish allies in northern Germany, and Gustavus Adolphus was forced to pull back his men to defend his friends. After months of skirmishing, Wallenstein's army defeated the Swedes in a pitched battle at Nuremberg in 1632, and over a third of Gustavus Adolphus' soldiers deserted and went home to Sweden. Gustavus Adolphus was rallying the rest of his men when an enemy bullet hit him in the chest and killed him.

Gustavus Adolphus. Under his rule Sweden became a major military and political power.

SHAH JAHAN: Nur Jahan 439 GUSTAVUS ADOLPHUS: Wallenstein 182

In gratitude for Cromwell's success, parliament used his portrait on the Dunbar Medal, a special medal given to the roundhead soldiers who had fought for parliament at Dunbar in Scotland.

CROMWELL, Oliver

English general and politician 1599-1658

After King **Charles I** disbanded the English parliament, civil war began between the "royalists" (the king's supporters) and the "roundheads" (those people loyal to parliament). Cromwell, a roundhead, formed a cavalry company and joined the fighting. His generalship was so brilliant that the revolutionaries made him their leader. He defeated Charles' army at the battle of Naseby in 1645.

After Charles' defeat, many people wanted the king executed. But Charles fled, and was not recaptured until 1648, after a second, brief outbreak of fighting. In 1649 Cromwell ordered Charles' trial for treason, and signed his death warrant. For four years he tried to keep parliamentary rule in Britain, but in 1653, tired of endless arguments, he disbanded parliament, just as Charles had done, and declared himself sole ruler.

Cromwell's official title was "Lord Protector". His rule was harsh but fair, and he abolished many of the unjust taxes invented by King Charles. Even so, people disliked the idea of Britain being a republic. They offered to make Cromwell king in 1657 but he refused, and two years after his death Charles' son succeeded to the throne, as King Charles II.

Cromwell and the roundheads at the battle of Dunbar in 1650.

CHARLES I

(ruled 1625-49)

British king 1600-49

Until Charles' reign, there had been little argument about who actually ruled Britain. The monarch made decisions and took responsibility; parliament was a gathering of nobles and leading commoners who gave advice. This system worked when kings and queens were sensible as well as powerful – but Charles was a fool. He demanded that parliament raise money to pay for pointless foreign wars – and when parliament refused he disbanded it and ruled without it for 11 years. Finally, in 1642, civil war broke out, and five years later Charles surrendered. He was tried for treason and beheaded.

CHRISTINA

(ruled 1632-54)

Swedish queen 1626-89

Christina's father, King **Gustavus Adolphus**, died when she was six years old, and she succeeded to the throne. Count Oxenstjerna, her father's former adviser, ruled the country in her name until she was 18.

Christina was fascinated by knowledge of every kind: as well as politics she studied science (her maths

CROMWELL: Charles I 42 CHRISTINA: Gustavus Adolphus 441 Descartes 342

An engraving of the Swedish queen Christina.

teacher was **Descartes**), languages, theology, literature, music and painting. She dressed as a man and learned the skills of an army officer: shooting, fencing, riding and planning troop movements.

When Christina was 27, she grew bored with power. She gave the throne to her cousin Charles Gustavus, and retired to live first in Brussels and then in Rome. She spent the rest of her life in luxurious exile, collecting paintings and financing the writers and composers she admired.

LOUIS XIV

(ruled 1643-1715)

French king 1638-1715

Louis XIV. His palace at Versailles was intended as a setting for the glory of the "Sun King", and it became a centre of attraction for artists, writers and musicians, French and non-French.

Louis inherited the French throne when he was only five years old, and throughout his childhood there was argument between his mother, who ruled on his behalf, and the parliament of nobles who wanted a share of power. When Louis was old enough, therefore, he disbanded parliament and said that he would be the only power in the land. He used the words *L'état, c'est moi*, "I am the state". He met every morning with a group of advisers, and between them they decided everything that should be done.

Louis ordered a magnificent palace to be built at Versailles – it was the biggest and most spectacular structure in Europe – and ruled there in such splendour that people nicknamed him *le Roi Soleil*, "the Sun King". Artists, musicians, writers and thinkers flocked to Versailles to enjoy royal patronage, and their work earned Louis' reign the same name as Queen **Elizabeth's** in England a century before: "the golden age".

So long as Louis and his advisers were young, the system of royal government worked well. But the older he grew, the more old-fashioned his ideas began to seem. His own nobles began to plot against him, and the other European nations made alliances against the French. Only Louis' diplomatic skill kept the French Empire from disintegrating.

When Louis was 64, he declared war on Spain, trying to win the Spanish throne for his grandson Philip, and the 11 years of fighting which followed (the "War of the Spanish Succession") bankrupted France. In addition to this public disaster, Louis suffered private grief. His sons and grandsons, his heirs, died one by one, until he had no one to leave the French throne to except his great-grandson, a child of five. But although Louis' last 25 years were clouded by such events, few monarchs, before or since, have ever equalled the magnificence of his younger days.

LOUIS XIV: Elizabeth I 436

KANG-XI (K'ang-Hsi)

(ruled 1661-1722)

Chinese emperor 1654-1722

In his youth Kang-Xi was a warrior-prince. He conquered the mountain peoples of north-east central Asia (the present-day Mongolian People's Republic in the USSR) and of the Himalayas to the south (present-day Tibet), making all China one vast, unified nation.

Once the country was at peace, Kang-Xi spent his time improving his people's lives. He ordered dams and irrigation channels to be constructed to control the flooding of the Yellow River, and built roads to make communication easier all over China. He encouraged architects, painters, potters and writers, and ordered a collection to be made of every Chinese book ever written. His finest surviving monument is the beautiful summer palace he built for himself at Jehol (modern Chengde).

Peter the Great, Tsar of Russia...

PETER I, THE GREAT (Pyotr)

(ruled 1682-1725)

Russian emperor 1672-1725

For most of the sixteenth and seventeenth centuries, the great age of European exploration and discovery, Russia had been an isolated, backward country. The Russians had stayed in their own vast lands, avoiding contact with outsiders. Europeans travelled west to the New World of the Americas, or south to Africa and India; very few ever went east to visit Russia.

Peter ended his country's isolation. He toured foreign countries to see how things were done in the West. Western writers, artists and thinkers were invited to Russia, and foreign books were translated into Russian. The power of the old Russian aristocracy was reduced, and the country was reorganized on the model of such Western monarchies as England, France or Sweden. Russian industry was modernized, and streamlined methods of farming and textile manufacture were introduced. Peter even enlisted secretly in the Dutch navy and used the knowledge gained in this way to reorganize the Russian army and navy along Western lines.

The emperor's reforms failed to please anyone in Russia, particularly the nobles whose power he was reducing. In 1698 there was a revolt

...disguised as a sailor. In one of his many disguises Peter the Great toured Western Europe and later introduced many Western ideas into Russia.

which he mercilessly crushed. He used the newly modernized army and navy to strengthen Russia's borders, in particular fighting the Swedes for access to the Baltic Sea. He lived in a magnificent new capital city in the Baltic, St Petersburg (now Leningrad), and filled it with buildings modelled on such Western wonders as Versailles, the palace of the "Sun King" – **Louis XIV** of France.

NADER SHAH

(ruled 1736-47)

Persian shah 1688-1747

Nader Shah saw himself as a mighty warlord, an heir to **Tamerlane**. His enemies regarded him as a bloodthirsty tyrant. He conquered much of what is now Turkey, the Caucasus, Iraq, Afganistan and Pakistan. His soldiers advanced into India, sacked Delhi, and carried off the Peacock Throne (which later became a symbol of the power of the Persian shahs).

Whever Nader's soldiers went, they took no prisoners, but instead lined their routes with skulls, as Tamerlane's men had done. The only place where Nader was vulnerable was home, and when he tried to enforce Sunni Muslim practices in Persia (a Shi'ite Muslim stronghold), he was assassinated.

Maria Theresa, Archduchess of Austria. Queen of Hungary and Bohemia.

MARIA THERESA

(ruled 1740-80)

Austrian empress 1717-80

In the mid-1700s people all over Europe were discussing the nature of political power: whether a country's citizens should have some say in the way they were governed, or if monarchs and emperors had a God-given right to absolute, sole, rule. Maria Theresa, empress of Austria, was determined to be seen to improve her empire. Although publicly she always gave the impression that she was in favour of shared decision-making, in fact every new law, every military decision, every proposal for improving people's lives, could be traced back to her. But she used her power to benefit, not to exploit, her people. She cut taxes, and ended the centuries-old feudal system which made peasants who worked the land virtually slaves of the aristocrats who owned it.

Maria Theresa also simplified and modernized the laws of the Austrian Empire, many of which dated back to the time of **Charlemagne** over 900 years earlier. She reorganized the army, the civil service and the tax system.

Elsewhere, the pace of political reform was speeding up. In France (where Maria Theresa's daughter **Marie Antoinette** was queen) and in America revolutions were brewing; in Britain political power was shifting from the monarch to the prime minister and parliament. The older Maria Theresa grew, the more she found herself opposing new ideas instead of encouraging them. She ended her reign not as a revolutionary but as a reactionary, trying to keep the future at bay. But in her youth she was a ruler to rank with **Elizabeth I** of England or **Louis XIV** of France, and her reforms made Austria one of the most forward-looking states in Europe.

PETER I: Louis XIV 443 NADER SHAH: Tamerlane 430 MARIA THERESA: Charlemagne 422 Elizabeth I 436 Louis XIV 443 Marie Antoinette 448

Afghanistan, the tiny fragment of the formerly vast Persian Empire inherited by Ahmad Shah Durrani.

AHMAD SHAH DURRANI

(ruled 1747-73)

Afghan prince c 1723-73

After the assassination of **Nader Shah**, the Persian Empire was divided. Ahmad had led Nader's soldiers in the south (modern Afghanistan and Pakistan), and was now made Shah (ruler) of that area. He followed Nader's bloodthristy ways, but concentrated on a smaller empire, ruling it with unsurpassed savagery. He regarded northern India, the old Mogul Empire, as his own private plundering ground, and several times invaded and looted its cities, including Delhi. He founded the Durrani dynasty, but his successors were feebler commanders than he was, letting enemies nibble away at his empire until little but Afghanistan itself was left.

Catherine II greatly increased Russia's power and influence in the world, but under her rule millions of Russian peasants were virtual slaves.

CATHERINE II (THE GREAT)

(ruled 1762-96)

Russian empress 1729-96

Catherine's husband, Peter III, was a weak, unpopular emperor, and after only a few months' rule he was murdered and Catherine took his throne. She followed the same policy as the earlier Russian Emperor **Peter the Great**, opening Russia up to the ideas and culture of Western Europe. Her court at St Petersburg (modern Leningrad) was one of the richest and most welcoming in the world, and attracted leading Western artists, musicians, writers and thinkers. Catherine went further and created schools and universities for studies of all kinds, especially medicine. She also encouraged the learning of such subjects as science, astronomy and maths.

Catherine knew the revolutionary French thinker **Voltaire**, and wanted to follow his ideas and turn Russia into a modern, well-governed state for the benefit of all its people. But her nobles blocked such changes, and threatened civil war unless she abandoned them.

Gradually, instead of being free and open, Catherine's state became ever more cruel and backward, and most people lost what few rights they had, becoming little better than slaves of the aristocrats and landowners for whom they worked. Catherine herself turned her attention to foreign wars, and her generals fought brilliant campaigns to strengthen Russian borders in the north, and also won territory in the west and south – "white Russia" from Poland, and the Crimea from Turkey.

AHMAD: Nader Shah 445 CATHERINE II: Peter the Great 444 Voltaire 344

George Washington crossing the river Delaware with his troops to capture Trenton, New Jersey, from the British in the War of Independence. The painting is by Emanuel Leutze (1816-68).

WASHINGTON, George

(held office 1789-97)

1st US president 1732-99

Washington's father, a rich farmer, died when the boy was 11, leaving him to be brought up by his step-brother. The young George Washington educated himself from the books in his brother's library, and also learned farming, hunting, riding and other skills. When his brother died in 1751 he ran the family estates.

In 1759 Washington married a rich widow, and between them they were the wealthiest couple in the area. By this time Washington had had military experience, leading British soldiers against the French (who challenged the British right to own territories in Canada). He was also a politician, and represented his fellow landowners in the "House of Burgesses", as the Virginian state parliament was called.

For the first 40 years of Washington's life, America was governed by Britain, and many Americans resented being ruled and taxed from the other side of the Atlantic Ocean. In the early 1770s, when discontent against the British flared into rebellion, Washington was given the job of recruiting farmhands and craftsmen and turning them into an army. He did this brilliantly, and although the British army was bigger and far better trained, he kept it fully occupied until France came to American aid in 1778. He finally defeated the British and forced them to surrender at Yorktown in 1781. There was fighting here and there but it was half-hearted and insignificant. The American Revolution was over and independence won.

After the war Washington was chairman of the group of people who discussed how the new country was to be governed and who was to do it. In 1789, having decided on a republic rather than a monarchy (rule by a king or queen), the committee unanimously elected Washington president. He served for eight years, and then retired from politics to run his estates. When he died, two years later, he left a will which gave freedom to all his slaves.

In all his portraits Washington kept his mouth closed because he had ill-fitting, painful, false teeth.

JEFFERSON, Thomas

(held office 1800-8)

3rd US president 1743-1826

Although Jefferson was known as a lawyer and politician, he had many other skills. He spoke several languages, including Latin, Greek and French, and had a good knowledge of maths, science and history. He designed his own house, Monticello, and much of his furniture, including a chair which revolved to follow the sunlight and a four-sided music-stand which allowed string-quartet players to sit in a circle and see each other as they played.

Jefferson went into politics at 26, and almost at once began working to win American independence from British rule. He helped to draft the Declaration of Independence, an official challenge to British power.

During the revolution Jefferson acted as an ambassador in Europe, winning other nations (for example France) to the American side. He was the first Secretary of State for the new republic, in charge of foreign affairs, and in 1800 was elected president. Under his administration the US government made the "Louisiana Purchase", buying a vast area of American land from the French Emperor **Napoléon I** at four cents per acre. He also abolished the slave trade with Africa.

Jefferson was re-elected in 1804, and retired in 1808. He spent his last 18 years working for the University of Virginia at Charlotteville: he raised money to found it, designed the buildings and furniture, and decided which subjects should be taught.

A painting made in 1876 to celebrate the centenary of American independence from colonial rule. The Declaration Committee are drawing up the famous document. Jefferson is on the left, Benjamin Franklin is standing in the centre.

MARIE ANTOINETTE

(ruled 1774-93)

French queen 1755-93

Marie Antoinette was the fourth daughter of the Austrian Empress **Maria Theresa**, and married the future Louis XVI of France when she was 15. From the moment she set foot in France, she was unpopular. Some claimed that her marriage was the first step in an Austrian takeover of the French royal family; others that she henpecked Louis and made all his royal decisions for him. People called her an empty-headed flirt, who squandered the nation's wealth on dresses, jewels and parties. The worse the political situation grew in France, with the people complaining about the gap between their own poverty and the wealth and extravagance of the nobility, the more this last accusation stuck.

In 1789, when the first blows were

Marie-Antoinette was famous for her rich clothes – and infamous for the lack of concern she showed for her subjects.

JEFFERSON: Napoléon I 451 MARIE ANTOINETTE: Maria Theresa 445

struck in the French Revolution, Louis wanted to give up supreme power and share rule with a people's parliament. Marie Antoinette made him change his mind. In 1791, after two more years of political turbulence, she tried to smuggle her whole family out of France in disguise. They were stopped at Varennes and returned to Paris. Rumours continued to circulate about Marie Antoinette's foolishness and ruthlessness. It was said, for example, that when she was told that the people had no bread to eat, she answered arrogantly, "In that case, let them eat cake." In 1792 a mob stormed the Tuileries, the royal palace in Paris, and Louis and Marie Antoinette were thrown into prison. Louis was executed in January 1793, and eight months later Marie Antoinette followed him to the guillotine.

During the French Revolution priests and aristocrats. Marie-Antoinette among them, were hurried to the guillotine. The poster demands that the revolutionaries' ideas be accepted – on pain of death.

MONROE, James

(held office 1817-25)

5th US president 1758-1831

Monroe was an ex-pupil and friend of **Jefferson**, and the president used him as a diplomat, sending him to France to settle the Louisiana Purchase with **Napoléon I**. In 1816 Monroe himself was elected president, and served for eight years. One of the greatest achievements of his presidency was to create the country of Liberia ("Freeland") in Africa, a home for freed American slaves. Its capital, Monrovia, is named after him.

Monroe is chiefly remembered today for "the Monroe doctrine". This was a warning he gave to the European powers in 1823 that the days of colonization were over in America, both north and south. The USA would keep out of wars in Europe, and in return European states should keep out of New World affairs. If any of them interfered with any Latin American country, for example, the USA would go to war.

The Monroe doctrine helped independence movements in many South American countries who were shaking off European colonial rule. It lasted into the twentieth century, when the allied powers requested US troops to fight in the First World War, and when the USA itself began to be accused of meddling in Central and South American politics.

MONROE: Jefferson 448 Napoléon I 451

ROBESPIERRE, Maximilien Marie Isidore de

French revolutionary leader 1758-94

Robespierre, one of the French Revolutionary leaders, who became a virtual dictator, and overthrew his rivals Hébert and Danton.

Robespierre, a lawyer, was elected to parliament in 1789, just as the French Revolution began, and quickly rose to become leader of the revolutionary Jacobin party. He believed that the only way to create a successful new state was to sweep away every reminder of the bad old days – and this meant reforming religion, law, politics and even the calendar: he gave the months new names. It also meant stamping out all opposition. Robespierre is said to have started what came to be known as the "Reign of Terror", in which more than a quarter of a million people were arrested without trial. Whether or not Robespierre was responsible, he was blamed, and in 1794 he himself was arrested and sent to the guillotine.

DANTON, Georges Jacques

French politician 1759-94

Danton was a lawyer, and his work often involved helping poor people suffering under harsh laws passed by the French king and his aristocratic advisers. He decided that the only way to bring true justice to France was through revolution. He urged ordinary people to take up arms against the aristocracy, and his powerful words attracted thousands of men and women to the cause.

After the revolution, when the king had been executed and the tyrannical old laws had been swept away, Danton thought the killing should end. But **Robespierre** and the other revolutionary leaders were determined to execute anyone who disagreed with them, rich or poor, guilty or innocent – and when Danton objected they rounded on him, too, and condemned him to the guillotine.

During Danton's ride to the guillotine he was pelted with rubbish and stones.

MEHEMET ALI (Mohammed Ali)

(ruled 1805-48)

Albanian soldier and ruler of Egypt 1769-1849

An orphan, Mehemet Ali was brought up by his army-officer uncle, and was sent to Egypt, to fight for the Turks against **Napoléon I**. In Egypt, he discovered that all the political groups were bickering for power. He bided his time, until in 1805 he was asked to become Pasha (ruler), as the only man who seemed able to keep the peace. He celebrated his new power by inviting 500 rivals to a banquet and butchering them.

Mehemet Ali modernized and strengthened the Egyptian army. At first he used it to keep his own people quiet, but in the 1820s he began wars of conquest – south into the Sudan, north-east towards Syria – and only agreed to abandon them on condition that he was allowed to found a royal dynasty in Egypt. Mehemet Ali ruled until 1848, when senility forced him to give up the throne. His royal dynasty lasted until King Farouk, last of the line, was deposed by **Nasser** in 1952.

DANTON: Robespierre 450 MEHEMET ALI: Napoléon I 451 Nasser 473

NAPOLÉON I

(ruled 1799-1813; 1815)

French emperor 1769-1821

Napoléon Bonaparte was educated in military schools and became an army officer. As a young man he sided with the French revolutionaries, and later led the French army against the Austrians and the British, who wanted to crush the revolution and bring back royal rule. His only defeat in ten years of campaigning was at the battle of the Nile in 1798, when **Nelson** destroyed the French fleet. Napoléon slipped back to France. By this time the members of the Directory (the French revolutionary government) were squabbling among themselves, and in 1799 Napoléon led a revolt against them, and seized power.

Napoléon wanted to make France the centre of a huge European empire, modelled on ancient Rome. He formed a senate, with himself as first consul (and, in 1804, emperor). He organized French laws in the same way as Rome's had been (the *Code Napoléon* or "Napoléon System" is still used today). He built a network of roads and bridges to give his army quick access to anywhere in France. He signed a treaty with the British to get his soldiers back from Egypt, and almost at once began attacking neighbouring countries, hoping to add all Europe to his empire.

As an army commander, Napoléon was a genius. But although he conquered the huge Austrian Empire, and for a few years ruled Italy, Switzerland and Germany, he found the rest of Europe more than a match for him. The British navy sank his fleet at Trafalgar in 1805, and on land the Spanish and Portuguese, helped by soldiers from many other European nations, kept his army pinned down for over six years in what was called "The Peninsular War". Napoléon turned to eastern Europe, and led half a million men into Russia. He looted Moscow in 1812, but on the way home his soldiers were unprepared for the terrible Russian winter, and over 400,000 died.

Seeing Napoléon's army so weak, the European states launched a united attack. In 1813 they defeated Napoléon at Leipzig and exiled him to the tiny Mediterranean island of Elba. In 1815 he escaped, went back to France and declared himself emperor once again. He ruled for 100 days, while the Europeans gathered their armies for a battle which would end his reign for good. This came in 1815, at Waterloo. Napoléon was sent into exile again – this time to the remote Atlantic island of St Helena, where he remained until his death.

The French Emperor Napoléon wanted to conquer the whole of Europe, and reached as far east as Moscow before most of his army perished in the winter of 1812.

NAPOLÉON: Nelson 192

O'CONNELL, Daniel

Irish patriot 1775-1847

Daniel O'Connell.

In the first years of the nineteenth century, the Irish people were struggling against British rule. Irish Catholics particularly hated the way the British oppressed their religion, putting no one but Protestants in positions of power. Many Irish people said that the only way to change things was to fight a war. Others, including O'Connell, said that peaceful discussion would work better.

O'Connell was successful in persuading the British to give Catholics and Protestants equal rights, and for a time the Irish hailed him as a liberator. But years passed and things grew just as bad as they had been before, with Protestants and British people taking the best jobs, whatever the law said. O'Connell fell out of favour with both sides. He went to live in Italy, and died a disappointed man.

JUÁREZ, Benito

Mexican leader 1806-72

Benito Juárez became the first Indian President of Mexico in 1861 and a national hero when he opposed, and defeated, the German prince – Maximilian.

Juárez was a Zapotek Indian, born in the Mexican state of Oaxaca. He studied to become a priest, but in his 20s he turned to law and politics instead. He defended poor people against the landowners who employed them, saying that plantation workers had just as much of a stake in their country as their employers.

In 1847 Juárez was elected governor of Oaxaca. At once he began reforming taxes, building schools and hospitals and using the state's laws to curb the power of the central military government. This brought him huge popularity with everyone except President (later Dictator) Santa Anna, who exiled him in 1853, along with all other supporters of people's rights. Four years passed before Juárez was able to return to Mexico, and another four years before he succeeded in being elected President.

When Juárez came to power, Mexico was crippled by foreign debts run up by Santa Anna and his cronies. In particular, the country owed billions to France, where Napoléon III was emperor. In 1866 Napoléon declared war against Juárez, sent in an invasion force of 28,000 troops and installed the German prince Maximilian as King of Mexico.

Once again, Juárez was forced into exile. But now the United States (which had until then kept out of Mexican affairs, being occupied with its own civil war), took fright at the idea of a large French colony on its southern border, and poured money and soldiers into helping him. In 1867 Maximilian was overthrown and executed, and Juárez returned to Mexico City to begin a second term as president.

Lincoln, Abraham

(held office 1861-65)

16th US president 1809-65

Lincoln, a lawyer, was well known for his work in land-cases – helping farmers whose land was being taken over to build railways – and in murder trials. He was also interested in politics, and his speeches, especially against slavery, attracted huge audiences. In 1856 he joined the Republican Party, which had been formed two years earlier to fight slavery, and in 1860 he was elected US president.

All though the 1850s, slavery had been a source of fierce political argument between north and south. The northern states were against it; the southern states approved of it. Shortly after Lincoln became president, the southerners declared themselves an independent country with their own government and laws. Lincoln ordered troops into action to prevent this, and the southern army resisted. In 1861 civil war began.

Like all civil wars, this one was bitterly fought. The slavery question split families, so that many people found themselves aiming guns in battle against their own fathers, brothers or cousins. Millions of men, young and old, enlisted on one side or the other, abandoning their businesses and farms to fight.

The civil war looked as if it would destroy the United States. But throughout the fighting, Lincoln spoke stirringly about the future. He said that as soon as the war was over, he would act as a political leader and "bind up the nation's wounds". In one of his best-known speeches, at the opening of a cemetery for the soldiers killed at Gettysburg in 1863, he called democracy the best and surest form of rule – government "of the people, by the people and for the people". In 1864 he was elected for four more years as president; in 1865 the south surrendered, and the civil war was over.

Lincoln now faced the hardest task of his whole presidency: to make friends and colleagues of people who had been at each other's throats only days before. But before he could begin, only five days after the surrender, he was shot dead in a theatre by the actor John Wilkes Booth. His death shocked the nation. People of both north and south, whatever their political views, joined to mourn him – the first united act of the whole country for half a dozen years.

Abraham Lincoln, the sixteenth American president who successfully ended slavery in 1863 and preserved national unity after the civil war.

CAVOUR, Camillo Benso di

Italian politician 1810-1861

Cavour worked for all parts of Italy to be independent and united. He did not agitate or rebel, but campaigned in favour of things like railway building, which would help in unification. He became a member of parliament and a minister. Cavour's clever political alliances (especially with **Garibaldi**) brought him his wish, a united Italy, in his last year.

Count Cavour, the "architect" of a united kingdom of Italy.

CAVOUR: Garibaldi 203

Cartoon of Bismarck from 1881, the "Iron Chancellor", with spiked helmet (for butting objectors).

BISMARCK, Otto Edward Leopold von

German politician 1815-98

Until Bismarck was over 40, he had little interest in politics. He was an enormously rich aristocrat, and spent much of his time hunting, feasting and travelling. Then he began carrying diplomatic messages on his journeys, acting as an unofficial ambassador between the princes, kings and queens of Europe. Soon he was an active politician, carrying out his own schemes as well as other people's. His ambition was to join all the German states into a single country, which would be ruled by his patron King Wilhelm I of Prussia. In 1871, after a long series of wars, conferences and treaties, Wilhelm was crowned Kaiser (emperor) of all Germany, and Bismarck was made the empire's political leader, with the title of Chancellor.

Bismarck's rule was strict, earning him the nickname "the Iron Chancellor". He believed in protecting the aristocracy and landowners, and passed laws to keep less well-off people in their place, and especially to limit the power of the new class of factory-owners enriched by the industrial revolution.

So long as Wilhelm I was Kaiser, Germany followed these ideas. But when his son Wilhelm II came to power in 1888, Bismarck's influence began to fade. In 1890 he was dismissed, went back to his old aristocratic way of life and took no more part in politics.

VICTORIA

(ruled 1837-1901)

British queen 1819-1901

For 60 years before Victoria became queen, Britain's monarchs had been a

An early photograph of Queen Victoria, pictured with European Royalty at Coburg in West Germany. Victoria ruled for 64 years.

disgrace. George III suffered from an illness whose symptoms were like madness; George IV was a drunkard; William IV fathered ten illegitimate children. Victoria's advisers were determined that if she ever became queen, she would be a very different kind of ruler. All through her childhood they taught her modesty, good manners and decent behaviour. They also worked to persuade her that a monarch was merely the official head of state; the real ruling was done by parliament.

When Victoria became queen at the age of 18, she showed great public spirit and a real interest in ordinary people. She shared her rule with the prime minister and parliament. She married her cousin Albert when she was 21, and they were idyllically happy. When Albert died in 1861, Victoria at first wanted to retire from public life. But her prime minister, Disraeli, persuaded her to stay on the throne for the good of the people, and she agreed. She ruled for another 40 years, and was one of the most accomplished and popular monarchs in British history.

During the Victorian age (as the nineteenth century is sometimes known in Britain), Britain was one of the most powerful nations of all. The British Empire was enormous, covering one third of the world. London was a centre for science and invention, and British-made goods, from iron to cotton cloth, were sold worldwide. At the heart of it all was the calm, comfortable figure of the Queen-Empress herself: Victoria. People all over the Empire regarded her not only as head of state, but as a kind of universal granny, kindly, honest and reliable.

CETSHWAYO: Victoria 454

CETSHWAYO (Cetewayo)

(ruled 1873-9)

Zulu king c 1826-84

Throughout Cetshwayo's youth, there were constant rivalries among the native peoples of Southern Africa, and between two groups of European colonizers, the British and the Dutch Boers (meaning "farmers"). The Europeans were fighting for control of the best land in the south of Africa, and for the gold and diamands that existed there in huge quantities. Cetshwayo's people, the Zulus, were sworn enemies of the Boers, who raided their territory and stole their cattle. When Cetshwayo became king, therefore, the British invited him to make Zululand part of the British Empire, and to swear loyalty to Queen **Victoria**. But Cetshwayo scornfully refused.

The British and the Zulus lived in uneasy truce for four years, until in 1877 a new British governor sent Cetshwayo an ultimatum: swear loyalty or fight. Cetshwayo at once attacked with 25,000 men, massacring the British at the battle of Isandhlwana and the siege of Rorke's Drift.

These defeats were more than the British could bear. They sent reinforcements armed with machine guns, and in 1879 defeated Cetshwayo's army at the battle of Ulundi. Cetshwayo was taken to London, where he met Queen Victoria and bowed to her authority He returned to Africa to rule in Britain's name, but his people never again trusted or respected him. He died suddenly and mysteriously in 1884, perhaps from poison.

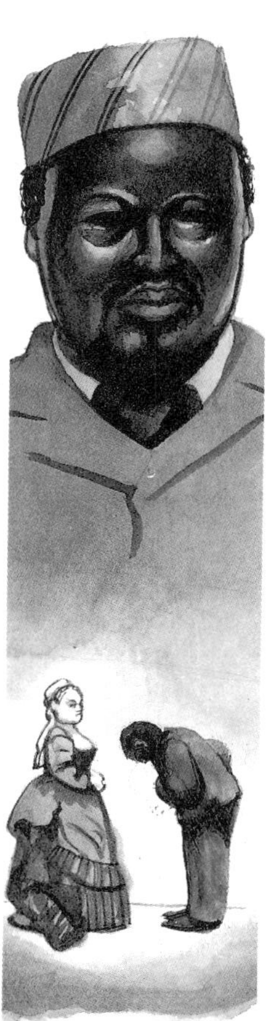

Cetshwayo, the Zulu king, meets Victoria, the British queen.

Geronimo and his Apache warriors, about to ambush a troop of soldiers. They were fighting for the desert and mountain territory of Arizona and New Mexico.

GERONIMO

Amerindian chief 1829-1909

Geronimo was the chief of the Apaches, one of many Amerindian groups encountered by whites when they began settling in the interior of the United States.

The arrival of the whites led to a number of fiercely fought battles: the Amerindians objected to strangers stealing their lands, while the whites regarded the Amerindians as savages. To stop each side attacking the other, the US government offered to divide the land between them. The Amerindians were given "reservations" – areas free from white interference. Even so, many Amerindians still objected. It was clear that the whites took all the best land, and they barred the Amerindians from their holy places, the homes of their ancient gods and spirits.

War between the two sides continued. But government troops hugely outnumbered the Amerindians, and were armed with modern weapons such as cannon and dynamite. One by one they defeated every Amerindian group. The last to surrender was the Apache people, led by Geronimo. He held out until 1886. Then, in despair at the slaughter of his people, he signed a peace-treaty with the whites and led his followers to become farmers in a desert region of the state of Oklahoma. In spite of this defeat, the Amerindians have never abandoned their demand for the return of their ancestral lands.

Geronimo, who finally surrendered in 1886, and ended the Apache wars.

TZ'U HSI

(ruled 1861-1908)

Chinese empress c 1834-1908

In 1851, aged about 17, Tz'u Hsi became a concubine (official mistress) of the emperor. She lived in the Forbidden City in Beijing. In 1856 she bore a son, and when the emperor died in 1861 she seized power, ruling in the boy's name. She was ruthless with anyone who opposed her. When her son came of age and seemed likely to want to rule for himself, he died mysteriously and she appointed another baby emperor, and ruled for him.

Tz'u Hsi believed that the old ways were best, and that modernizing China was wrong. She particularly opposed the ideas of the Western industrial revolution. Her 40-year stranglehold on China meant that by the end of the nineteenth century her

Tz'u Hsi, the Chinese Dowager Empress.

The Boxer Rebellion began as a peasant revolt against the ruling dynasty, which then turned against Western traders, diplomats and missionaries. Tz'u Hsi may have ordered the murder of many foreigners. Forces from Europe were sent to stop the killings, and the rebels themselves were executed.

country was one of the most backward in the world.

In 1900 a group of fanatics, the "Boxers", started murdering Westerners, and the European nations sent warships to end the slaughter. "The Old Buddha", as Tz'u Hsi was nicknamed, disguised herself as a peasant and fled for her life. But it was too late: revolution was in the air. In 1912, four years after Tz'u Hsi's death, revolutionaries (inspired by **Sun Yat-Sen**) threw out the last emperor and made China a modern state.

YAA ASANTEWA

Asante queen c 1840-1921

As queen mother of the Asante nation (in what is now southern Ghana), Yaa Asantewa was almost as powerful as the king. In the nineteenth century Asante leaders began squabbling about who was the rightful king, and the British seized their chance to try to impose British rule. In the 1880s they made a treaty with King Prempeh II, then accused him of breaking it and exiled him. They built a fort at Kumasi, the Asante royal capital, and tried to force white government on the people.

At this point Yaa Asantewa, by then in her 50s, began organizing resistance. She called on the Asante chiefs to band together to save their nation, and besieged the fort. She led such a successful guerrilla campaign that it took five months, and thousands of British lives, before she was finally captured. She died in exile 20 years later.

Although the British went on to rule Yaa Asantewa's country for 60 years, until independence in 1957, her courage was never forgotten, and she is still regarded as one of the greatest leaders in Asante history.

MOHAMMED AHMED (Muhammad Ahmad)

Sudanese leader 1844-85

Some Shi'ite Muslims believe that the last descendant of **Mohammed**, the Mahdi ("guided one"), will return to Earth to bring about the end of the world. Several people have claimed the title Mahdi. The best known is the Sudanese sheikh Mohammed Ahmed. He proclaimed himself Mahdi and began a holy war against the Egyptians, who at that time ruled the Sudan. In 1884 he and his fanatical followers attacked and captured the city of Khartoum, which was defended by British troops. But before he could go on to further conquest, he fell sick (perhaps with typhus from a wound) and died.

TZ'U HSI: Sun Yat-Sen 458 MOHAMMED AHMED: Mohammed 332

Ludwig II and one of his fairy-tale castles in Bavaria.

LUDWIG II

(ruled 1864-86)

King of Bavaria 1845-86

Ludwig had no interest in politics or rule: he lived his life like a spoiled, rich child, doing exactly as he pleased. His real passions were architecture and music. He thought that no more beautiful buildings existed than the castles in fairy-tales, and ordered his architects to build real ones, in fairy-tale style, on steep hillsides and jutting crags beside the river Rhine. His musical passion was the operas of **Wagner**, and he poured money into financing them.

But Ludwig's activities, and his neglect of state affairs, bankrupted Bavaria. People were also shocked by the many rumours about his private life. In 1886 his doctors declared him insane, and soon afterwards he was found drowned – either by accident, suicide or murder.

CHULALONGKORN

(ruled 1868-1910)

Siamese king 1853-1910

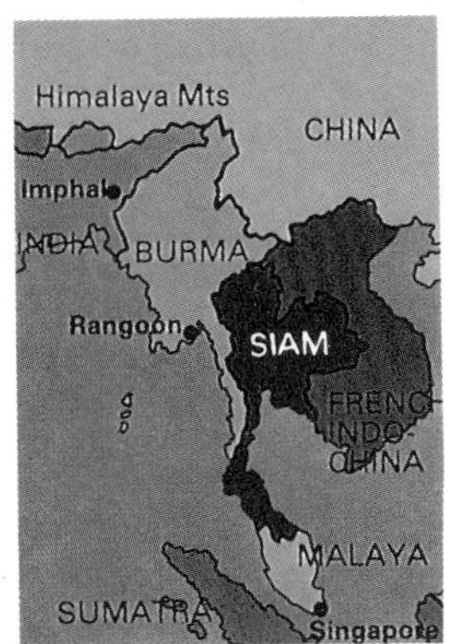

Siam and its neighbours in Chulalongkorn's time.

Chulalongkorn's kingdom, Siam (modern Thailand), lay between two areas colonized by Europeans – British-run Burma and French-run Indo-China (Vietnam). He decided that the only way to rival them in trade and prosperity was to teach his people Western ways. He abolished slavery and replaced harsh, centuries-old laws with new ones based on the French system devised for **Napoléon I.** He ordered the building of roads, railways and up-to-date irrigation systems. He also proclaimed that everyone in the kingdom was to be educated, and set the fashion by bringing an English governess to teach Western ways to his many wives and children. (Her story was later made into a favourite **Rodgers and Hammerstein** musical *The King and I*.)

SUN YAT-SEN

Chinese revolutionary leader 1866-1925

Sun Yat-Sen was educated in Hawaii, as a Christian and a doctor of Western medicine. When he was a student, he read **Marx** and became eager for revolution in China, which was ruled at that time by the corrupt empress **Tz'u Hsi**. He began making speeches and writing articles encouraging rebellion, and Tz'u Hsi sent assassins to hunt him down. He escaped to England, and later to Switzerland, where he met **Lenin**.

While Sun Yat-Sen was abroad, he continued to encourage revolution. He proposed that China should be a republic governed by three principles: Nationalism (freedom from foreign interference), Democracy (rule by elected politicians) and Livelihood (the creation of a welfare state to benefit all citizens).

In 1912, after ten attempts, the revolution succeeded. The last emperor (a child) was deposed, democracy declared, and Sun Yat-Sen invited to be the republic's first

LUDWIG II: Wagner 36 CHULALONGKORN: Napoleon I 451 Rodgers 269 SUN YAT-SEN: Lenin 460 Marx 369 Tz'u Hsi 456

Sun Yat-Sen, presiding over the first Chinese parliament in 1912.

Mahatma Gandhi.

president. But he was opposed by General Yun Shih-Kai, and was exiled during another 11 years of civil war. It was not until 1923 that peace was restored, and Sun Yat-Sen once more became president of the republic his ideas had helped to make.

GANDHI, Mohandas Karamchand

Indian politician 1869-1948

Gandhi started his career as a lawyer, working in London and Bombay, and then spent 11 years in South Africa. In 1914 he went home to India to win political rights for members of the Hindu faith known as the "untouchables", who were regarded as outcasts by other followers of the religion. Soon he began a second political struggle – to win India's political struggle – to win India's freedom from British imperial rule.

Instead of using force in the independence struggle, Gandhi preferred "non-cooperation". He and his followers refused to pay taxes to the British, to have their children educated in British-run schools, or to buy British goods. When the authorities used force against them, Gandhi's followers replied with "passive resistance". They sat quietly where they were, politely refused to do as they were told, and offered flowers and handshakes to the soldiers sent to arrest them. When the British tried to argue with Gandhi, he responded by going on hunger-strikes, threatening to starve himself to death unless his requests were heard.

Although the authorities regarded Gandhi as a nuisance, most people treated him as a kind of holy man. They called him Mahatma ("Great Soul") and gathered in millions to hear him speak.

Eventually, in 1944, the British were prepared to hold serious independence talks. By now Gandhi foresaw new dangers: that Hindus and Muslims would fight each other after independence, and that India would be torn by civil war. There was even talk of a new state, Pakistan, which would be Muslim while the rest of India was Hindu. Gandhi preached that all people should live in peace, with no barriers between them. But the authorities went ahead regardless. India and Pakistan were declared separate states – and rioting broke out. One riot happened at a prayer meeting in Delhi in 1948, and during the confusion an assassin shot Gandhi dead.

LENIN, Vladimir Ilyich

Russian leader 1870-1924

When Lenin (originally called Vladimir Ilyich Ulyanov) was a student, he read the works of **Marx**, the founder of modern communism. He made up his mind to end the tyrannical rule of the Tsars and other Russian aristocrats, and to give political power to the rest of the people. In the 1890s he joined the newly formed Social Democratic Party, and soon became the leader of one of its main groups, the Bolsheviks ("majority").

In 1905 the Bolsheviks organized strikes and demonstrations against the government – and the authorities replied by imprisoning or banishing their leaders. Lenin lived in exile in Switzerland until February 1917, when there was a second revolution in Russia, the Tsar was removed from power, and it was safe to return home. For several months there was a power struggle between the army, the old government officials and the revolutionaries, led by Lenin. Finally, in October 1917, the Bolsheviks won control.

The next few years were agonizingly difficult for Lenin. No one had ever created a full-scale Marxist state before, and the Bolsheviks' plans to take over all privately owned land, factories, banks and businesses and to redistribute them to everyone (called "communal ownership" or "communism") not surprisingly provoked violent resistance from the original owners. For four years there was civil war, fanned by the troops of over 30 other countries, sent to Russia to destroy the Revolution. Hundreds of thousands of people died; millions went into exile; there was famine, poverty and misery even greater than before the Revolution. But at last, after appalling suffering, the new political system was established. The vast nation of Russia, the largest country in the world, was organized as a federation of 15 communist republics, each led by a "soviet" or workers' parliament.

In 1922, soon after the end of the civil war, Lenin had the first of a series of crippling strokes, and 18 months later he died. His body was embalmed (preserved), laid in a glass coffin and placed in a huge tomb in Moscow's Red Square. Throughout the USSR he is hailed as the nation's founding father.

Lenin, the Russian Revolutionary leader, speaking in Moscow. Just beneath him is Leon Trotsky who became leader of the Red Army. Lenin is a national hero in the USSR. His statues are in every town and there are paintings or photographs of him in every public building.

LENIN: Marx 369

SMUTS, Jan Christiaan

South African soldier and politician 1870-1950

Smuts fought as a guerrilla leader in the 1899-1901 war between the Boers and the British, and after the war began a career in politics. Although he was a leader of the Afrikaans-speaking South Africa Party, he supported the British and kept South Africa in the Commonwealth. He worked ceaselessly for world peace, supporting the League of Nations and later the United Nations.

From 1919 to 1924 Smuts was Prime Minister of South Africa, and in 1939, when the Second World War broke out, he was elected prime minister at the age of 69. Three years after the war he campaigned for a second term of office, but was defeated by the group of South African whites who believed in apartheid – separate development for people with different skin-colours – an idea which Smuts detested.

Winston Churchill making his famous victory sign outside 10 Downing Street in June 1943.

CHURCHILL, Winston Leonard Spencer

English politician and writer 1874-1965

Churchill began his career as a soldier, and then acted as a war reporter, sending news to London papers on the Boer War in South Africa. When he went home he began a career in politics, and was elected a Member of Parliament at 26. In 1911 he became First Lord of the Admiralty, in charge of Britain's navy, and he held this post until 1915.

In the 1920s Churchill disagreed more and more with his fellow-politicians. He disliked the way they were handing over British power in India, and later he was more anxious than they were about **Hitler's** growing power in Europe. Churchill retired to his country house, where he spent most of the 1930s writing books (chiefly on history), painting and indulging in his favourite hobby, bricklaying. But in 1939, when parliament at last realized that fighting Hitler was the only way to stop him taking over Europe, Churchill returned to London and in 1940 was elected prime minister.

Churchill led the British people throughout the Second World War, inspiring them to fight by his own personal courage and by making magnificent speeches, many of which were recorded and can still be heard.

After the war there was a general election and Churchill's party lost. But in 1951 they returned to power, and Churchill was prime minister for four more years. He went on working until he was over 85. When he died he was given a state funeral.

Below: a cartoon of "Winnie" by Bert Thomas, c 1918.

ADENAUER, Konrad

German politician 1876-1967

For most of his long life, Adenauer worked in local politics. He was mayor of Cologne from 1917 to 1933. When the Nazis took power he was removed from office and twice imprisoned. After the Second World War he was made chancellor of Germany and rebuilt his country, both politically and financially. West Germany's "economic miracle" began with him.

Konrad Adenauer, chancellor of West Germany 1949-63.

CHURCHILL: Hitler 466

Left: Jinnah in Western clothes (a rare thing in his time for a Muslim leader).

JINNAH, Mohammed Ali

Indian/Pakistani politician 1876-1948

Jinnah studied law in London, and worked as a lawyer in Bombay. In 1906 he began taking part in politics, and ten years later he was elected president of the Muslim League, founded to give Muslims political power in India. For some years he worked alongside the Indian National Congress Party, campaigning to end British rule in India. But he disagreed with **Gandhi's** idea of civil disobedience, and he began to think that the Congress Party was too concerned with the interests of Hindus and that Muslims might do better on their own.

In the 1940s, when India and Britain were negotiating to end British rule, Jinnah fought hard for a separate Muslim state – Pakistan. When it was created in 1947 he was made its first governor-general. He is revered as the founder of the nation, and is given the honorific name Quaid-i-Azam, "Great Leader".

STALIN, Joseph

Russian dictator 1879-1953

Stalin, meaning "steel", was the political nickname of Joseph Vissarionovich Djugashvili. He fought vigorously and ruthlessly in the 1917 Russian Revolution and the civil war which followed. In 1922 he was made General Secretary of the Communist Party, one of the highest political offices in the Soviet Union. In 1924, after **Lenin's** death, he was one of a group of leaders who took supreme power, and in 1929 he became sole party leader. He rid himself of those of his fellow-revolutionaries who now opposed him, in a series of "show trials" which led to their execution.

Soon after Stalin became dictator, he began rebuilding Russian industry and agriculture. To make farming more efficient, he forced the peasants to join "collective farms", huge areas of land worked jointly by thousands of people. Many peasants objected, and Stalin sent in his troops to quell resistance. In the early 1930s alone he is thought to have ordered 20 million deaths. But his brutal methods worked, and Russia did become a powerful nation, a match for any country in the world.

Despite Stalin's pre-war brutality, in the Second World War he became a symbol of Russian resistance to Hitler.

Stalin's non-aggression agreement with the Nazis was broken when German tanks invaded Russia in 1941. But the German army was crippled by the harsh Russian winter and the bravery of the Russian troops, which helped to win the war.

JINNAH: Mahatma Gandhi 459 STALIN: Churchill 461 Hitler 466 Lenin 460

Just before the Second World War, Stalin signed a non-aggression pact with **Hitler**. But two years later the Nazis treacherously invaded Russia, and Stalin joined Britain and the USA in a military alliance against Germany. The bravery of Russian soldiers on the eastern front, where over 20 million died, helped to win the war.

Almost as soon as victory was declared, Stalin ended his alliance with the West. The Russians had freed a dozen Eastern European countries (including Poland, Czechoslovakia and Hungary) from Nazi rule; now Stalin bound them together as a "Soviet bloc", loyal to the USSR and opposed to capitalist Western ways. In the 1950s emigration stopped between East and West. As **Churchill** put it, an "iron curtain" separated Russian-dominated countries from the Western world. The so-called "cold war" (that is, a battle of words and sneers, without actual fighting) has continued ever since.

Millions of young people had been killed in the "Great Patriotic War" (as Soviet citizens call the Second World War), and the country had all but bankrupted itself to pay for it. Stalin in the late 1940s and early 1950s made even tougher plans to rebuild national wealth. Once again he eliminated all opposition, sending dissidents – those who disagreed with him – to forced-labour camps or to exile in Siberia.

Stalin died in 1953, and ever since then the Soviet Union has been trying to shake off the effects of his dictatorship and its worldwide reputation for repression of human rights.

ATATÜRK (Mustafa Kemal)

(ruled 1922-38)

Turkish leader 1881-1938

After the First World War, the Greeks besieged Turkey, and Kemal led the armies which fought to keep them out. In 1922, when peace was declared and Turkey became an independent nation, Kemal was made its first president. He abolished the law making Islam the state religion, and set about turning Turkey into a modern industrial country. He ordered factories to be built: the first industry many Turks had ever seen. He insisted on mass education, and ordered that the Western alphabet and numerals should replace the thousand-year-old symbols Turks had used till then. And, for the first time in Turkish history, women were declared to be equal to men.

In 1934 Kemal took the honorific title Atatürk, "father of Turkey" – one he well deserved, for he had re-created a nation and given back his people their pride.

The War of Liberation Medal presented to Commander-in-Chief Kemal for his part in Turkey's independence.

This illustration is from an official painting of Atatürk speaking to his people from the balcony of the Turkish Grand National Assembly.

ROOSEVELT, Franklin Delano

(in office 1933-45)

32nd US president 1882-1945

Roosevelt, a lawyer, went into politics in his mid-20s and quickly rose to high office. He was elected senator for New York, served for seven years, as assistant secretary for the navy, and stood (unsuccessfully) for election as vice-president. Then, in 1921, he was a victim of polio, and was crippled from the waist down. This setback would have ended many men's careers. But Roosevelt began a daily routine of physiotherapy, to make his muscles as healthy as possible. It was so successful that he was able to appear in public without many people ever knowing that he was paralysed. He was elected Governor of New York State in 1928 and President of the USA in 1932.

In the early 1930s the USA was in crisis. After the 1929 "Wall Street Crash", when the American stock market collapsed, companies were going bankrupt all over the country. Millions of people became unemployed, and there was no welfare system to provide even the bare necessities of life. Despair, crime and misery were everywhere. Roosevelt fought this Depression, as it was called, with what he termed a "New Deal". He poured national money into building work: new dams, irrigation schemes, roads, city centres and, above all, houses. The construction companies had jobs to offer the unemployed. Recovering from the Depression took years, but by the end of the 1930s the New Deal had worked and the USA was prosperous again.

Roosevelt photographed in front of a gigantic US flag – a favourite wartime picture.

In 1939, when the Second World War began, Roosevelt at first kept the USA out of the fighting. Then, in 1941, the Japanese (allies of Germany and Italy) bombed the US fleet in Pearl Harbor, Hawaii, and Roosevelt declared war. American money, men and weapons flooded across the Atlantic to help the European countries opposed to **Hitler**, and US forces fought the Japanese in the Pacific.

All through the war, in stirring public speeches, many of them filmed for newsreels, and in radio "fireside chats", Roosevelt would tirelessly encourage the Americans to fight for freedom as they had fought in the Depression for prosperity. Tragically he died of a stroke in 1945 – only three weeks before the end of the war in Europe.

Roosevelt was the only president in US history to be elected four times.

ROOSEVELT: Hitler 466

Right: Mussolini rallying his Fascist supporters in Rome.

MUSSOLINI, Benito

Italian dictator 1883-1945

Determined to make his career in politics, Mussolini joined the Socialist Party. But, against party policy, he wanted Italy to join in the First World War, and the socialists threw him out. In 1919 he formed a new party, called the Fascists after their symbol, a bundle of sticks tied round an axe (*fasces*) which used to be carried before the consuls in ancient Rome. The party grew quickly, and was soon one of the most powerful in Italy.

Mussolini liked to put on what he called his "Roman emperor" face for official portraits.

In 1922, modelling himself on **Julius Caesar** 2,000 years before, Mussolini marched on Rome and demanded a share in the government. He was made prime minister, and in 1929 declared himself dictator. He made grand speeches offering the people the same living conditions as those enjoyed by the citizens of ancient Rome – firm government, clean streets, law and order and what he called "social discipline". He also copied the rulers of ancient Rome by trying to build an empire, sending armies to Abyssinia in Africa (modern Ethiopia) in 1935 and to Albania in 1939.

In 1940 Mussolini made an alliance with **Hitler**, and declared war on France and Britain. But his soldiers lost battle after battle, and in 1943 Mussolini's own supporters forced him to resign. Hitler promptly reinstated him, not as dictator but as regional ruler of northern Italy. In 1945 the Italian Resistance captured him and shot him. They hung his body upside-down from a roof, and people marched up and down in front of it, mocking it with the fascist salutes Mussolini had always claimed were his royal right.

David Ben-Gurion, the first prime minister of the Jewish state – Israel.

BEN-GURION, David

Israeli political leader 1886-1973

Ben-Gurion was born in Poland, but emigrated to Palestine in 1906. He worked first as a farm labourer, then as a trade union official and finally as leader of the Jewish Labour Party.

All through Ben Gurion's early life the Jews were fighting to have Palestine, their Biblical homeland, restored to them, and when the State of Israel was created by the United Nations in 1948, Ben-Gurion became its first prime minister. He stayed in office, except for a few months, until he retired in 1963, and his calmness and political skill did much to keep the peace between Jews and Arabs (who challenged the Jewish claim to Palestine) and to build Israel into a prosperous state.

MUSSOLINI: Caesar 415 Hitler 466

HITLER, Adolf

(ruled 1933-45)

German dictator 1889-1945

In the early 1920s Hitler joined the tiny National Socialist (Nazi) party, an extreme right-wing group which at that point had only six other members. He spent the next ten years building it into one of the largest political parties in Germany. He was a brilliant public speaker and drew eager crowds to every meeting he addressed. His oratory converted many people to the Nazi beliefs: anti-communist, anti-Jew, and anti-government. The 1920s were a time of poverty and unemployment, and when Hitler promised full employment, claiming that the National Socialists were the only party which would make Germany great and rich again, hundreds of thousands of people believed him.

In 1932 Hitler stood as a candidate in the German presidential election. Although he lost, parliament thought that he was too powerful to overlook, and gave him the important job of chancellor. One year later, the Nazis called a general election, and won. From then on, Hitler was supreme. He proclaimed himself Führer ("leader"), and abolished all opposing political parties. He created a force of secret police, the Gestapo, whose actions could not legally be questioned. Above all, he spoke with spell-binding power of Germany's future, saying that he would create a 1,000-year empire like that of ancient Rome, and that the way to begin was by removing communists, Jews, homosexuals and intellectuals from positions of any power and influence.

By 1936 all Germany was under Hitler's spell. He began building up the army, navy and air force, announcing that soon Germany would conquer the world. In 1939 his troops invaded Austria, Poland and Czechoslovakia; in 1940 they took over Denmark, Norway, Holland, Belgium, France, Romania and Greece.

Until these attacks began, people in other countries had watched Hitler with distrust but not alarm. But after the invasion of Poland in 1939, Britain declared war, and in 1941, when the Japanese (Hitler's allies) bombed the US fleet at Pearl Harbor in Hawaii, the Americans joined the fighting. This was the Second World War.

By 1944, after millions had been killed on all sides, it was clear that Germany's opponents were winning.

Hitler had been a corporal in the First World War and, as the Nazi leader, he liked to dress in uniform, with an Iron Cross (awarded for bravery) pinned on his chest, to rally the people.

They marched into countries formerly occupied by the Nazis, and liberated them one by one. In 1945 they began advancing through Germany itself, and in April reached Berlin. Realizing that all was lost, Hitler committed suicide.

After the war, the leading Nazis were put on trial at Nuremberg, and the details of their crimes horrified the world. The Jews, gypsies, communists and others who had "disappeared" had not, as Hitler's propaganda-chief **Goebbels** had claimed, been resettled in other parts of the German Empire. In fact they had been starved, tortured or gassed to death in concentration camps. Over six million men, women and children had been murdered in such places as Dachau and Auschwitz. This is now known as the "Holocaust" (a grim word meaning "multi-sacrifice"), and it, even more than his political plotting or the devastating war he began, is what makes people curse Hitler's memory.

NEHRU, Jawaharlal

Indian politician 1889-1964

Nehru was educated as a lawyer, but his real interest was politics. He wanted to free India from British rule. He joined the National Congress Party and became its leader in 1928. He supported **Mahatma Gandhi's** ideas of civil disobedience and passive resistance. But he also made fiery speeches against the British, who responded by jailing him as a troublemaker. Between 1921 and 1942 he spent 18 years in prison.

In 1947, when India at last broke free of Britain, Nehru became prime minister. For the next 17 years he was one of the main leaders in the Commonwealth (the group of former British colonies), and he also led the group of "non-aligned" countries, which deliberately made no alliance with either of the great world powers.

Nehru, with his daughter Indira Gandhi and grandson Rajiv Gandhi: three generations of the same family, all to be leaders of their country.

In India, Nehru worked to reform the caste system, to give women equal rights with men, and to make the whole vast country a single, self-sufficient state, able to feed and clothe its people without relying on imports. He encouraged industries such as mining and steel-making, and ordered the building of thousands of kilometres of roads and railways, and of irrigation schemes to improve agriculture and at the same time provide hydroelectricity.

Nehru died in 1964, and two years later his daughter **Indira Gandhi** succeeded him as Congress Party leader and then Indian prime minister. She in turn was followed by her son **Rajiv Gandhi**

HITLER: Goebbels 470 NEHRU: Gandhi, I 472 Gandhi, M 459 Rajiv Gandhi 476

Cartoon of de Gaulle in his army coat and cap, taking the salute.

DE GAULLE, Charles André Joseph Marie

French soldier and politician 1890-1970

After fighting in the First World War, in 1921 De Gaulle published his idea of combining air and tank forces in attack. His suggestion was ignored by his superiors, but was developed by Germany, and became the basis of the "Blitzkrieg" air attacks (total bombardment by bombers) which the Germans launched against many European cities in the Second World War.

When the Germans invaded France in 1940, De Gaulle escaped to Britain, from where he organized the "Free French" movement of people who opposed German rule. He became leader of the French Resistance, battling against the occupation of his country. In 1944 he returned triumphantly to Paris with an army which freed the city from German rule, and was made head of the new French government.

De Gaulle found politics personally unsatisfying, and after two years in power withdrew to his country home, leaving the large "Gaullist" party leaderless. But in 1958 he agreed to return to power, this time as all-powerful President of France. He served for 11 years, and became a leading spokesman for France's power and independence from US control. He granted self-rule to former French colonies including Algeria (which had been fighting a long and bitter war of independence), and helped to re-establish France as a leading state in both European and world politics.

HO CHI-MINH

Vietnamese politican 1892-1969

Ho Chi-Minh was one of the founders of the international Communist Party and led a rebellion against French colonial power in his country. After his troops captured the stronghold of Dien Bien Phu, he declared himself president of North Vietnam. He went on fighting the South Vietnamese, who were supported by the USA – and won. When South Vietnam fell to the communists in 1975, its capital, Saigon, was re-named Ho Chi-Minh City after him.

FRANCO, Francisco

Spanish soldier and dictator 1892-1975

Franco had a distinguished army career, and in the 1930s was made commander of the Spanish Foreign Legion in north Africa. But soon afterwards civil war broke out in Spain, between the ruling Republicans (who believed in a socialist, democratic state) and the Nationalists (who believed in keeping the power of the aristocracy, supported by the army). In 1936 Franco flew home to command the

The dictator, General Franco.

Nationalists. He was supported by **Hitler** and **Mussolini**, who sent him money, planes and bombs. The Republicans, in turn, were supported by the "International Brigade", socialists and communists from all over Europe.

As in all civil wars, the fighting was bitter and bloody, and it lasted for three terrible years, during which Franco outraged his enemies by bombing civilians – one of the first times in history this ever happened. By 1939 the Nationalists had won the war. Franco set up a one-party state with himself as El Caudillo ("The leader", a Spanish equivalent of Führer, Hitler's title in Germany), and began executing or imprisoning as many political opponents as he could catch.

Franco's dictatorship lasted for 36 years. He ignored the anti-fascist fury in Europe which followed the Second World War, and kept his country under firm military control, despite assassination attempts by poison, bomb and bullet. He kept Spain on the sidelines of international politics, and discouraged "modern" ideas in education, agriculture and industry.

At the end of his life Franco made plans to be succeeded by **Juan Carlos**, a member of the Spanish royal family. When he died, Juan Carlos duly became king, but instead of keeping things as they were he immediately set about guiding Spain in a return to democracy.

TITO, Marshal (Josip Broz)

Yugoslav soldier and politician 1892-1980

Tito was head of the Yugoslavian Communist Party during the Second World War when the Axis powers (Germany and its allies) invaded his country. He led the Partisans (the heroic resistance movement) with spectacular results and became leader of Yugoslavia in 1945. He refused to join either the Eastern or Western power blocs, and supported **Nehru's** idea of non-aligned nations.

Right: Marshal Tito, president of the independent Yugoslavia from 1953 until his death in 1980.

FRANCO: Hitler 466 Juan Carlos 475 Mussolini 465 TITO: Nehru 467

MAO ZEDONG (Mao Tse-tung)

Chinese leader 1893-1976

Mao Zedong was one of the founders of the Chinese Communist Party. At that time, communists all over the world were excited by the success of the Russian Revolution (see **Lenin**), and Mao wanted to lead a workers' revolution in China too. His political opponents savagely attacked his communist ideas, and when he set up the first Chinese Marxist state, in the southern province of Jiangxi (Kiangsi), they turned from insults to war. Led by Jiang Jie Shi (Chiang Kai Shek), they sent soldiers to kill every communist they could find.

Mao Zedong, first chairman of the People's Republic of China. He prepared a "Little Red Book" of his ideas, which was issued free to every Chinese citizen.

By 1934 Mao's enemies were ready for a final onslaught. His followers seemed doomed. But he decided on a daring escape plan. With a vast group of people, 80,000-100,000, he set out, quite simply, to walk to safety. The "Long March", as it came to be called, lasted for 12 months and covered 10,000 kilometres. The marchers climbed mountains, crossed deserts and bridged torrents, ambushed at every step by Jiang Jie Shi's soldiers. In the end, after a year's hardship, 30,000 survivors reached safety in Ya'nan (Yenan), and set up new homes there.

Mao and his communist followers – men, women and children – on the Long March.

Throughout this time of civil war, the Japanese had been quietly conquering Chinese territory in the east. By 1938 it was clear that the Second World War was about to start in Europe, and that the Japanese – allies of Germany – would take advantage of the struggle, if they could, to seize control of China.

Faced with this danger, the Chinese communists and nationalists made a truce to fight the Japanese. But in 1946, as soon as the Second World War was over and Germany and Japan had lost, the Chinese civil war broke out again. The Americans supported Jiang Jie Shi and the nationalists; the Russians supported Mao and the communists.

After three years' fighting, the nationalists lost, and Jiang Jie Shi and his followers went into exile on the island of Formosa (now called Taiwan). The communist People's Republic of China was born, and Mao became its first leader.

GOEBBELS, Paul Joseph

German politician 1897-1945

Goebbels became **Hitler's** Minister of Enlightenment and Propaganda in 1933. Propaganda is information, true or false, designed to keep a country's people loyal and cheerful. Goebbels controlled all information in Germany for the next 12 years. He censored books, newspapers, films, radio broadcasts – even advertisements and sermons.

In the Second World War, Goebbels' job was crucial. He allowed nothing to reach the German

MAO ZEDONG: Lenin 460 GOEBBELS: Hitler 466

people that might make them distrust Hitler and the Nazis, and in particular kept from them the existence of concentration and extermination camps, saying instead that the Jews and other people who disappeared had been "relocated" elsewhere in Germany. In 1945, realizing that Germany had lost the war, he shot his six children dead, and he and his wife took poison.

Right: Hirohito, in official dress – the 124th emperor of Japan.

Golda Meir.

MEIR, Golda

Israeli political leader 1898-1979

Meir was born in Russia, but went to live in Palestine (the country which later became Israel) in 1921. She worked on a farm, and also took part in politics, working closely with **Ben- Gurion**. After the state of Israel was created in 1948, she became a member of the government. She formed the Israeli Labour Party in 1957, and was prime minister from 1969-74.

HIROHITO

(ruled 1926-1989)

Japanese emperor 1901-1989

Hirohito was born at a time when many Japanese still believed that their emperors were direct descendants of Jimmu, founder of the unbroken imperial line, 2,600 years ago. But as an adult he was more interested in the present than the past. He was the first Japanese prince to visit Europe and the USA, and studied modern science (botany and marine biology).

As emperor, Hirohito had the people's respect but no real power, and he did nothing to stop the careers of military men, including General Hideki Tojo (1884-1948), who were determined to conquer the whole of south-east Asia. During the Second World War Japan was allied with **Hitler**, and in 1945, after the Americans dropped atom bombs on the Japanese cities of Hiroshima and Nagasaki, Hirohito forced Tojo to agree to unconditional surrender. He gave up his claim to divinity and spent the rest of his life out of the public eye, presiding on official occasions as head of state but taking no part in politics.

ALLENDE (Gossens), Salvador

Chilean politician 1908-73

In 1970 Allende became the first Marxist president in the Western hemisphere to be freely voted into office. His socialist policies alarmed the rich in Chile and the powerful Central Intelligence Agency (CIA) in the USA. In 1973 he was killed by unknown attackers during a revolution by the CIA-backed Chilean armed forces. They, under General Pinochet, have since made Chile one of the harshest military dictatorships in the world.

MEIR: Ben-Gurion 465 HIROHITO: Hitler 466

Willy Brandt, former chancellor of West Germany.

BRANDT, Willy

German politician born 1913

When Brandt was 20, he fled from the Nazis and worked in the Norwegian and German underground movements against them. After the war he went back to Germany, and had a long political career. He was made chancellor in 1969. In 1971 he was awarded the Nobel Peace prize for his work in improving the atmosphere between Eastern and Western Europe. He resigned from German politics in 1974, and headed the committee that produced the Brandt report. This recommended ways in which the prosperous nations of the world (mostly in the north) should help, not exploit, the poorer south.

KENNEDY, John Fitzgerald

(held office 1961-63)

35th US president 1917-63)

Kennedy was elected US president at the age of 43 – the youngest person, and the first Roman Catholic, ever to reach office. He belonged to a rich, famous family, and was as well-known as any film star or pop singer. Some older US politicians objected that he had no experience of government. They said that his presidency would be like a firework display: impressive while it happened, but of no lasting use.

Kennedy quickly proved his critics wrong. He tried to make Congress (the US parliament) pass a law forcing all schools and universities to admit blacks and whites equally, and to give equal voting rights to all. He proposed laws to help the poor, sick and unemployed. He condemned the newly built Berlin Wall, and in 1962 insisted that the Russians remove nuclear weapons from Cuba.

Soon, instead of condemning Kennedy, many Americans, both Democrats (his own supporters) and Republicans, were saying that if he were selected for a second four-year term of office, he might turn out to be one of the finest presidents the USA had ever had. Unfortunately, time was denied him. In 1963, when he was driving in an open-top car in a political procession in Dallas, Texas, he was shot dead – and to this day it is not certain who his killer was.

After Kennedy's death, Lyndon Baines Johnson (1908-73) became president, and carried out many of Kennedy's proposals for equal rights and social welfare.

The headline that shocked the world.

PRESIDENT SLAIN

Texas Assassin Hits Kennedy in Automobile

News Call Bulletin

SAN FRANCISCO'S EVENING NEWSPAPER

Volume 5, No. 90 FRIDAY, NOVEMBER 22, 1963 Phone EX 7-5700 Price 10c

DALLAS—President John F. Kennedy is dead.

He died after an assassin fired on his car leading a motorcade into Dallas, third stop on his Texas tour.

DALLAS (UPI)—President John F. Kennedy and Gov. John B. Connally of Texas were cut down by an assassin's bullets as they toured downtown Dallas in an open automobile today.

Mystery San Carlos Gun Battle

Gunfire blazed in a quiet residential section of San Carlos early this morning as an apartment house dweller

PRESIDENT JOHN F. KENNEDY

GANDHI, Indira

Indian political leader 1917-84

Gandhi was **Nehru's** daughter, and worked to win Indian independence from Britain. She was a member of

GANDHI: Rajiv Gandhi 476 Nehru 467

the Indian National Congress Party, and was elected prime minister in 1966. She served from 1966-77, and then again from 1980. But her opponents said that she behaved more like a dictator than an elected leader, that her family took bribes and that she was unfair to religious minorities, especially Sikhs (some of whom wanted to break away from India and form a separate state). Sikh extremists murdered her in 1984, and her son **Rajiv Gandhi**became prime minister in her place.

REAGAN, Ronald Wilson

(held office 1981-9)

40th US president born 1917

Reagan was a film actor. His hobby was politics until 1964, when he made it his full-time career. He was elected US President in 1981, and served for eight years. He was famous for his easy-going manner, and for his right-wing ideas (which were nicknamed "Reaganomics") on cutting taxes and reducing state control. Although he once declared the USSR "an evil empire", he later made the breakthrough with President **Gorbachev** which both men hoped would lead to the end of the threat of nuclear war.

REAGAN: Gorbachev 76

NASSER, Gamal Abdel

(ruled 1956-67)

Egyptian soldier and politician 1918-70

Like many other Egyptians of the time, Nasser was appalled by the corruption of King Farouk of Egypt and his courtiers, who lived in luxury while millions of their people starved. In 1952 Nasser master-minded a military coup which dethroned Farouk. Egypt became a republic, with General Neguib as its president and Nasser as its first prime minister.

Two years later, in 1954, Nasser organized a second coup, dismissed Neguib and took presidential power himself. At once he nationalized the Suez Canal, saying that since it lay in Egyptian territory, it should be controlled by Egypt and should not be a neutral zone, managed by the British, as it had been till then.

Nasser's ambition was to make Egypt the heart of a single state (the United Arab Republic, or UAR), which would unite all the Muslim peoples of north Africa and Arabia. Syria, the Yemen and Iraq signed treaties with Egypt. But in 1967, after defeat in the Six-Day War with Israel, the Arab nations quarrelled, and Nasser's dream of Arab unity has never been fulfilled. Even so, the self-governing, democratic republic of Egypt, which he created, is still a leading power in Mediterranean and Arab politics.

Indira Gandhi. She was assassinated by members of her own bodyguard in 1984.

Gamal Nasser.

Anwar Sadat.

SADAT, Muhammad Anwar al

(held office 1970-81)

Egyptian president 1918-81

In 1952 Sadat was one of the group of officers who deposed the corrupt King Farouk. He served for many years as a minister in the republican government, and was elected vice president in 1964 and 1969, and president in 1970. In 1977, to the horror of Arabs who believed that the State of Israel had been created on land stolen from the Palestinians, and had no right to exist, he went to Israel, spoke in parliament there, and signed a peace treaty in 1979. This effort won him the Nobel Peace prize (shared with Israel's prime minister Menachem Begin) – and also the fury of his political enemies, who assassinated him.

Eva Perón always managed to look every bit the glamorous film star, even as a leading politician.

PERÓN, Eva Maria Duarte de

Agentinian actress and politician 1919-52

Eva Ibarguren was one of the most popular actresses in Argentina. But she was also interested in politics, and when she was 26 she retired from the stage and married Vice-President Perón. At the time he was out of favour with the rest of the government, because he approved of such "revolutionary" ideas as allowing trade unions and giving women the vote. In 1946 Perón was imprisoned, and Eva organized strikes and protest marches until he was released. A general election followed, and Perón was elected president with a landslide majority.

Although Perón was president, everyone knew that Eva was his inspiration, and that he relied on her political and common sense. She worked ceaselessly to improve the lives of the Argentinian people. She and her husband Juan persuaded parliament to pass a law giving women the vote. They legalized trade unions, and made laws to shorten working hours and improve factory conditions. Eva encouraged mass education, and formed the Eva Perón Social Aid Foundation to help the poor.

Eva Péron died in 1952, aged 33, and without her guidance her husband began to make disastrous political mistakes. In 1955 a group of officers rebelled against him and sent him into exile. The reforms inspired by Eva Perón had lasted for less than a decade. But people still think of her as one of the great benefactors of her country, and look back on her time as a political golden age.

Fidel Castro, in stirring mood.

CASTRO (RUZ), Fidel

Cuban politician born 1927

Castro's political activities began when he was a law student. In 1953, he was sentenced to 15 years' imprisonment, but was later released in an amnesty. He trained with other Cubans as a guerrilla in Mexico, and his band "invaded" Cuba in 1956. Only 12 of them, including Castro, survived. They hid in the mountains from the army of the dictator Batista, a man so hated that people flocked to join Castro. In 1959 Batista had to flee for his life, and Castro became president of Cuba and leader of the Cuban Communist Party. He has since survived economic crisis, an American-supported invasion (the "Bay of Pigs"), and the Cuban missile crisis (in 1963 the USA and USSR almost declared war over missiles stored in Cuba by the USSR, within range of major US cities).

Julius Nyerere.

NYERERE, Julius Kanbarage

Tanzanian politician born 1922

From 1954 Nyerere worked for Tanganyikan independence from Britain. He became Tanganyika's first prime minister in 1961, president in 1962 and then president of Tanzania, a union of Tanganyika and Zanzibar. He has tried to keep Tanzania self-reliant, especially in food production. The country consists mainly of farms and scattered villages, but Nyerere has tried to bring the benefits of education and medicine to all. Nyerere has translated **Shakespeare's** *Merchant of Venice* into Swahili.

JUAN CARLOS I

Spanish king born 1938

Juan Carlos is the grandson of Alfonso XIII of Spain, who left the country in 1931. He was given a military education and in 1969 the dictator **Franco**, impressed by him, nominated him as the future king. Two days after Franco's death in 1975, Juan Carlos succeeded to his throne, and the Spanish monarchy was restored. But he has not continued Franco's strict rule. Instead, Juan Carlos has encouraged democracy, in spite of political and military difficulties including two attempted coups (take-overs).

NYERERE: Shakespeare 16 JUAN CARLOS: Franco 468

GLOSSARY

Abdicate To resign from being ruler.

Administration The term used to refer to the government.

Amnesty A general pardon, or an agreement not to prosecute people (for example if they hand in illegal guns), or to free prisoners from jail before their sentences are served.

Aristocrat A person whose family is powerful, rich or noble.

Capitalism A political and financial system where private individuals (not the state) lend others money to make things, and then take profits.

Civil war Fighting between two or more groups of citizens of the same country.

Communism A political system in which the state takes control, and each person works for the benefit of everyone else, giving as much as he or she can and receiving as much as he or she needs. Communism is the opposite of capitalism.

Concubine A ruler's assistant wife, or an official mistress.

Coup A sudden, often violent, takeover of government power by a group of people.

Crusades The wars fought from the twelfth to the fourteenth centuries by Christians trying to win the Holy Land (Palestine) from Muslim rule.

Democracy A political system in which all people vote to say what should be done, and who should rule them.

Depose To remove a king, queen or president from power.

Dictator Someone who rules by force.

Dynasty A sequence of leaders of the same powerful family. Power is passed on from one generation to the next.

Exile Being forced to live outside your own country.

Fascism A right-wing political movement begun by Benito Mussolini in Italy. The Fascists modelled themselves on the leaders of ancient Rome, with strict state control.

Fanaticism Wild, unreasoning support for something, usually a religion or political belief. The word "fan" comes from it.

Garrison The group of soldiers left behind by a conqueror to run a captured city or country.

Guerrilla A fighter who is not part of the official army.

Imperial Belonging to an emperor or empire.

Independence Political freedom to run your own affairs.

Medieval From the time of the Middle Ages: from the fifth century to the middle of the fifteenth century.

Monarch (Greek for "sole ruler".) King or queen.

Non-aggression pact An agreement between two or more states not to attack one another.

Parliament (from the French for "to talk") The assembly of lords, ladies and ordinary people chosen to help rule a country.

President The elected head of state in a republic.

Reactionary Someone who thinks that past ways were better than those of the present, and so reacts against change.

Regent Someone who rules for a child monarch, until the child grows up.

Renaissance A word meaning revival or rebirth. It often is used to describe the period in European history from 1400 to 1650, a time when people were rediscovering the arts and civilization of ancient Greece and Rome.

Republic A country without a monarch which is ruled solely by elected representatives, such as modern France, or the USA.

Revolutionary A person who believes that change can only come by overturning the way things were done before.

Sack You sack a city by looting its wealth, burning and wrecking its buildings and killing or enslaving its people.

Sheikh Muslim ruler of an Arab people or state.

Shi'ite Muslim The Shi'ites, 13% of all Muslims, live mainly in Iran. They are stricter than **Sunni Muslims** (85% of all Muslims), and despise 20th-century Westernized ways.

Socialist One who believes that the state should rule people's lives, helping those in need.

Subjects The people ruled by a monarch or emperor.

Treason Betraying your ruler or country.

Ziggurat A rectangular temple tower or stepped mound built in ancient Mesopotamia.

INDEX

ILLUSTRATORS:

Peter Bailey 22 (top); **Damon Burnard** 7 (centre), 16, 35 (btm), 50 (top), 85 (top), 96 (btm), 106 (left), 115, 129 (btm), 139 (rgt), 154, 157, 168, 180, 187 (btm), 190 (top), 193 (btm), 197 (btm), 231 (top), 247 (btm), 248 (btm), 253, 286 (btm), 290 (rgt), 291 (left), 333 (top), 352 (btm), 358 (inset), 372 (btm), 395 (top), 424 (left), 432 (btm); **Steve Carey** 21 (btm), 22 (btm), 66 (left), 75 (btm), 76, 77 (top), 184 (left), 213 (btm), 226 (rgt), 232 (btm), 233 (btm), 236 (left, both), 237 (btm), 263 (btm), 264 (btm), 266 (btm), 281, 295 (left), 392 (left), 394 (top), 395 (btm), 436 (btm), 465 (btm), 469 (top), 471 (left); **Jonathan Clement** 34 (rgt), 74 (top); **Jeff Cummins** 43 (top); **Richard Draper** 8 (top), 23 (top), 27 (btm), 30 (btm), 86 (btm), 101 (top), 105, 116 (btm), 117 (top), 120 (top), 123, 132 (top), 135 (btm), 137, 139 (left, both), 141 (btm), 142 (centre), 144 (rgt), 146-7, 149 (btm), 150 (top), 153, 155 (rgt), 169 (top), 189, 199 (top), 206, 209, 228 (top), 279 (top), 307 (btm), 334 (top), 350 (btm), 356 (btm), 386 (centre), 388, 390 (btm), 405, 406 (top), 409 (btm), 410 (btm), 414 (btm), 421 (top), 427 (left), 428 (btm), 430 (btm), 440 (top), 441 (btm), 446 (top), 448 (btm), 452 (btm), 458 (top), 462 (top), 465 (rgt), 473 (rgt, both), 474 (btm); **Mike Kirby** 287 (top); **Robin Lawrie** 52 (btm); **P J Lynch** 234 (top); **Tony Miller** 17 (btm, rgt), 25, 31 (btm), 36 (btm), 38 (btm), 59 (btm), 86 (top), 93 (btm), 97, 108 (btm), 113 (top), 118 (btm), 126 (btm), 128 (btm), 136, 164, 166 (left), 167 (rgt), 172-3, 175, 176, 181 (top), 185 (top), 186, 197 (top), 200 (btm), 203 (btm), 205, 213 (top), 221, 223 (left), 225 (left), 227, 234 (btm), 286 (left), 302 (btm), 339, 340 (rgt), 350 (rgt), 351 (top), 365 (top), 367 (top), 384 (btm), 392 (centre), 393 (btm), 394 (left), 404 (top), 407 (btm), 410 (top), 413 (btm), 414 (top), 419 (top), 420, 422 (top & rgt), 423 (left), 426 (left & btm), 427 (btm, rgt), 428 (top), 429 (left), 430 (top), 431, 433 (top), 441 (top), 444, 445 (top), 449 (btm), 451, 453 (top), 455, 457, 459 (btm), 460, 463, 466 (btm), 469 (btm), 470, 475 (top); **Peter Morrison** 274 (top); **Lyn O'Neill** 10 (top), 33 (btm), 59 (top), 62 (top), 70 (btm), 72 (btm), 84, 101 (centre), 112 (btm), 121 (top), 183 (rgt), 185 (left), 198, 207 (top), 208 (btm), 218 (btm), 230-1, 232 (top), 244 (top), 245 (top), 252, 284 (top), 333 (btm), 341, 381 (btm), 382 (left), 391 (top), 417, 418 (top), 424 (top, rgt), 434 (rgt), 435 (btm, both), 447 (btm), 450 (btm), 468; **Ann Winterbotham** 111 (centre), 119, 122, 124-5, 130 (top), 165 (top), 170 (top), 171, 443 (btm), 468 (top).

Note: Some of the illustrations in this volume have appeared in the Granada Guides series, previously published by Granada Publishing Ltd.